Framing Portraits, Binding Albums: Family Photographs in India

Supported by the
MurthyNAYAK Foundation

Over the last 200 years, the study of humans and their cultures has benefited from the addition of a new resource: photography. At first an intrusive tool in the hands of the colonizer, there perhaps was more truth than superstition to the fear that the camera would 'steal the soul' of the subject. But thankfully the pleasurable choice to have formal photographs made to commemorate special occasions soon followed. And then there were cameras in the hands of home hobbyists, who brought about an acceptance of informal snapshots for remembrance.

PhotoSouthAsia is proud to support the printing and production of *Framing Portraits, Binding Albums: Family Photographs in India* edited by Shilpi Goswami and Suryanandini Narain. These academic examinations of family photographic archives recognize them not only as witnesses to these specific people, in these specific places, at these specific times, but also bestow value on photo albums and shoeboxes in attics, cedar chests, and flea markets around the world, bursting to tell their stories: the stories of other people, in other places, perhaps occasionally at the very same time.

Framing Portraits, Binding Albums

Family Photographs in India

Editors
Shilpi Goswami
and
Suryanandini Narain

zubaan

ZUBAAN
128 B Shahpur Jat, 1st floor
NEW DELHI 110 049
Email: contact@zubaanbooks.com
Website: www.zubaanbooks.com

First published by Zubaan Publishers Pvt. Ltd 2025
The publication of this book is supported by *PhotoSouthAsia*.

We are grateful to Dayanita Singh for generously providing the cover photograph by Noni Singh.

10 9 8 7 6 5 4 3 2 1

ISBN 978 93 90514 92 2 (paperback)
ISBN 978 93 90514 74 8 (ebook)

Zubaan is an independent feminist publishing house based in New Delhi with a strong academic and general list. It was set up as an imprint of India's first feminist publishing house, Kali for Women, and carries forward Kali's tradition of publishing world quality books to high editorial and production standards. *Zubaan* means tongue, voice, language, speech in Hindustani. Zubaan publishes in the areas of the humanities, social sciences, as well as in fiction, general non-fiction, and books for children and young adults under its Young Zubaan imprint.

Typeset by in Baskerville 11/13 by Jojy Philip
Printed and bound at Chaman Offset.

Contents

4
TIES (RE)INVOKED:
ARCHIVES IMAGINED, BORROWED AND LOST:

5
FAMILIES (RE)CALIBRATED:
VISUALISING CLASS AND CASTE HIERARCHIES:

6
IDENTITIES (RE)CENTRED:
NEGOTIATING ETHNIC MARGINS:

7
BELONGINGS AND ALBUMS (RE)VISITED:
VISUALISING MATERIALITY:

Introduction

Shilpi Goswami and Suryanandini Narain

> 'What gets left out of dominant discourse isn't neutral or accidental, but a result of the structures that produce and preserve them.'
>
> (Kristen Lubben, 2018)[1]

The essays in this book address the absence of family photographs in academic discourse in India and dwell on their importance and visual omnipresence in our daily lives. Family photographs have belonged to the 'vernacular'[2] material of visual culture, more seen and lived with, less written and consciously thought about. This book is an attempt to retrieve family photographs from a space of neglect and bring them forth as fundamental to the microhistories of a nation, suggesting counter-narratives to the dominant strains in an emerging discursive space.

The aim of this anthology is to analyse family photographs for the contribution they make to the histories of photography, marginality and family in India. While studies on family photographs from South Asia are very limited, there is significant international scholarship in the domain (Brown and Phu 2014, Hirsch 1997 and 1999, Bourdieu 1996, Langford 2008, Rose 2016 and Kuhn 1995).[3] The production of family photographs has been a generic reason for the camera's existence in the lives of people, where it played the role of a mediating agency for interpersonal relationships. The essays herein do not claim to be a comprehensive survey of all types of family photographs in India, as much as they are focused insights into chosen areas of interest by the contributing authors. Collectively, they embrace the intersectionalities of gender, caste, class and regional trajectories in their engagement. Contestations between historical and affective memorialisation surrounding

---

[1] Lederman, Russet, Olga Yatskevich and Michael Lang. eds.2018. *How We See*, 16, 10 x 10 Photobooks.

[2] Batchen, Geoffrey. 2000. 'Vernacular Photographies'. *History of Photography*, 24(3): 262–271.

[3] Bourdieu, Pierre, Shaun Whiteside (tr.). 1990. *Photography: A Middle Brow Art.* Stanford University Press: Redwood City, CA; Brown, Elspeth and Thy Phu. eds. 2014. *Feeling Photography.* Duke University Press: Durham, NC; Kuhn, Annette. 1995. *Family Secrets: Acts of Memory and Imagination.* University of Michigan Press: Ann Arbor, MI; Langford, Martha. 2008. *The Afterlife of Memory in Photographic Albums.* McGill-Queen's University Press; Rose, Gillian. 2003. 'Family Photographs and Domestic Spacings: A Case Study'. *Transactions of the Institute of British Geographers.* 28(1); ———. 2010. *Doing Family Photography: The Domestic, the Public and the Politics of Sentiment.* Routledge: London.

family photographs centrally inform the 21 essays here, as they accept and negotiate a terrain shared by both types of narrativisations.

The photograph as a visual, material and/or virtual artefact fulfils the family's desire of completeness and memory-making, while revealing the scaffolding of kinship beneath the flesh of affective relationships. The oral recollections surrounding family photos need documentation and analysis in order to draw larger inferences about relational realities of family life in India. An important purpose of this book is to dwell on the notion of the 'ideal' family and thereafter examine its modular transformations in response to shifts in society and politics. We hope to uncover the visual conventions within photography that respond to sociocultural aspirations for the 'ideal' family. One such convention concerns the replication of photographable moments in families across social categories, counterbalanced by the specificity of interpersonal relations. This is what leads to categorisations such as 'wedding photographs', 'baby photographs', 'holiday photographs' to be standardised under the larger theme of family photographs, challenged by the more individual engagements of, say, selfie culture enabled by mobile phone photography. Subsequent deviations from the ideal familial type are also of interest, as family photos become the via media for gleaning important gaps in continuity, unexpected moments of instability and an obvious effort towards the constructedness and continuity of the family. Hence queer identities, feminist voices, diasporic tensions and challenged childhoods that have had visual traces and contestations within family photographs, become of special interest. The essays also trace the abstractness of personal photographs, where meaning and memory are beyond the certainty of comprehension, or as Susan Sontag has said, 'The quickest, driest way to convey the inner commotion caused by these photographs is by noting that one can't always make out the subject, so thorough is the ruin of flesh and stone they depict' (Sontag 2003:4).[4]

We recognise the multiplicity of meanings that the same image or set of images may carry for a viewer. In Barthesian formulation, there are three participants who experience a photograph—the photographer as 'Operator', the subject as 'Spectrum' and the viewer as 'Spectator'.[5] Bound by an unstable power dynamic, they differentially determine meaning-making around images. Sontag, in her book *Regarding the Pain of Others*, writes, 'Whether the photograph is understood as a naïve object or the work of an experienced artificer, its meaning—and the viewer's response—depends on how the picture is identified or misidentified, that is, on words. The organising idea, the moment, the place, and the devoted public made this exhibit something of an

[4] Sontag, Susan. 2003. *Regarding the Pain of Others*. Picador: New York. p. 4.

[5] Barthes, Roland. 1999. *Camera Lucida: Reflections on Photography*.9. Farrar, Straus & Giroux Inc.: Paris.

exception'[6] (Sontag, 2003:29). Giving in to these possibilities of 'identification' and even 'misidentification', our contributors have engaged with the process of textualising family photographic narratives in unusual and experimental ways. The critical charge of the essays in this volume variously approach the following questions: what role does photography play in encoding the ideal family, what are these codes, and in what ways are the cracks visible? How are the dominant family-owned narratives of photographs challenged by counter-narratives of history and vice versa? How do intersectional identities inscribe themselves onto the codes of ideal familial configurations? For instance, taking gender as identity, do men and women appear differently as subjects and photographers in their families, and do they read family photographs differently? How does the family as a social institution interact with other systems of society and can these relationships with the outside world be gleaned through photography? What is the significance of the materiality of family photographs and their sites of display in albums, homes, archives, exhibitions? What is the place for memory and orality which is affective, personal, contingent and fickle? How are the standards for such an archive of memory and fact of history reconciled to create a cogent past? Is there an afterlife of family photographs?

Answers to these questions lie in the deeply complex nature of family photography, yet to be academically explored in South Asia. The making, preservation and historicisation of these photographs has long needed attention. In the absence of any precedent that could inform our project, we as editors felt the need to bring our contributors in dialogue with each other. This was enabled by a roundtable discussion on family photographs at the School of Arts and Aesthetics, Jawaharlal Nehru University, in 2019, headed by the steering committee of the Family Camera Network (FAMCAM, www.familycameranetwork.org/), based out of Toronto. Their work has manifested in major conferences and exhibitions (2017–19) bearing dialogues on diasporic, racial and queer identities through family photographs in Canada. FAMCAM's articulations have fundamentally influenced our book and Deepali Dewan, Thy Phu, Sarah Parsons and Elspeth Brown have guided our work with their advice. Their publication *Feeling Photography* (2014) crucially sensitised us to think about the question, 'What might it mean to feel photography?'[7] (Brown and Phu, 2014:2). Thereafter, supported by the India Foundation for the Arts (IFA), we organised three online closed-door workshops for our contributors, with Urvashi Butalia of Zubaan Books, Surojit Sarkar formally of Ambedkar University, Delhi, and graphic novelist Sarnath Banerjee. These were held across the winter of 2020–21. Each workshop was a closed-door session in order to maintain the space for free, unselfconscious exchange of thoughts and to protect emerging ideas. The three resource persons were extremely generous

[6] Sontag, Susan. 2003. *Regarding the Pain of Others*. Picador: New York. p. 29.

[7] Brown, Elspeth and Thy Phu. eds. 2014. *Feeling Photography*. Duke University Press: Durham. p. 2.

with sharing their experiences in the domains of writing, archival work and field work in the visual realm, and they interacted with all the contributors, addressing queries and offering advice.

In the workshops, we wanted to engage not only with well-known frameworks of photography but with alternative intermedial concerns of production and authorship, circulation, archiving, revisions and textual reflections, and we tried to open up new ways for us to think about all-too-familiar material. An important outcome of these workshops was the abetment of diversity in method and approach amongst the contributors. Each of the presenting contributors had not only very unique subject matters at hand, but also issues of access, personal positioning and reflexivity, and an awareness of the temporal specificity in their respective research areas, making it impossible to have a one-size-fits-all approach from an editorial perspective. If one author focused on interviews, another worked with an archive, while one had too many photographs to include and had to have much of the material edited out; another had to deal with gaping absences in data. The writing that ensued from these workshops showed great diversity in method and approach, ranging from the theoretical to the journalistic, the conversational to the poetic. As editors, we were open to receiving these heterogenous texts, with the understanding that individual interpretive subjectivities were key to family photographs. Through these workshops, we also opened opportunities for future one-on-one conversations between the participants, as they developed their own networks of intellectual exchange. It is our hope that these networks will outlast the book itself and flower into more collaborative efforts in the field in the future.

On 16 and 17 July 2021, we held a final online conference for all the contributors. This conference came at a time when we were working on writing our essays from the research conducted over the past year, or longer. Our two experts, Prof. Tapati Guha-Thakurta and Prof. Malavika Karlekar, have engaged with these themes in their well-established scholarship in the field of visual culture, and they made important connections, observations and suggestions to the participants after each panel's presentations. The conference was replete with rich visual imagery and clinched our multi-pronged effort to bring family photographs into the discursive space of scholarship. Members of the IFA, our workshop resource persons and the funders of our book from the MurthyNAYAK Foundation were also invited. The format of the conference entailed grouping similarly themed research areas together, making a total of eight panels, the participants engaging in prior discussion with each other regarding their thoughts. These panels, in fact, correspond to the eight sections in this book. The panel/section titles bear a repetitive use of the prefix 're' as an articulation of new photographic responses to historical matter in the familial context. Even though family photographs have not been theorised until now, their ubiquitous presence—and banality even—are challenged herein by fresh inquiries into their importance.

The essays in this volume can be organised in various ways and no section is exclusive of the others. The eight categories dividing the essays are fairly narrow, addressing the texts partially rather than holistically, in their central thematics. Their ideas and arguments overlap with each other, resonating with common experiences. Hence, in the first section, Ajay Salunkhe, Annalisa Mansukhani and Diya and Jayanti Dutta have been brought together for their intergenerational dialogues that enliven or 're-imagine' the family through photographs. As a well-established narrative around personal photographs, this reimagination entails multiple personal views about the timing, contexts and meanings that photos bear, often appearing as variable in each narration. All three essays focus on the maternal figure as the subject, narrator and proprietor of the family photographic archive, while also dwelling on the irony of loss and absence amidst familial plenitude.

Photographs recall absences and instability in the next section on migration, displacement and diaspora, where the motherland, so to speak, comes into question. Adira Thekkuveettil has an active project on the Anglo-Indian archives (www.angloindianarchives.com/) that attempts to retrieve histories, genealogies and kinship connections across time and continents. However, migration and displacement are usually accompanied by the loss of memorabilia such as photographs and their associated history, as illustrated by Aditi Gupta in her essay on memories of the Partition of 1947. The culling together of previously lost archives is again seen in the essay by Sarojini Lewis, as she returns to her roots in Suriname to uncover the politics of gendered histories from the region.

The lost or absent archive makes a stronger appearance in the fourth section, with stories of displacement casting long shadows across generations. Nadia Nooreyzdan inquires into a dispersed Iranian community through photographs she accidentally discovered at home, while Shilpi Goswami dwells on the irretrievability of personal history when photographs have not been taken at all, or lost or worse, when they have been purposefully misplaced. Intersectional identities of sexuality, class and caste centrally condition family photos and their narratives in the third and fifth sections of the book, with Charan Singh and Hardik Brata Biswas directly addressing queer and feminine subjugations and visual countermeasures of subversion. They are followed by inquiries by Divya Gauri, Rajyashri Goody and Vijay Kumar into caste-based marginality in the form of servitude and Dalit identity manifesting itself in family photographs. Ethnic marginalisation of a religious nature is investigated in the sixth section with Uzma Mohsin's essay on the modern Muslim identity in Aligarh, while Anna Sireiliu Charenamei and Ranu Roychaudhuri's inquiries are located in a troubled Northeastern hinterland. The latter follows Sharbendu De's artistic intervention in representing the Lisu family idiom, and Roychaudhuri's essay is critiqued in a statement from the artist himself. The Indian State appears again, not in its imagined paternalistic role, but as a repressive force in the essays by Jigisha Bhattacharya on the anti-CAA protests and Dipti Tamang and Ruchika Gurung's study of the Darjeeling political agitation of 1986. Women appear to redefine familial narratives as they rescript feminine participation at difficult moments in Indian history. These essays evoke Ariella Azoulay's *The Civil Contract of Photography*, wherein she has raised pertinent questions like: how do photographs function as argumentative fragments within a larger discursive economy or 'regime of statements'?[8]; how should spectators of political violence experience and witness photography so as to articulate an 'emergency claim' as a way of defining rhetorical exigencies?[9]

We hope that the essays in the book can extend such theoretical inquiries, and family photographs can suggest some areas of resolution. Occupying a small but important space within the discourse on family photos are the essays on more celebratory moments, such as family holidays by Suryanandini Narain and the purchase of new cars by Chinar Shah, that never go unaccompanied by the camera. Mallika Leuzinger explores the new figure of the woman photographer and her unparalleled perspective into privacies of the family in her text on amateur photography from the early 20th century. This range of essays maps a fairly large terrain of personal photography, yet it is not exhaustive, and future possibilities of research can be easily identified. In this anthology, a conscious attempt has been made to tap into the 'fragmented memories'[10] (Saikia 2004) of common folks whose stories fall through the cracks of time, like 'The Common Man', that silent presence anchoring R.K. Laxman's daily 'You Said it' cartoon strip in *The Times of India*, who has been an iconic figure of Indian political commentary for over 50 years. 'Despite charting India's changing times since 1951, the Common Man has remained remarkably unchanged… While Laxman's Common Man is a silent spectator in the world of politics, his alter ego, the *aam aadmi*, the ordinary person or Everyman, is vocal and active.'[11] (Baviskar and Ray 2011).

Framing Portraits, Binding Albums highlights some of the definitions that compose the family in India, the camera playing its own crucial role in 'producing' the family for the lens. As much as visual representation is a means towards framing the family, it is also a via media of reflecting upon its points of strength and fissures of weakness, the 'unframing' and 'unbinding' of humanity's fundamental social institution. Photographs perform the role of covering cracks, smoothening personal differences, while also touching upon the precarious nature of the family that is challenged by larger intersectional forces. In this light, we must acknowledge the sensitive timing of this book. To begin with, 5 January 2020, the date for a Delhi-based conference on pedagogy

[8] Azoulay, Ariella. 2008. *The Civil Contract of Photography*. Zone Books: New York. p. 191.

[9] Azoulay, Ariella. 2008. *The Civil Contract of Photography*. Zone Books: New York. p. 145.

[10] Saikia, Yasmin. 2004. *Fragmented Memories: Struggling to be Tai-Ahom in India*. Duke University Press: Durham.

[11] Baviskar, Amita and Raka Ray. eds. 2011. *Elite and Everyman: The cultural politics of the Indian middle classes*. Routledge: New Delhi. p. 1.

in the field of photography, held by the MurthyNAYAK Foundation, was when we first got a sense that our work may see the light of day. The Foundation had readily agreed to financially support the production of this book. It was also a landmark date that saw two important events in the world, one of which was an incredibly violent attack on a peaceful student meeting at Jawaharlal Nehru University that blotted out an understanding of democracy from the history of this country. It made clear the need for young voices, braving right-wing assault, to have fora for documenting the histories that remain unheard and unwritten, and for them to feel that they will be heard. 5 January 2020 is also the date that the genetic sequencing of the coronavirus was discovered by scientists in Wuhan, China. That discovery confirmed the essential nature of the COVID-19 pandemic that swept the world in the months to come. In direct ways, these events have affected our project and have been woven into its fabric. They have made urgent the need for alternative histories and personal domains to be introspected, both visually and textually. Family photographs from this time only bring to relief the importance of micronarratives—with all our lives marked in various ways by the pandemic even as we attempted to bring them to the fore.

More specifically, the project would have had a very different form had it not coincided with the pandemic so closely—both project and pandemic commenced and concluded at the exact same time. This has been a time when we have been pushed further into interiorities, bringing the family into greater focus than ever before, impacting the very core subject matter of our project. We have had to be deeply empathetic, flexible and sensitive to our participants, who, in various ways, suffered terrible losses and obstacles to their work. Many of us lost friends, family and colleagues, stalling our lives and all aspects of work. Some of us lost access to the archives that we were depending upon, hence having to change the focus of our research and look at other available material. Our online conference, first scheduled for the third week of April 2021, had to be shifted by three months due to the onset of the deadly second wave of the virus. Several of us had to head home from cities to rural interiors, the sites of our ancestral homes and problems of infrastructure such as electricity and the internet slowed down our work. We are grateful to our supporting agencies for understanding our situation and granting us several deadline extensions.

Our greatest loss has been the withdrawal of two of the initial participants in the project for entirely personal reasons. As such, we have had to be open to these reconfigurations due to unforeseen reasons and the extreme challenges of this time. We had to make allowances for these organic changes, in order to carry on with the project. As a result, we now have 21 instead of 23 contributors to the volume, unlike initially envisioned.

As editors, our individual journeys with photography over the last couple of decades have seen constant renegotiation and navigation amidst established frameworks of understanding South Asian visual culture. Departing from the realms of nostalgia and linear narratives in the history of photography in India—indeed 'unframing' and 'unbinding' them—has been very unsettling. With this volume, we have tried to make an attempt to see the in-betweens, going beyond the family from being a mundane sociological demographic to a centrally impactful social organ. Our conversations with the book's congregation of thinkers have been very reassuring in this endeavour. It has been a privilege to academically engage with each one of our writers who challenged the established agencies, patterns and conventions in academic research. We both earnestly thank all our fellow travellers on this journey.

1

Families (re)imagined: Postmemory and intergenerational dialogues

My Mother's Stories

Access, Absence and Archive in the Making of Family Albums

Ajay Salunkhe

> '*Mala tumche photo kadhayala khoop avdayche*
> (I liked to have you photographed).'[1]
>
> – Radhika Salunkhe, 2020

My mother, Radhika Salunkhe, told me how much she liked to have me photographed in response to my question of why our family photos are mostly random ones of my brother and me growing up. I remember seeing far fewer photos from her wedding and other similar social occasions. Pondering on her reply, I realised she actually liked to take photos of herself and of us as well, although she is reluctant to admit to the former. I remember one such instance of her taking me to a studio to get photographed when I was in the fourth grade. She picked me up from school on a Saturday at half-day, and we walked to a small neighbourhood photo store-cum-studio in the bazaar of our locality in the Mankhurd area of suburban Mumbai. It was a popular studio where each wall had a different wallpaper to serve as different backdrops. It was the kind of space that visual anthropologist and art historian Christopher Pinney called 'chambers of dreams' in his seminal articulations on India's popular studio photography.[2]

I was asked to keep my school bag down and put talcum powder on my face. There was also a mirror in the corner and a comb to fix your hair. My mother used all these available accessories on me and asked me to stand against one of the backdrops. The photographer then threw away his *bidi*, corrected my posture, went behind a serious-looking camera, gave me instructions to look in a particular direction, and then there was a flash and a clicking sound. In hindsight, the camera was probably a semi-automatic analogue, which was commonplace in these neighbourhood photo studios of the 1990s and early 2000s. I distinctly remember how the flash blinded me for a few seconds. Then

---

[1] Interview with Radhika Salunkhe, Mumbai, 2021. Radhika Salunkhe's interview was in Marathi and was translated by the author into English.

[2] Pinney, Christopher. 1997. *Camera Indica: The Social Life of Indian Photographs*. London: Reaktion Books.

came the special moment that has allowed me to retain this little memory all these years later. The photographer came up to me and put a tie on my neck and gave me a coat. I remember feeling really nice wearing these accessories, which gave me an entirely different sensation from my own regular attire. Then he clicked a few more shots with and without the coat. My mother had a short discussion with him, and then we left the place. I was elated after receiving the processed photograph a few days later. The final image was a composite print depicting me with and without the coat, simultaneously (Figure 1).

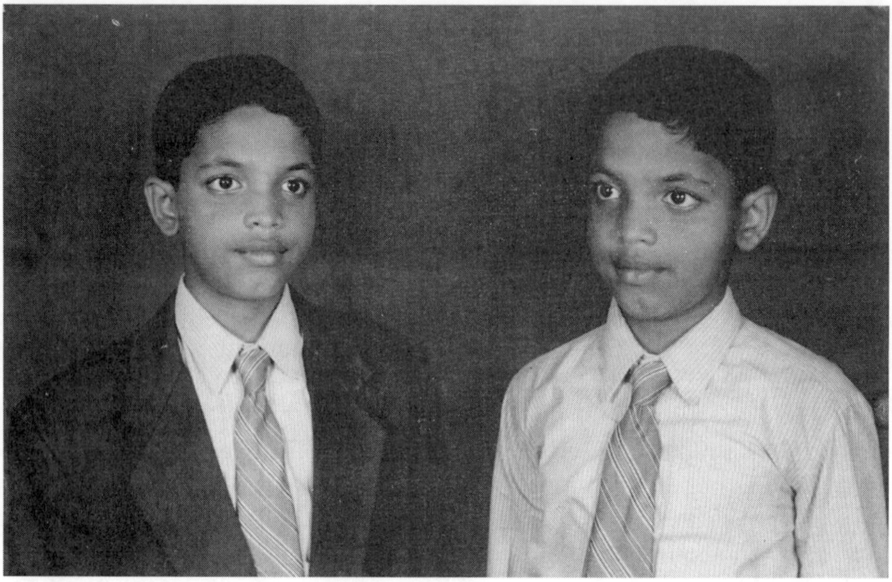

Figure 1. The author as a fourth grader in a composite print. Mumbai, 2002.

This composite print became my mother's favourite photograph of me. She later framed a copy and put it up on the wall facing the main door of our ancestral house in the village named Satar, in Satara District, Maharashtra, for relatives and visitors to see. It became one of her cherished image-objects. That wall also had her other favourite photographs, all framed, mostly of us as children and pictures of gods, arranged in a row. Family photographs are often deployed (shown and/or talked about) in series; pictures get displayed one after another, and their selection or ordering is as meaningful as the pictures themselves. 'The whole, the series, constructs a family story in some respects like a classical narrative.'[3] The memories of my family could be constructed by the narration emerging from these serialised photographs. There was another photograph, not traceable now, of my brother and I in our school uniforms, both younger than I am in Figure 1. We are with our pet parrot, Vithu, in a cage between us. Vithu later died of snakebite during the monsoon of 1999,

[3] Kuhn, Annette. 2002. *Family Secrets: Acts of Memory and Imagination*. Verso Books. p. 19.

when our house in a Mumbai slum near Ghatkopar flooded with water from a drain next to it. Even though my father killed the snake, eventually, we lost our beloved parrot who would greet my brother and mother by their names. Vithu was a family member and my mother would tell stories of him calling her name to almost all new visitors, and how we lost him to the flood. The wall opposite the entrance of our village home was nothing short of a hall of fame for my mother to showcase photos of her family. Unfortunately, she lost access to the wall and countless other prized photographs in that home after she separated from my father when I was 15 years old.

Subsequently, a remarkable shift occurred in the kinds of photos that were made and preserved in my family. As an adult, I never went to a studio for a portrait, except for passport photos for official purposes, or as part of family group photos. Losing the photographs at our ancestral place was an immense personal loss for my mother. In our general conversations, she finds ways to refer to them even today, as she talks about specific photographic and extra-photographic details and then expresses her grief over losing them. Family photographs that survive in my mother's humble collection were curated at the behest of people from the previous generation. My mother's and my own recollections of the past made me wonder why she remembers so vividly the photographs she has not seen in years, and what role they continue to play in shaping memories of my family even after our losing physical access to the majority of them.

As everyday tangible objects, family photographs and albums contain specific meanings, even while they remain semiotically fluid and capable of inventing infinite new meanings. This is where photography and memory intersect.[4] Family photographs not only allow us to observe records of the past and images of people from the past, but they also let us take a closer look at the construction of specific family histories.[5] This essay explores how photographs, both present and absent, constitute my mother's own biography and the narrative of our family. I regard my family photographs as specific productions that reveal and conceal parts of our history, and examples of financial and emotional investments made by my mother as the chief archivist. Allan Sekula, in his 2003 article, 'Reading the Archive: Photography Between Labor and Capital', defines an archive as a quantitative ensemble of photographs and distinguishes between numerous sorts of archives, including museums, institutional archives and family albums. These archives, according to Sekula, are not neutral repositories. Instead, they are representations of the politics and systems that operate them. Apart from providing evidence of

[4] Kuhn, Annette. 1 December 2007. 'Photography and Cultural Memory: A Methodological Exploration'. *Visual Studies* 22:3. p. 285. doi.org/10.1080/14725860701657175.

[5] Erkonan, Şahika. 2016.'Photography and the Construction of Family and Memory'. *Politics, Civil Society and Participation: Media and Communications in a Transforming Environment* (ed. Leif Kramp et al.). Bremen: edition lumière. p. 261.

what is selectively preserved by institutions, they also represent what is absent.[6] According to Enwezor, the desire to take a photograph and capture an event is inextricably linked to the need to create an archive, which he refers to as 'archival madness'.[7] I write this essay as an act of restitution of power to my mother as the archivist of our family photographs, tracing the losses and gains in the process. Looking at the narrations that emerge from our conversations as a source of oral history, my attempt is to 'enable us to document certain aspects of experiences that are often missing from other kinds of historical sources', as the ones that 'talk back to the historian, confronting, disrupting, and sometimes resisting the historian's understanding of the past.'[8] I write from the belief that family photos and the memories attached to them are not fixed entities; both collection and the narration around family photos are dynamic and prone to change over time.[9]

But what kind of archive do family photographs/albums constitute for writing microhistories of families and/or social histories of time and/or photographic histories of image-objects?

The popularisation and eventually democratisation of photography gave rise to a 'pictorial generation' and an intense accumulation of photographs by people of all socioeconomic backgrounds. Of course, the narrative of this widespread practice was never uniform and was always conditioned by historical differences.[10] What makes family photographs and family albums archival? Domestic images conjure up meanings that let us return to the past. As a result, photographs of any family are essential historical and anthropological sources in addition to functioning as a family memory. It is an archive and a key to 'historical experiences' since it is 'a site where society and its habits are given shape'.[11]

> A photograph is not just a recording: it constitutes the event … the photo you take of your family: it makes a record of that little group, but it also occasions it. The reality we record and the way in which we record, are induced by socio-cultural factors. Each influences the other.[12]

---

[6] Sekula, Allan. 2019. 'Reading an Archive: Photography between Labour and Capital'. *The Photography Reader* (ed. Liz Wells). Second Edition. London and New York: Routlege. p. 444.

[7] Enwezor. Okwui. 2008. 'Archive Fever: Photography between History and the Monument'. *Archive Fever: Uses of the Document in Contemporary Art*. 1. p. 12.

[8] Chowdhury. Indira. 2014. 'Speaking of the Past: Perspectives on Oral History'. *Economic and Political Weekly*. 49:30. p. 40.

[9] Erkona. 'Photography and the Construction of Family and Memory'. p. 263.

[10] Ranu Roychoudhuri proposes to differentiate between popularisation and democratisation, and argues how India never really had a Kodak moment. See Roychoudhuri, Ranu. 2015. 'The Public Lives of Photographs: Visual Convention and Social Change in Twentieth-century India'. Unpublished PhD Dissertation. The University of Chicago.

[11] Enwezor. 'Archive Fever: Photography between History and the Monument'. p. 40.

[12] Ketelaar, Eric. 1 June 2001. 'Tacit Narratives: The Meanings of Archives'. *Archival Science*. 1:2. p. 134. doi.org/10.1007/BF02435644.

Family photos are often the only way to experience the past that produced them. Despite being significant archives, they remain underdiscussed within institutional and disciplinary structures. For example, my family photographs would probably never make it to institutional archives. They are an otherwise banal record of the lives of a low-income Hindu Maharashtrian family. Yet they are significant sites where the social is constructed and translated into the visual.

My family's collection includes somewhat conventional photographs of birthdays, baby portraits and studio photographs of family members. There is also another type of imagery that often falls through the cracks between family photography and documentary photography. These are photographs produced as a form of documentation by NGOs and local housing authorities, whose social welfare projects included my family and featured us in group photographs. My mother keeps these 'welfare photographs' in the same box in which she treasures other photographs of family events along with our studio photographs. Thus, the 'social welfare' photographs are very much part of her—and our—visual memories just as any other photograph. My family photos are individual prints that are stored in a box and represent the traditional idea of a middle-class family album, but they are not organised or presented in a typical album format. Most of them are small-size prints, with only one exception that is framed and displayed in our home. Information and memories about what the photographs in the box depict come from my conversations with my mother as she reflects upon those photos, and from my own memory of these images.

My mother, Radhika, commissioned photographs on various occasions, collected them from numerous sources and consciously preserved them with an aim to build a story that would otherwise be lost even to her own children. For my brother and me, many of these photographs and the stories associated with them form what Marianne Hirsch calls 'post memory', as a relationship with the past through a 'memory distinguished by generational distance and from history by deep personal connection'.[13] Even though we were also part of the creation of some of these photographs, I was too young to remember every detail at the time, and most of them are mediated by my mother's narrative of my/our childhood. The memory gaps in my recollections are filled with hers, almost making it someone else's memory altogether. Such a memory with missing links is 'shot through with holes', [14] where details of times before and after the photograph, the exact moment of its production, etc., are often lost. Visual critic and cultural theorist John Berger argues, like several other commentators before and after him, that photographs are ambiguous, but for

[13] Hirsch, Marianne. 1992. 'Family Pictures: Maus, Mourning, and Post-Memory'. *Discourse*. 15:2. p. 8. www.jstor.org/stable/41389264.

[14] Raczymow, Henri and Alan Astro. 1994. 'Memory Shot Through With Holes'. *Yale French Studies*. 85. p. 101. doi.org/10.2307/2930067.

him the ambiguity does not lie in the production of the photograph or at the moment of creation. Instead, '[t]he ambiguity arises out of that discontinuity which gives rise to the second of the photograph's twin message. The abyss between the moment recorded and the moment of looking.'[15]

I contend that the memories inhabiting the photographs from my mother's collection are as distant to us as that of a previous generation's, which we recollect through myths surrounding them, passed down to us via retellings by our mother. H. Raczymow identifies such a memory as 'nostalgia' which is 'an ambiguous sentiment, rife with mythology about a lost paradise'.[16] Raczymow also establishes another type of 'nostalgia' that is 'devoid of content' and is 'motivated by the very fact that the world we long for, is no more'.[17] This 'devoid' world or the 'gap' in content in our case, is the outcome of my parents' separation in 2005. Most of the images that my mother had collected and arranged for display were lost to us forever in that moment of rupture, left behind in my paternal ancestral home in Satar. I did not see these images for most of my adult life and soon they became remembered fragments of my childhood. We were left with select copies in Mumbai by accident. With the loss of these images, I experienced the irretrievable loss of my familial unit that would never be whole again. The inaccessibility of our photographs was representative of a severance from my paternal family, a break in our biography, sealed by the images that we would never see again.

But what makes someone like my mother commission and treasure photographs in the first place? My family lived in a slum, on an income as low as ₹700 a month. Despite such adverse financial conditions, what made my mother to go to a photo studio and pay for photos to be made, before and after her separation from my father?

While reflecting on my brother's photo as a toddler (Figure 2), that my mother commissioned from a local photo studio, she said,

> He [the photographer] charged me 15 rupees for three copies. I used to save a few rupees out of the daily household expenses and sometimes even my mother used to lend me some money in times of need.[18]

Why choose to spend money on photographs that are apparently non-essential and expensive? My mother replied,

> I wanted to have this memory of my child starting to crawl. I feel that had I been an educated woman, who could read, I would have been a better mother. It felt great—like an achievement—for my child, without any proper nourishment, to crawl this early and everyone felt really happy. That's why I decided to have it

[15] Berger, John and Jean Mohr. eds. 1982. *Another Way of Telling*. New York: Pantheon Books. pp. 88–89.

[16] Raczymow and Astro, p. 101.

[17] Raczymow and Astro, p. 101.

[18] Interview with Radhika Salunkhe, Mumbai, 2021.

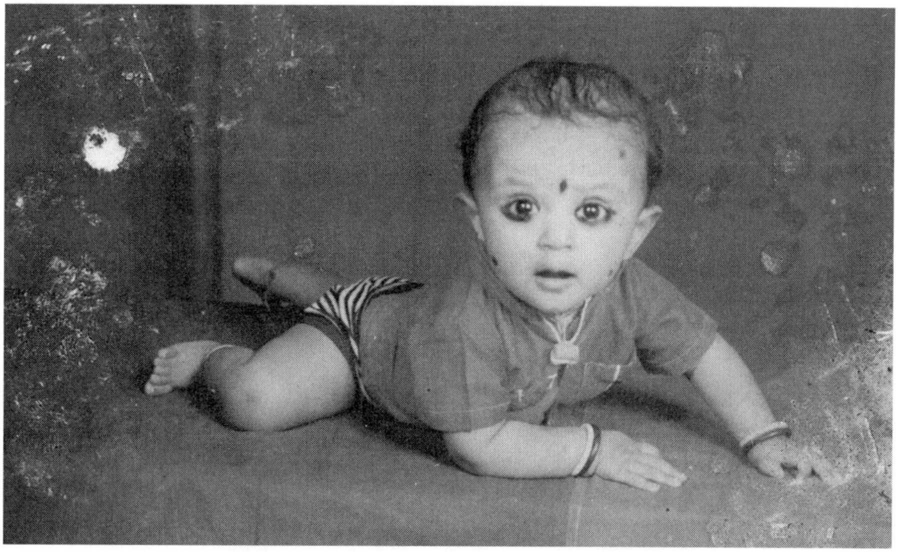

Figure 2. My brother, Vijay Salunkhe as a toddler. Mumbai, 1992.

clicked.[19]

This conversation helped me realise the magnitude of photography as a social phenomenon. It has been historically recognised as a 'democratic visual sphere'[20] as it 'makes it possible to mass-produce an aesthetic'[21] object as a mnemonic device. For us, it was a marker of survival in the face of great adversity; a comment on how the human spirit triumphs against extreme ordeals.

The oldest photo in my mother's box is that of my maternal grandparents with their children (Figure 3). It was taken at a photo studio during their visit to Mumbai in the late 1980s. The small colour print does not bear the name of the studio, but it does embody the widespread, popular studio style of family portraits in its use of a patterned backdrop and the careful arrangement of figures in a montage. Simultaneously, the image encodes memories specific to my mother's life. Her early years may not be unique or remarkable compared to others in similar situations, but how she positions this photograph in the arc of her life gives significant meaning to this photo-specific relationship between memory and her impulse to archive. Indeed, the photograph seems to mark a watershed in the microhistory of her life. It was preserved by my mother as a memory of two things: first, it shows her parents and younger siblings in their early years, but there is an undertone to the verisimilitude.

[19] Interview with Radhika Salunkhe, Mumbai, 2021.

[20] Appadurai, Arjun. 1997. 'The Colonial Backdrop'. *Comparative Technology Transfer and Society*. 24. pp. 4–7.

[21] Pinney, Christopher. 2008. *The Coming of Photography in India*. Panizzi Lectures. British Library. p. 135.

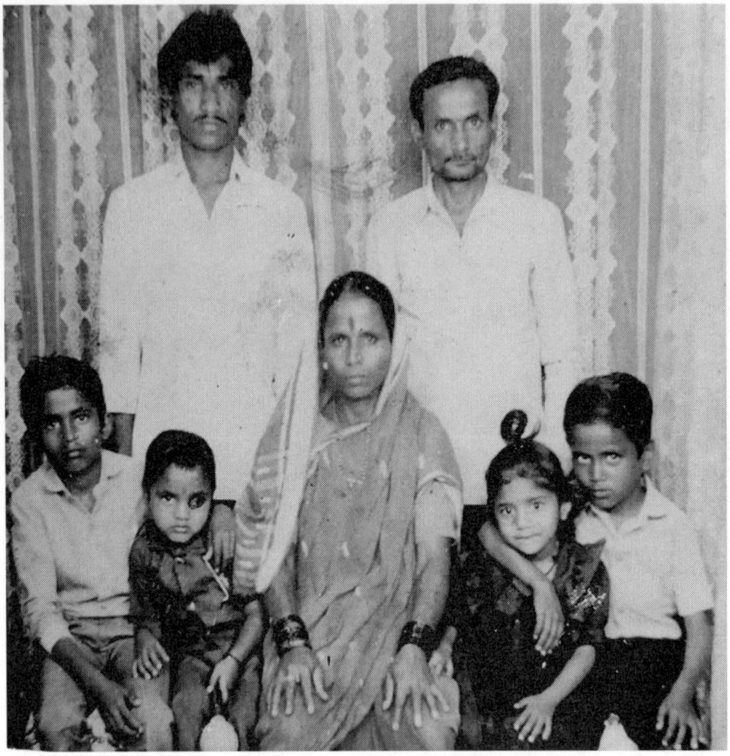

Figure 3. My maternal grandparents with their kids. Mumbai, 1989.

My mother recollects,

> Two of my younger brothers used to stay with my father in Mumbai for their education. They used to go to the local municipal school. This photo was taken when my mother was visiting my father and the two children. They all went to watch a Marathi movie also on that day. My mother (*Aai* as we all call her), came back to the village and told me about all the fun they had. That was also when they chose your father for me and fixed the marriage (her voice getting lower towards the end).[22]

Thus, a supposedly innocuous-looking family portrait of a lower-income Maharashtrian family from the late 1980s, complicates a now classic reading of the democratisation of technology and the aesthetics of the materiality of studio photography in postcolonial India. It is also a portrait that holds concealed strains and submerged emotions in relationships. For the grandchild in me, it is a portrait of my grandparents. But for my mother, it holds a memory of injustice she endured for being a girl. She keeps telling us how she always wanted to go to school, to read all the things she cannot. It was this decision of my grandparents to not educate either of their girls, who were older than all

[22] Interview with Radhika Salunkhe, Mumbai, 2021.

the boys, that my mother could not forgive.

My mother saw my father for the first time on her wedding day. She was hardly 15 years old, while my father was 21. It became apparent to my mother that it was a mistake from day one, when my father started hitting her on their wedding night. But it was too late. What followed was a physically and mentally abusive relationship that ended in a bitter separation, 15 years later. For my mother, this photo of my grandparents is also a reminder of everything that went wrong in her life. Such an innocent-looking photo has proven to be deceptive in the partial portrayal of who and what is present against what is absent.[23] A closer scrutiny of my family's images reveal complex interrelationships and controversies that thread through 'the soap opera of personal life'.[24] Modifying Pinney's theorisation of studios as 'chambers of dreams' that offer possibilities of reinventing selves and identities, I would argue that this process of self-representation encodes narratives of unfulfilled dreams, unrealised desires and memories of trauma. Looking at loose prints of studio photographs as family albums opens up possibilities of recovering supposedly mundane lives and 'small voices of history'.[25]

Even the photographs that evoke hopeful memories for my mother are reflective of the challenges and trauma she endured. Figure 4, depicting her during a puja, goes beyond being a simple portrayal of a religious ritual; it also contains elements that contributed to the eventual manifestation of violence in her life. Looking at this photograph is akin to how Barthes saw specific extra-photographic future outcomes in his mother's now-famous 'Winter Garden Photograph'.[26] Before discussing Figure 4, an elaboration on the events leading up to this photograph would help contextualise the image and the uncertain future that it signals.

My parents lived in a suburban slum next to a railway track in the Ghatkopar area of Mumbai, which used to be frequently bulldozed by the local redevelopment authorities. An NGO named SPARC: Society for The Promotion of Area Resource Centres, works towards uniting the urban poor and slum-dwellers living under the threat of evictions and slum demolitions, by providing them with the tools to engage with the state and the city to secure permanent housing.[27] They also unite women under their programme called 'Mahila Milan' ('Women Together'). It is a decentralised network of

---

[23] Hall, Stuart. 2021. 'Five Reconstruction Work: Images of Post-War Black Settlement'. *Writings on Media: History of the Present*. ed. Charlotte Brunsdon. Duke University Press. pp. 78–94, doi.org/10.1515/9781478022015-007.

[24] Wells, Liz. ed. 2011. *Photography: A Critical Introduction*. Fourth edition. Taylor & Francis. p. 153.

[25] Guha, Ranajit and Partha Chatterjee. eds. 2002. *The Small Voice of History: Collected Essays*. Delhi: Permanent Black.

[26] Barthes, Roland. 2006. *Camera Lucida: Reflections on Photography*. trans. Richard Howard. 26th edition. New York: Hill and Wang.

[27] 'SPARC: Society for The Promotion of Area Resource Centers'. n.d. www.sparcindia.org/.

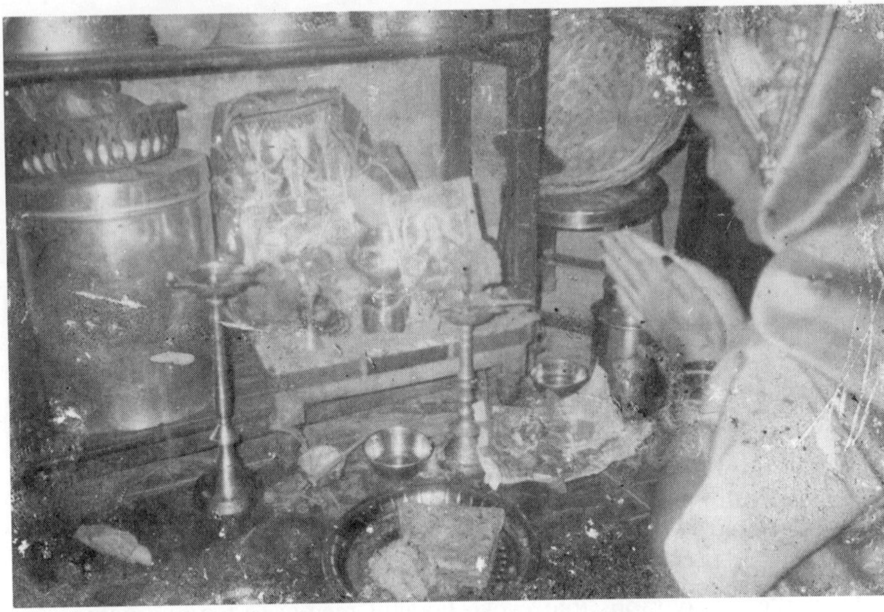

Figure 4. My mother offering puja during Santoshi Mata Vrat Udyapan. Mumbai, 2001.

poor women's collectives that manages credit and savings activities in their communities. Thousands of women, including my mother, used this scheme to save even the smallest amounts such as two, five, or ten rupees per day.

The photograph in Figure 5 is of one such meeting of the Mahila Milan. The woman on the extreme left in the front row, with her hand placed on her hip, is my mother, and the accompanying child is my elder brother. This photo is part of the documentation done by SPARC to indicate participation and the strength of numbers, both important agents of popular movements. My mother managed to get this photo from her father, as he was an active member of SPARC and used to organise community gatherings in our locality for them. All these women used to attend the meetings out of fear of losing their homes due to changing government policies for urban development. The women are posing for this group photo (Figure 5) with complete awareness of its purpose of documentation. This photo in my family's collection is a tiny fragment of the democratic life of an active citizen that my mother and thousands of women once led, under the guidance of an NGO. The head of the National Slum Dwellers' Federation (NSDF) under SPARC, Mr Jockin Arputham, with whom my mother had a personal acquaintance, went on to win the Ramon Magsaysay Award for Peace and International Understanding in 2000 for his work with the urban poor. He had helped many families in our locality get a house under the Slum Rehabilitation Authority (SRA) of Mumbai. For the art historian Geoffrey Batchen, the memory associated with photographs is 'less about the detailed recall of appearance and more

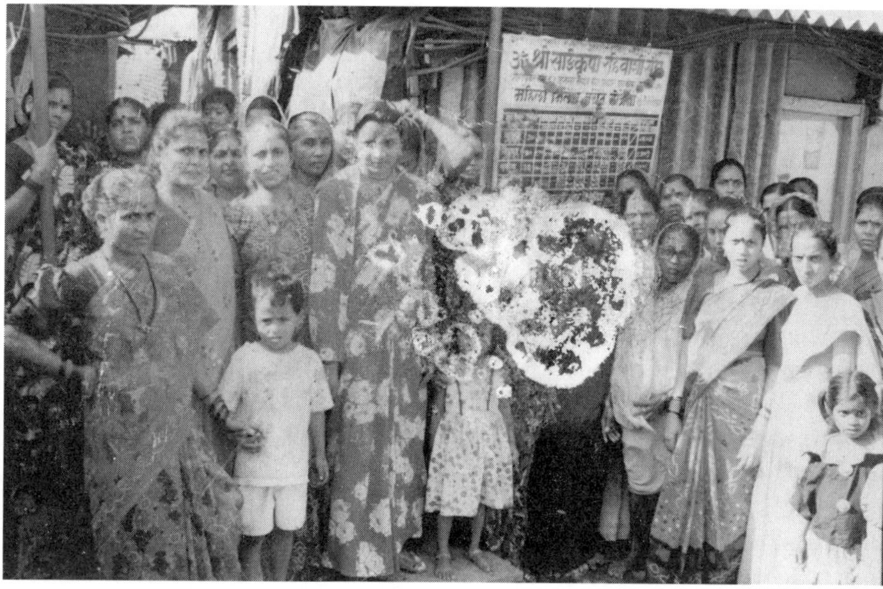

Figure 5. A meeting of the Mahila Milan. The author's mother is on the extreme left. Mumbai, 1996.

about the extended act of remembrance and a state of reverie. For us today the photographs from the past are more associated with one particular type of memory—nostalgia.'[28] Along similar lines, David Bate calls photographs a 'time machine'; a device for remembering.[29] However, unlike others, he does not limit the relationship between photographs and memory to private family albums, but expands the debate to thinking about 'collective memory'. He proclaims,

> ... the invention of photography has not only changed the means through which we individually recollect and remember things, events and people, including our experience of them, but it has also completely transformed the entire social relations of any 'collective' or social memory.[30]

Bate further contends that in modern cultures, there is a growing tendency to express ourselves visually through photographic images. To comprehend public memory effectively, it's crucial to grasp the articulation and impact of these images. I regard this group photograph as an example, initiating collective memory even while it holds significant personal meaning to me and my immediate family.

---

[28] Batchen, Geoffrey and Rijksmuseum Vincent van Gogh. eds. 2004. *Forget Me Not: Photography & Remembrance*. Amsterdam: Van Gogh Museum. p. 14.

[29] Bate, David. 23 August 2010. 'The Memory of Photography'. *Photographies*. 3:2. p. 243. doi.org/10.1080/17540763.2010.499609.

[30] Bate, David. 2009. *Photography: The Key Concepts*. Oxford: Berg. p. 10.

The photograph in Figure 4 is intimately connected to this history of urban development in Mumbai's suburban slums. There was a time when this rehabilitation was not certain and my parents were not sure of their future in Mumbai. My father started pressuring my mother to sell their current house in the slum for whatever money they could get, and to permanently relocate us to our ancestral village. My mother was determined to stay on in Mumbai for our education. She was certain that if we moved back to village, both her children would lose the opportunity for a better education and future, just as she had. This created further strain in her marriage, and my father unleashed all his anger by hitting us, just to make us leave. My mother used to go to meet Jokin Arputham and beg him to get a house allotted to her, explaining how otherwise her children will have to go back to the village and stay uneducated. This was when my mother learned about a new religious ritual from our neighbours called the 'Santoshi Mata Vrat'.[31] One has to worship the Goddess Santoshi, a non-scriptural, popular incarnation of Goddess Durga, and fast for sixteen consecutive Fridays. On the last Friday, one has to do an '*udyapan*' or a concluding ritual. My mother was told that this worship and fast will fulfil all her desires and remove all obstacles from her life. Being an ardent theist, my mother performed this vrat diligently. To her gratification, by the sixteenth Friday, my parents were allotted a flat in a building in the Mankhurd area in suburban Mumbai, under the slum redevelopment plan, and she still proudly tells me this story. This, however, was a fleeting joy, as my father sold the allotted house and separated from us within a few years.

Through our family photographs, the story of this conjugal separation is performed in my house every day on the visual plane. As part of the documentation for the housing allotment, photos were taken of each family occupying the houses granted under the slum redevelopment project. My family also had to take one such photograph. The photograph in Figure 6 was taken in the flat in Mankhurd, which my mother managed to beg and get from the SRA. But, as my mother refused to leave Mumbai, my father gave her an alternative option to allow him to separate and remarry. She agreed to take up the responsibility of educating and supporting two children and chose to put an end to her marriage. Years later, the photograph in Figure 6 remains framed and displayed on the wall in our house, but with a slight change. My father is no longer in it.

Any family's relationship with its photographs and the practices of archiving and display are important in the construction of its family history. Apart from

---

[31] For scholarship on how the new deity was invented by Bollywood but has now become academic common sense, see Pinney, Christopher. 1992. 'The Iconology of Hindu Oleographs: Linear and Mythic Narrative in Popular Indian Art'. *RES: Anthropology and Aesthetics*. 22. pp. 33–61; Lutgendorf, Philip A. 2002. 'A Superhit Goddess/A Made-to-Satisfaction Goddess: *Jai Santoshi Maa* Revisited'. *Manushi*. 131. pp. 10–16, 24–37; Knauss, Stefanie. 22 January 2020. 'Religion and Film: Representation, Experience, Meaning'. *Brill Research Perspectives in Theology*. 4:1. pp. 1–103, doi.org/10.1163/24683493-12340009.

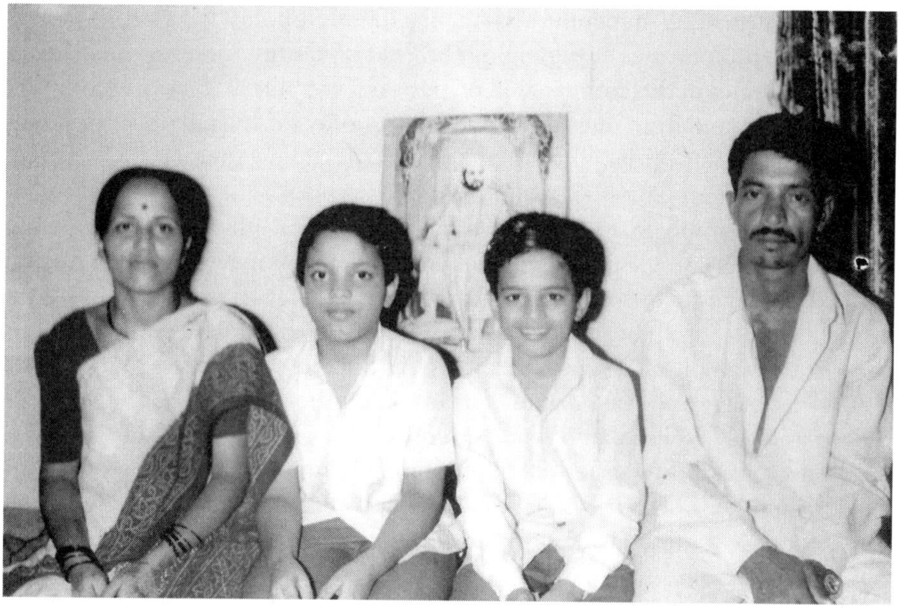

Figure 6. My parents, my brother and I in our new apartment allotted by the SRA. Mumbai, 2002.

framing, collecting, preserving, editing, reshaping and destroying them, the photos are also part of living, ongoing familial practices. Using the example of a 'demonic' diva who is alive, and a photograph of a deceased grandmother, Siegfried Kracauer claims that 'were it not for the oral tradition, the image alone would not have sufficed to reconstruct the grandmother'. According to Kracauer, a photo replicates 'reality', but only as the spatial fixation of a past moment, whereas memory images are capable of making up the 'history' of a person due to the 'historical significance' that they retain. According to him, individuals retain memories because they are significant. But they are organised differently from the way photographs are organised. The meaning of memory images is linked to their truth content, hence the last image of a person (in memory) is that person's history. Photographs do not contain this meaning.[32]

For John Berger, photographs are a 'memento of the absent' which we create out of our 'desire to record and remember.'[33] My parents' separation and the history of their unhappy married life informed my mother's choice to alter our family portrait and to frame it, excluding the person who was once her husband. For her, this act of erasure through an alteration of the original photograph by editing my father out 'legitimises the separation and

[32] Kracauer, Siegfried. 1995. *The Mass Ornament: Weimar Essays*. trans. Thomas Y. Levin. Cambridge, MA: Harvard University Press. pp. 48–51.

[33] Berger, J. and G. Dyer. 2013. *Understanding a Photograph*. Penguin Modern Classics edition. London: Penguin Books. p. 20.

even validates it permanently'. Reshaping family photos is as important as preparing an album, as it highlights the role of family members and intra-family dynamics in the construction of personal memories. This act of cutting away her husband from our family photo is not only for the purpose of erasing his visibility from our daily lives, but 'to construct a new memory' of a happy family of three—my mother, my brother and myself.[34]

The photograph in Figure 7 was taken at a local photo studio after my mother become a single parent and an independent woman with her own sense of identity. While she still carries the *sindur*, a vermillion powder applied on the forehead to mark her married status, this photograph marks my mother's corporeal assertion of a sense of liberation. She was no longer bound by an abusive marriage and was earning her own living working as a housemaid. On the occasion of Rakshabandhan,[35] she dressed up in her best and went to a local photo studio to get herself photographed (Figure 7). The photographer liked my mother's photo so much that he asked her if he can display the photo in his shop. My mother asked my uncle (her younger brother) as the studio was located near his residential place, but he disagreed and told her it was an inappropriate thing for women to do. He said it would reflect badly on their family, especially after her recent separation from my father.

This was not the first photographic portrait that my mother had commissioned in a studio on her own. But it was the first print that she possessed. Talking about getting photographed in a studio as a young woman, my mother recollected the following:

> Before my marriage, I, along with my few female friends had decided to get a group photo clicked. We were curious to see how we would look in a photo. So we walked a really long distance to Dhebewadi.[36] Back then, each copy would cost ten rupees, and that was too expensive. I used to manage my household on a rupee or two in a week; ten rupees was an amount we never even saw at once. So for me, it was not possible to get my own copy of the photo. So my friend, who had money to pay for one copy, asked me to join her for a photo and got a copy for herself. But I always wanted to have my own photos. I used to look good; people also used to tell me so. But I don't have photos to remember my younger self. You can do that now.[37]

---

[34] Erkonan, 'Photography and the Construction of Family and Memory'. p. 270.

[35] Rakshabandhan, a Hindu festival celebrating the brother-sister relationship during which the sister ties a *rakhi* (a sacred thread) around her brother's wrist, who in turn promises to protect her and gives her gifts. The photo in Figure 7 was taken when my mother visited her brother on this occasion at his home in Navi Mumbai (a planned city near Mumbai) in 2006.

[36] Dhebewadi is a town in the Satara district of Maharashtra. It used to host the weekly market for the entire region. It was the only marketplace for villages as far as 30–40 kilometers away. My mother's home was 37 kilometres from the town. People used to walk to and from the town, as modes of transport were scarce and expensive. People in general did not have money to spend. Only things that could not be produced or sourced locally, like salt and tea leaves, were purchased using cash payment.

[37] Interview with Radhika Salunkhe, Mumbai, 2021.

Conclusion

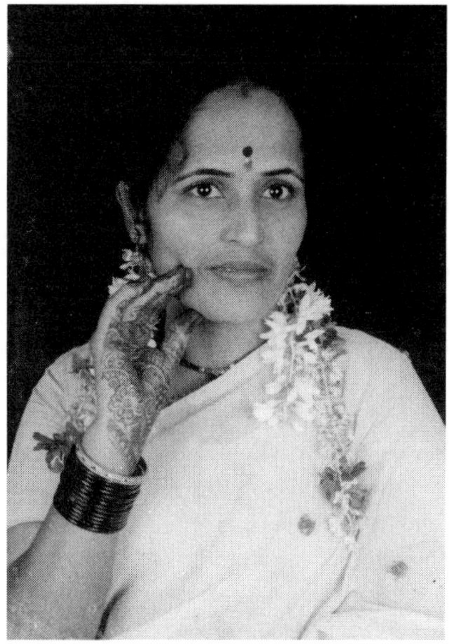

Figure 7. Radhika Salunkhe, studio portrait of the author's mother made in a neighbourhood photo studio. Navi Mumbai, 2006.

My mother loves the concept of photography. It is evident from her attempts to get important moments from her children's lives photographed, to collect and preserve them by getting them framed and displaying them on the walls of our home. Reflecting on her personal photo-archive, this essay meditated on questions of the survival and absence of conventional photo albums in my family. While searching for reasons for not having a family album, I discovered that loose photo prints play an important role in my family's memories. They may not look like a conventional album, but my mother's stories suture these loose photographs into a coherent curated album of family memories and connect the microhistories of my family with historical processes in modern India. The surviving photographic images of my family have provided important evidence of developments in suburban low income communities through the late 1990s and the 2000s. They provide testimony to gender discrimination, as seen in the case of my mother as a girl child born into a poor rural Maharashtrian family, forced into an abusive and exploitative marriage that ended in an unfair separation. All these traumas and social injustices have categorically gone undetected by any legal prosecution or statist documentation. The small tin box that now holds photographic images of my family, the photos that were a part of public documentation but now play an important role in my family's attempt to trace its origin, and the altered and framed family portrait on my wall comprise the photographic archives representing the politics of patriarchal social systems that have produced them. My mother's inability to regain access to a large number of photographs that she had selectively ordered, framed and displayed in our ancestral village home, and the fact that only a few of the images from our family's past were selectively preserved, highlights the paradoxical ability of images to represent what is absent by virtue of their own sparseness. Therefore, while comprehending what a family album really is, one needs to consider not only the images that are preserved in the folios of a complete album, but also a tin box, a wall, any official photographic documentation, their usage, and even a memory of lost photographs—their surviving narration and their absence being as important as the thriving images that make a family album.

References

Appadurai, Arjun. 1997. 'The Colonial Backdrop'. *Comparative Technology Transfer and Society*. 24. pp. 4–7 (Print).

Arnheim, Rudolf. 2009. *Art and Visual Perception: A Psychology of the Creative Eye; The New Version*. Berkeley, California: University of California Press.

Barthes, Roland. 2006. *Camera Lucida: Reflections on Photography*. Translated by Richard Howard. 26th edition. New York: Hill and Wang.

Batchen, Geoffrey and Rijksmuseum Vincent van Gogh. eds. 2004. *Forget Me Not: Photography & Remembrance*. First edition. Amsterdam: Van Gogh Museum.

Bate, David. 2009. *Photography: The Key Concepts*. Oxford: Berg.

———. 23 August 2010. 'The Memory of Photography'. *Photographies*. 3:2. pp. 243–57. Online. Accessed 3 June 2022. doi.org/10.1080/17540763.2010.499609.

Berger, J. and G. Dyer. 2013. *Understanding a Photograph.* Penguin Modern Classics. Penguin Books Limited.

Berger, J. and Jean Mohr. eds. 1982. *Another Way of Telling*. New York: Pantheon Books.

Chowdhury, Indira. 2014. 'Speaking of the Past: Perspectives on Oral History'. *Economic and Political Weekly*. 49:30. pp. 39–42. Online. Accessed 3 June 2022. www.jstor.org/stable/24479737.

Enwezor, Okwui. 2008. 'Archive Fever: Photography between History and the Monument'. *Archive Fever: Uses of the Document in Contemporary Art*. 1. pp. 11–51. Online. Accessed 3 June 2022. sites.duke.edu/vms565s_01_f2014/files/2014/08/enwezor2008.pdf.

Erkonan, Sahika. 2016. 'Photography and the Construction of Family and Memory'. *Politics, Civil Society and Participation. Media and Communications in a Transforming Environment*. ed. Kramp, L. Nico Carpentier, Andreas Hepp, Richard Kilborn, Risto Kunelius, Hannu Nieminen, Tobias Olsson, Pille Pruulmann-Vengerfeldt, Ilija Trivundza, and Simone Tosoni. Edition lumière. pp. 257–72.

Foucault, Michel. 2002. *Archaeology of Knowledge*. Translated by A.M. Sheridan Smith. Routledge Classics. London and New York: Routledge.

Guha, Ranajit and Partha Chatterjee. eds. 2002. *The Small Voice of History: Collected Essays*. Delhi: Permanent Black.

Hall, Stuart. 2021. 'Five Reconstruction Work: Images of Post-War Black Settlement'. *Writings on Media: History of the Present*. ed. Charlotte Brunsdon. Duke University Press. pp. 78–94. Online. Accessed 3 June 2022. doi.org/10.1515/9781478022015-007.

Hirsch, Marianne. 1992. 'Family Pictures: Maus, Mourning, and Post-Memory'. *Discourse*. 15:2. pp. 3–29. Online. Accessed 3 June 2022. www.jstor.org/stable/41389264.

Ketelaar, Eric. 1 June 2001. 'Tacit Narratives: The Meanings of Archives'. *Archival Science*. 1:2. pp. 131–41. Online. Accessed 3 June 2022. doi.org/10.1007/BF02435644.

Knauss, Stefanie. 22 January 2020. 'Religion and Film: Representation, Experience, Meaning'. *Brill Research Perspectives in Theology*. 4:1. pp. 1–103. Online. Accessed 3 June 2022. doi.org/10.1163/24683493-12340009.

Kracauer, Siegfried. 1995. *The Mass Ornament: Weimar Essays*. Translated by Thomas Y. Levin. Cambridge, MA.: Harvard University Press.

Kuhn, Annette. 2002. *Family Secrets: Acts of Memory and Imagination*. Verso Books.

———. 1 December 2007. 'Photography and Cultural Memory: A Methodological Exploration'. *Visual Studies*. 22:3. pp. 283–92. Online. Accessed 3 June 2022. doi.org/10.1080/14725860701657175.

Lutgendorf, Philip A. 2002. 'A Superhit Goddess/A Made-to-Satisfaction Goddess: *Jai Santoshi Maa* Revisited'. *Manushi*. 131. pp. 10–16, 24–37. Online. Accessed 3 June 2022. www.manushi.in/culture--faith-traditions/a-superhit-goddess-jai-santoshi-maa-and-caste-hierarchy-in-indian-filmspart-one.

Pinney, Christopher. 1997. *Camera Indica: The Social Life of Indian Photographs*. London: Reaktion Books.

———. 2008. *The Coming of Photography in India*. Panizzi Lectures. British Library.

———. 1992. 'The Iconology of Hindu Oleographs: Linear and Mythic Narrative in Popular Indian Art'. *RES: Anthropology and Aesthetics*. 22. pp. 33–61. Online. Accessed 3 June 2022. doi.org/10.1086/RESv22n1ms20166853.

Raczymow, Henri and Alan Astro. 1994. 'Memory Shot Through With Holes'. *Yale French Studies*. 85. pp. 98–105. Online. Accessed 3 June 2022. doi.org/10.2307/2930067.

Roychoudhuri, Ranu. 2015. 'The Public Lives of Photographs: Visual Convention and Social Change in Twentieth-century India'. Unpublished PhD Dissertation, The University of Chicago. Online. Accessed 3 June 2022. doi.org/10.6082/M1T151V4.

Sekula, Allan. 2019. 'Reading an Archive: Photography between Labour and Capital'. *The Photography Reader*. ed. Liz Wells. Second Edition. pp. 243–52. London and New York: Routledge.

'SPARC – Society for The Promotion of Area Resource Centers'. Online. Accessed 3 June 2022. www.sparcindia.org/.

Tagg, John. 1988. *The Burden of Representation Essays on Photographies and Histories*. New York: Palgrave Macmillan.

Wells, Liz. ed. 2011. *Photography: A Critical Introduction*. Fourth edition. Taylor & Francis

The Words We Wrote in Other Years[1]

My mother in her likeness, imaged

Annalisa Mansukhani

My earliest memory of myself is from when I was two or three years of age, standing in the living room of a house we lived in for a while. The room was small, sunlit, with a mosaic floor that was cold beneath my socked feet. I remember the feeling of my mother's presence, her body silhouetted against the sunlight, her shoulder-length hair, her clothes dull pink and paisley-printed, her feet firm on the ground.

Somewhere, against the sunlight, she turned and her words were lost to me forever.

This memory in itself is centred around a peach held in my hands at the time. I remember its soft downy fuzz, dimpled by the heat of my palm; I remember my eyelids shutting against the light. Whenever I think of that memory and that day, I watch myself release the peach into a small stainless steel bowl on a square wooden table—again and again and again. Like a setting sun of my own, the horizon bending.

Whenever I think of this memory, I watch my child-self stand by the square wooden table—one that would remain with us for years after—my child-arm holding the bowl with the dimpled peach, child-ears listening to, and for, my mother.

In 2017, my mother and I moved out of the house we shared with my father in a violent uprooting of our domestic lives. While moving out, we took more than we left behind; at least that is what we convinced ourselves was true. I had lived two decades in Delhi by 2016, and up until then, the multiple transitions made between houses was a way of life. Each move meant carving out a familiar space over and over again. Each move was always wishful; a hopefulness directed at a desire to finally settle our lives and our aspirations as a family. However, 2017 disproved that for me, to the point that I would personally shift across three cities and four houses with a heavy accumulation of sentiment across a variety of spaces.

This memory-image of myself has come back to me in every new living

[1] K. Le Guin, Ursula. 2018. 'Leaves'. *So Far So Good: Poems 2014-2018.* Copper Canyon Press. The title is inspired by a line in the poem, 'Leaves': 'Might as well say I am the words she read or the words I wrote in other years / flicker of shade and sunlight as the wind moves through the leaves.'

room I have unpacked in. It is a slow-growing image; a blurry conjuring that seems like the last, desperate reverberations of a dying echo. Outstretched hands, a moment in time, very vaguely frozen in the sickly warm sunlight of what was probably a fading Delhi winter giving way to spring.

It is a routine I have internalised—the memory-image and the act of moving—bequeathed upon myself, taught, retained, remembered fiercely in a very potent, possessive way. The creak of old cardboard, the weight of memory. The ear-splitting shriek of plastic tape, residue that sticks to wood and skin alike. Unrelenting, merciless in the way it reminds you of change. Each time it would return, this memory would disappear for a while, and I would be left with a dull ache as though I were failing to grasp at something without knowing what it was. However, the memory—and all the times it has rebuilt itself in my head—has always been about the anticipation of space. Familiar space. Of to-be-familiar space.

In all of this charting and moving, there was always something that moved with us: our family photographs. A disordered collection of images, a significant portion of which were not in albums; packed in resealable plastic bags, stored and transported hastily, a portability of association that travelled with us, easily grabbed and placed into various cardboard boxes or carried in person to a new house. Within this expansive archive of our family, the one set of photographs that found their way into neat albums were photographs of my childhood that had been taken by both my parents. Other photographs that form part of this family archive include pictures of both sets of my grandparents, photographs from my mother's childhood, images of her family in Kerala, as well as photographs of her life across several cities in India. A tiny fraction of this collection are photos of my father and his life. There were photographs of him in an album my mother curated for them in the early years of their courtship; there were photographs of him from my childhood, and there were some images that I had personally taken, later, with our family camera. My associations with this larger, chaotic archive of photographs were predominantly and primarily linked with images of my mother and her family. These bonds—with the images and the people in them—strengthened over the years as I spent more time in Kerala and with the fact that as I grew older, my relationship with my father grew more and more estranged.

After 2017, all the photographs fell silent. The prefix of 'family' was an uneasy one to attribute to them, and I relegated any thought of engaging with them to the back of my mind. The suffocations of the pandemic in 2020 reminded me of their presence again. Plastic can definitely sustain the tangibility of memories, and the photographs were still intact, sealed inside those resealable bags. They were still disordered, they were still primarily of my mother, and that is how they would remain. My time was spent sorting through these photographs, buying translucent storage boxes for them and reading up on the painstaking process of digitisation, also included thinking of the ways in which I could place them in structured relationships with each other—and to myself—and also decide on categorisation. Choosing to categorise them in a manner that would centralise visuals of my mother, I decided to segregate them on the basis of my mother's relationships with the people in the photographs, both filial and otherwise. This explains why I now have yellow envelopes of photographs titled 'Appapa and Ammama' (one of the many Malayalam colloquialisms for grandparents), 'Maa & her Schools', 'Maa & Family', and the most important envelope of them all: 'Maa, Solo'.

Ritualisms or ritual practices are a key component of how we develop associations with the human countenance within portraiture across mediums. 'Ritual' could mean the things we do to remember the imaged, the enactments we repeat each time to further contextualise our remembrance of them, and to summon Walter Benjamin here, despite photography's reproducibility and its espousal of exhibition value, it is the cult of remembrance that drives home the singularity of the value we ascribe to a photograph of a human face.[2] Thinking about the dynamic that comes into play when we are faced with the camera, the solitariness of the subject and the fantasy of the self that emerges, the imaginative freedoms we allow ourselves in that space of making are truly fascinating. Pairing this curiosity around the rituals that subsist within and sustain photographic portraiture, with my deep desire to read and analyse the ordered dimensionality of family photography, this essay follows what it means to read narratives around portraits and presences that intervene, disrupt and completely overturn the imposed structural normativity of family albums that determinedly convey an alleged narrative of coherence.

Family photography is a performance of the ideal of familial togetherness. This ideal is portrayed in the way family photographs are composed, and it persists in their assimilation, categorisation, preservation and also in the way these images 'gather' to represent the cohesive family unit.[3] Grief and trauma are incoherent; both are cyclical in their onslaught, and they never subscribe to the linearity we wish they would. The grief of losing the presence of a parent entails acknowledging not just their absence in your life but a more disturbingly inconsolable irretrievability. My associations with my family photographs after the rupture in 2017 have been situated around a sense-making, a dialoguing with—sometimes a denial of—grief and the inescapability of trauma that stays long after; a residual remnant indexing the preexisting disorder of my family photographs against the order I wish they had.

The questions we ask of family photographs are always intensely personal.[4] This essay thinks of the photograph as raw material—malleable, fallible and

---

[2] W. Jennings, Michael, Brigid Doherty and Thomas Y. Levin. 2008. *Walter Benjamin: The Work Of Art In The Age Of Its Technological Reproducibility and Other Writings On Media.* Cambridge, MA: The Belknap Press of Harvard University Press.

[3] Rose, Gillian. 2010. *Doing Family Photography: The Domestic, The Public and The Politics Of Sentiment.* England: Ashgate Publishing Limited. p. 45.

[4] Hirsch, Julia. 1981. *Family Photographs: Content, Meaning And Effect.* New York: Oxford University Press.

verbose—an attribute that allows me to frame them almost as palimpsests, with the capacity to both rewrite and be rewritten, evoking and indulging vulnerabilities that otherwise go unarticulated in the coherence that families like to record, remember, and be remembered. For this essay, I have chosen to write alongside portraits of my mother that include single, separate, still photographic portraits of hers from various time periods in her life that she reclaimed, salvaged—quite literally, stole—from the houses and albums of other people. The photographs I choose to rewrite also include photographs of my mother that ended up in two albums—one, as I mentioned, my mother made for my father, and the other that my father made for her—that are products of acts of love and acts of remembering, annotated not just with what they both had to say to and about each other but also, according to me, inscribed with the possibility of an overwriting in the present moment.

I chose to situate my readings of these photographs within and in conversation with the frameworks and paradigms put forth by Marianne Hirsch and Gillian Rose in their seminal works on family photographs. As an attempt to record my sit-down with the photographs I exhumed from my family archive, this essay unfolds alongside Hirsch's engagement with what she calls, 'the structure of looking',[5] a system of exchange between the self and the familial subject that takes place, outlining how the self comes to be constructed in relation to what it encounters as the familial. Her larger argument in *Family Frames: Photography, Narrative and Postmemory* sites the indexical nature of the family photograph as written by Roland Barthes, in a realm that expands upon its subjectivity as material trace.[6] For this essay, it was important for me to find a way to speak about the photographs of my mother, taking cognisance of how idealistic imaginations of family and family photographs often rely on inherited cultural significances, and to be able to break away from these. Hirsch's work brings the coded conventions of family photos into contexts, vocabularies and contestations that resist their ideological power, especially through her rigorous 'theoretical, critical and autobiographical' registers.[7]

With Gillian Rose in *Doing Family Photography: The Domestic, The Public And The Politics Of Sentiment*, 'doing' became a verb, word and sentiment I began exploring very closely, finding intersections with her work on women and their roles in family photography, and my own attempts to subvert the ideal of togetherness that permeates the same. Rose's field research brings her interviews with women, particularly mothers, into her theoretical underpinnings around family photos, seeking to understand what it means to 'do' family photography. In looking at how she construes such a 'doing', extending beyond the limitations of the action itself and into subliminal examinations of the spatio-temporality

[5] Hirsch, Marianne. 1997. *Family Frames: Photography, Narrative And Postmemory.* Cambridge, MA: Harvard University Press. p. 9.

[6] Ibid. p. 6.

[7] Ibid. pp. 10–15.

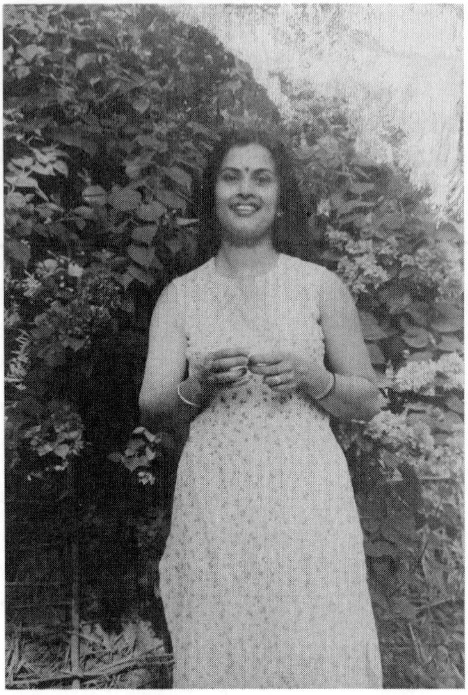

Figure 1. This was me on my winter break from Mussoorie. I used to travel to Delhi by bus, and then take the train to Kochi from New Delhi Railway Station. Winter break was two-and-a-half months long, and I really looked forward to it. Njarackal, 1985.

of familial togetherness, it was important for my readings to parley with how the critical complexity of domestic space remains an entanglement, rather than an irrefutability.[8]

The entire set of images—albums included—is a range of photographs taken between 1982 and 1990, spanning the cities of Mussoorie, Hyderabad, Kochi and Delhi. My readings of these photographs are primarily about how the inheritance of memory around a parental past can lead to erasures in the present; erasures that demand a necessary rescripting in order to negotiate with the cyclicality of trauma and grief. Upheaval that often goes undocumented, unaddressed and wordlessly put aside. The wordlessness that tends to characterise filiality, in particular, has been combatted here through embedded points of encounter and departure that this set of photographs permits me, as they stitch together a significant time in my mother's early adulthood: her late-twenties, on the precipice of marriage and immediately after. There are a variety of claims to authorship around single photographic portraits in this set of images, which further made me think about how intention is often an attempted finality that doesn't always make it through other readings and ascriptions. Afterlives can be disruptive, and by moving beyond the limitations of dictated intention and authorship around these photographs, into a freer, more haptic and sensorial assimilation of feeling as affective response, I have written this essay as an act of rewriting and overwriting, alongside my own reclamatory associations of what are now personal histories shared between my mother and me.

Choosing to engage with family photographs does not mean I have abandoned the politics of the medium in my analysis of family photography. The domestic is deeply political, especially with regard to the performance of gender within its milieu as well as how labour-intensive the making,

[8] Rose. 2010. *Doing Family Photography.* p. 49.

documenting, and archiving of family life is, in the routines and circuits it establishes and expects.[9]

The possesiveness that we perform towards family photographs, engenders an attachment to the weight we feel these photographs hold. A gravitational yearning that is choreographed, narrativised or dismissed entirely, in the name of family. As raw material being responded to via emotional registers, I have been able to read these photographs as objects of memory that are in the process of being redefined in their objecthood. This has allowed me to activate the photograph's talismanic, commemorative, violent, unforgiving and evidentiary qualities; where my act(s) of (re/over)writing have further led me to silhouette my relationship with my mother and her memories—shared with me over my two and a half decades with her—against a landscape of loss, love and the silences of familial trauma.

Familial subjectivity is relational, and within the space of the family and its representations, we are both self and other-ed; we are both subjected and objectified.[10] This essay considers my personal endeavour to organise and preserve photographs of my mother as an act of identity-making, rooted in developing its own conceptualisation of familiality. Marianne Hirsch's tact and sensitivity in speaking of the social constructedness of the family has proved immensely useful in my readings of these photographs.[11] Hirsch identifies the family as a social construct that has invisible structuring elements, wherein its visuality is determined by the 'familial gaze'. She introduces us to the tussle between the gaze and the 'familial look', where the former is myth-making—constructed to present the institution of family as cohesive and coherent—and the latter is contingent, mutual and reversible.[12] Framing the process of familiality as one that is created through the exchange of 'looks', Hirsch believes that any act of portraiture, especially of and within the space of the family, reveals the imaged self as a relational entity—bound to the additions, editions and extensions of selfhood as it emerges. If read in similar light, a portrait of a mother—my mother, in this case—would always include certain contradictions that present her as so much more than just her image. My mother and her likenesses are built out of these familial oppositions; she is imaged alongside that which both buttresses her selfhood and that which reminds her constantly of its demise. In its constitution, this makes the (self-) portrait an image that is both autobiographical and impersonal, fragmented and whole, opaque and timeless.

What does it mean to read a single, still portrait over a refrain of encounters? What does an established familiarity with the photographed subject and her subjectivity permit me? Reading isolated images becomes a work of over-reading,

---

[9] Ibid. p. 32

[10] Hirsch. 1997. *Family Frames.* p. 9.

[11] Ibid.

[12] Ibid.

conditioned by our own familial relationships with them. In accepting an image as familial, we extend a readerly or spectatorial look, an *affiliation* through which we are 'sutured' into the image, absorbing it into our own narratives of belonging.[13]

Remembrance and sentiment as affective engagements chart some of many encounters with the photograph, and much like the oscillations of the memorial, the photograph, too, expands and contracts in relation to the frame of its materiality. This essay is a mode of remembering my mother as she lives alongside my collected memories of her. In following through with that line of thought, I am urged to think of the implications of the kinds of processes of archiving in such an endeavour. Are all archival processes constituted with such a capacity, with the room to overwrite? What does it mean to locate a family archive in an intergenerational space of remembrance?

In *Doing Family Photography*, Gillian Rose interviews women with young children about their family photographs. Thinking about family photography as a social practice, as 'something that people do', Rose centralises not just the dating, storing, displaying and circulating of these photographs but also the act of looking, in her definition of 'doing' family photography.[14] Looking is routine, and the mothers that Rose interviews hint at a subliminal sentimentality that characterises their subjective relationships with their family photographs. This subjectivity keeps the images rooted in their daily lives, it keeps them present and alive. In their day-to-day relationships with these images, the photographs enact an integration of sorts within the familial spaces that they inhabit. Immediate and extended, the ideal of the family is bound together by photography acting as a medium of affiliation; family photographs are sent to members of the family, they are received by several others, they are shared, saved and preserved.[15] The image is a qualifying attribute in itself. It states that you are integral and integrated.

Photography can facilitate the exchange and convergence of familial processes of loss, mourning and celebration, structuring the ways in which we acknowledge each other, our anxieties and our perceptions of ourselves. It can attempt to contain us but still be resisted through acts of intervention that do not fall prey to the wiliness that often prevails in the tussle between truth and fiction that besets the photograph.[16] Hirsch speaks of the photograph as central to a writing of histories—autobiographical and otherwise—and by doing so, she removes reductionist understandings of the photograph as a mere accompaniment to something, including critique. Rose extends the integrative social practice of family photography to also suggests that within the spatio-temporality of the domestic, family photos articulate absence, emptiness and loss as well as togetherness.[17]

---

[13] Ibid. p. 93.

[14] Rose. 2010. *Doing Family Photography*. pp. 35–36.

[15] Ibid.

[16] Hirsch. 1997. *Family Frames*. p. 177.

[17] Rose. 2010. *Doing Family Photography*. p. 46.

The rescripting that I undertake around the photographs of my mother confronts the fallibility of the photograph head-on, locating it within trajectories of meaning that suffuse imaginations of the familial. In conversing with these 'difficult images'[18] through the scope of this essay, I wish to—in some way—also think about resisting the conventional modes of (auto)biography that family photographs champion.[19] Deployed discursively, the photographs of my mother are a starting point for the critical rereading and rewriting of a microhistory of the personal and the familial as it evolves before me and through me.

The sections that follow present two kinds of rewriting. The first is a rewriting alongside single, still portraits of my mother that became part of our collection of family photographs owing to her retrieving them from different spaces and places. I look at the material singularity of these portraits and how it allows me to fabricate an autobiographical act of interpretation and narrativisation. As I rewrite, I think of what it means to encounter them in the present—as reader, viewer, daughter—to listen not just to her anecdotes but also to the photographs themselves and the acts of reclamation that ground them. The second section extends the rewriting process into an act of overwriting the narrative that underlies the two albums exchanged between my parents, harnessing the potency of erasure towards the conjuring of a counter-affiliative posterity of reparation.

Maa, Solo

Which childhood?
The one from which you'll never escape? You,
so slow to know
what you know and don't know.
Still thinking you hear low song
in the wind in the eaves,
story in your breathing,
grief in the heard dove at evening,
and plentitude in the unseen bird
tolling at morning. Still slow to tell
memory from imagination, heaven
from here and now,
hell from here and now,
death from childhood, and both of them
from dreaming.

– Li-Young Lee, 'A Hymn to Childhood'[20]

---

[18] Fahd, Cherine. 2019. 'Difficult Images: A Family's Hidden Photographs Of Grief And Mourning'. *Photography And Culture*. 13:1. pp. 3–27. doi:10.1080/17514517.2019.1571732. p. 12.

[19] Schmahmann, Brenda. 2012. 'Developing Images Of Self: Childhood, Youth And Family Photographs In Works By Three South African Women Artists'. *African Arts*. 45:4. pp. 8–21. doi:10.1162/afar_a_00024. p. 9.

20 Lee, Li-Young. 2008. 'A Hymn To Childhood'. *Behind My Eyes*. W.W. Norton & Company Inc.

Personifications of togetherness and familial integration, family photographs are made in the image of an ideal.[21] However, Gillian Rose writes that though the image allows us to somewhat gauge a superficial filial cohesion at its surface, it is the enactment of relationships, it is what families 'do' with their photographs that define this togetherness that is so desired. In her research that looks at the 'doing' of family photography in families in the UK, Rose returns continually to the haptic engagement that is a crucial part of making these images. Her interviewees date, number, file, print, paste, arrange and store the photographs they take, creating devoted vocabularies that sustain the memories and value ascribed to them.[22] While family photographs form a specific kind of image, representing a particular subject matter, their content becomes only one part of what makes them so special. Of equal or more importance is what is done with them—actions, meanings, values, ascriptions—and how these specificities of association become practices of engaging with the photographs.[23] Challenging literature that criticises family photographs as being overtly banal, repetitive, conventional and predictable, Rose urges her readers to look at how the sentimentality of family photographs can become a reason to remain curious about their role and function in our lives instead of outrightly dismissing them.[24] She highlights the importance of focussing on the social practices in which family photographs are embedded, moving beyond readings that limit themselves to interacting only with subject matters of the photographs.

The genesis/birth of the yellow envelope titled 'Maa, Solo' was, first and foremost, an act of redefinition. Rejecting what would have been the more obvious choice of aligning our family photographs in an order that would ensure a placid narrative of coherence and contentment around celebration and ceremony, I chose to overhaul this classification. Focussing it instead around the figure of my mother, this became a negotiation of familiality that not only foregrounded her as the centre, but also streamlined my associations with her as central to this reorientative exercise. The iconicity of the single still photographic portrait of my mother was undeniably exciting; it obstructed the policing process of family albums that often leave out portraits of the individual as disruptive to the ideal of togetherness; to the 'unit' of the family. These portraits taken during her years in Mussoorie (1982–87), her intermittent sojourns back home in Kochi, her life in Hyderabad (1987–93) and her occasional trips to Delhi before she began living in the city in 1994, marked an errant discontinuity where the offensiveness of an unattached woman, her aspirations, her decisive independence in the face of societal silencing were merely expressions of her individuality. Silhouetted against different backgrounds, with poses and stylistic

[21] Rose. 2010. *Doing Family Photography*. p. 41.

[22] Rose, *Doing Family Photography*, 16

[23] Ibid, 14

[24] Ibid, 12.

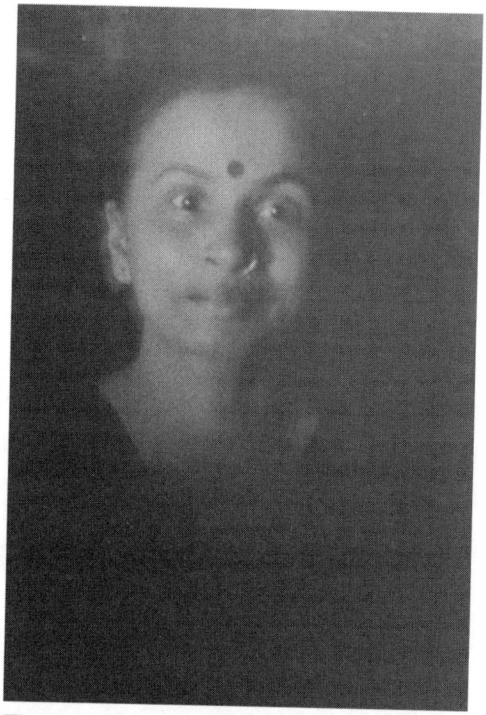

Figure 2. I got my nose pierced in Dehradun right before Joe's (my mother's older brother) wedding. Mussoorie, 1984/85.

choices peculiar to the time, these images were retrieved from various sources by my mother—a sieving of the self, fragmentary as ever. To me, these photographic portraits present a veracity of autonomy, simply in how their 'doing' brought them into my family archive, over years of collating and collecting, slowly corroding any imposition of seriality and indistinguishability.

Thinking of family photographs as 'assemblages' of complex objecthoods and socially instituted practices of representation, Rose reiterates Pierre Bourdieu's work that regards the family photograph as reinforcing the solidity and impermeability of the familial institution itself.[25] With the portraits that constitute 'Maa, Solo', I was drawn to the trajectories of each image, implied by their journeys right down to being part of this folder, this classificatory process of identification and its consequences for their afterlives. In conversations with my mother, she recollected how each photograph was made; some were taken by her siblings, some by colleagues, some were commemorative of an event—nose piercing made the cut—and some were simply a record of a day well-spent in the lap of nature. While leisure is a theme that enters the idealistic expanse of a family album, the audacity of the individual portrait suggests something else. It is emotive, it is passionately undisciplined, spontaneous and does not confine itself to documenting an event; instead, the lens and the frame of the photograph spotlight a version of the self that is imaged, free of the confines of genre-category: a persona, an aspect of personality, the selfishness of whim and fancy. The significance of family photographs extends into the realm of affect, created and enhanced by the tangibilities and tactilities that build our understandings of the material lives of such images.

A number of the critics that Rose references, fail to understand why family photographs hold such sway over people, and this is because they are in some way limited to viewing the image as one-dimensional.[26] What becomes evident

[25] Ibid. pp. 12–13.

[26] Ibid. p. 15.

through Rose's research is the role of the photograph-as-object, located in a circuitous social practice of meaning-making, where affectivity is cultivated and disseminated through the way these photographs are shared—digitally and/or in print—as stimuli cementing deeper familial association.[27] What is fascinating about these portraits of my mother has also to do with the modes of retrieval that add to their redefinitive capacity. Across their many makers and keepers, these photographs of my mother were actively retrieved by her to be brought back to her personal archive of herself. Reading these photographs and writing alongside them has allowed me to view and acknowledge their responsiveness as reclaimed objects of the/her self, as key factors in the process of reifying what the familial space means to me, and the role(s) that my mother performs, engirds and unravels as a fulcrum within it.

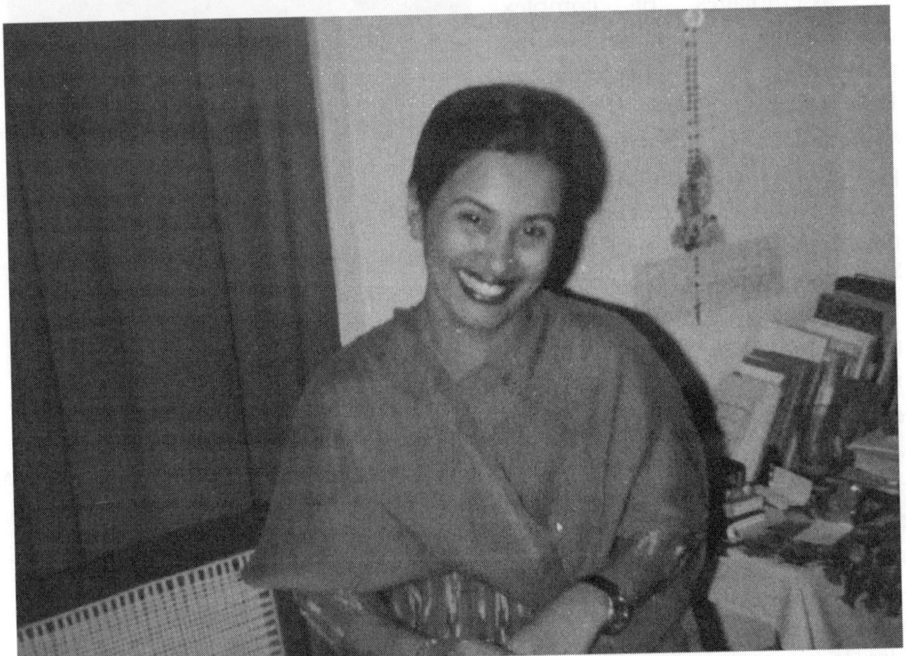

Figure 3. We would get ready in my room and we'd spend a lot of time planning for the weekend. This was taken by Rema (my mother's friend and colleague at Mussoorie Public School), using my camera. Mussoorie, 1984.

Through their visual, material and presentational forms, photographs are encountered by viewers, makers and readers in ways that augment the material qualities of images. Elizabeth Edwards calls these qualities 'affordances'—attributes outlining the possibilities ensconced in certain objects that determine their future use and functionality—and Gillian Rose takes this attribution a step forward. She juxtaposes Edwards' phraseology in conjunction with actions that

[27] Ibid. p. 17.

are taken with and around photographs, building on and extending Edwards' argument. Rose writes that the affordance of a photograph is often enlivened only in part, and it depends on the material existence that the photograph occupies; certain dimensions entail a specific kind of storage and certain paper and print qualities imply longer endurance than other kinds.[28] The affordance of these portraits of my mother is activated by their material singularity. What can be done with them is wholly dependent on their emblematic nature as images, on their presence as single photographs, unserialised and disordered, yet seemingly more in sync with insinuations of the filial than the ordered state of any album. If read as objects 'recording' my mother, these photographs are deeply embedded within self-imaginations that fuel a vulnerable visibility. In becoming visible, my mother in these photographs relinquishes, in some part, the 'objectifying effects' of the familial gaze.[29]

The acts of reclamation that define the photographs within 'Maa, Solo' are further enlivened by the diversity that seeps through their material existence as photographs. If an album is an accumulation, these portraits of my mother are equally assimilatory, even though I do not wish to establish an equivalence with the hegemony of the former. They congeal with her memories, they bleed into one another, they resist the chronological dictation of the time-stamp and remain decidedly fragmented. This fragmentation is purposeful; it complicates their presence within the family album and as fragments, they stitch together so much more than what the confines of an imposed narrativity could ever accentuate. The kinds of subjectivities and relationalities that develop in intimate encounters with such images and what they represent, indicate and instigate a *becoming* that is imminent—a tussle brewing between conventions of the family and the ways in which it

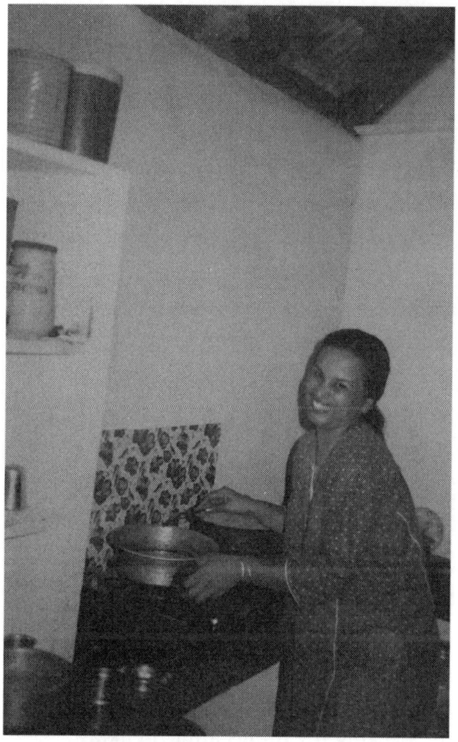

Figure 4. I had come home from Bengaluru, after spending time at Joe's. I spent the day cooking. I loved this kitchen. Njarackal, Vypin Island, Kerala, 1991/92.

[28] Ibid. pp. 17–18.

[29] Hirsch, 1997. *Family Frames*. p. 184.

is eventually remembered.[30] Family photography as a social practice deploys consistent methodologies, gestures, ascriptions and emotions. Affect is crucial to the more emotional, intuitive responses people have to family photography as a practice, and as a creator of objects of memory that sustain long after moments—and in a lot of cases, people—have passed. Affectivity becomes a cardinal register, immersing makers, viewers and keepers alike, stretching across the sanitised distance that is often maintained by the medium of photography.[31]

Marianne Hirsch reads Roland Barthes's description of his mother's death, his mourning as well as his anticipation of his own death, and we find each subject—both Barthes and his mother—being constituted by the relationship they shared with each other. Getting beneath the surface of conventional family photographs, one can make space for the revisions of social roles and positions, and in doing so, *re*read and *re*write the frames through which the ordering narrativisation of the familial gaze is filtered. As a form of resistance, rewriting not only contests the dominion of gaze and the album, but also reveals the manipulative possibilities of photography as a technology of personal familiality.[32] The roles and interactions that we presume and assume within the space of the family are negotiable, and Hirsch's writing on family photographs replaces the regime of the familial 'gaze' with the field of the familial 'look'. To reiterate, the space of looking is a space of mutuality, where the 'looks' exchanged between viewer and the photographed subject are affiliative, identificatory, and recognitive.

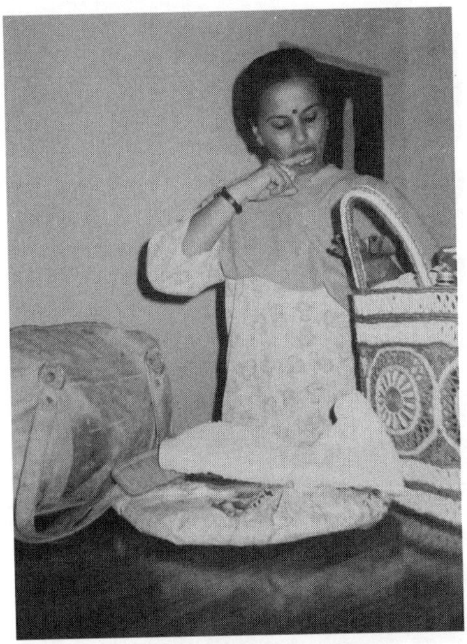

Figure 5. I came home for Jessie's (my mother's younger sister) wedding, travelling from Hyderabad. This was me packing my things after breakfast, probably in the middle of some last minute checks. I remember buying this bag from the Kairali Emporium in Ernakulam. Njarackal, 1990/91.

Reconstitution is possible and inevitable. In the affordances that get activated as a result, each encounter with these portraits of my mother formulates different subjectivities that get attached to the material

[30] Rose. 2010. *Doing Family Photography*. p. 21.

[31] Ibid. p. 19.

[32] Hirsch. 1997. *Family Frames*. p. 194.

existence of these photographs.[33] Here, the single still photographic portrait can be seen as a 'form of suture', traversing the gap between the subject gazing at her own image and the fluidity of the familial look as reparative, palliative and illustrative of more than one self, more than one subjectivity.[34] As such, the cyclicalities that govern family photography extend beyond rituals of composition, posing and display into ever-widening, oft invisibilised orbits of representation that manifest in several realignments of the domestic. By incorporating these photographs of my mother within a reality of imaging the constitutive essence of my family, I adopt an idea of the familial that is fundamentally defined by maternity. This act of adoption overrides spatio-temporal, socio-cultural chasms that separate me from her many selves imaged in these photographic portraits, across non-linear timelines. This act of adoption is also transferential, enabling an inheritance of imagination to be passed down to me. Instrumental in formulating a kind of self-knowledge within the familial space, what we decide to observe as family photographs foster, in turn, a space of identification and representation that in some cases like mine, can further abet its own destabilisation.[35] In its desire to redefine, my

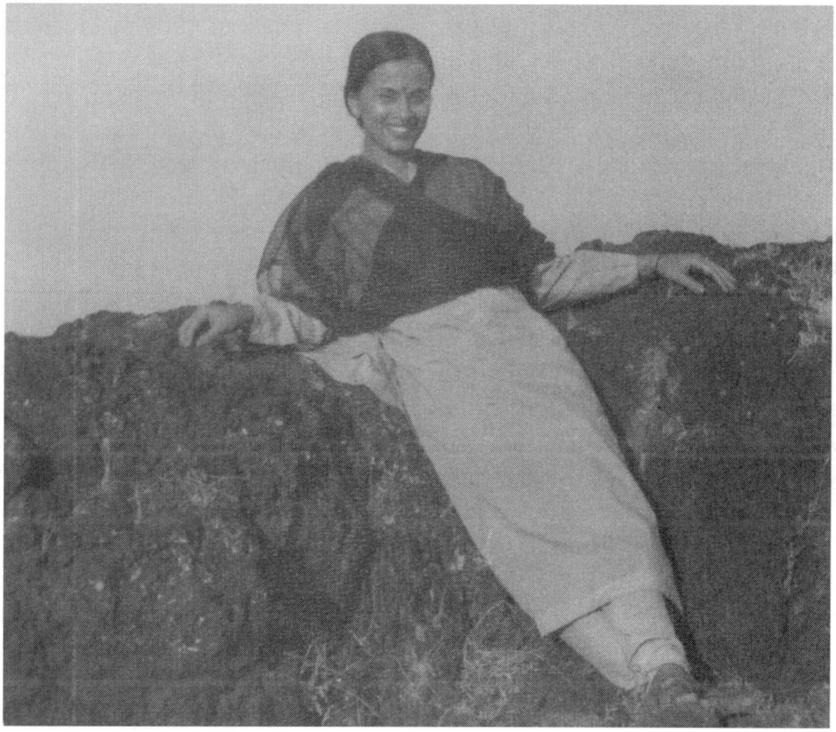

Figure 6. This is one of the photographs with an inscription at the back. The inscription reads, 'Lucky year, 1985.'

[33] Rose. 2010. *Doing Family Photography*. p. 23.
[34] Hirsch, *Family Frames*, 197
[35] Ibid, 83

act of rewriting alongside these portraits of my mother is admittedly a critical fabrication, stemming out of these available photographic fragments of my mother; 'pieces' that acknowledge in turn the splintering implicit in any act of 'piecing' her—and myself—together again.

The Albums

> 'Language is what eases the pain of living with other people, language is what makes the wounds come open again.'
>
> – Anne Carson bot (@carsonbot) on X[36]

> 'What parents leave you / is their lives.'
>
> – Frank Bidart, 'Lament for the Makers'[37]

> 'I always knew that grief was something I could smell. But I didn't know that it's not actually a noun but a verb. That it moves.'
>
> – Victoria Chang, 'OBIT'[38]

> 'Albums are very selective visions of [their] family life.'[39]
>
> – Gillian Rose

There is a photograph of my mother, a portrait taken in 1984 in Mussoorie, with the gentle slope of a hill visible in the background, tall poplars descending, dense shrubbery fading into the greys of the black-and-white image. My mother is smiling in the photograph, head tilted, hair parted, eyes crinkling in the light, her right shoulder bare, her left shoulder covered by the printed cotton of her sari *pallu*. The frame ends a few inches below her collarbone; the landscape looms behind her.

It is a beautiful image, undoubtedly one of my favourites of hers.

As a teenager, I took to writing poetry, enamoured by its free and anarchic form. Surrounded by bookshelves that stocked the Romantics, Modernists and Harlem, as well as more contemporary poets, I grew to appreciate the urgencies of language that broke through in poetic verse. Gradually, I began my own traipsing, finding echoes of familiarity in the works of Li-Young Lee, June Jordan, Wallace Stevens, Rita Dove, Fatimah Asghar, Timothy Liu and Robert Bly, to name just a few, even during my years as a student of art history. As my fixations with the history of photography expanded, so did my poetry reading list. Somewhere, somehow, poetry made sense; it was absorptive and interruptive, a prick in the side of academic vocabularies that threatened to overwhelm. Continuing to read and work with photographs,

[36] The Anne Carson bot (@carsonbot). 19 July 2021. 'I weep, I melt, I grieve'. x.com/carsonbot/status/1417001694718828544.

[37] Bidart, Frank. 2006. 'Lament for the Makers'. Star Dust. New York: Farrar, Straus and Giroux.

[38] Chang, Victoria. November 2019. 'OBIT'. Poetry. www.poetryfoundation.org/poetrymagazine/poems/151141/obit-5d8d0cffc5885.

[39] Rose. 2010. *Doing Family Photography*. p. 13.

I began encountering more and more often the slipperiness common to both image and verse, leading me to realise and acknowledge the mutual enrichment with which each infused the other. I eventually understood my relationship with both poetry and photography as defined by the affective encounters they comprised and incited. Navigating the minefield of family photographs alongside the possibilities residing in creative poetic expression, I noticed the complementarity of affect accentuated by this pairing, particularly as this juxtaposition performed translations of feeling as both linkage and abrasion. To speak of catharsis as a journey, of healing as a process, is to also acknowledge in some part the excess—of feeling—that accompanies us along the way, especially in reading difficult associations with difficult images.[40]

The image of a family that is assembled within an album is an earnest falsification. It is ironic in that the 'truth' it conveys is in fact manufactured; it is an imagination arranged carefully and curiously for the sake of evidence, to show as record that 'this is as it was and shall be forever'. Family albums are storehouses of erasure. Conflicts of death, sorrow, grief, mourning, loss are imperceptible; invisible within their pages, and more often than not, family albums describe and represent the epitome of contentment. Cohesion and coherence twins in the triplet they form with continuity.

Exchanged as gifts in the years between 1984 and 1987, two albums—one, a small black book put together by my father, and the other a plastic semi-accordion fold out curated by my mother—as part of my family photographs are oddities in their own right. As family albums go, they seem out of place amid the rest of my family photographs that comprise grandparents and relatives, celebrations, funerals and my entire childhood, right up until the digital camera exploded onto our family scene in 2008. Devotedly personal dedications, these albums made for increasingly riveting objects in the manner that they archived my parents, as seen through each other's eyes. Sitting down with these albums over the years placed me as a viewer/reader/daughter firmly outside the relationship that they immortalised—an unsettling feeling, characterised by the realisation that you are watching something that has already taken place, unfolding before you all over again—within their sticky plastic, the creaky inner leafing, the inscribed poetry, the memories and most importantly, the associations, preexisting and impending, milling around them.

As accumulations of memory, these albums have rarely been stored apart from each other. In the case of family photographs, it is the objects surrounding them that further substantiate familial connections, and more often than

[40] Zia, Ather. 2019. *Resisting Disappearance: Military Occupation and Women's Activism in Kashmir*. Seattle: University of Washington Press. p. 27. It talks of ethnographic poetry as a moment of surfeit as well as a catharsis of the excesses that ethnographers have to engage with. She speaks of how occupying the role of an ethnographer-poet is similar to holding a wound that is both in your body and in the body of the 'other', creating a doubly layered understanding of pain. Zia's book is also interesting in its incorporation of poetry at the beginning of each chapter, almost as markers of her process(ing) of witnessing Kashmir and its many resistances.

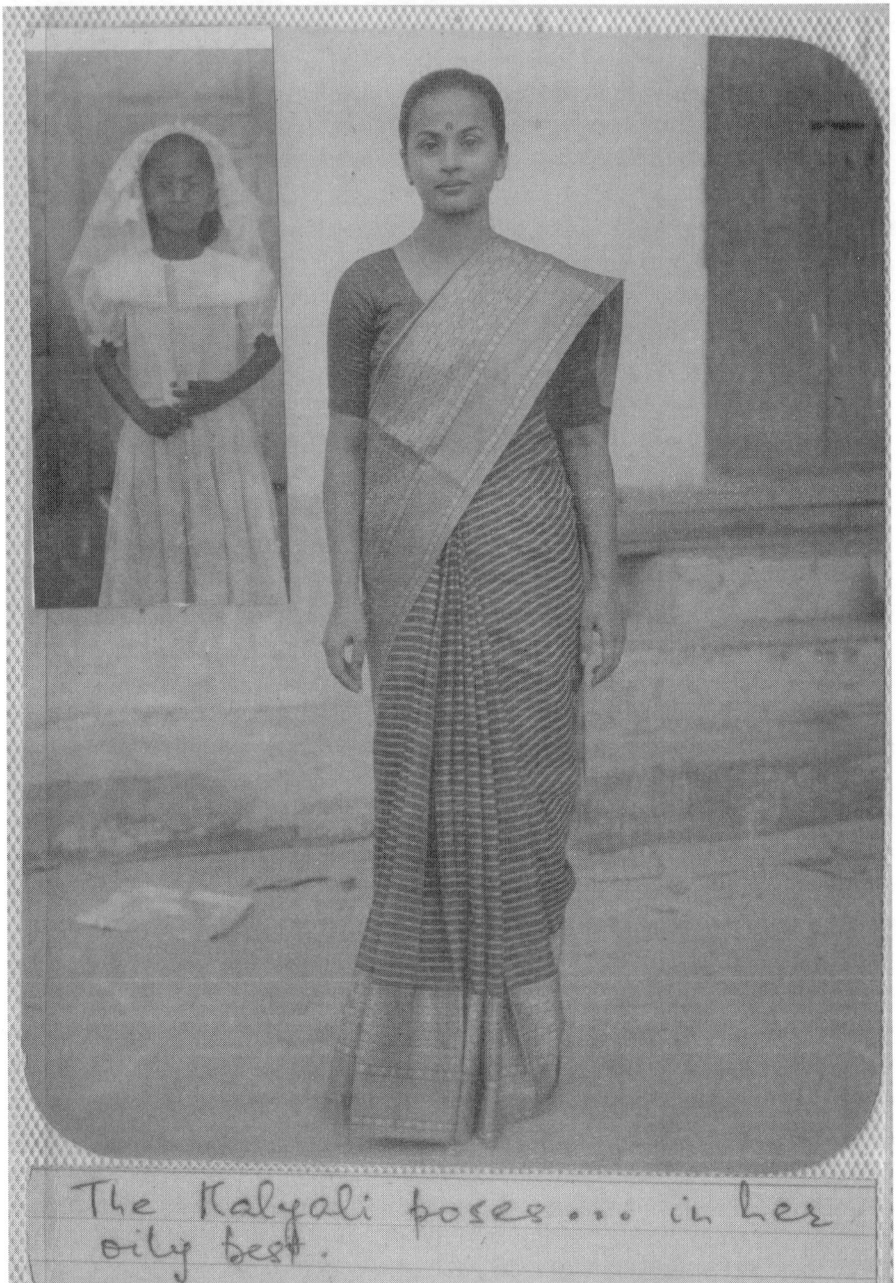

Figure 7. The first page of the album my father put together. The caption reads, "The Malayali poses…in her oily best." The full length formal portrait of my mother is accompanied by a small cut-out of her at her First Holy Communion in 1963, a Catholic ceremony to mark a child or adult's first reception of the Sacrament of the Eucharist.

not, the objects around family photographs are simply other photographs.[41] Proximity becomes a mode of 'gathering' the family and its images, inviting into creation the boundedness of the domestic space and its conventions. The two albums exchanged between my parents consist of black-and-white photographs—some taken by both of them of each other, some taken by other people—single portraits as well as portraits of them as a couple, annotated with captions and scribbles. Across both albums, there are several similarities in the kinds of photographs they contain. Some are identification photographs, some photos have them in formal poses; but a significant portion of them are candid photographs, visibilising the intimate gaze of a personal relationship. There is also the occasional photograph where they are accompanied by another person, and these include friends and colleagues—but also three instances in which they are photographed with a parent. In the album put together by my father, each page has a caption on a small slip of paper separating two photographs of my mother; the photographs, most of them taken by him, portray her against the scenic landscape of Mussoorie, where they first met, but also include glimpses of Dehradun and Rishikesh. Interestingly, in this album he also chose to include photographs of her that she had probably sent to him. I deduce this by identifying what are evidently cut-outs of her taken from photographs where she is pictured with other people, and those that are also present as whole photographs elsewhere within our collection. These fragments of her are fitted into columns of space on certain pages, and I am unsure whether these were afterthoughts or conscious additions during the process of making this album.

The smaller of the two albums was made by my mother, and it contains photographs of both my parents—though my father features more prominently in it—with a slightly more haphazard annotative practice. Though mostly on slips of near-translucent paper, the captions sit next to a few of the photographs, there are also several images that have inscriptions on the back. What stands out to me in this album is my mother's decision to include photographs of herself—more often than not, single still portraits of hers. Deepening my reading of this act, it seems as though a number of these portraits of my mother were taken by my father, and so in the soldering of their relationship that emerges across the pages in this album, my father is sighted and sited even in sole portraits of her. I read the intermittence of these photographs—each kind dispersed across the other, the person of each melding into the other—as an ironic synecdoche, a mutuality sanctified within these pages but far removed from the circumstances without. The captions in both always drew me in each time I saw them; the act of annotating is intensely personal, and in the case of these albums, the captions with their warmth and softness exacerbated the pain of rereading them in the present. Almost agitative, these captions grew to be coloured by the fact that we had long since left the reality they alluded

[41] Rose. 1997. *Doing Family Photography*. p. 43.

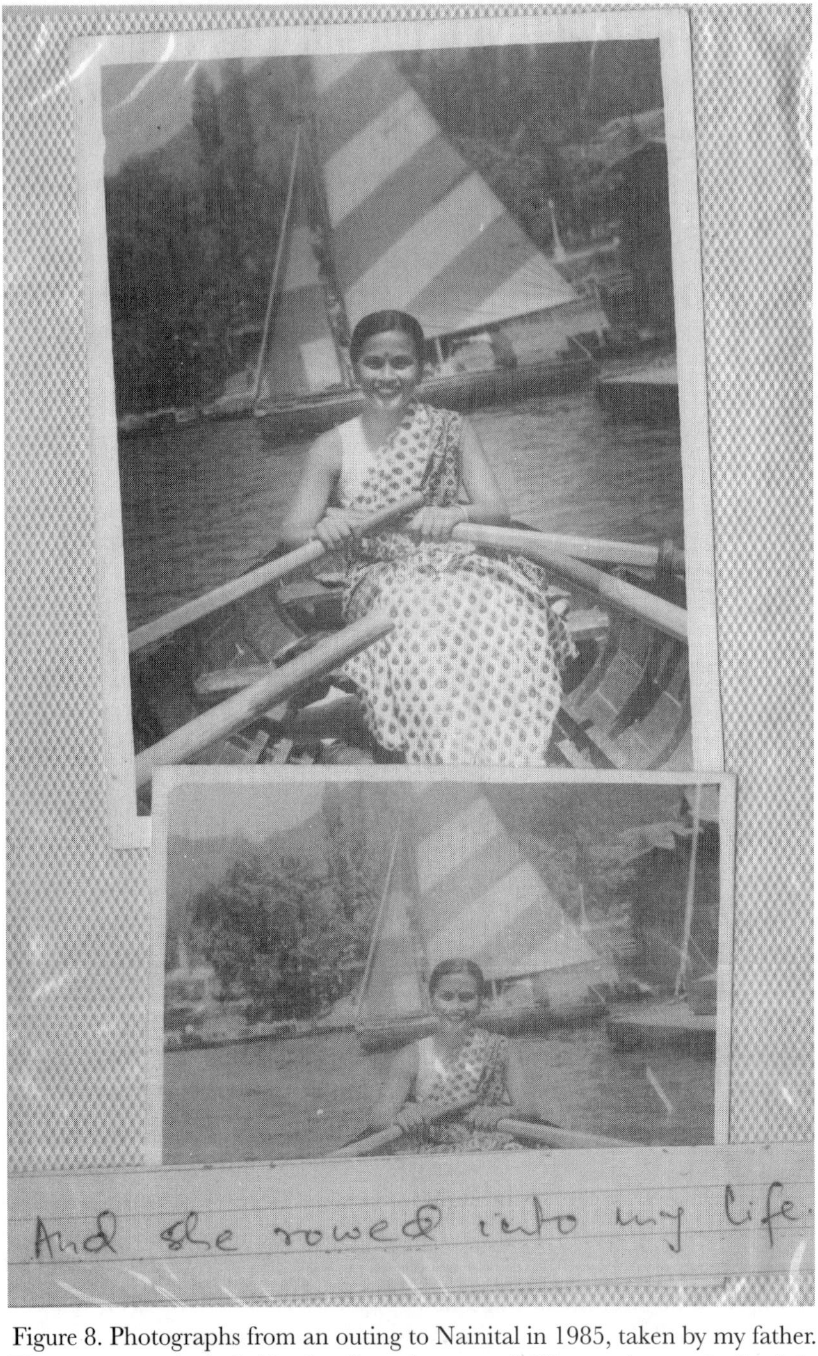

Figure 8. Photographs from an outing to Nainital in 1985, taken by my father. These too, were included in the album he curated. The caption reads, 'And she rowed into my life.'

to, and more often than not, prevented me from viewing these portraits of my mother as part of the family archive I was so intent on (re)creating.

In beginning of the process of re-categorising and digitising our entire collection of photographs, I wondered aloud about the possibilities and potencies residing within acts of erasure. What would it mean to extend my desire to rewrite a history as a drastic reinvention, a more severe contestation to the burdens of the past? What would it mean to *over*write the reality within these albums as a means to rescripting our lives, and more importantly, our memories? Thinking of the disruptiveness of such an exercise alongside the more curative acts of digitisation and preservation became a way of re-inscribing the albums and their space(s) of memory with revisions and interventions, bent on processing in some way the heaviness of grief and rage. Erasure allows the act of overwriting to centralise the albums in providing me points of departure from a painful past towards a resistance staged through manipulation—of photographs and relationships—to interpellate a future past I want to choose.[42] By framing and asserting a redefinitive posterity for myself and for these portraits of my mother, I consciously overwrite and vigilantly rescript what already exists as material record of a family, into a counter-affiliation, centred around and directed solely at my mother.

Countering the swathes of sentiment that cloak these albums, my mapping of erasure through the act of overwriting entails a concerted forgetting, coded through acts of insertion and removal. The act of erasure, of overwriting, exhumes her portrait from the album, and in removing her from its narrative, seeks to relinquish the existing narrative order. Dethroning the desire for manufactured pretence to convey the ideological representation of familiality and its gaze, I choose to supplement her acts of retrieval with my own, taking her—and myself—back from that which is no longer there.

However, I remain wholly aware of the fact that family photographs do not change, only the stories we (re)tell around them, do.[43] With 'new threads in an old weave,' the desire to overwrite functions also as an imaginative exercise, bordering on the delusional in what it reminds me to forget, but also interrogative in the misremembering it orchestrates. For the purpose of this

[42] Hirsch, *Family Frames,* 197. Hirsch references Jamaica Kincaid's first novel, *Annie John,* that is composed of a number of stories originally published in the New Yorker. The book tells the story of the narrator Annie's childhood and adolescence on a Caribbean island that she later leaves for England. The protagonist, Annie, is a reader of the family photographs in her night stand, gradually developing complex confinements and confrontations with the space of the photographs and her relationships to her family. Eventually, Annie 'intervenes' in the photographs, breaking with her past, giving the photos a 'feverish bath' in an attempt to erase and consequently reinscribe herself and her new life. Doing so, Hirsch believes, changes her relationship to her past and in turn to a future that she can actively choose to spell out. In Kincaid's narrative, erasure creates the space for reinvention, an *opening* or 'space-off' that Annie carves out for herself from the grasp of posterity.

[43] J Hirsch, Julia. 1981. *Family Photographs: Content, Meaning And Effect.* New York: Oxford University Press. 5

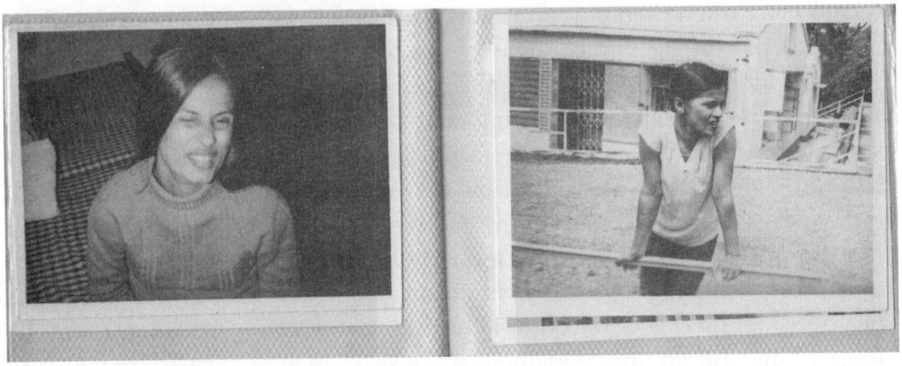

Figure 9. This is a spread from the album my mother curated for my father. Both pages had one photograph each of them, and I placed the two photographs of her over the photographs of him. Rishikesh, 1984.

essay and its exploration, I chose to read the albums with and against the grain they proffer; in part, I disinterred the photographs of my mother from the dirge-like existence of the albums, reading them as images overlapping with other single still photographs of her, inserting them into the sanctum of 'Maa, Solo'. The process and this act were both fuelled by an adamant refusal on my part to accept into the archive the triggering realities impeccably preserved within the albums, painfully contrary to the jagged edges of my present. Foregrounding fragmentation—mirrored in my own reality—my readings of these albums and my active intervention in their material existence are structured around repairing and resisting continuous rupture. The upheaval that marked our lives was in itself a wounding break, and in pushing back against the coercive tendencies that dictate how one is expected to remember the familial, I negate through the counter-affiliative. Negation is political. It is unapologetic; and in refusing to deny the evident cyclicality of grief caused by ruptures in a family, this negation is exercised as building on the foundational role of photographs as keystones in the arch of remembrance and memory-making. Negation is catalysed by anger and the force of mourning an absent present, motivating a reorientation of self-definition and belonging.

What happens when the indexical nature of the image is exactly what allows one to rescript filial affiliation?[44] The social practice of integration that underlies family photography is also what destabilises it, for in its 'doing', family

[44] Rose. 2010. *Doing Family Photography*. p. 38. Rose writes that 'family snaps' picturise members of a family happily at leisure, and they are dated, stored, displayed, looked at and circulated according to the rules of the integrative practice that is family photography. The perceived affordance that makes all that work possible is the indexical nature of the image. It is because the photo is a true record of what was there when the shutter snapped—a physical trace of the bodies made visible, 'a relic of the body of the beloved person'; that the photo is almost impossible to throw away and that it is worth looking at, displaying in one's own home and sending to others. The materiality of the photo allows these activities to happen.

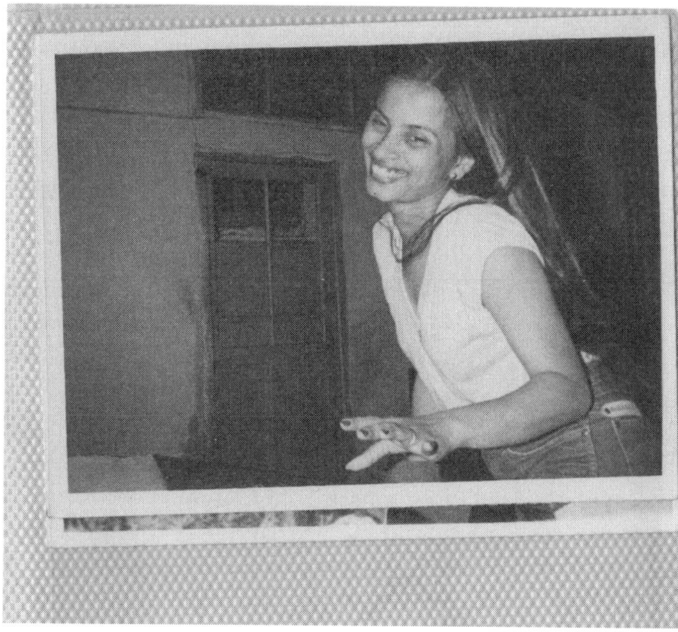

Figure 10. A page from the small fold-out album my mother put together. The page had a picture of each of them, and I placed her photograph veiling his. One can faintly make out an inscription at the back of the photograph on the next page. Rishikesh, 1984.

photography defines the family by acts of inclusion, and by extension, exclusion. Instead of being read as a simplistically unifying practice, family photographs are also divisive in the remembrance they frame. It is the materiality of the photographs that allows this to happen; family photographs are also subjected to intervention; people are 'removed,' 'forgotten' and cast out in different ways, but the photograph persists through all of this as an unsullied object of memory. Considering the facets of erasure and its possibilities at this moment, I am also reminded of its superficiality. Erasure is also a form of mark-making. In fact, it is exactly that. It does not oppose the mark, it scores it even deeper. Wiping a slate clean is violent. A surface can only hide, it can only conceal, it can never truly erase, because that is what surfaces are meant to do.

Marianne Hirsch asks, can words empower us to imagine what is behind the surface of the image?[45] In *Camera Lucida*, Barthes produces his mother's picture through the words he uses to describe it and his reaction to it, creating what W.J.T. Mitchel called an 'imagetext' and what Hirsch calls a 'prose picture'. Words undo the objectification that follows a still photograph, taking it out of stasis and into a liveliness.[46] 'Writing the image' like Barthes and Hirsch catalyses a meditation on the phenomenology of the image but

[45] Hirsch. 1997. *Family Frames*. p. 2.

[46] Ibid. p. 3.

it is in fact, the collaboration between text and image that coalesces to (re) tell loss and longing for both.[47] My act of writing alongside these images of my mother allows me to sight/site them as objects of memory—fluid in their meaning and alive in their inherent affiliations—that respond to my act of rewriting in turn. The reparation that Barthes seeks is performed through his prose pictures, though his writing is central to family and photography. As Hirsch writes, ultimately, it is not the detail of the picture that is the *punctum* for him: it is time itself.[48]

What Hirsch makes available in her writing on family photography is the concept of the meta-photographic text that emerges as a frame of encounter, placing family photographs in narrative contexts, through reproductions and descriptions that take a variety of forms across media. These 'textualities' allow us a route to possibly resisting the conventions of family and family photography, breaking away from monolithic narratives and ways of looking at family photographs.[49] As photographs are often situated between myth-making and lived realities, meta-photographic textuality can assume a self-reflexivity that reshapes the desire to see and be seen in family photography. Taking this a step further, I believe the meta-photographic text can also offer a re-siting of sight, reconvening the domestic to be constituted around those looks that belong with each other, steering the familial as an institution and as a body, towards how I wish my family to be seen and remembered.

The 'clustering' of family photographs also articulates the spatial dispersion of contemporary family life. As families are often scattered, the act of grouping family photographs—extending the discursive argument about proximity and gathering—also reiterates closeness/distance as well as presence/absence. As photographs index a presence as a reminder of absence and distance, the gathering or grouping photographs definitely ameliorates the pain of separation. However, Rose deftly inserts a corollary: in salving absence, they also depict it in the gaps that exist between different photo-frames; in the fractures that may not be visible but are still tactile memories, and also in the dispersion of these photographs across domestic space. Though integrative and assimilatory, the space of the domestic is haunted by the perpetual spectre of disintegration.[50]

There is a photograph of my mother, a portrait taken in her room in Mussoorie. She is facing a long, rectangular mirror, held in place by a wooden frame, and a dresser holding what seem to be perfume bottles and a hairbrush. She grasps her waist-length hair with her left hand, comb in the right, arms bare in a sleeveless checked shirt worn over jeans. To the right of the mirror, towels hang off wall hooks, and a bed is reflected in the mirror,

[47] Ibid. p. 4.

[48] Ibid. p. 3.

[49] Ibid, 8

[50] Rose, *Doing Family Photography*, 49

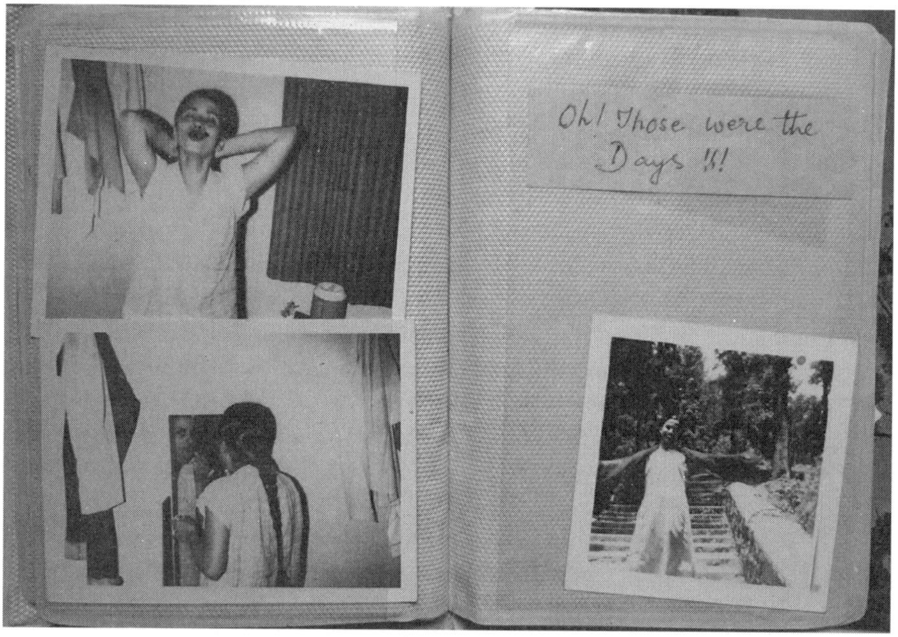

Figure 11. A double spread from the album curated by my mother. It has three photographs of hers, and in place of the fourth photograph, a small slip of paper reads, 'Oh! Those were the Days!!!' [sic]

a pillow visible with soft indentations. Her face is lost in the shadows of the reflection but I can make out her eyes, nose and lips under the teeth of the comb that she aims at her hair. The frame of the photograph slices through her hair before it ends, the dark length of it gleaming in the flash of the camera.

There are two of these photographs on the same page of the album, and they are identical in every way, even in their state of preservation, save for a slight difference in contrast. Mirrored and in multiples, this single album page with the two identical photographs turns my mother and her likeness(es) into objects—in the archive—and subjects of her own making. To live a memory is to re-enact that which is both there and gone, and in reading these photographs of my mother, I find that which adheres me to her.[51]

It is a beautiful image, undoubtedly one of my favourites of hers.

Hidden away on the last page of one of the two albums is a thin, torn piece of parchment paper with tiny slivers of photographic portraits of my mother stuck to it, arranged around the sides. The piece of paper is a fragment, the photographs themselves are fragments, and in the middle of the piece of paper, surrounded by the photographs, the numerical representation of the year '1982' is written in blue ballpoint. A strangely fragile 'object', it rests unaccounted

[51] Mavor, Carol. 2012. *Reading Boyishly.* Durham: Duke University Press. pp.140–143.

for between the last page of the album and its hardbound cover, straddling indecisions of archival category, intended purpose and uncertain afterlives.

In this act of rewriting my mother, I find myself thinking of the origin(al) as a genealogy of emotion—edges blurred, inescapable attachment, fearful sentiment—making the (photographed) self one of many memorised retellings, much like the odd assemblage. Through my readings of them, my mother's images seek and find the words that bring her home, and in them, she writes of summer in the hills, a holy bible of expectation, hope and hopefulness, a wish and wishfulness, tall trees after sunset, the long shadows of love. She writes of belief and faith—unwavering, callously trusting, patient, selfless, warm.

In a conversation around the time I began sifting through these photographs last year, my mother remembered that the reason why the strange assemblage of photographs existed in the first place was because she meant to *make* it as a 'portrait' of her, imaged over the years, to be remembered as such by whoever would receive it.

Her statement put into motion what grew to be an understanding of the familial as an interstice—precarious, awkward, fiercely redefined—and it reminded me of the last two lines of 'Matrilineal Descent,' a poem by feminist poet, journalist, editor and activist Robin Morgan, which read:

'Mother, in ways neither of us can ever understand,
I have come home.'[52]

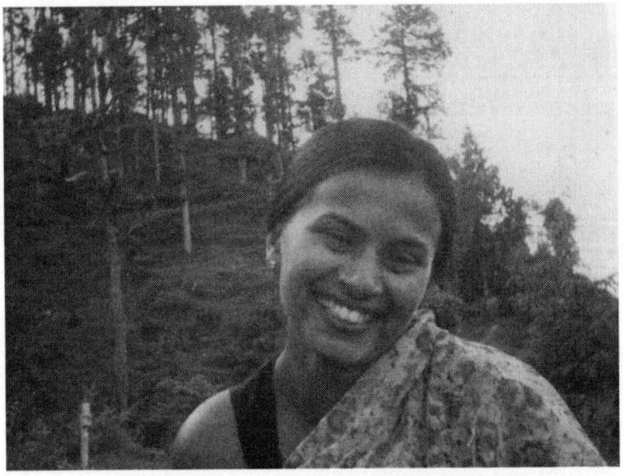

Figure 12. Mussoorie, 1983.

[52] Robin Morgan, "Matrilineal Descent" from Monster. 1972 www.poetryfoundation.org/poems/90823/matrilineal-descent. Accessed July 2021.

From Grief to Reminiscences

Memories of My Mother's Early Travels and Family Life

Jayanti and Diya Dutta

Just as we thought that 2020 was the worst year in our lives and thanked our lucky stars that we had survived the deadly COVID-19 pandemic unscathed, 2021 dawned with its own set of twists, turns and heartbreaks for my family. My mother lost her husband and I, my father in May 2021 due to complications arising from a tumour in the brain. It coincided with the peak of the second wave of COVID-19 in India and Delhi-NCR was particularly badly affected.[1] *The entire health infrastructure collapsed; there were no ambulances to take my father to the hospital, OPDs were shut and no hospital beds* [were] *available for non-COVID-19 patients. The doctors fought valiantly, trying to deal with my father's health condition remotely. But the suffering was great and in the end, my father succumbed on 4 May 2021. So terrible was the situation in Delhi, my mother and I made up the lonesome pair who took my father to the Lodhi Road crematorium, devoid of friends and family who could not join us in his final journey, for fear of contracting the deadly virus.*

All this left us feeling terribly lonely and traumatised—there was so much we couldn't do for him; our helplessness; his pain and trauma; the sheer impossibility of the situation. Never one to succumb to sorrow and one of the strongest women I know, my mother turned her attention to constructive and creative activities to distract herself from her grief. She discovered the joys of writing and started narrating stories of herself and her husband, from their journey as a young couple [when] *they first moved to Chennai (then known as Madras), a few months after their marriage in 1975. Since the twenty-first century, social media has been a space of tremendous democratisation, where one can express one's feelings and creativity. My mother chose to share her reminisces on Facebook. Not only did we discover a writer in our family, but tributes and generous words of encouragement started pouring in from all quarters. At first, we thought that close family and friends were empathising with our situation and our grief. But when my friends and colleagues, totally unknown to my mother, started sharing their appreciation for her writing, we realised that there was more to these stories than mere empathy for our loss. For one, these stories have a simplicity and candour which I think many readers related with. It also told a tale of a common man's life in the 1960s and 70s in India, when the life was modest but endearing. Simple things brought tremendous joy and a great sense of achievement. Just like my parents, many of their friends were also newly married then, and setting up homes in new cities. The security of living with their middle-class*

[1] The official statistics recorded 250,000 deaths from COVID-19 during the second wave, all over India (*TOI*, 14 July 2021). However, experts surmise that many more people died during this time than what was officially quoted (Harsh Mander, *Scroll*, 22 February 2022).

families in familiar surroundings had to be given up, the warmth of their native city [sic] *left behind—the comfort of the known had to be foregone. But new adventures and a new life lay ahead, whose triumphs and tribulations make for interesting narratives about middle-class cosmopolitan life in India.*

Ma's writings have been greatly healing for both herself and me. What we have put together in this essay concerns events which took place much before I was born. Though these stories have been told and retold many times, they helped me discover new facets of my parents' lives. My excitement at reading them was as intense as when I had first heard these stories.

Bengalis and their wanderlust is well-known. My family was no exception. Nevertheless, middle-class families in the 1960s and 70s did not have too many opportunities to travel long distances. They devoured travelogues[2] *and travel stories and travelled the world through their authors' eyes. My mother's stories, as presented here, share the joy and excitement of a teenager stepping out of the confines of her Kolkata home for the first time in 1968, on a long journey to Delhi and beyond. It also attempts to share with the readers the excitement of immense possibilities that she saw laid out before her. Her subsequent travels only added more excitement to her first journey.*

My parents lived modest lives. For a twenty-year-old, a newly married woman's daily life could be quite uneventful when living far away from her home and city. Yet, my mother's indomitable spirit and inquisitiveness took her much farther than what life would have normally allowed. My parents found joy in simple pleasures, such as short holiday trips to places in and around Madras and the adventures they encountered on their journeys. None of these are out-of-the-world, spectacular experiences. On the contrary, they are quite common, relatable and realistic.

Delhi Diaries

Quite a few of my readers requested me to write about when we were posted in Delhi. Before doing that, I wish to share the tales of my first visit to Delhi.

It was most probably October of 1969—which would make me fifteen years old, the ripe time for falling in love—when I fell in love with Delhi. It is an unique time in one's life when you have left childhood behind but are still not a full adult (though we considered ourselves very adult and mature). To me, having lived a very sheltered life in Calcutta, Delhi was like glimpsing the wide open world with all of life's possibilities laid out, as if I was witnessing it from the confines of a closed room with one window open to see it all. It was a brief time when mundane life took a bow and left the stage open for discovering fun, adventure, travel, new places and new ways of life. I knew full well there were years and years more of mundane life ahead of me, once this magical time vanished. But it still managed to leave behind a yearning for a dreamlike life, where all was sunshine, success and happiness. Now that I am in the waning years of my sixties, most of my active life behind me and having achieved very

---

[2] Some popular Bengali travel writings of the time were the Rammaniviksha series by Subodh Chakravarty; books by Syed Mujtaba Ali and Uma Prosadh Mukhopadhyay.

little of the possibilities I had glimpsed or imagined, I realise that it was the time to dream and the rest of my life was the time to wake up! Let me give you a background of how this magical time came to pass.

In the summer of that year, one of my aunts, my mother's elder sister, came to visit Calcutta with her family. Her husband was my Dilip mesho and her children, my two cousins, Dolludidi, eight years older, and Kutush, who was almost the same age as me. They were staying at their aunt's house on Lansdowne Road. We met a few times and the bond that was forged between all of us has endured till now. They most fervently encouraged my mother and me to visit them in Delhi, where my mesho worked at a government office. I had very little opportunity to travel until then, and so did not like the idea of travelling without my father, who was a couch potato and never liked to travel. I still remember that the house where my aunt was staying had one of those grand staircases, and as I was coming down with Dolludidi on our last visit before they left, I accepted her invitation to visit them around Durga Puja. They were uniquely warm and welcoming. The decision itself was very exciting as I had not been on a long train journey before, and now Delhi beckoned with its history and glory, past and present.

At this point, I must introduce to you one more family. My grandmother's cousin, the late Amiya Kumar Basu was an extremely well-known barrister in those days. He was close to my father's age and the two of them were the best and closest of friends. Amiyada's three children—Bubai, Buro and Buri—and I grew up together, considering each other's houses as our second homes. So when they heard that we were going to Delhi, the siblings lamented that though my granduncle made frequent trips to Delhi, they had never been. Eventually, it was decided that they, too, would go on a holiday to Delhi at the same time as us. What could be more exciting or fun! To make it even better, it was decided that my mother, I, Bubai, Buri and their mom (Meenadi to me), would travel together in the Rajdhani Express. This superfast train between Calcutta and Delhi had been recently introduced and elicited great deal of excitement for its air-conditioned chair car—a whole new way to travel by train.

The intervening months passed as usual, busy with the final exams of the school year which were held before the Puja holidays. By then, all arrangements for the trip were complete, including train tickets, our stay at my aunt's, and a visit to my maternal uncle, who was then staying in Chandigarh. The packing was done by my mother, with the usual arguments about what to take or not. Finally, we were onboard the Rajdhani Express, our heavy luggage booked into the luggage van and smaller pieces with us in the compartment. Bubai, Buri and I sat in a row of three adjacent seats, our mothers across the aisle from us. In those still-early days, food served on the Rajdhani was great in terms of variety and quantity, and was served elegantly. Tea and snacks, dinner and then the second day's breakfast were served during the journey. Everything seemed very new to us and we laughed and chatted through the evening. As a concession for being teenagers, we had been allowed to use lipstick and I

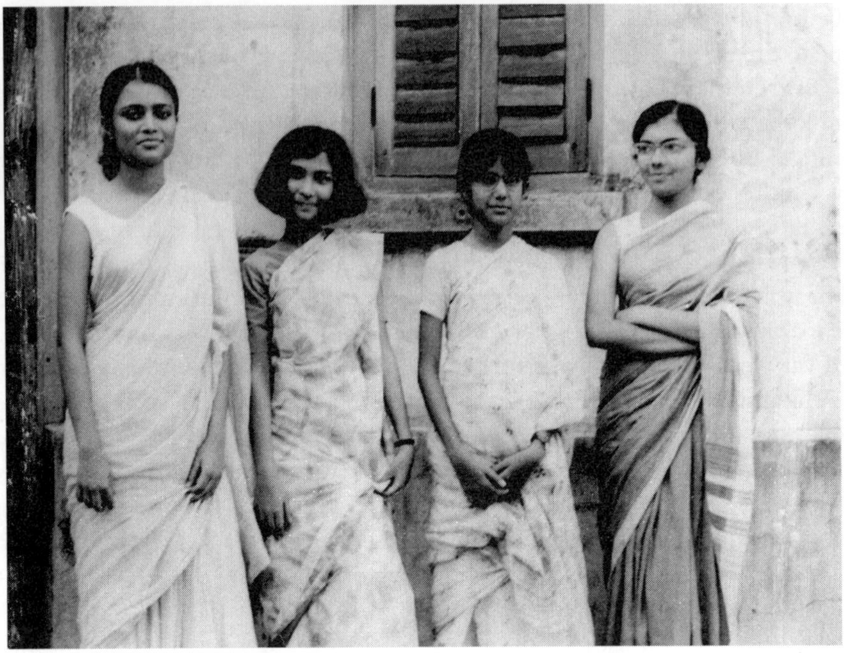

Figure 1. Left to right: Bubai, Myself, Buri and my other aunt, Bulipishi.

remember we kept reapplying it every once in a while, with the excuse that are our lips were getting dry! In reality, it was just a time when everything was fun. We hardly slept during the night; we were too excited. Finally, around eleven the next morning, the train entered the New Delhi Railway Station Platform 1, on what is now called the Paharganj side. At that time, this was the only way into the station and Platform 1 meant one didn't have to climb the overbridge to exit the station. Here we had to part ways, for my mesho had come to collect us and Amiyada had sent a car for his family. They were bound for Greater Kailash-I (GK-I), where Amiyada had arranged for an apartment for them. We, on the other hand, were headed to my aunt's house, near Panchkuian road. Reuniting with Pollymashi, Dolludidi and Kutush was great and their household was also in a state of high excitement and joy because Dolludidi's wedding had been fixed and was going to take place in a couple of months. Since we were going to be there for nearly a month, there was no hurry to sightsee. The first couple of days were spent eating, resting and talking non-stop. My mesho took me around on his scooter, which was a fun new experience for me. The only disappointment arose from the discovery that GK-I was very far from where we were staying and therefore going sightseeing together with the Basus was rather impossible. Then, one evening, Amiyada and Meenadi came over to my aunt's house and proposed that we move in with them for a few days to go sightseeing in Delhi and then go to Agra on a day trip. My mashi and mesho being the most easygoing of hosts, had no issues with this arrangement and so we left after packing, for a few days. I still remember the drive from my aunt's house to GK-I; it seemed never-ending. We Calcuttans were not used to driving such long distances! Today, after so many years of coming to Delhi regularly, even longer drives have become routine. Anyhow, reaching their GK-I residence and reuniting with Bubai and Buri was even more joyous. Now we were all set for our Delhi adventure!

Let me give a description of the apartment we were staying in. It was on the main road, right opposite the market. GK-I was one of the relatively new and upmarket South Delhi colonies at the time, and as is standard for any residential area in Delhi, there was a local market with shops selling daily essentials, one or two bakeries, and maybe a couple of restaurants. The idea was to make every area self-sufficient and not allow shops to open outside the designated market area. This arrangement was also totally alien to us, since in Calcutta, there were shops scattered everywhere and local markets were mainly for meat, fish, vegetables and groceries. The apartment was on the first floor of a two-storeyed house, with a veranda overlooking the road. The concept of a drawing–dining area, now so commonplace, was still not as common in Calcutta at the time. This apartment had a largish drawing–dining room with sofas and chairs grouped on one side and a big dining table with a sideboard arranged on another side. This is the usual setting in most homes today, but through the eyes of a fifteen-year-old girl coming from a middle-class environment in Calcutta of the sixties, it felt like a wonderland. There was also a TV—still not available in Calcutta—and carpets and ornaments to enhance the beauty of the place. Then there were two very large bedrooms, one of which Amiyada and Meenadi had occupied. We piled into the other bedroom, which of course, soon started to look like a madhouse. But every day, we came back in the evening to find that some order had been restored to the room by the caretakers. Seeing our toothbrushes kept in order in the bathroom made us laugh aloud because we were not used to the luxury of being waited upon. Meals were served with proper place settings and serving bowls and correct cutlery, napkins—the whole works. To me, at least, it was a whole new way of living; the first awakening to the concept of a lifestyle.

Now for the sightseeing. Delhi has too many monuments for anyone to see in one visit. But the main ones, like the Red Fort, Jama Masjid and Old Fort, which also houses the Delhi Zoo; Qutub Minar and Jantar Mantar, to name a few, must be visited by any newcomer. It was decided we would take the guided tours being offered by Indian Tourism Development Corporation (ITDC), which included commentary on the history of these places. I think there were two tours which covered the entire itinerary and they could be taken on the same day during the morning and afternoon. As impressions went, the royal quarters inside the Red Fort made me feel they were rather small for the Mughal Emperor and his family. The lack of privacy also struck me as incongruous. At the Qutub Minar, we were allowed to climb up to the first balcony and the view from there was quite awesome. For people with vertigo, it was a misery. The light and sound show on the grounds of Red Fort, held during the sunset hour, felt unique, as it was the first of its kind in India as well as the first time I witnessed it. The Urdu version sounded better, but that first time, we saw the English version. Walking down what used to be the Meena Bazar, where royal ladies shopped and gossiped and made plans for assignations, one felt as if we had been transported to another age; amidst the sweet echoes of tinkling bangles mixed with the laughter of Mughal ladies.

The next little adventure happened on 8 October, which is Buri's birthday. Amiyada decided to treat all of us at The Oberoi hotel, where he always stayed when he came for work. We had never been to a five-star hotel before, so with great excitement, we dressed up for the occasion—maybe overdressed, as teenagers often do. We had a grand meal and then on the elevator down, I remember we somehow pressed the wrong button and reached the wrong floor. In trying to rectify this, we ended up going up and down in the lift several times before finally managing to exit from the ground floor. All this was accompanied by much giggling and fun. Since there was one car for our use and we were too many people the elders decided to take a taxi home and we were to follow in the car. Once inside, we suddenly felt the urge to see Connaught Place (CP) at night and asked the driver whether we could take a detour. He was quite willing but we knew fully well how this delay would cause anxiety and bring down the wrath of our parents upon us; still, we felt very adventurous and decided to take the plunge. So a drive through CP late at night was achieved, our fear making it even more exciting! When we finally reached the house in GK-I, all the elders were standing on the pavement, surely most anxious about our fate. But fortunately, the scolding was not so bad; Amiyada was in one of his magnanimous moods and let it go, attributing it to the high spirits of youth.

One morning, we were strolling through CP and saw some booksellers selling their wares on the footpath. All three of us were avid readers and stopped to see if any new book was on offer. We found *Exodus* by Leon Uris (1986),[3] about which we had heard a lot but had not managed to buy. We bought it and Bubai, being the eldest, promptly announced that she will read it first. Then came my turn. The book gave me a glimpse into a wider world which left a lasting impression on me, and I became an ardent admirer of Israel's history. One evening, we had a meal at the Moti Mahal restaurant in Daryaganj, and I was introduced to Chicken Butter Masala, which remains my favourite dish till date. One other excursion I remember was to the airport, where one of our relatives was a ground engineer with the Indian Airlines and had made arrangements for us to see the inside of an aircraft, including the cockpit. This was very exciting for me, since I was greatly interested in airplanes and their mechanics.

The holiday seemed to be flying by with daily activities and fun and laughter. There was one excursion still left, and that was the visit to Agra via the Taj Express. This was also a guided tour; once in Agra, a bus took the entire group

[3] Uris, Leon. 1986. *Exodus*. Bantam Books.

around and then would bring us back to the station for the return journey by the Taj Express. Agra, the city of Taj Mahal, that wonderful memorial to an emperor's love for his wife. I was truly awed by it on that first occasion, and it still awes me the same way after many more visits. This most beautiful monument is a white marble edifice, with precious stones set in marble in leaf and flower motifs, glowing like jewels in myriad colours. The Agra Fort was as interesting as forts go, but the most amazing thing there for me was a small mirror set on a wall in which the reflection of the Taj Mahal can be seen with some twisting and turning of the head. Why Emperor Shah Jahan chose to view his beloved monument in this fashion when it was clearly visible across the river puzzled us to no end.

Then on to Fahtepur Sikri, another Mughal palace built and later abandoned due to shortage of water. Its red sandstone architecture was marvellous; entering through the Buland Darwaza into the huge layout of the complex, actually built like a city. We saw the building which was Akbar's personal palace, where he lived with Jodhabai and his other queens. In front of this building is a courtyard paved with black-and-white-coloured stones, creating a chequered look. There is a fountain in the middle of this courtyard from which the story goes that rose-scented water was sprayed forth on special evenings, and the chequerboard floor was used for playing a game called '*Pachisi*', which is more or less like chess, with ladies being used to represent the chess pieces. Romantic, oh so romantic, to fifteen-year-old me! Now a feminist, the lives of those slave girls no longer seem romantic to me, but rather pathetic. Inside the main courtyard of the palace is the small tomb of Salim Chisti, a Muslim sage, where people come from faraway places to tie coloured threads and hope to have their wishes fulfilled—mainly pertaining to begetting children.

Thus came to an end a day of hectic but most satisfying sightseeing in Agra. Back on the Taj Express for our return journey to Delhi, we encountered a dining car, known to us through Satyajit Ray's movie *Nayak* (1966), in which we had dinner. Railway catering being of high quality in those days, I still remember the mutton curry, rice and caramel custard pudding we had. Now, the Railway Mutton Curry has become a delicacy offered at certain restaurants! After Agra, separation again loomed. It was time for my mother and me to proceed to Chandigarh, as planned. Bubai and Buri were quite crestfallen that such a lovely holiday was coming to an end. Amiyada, usually a rather stern and unapproachable parent, could at times be extremely soft and loving. So it was decided overnight that they would follow us to Chandigarh by car; another car was procured for this outstation trip. Hearing this, every face was wreathed with smiles.

Though my mother and I reached Chandigarh a day or two ahead of schedule, it gave us time to spend time with Ahimama, Barshamami and my three cousins. Barshamami was one of the warmest persons I have known in my life; she was also beautiful and always dressed well. Once the Basus also arrived, they were welcomed most warmly into my *mama*'s home. Durga puja had started by then and they were very involved in their *pujo*, so evening always meant dress-up time. Since we were not carrying suitably formal clothes, I remember Barshamami opened her cupboard and offered the three of us her sarees; she also did our makeup. With our mothers not being particularly fashion-conscious, this was like heaven to us—an elder helping us dress up; a very different scenario from the usual scolding and chastisement meted out to us whenever we dressed up. Conservative family elders had this idea fixed in their heads that young girls dressed up only to attract boys' attention and I could never make them understand that at that age, if we were not allowed to follow fashion trends, we felt out of place and lacked confidence.

The next excursion was to see the Bhakra dam. It was about a two-hour drive from Chandigarh, maybe a little more then as the roads were not what they are now. First came the Naya Nangal rest house and we went in to order lunch before proceeding to Bhakra. The main dam was a gorgeous sight, with water gushing down the spillways in foaming glory. We first went down to the powerhouse level, and from there, an express lift took us up to the highest point. The road over the dam offered a view of both the reservoir and the river downstream. In the 1960s, hydel power projects and dams were considered engineering marvels of independent India on its way to achieving self-sufficiency. To me, an ardent student of science, the whole place appeared awe-inspiring. Then we came back to the rest house for lunch, where I first heard of and tasted chocolate soufflé, a dish I later learned to make and till now enjoy whenever it is on offer—an all-time favourite.

So we were back in Chandigarh; now what? End of holiday for the Basus? Oh no, on impulse, Amiyada decided to take all of us to Shimla. For me, this was the first hill-station visit of my life which then became my favourite holiday destination thereafter. We started making the climb to Shimla in a heavily loaded Ambassador—three girls, three parents and two drivers squeezed into the vehicle. My mama and *mami* had warned us of nausea and vertigo and gave us lemon slices to suck on. As the road wound upwards and no uncomfortable feeling hit, I kept thinking the worst part of the road still lay ahead. In this manner, without any feelings of discomfort, we reached Shimla. In those days, one had to climb up to the mall road on foot; the lift was still a long way in the future. We stayed in an old heritage-type hotel with huge rooms. We got the hotel staff to light a fire in the fireplace, where we tried to roast some chestnuts we had picked up on our way; Amiyada looked in and remarked, 'Oh, pulling the chestnuts out of the fire!' We stayed for a couple of nights in Shimla. The town exhibited its Raj ambience and walking up and down Mall Road was *the* thing to do. We did some sightseeing in the surrounding areas as well, but I don't remember exactly where we went. After that, we came back to Chandigarh, and after a day or so, to Delhi. I went back to Delhi with the Basus first, while my mother returned later with some other relatives, who were also visiting Chandigarh at the time.

Now that the holiday was finally ending, on the last evening in GK-I, we sat on the veranda and talked late into the night. Next day, my mother and I were to go to Pollymashi's to spend our remaining days in Delhi with them, and then we were to return to Calcutta. But what a holiday it had been—a lifelong memory, a time when new ideas and perceptions were formed, along with a love for travelling. The holiday was unique in the way it got extended time and again, including new places and giving us new joy and happiness. The rest of our stay in Delhi was also exciting and filled with joy, given Dolludidi's engagement, but that's a story for another day.

What strikes me most while reading this narrative is the important role that extended families played in middle-class lives in those days. The relative who hosted my mother and grandmother in Delhi, Amiya Kumar Basu, was my mother's grandmother's first cousin; thus thrice removed from my mother's generation. Yet his children and my mother grew up like a family and stood by each other through thick and thin, just like one's immediate family. The way Amiyada took my mother and my grandmother under his wing and shared his life and pleasures with them, is unthinkable today. There was a definite class difference between the two families. Amiyada was a well-known barrister at the peak of his career. His lifestyle was akin to upper-/upper middle-class families. My grandfather was a professor of very modest means. My mother grew up in a rather middle-class setting. Dining out was reserved for special occasions; a five-star restaurant was entirely unthinkable for her and her family. Yet, in the intimate social arrangement described above, Amiya Basu acted as a senior family member and effortlessly took charge of my mother and grandmother, sharing with them all the pleasures enjoyed by his own family. My grandfather also gracefully accepted this without any sense of inadequacy. It was a reflection of a time when economically better-off family members included their cousins, who could afford less, sharing their generous lifestyle. The other side also embraced it gracefully without class bias coming in the way. It is indicative of the social ethics of those times, and also indicates a certain class parity in terms of lifestyle between the well-off and the middle class—that is to say that the sharp class differences we witness today were somewhat blunted then by more humane familial and social networks of affection that brought people together. This allowed for seamless interactions between different families of different economic statures.

An interesting development followed when Ma posted this on Facebook—it triggered a renewed sharing of stories. Her cousins, Dolludidi and Barshamami's daughters, Malu and Gutul, shared similar stories of Barshamami's generosity in helping the younger generation 'grow up'. Dolludidi shared how Barshamami had bought her an entire makeup kit just before her marriage. She was thrilled to bits because she had never been exposed to such adult things that every young girl dreamed of possessing. Barshamami also taught Dolludidi how to use the makeup. Malu recalled that Barshamami had once won at a Tambola event and used the prize money to buy the makeup kit for Dolludidi—such were her impeccable planning capabilities and generosity! Gutul remarked how she could relate to these stories as she had grown up seeing her mother's generous character, helping one and all in whatever way she could.

Social media platforms like Facebook bring families and friends closer in times when all are so widely dispersed. What a beautiful and seamless, easy way to share old memories and stories with each other, and engage in dialogue in real time!

Lucknow Diaries

Fast forward to the beginning of 1975. I had just finished my graduation part-II exams, and for the moment, was at loose ends. I was twenty years old and had suffered my first major disappointment in life: I had been offered admission at IIM Calcutta but was unable to accept due to the delay in my university exams. I was really standing at a crossroad in life—continue studying or get married, as my parents were urging me to. I also had a couple of flirtations, so an interest in boys which had been absent while I was on my Delhi holiday, had raised its head by this time. That summer, I was invited by my eldest cousin sister on my mother's side, Banshididi, to visit her in Lucknow. Banshididi and her husband, Arun Kumar Ghosh (Montuda to us), their little daughter Mona, and her mother, my eldest *mamima*, lived together in Lucknow. They had come to Kolkata the previous year, and a close bond had formed amongst us, but Montuda and I met for the first time only after my arrival in Lucknow. On the journey there, I was accompanied by our neighbour—they were like family and they also had relatives in Lucknow, so it all worked out very well.

Lucknow is a city with a dominantly Islamic architectural flavour, with buildings sporting domes, minarets and arches. The main road is called Hazratganj, and old relics like the Imambara, Bhulbhulayia and others, stand as reminders of that Islamic era of its history. It was also one of the cities affected by India's first uprising against the British that took place in 1857, the famous Sepoy Mutiny. The overt cause of this uprising was a widely believed rumour spread amongst the Indian sepoys of the East India Company that the bullets which they had to tear open with their teeth before each use, were greased with pig and cow fat, thus offending the religious beliefs of both Hindus and Muslims. The British colonial power seat, known as the Residency Building, was attacked during the uprising and the bullet marks inside the building were still visible then, and were a tourist attraction.

Eventually, during my two weeks' stay, I visited all these historical sights but my memory of them is rather hazy now. Banshididi and Montuda were a strikingly handsome couple, both tall, fair and very good-looking. They were the most light-hearted and fun-loving couple I have ever come across. As foodies they loved good and exotic food! Biryani and kebabs were the most commonplace dishes in their house, with even more exotic items coming out of the kitchen regularly. I remember they hadn't employed any cooks—my aunt and Banshididi did all the cooking. One recipe I particularly remember was as follows: Ribs of lamb were marinated in curd and other exotic spices, and were cooked on a slow fire to make them tender as well as to up any extra juice. Once dry, the meat was taken off the fire and allowed to cool. Then the lamb pieces were dipped in egg, coated with breadcrumbs and deep fried in oil. What a taste and crunchy texture, when you bit into it! It was truly fusion food, even though that concept was still unknown to us. For the two of them, it was no big deal cooking up something as complicated, and they did not even spend all their time in the kitchen.

Banshididi was an avid knitter and when not in the kitchen, her hands were most often occupied with her knitting needles. She often made garments in Fair Isle design, which needed multiple balls of different-coloured yarns. Knitting a frock for her five-year-old daughter was a cakewalk for her. Although I couldn't cook, my paternal grandmother and aunt had taught me knitting from a very young age, and as a proficient knitter myself, I appreciated my sister's work all the more.

After a lunch of exotic dishes, on most evenings, we went out strolling and window-shopping in Hazratganj, and quite often, had dinner at a restaurant. This was a way of life totally unknown to me, as our eating-out was confined to about three or four times a year. To my twenty-year-old self, this was pure fun, again a sliver of time never to repeat. After coming home, I would go and lie down with Banshididi and Montuda for sometime, before going to sleep next to my aunt. This was when all kinds of adult subjects, specially those concerning boys, dating, marriage and even sex, were discussed. They were very open about all my questions, but gave very considerate and nuanced answers. It was fun but a time for learning also, and at that age, older cousins are of great value. Curiosity which can't be satisfied by people of the parental generation, can be quelled with fun and laughter with cousins such as my Banshididi and Montuda.

Another memorable and fun holiday was drawing to a close. The last bit of excitement left now was going back to Calcutta on my own. It was decided that Montuda would drive me to Kanpur and see me off on the Rajdhani Express coming from Delhi. Once on the train, I would be on my own till I reached Calcutta, where I would be picked up by my parents. Having never travelled alone on a train, the prospect was exciting, though nothing extraordinary happened during the journey. But for ever afterwards, whenever I travelled alone on a train, I always felt a lightening of the self—expectations and restrictions that were put on one's shoulder by parents, my husband, social norms and such, seemed to fall away and I was free to be my own self for the duration of the journey. Soon after this, my marriage with Sabyasachi was fixed and still in the daze of the joyful time I had spent with a young and fun-loving couple, I said yes to the match—digging my own ditch and forever regretting giving up on my bright career prospects. To my young readers, let me say that early marriage is like closing doors on your own possibilities and capabilities, so give yourself time to get to know yourself, find your own niche in life and only then think of settling down.

I asked Ma what was the lasting impression on her from this trip or its memory. In reply, she rued her naïveté. Banshididi and Montuda were, in many ways, a match made in heaven. They were perfect for each other. In a young twenty-year-old's imagination, this became the epitome of love and conjugal bliss. She believed all marriages were as perfect as theirs. To her young, impressionable mind, it did not occur that marriages are but social constructs; they require tremendous adjustment, involve disappointments and a constant realignment of one's

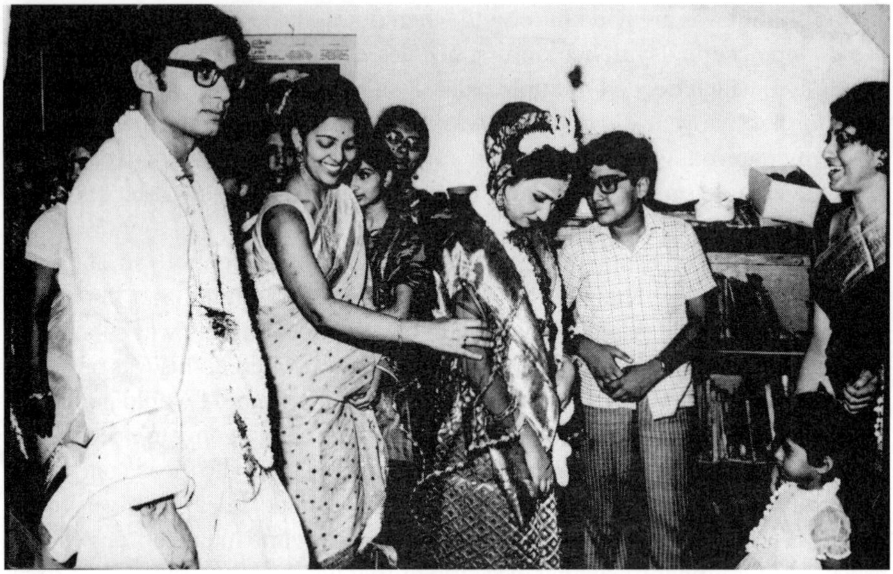

Figure 2. On my wedding day, Banshididi guiding me (a young bride) through the seven rounds (pheras) of the Hindu marriage ritual.

expectations. Marriages need to be worked on, and not all are lucky enough to find themselves in well-adjusted marriages. The same year that my mother visited her cousin in Lucknow, she got married at the young age of twenty, and hence was thrown into a complex web of adjustment, heartbreak and reconciliation early on. She forever searched for love like the great love of her cousins—she found some and lost some. Her young self learnt the realities of life the hard way and early years of great dreams and ambitions were eventually humbled over the years.

In those days, very conservative families that preferred an early marriage for their daughters, took time to prepare them for some of the adjustments expected after marriage. But in my mother's family, education for women was paramount and girls were taught to think for themselves and be independent. Hence, when suddenly, my mother was married off just after her graduation, she had no time to mentally prepare for married life. Hers was a generation that was at the cusp of transition between arranged and love marriages, and there were a few exceptions which fell through the cracks. Hers was one such—she married in search for love but in an arranged setting, where neither party had been given enough time for courtship so they could get to know each other. As a result, they were left spending their entire lives merely adjusting to each other.

Chennai Tales

The first love we discovered in our married life was travel. Sabyasachi and I—and later our daughter, when Diya came along—loved to travel. The conversation around travel started even before we had got married. Sabyasachi asked me, one day, 'Where would you like to go for our honeymoon?' and I

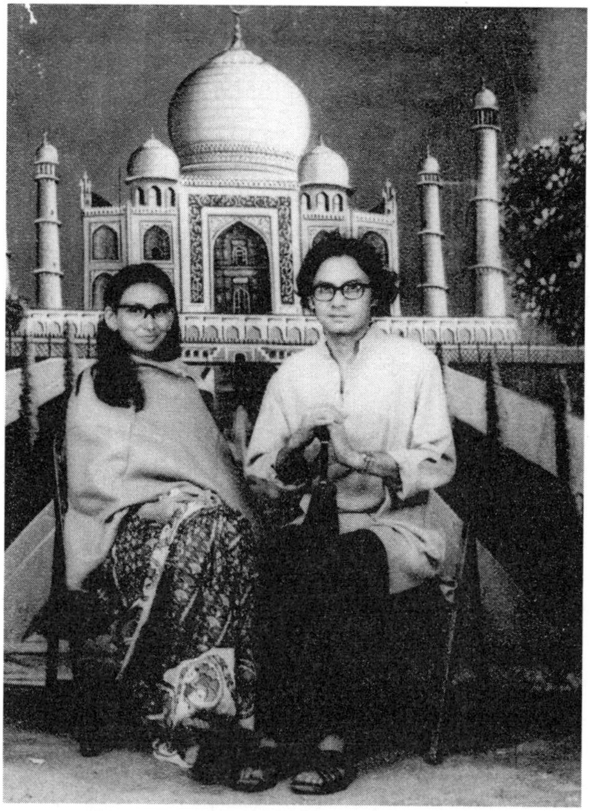

Figure 3. Myself and my husband Sabyasachi on our honeymoon to Darjeeling at a photo studio with the image of Taj Mahal as a backdrop.

replied, 'It doesn't matter where because I have had very little opportunity to travel so far, but I would love to travel a lot,' leaving the choice of our honeymoon destination to him. Ultimately, he decided on Kalimpong, with the last two days in Darjeeling, seemingly a rather mundane choice—but imagine, I had never been to either place before that! In Kalimpong, we stayed at the Tourist Lodge, which for many years, remained our standard choice of accommodation. The place was near the market area, at an easy walking distance from restaurants and shops. I remember it was a very pretty town but I don't remember much of the sightseeing we did. What I do remember is the aroma of Darjeeling tea in the morning, which used to be served on a veranda, if I remember correctly. One could—and did—drink cup after cup of that tea, which has since become my favourite. And then the green chillies, I could never forget them—they were the short and roundish hill country type and oh so hot! Me, the one who could never eat spicy food, couldn't even eat the salad where one sliced green chilli had been placed on top! Sachi, who could eat any amount of hot food, enjoyed my discomfort but asked the waiter to omit the chilli from my salad.

The journey from Kalimpong to Darjeeling is a picturesque winding route, which in those days, was rather narrow. We travelled in a shared jeep, where we were offered the front two seats, next to the driver. To my utter amazement, I found that the driver was carrying a bottle of some country liquor and taking regular swigs from it. I must have kept giving him worried looks because sometime later, he gave me a broad smile and said '*Behen daro mat, safely pahunch jaoge*' ('Don't worry, sister. You will reach safely'). He was Nepali and didn't speak Bengali. At last, we arrived at Darjeeling, the famed hilltown with a view of the Kanchenjunga. Alas, the whole place was shrouded in mist and clouds that afternoon, much to our disappointment. We selected a hotel on Mall Road with bay windows, an old heritage-type building. Because of the rainy weather, Sachi bought an old-style men's umbrella. One day, while carrying it like a walking stick, as we were walking down a lane, he suddenly noticed a small photo studio and entered it. To my surprise, since he was already carrying his Nikon SLR with him, he simply asked the owner, 'Can you take a picture of us?' He answered in the affirmative and we were taken to a small inner room, where to my even greater surprise, there was a large picture of the Taj Mahal as the backdrop. The picture was shot and duly collected the next day. In the picture, Sachi was sitting with his hands folded on top of the umbrella, like men two generations before him. Sachi then said, 'Now you can say you have been to both Darjeeling and Agra!' Such was his sense of humour.

We had a disappointing stay otherwise, for the sun never came out and there was a constant drizzle, with no chance of a glimpse of Tiger Hill or the Kanchenjunga. But then, June was never the best time to visit Darjeeling.

Our next holiday was a few months after we took up residence in Madras. Sabyasachi's colleague and friend Kamal and his wife Tutun, along with their little daughter, decided to visit a few places in South India, so we planned a joint trip with them to Ootacamand or Ooty, in the Nilgiri Hills. It doesn't quite feel right to call them friends because for many years now, we have lived like family. Anyhow, Kamal had managed to snag a discount, so we were putting up at The Savoy, an old Raj-style hotel, normally rather expensive. One had to catch an overnight train to Coimbatore and from there, take the toy train up to Ooty. Toy train rides take time but one gets to really enjoy the scenery. I remember our coach had a glass wall running up to the ceiling, and the view was simply awesome. In Ooty, there is a lake where one can enjoy boating, which we did. I remember there were some pictures taken as well, but Sachi had suddenly decided to shoot slides—I really don't know why because we didn't have a slide projector at home. But that was Sabyasachi, practical considerations never meant much to him. It was a lovely break for us, with long walks in the mornings and evenings spent in good old *addas*[4] around a wood fire, with a splash of rum.

---

[4] *Adda* is a Bengali term for the tradition of casual debate and discussion in Bengali culture. It implies a place and an environment in which friends and acquaintances can gather to freely exchange ideas on a wide variety of issues—economic, political, social, artistic and cultural, etc.

While in Madras, our annual holiday had to be spent in Calcutta, as both our parental homes were there. Travel for sightseeing had to be short, usually over the weekends with one or two days leave added to either end. Travelling modes varied—there was train, of course, but also bus travel. Fortunately, from Madras, there were many places one could visit close by, often two or more places being clubbed together. Once, I remember, we had gone to Kanyakumari by bus, and in those days, luxury air-conditioned buses were few, so often one had to take ordinary local State Transport buses. In the middle of the journey, it suddenly started to pour. Such was the fury of nature that the bus had to halt till the rain stopped. Quite a while later, we were on our way once again, but it was much later than expected and pitch dark. Suddenly, the bus stopped after some time and the driver said we all had to get down, he won't go to the bus stand because he was late, or the road was waterlogged, or some such thing.

What were we to do—with luggage, getting down in the middle of nowhere, how were we to reach the Tourist Lodge? Then someone told us that the boundary wall right where we had stopped was that of the Tourist Lodge, but to reach the gate by road would be quite a walk. It was suggested that we scale the hedgerow and then walk through their grounds to the lodge, which would be much quicker. Sachi tried to reason with the driver but knowing almost no Tamil, could make little headway. With no other solution in sight, we got down, collected our bags and walked a little to where the wall gave way to the hedgerow, and somehow climbed over to the other side. It was an unkempt uneven ground and till today, I don't know how we reached the building, carrying our bags, all soaked and bedraggled.

Another time, the problem was the reverse. We had to catch a very early morning train, at around 5 a.m. or so. The evening before, we asked the reception how we could get to the station that early. The receptionist shook his head and said no vehicle of any kind would be available then and we would have to walk. The station was close, one could even see the platform lights, but still, we wondered how we'd reach there in pitch darkness, carrying our luggage! Remember that there were no trolley-type suitcases we could roll behind us. We walked away and were looking very dejected when a man came up to us and said, 'I was listening to your problem. I have a car, I have to drive my boss, the manager of Usha Company, to the station, so I can take you, too—if only you can wake me up. I will be sleeping in the dormitory.' This was like manna from heaven and we gladly accepted his offer. Sachi went and woke him up the next morning, and we reached the station in time. Sachi asked the driver, 'How can I compensate you for your trouble?' To which, he answered, 'No trouble, if you want to buy a fan, here's my name, ask for me at the office and I will get you a good discount!' We learnt then that sometimes, a good thank you is all that is needed.

One more incident comes to mind. One of Sabyasachi's childhood friends, Arya Gupta, was once posted in Cochin. His father was a senior marketing executive and his company was holding some sit-'n'-draw competition as part

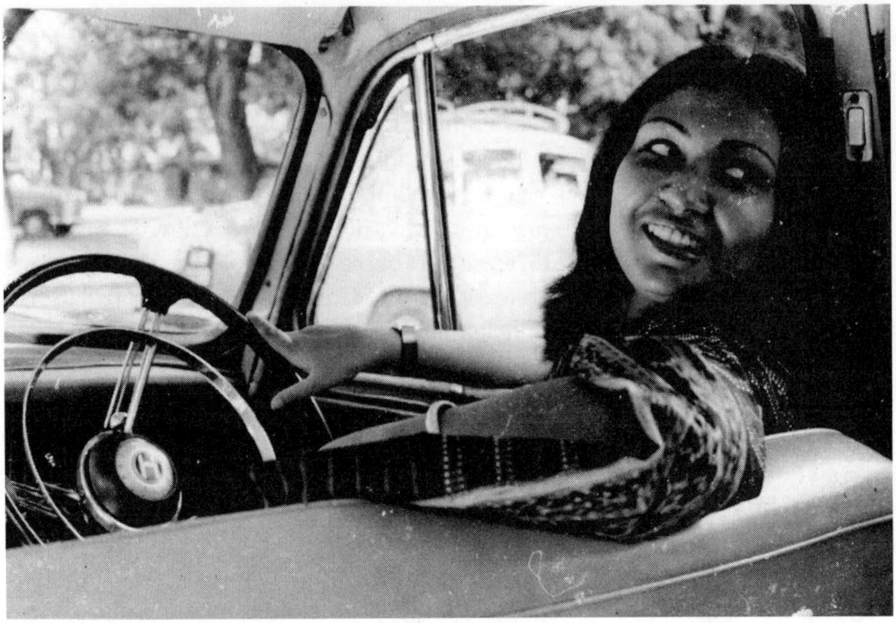

Figure 4. In my early days of marriage I learnt to drive our Ambassador car. A rare picture of myself seated on the driver's seat taken by my photographer husband, Sabyasachi.

of a product launch in Coimbatore. He promptly engaged Sachi to be the judge and told someone that being newly married, he never went anywhere without his wife. If only the judge truly ever thought so! So the long and short of it was that two tickets were procured for a Madras–Coimbatore–Cochin flight—one for me to travel all the way to Cochin, while Sachi got down at Coimbatore, and came to Cochin with senior Gupta the next day. In those days, we had only two suitcases—one larger, used by me (ladies needing more space) and the smaller one used by Sachi. At that time, these feeder flights operated with small aircrafts which stored luggage inside the cabin. When the plane landed at Coimbatore, Sachi got down while I looked on from my window seat. Suddenly, I saw that the bigger suitcase had been offloaded and was sitting on the tarmac. Aghast, I ran to the door and started shouting, 'Wrong bag, wrong bag!' in a mix of Tamil and English. People nearby were startled until the problem was understood and rectified. We enjoyed a couple of days of stay with Arya, Radhika, Mashima and Meshomashai. There was a cricket match one day, for which a gala cricket lunch was planned and prepared by Radhika to perfection.

Another memorable trip we took was through Bangalore, onward to Belur, Halibid, Hasan and Shravanabelgola, all ancient temple towns in Karnataka. This trip came about like this. In those days an advertising agency then called Ogilvy Benson and Mather, popularly known by its shortened form OBM,

Sachi's company, didn't have an office in Bangalore but they had some clients there who were handled by the Madras office. One client wanted to have a meeting on a Friday before a long weekend. The manager, Chandru, was supposed to go for the meeting but on that day, there was a very important cricket match in Madras. So Chandru told Sachi, 'You take the car and take Jayanti with you, attend the meeting and then make use of the long weekend to take a trip around.' When Sachi told me, I was in seventh heaven because going on a roadtrip held its own charm and didn't happen often. We visited all the old ruined temples in these towns, but a problem arose when we reached Shravanabelagola. There is a monolithic statue of Gommateshwara high up on a hilltop, which one had to climb to see. Now, I always felt breathless when climbing, so I opted to sit at the base of the hill. Dorai, our driver, was very unhappy about this—he told me people came from such faraway places to see the statue and there I was, refusing to climb. 'Please come with me, I will help you,' he offered. Thus, I began the ascent with him, Sachi having already gone ahead. After sometime, the rock-cut steps became steeper and I started feeling breathless. When it became impossible for me to go on, I told Dorai, 'You go ahead, I will rest and then slowly go back down'. So I sat down on a step, my face very red from the effort and the hot sun. People going up and down gave me concerned looks till I managed to get down and reach the base. Sachi, unaware of my misadventure, came down wearing a satisfied look.

We covered quite a few of the southern attractions, at one time even visiting Trivandrum and Kovalam beach, then known as a high-end tourist attraction. But we never got to watch the Onam boat race, which we very much wanted to. Our daily budget for these trips was ₹100, excluding tickets. Since there were no ATMs, no core banking and no credit cards, the only recourse was to carry the entire amount in cash or buy State Bank of India traveller cheques. The latter, I found to be very convenient, since Tourist Lodges accepted them and quite often exchanged a couple for cash. But the problem was that there was hardly any cushion for emergencies, and hence Sachi's diktat was that shopping was to be done only on the last day.

I remember in 1978, near the end of our stay in Madras, Sachi was sent to Singapore on a three-month training programme and I joined him there during the last month. As had been our routine when we first arrived in Madras, here also I met Sachi for lunch, then he went back to work and I went to roam around the shops till he finished work and we met again. One day, on my way to lunch, I saw a shop where they were selling Philips hair dryers at a reduced price, and a stack of them was lying on the pavement and selling like hot cakes. I almost ran to meet Sachi and knowing his dislike of shopping in the middle of our stay, I timidly but earnestly pleaded my case. He agreed and took out SG$20 from his purse. I almost ran back to the shop and bought a very useful hair dryer for about ₹80. I possibly didn't get much of a lunch after, but was so happy, it didn't matter. Such joy and pleasure for such small things. Singapore was my first visit abroad and I had travelled alone; there was a layover at Bangkok. Great food was served on both flights. When I fly abroad today and get the most unpalatable meals onboard, I always think back to my first flight. The term 'cattle class' hadn't been invented yet.

That one month in Singapore was a wonderful experience; we spent part of it with a Chinese family and the rest at an upmarket hotel. Singapore is known as a shoppers' paradise. The city had malls then like the ones we have now. To my young self, it was like Aladdin's cave. Every weekday afternoon, between lunch and early evening, was my time to saunter around the malls filled with goods heard of but never seen in India. Kitchen gadgets were part of one such category. One day, I bought a measuring cup made of thick glass, which is still used in my kitchen to this day. Same as a hand beater, so essential for baking but unavailable in India for many years, which also I bought there and it still works. The chocolate section of departmental stores got my most careful attention and usually, saw my only purchase of the day. On weekends and in the evenings, we explored the city. On the sea front, there is a statue of the Singapura Lion, the country's emblem, with lighting and a promenade. It was a nice place to visit in the evenings.

Then there was the day trip to Sentosa Island, which was connected to the main island by a ropeway. Though I am rather scared of ropeways, Sabyasachi's enthusiasm for it made it impossible for me to refuse. We had a safe crossing, but a couple of years later, we heard there was a horrible accident on the same ropeway! Sentosa had been developed as an entertainment park with rides, food joints and other enjoyable activities. I remember we enjoyed our day very much. Jurong Bird Park was another attraction we visited and it was full of such

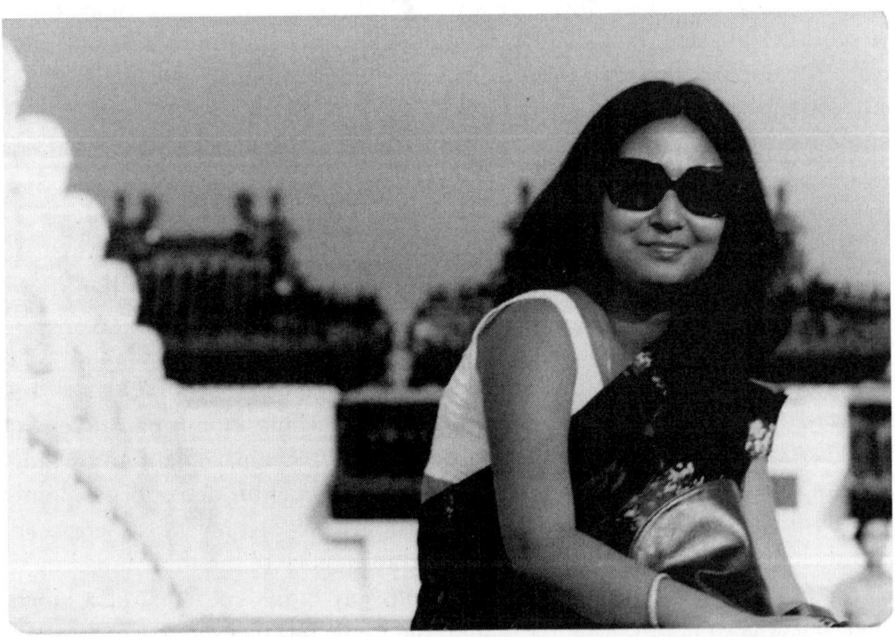

Figure 5. Myself in Singapore, photographed by Sabyasachi.

exotic colourful creatures. Then, of course, Orchard Road, the Chowringhee (main shopping street of Calcutta) of Singapore. The upmarket hotels were mostly located here—the famous British-era Raffles Hotel, a beautiful old building, was nearby. When we were staying in another hotel in the same area, we used to stroll down Orchard Road in the evenings, all lit up with neon signs for cinemas, theatres, restaurants, cafes and bars. Though there were plenty of upmarket restaurants, good-quality cheap food was also easily available. At various places in the city, there were food courts, but not fancy ones like those in the malls of our metropolitan cities now. These were paved and covered courtyards where individual stalls served variety of food items. From Indian chicken curry to Chinese chilli chicken, to momo and thukpa, the choices were plentiful. When it came to soft drinks, the variety was much more than what was available in India then. Sabyasachi, always one for trying out new things, would buy a different one each day, while I stuck to my Coke, which had sadly been banned in India at that time. And then there were the McDonald's burger joints. I loved a hamburger with French fries, which we would often have for lunch. On the last day of our stay, Sabyasachi's colleagues treated us to dinner and drinks at a fancy restaurant, so that experience also came our way.

We also took a trip to Malaysia, covering Genting and Kuala Lumpur, mainly. I admired the winding road up to Genting, since our hill roads then were very poor in comparison. My first experience of going to a casino was at Genting; we, of course, played only on the slot machine, but encashing our small winning was also fun. Here again, we encountered a cultural difference. At the dining table, the all-Chinese group would take their rice or noodles in a bowl and pick from the side dishes with their chopsticks, time and again. We could neither use chopsticks, nor were we used to people eating from the same dish. Sensing our difficulty, the others at the table told the waiters to give us spoons and forks and also invited us to serve for ourselves before they dug in. I have seen time and again that if one is respectful of other people's cultures, they go out of their way to make you feel welcome.

Hence, a very memorable sojourn came to an end. The journey back to Calcutta was also something to remember. The flight from Singapore to Bangkok on a Thai Airways flight passed without incident. There was a night halt in Bangkok, but we arrived rather late and were taken to a hotel by airline transport. Next morning, we went back to the airport for our flight to Calcutta. Here, things started to go wrong. There was a long delay, after which the flight took off, but soon, it felt that it was not gaining height as it should. I pointed this out to Sachi, but he didn't think anything was amiss. A few minutes later, there was an announcement from the flight deck, telling the control tower that one engine was not giving enough power and the pilot had requested permission to return and land. By then, we had started feeling scared, but the plane landed back safely in Bangkok. We were offloaded and taken to a lounge, which got crowded with all the passengers from our flight. There, we waited and waited with no food or drink. Finally, after protesting to the airline officials, food and drinks were served. By this time, we were running late by several hours of our scheduled arrival in Calcutta. It was a time when international calls were not so easy so we couldn't inform anybody back home about what had happened. After a few exhausting hours, we reboarded and the flight took off and eventually landed in Calcutta. But there was more—while still taxiing on the runway, the aircraft came to a sudden stop with a mighty jerk; there was some problem with the breaks! The Calcutta passengers were asked to deboard on the tarmac itself and brought to the terminal in a bus. After clearing immigration, we were finally out of the terminal, but by then, it was late afternoon. My parents had been waiting since the morning at the airport and endured a great deal of anxiety as no proper information about our delay had been given to them. But all's well that ends well!

Soon afterwards, we were posted to Delhi and a new chapter in our lives began.

When my mother started penning her reminiscences, she had no intention of publishing them, nor pairing them with photographs. Hence, this narrative was not built around the photographs, but rather, suitable photographs have been retrospectively added from the family archive. One thing needs mentioning here that in the 1960s and 1970s, photography was a very different proposition. First, only people particularly interested in photography as a hobby possessed a camera, and to get a finished picture, one had to go through a long process. Those who didn't have a camera, used the services of professional photographers, who would come and take pictures on special occasions. So photos were mostly of family groups arranged in some sort of conventional order, or newly married couples in various predefined poses. Candid photography really took off only once point-and-shoot cameras became easily available. And then, the digital revolution made photography an everyday activity to the extent that cellular phones now sell based on the merits of their cameras!

My grandfather was a keen photographer and had a camera; the group picture of my mother with the Basu children was shot by him (circa 1970) (Figure 1). Since Amiya Basu did not have a camera, there are no pictures of their Delhi trip, but I find my mother's textual description to be highly visual. Similarly, there are no pictures of her Lucknow stay, but amongst my mother's wedding pictures, we found the one with Banshididi (Figure 2). My father was an even keener photographer, possessing very sophisticated camera equipment. Being a creative person by nature, he specialised in different sorts of pictures at various stages in his life. In the early years of their marriage, he shot some beautiful portraits of my mother. Some pictures might have got lost in transfers. No picture of any trips taken from Madras could be found, but a picture of my mother in Singapore, shot by my father (Figure 5) has been included. And then, of course, the delightful picture shot at a studio in Darjeeling (Figure 3).

2

Families (re)located: Migration, displacement and diaspora

The Anglo-Indian Archives

Setting up a Community Photographic Archive

Adira Thekkuveettil

Introduction

Dileep Prakash, Sheik Mohamed Ishaq and I are not Anglo-Indian, although we run a small, independent archive called *The Anglo-Indian Archives*. At present, this is a digital collection of family photographs from the Anglo-Indian community in Chennai and Guwahati, India. Through this essay, I chart the story of this archive—from what we intended it to be, how it came about, to where it is now. Taking a critical approach, I introspect on both the conceptual and the practical dynamics of setting up a community archive, while also reflecting on the tensions that emerge when negotiating questions of ethical responsibility, representation and power within an archival context.

In early 2018, when Dileep first approached me with a nascent plan to create an archive of Anglo-Indian family albums, I had recently graduated from a master's programme in photography from the National Institute of Design (NID). My own work examined questions of identity, histories and representation through the lens of the family, and I was also very interested in exploring vernacular photographic histories of the subcontinent. But up until that point, I had had no experience of setting up an archive. More significantly, I had not interacted with the Anglo-Indian community considerably, and my first proper exposure to their images had, in fact, largely been through Dileep's own work on the community, through his 2007 photobook titled *The Anglo-Indians*.[1] The book, as well as its introduction by noted Anglo-Indian writer Irwin Allan Sealy, was what had provided me with the first framework to understand the Anglo-Indian community. Our shared interest in the histories of photography and Dileep's long engagement with the community was what brought us together in our first conversations around possibly collaborating on a project to help archive an Anglo-Indian photographic history that was fast disappearing from the consciousness of the subcontinent.

In this essay, I first briefly trace the history of the Anglo-Indian community through the colonial and post-colonial periods, focussing on the coming together of a community within the precarious circumstances of a divisive colonial context, and the changing identities Anglo-Indians later adapted,

[1] Prakash, Dileep. 2007. *The Anglo-Indians*. New Delhi: Photoink.

as citizens of independent India and as members of a global Anglo-Indian diaspora. Following this, I consider the circumstances that informed our approach in setting up *The Anglo-Indian Archives*, reflecting especially on the conceptual and methodological concerns that arose through our centering of the family album within the archive. Drawing next from our fieldwork with Anglo-Indian families in Chennai, I focus on our experience of interviewing Margaret Dawson and Russell Lowe,[2] and archiving their collections, paying close attention to how our methodology evolved with each family we interviewed. Finally, I chart our experience of exhibiting a curated selection of photographs from our fieldwork at the 11th World Anglo-Indian Reunion in Chennai in 2019, reflecting on the community's response to the photographs in the collection and more broadly, to the archive. I close the essay with a brief deliberation on the most critical learnings we acquired through the first year of this archive's existence.

Who Were/Are the Anglo-Indians?

The term Anglo-Indian has been in vernacular use since at least the early nineteenth century, but up until 1911, it was generally understood to denote Europeans, specifically British officials, state functionaries, bureaucrats, traders as well as private individuals and their European families, who had been born and raised in India, or domiciled in India for much of their lives.[3] In 1911, the term's meaning was officially redefined in the Census of India[4] to henceforth refer to children of European fathers and Indian mothers, and the children of their offspring through the male line living in India.[5] Before the community's official recognition, the Anglo-Indian community had long been identified both officially and unofficially through terms like

[2] Margaret Dawson, b. 1943, was the first person from the Anglo-Indian community we interviewed for the archive. It was through this interview that we began to think about questions of trust, understanding and sharing more seriously within an archival process. Our interview with Russell Lowe (b. 1953) was especially important as he was an avid family archivist himself, who shared with us a wealth of deeply researched information as well as methodologies for the organisation of his own archive.

[3] Through the nineteenth and early twentieth centuries, the word Anglo-Indian was also used to refer more broadly to concepts relating to the British presence in India, as well as to the evolving English language of British India, which also evolved through the influence of Anglo-Indians. See: Sealy, Allan in Prakash, Dileep. 2007. *The Anglo-Indians*; Arondekar, Anjali. 2001. 'Too fatally present': The crisis of Anglo-Indian literature. *Colby Quarterly*. 37. pp. 145–163.

[4] *Census of India*. 1911. Volume 1. Part 1. p. 139. Within the census, it was also noted that the marked increase in the community's population from the previous 1901 census was largely due to the official recognition of the term Anglo-Indian to denote this community, as opposed to earlier terms such as Eurasian, which had long been considered derogatory within the community.

[5] This definition was further solidified in the Indian Constitution in 1949. Although Anglo-Indians who are part of the larger global diaspora since Independence are not 'officially' recognised, the term is still considered as a broad cultural identity.

'country-born', Eurasian[6] and East Indian, which were unpopular within the community; together with more disparaging terms bordering on racist slurs which emphasised their identities as being split in two, hybridised, or not being whole. It is especially telling that Anglo-Indians were only acknowledged by the colonial government with an official term close to four centuries after the first Indo-European communities began growing along India's coasts in the sixteenth century.

A Brief History

The Portuguese were the first Europeans to start setting up trading stations along India's southern coasts in the early sixteenth century, a few decades before the establishment of the Mughal Empire in North India.[7] These early colonial traders, almost all of whom were men, soon began entering into relationships and even marrying local women, leading to the first generations of Indo-European[8] children. Over the next two centuries, traders belonging to British, French, Dutch and Danish nationalities also began setting up factories, trading posts and settlements across the country. Like the Portuguese, they too established relations with local women, and—by now, more commonly—with the descendants of previous unions between Europeans and Indians. As S. Muthiah and Harry MacLure have noted, 'Fathers from a dozen European nations sired the community in wedlock and out with mothers from every country of the region where a European flag was planted.'[9] The fates and fortunes of these children depended heavily on the class of society they were born into, especially their fathers',[10] as well as the constantly shifting attitudes

---

[6] Although the terms Eurasian and East Indian were widely used by both the British as well as Anglo-Indians throughout the nineteenth century, it grew increasingly unpopular as the century waned.

[7] Byrne, John. 2011. 'The Luso-Asians and Other Eurasians: Their Domestic and Diasporic Identities'. *Portuguese and Luso-Asian Legacies in Southeast Asia, 1511–2011*. Vol. 1. *The Making of the Luso-Asian World: Intricacies of Engagement*. ISEAS–Yusof Ishak Institute. p. 131–154.

[8] Within scholarship on Anglo-Indian history, there continues to be much debate on the veracity of terms such as Indo-European, mixed-race, hybrid etc., some of which also have the potential to be offensive to the community. See also Lionel Caplan for a similar concern with terminology: Caplan, Lionel. 2003. *Children of Colonialism*. Routledge. p. 18.

[9] Muthiah, S. and Harry MacLure. 2014. *The Anglo-Indians: A 500-Year History*. New Delhi: Niyogi Books. p. 11.

[10] There is markedly more scholarship on the fates of children of upper-class European men through the eighteenth and early nineteenth century, who were often sent away to Europe at very young ages and either remained there throughout their lives, or returned to India as adults to work for the colonial powers. However, a majority of European fathers either could not afford to, or preferred not to, care for their children from native unions. So a network of orphanages were established to educate and care for these children. See: Chatterjee, Indrani. 'Colouring Subalternity: Slaves, Concubines and Social Orphans in Early Colonial India' in Bhadra, Gautam. 1999. *Subaltern Studies X*. New Delhi: Oxford India Paperbacks. p. 76. Much of the historical as well as ethnographic scholarship on the community has also reflected on the lack of identifiable female Indian ancestors for a majority of the community. For a more

of various European powers regarding these unions and the children born of them.[11]

As Britain emerged as the dominant colonial power through the latter half of the eighteenth century, communities of Indo-European descent who had thus far been widely heterogeneous with different linguistic, cultural, religious and social norms, increasingly began to be brought under a British sphere of influence.[12] British colonial cities and their territorial domains provided opportunities for the anglophone and educated among these populations, with men often finding employment in subsidiary positions in the East India Company, and women gaining security through marriages to European men or men of similarly mixed ancestry.[13] However, both Anglo-Indian and other scholars[14] seem to agree that the emergence of a distinct Anglo-Indian *community* through the late eighteenth and early nineteenth centuries was not necessarily as a result of opportunities within the British colonial world, but was rather facilitated through a long series of 'proscriptions'[15] enforced by the British government in its Indian territories, that effectively disenfranchised and othered these communities while continuing to leave them officially unacknowledged as active subjects. By the turn of the nineteenth century, Indo-European communities which had thus far been territorially spread out and culturally diverse, were coerced into being largely confined to presidency capital cities[16] under British surveillance, spatially and culturally isolated from

---

detailed analysis, see: Caplan, Lionel. 2003. *Children of Colonialism*. p. 23; Muthiah, S. and Harry MacLure. 2014. *The Anglo-Indians*. p. 13–30.

[11] From the sixteenth to the early nineteenth century, the Portuguese, French and British oscillated in their views on unions between local women and European men, initially encouraging such unions to spread Christianity among the native population. See Hedin, Elmer L. 1934. 'The Anglo-Indian Community'. *American Journal of Sociology*. 40:2. pp. 165–79. Accessed 23 July 2021. www.jstor.org/stable/2768058. For a more in-depth analysis of progressively hardening colonial policy, see Anderson, Valerie E.R. 2011. *The Eurasian problem in nineteenth-century India*. PhD Thesis, School of Oriental and African Studies. eprints.soas.ac.uk/13525.

[12] Anthony, Frank. 1962. *Britain's Betrayal in India*. New Delhi: Allied Publishers. pp. 2–3.

[13] The securing of positions within the company was, however, heavily reliant on the social class into which he had been born. See Anderson, V. 2011. *The Eurasian Problem*. p. 164. Also see Ghosh, Durba. 2003. 'Making and Un-making Loyal Subjects: Pensioning Widows and Educating Orphans in Early Colonial India'. *The Journal of Imperial and Commonwealth History*. 31:1. pp. 1–28.

[14] Anthony, Frank. 1962. *Britain's Betrayal*. p. 20; Hawes, Christopher J. 1996. *Poor Relations: The Making of a Eurasian Community in British India, 1773-1833*. Richmond: Curzon Press. p. 73.

[15] Some of the notable proscriptions included: the 1786 Court of Directors Directive which barred illegitimate children of European officers from being sent to Britain; Court of Directors Minute of 1795, which barred Anglo-Indians from combatant roles in the EIC military. The Charter Act of 1813 demarcated Hindu, Muslim and British laws as applicable only to said populations, leaving confusion as to which laws governed Anglo-Indians. For a more detailed analysis of the laws and their impacts, see Anderson, V. 2011. *The Eurasian Problem*. pp. 35–60.

[16] A ban on land ownership by Europeans and Anglo-Indians from 1790–1837 ensured that the community became largely confined to the British colonial cities of Calcutta, Madras and Bombay, unless in native states. Anthony, Frank. 1962. *Britain's Betrayal in India*. p. 18.

native communities and largely relegated to the borders of European society. Although many actively resisted and petitioned against these British laws, a shared sense of support, assistance and community also grew among the population during this time,[17] and slowly through the early nineteenth century, a distinctly urban, anglophone, cosmopolitan Christian community with close cultural ties to Europe, and more specifically to Britain, began to take shape.

The severe curtailment of the community's agency to access opportunities and lead independent lives outside of the British colonial state created a situation where Anglo-Indians increasingly came under the direct supervision and control of the British through the nineteenth century. As British hegemony became firmly established, the state's concern with the community's loyalty to its interests as well as their religious and moral attitudes grew. The colonial government, prominent individuals and civil society organisations began investing heavily in setting up and running schools, Christian religious institutions and orphanages, where young wards of European and Anglo-Indian soldiers, company officials and others could be educated and moulded into 'useful citizens who could serve the government in various subordinate roles, who would represent a return on their investment'.[18] As control of India went from Company to Crown in the mid-nineteenth century, opportunities for 'public service' emerged for Anglo-Indians within the rapidly growing realms of infrastructure, transport and communication, through the Indian Railways, Post and Telegraph, as well as intermediate positions in various government agencies.[19] Anglo-Indians were generally preferred for positions that native Indians could not be trusted to occupy (like engine drivers in the railways), but which were still beneath positions held by Europeans.[20] As the anthropologist Ann Stoler has noted of similar populations in the colonial context, Anglo-Indians were 'subject to a frequently shifting set of criteria

---

[17] Frank Anthony describes how the community essentially came together through 'bonds which distinguish them from other communities and identify them with each other'. Ibid. p. 7.

[18] Anglo-Indian children were often separated by force from working-class families and entered as wards into state-sponsored institutions and orphanages, where they remained cut off from their families for at least a decade, making it incredibly difficult for families to be reunited after the children grew up. Anderson, V. 2011. *The Eurasian Problem*. p. 167.

For a detailed analysis of these schools and institutions, see D'Souza, Austin A. 1976. *Anglo-Indian Education: A Study of its Origins and Growth in Bengal up to 1960*. Delhi: Oxford University Press.

[19] For shifts in employment patterns among the Anglo-Indian community through the nineteenth century, see Younger, Coralie. 1987. *Anglo-Indians: Neglected Children of the Raj*. New Delhi: B.R. Pub. Corp.

[20] Anglo-Indian employment in the railways was so widespread that it led to an almost separate 'railway caste' to develop within the community. For a thorough examination of the circumstances of Anglo-Indian presence within the railways, see Bear, Laura. 2007. *Lines of the Nation: Indian Railway Workers, Bureaucracy, and the Intimate Historical Self (Cultures of History)*. New York: Columbia University Press. For analysis specific to Madras, see Caplan, Lionel. 2003. *Children of Colonialism*. p. 29.

that allowed them privilege at certain historical moments and pointedly excluded them at others',[21] thereby placing the community in a constant state of precariousness. Even with the rise of more secure employment, the community continued to face considerable economic insecurity, as they were expected by the British to maintain a European lifestyle with far less pay than was provided to Europeans in similar professions. Supplemental income and even primary income in many cases thus often came from Anglo-Indian women entering the workforce. Many took up jobs as nurses, teachers in schools and institutions, and governesses, as well as set up their own enterprises like 'dame schools'.[22] Through the late nineteenth century, the Anglo-Indian community spread and settled across the country, following the railways to smaller towns and junctions, but largely continued to remain confined to enclaves adjacent to, or alongside European neighbourhoods, at some distance from the local native population.[23]

By the early twentieth century, as nationalist politics gained momentum across India, the ongoing liminal position the Anglo-Indian community had been forced to occupy proved to be especially difficult to negotiate. Official recognition by the British did little to provide clarity on the community's place within the heavily contentious political and social spectrum of late colonial India.[24] The Anglo-Indian community was also often seen through an essentialist lens by the broader Indian imagination, as being in cahoots with the British, and against Indian interests.[25] As India gained independence, most Anglo-Indians found themselves having to renegotiate a place for their community within a newly forged sovereign state. Although prominent Anglo-Indian politicians and leaders lobbied[26] strongly to ensure continuing

---

[21] Stoler, A.L. 1989. 'Rethinking Colonial Categories: European Communities and the Boundaries of Rule'. *Comparative Studies in Society and History*. 31. pp.134–61.

[22] In his essay, 'The Anglo-Indians', Allan Sealy details how Anglo-Indian women ran informal schools to provide English education to children, going back to the earliest years of British colonial influence. Sealy, Allan in Prakash, Dileep. 2007. *The Anglo-Indians*.

[23] For a deeper analysis on the gradual enforcement of Anglo-Indian enclaves through the nineteenth century and especially in railway colonies through the latter nineteenth century, see Bear, Laura. 2007. *Lines of the Nation*.

[24] When asked to clarify on the community in the House of Commons in 1925, the Under Secretary of State for India declared the following: 'For purposes of employment under government and inclusion in schemes of Indianisation members of the Anglo-Indian and Domiciled-European community are Statutory Natives of India; for purposes of education and internal security, their status, so far as it admits of definition, approximates to that of European British Subjects.' Winterton, Earl. House of Commons Debate. 21 December 1925; Hansard. Vol. 189. cc. 1925–6.

[25] For a thorough analysis, see D'Cruz, Glen. 2006. *Midnight's Orphans: Anglo-Indians in Post/Colonial Literature (Studies in Asia-Pacific 'Mixed Race')*. New edition. Switzerland: Peter Lang AG.

[26] Henry Gidney and Frank Anthony were among the two most prominent Anglo-Indian politicians of the twentieth century, both of whom worked to ensure representation and recognition for the community in the years leading up to Independence, with Anthony being prominent in post-colonial Indian politics as well.

job security for the community, as well as recognition as a minority in the Indian Constitution, many within the community chose instead to emigrate, with the first wave of post-Independence migrants choosing to move to Britain throughout the late 1940s to the early 1960s. As countries like Australia, New Zealand and Canada opened up to South Asian immigration in the latter half of the twentieth century, subsequent waves of Anglo-Indian families chose to settle in these countries.[27]

Today, those remaining within India constitute a fraction of the global Anglo-Indian population, and while cultural and religious ties within the community have largely remained strong, Anglo-Indians in India form an incredibly diverse population, who are now in many ways culturally indistinguishable from a broader upwardly-mobile westernised Indian population, especially in the decades since the economic liberalisation of the early 1990s. Among the global Anglo-Indian diaspora, too, ideas of who can and cannot claim an Anglo-Indian identity have increasingly been debated and challenged, both within scholarship as well as through the lived experiences of younger generations, who have had to negotiate the claims of more varied intersectional identities. The debates around the histories and experiences of people of mixed descent in post-colonial scholarship have also been evolving as the frameworks of identification and the choices of people to claim or disclaim specific identities have been reevaluated and examined more critically.

The Familial within the Archive

How does one archive a community's history through its family albums? And what are we really seeking to 'archive' through family photographs from the Anglo-Indian community? From our very first conversation, these constituted some of the looming questions Dileep and I grappled with as we attempted to formulate a plan for setting up the archive. The initial impulse to begin this project came from a place of both interest and concern—as the Anglo-Indian community continues to dwindle in India, with their descendants becoming part of wider diaspora communities, their family photographs have often been dispersed across the globe, with physical albums sometimes getting lost, destroyed and even discarded in the process. What we wanted to do seemed simple—undertaking fieldwork among the community in India, we would interview families through the perspective of their albums, then digitise the photographs with the aim of creating an online repository, which younger people from the community as well as a wider audience of scholars, researchers and others could then access. As I proceed through this essay, I will reflect on and unpack the strategy we employed and its methodological and epistemological implications on the resulting archive.

---

[27] For more detail on British and Australian immigration laws that influenced the community's choices for migration, see Caplan, Lionel. 2003. *Children of Colonialism*. pp. 133-135.

Soon after Dileep and I began our first discussions, he introduced me to the Anglo-Indian publisher and filmmaker Harry MacLure. Harry runs a Chennai-based independent publishing house called Anglo-Ink, which has been instrumental in publishing contemporary Anglo-Indian writing from across the globe. He also edits and publishes a quarterly magazine, *Anglos in the Wind*, which caters to a wide readership both within the community and beyond. When we began conversing in early 2018, Harry was also organising the 11th World Anglo-Indian Reunion, a major event held in a different city around the world once every three years,[28] that brings the community together for a series of events. Its upcoming edition was set to take place in Chennai in January 2019, and we were considering it as the ideal setting for us to possibly present our idea for a visual archive before a wider Anglo-Indian audience, gain feedback on the project and explore further possibilities.

The Conceptual Problem of the Archive

As we began working on our initial frameworks, aims and objectives, Dileep also sent me a set of scans of Anglo-Indian photographs from families, which he had curated in collaboration with Harry for an exhibition in Chennai in 2006. Although the exhibition itself had featured details of each photograph, including information about their subjects and the families to whom they belonged, the scans themselves did not carry this context, and in my first encounter with them, I read them almost as though they were found images.[29] These photographs seemed to me to be far removed from images I had seen more generally of middle-class families in twentieth-century India,[30] depicting men and women dressed in Western fashion, and showing distinct ease and familiarity with the camera. Seeing them as an outsider with only a vague understanding of the community at this point, I very quickly found myself inadvertently trying to place them within 'representations' of some undefined Anglo-Indian identity, contrasting these images with other visual material and even literature on the community I had come across in broader

---

[28] For a more detailed look at the Anglo-Indian Reunions, see Andrews, Robyn. 2012. 'Anglo-Indian reunions: secular pilgrimages?'. *South Asian Diaspora*. 4:2. pp. 159–173. DOI: 10.1080/19438192.2012.675723.

[29] The lack of context like dates or names of subjects alongside these images made them, in effect, purely visual surfaces, making it difficult for me to infer meaningful information about the photographs.

[30] Looking at my own initial reading and comparison between what I had seen more 'generally', I noticed how my own expectations had been deeply defined by the broader imagination of Indian family photography being confined to largely Hindu, homogeneous, nuclear or joint families, depicting men and women in traditional gender roles and poses. Indian Christian families of a certain class or even upper-class Hindu or Muslim families with Western tastes would probably have had similar family albums, but this, too, did not immediately occur to me as an initial reference point.

media.[31] Without any accompanying context, the fact that they belonged to Anglo-Indian families became their sole identification for me, and I struggled to read them without coming up against long-established stereotypes and misrepresentations of Anglo-Indians.[32]

As I looked and re-looked at these photographs, I also began to sense a looming problem that might arise with a community photographic archive largely gleaned from family albums. Family photographs are richly imbued with memories and markers that are activated within the private and intimate environments of the kinsmen who encounter them. An archive that holds a digital copy of the image retains only a few of its original contexts, usually whatever little is learnt from interviewing its keeper. However, once the image is in an archive, it is also imbued with ethnographic meaning—the event depicted (a birthday, or a wedding); the community (Anglo-Indian parties at the Railway Institute); the time and place of their making (Chennai in the 1950s, women's fashion in post-independence India)—with each of these meanings further removing the photograph from its original intended context as a record of memory within a family. Inside an archive, all these images inevitably stand to represent the community in some way, although they never originally intended to, given that the primary reason for their inclusion is the fact that they belong to Anglo-Indian families. They acquire larger identities of historical or sociological interest, becoming more generalised in their purpose.

These are concerns that are inherent to any archival project. The archive, by its very nature, is simultaneously rooted in both 'preservation and cancellation'.[33] According to Foucault, 'The archive is first the law of what can be said, the system that governs the appearance of statements as unique events. But the archive is also that which determines that all these things said do not accumulate endlessly in an amorphous mass, nor are they inscribed in unbroken linearity, nor do they disappear at the mercy of chance external accidents; but they are grouped together in distinct figures, composed together in accordance with multiple relations, maintained or blurred in accordance

[31] The portrayal of the Anglo-Indian character Mrs Mainwaring as an overly sexualized woman in Mulk Raj Anand's famous 1936 novel, *Coolie*, was a prominent example of stereotyping of Anglo-Indians I had been exposed to, early on. A more recent portrayal of the community in Anjan Datta's 2004 film, *Bow Barracks Forever*, fell into a similar trap of stereotyping the community.

[32] Allan Sealy, an early mentor to our project pointed out how in an early proposal for the archive, I had spoken about the pervasive stereotypes around the community by wider media, and yet the images I had used in the proposal had largely been of Anglo-Indian musicians and photographs made at dances, which was very much a stereotypical way of depicting the community, mostly as entertainers or 'fun-loving' and therefore 'loose'. It was very striking to me then how deeply a negative stereotype can unconsciously run.

[33] Family photographs are simultaneously 'historical documents', and 'aesthetic objects' while also existing 'simply for their own sake', always creating a deep dilemma in their reading. Sekula, Allan, "*Reading an Archive: Photography between Labour and Capital*" In Wells, Liz (ed.). The Photography Reader, Routledge. 2003

with specific regularities.'[34] Fairly early on in our discussion, both Dileep and I came to realise that what we were attempting to do would never result in a simple repository of images with an inherent organisational hierarchy, a representational bias and perspective, by virtue of which photographs were excluded from the archive. The archive could come into being only through its own unknown, emergent logic, and given that neither of us belonged to the community, we remained concerned about how our location as outsiders would influence its structure.

By involving the community as much as possible in the archive's creation, and by being very clear in our role in this project as initiators to put together the first collections of images and gather as many stories as we could, we hoped to build the foundation for a space which could then evolve and grow independently. An archive that is open for active engagement also has the potential to function as a space to explore and understand a much more nuanced and personal history of a community. Given that a majority of the community has now, for many generations, been part of a vast global diaspora, a digital archive that could be accessed by younger Anglo-Indians as well as others, could also open up more conversations around their visual history on their own terms.

The Practical Problem of the Archive

To effectively consider the archive's conceptual concerns and address them methodologically, we needed a team of collaborators and experts to come onboard the project in various capacities, including researchers and scholars of the community and beyond, who could help us with planning and research, as well as a technical team for digitising images, recording interviews and organising the collections. However, funding proved to be the deciding concern around which we had to negotiate all our plans.

We had been unable to bring an Anglo-Indian researcher or a scholar of Anglo-Indian studies onboard since at this stage, we had no funding or even a solid plan to propose. Over many months, as Dileep and I went through numerous funding applications to institutions and grants, we gradually came to understand the difficulty in convincing a funding body to support an independent, community-centred archive without providing a sense of what the archive could potentially contain. We realised that if we could generate a minimal amount of funding, it would make more sense for us to first attempt a pilot project with a few families; through that process, we would also be able to better gauge what our fieldwork would look like. A successful pilot would also enable us to be better-placed when applying for funding for the larger archival project. We decided to conduct our first field visit in Chennai, as we already had the support of Harry, who had also offered to connect us to families we

[34] Cassar, Ignaz, "Photoworks," *Philosophy of Photography*, Vol.1, No 2 (2010), p.202

could meet and potentially interview. As the 11th World Anglo-Indian Reunion was slated to be held in Chennai in a few months from then, it made sense for us to first focus our fieldwork there.

At this juncture, community organisations such as the Australian Anglo-Indian Association, as well as Harry MacLure through Anglo-Ink, generously came forward to support us. Through this collective fund, we were able to organise a five-day fieldwork visit to Chennai with a plan to interview as many families as we could, along with digitising the photographs they agreed to share with us for the archive. This fund also allowed us to add Sheik Mohamed Ishaq, who was based in Chennai, to our team as the technical expert for digitising the albums and ensuring our interviews with the families did not suffer technical issues. Once we thought we had our practical details in place, I travelled to Chennai.

Harry and I met at his Anglo-Ink office on the afternoon I arrived, and along with Ishaq, we fleshed out a strategy for scheduling our interviews with the families Harry had already got in touch with. That same day, I was also introduced to Richard O'Connor and Dominic Johnson, who were interested in our project and offered to help us with fieldwork in their spare time. I was already familiar with Richard through the popular YouTube documentary series he was making with Harry, called the *Anglo-Indians of Madras*,[35] a series that I had found immensely informative as I prepared for fieldwork. Dominic was acquainted with most of the families with whom we were to meet, and he also helped us schedule interviews in specific areas on each day, so we could minimise the time spent in commuting across the city to keep our appointments. We had an ambitious plan to meet with at least three families each day over the four days I could be there, and so, early next morning, Richard, Dominic, Ishaq and I set off to visit Margaret Dawson.

Margaret Dawson

Margaret had lived in an old bungalow on St Thomas Mount for decades. The area had long been an Anglo-Indian neighbourhood, but in recent years, many families had migrated and its demographic had changed considerably. When we arrived, Margaret greeted us warmly but with some hesitancy. Although we had spoken briefly over the phone and she was happy to have us visit, she was not sure why we wanted to see her family photographs and archive them. I introduced our project and explained what we hoped to do in more detail and Richard, who had known Margaret for a long time, asked her if she had any photographs she could show us. As we sat down around a little table on her front porch, Margaret brought out a total of four colour photographs and

[35] Harry MacLure and Richard O'Connor directed a series of YouTube documentary films on the Anglo-Indian community of Madras (Chennai), two of which focus on the community in St Thomas Mount: www.youtube.com/watch?v=wzyMKC6XzsA. Last viewed on 9 August 2021.

placed them on the table, saying she had given most of her other photographs away. She mentioned that after Richard had called her, she had thought about the 'brief'[36] he had given her and kept aside the only photographs she still possessed of her family.

We all fell silent as we considered the four little photographs on the table. Somehow, I had made the assumption that the families we met would have multiple photographs and albums, that too in print, which they would be willing to show and share with us. I asked Margaret if she could tell us more about the pictures and she explained who the people in the photos were, and pointing to their backgrounds, mentioned that they had all been taken at the home we were at presently. As Ishaq prepared to digitise them, Richard teasingly asked her why she had not kept any of her other photographs, to which Margaret replied, laughing, 'I don't need to look at photographs, Richard! I'd rather my friends were here, all the mischief we used to do, all that I remember. So, photos I don't really need.'[37]

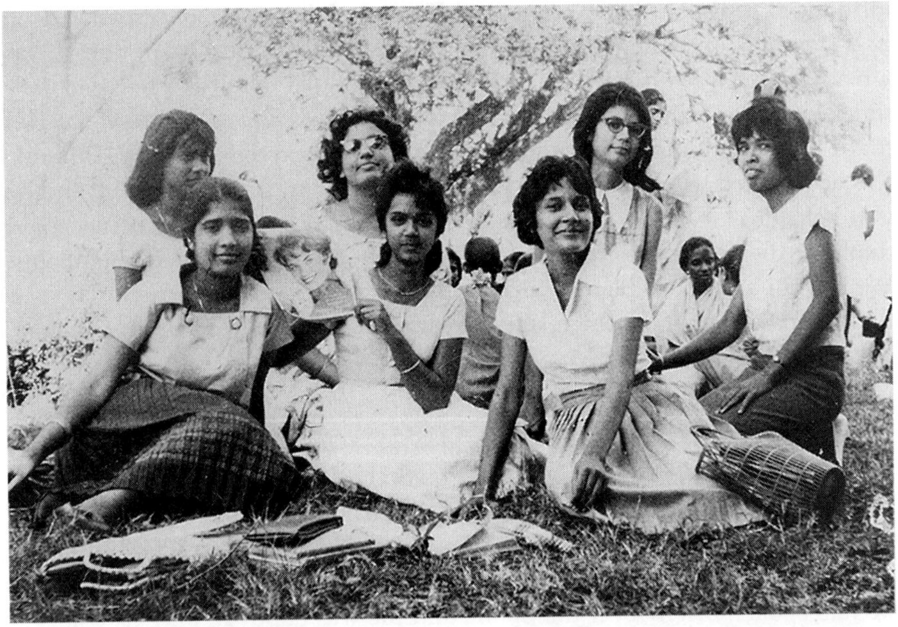

Figure 1. Margaret, second from left in back row, with friends Joyce Anderson, June Edmonds and others, Stella Maris College. Chennai, 1963–64.

---

[36] It was the word Richard had used when he had spoken to Margaret. It is interesting that as I look back, the word does seem to reflect how that exercise may have appeared to many of the families who were told a team of researchers were coming to talk to them about their family photographs, and had spoken to us only briefly before we visited them.

[37] Excerpt from our interview with Margaret Dawson. Source: AIA_2018_Chennai_MargaretDawson_00.mp3 [audio] courtesy *The Anglo-Indian Archives.*

On further probing by Richard, Margaret began reflecting on how she had not been raised to be very sentimental or very attached to material things.[38] Growing up in a very tight-knit family with her parents and brother near Shimla in the early 1950s, she had not interacted very much with her extended family and had made close friends only after she had returned to Madras for higher studies. She didn't have any children and her husband had also passed away. Now she had no close family remaining, and so felt no need to hold onto objects such as photographs. When I asked her when she had given her albums away, Margaret said it had been about two years ago. But then she mentioned that she did in fact have lots of other photographs around the house, and could show us if we wanted, but she was not too sure what we would think of them.[39] Richard and I immediately responded that we would indeed like to see them, if possible, and it was at this point that Margaret invited us into her home and beckoned us to her dining table. As we settled around it, she brought out a box full of black-and-white prints of various sizes and set them before us.

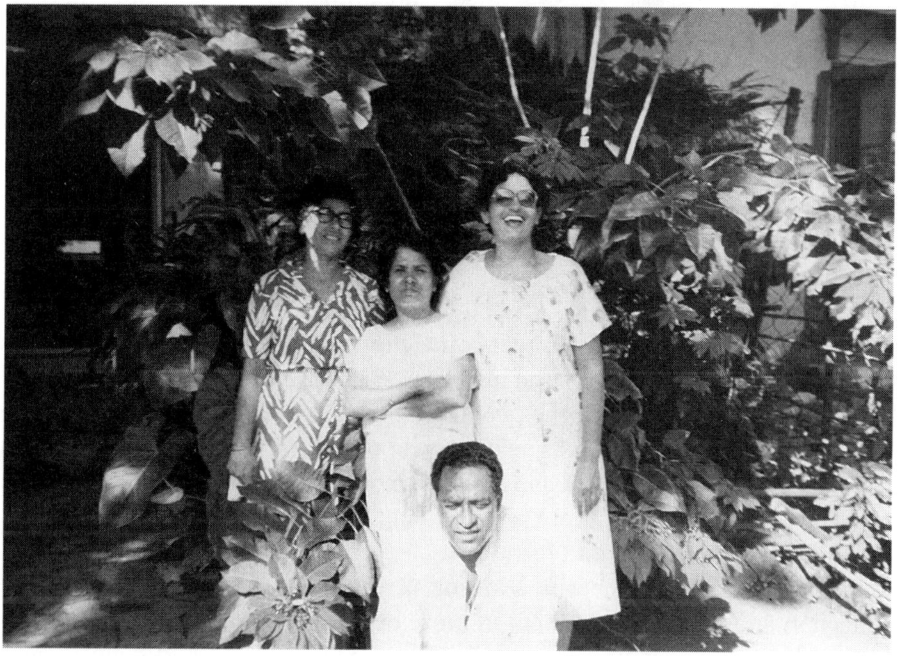

Figure 2. Left to Right: Theresa Marie, Beryl Lanson, Margaret's niece (standing, centre), Margaret and her husband Bobby at her home, early 1990s.

Over the next hour and a half, we went through each of them, with Richard and I taking turns to ask Margaret about the people in the images, when and why they were taken, our questions leading to stories about her childhood in

[38] Ibid.

[39] It was interesting how she looked at family photographs as material things, like furniture or books, but did not necessarily see them as objects imbibed with memory.

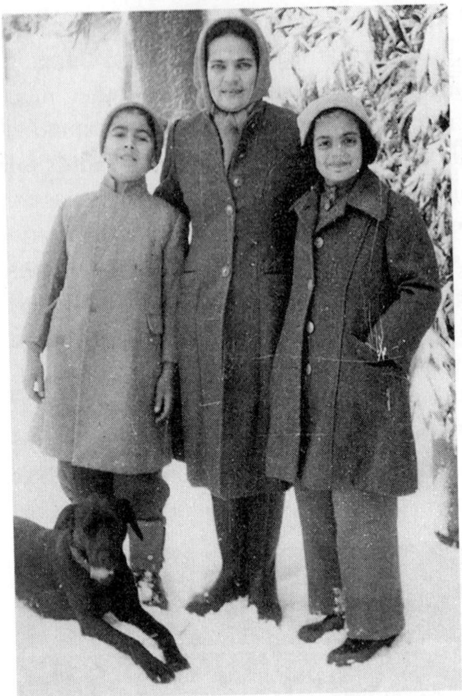

Figure 3. Left to Right: Margaret's brother Terrence D'Silva, her mother Thekla D'Silva (née Schonberg) and Margaret with their dog. Near Shimla, 1950s.

the hills near Shimla, her youth and college days in Chennai in the 1960s; the photographs acting as conduits for the stories. The stacks contained many pictures from her childhood, of her parents, her brother and her friends, and as I looked at them, I began to sense that perhaps our approach of entering her home and asking to see her family photographs immediately upon meeting her, had been very misplaced.[40] Margaret had not been sure of what we were looking for, how we understood 'family' and 'family albums' and did not immediately understand that she was to bring out photographs from her early childhood and youth and talk about her life through them.

Richard was an expert interviewer and seeing me struggle through the first ten minutes with questions, had immediately taken the lead. Margaret too seemed to be more comfortable talking to Richard, as they had many mutual connections, including friends, and as we discovered over the course of the interview, even distant family. Both Richard and Dominic knew many of the people in the photographs, and also knew the contexts and histories around specific neighbourhoods, places and institutions Margaret spoke of. It was a familiarity I could never have been a part of not simply because I was not Anglo-Indian, but also because I was entirely unfamiliar with Chennai and its history.

As soon as Margaret began showing us the photographs from her larger collection and talking about them in more detail, I realised that we had failed to be adequately prepared technically. Ishaq, Dileep and I had been largely concerned with making sure we had everything we needed to digitise the images as efficiently and quickly as possible inside the homes of the families.

[40] In the interview, she said, 'maybe it's because it's my family that the pictures are so…' indicating she did not think her family photographs fit into some expected mould and had therefore been reluctant to show them to us. But as we went through the photographs and Margaret spoke more about her life, it became clear that she had been hesitant to show us the photographs because they were very personal to her, and she had not initially been keen to talk about her life with us.

However, we had not accounted for our need to make video recordings of the interviews or make videos of the prints as they were shown and described to us. Without the latter, it was obvious that it would be very difficult for us to correlate our audio interviews with the pictures themselves. I resolved this as best as I could by taking videos of the pictures with my phone, but this was not ideal.

As the interview gradually wound to a close and Ishaq finished digitising the photographs we had set aside with Margaret's permission, we helped her put the prints back into their original boxes. The atmosphere around the table was now much more intimate. The act of sitting together and looking through the pictures, talking about them and about Margaret's life, had allowed for a sense of trust to grow, and Margaret continued to tell us stories about her house and other experiences as we put the photographs away. Leaving Margaret's home and walking across the street for our next interview, Richard and I spoke about how photographs are activated only when there is a sincere and honest desire to see them, and opening up about one's family to a group of strangers inside one's home is immensely difficult unless trust and a sense of ease are established early on and maintained continually. Within our fledgling archive, Margaret's images would now be perfumed by what we had spoken of during our interview. Our tone, turns of phrase and sequence of questions would all potentially impact the way the image was read by someone in the future. Slowly, I realised that we were part of the archive, too; a realisation that seemed obvious but one I had thus far not considered.

Russell Lowe

It was late afternoon on our third day of fieldwork when we visited Russell Lowe at his home in Madhavaram, Chennai. Russell was to be the sixth person we interviewed, and over the past three days, every individual and family we had spoken with had been incredibly warm and generous with their time and their stories. Although we had been able to digitise hundreds of photographs without much trouble, the problems around conducting video interviews remained as we did not have the time, resources or the budget to immediately rectify it. Richard had also been unable to accompany us to visit any more families after we visited Margaret, however Dominic had been with us throughout our fieldwork and continued to assist us through all the introductions and interviews with the families. The only problem we continued to face was that of time. In our attempt to reach as many families as possible with the limited resources we had, we had stretched ourselves thin, meaning that we had little time to properly process our experience and learnings from each interview.

As we drove across the city to make it in time for our meeting with Russell, the effects of what had so far been our busiest day were already beginning to show on our team, and we were tired. But the moment Russell cheerfully

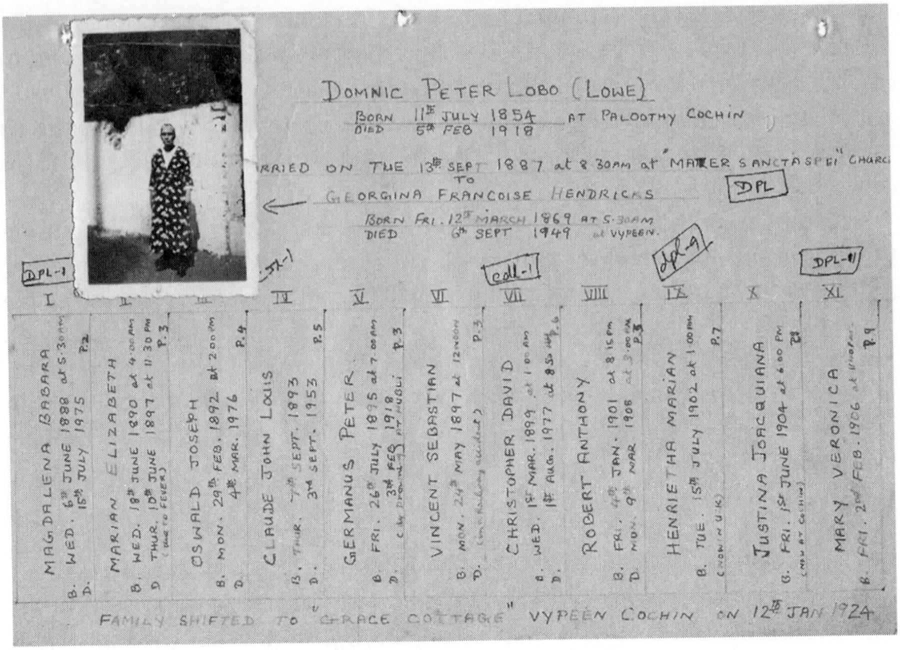

Figure 4. Excerpt from an extended copy of Dominic Peter Lobo's original family ledger, made by Russell in Cochin, 1979.

ushered us into his neat and bright home, something shifted. Russell was very friendly and welcoming as he settled us down on his couch and expressed deep interest in knowing more about our archive and our process. After we gave him a brief introduction, he told us he had been keen to speak to us as he had been archiving his own family history for several years. He then brought out his laptop and began showing us a series of documents containing meticulously detailed family trees.

The archive Russell and his family had put together tracing their history was stunning. As the interview commenced, Russell began with a scan of an old handwritten family tree, on which he pointed out the name of his great grandfather, Dominic Peter Lobo. In 1979, when Russell had freshly graduated from college, he went to visit his ancestral family home in Vypin, near Cochin. There, he happened to find an old ledger that had been maintained by his great grandfather, which contained a carefully detailed family tree, marking out the births, deaths and marriages of every family member, down to the date and time each had taken place. After Dominic passed away in 1918, the ledger had remained in his home until Russell chanced upon it and copied out its contents. This discovery sparked his interest and led him to seek more about his history by contacting older relatives, friends and acquaintances. Gradually, some of his cousins and other relations, too, got involved in tracing the broader history of their family, and over the next four decades, a rich tapestry of information was gathered.

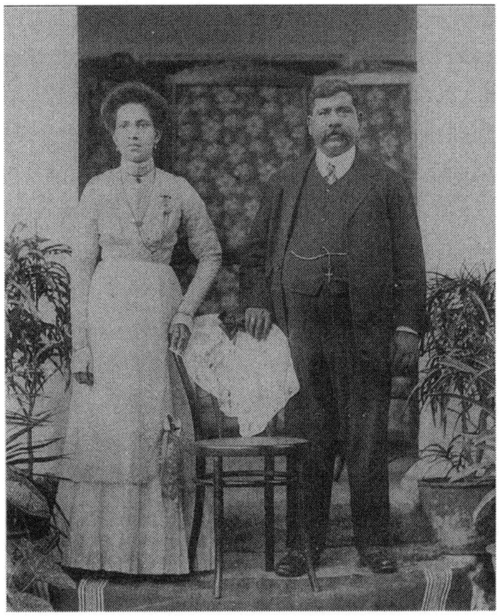

Figure 5. Agnes Dias and her husband Leander Rebello. Cochin, circa 1910s. Leander and Agnes are Russell's paternal grandmother Evelyn's parents.

Through the interview, Russell speedily took us through a broad selection of his archive. Although there were a few scanned photographs in his collection, many of which were from the early twentieth century, the bulk of his archive consisted of very detailed family trees, much in the tradition of his great grandfather's ledger. Russell had traced both his paternal line of the Lowe family, as well as his maternal, Rebello family, in careful detail and through them, had also collected a wealth of information about his extended family. This included the Scolt, Alwyn, Meyn and Fernandes families, all of whom had originated in Vypin, Cochin and had regularly intermarried across generations. Each document also included anecdotal information on family members, including an intriguing reference to Edith Scolt, who had lived and worked in Calcutta as a teacher and had been a possible inspiration for the character of Ms Violet Stoneham in the famous Aparna Sen film, *36 Chowringhee Lane.*[41] Russell explained to us that most of these families had Portuguese roots, and one of the most interesting details we learned was how family names were anglicised through the late nineteenth century in order to secure better employment opportunities.[42] Thus, Russell's grandfather Claude Lowe changed his family name from Lobo to Lowe, and Claude's uncle Thomas changed it to Lobow while another uncle Alexander retained the original Lobo. Similarly, the Scolt family originally had the amalgamated Dutch-Portuguese name of Scolta-D'costa which was also later anglicised.[43]

[41] Margaret warmed up to our presence slowly and was more comfortable since Richard had taken the lead in the interview. Asking to see someone's private family albums is far more intimate than simply doing an interview about their life, and we had rushed into making our initial request to see photographs within the first five minutes of meeting her.

[42] Document from Russell's archive detailing Alexander Lobo's descendants contains a listing for Edith Scolt, also referred to as Hedwig and Edie, and notes an excerpt from an email by Ben Scolt on 4 April 2014, reading, 'My aunt Edie was quite a character. One of Edie's students, Aparna Sen, directed a movie *36 Chowringhee Lane*, based on Aunty Edie's life.' Alexander Lobo's Descendant's Report, courtesy *The Anglo-Indian Archives*.

[43] Detailed in a letter to Russell Lowe by an elderly relative named Allen Scolt in 1988. Courtesy *The Anglo-Indian Archives*.

As Russell got deeper into each family tree, his complex map-like documents gradually began to open up to us. Thus far in our fieldwork, we had interacted with families who either had physical photo albums or other materials with them in their homes which we were able to digitise once they had agreed for them to be a part of the archive. Russell, however, had offered to share with us an already researched, compiled and fully digital archive, made through four decades of collaborative efforts by his family. How would this wealth of material, which was largely textual, change the predominantly photographic archive we had initially imagined? And how would these family trees, which carefully detailed the lives of hundreds of people across more than two centuries, interact with the collections of other families?

Although it was not immediately obvious to us as we sat in Russell's living room looking through the detailed documents, as we later organised the material within the archive, we were able to see more clearly how his family trees could find connections with the stories of other families in Cochin whose narratives could be a part of the archive in the future, or even link to Anglo-Indian family histories from Asansol and more recent stories from Anglo-Indians living in Australia. We could also see his collection being of immense value to a potential researcher studying Anglo-Indian histories of Cochin through the nineteenth century or migration patterns in the twentieth, as well as the impact of colonial laws on employment prospects for Anglo-Indians, as a few possibilities.

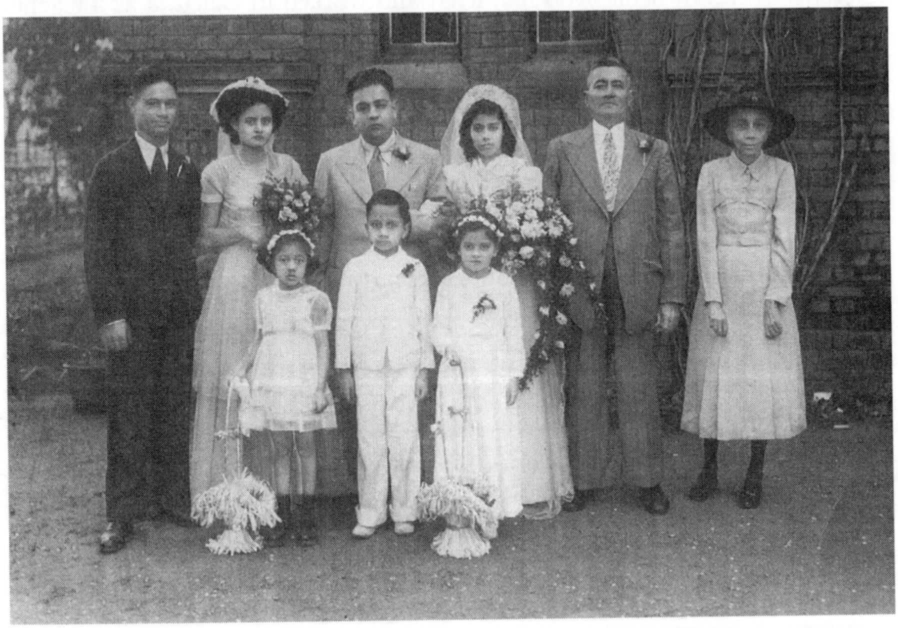

Figure 6. Top Row, Left to Right: Oscar Montaut, Edna Montaut, Robert Lowe and Zona (Montaut) Lowe, Adolphus Montaut and Magdalene Lowe. Bottom row: Cletty D'Souza, Keith Gill and Ursula Montaut. Photograph from Robert and Zona's wedding day. Asansol, West Bengal, 1949.

As Russell put together all the documents and images into a folder to share with us, I also thought about the role of trust, which was so central to this project. Every family we had visited thus far had readily shared their albums with us, telling us about their lives and the histories of their families in rich detail, trusting that their stories would remain in the archive as they had told them while aiding a community effort to preserve a part of their history. It remained to be seen how each family's story would influence the larger archive, but Russell's decades-long archival project clearly demonstrated the value of tracing larger histories through the very personal.

The Archive at the 11th World Anglo-Indian Reunion

As we wrapped up our first round of fieldwork in Chennai in late November, less than two months remained before the commencement of the 11th World Anglo-Indian Reunion in Chennai in January 2019, where we were scheduled to put up an exhibition and a presentation of the archive for the broader Anglo-Indian community. For this, we created a series of short slideshows from the photographs we had digitised for the archive, incorporating snippets and contextual information from the interviews and other material. These were to be presented in conjunction with a physical exhibition of images from a 2006 Chennai exhibition Dileep and Harry had co-curated, of Anglo-Indian family photographs from an earlier archival exercise. The reasoning for this was largely practical, as we only had permission to play the slideshows for a stipulated period in the Loyola College auditorium, where our project was to be presented. So it had been decided that the older exhibition was also going to be put up outside the venue to have a more lasting presence through the duration of the reunion, as more families and other visitors could get to know about the existence of the archive.

In Delhi, in early December, Dileep and I worked through all the material we had gathered through fieldwork and prepared the slideshows. Overall, we had interviewed ten families and had digitised the albums and collections of nine. Already, we were working with over a thousand photographs and hours of audio and video footage, as well as other material such as documents and records. The slideshows were to include images from all the family archives, and the logic behind their curation was discussed extensively. There were two ways we could go about its organisation, the first being to arrange them as per family and present the archives as they had been originally catalogued. A second approach was to find other links among the images and curate them by subject, event, location or other markers instead. Unsure of what would work best to convey the nature of the archive and wanting to engage with the community audience in multiple ways, we decided to try both approaches and made two versions.

On the afternoon of the screening at the reunion in Chennai, the attendees gathered in a small auditorium in one corner of Loyola College, where, after a short introduction to the archive by Richard, both slideshows were projected in a loop. Many of the families we had interviewed were present for the screening, and as the slideshows played, some from the audience recognised the subjects in the photographs, and soon conversations began between the families and members in the audience as friends and extended family members were identified in the photos, along with events, locations, buildings in the backgrounds and other details. Soon, the atmosphere in the auditorium began to resemble a large informal family gathering, and the slideshow almost faded into the background as conversations went from the photographs to inquiries about the health and wellbeing of relatives, friends and acquaintances. The photographs seemed to act almost like hyperlinks or conduits for other stories and conversations to be exchanged among the audience.

We had imagined that there would be a difference in the engagement of the audience to the second, shorter projection which was curated more thematically, mixing images from different archives within its sequence.[44] However, as the first slideshow concluded and the second began after a short pause, the response from the audience did not shift a great deal and the altered curation went largely unnoticed, except for a few keen observers who later came up to us to discuss the archive and the project in more detail. The informal atmosphere in the auditorium remained as the slideshows continued to play, and the audience filtered in and out, some taking the time to look at the print exhibition outside. As evening approached, we wrapped up the screenings, and although we had engaged with many families through the course of the day and spoken at some length about the archive with various people, it was interesting how the photographs themselves had not really been the core point of these discussions.

The reaction we received to the exhibition as well as the archive by attendees from the community, was different from what we had initially expected. Looking back, it seems more obvious to us that as the reunion was held in Chennai, many Anglo-Indians with origins in the city would have chosen to visit that year. Since our fieldwork had focused exclusively on families in the city, it is not particularly surprising that many in our audience had found personal links to the photographs screened. In fact, it was the print exhibition of photographs on display outside the venue which was received more as an 'archive' of images by the audience. The immediate ties of kinship and family were less prominent to the audience who engaged with these images, and here, they were read more as photographs of the community, with details in the images like fashion and pose more remarked upon and noticed.

[44] As we began to look at the archive more cohesively and outside of the family structures, various photographic themes began to emerge. These included group photos, individual portraits, photos of children, couples, photos of events like birthdays or Railway Institute parties, weddings, casual snapshots, etc. In a second—and more thematic—curation of the archive, we organised it within these broader themes rather than familial arrangements, prompting different interpretations.

Somehow, this was closer to the reaction we had expected from our audience to all the photographs, to see them as we had seen them, as *representing* the community. As outsiders to the community and more specifically to the families we had interviewed, we could not help but read all the photographs within the archive as representative of the community at large. But the subtle difference in the reactions of many in our audience made visible how despite being in an archive, and even when decontextualised from the family albums the photographs had originally come from, the images remained distinctly tied to their families and remained ready to be activated within that context.

Learnings and Conclusions

Our experience through the first year of the archive's existence has gone on to significantly shape the decisions we have taken around it as we have moved forward. Through our first round of fieldwork with families in the community and the experience of showing the archive in a public context, we became acutely aware of the multiple and shifting contexts around family photographs that need to be continually negotiated within the archive. As we have progressed with carrying out fieldwork with families in Guwahati, Assam, we have continued our discussions, exploring more possibilities of collaborations with individuals and scholars from within the community and outside it. We have gradually begun to understand more clearly how within a community archive, while collections of private and intimate familial histories do remain largely intact, they also cannot escape their role as documents representing community histories, identities and narratives. And since this latter role becomes more primary and obvious when the archive is approached as a research tool or a space for learning, the inclusion of more diverse and nuanced perspectives of Anglo-Indian experience within the archive becomes crucial. Given that the archive is primarily centered on photographs, it has also been very important for us to have a broad-based approach to defining what really constitutes family photographs.

The reading of an archive and the material it holds is also significantly defined by how and where the archive is shown, who curates and shows it, who engages with it and in what way, and the quality and quantity of the information embedded within it. We have gradually understood and negotiated each of these factors at every turn of the archive's evolution, and as we have moved to organise the archive more systematically in an online space, the concerns around metadata tagging, captioning of images, the nature of contextual information embedded within the images, as well as how publicly accessible it can and should be, have all been important and ongoing areas of concern and consideration for us. The process of digital organisation and categorisation of the images has also thrown up more conceptual questions for us, centred around information hierarchies. Since the stories around each image in the archive were relayed to us only through one, or perhaps two people from a family, the archive holds only these specific perspectives of the photographs, and the scope for more interpretations of the images to emerge if more members of a family or even a scholar or researcher were to add another layer to its reading, always remains.

Over the last three years, in setting up and creating a space for this archive, it is the continuing support, collaboration and encouragement of the Anglo-Indian community which has allowed it to grow despite the real logistical and financial constraints it has constantly been under. Since we set up a more substantial online presence with a website in 2020,[45] we have gradually seen interest in the project growing among researchers and individuals exploring histories of colonisation and the post-colonial worlds, other archives in Asia, and most importantly, the broader Anglo-Indian community in India and abroad, who have been able to find us independently and connect with us. Although it has continued to be an enormous challenge to secure financial assistance to keep this project going—resulting in limited and slow progress with fieldwork and expansion of the archive, opportunities to collaborate and build networks with other community archives—individuals from the community and scholars have helped us keep the archive running and gradually growing.

[45] www.angloindianarchives.com

Photographing Trauma, Repatriation and a New Life

Re-Remembering the Family during the Partition of 1947

Aditi Kumar

This essay will explore the visual archives of displaced communities from Mirpur, a city that is in contemporary Azad Kashmir, Pakistan. I study the case of a repatriated Indian woman named Fatima Bibi (b. 1930) from undivided Jammu and Kashmir, who was left behind in Pakistan-administered Jammu and Kashmir (hereafter PAJK) in the year of India's partition in 1947. She breathed her last among her children in 2008, who are now settled in the United Kingdom. Led by her son Zualfqar Ali, they have contributed to the interviews informing this essay. Another photographically induced family narrative contemporary to Fatima Bibi belongs to Bansa Devi, whom I address at the end of the essay through oral interviews with her son K.L. Balgotra. The visual materials for my research are in the form of personal photographs and oral memories that evidence the construction of an alternative history and culture of a displaced community.[1] I chose feminine narratives as these women have changed identities in correspondence with the changing history of the Indian nation. Parts of their personal histories have been lost forever, just as Mirpur became a forgotten city, submerged in the Jhelum River after the construction of the Mangla Dam in 1962.

Mirpur's submersion not only resulted in the large-scale loss of home and hearth but also the obliteration of a cultural ethos associated with the physical site that had been a geographical marker of identity for many. While conducting oral interviews with these displaced families between the years 2016–2019, most of them reiterated the fact that in their sudden displacement, they had been forced barefoot and penniless into a new country. The only thoughts that occupied them were whether they would get anything to eat, and where they would live. At such a time, preserving photographic albums or getting fresh photographs taken was a luxury unthinkable for many. In their transition from PAJK to the India-administered part of J&K, they had left

---

[1] The political status of PAJK displaced communities till date remains problematic as the Indian state still recognises them as a part of the larger state of Jammu and Kashmir. Before 1947, PAJK was a part of the undivided state of Jammu and Kashmir. Therefore, if recognised as 'refugees', it leads to a conundrum for the Indian State. Because it would mean accepting that a part of Jammu and Kashmir State is indeed under Pakistan's administration.

wounded and dying relatives behind, unable to carrying anything apart from themselves across the border. They were starving refugees, thirsty for days on end. Most of the valuables they carried were either sold or distributed among the people who needed them the most. Even the clothes that they were wearing were torn. They were only concerned with saving their lives and reaching safely to the other side of PAJK. The larger socio-cultural and historical contexts of the idea of families during Partition become important while documenting photographs for my study. There was a dearth of family photographs to inform my research among the displaced families from Jammu and New Delhi. Even the families who were more privileged, such as those who were rescued in army trucks or aircrafts, preferred to carry with them only utilitarian items, kitchenware, jewellery or valuables. Most of the families in my research had photographs or albums that were made post 1947. In any case, the taking of photographs was thought of as a privilege or reserved only for special occasions till the mid-twentieth century. Photography was a new phenomenon, even to the Indian urban middle class, and not easily accessible to most people until the late twentieth century. Where then, was the scope of carrying family photographs and tending to them at this moment of deep rupture?

The wide range of images that can be broadly classified as 'family photographs' invite the reader to reflect on the different types of relationships they depict. For example, individual poses and gestures by bodies within the frame, the display of material objects and choice of location, express family dynamics and interpersonal relationships (Hirsh, 1981).[2] A family photograph bears the potential to display the dynamics of power and economic relations within as well as outside the structure of kinship. However, the viewer needs to be careful of this inside-outside division as it can be deceivingly porous.[3] Family photos are considered 'non-state institutionalised', taken from intimate spaces of domestic life. But domestic photographs too follow social norms, a system that is 'rule governed and engaged in a socially patterned communicative process, which though implicit, still constitutes a social institution'.[4] These norms become evident when the photographs are explained to an outsider through a process of narrativisation, which marks the difference between the construction of meanings by an insider and an outsider. However, it is believed that despite competitive subjective interpretations, the common world of shared meanings ensures an intersubjectivity of interpretations. Therefore, while personal experiences determine the meanings of photographs, they are nonetheless understandable from other positions via their narrations.

---

[2] For family photographs and dynamics, see Hirsch, Julia. *Family Photographs*. P. 3.

[3] See Bourdieu, Pierre et al. 1990. *Photography: A Middle-brow Art*. Trans. Shaun Whiteside. (Cambridge: Polity Press).

[4] Musello, Christopher. 1980 'Studying the Home Mode: An Exploration of Family Photography and Visual Communication'. *Studies in Visual Communication*. Vol. 6. No. 1 (Spring). p. 23, 28.

From the case studies discussed below, the process of narrativisation as well as the connection between inter-subjectivity and family photographs becomes evident. Photographs that already existed as part of family memorabilia, and those that were taken while archiving the social lives of survivors of displacement, collectively comprise the category of 'family photographs' in this essay. For understanding the aspect of intersubjectivity, I will be referring to key arguments by Lusia Passerini on 'the primacy of intersubjectivity'.[5] Intersubjectivity asserts that the photograph is itself a form of negotiation, a form of communication that does not exist outside of a context. We communicate 'with people', to construct shared meaning/s. On the heels of theorists like Luisa Passerini (2007) and Paul Ricoeur (2000), Phil Sandick states in an unpublished doctoral dissertation that, 'while oral history is a distilled and temporal act of narrativisation, photography is a distilled and ex-temporal act of narrativisation'.[6] In the course of documenting narrativised family photographs both in Jammu and New Delhi, I realised that both oral and visual media shared a dialogic relation that is often (re)negotiated and (re)constructed during 'narrative concatenation' (Ricoeur, 2000) to create meaning; a meaning that is understandable and relatable in the present socio-cultural and historical environment from an intersubjective standpoint.

The images used in this essay are photographs of first-generation Indo-Pak Partition survivors from Mirpur, that were taken as part of the documentation of their social mobility as citizens of post-Independence India. These photographs in turn become points of entry to question the identity, agency and socio-cultural locations of the erstwhile residents of Mirpur. I will be drawing on the critical framework in the writing of Ariella Azoulay (2008) to understand questions of citizenship, state-controlled photography and vernacular visualisation by citizens, including women. The Palestinian community that she works with has experienced similar forms of displacement as the ones I examine in the context of India, giving an opportunity to Azoulay's notion of 'deterritorialised citizenship' to manifest in both places. While examining the works of Roland Barthes (1980) and Susan Sontag (1977), Azoulay engages her readers with an insider-outsider perspective, journeying from the photographer

[5] 'While objective reality comprises empirically verifiable external "facts", one's first-person experience—the internal landscape of truth claims—is the subjective reality of that individual. Starting from a social constructivist stance, intersubjectivity looks at the underlying cause of those internal truth claims. It posits that one's subjective beliefs are shaped not only by the historic-cultural contexts of that particular individual ... but also by that individual's dialogical position within an ecology of other individuals and groups. It recognises that these external actors have their own potentially competing truth claims, the negotiation of which is a crucial ingredient in the intersubjective multiplicity of self that is bound up into a single human being'. Sandick, Phil. 2009. 'Intersubjectivity in Photography and Oral History: Toward Ethical Creation and Production' (PhD Dissertation, Columbia University). www.philsandick.com/Intersubjectivity/Photography.pdf.

[6] Ibid. p.10.

to the photographed, where although the source of power lies with the former, the image itself evokes civic engagement by the latter.[7] A comparison can be drawn here between the rights that are given to the state subjects of Jammu and Kashmir and those who do not have them, despite belonging to the extended areas of the state now under PAJK. Drawing upon Azoulay, one can infer that the state re-territorialises citizenship, wherein state protection and facilities are provided to those who are declared as 'citizens'[8], while it discriminates against the 'non-citizens', who occupy the same territory and are ruled by the same power. In Jammu, such examples can be witnessed on the outskirts of the city, in the informal settlements of R.S. Pura and Simbal Camp—where roughly 25,000 to 30,000 new migrants to the city have conglomerated. The family albums and photographs obtained from the people of such informal settlements can be studied as 'social biographies' (2012),[9] horizontal narratives that contain both 'epic and anecdotal dimensions' of a major political moment in the subcontinent. The same structure of culling stories from oral memory applies to family albums, building upon 'photographic memories' which are used in a 'performative oral tradition' (2001).[10]

I find this model to be quite evident in the archival collection of Mr. Zualfqar Ali, whose family photographs reference various occasions that mark both

---

[7] 'In photography—and this is evident in every single photo—there is something that extends beyond the photographer's action, and no photographer, even the most gifted, can claim ownership of what appears in the photograph. Every photograph of others bears the traces of the meeting between the photographed persons and the photographer, neither of whom can, on their own, determine how this meeting will be inscribed in the photo.' Azoulay, Ariella. 2008. *The Civil Contract of Photography* (New York: Zone Books). p. 11.

[8] In his work on civil contract of photography in India, Christopher Pinney explains and further develops on Ariella Azoulay's idea of the 'civil contract of photography'. He says that the nineteenth century, State-controlled photography gradually evolved to possess an unpredictable potential. This potential seems more of a political struggle, especially during early twentieth-century British India. For example, in the case of the Amritsar Jallianwala Bagh massacre of 1919, the aftermath of the massacre was documented by a Bombay-based photographer, Narayan Vinayak Virkar. These photographs were a part of the Indian National Congress Punjab Inquiry report in 1920 (reproduced anonymously). This resulted in a mass furor both in India and London.

The images included deep bullet holes in the walls of Jallianwala Bagh, people with amputated limbs, among others. These images were later published in London, in *Our Daily India* by B.G. Horniman, who compared them with a report on Congo atrocities. This also marked the shift in ownership of these photographs. Thus, mobilising photography's 'civil contract'; from state-controlled—to the wider public. This, Pinney infers, created an anxiety crisis in twentieth century photography in India that destabilised the control of photography from the hands of the state; the slipping of the 'indexical authority' in India's *colonial habitus*. See Pinney, Christopher. 'Civil contract of photography in India 1' in *Media and Utopia*, p. 23, 26, 33 (Routledge, 2017).

[9] 'Social biographies' is a conceptual framework that was developed to use the conceptual framework developed by Elizabeth Edwards. To read further, see Edwards, Elizabeth. 2012. 'Objects of affect: Photography beyond the image'. *Annual review of anthropology*. Vol. 41. p. 221.

[10] Langford, Martha. 2001. *Suspended conversations: The afterlife of memory in photographic albums* (Canada: McGill-Queen's Press-MQUP). p. 175.

struggles and achievements among the displaced community of Mirpur. The images act as social and emotional signifiers that give meaning to their new, post-traumatic, resettled life. According to Erkonan, family photography needs to become a lived proof of family memory that is successful in creating the 'concept of family' with its inherent past, and this helps in creating a family image that represents belongingness.[11] The creation of a sense of belongingness via photographs can be understood better through the narrative recollection of Zualfqar Ali. Through Ali's family photographs, I have chanced upon the personal narratives of displacement that belonged to thousands of women beyond Mirpur, who were subjected to a 'double violence' during Partition; raped or abducted by men of another religion, later forcefully married to them, and then repatriated to their former families and countries. Violence was thus perpetrated by the governments of both India and Pakistan, who in a second step, had uprooted these abducted women after several years in a bid to reinstate them to their roots, not heeding to the fact that they had by now fostered a family in the new country that they had come to accept as their 'home'. Pain here becomes a political instrument for wielding power, and the bodies of women become the 'property' of men, families or even governments, as the surface on which political programmes are inscribed. Pain becomes the medium through which society claims ownership of 'individuals'.[12] Hence, the separation of mothers from children, wives from husbands, and siblings and parents in the hands of sexual and reproductive violence, cannot be seen only within the discourse of family, but also needs to be understood in terms of politics and nation-making.[13]

---

[11] Erkonan, Şahika. 2014. 'Family Photographs: Exploring The Role of Photography in the Construction of Family Memory With the Ethnographic Method'. *Moment Journal*. Vol. 1. No. 2. doi:10.17572/mj2014.2.122147.

[12] In this case, the individuals are women who remember the historical wrongs done to them through the memory of pain that has been inscribed on their bodies. The marks on the bodies incurred due to violence become an obstacle in forgetting the traumatic past and the body of women; a 'memory'. While explaining the non-existent agency of women in war/post-war situations, Das refers to 'state' as a purely masculine space that reestablishes authority in the familial space through the father, brother or husband. She says that the state is not interested in the 'legal rights of women citizenship' but women as 'sexual and reproductive beings'. Both the honour of the state as well as the family lies in the bodies of women (as for both state and family, bodies become the living testimony for inscription of violence/shame). Taking a departure from the work of Elaine Scarry, *The Body of Pain*, she argues that the victim-subject position of women during the Partition was not fully determined by them. Drawing on the works of Ludwig Wittgenstein, Das elucidates how violence of Partition percolated into the everyday life of women; the silence around Partition created a 'force-field' within which women's narratives moved and slowly, they found their voice. A voice that helped them navigate within the realm of the domestic through the process of re-narrativisation. See Das, Veena. *Critical Events*, pp. 15–26.

Das, V. and Singh, B., 1995. *Critical events: an anthropological perspective on contemporary India* (Vol. 7). Delhi: Oxford University Press. p. 26.

[13] Ibid. p. 68.

Family Photographs and Collective Remembering: The Case of Fatima Bibi

Family photographs are repositories of family memories. In one of the most celebrated works on collective memory, Maurice Halbwachs (1992) said that family memory must be viewed as a part of collective memory, something I extend to understand as community memory. One cannot conceptualise memory only within the scope of an individual's recollection, and family memory needs to be understood in an inclusive social context. In similar parlance, Jan Asmann (1995) proposes that memory should be seen in its cultural context. He suggests that there are two kinds of memory: cultural memory and communicative memory. Cultural memory is constructed through various ritualistic practices and customs that have had a long-lasting impression on a community or a family. On the other hand, communicative memory is temporary and has limited scope. Cultural memory includes communicative memory, whereas the latter refers only to a recent past—memory which can only be perceived within a single generation. So when that generation disappears, the constructs of that specific memory are inevitably susceptible to disappearance. According to Astri Erll, 'Family memories belong primarily to the field of communicative memory, with its focus on everyday life, face-to-face interaction, oral communication and its restricted timespan of about three to four generations. However, communicative memory is linked to cultural memory and cannot be separated from the latter's myths, and there is always a possibility of inherited meaning in the notion of family memory'.[14]

This, I refer to as a process of 're-remembering', where a specific memory is recalled, reconstructed and recreated by the family in a dynamic space, where they work with the photographs. Annette Kuhn has worked extensively on the notion of familial autobiographical memory (1995). She feels that in studying family photographs, it is necessary to deconstruct memory as well as the image of a family. Thus, for her it is important to locate such photographs in their own sociocultural context, as well as to question them within other contexts of representation. She says that the arrangement of images, their display (pictures as shown, discussed or talked about) in series, and the ordering of these images are as meaningful as the pictures themselves. The display of images in a series constructs a family's story in a form that appears to be a 'classic narrative'[15]. According to Marianne Hirsch, 'photographs locate themselves precisely in the space of contradiction between the myth of the ideal family and the lived reality of family life.'[16] Often, non-serialised images reflect the silences within family histories.

---

[14] Erll, Astri. 2011. 'Locating Family in Cultural Memory Studies'. *Journal of Comparative Family Studies*. Vol. 42:3. doi:10.3138/jcfs.42.3.303.

[15] Kuhn, Annette. 1995. *Family Secrets: Acts of Memory and Imagination* (London: Verso). p. 17.

[16] Hirsch, Marianne. 'Family frames: Photography, narrative and post memory' in Erkonan, Sahika. *Family Photography and construction of memory*. p. 262.

The photograph which appears to be silent is in fact imbued with meaning; a meaning that resurrects or is reconstructed when viewers are provoked to recall the circumstances under which they were made. The 're-remembering' of past experiences by families sometimes includes specific dynamics such as migration, separation issues or traumatic events. Erll further adds, 'family memory is not simply "there"—it is not a mnemonic content stored in a family archive; instead, versions of the familial past are fabricated collectively, again and again, in situ, through concrete acts of communication and interaction.'[17] So in their retrieval, family memories are made and remade according to the contexts and agencies of their meaning-making.

Zualfqar Ali, a current resident of Birmingham, has carefully preserved the last traces of his family memory, which comprise a single, framed family photograph, a portrait photo of his mother,[18] and identity (ID) photos of both his parents. It is interesting to observe how various photographs comprising the broader category of 'family photographs' are mediated through socially constructed affiliations of kinship, nationhood and religion. There are multiple layers which disentangle as one views and analyses a particular photo, specific in time and space; it's the performative index that acts out in both private and public spheres. Ali's stepmother, Ved Kumari aka Fatima Bibi, belonged to the city of Mirpur in PAJK. She was separated from her family during the communal violence of November 1947, thereafter building a new life in independent India until she passed away in 2016. Her story was recounted by Ali, who as a young boy, witnessed his and his sibling's separation from her, their biological mother. He later played an instrumental role in reuniting her with her Hindu family back in Jammu. The majority of the second-generation inhabitants of such displaced families, now living in Jammu or Delhi, did not want to disclose the names/new identities of the women relatives that had been left behind in PAJK. Zualfqar Ali, was one of the rare interviewees who narrated at length the true story of his mother, premised on her fragmented life.

Ved Kumari was born in a Hindu family and was separated from them in 1947 at a young age. She converted to Islam in PAJK, and changed her name to Fatima Bibi, and stuck with this identity till the end of her life. My telephonic interview with Zualfqar Ali was followed by emails with attachments of passport-sized photographs of his parents, carefully preserved from ID cards and passport booklets. These ID photographs either bore stamp marks or were overwritten with signatures. One of the pictures was taken almost two decades after his mother's relocation to London in 1955. In the photograph, Zualfqar is seen as a young adult, accompanied by Fatima Bibi and his youngest sister (Figure 1). He can be seen sitting on a stool in formal attire. His sister Noreen is gleeful and seated on a high stool in the centre. Placed between her and his

[17] Erll. *Memory in Culture.* p. 313.

[18] Zualfqar's mother left PAJK for London in order to escape her extraction under the Repatriation Act that was signed between India and Pakistan (1950–1951).

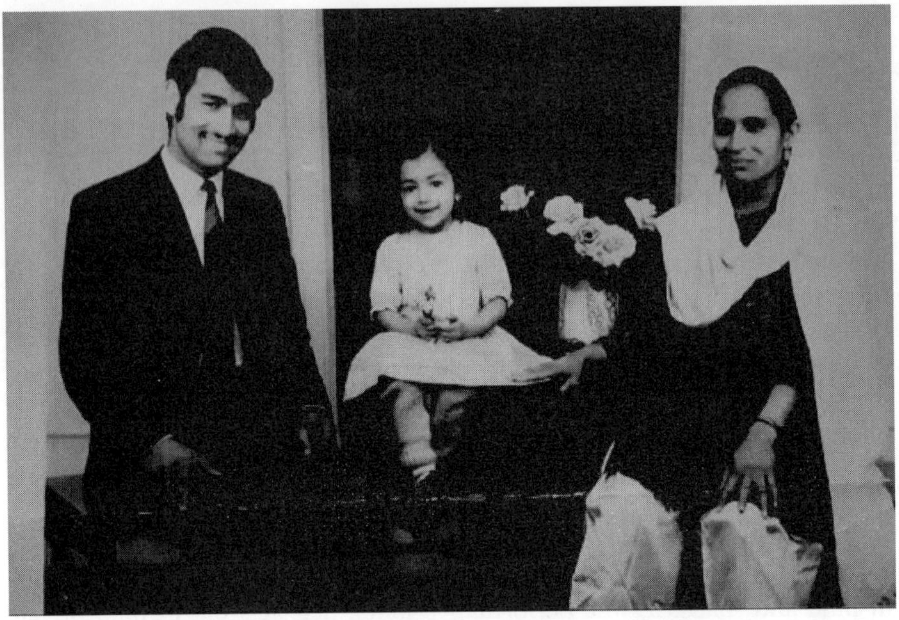

Figure 1. Zualfqar accompanied by his mother and sister. Birmingham, 1958 (© Private collection of Zualfqar Ali).

mother is a full flower vase, on the right-hand side. Zualfqar's mother is seen seated on the right-hand side, dressed in a traditional *salwar kameez*, with her head covered with a white dupatta and wearing golden *jhumkas* (chandelier-style earrings). He also shared the few letters that she wrote to her brothers in Jammu in the years immediately after her separation in 1947. On inquiring about the details of his mother's life history, he said that she used to repeatedly recount her life story to him in his childhood, thereafter deeply etched in his memory. He even remembered the names of the places and the people she met while fleeing from the government officials, who had come to extradite her from PAJK and return her to her Hindu family in Jammu.

The earliest passport photographs of Fatima Bibi are from the year 1959 (Figure 2). In 1947, his mother was only fourteen years old. As Ved Kumari, she, along with her parents and three brothers, Om Prakash, Bansilal and Bal Krishan, had been staying in a place called Dadyal, which was part of Mirpur district before Partition. After the communal riots of 1947 broke out in her region, she was separated from her family. She was abducted by an elderly Muslim man and brought to be a part of a new family in Pothasher. Burhan Ali was double the age of Kumari, and his mother was ardently religious. Kumari was converted, renamed as Fatima Bibi, married to Burhan Ali, and within a year, her son Zualfqar Ali was born.

When the repatriation act of 1950–51 was signed between the governments of India and Pakistan, repatriation officers accompanied by policemen were sent to Burhan Ali's house[19] to extradite his wife. Fatima refused to leave her family behind, though she was required to comply since these orders had been issued by the government of Pakistan. Between 1947–49, Fatima had given birth to two more children, Zualfqar's younger brother and sister. In 1958, at the onset of a military dictatorship in Pakistan, Fatima came back to Mirpur- Pothasher, and took her daughter back with her to England. During her ordeal with the repatriation officers who had come to extradite her from her new house at Pothasher in 1951, Fatima had secretly taken note of her Hindu family's Jammu address.

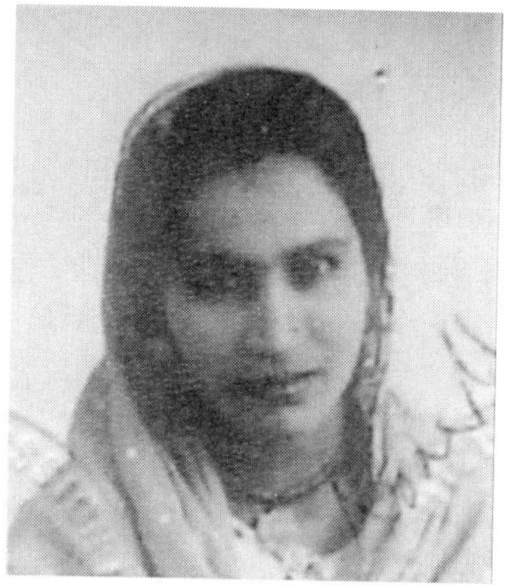

Figure 2. Identity photo of Fatima Bibi. Birmingham, 1959 (© Private collection of Zulfi Ali).

After some time, she mustered up the courage to write her first letter from London to her eldest brother, Om Prakash, who was then a practising dentist in Kathua. In 1987, she was finally able to visit her brothers in Kathua after forty years of separation.[20] A colored family photograph of this moment shows Zualfqar's youngest aunt and mother in Jammu (Figure 3). Thus, an apparently banal-looking family photo is imbued

[19] She left with the policemen carrying her infant daughter, leaving her two sons, husband and extended family behind. At night, she was housed in old Mirpur's famous advocate Laurasat Ali Khan's home. Fatima requested his wife to allow her to escape from their house the next morning, so she could reunite with Burhan Ali and her children. The advocate's wife felt sympathy for her and made arrangements for her escape. Fatima's brother-in-law's friend's house was at the outskirts of Mirpur city, in a village called Jhang, and popularly known as the Khad area. At night, Fatima, along with her infant daughter, left on foot for this place. Zualfqar remembered an incident his mother had recounted several times. During her journey, she was praying to Hussain to protect her and her infant daughter. Suddenly, in the thick of the night, she mystically encountered an old man in white dress. He guided her till the brink of the city and disappeared, much like a semi-divine figure, or *farishtah*. On reaching Jhang village, the friend's family was shocked, but received her with warm blankets and food. A message was sent secretly to her husband about her well-being. The same night, her husband and brother-in-law took her to their sister's house in Samloth in *zila* Gujjar Khan. She stayed at Samloth with her family for two or three years, thereafter leaving for Karachi. From Karachi, they moved back to Pothasher in 1950. Zualfqar's father left for England in 1952 and Fatima followed him in 1955 leaving her children behind with relatives, in order to avoid extradition from PAJK under the repatriation act.

[20] On reaching Jammu, she discovered that her eldest brother had not married since he did not want to marry in his sister's absence. Fatima Bibi chose a bride for him and in her presence, got her brother married. From Jammu she wrote a letter to her Zualfqar Ali in England accompanied with a small note from his uncle Om Prakash in Urdu. Her two brothers Om Prakash and Bansi Lal are no more. Fatima Bibi died in 2016. Telephonic interview, Zualfqar Ali, January 2019.

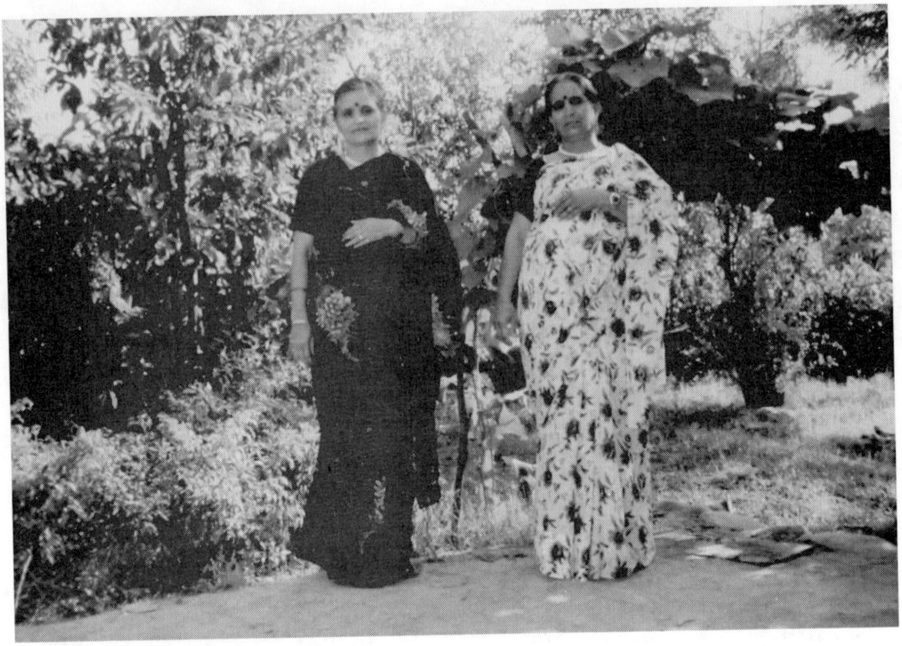

Figure 3. Fatima Bibi with her sister. Jammu, 1987 (© Private collection of Zulfi Ali).

with complex life histories and kinship memories amidst nations and identities in the making. In her work on family photographs, Julia Hirsch (1981) urges the viewer to look more keenly at the mundane family photograph.

A family photograph does not only portray family relationships but acts as a performative space where a social system of standard rules are played out. Zualfqar's photograph with his mother and sister shows them relaxed and joyful (Figure 1). Such family photos that are conventional recordings of domestic life remain ubiquitous in our world, urging the viewer to overlook a violent past. Evident in the joyful faces of the portrayed subjects, their dress and direct gaze is at the hope for a better life in a new country and a new 'home'. This, according to Margaret Olin (2012) is the 'performative index' of family photographs that helps to visually reframe and re-remember a violent past with the promise of a better future. It is visible in a majority of the family photos belonging to PAJK families, who consciously pose for the camera with brightly lit faces, often dressed in their finest clothes and accessories.

Zualfqar's fourth photograph was a black-and-white image of his mother standing (Figure 4). The picture was taken in London during the late 1950s. It appears strikingly different, for she is dressed in one of her finest garments, in direct contrast to the ordeals she had recently faced in PAJK. This portrait is emblematic of the new life she had built with her husband in London. The display of cultural signifiers such as jewellery and decorative items in the picture reflect a consciously constructed image for public viewing, blurring

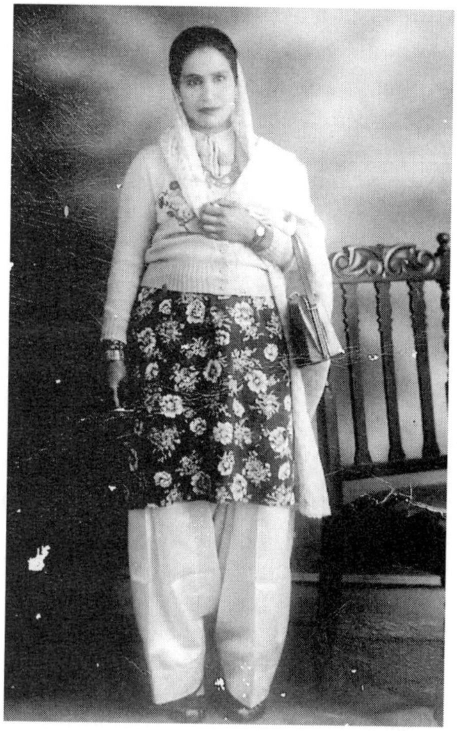

Figure 4. Self portrait of Ved Kumari aka Fatima Bibi. Birmingham, 1970 (© Private collection of Zulfi Ali).

the public–private divide in family photographs. In the picture, Fatima is seen standing with partially folded arms, clasping the fold of her white *dupatta.* The presence of a chair in the photograph might be an added cultural accessory, the wooden design on the back of the chair making it one of the typical modern dining chairs found in middle-class Indian households of the time. Her crisp, ironed *salwar kameez* with a floral print stands out in the picture, as do the polished shoes, a necklace worn over a cardigan, a hand purse, and a gold *kada* (bracelet)—all signifying a good standard of living that Fatima had acquired after relocating to London. In some senses, the photograph freezes time as a testament to joyful memories of domestic life. Framing it can also be seen as an attempt to remember a specific part of family history. Fatima's dressing-up also signifies the social mobility of her family and her portrait acts as a representative image for other middle-class families that relocated to London after the construction of Mangla Dam in Mirpur district.[21]

The careful preservation of Fatima's photograph by Zualfqar is similar to Barthes' discovery of his mother's image, 'the Winter Garden Photograph', after her death. The photograph helped Zualfqar mediate through a period of loss and mourning after Fatima's demise. He explained, 'my grief wanted … an image which would do both justice and be accurate'. Most of the photographs he had found initially 'were merely analogical, provoking only her identity, not her truth.'[22] Like Barthes' search guided by a visceral longing, Zualfqar preserves his mother's photograph as 'a material vestige',[23] embedded in the photographic index that provides him a link between corporeal reality and his deceased mother. This link ceases to exist beyond the image. As noted by

[21] During the mid-1950s and 1960s, Mirpur district of PAJK witnessed a mass migration of people to the United Kingdom due to the construction of Mangla Dam, that entirely submerged Mirpur and its 400-plus villages.

[22] Barthes. 1980. *Camera Lucida*. p. 71.

[23] Ibid., p. 80.

Margaret Olin, 'Barthes uses the photograph to satisfy his desire to possess or commune with his mother, to absorb her into himself and preserve her there through his identification with her.'[24]

Zualfqar also shared his parents' ID photographs. As mentioned earlier, all of them were either stamped or had signatures across their surfaces. These photographs were removed and preserved separately from their respective identity cards or passports. The assimilation of ID photos in the intimate preserve of private collections refutes the primary reason of their production as identity photo documents meant for state surveillance. The ubiquitous ID photo remains a common visual form that is found in several family montages, and in albums. In a few cases, they are the only tangible visual memory that informs a family's process of photographic memorialisation.

A primary difference between such ID photographs and other family photographs in Zualfqar's collection, was that the 'familial gaze'[25] in these photos was addressed by a stern and wide-eyed subject, with a grim-looking face devoid of any facial expressions. While elucidating the purpose of refugee ID photos within the private sphere of family photos in the case of Vietnamese diaspora, Thy Phu says,

> the inclusion of refugee ID photos within the discourse of diasporic family humanises subjects in a way that mirrors the logic of neoliberal humanism … exposes an underlying tension between the surveillance of subjection and identity politics … At the same time, the inclusion of refugee ID documents as family photos intersects with the discourse of neoliberal humanism. The implicit before/after structure that upholds self-fashioning as a counter to the violence of subjection invokes a controversial form of identity politics.[26]

According to her, the inclusion of ID photos in family albums or collections humanises the subject in the photograph, hence challenging the hierarchical structure for which it was produced in the first place. The ID photograph acquires a different meaning in the space of 'civil identity defined by the state',[27] a symbol of a new identity that is reimagined, appropriated and re-mediated in public or private realms.[28]

Surprisingly, Zualfqar had no portrait image of his father, apart from three ID photographs from the year 1955, 1971 and 1979. Here, too, the refactoring

---

[24] Olin, Margaret. 2012. *Touching Photographs* (Chicago: University of Chicago Press). p. 69.

[25] Hirsch, Marianne. ed. 1999. *The Familial Gaze* (Hanover, NH, and London: Dartmouth College).

[26] Phu, Thy. 2014. *Diasporic Vietnamese Family Photographs, Orphan Images, and the Art of Recollection* (Ann Arbor, MI: Michigan Publishing, University of Michigan Library).

[27] Edwards, Elizabeth. 2012. 'Objects of affect: Photography beyond the image'. *Annual review of anthropology*. Vol. 41. p. 227.

[28] The Muslim diaspora population that migrated from Mirpur to London during the late 1950s and 1960s was offered British citizenship. Few of the families from Mirpur forfeited their Pakistani citizenship and acquired British citizenship. Zualfqar's family was one of them.

of ID photos counters the state's purpose of 'dehumanising' the subject by neoliberal logic. Instead, the image is a trace of family memory that helps to mediate through lived experiences of first-generation survivors and their oral narratives in understanding familial relationships. The ID photo of Burhan Ali acts as a trace of his life's journey. For Zualfqar, he is the provider who moved to London to start a new life and give his wife a new home; a home she could never have had in PAJK under the threat of extradition by repatriation officers. ID photographs in this case, demonstrate how new identities can be formed, re-imagined and appropriated from a public domain to speak to a private realm, forging new meanings in a social space that they come to occupy. I agree with Janet Hoskins, who says that photographs have the potential for 'a process of enactment and rhetorical assertion and act as nodes where various discourses temporarily intersect in particular ways'.[29] These photographs are not mere surrogates for the absent person but also play an active role in the construction and experience of social space, and therefore, are a form of 'partible self'.[30]

The social efficacy or meaning of a photograph is not only limited to the visual realm but is a convergence of several sensory responses. Several scholars such as Elizabeth Edwards (2006), Martha Langford (2001), Christopher Pinney (1997) and W.J.T. Mitchell (2005) argue that the efficacy of a photograph is made possible by its multisensory modalities. It includes everyday performative embodiments and negotiates between the past and the present. In such senses, photographs act as relics, and connect the living with the dead. Thus, a photograph is embedded in a system of social relations, performative enactments and 'patterns of affect' that need to be understood in relation to different space and time trajectories.[31] The multi-sensorial aspect of photographs is highlighted by the anthropologist Michael Taussig, who argues that while describing photographs, one cannot overlook their relationship with orality and sound. This is further augmented by Edwards, who says that people use photographs as a focus to tell their stories, 'claim histories'—and she calls this a work of 'visual repatriation'.[32] In a way, they not only supplant various processes of identity formation but also form a connection between memory and history.

Multi-sensorialism adds another layer to the subjective meaning-making of photographs. It also means that photographs become differently related to the present via memory and practice. Photographs therefore become memories in progress; meaning-making itself being a constant process of construction by which people create a story of their family's past in the present. Thus,

[29] Hoskins, Janet. 2013. *Bibliographical Objects: How Things Tell the Stories of Peoples' Lives* (London: Routledge).

[30] I borrow this term from Elizabeth Edwards, who believes that photographs are powerful actants in a social space 'intertwined with a larger process of maintaining different forms of sociality and personhood'. See Edwards. 2012. *Annual review*. p. 229.

[31] Ibid. p. 222.

[32] Ibid. p. 229.

photography becomes an important means to enable the creation of a family's self-image through a memorial process, which embodies different time frames both of the past as well as of the future. As enumerated by Katherine Hoffmann,

> Family images may provide some sense of immortality of bloodlines; family images may call up pleasant and/or unpleasant memories or current situations. But there can always be a 'journey' to 'see a newer world' that may be clearer and richer as a result of having looked at and been moved by images of others and thereby to understand our own individual identities and the families we are a part of or close to.[33]

Elaborating Katherine Hoffman's idea of individual identities, I would like to discuss how intersubjectivity in the case of family photographs can be seen as intercorporeality.[34] Departing from 'subjective idealism', I would like to emphasise the interconnectedness of relations/bodies in a family frame, through poses, gestures, etiquettes that define the nature of relationships in a family photograph. Thus, the photograph acts as synecdoche for its temporal and spatial occupation and generated social meaning.

Family Memory and Trauma in Photographs: The Case of Bansa Devi

The family album of K.L. Balgotra memorialises and preserves landmark achievements in his family after their displacement from Mirpur and subsequent resettlement in Delhi. These photographs bear witness to a new life that K.L. Balgotra built for himself, marking the ascent of his family from makeshift refugee camps in Sabzi Mandi, Old Delhi to *pakka* (permanent) houses in Lajpat Nagar. The photographs included in the album are commemorative photographs, portraits of family members and group photographs (Figures 5, 6). For instance, there are images from the graduation ceremonies that belong to K.L. Balgotra's sisters, taken after their displacement to Delhi. Most men in the family joined commercial businesses while the women were married off at an early age, making the women's postgraduate education an exceptional occurrence (Figure 7).

The other notable photographs in his collection were portraits of Balgotra's mother and aunt. Their stiff bodies and fixed gazes hide their larger, more

---

[33] Hoffmann, Katherine in Erkonan. 2014. *Family Photography*. p. 262.

[34] The notion of intercorporeality was introduced for the first time by Merleau-Ponty, who defines it as a process of social cognition wherein individuals reciprocate certain gestures or actions in relation to each other. He illustrates it with an example of the 'perception–action' loop such as smiling, yawning etc. that have contagious effects on individuals, who willingly or unwillingly reciprocate these gestures. Also, according to the phenomenological approach, the social interaction of individuals does not start in isolation but from intercorporeality. The interaction between individuals is visible in various elements of embodiment such as gestures, body image, language, touch, etiquette etc. For Intersubjectivity and Intercorporeality, see Thomas J. Csordas, *Embodiment and cultural phenomenology*. na, 1999.

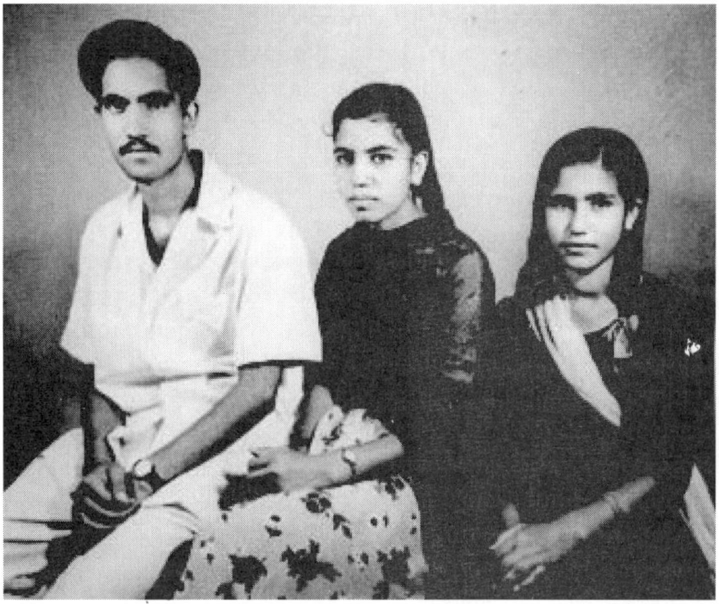

Figure 5. K.L. Balgotra with his family. New Delhi, 1950 (© Private collection of K.L. Balgotra).

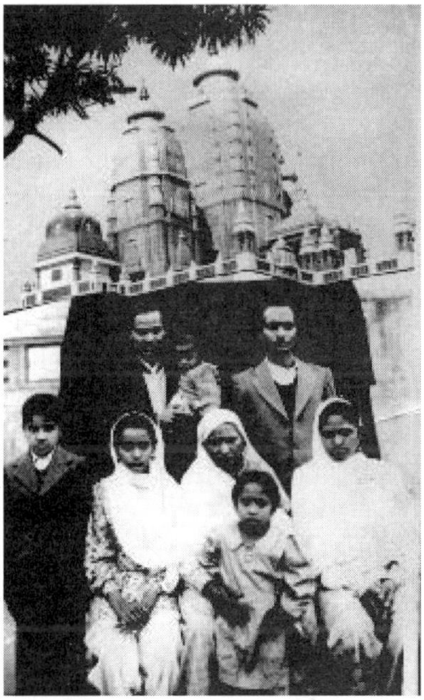

Figure 6. K.L. Balgotra with his family outside Birla temple. New Delhi, 1952 (© Private collection of K.L. Balgotra).

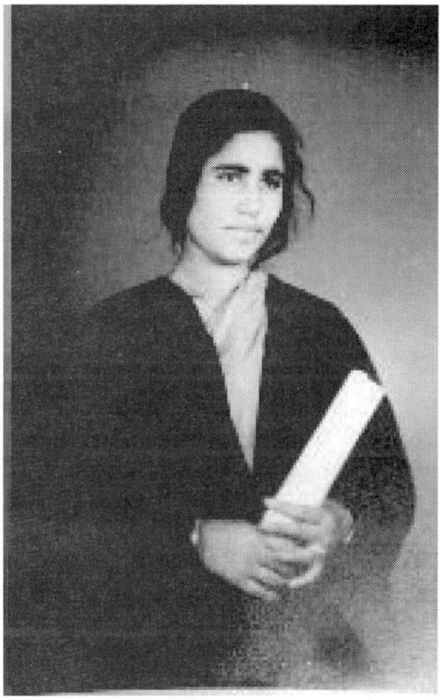

Figure 7. K.L. Balgotra's sister after her graduation ceremony. New Delhi, 1962 (© Private collection of K.L. Balgotra).

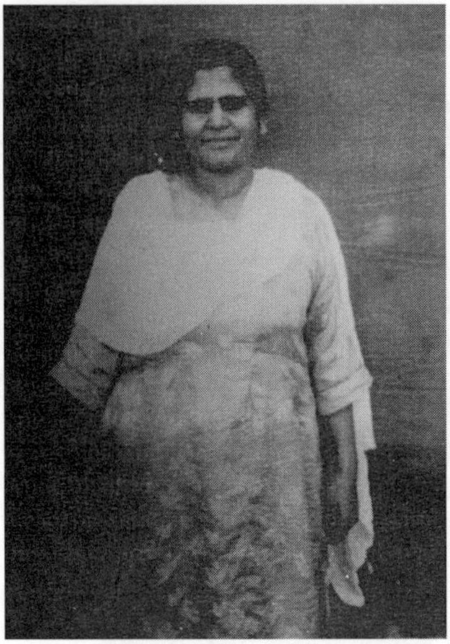

Figure 8. K.L. Balgotra's aunt Bimbla Devi. New Delhi (© Private collection of K.L. Balgotra).

complex stories and tumultuous histories. My interview with Balgotra revealed that the two women had been abducted during the Partition riots, and one of them attempted to immolate herself but survived the burns (the marks near her neck are visible in one of the photographs). They stayed in refugee camps and three years later, were reunited with their family members in Delhi (Figure 8).[35]

The late Bansa Devi was K.L. Balgotra's aunt, who, while fleeing from Mirpur, had been held captive by an Afghan in a thatched-roof room. Balgotra elucidates that Mirpur city was looted by Afghan tribals after the city's evacuation. During her captivity, Bansa Devi had retaliated against her captor's attempts at assault, and incurred several injuries on her body. She tried to immolate herself but survived, and her wounds later got infested by maggots. Balgotra described it thus, '*Mata ji ke gale ke zakhm mein keede pad gaye the*'. The burn marks that she incurred are visible on the right side of her neck, just below her face in the photograph. Somehow, she was fortunate enough to escape and was finally rescued by the Red Cross, after which she was reunited with her family members in Delhi. The photographic image does not bear direct testimony to past events, but bears certain traces or signs that only come alive to a viewer with accompanying oral narratives. Bansa Devi's portrait appears as a mundane photograph of a middle-aged woman, wearing a *salwar kameez* and a white dupatta. The only marker of the past that draws the attention of the viewer is the burn on her neck as it remains the only tangible memory permanently embodied by her. Balgotra explains that if she were still alive, she would have never recounted her traumatic experience to anyone. It was only after her death that her traumatic past was discussed by the family.

The psychologist Dori Laub, whose primary research is based on the testimonies of the Jewish Holocaust survivors and the relation between trauma and narratives, has suggested that in the case of Holocaust witnesses, there is a severing between the 'I–Thou' relationship. The severing of the I and Thou results in the survivor's inability to narrativise.[36] Laub further writes that the

[35] K.L. Balgotra. Interview with the author. June 2017.

[36] 'The traumatic event became an "absent" experience because at the core of the executioner-victim interaction all human relatedness is undone. The internal other, the "Thou"

disjunction between the I and Thou reflects the fracture in the narrative of a victim who has undergone massive trauma. In such cases, people (here, family members) refrain from asking the victims or survivors about their traumatic experiences. The thought of not asking the victim about the past, thinking it might upset her/him, is the opposite of what is most needed.[37] On analysing Bansa Devi's photograph, it can be inferred that she buried the trauma of her past by negating it. It is, in a way, negating the pain she must have gone through. In Sarah Ahmed's formulation, the 'affect' of the photograph on its viewer evokes a sense of empathy and throws light on the visible traces of pain. The impression or sensation of the fire left its trace on the surface of her skin, and it was through encounters with other bodies or objects creating discomfort that she recognised that her body has a 'surface'. The recognition and reading of this sensation transform it into a 'feeling of pain'.[38] In simpler words, what separates 'us' from 'others' is also what connects us to others.[39] This, I feel, is the cathartic effect of the process of narrativisation. Looking at the array of photographs that form K.L. Balgotra's collection, one recognises that the life that surrounds the image comprises the sociocultural 'ecosystems in which pictures come alive'.[40] The picture or group of pictures have an intrinsic value that is generally imposed by the viewers who see the 'living image as an apt metaphor' for a subject's historical or social life.[41] They also become the means by which values are intergenerationally transmitted.

---

to whom one can address one's plea, tell one's story, no longer exists. Therefore the "story" is never known, told, or remembered. The frozen image, recorded in a different part of the brain, is all that remains and is retained for life. No perception of the traumatic event is translated into symbolising words; no narrative is formed. In a very important sense, the event has not yet been experienced. What the giving and receiving of testimony does is to set in motion a dyadic-dialogic process. The listener-companion, in his or her total presence, offers the possibility and the protected holding space, within which the internal other, or Thou, can be re-established, necessary to face the traumatic event. The story is told both to the listener and to oneself, and the process of narrativisation unfolds.' Laub, Dori. 2005. 'From speechlessness to narrative: The cases of Holocaust historians and of psychiatrically hospitalised survivors'. *Literature and Medicine*. Vol. 4. No. 2, p. 257.

[37] Ibid.

[38] 'It is through the intensification of pain sensations that bodies and worlds materialise and take shape, or that that the effect of boundary, surface and fixity is produced. To say that feelings are crucial to the forming of surfaces and borders is to suggest that what "makes" those borders also unmakes them.' Ahmed, Sarah. 2013. *The cultural politics of emotion* (New York: Routledge). p. 24.

[39] She further elucidates the concept of 'us' and 'others' by stating that this 'paradox is clear if we think of the skin surface itself, and begin to think of the skin as a surface that is felt only in the event of being "impressed upon" in the encounters we have with others.' Ibid. p. 25.

[40] Mitchell, William J.T. 2011. 'Migration, law, and the image: Beyond the veil of ignorance'. In *The Migrant's Time: Rethinking Art History and Diaspora*. ed. Saloni Mathur (Williamstown, Massachusetts, U.S.A: Sterline and Francine Clark Art Institute). p. 203.

[41] Mitchell. 2011. 'Migration, law, and the image'. p. 203.

After viewing these family photographs, one deduces that these photographs hold a significant role in constructing an ideal family and its memory, fostering unity and reflecting social dynamics. They also act as social documents that reflects on social class, gender as well as interpersonal relationships.[42] However, they also reveal the ruptures within the projection of an 'ideal family'. These photos prompt family members to remember forgotten pasts, highlighting pain and trauma experienced by women. Some endured violent separations from their families, while others faced challenges due to belonging to older family structures, as seen in the photographs of Bansa Devi or Fatima Bibi. The question arises: how their portrait photos reflect these moments of pain and rupture?

In families with traumatic histories and permanent displacement, family photography showcases the desire for a 'normal' family life. These photographs serve as symbols of completeness and rootedness, reinforcing the narrative surrounding the idealised family image. This attention to maintaining the family narrative contributes to the unity of the family and stability within society.

---

[42] Erkonan, Şahika. 2014. 'Family Photographs: Exploring The Role of Photography in the Construction of Family Memory With the Ethnographic Method'. *Moment Journal*. Vol. 1. No. 2. doi:10.17572/mj2014.2.122147.

Interpretations of Personal Family Photographs in Suriname

Female Emancipation Through Cultural Intermixing

Sarojini Lewis

Travelling along the coastline of French Guiana, I was contemplating the passage of time while observing the waterways, the sea intermingling with the river running through Suriname. During different periods in my life, the sea has been present to provide a source of energy; the movement of the waves, the salt in the water being the only things that are constant as life around me changes. Coming from a family of different religions and ethnicities, I seek spiritual solace from the movement of the sea and its salty seawater.

The Atlantic Ocean and Marowijne River intermingle with each other to form a wide span that separates St. Laurent in French Guiana from Albina in Suriname. In 2020, after showing my passport to the French immigration control in Guiana, I was allowed to cross the French-colonised border of St. Laurent situated near Marowijne, on a small wooden *corjal* (boat) to Suriname. There was a lot of uncertainty about whether travel by boat was legal during the recent outbreak of the COVID-19 pandemic. According to the locals, the boats were only transporting small groups of people. The moment I boarded the small river boat, there was nobody around except for a local Afro-Surinamese boatman. He did not speak much and made gestures to instruct me how to get into the boat and the amount of money I should pay.

This was the journey made by my Indo-Caribbean ancestors from the eighteenth century to the Surinamese landscapes that overlook part of the Amazon Forest and its complex river webs, which are, at present, visible from the window of an airplane. This time, I had travelled from Cayenne in French Guiana by local transport and by foot overland, until I could cross the river to Suriname. My solitude and the breadth of the Marowijne made me realise how fragile we were in the wooden *corjal*, yet at the same time I felt fascinated by the power of the water's current, the breeze blowing though my hair. The river was looking dangerously deep and its current seemed wild and restless. I remember staring at it and gazing at the distant shore, recalling what I read about the excitement of the indentured migrants when they arrived by boat and saw a similar view. Arriving by boat, retracing the footsteps of my ancestors and arriving on Surinamese land by waters in a tiny wooden *corjal* was something special.

In this essay, I trace different family lineages of the Afro-Surinamese and Hindustani diaspora in Suriname and how they underwent cultural intermixing. By combining photographs and missionary reports, the passage of female migrants becomes the 'real evidence' that I dwell on. Even though colonial photographs don't show the daily lives of people on the plantations in any detail, nor does it differentiate their lives from that of the enslaved, I wish to re-examine these photographs as potential evidence. Marina Carter reminds us that, 'The history of the indentured labour diaspora is one of individuals engaging with, renegotiating, and transcending the limitations suggested by their ascribed status and imagined identity.'[1] She describes the 'complexity and multiplicity' of identities as bearing the potential to reimagine images from photographic archives, leading to clearer perceptions on individual identities and personal experiences.

My chief entry point into building a new hypothesis of gendered cultural intermixing rests on some photographs taken during the 1920s and onwards, when indentured labour in Suriname came to be abolished. Indo-Caribbean indentured labourers first migrated from Barbados in 1863, where they would have commenced with their first contractual labour periods after having arrived from India. The first ship *Lalla Rookh* departed from Calcutta in 1873 and arrived three months later in Suriname. Photographs are testimony to the fact that there was a significant difference in the social lives of women in this period when compared to the freedom enjoyed by first-generation indentured migrants that arrived from Calcutta at the end of the nineteenth century. In the second- and third-generation of the Indo-Caribbean female migrants, they worked for family members, rather than as labourers on plantations. This heralded a period for the reconstruction of caste patterns and education in religious 'Hindu' schools. As such, there was incremental conservatism in the Indian diaspora in Suriname. By looking at changes in feminine clothing and styles in archival photographs, I hope to trace the changes in identity formation along gender patterns in mid-twentieth-century Suriname. I attempt to understand the journeys these women made and how they were transformed by diasporic experiences, as has been noted by Bikhu Parekh.[2]

From my mother's sister Sita's family photographic archive by the names of 'Gajadien' and 'Bissumbhar', I shall trace the transformations in women's dressing among intergenerational migrants from India to Suriname. My study will revolve around photo albums that were collated by Sita, consisting of images taken from 1954 until the 1970s. The women are seen wearing a range of garments, including tight blouses and long skirts or knee-length, Western-style dresses, akin to *lehengas*, as worn by women in several

---

[1] Carter, M., & Flynn, D. (2017). Pulled through Time: Art and the Indian Labour Migrant. *South Asian Studies*, *33*(1), 85–104.

[2] Parekh, Bhikhu(1994) Some reflections on the Hindu diaspora, *Journal of Ethnic and Migration Studies*, 20:4, 603-620.

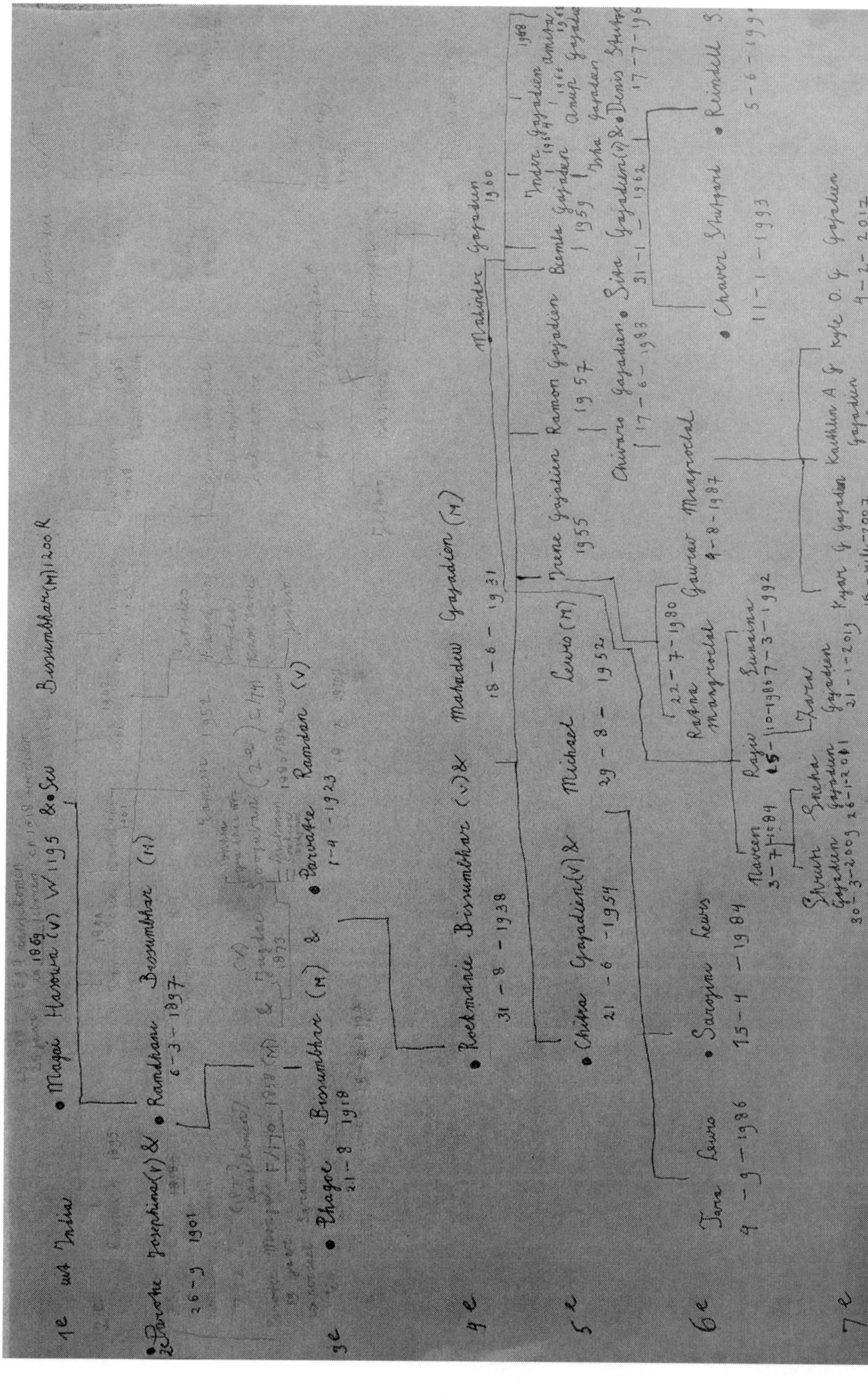

Figure 1. Lewis, Sarojini (2020) Bissumbhar Family Tree. Paramaribo Suriname. Sketch with pencil.

farming communities in India. Saris were meant for traditional occasions, during wedding ceremonies or *pujas*. I seek to read the cultural codings of women's dressing through these albums, but more important are the multiple ethnicities that are part of one family; hence, I hypothesise a larger claim on their changing social status. Since Bhojpuri females belonged to villages characterised by different North Indian traditions, how did these remain or change within the diasporic process of adapting to diverse ethnicities in Suriname, leading to multiple identities?

This essay than seeks to address the ethnic mixture and reinvention of cultural patterns as diverse cultural influences become traceable in photographs, illustrating sartorial changes. I argue that by having an understanding of the complexity of the cultural and ethnic diversity apparent in these photos, we can identify visual traces that may indicate the emancipation or conservatism towards female Bhojpuri migrants. In time, how does my practice deal with this visual inheritance, and how do my interventions as a woman photographer–artist impact these narratives?

As Véronique Bragard has noted, after the the Négritude movement and the understanding of Caribbeanness existing beyond island boundaries, after créolité that reclaims popular culture of the Afro-Surinamese, comes coolitude, which endeavours to validate coolie history and culture, to be able to cope with the entangled past of the shameful bondage of ancestors.[3] Contemplating on Khal Torabully's's[4] writing, Bragard suggests that coolitude is actively participating in créolité, furthering creolisation and cross-cultural exchange. The concept of coolitude is based on the term 'coolie', meaning unskilled worker, a term which can also apply to other indentured labourers such as the Chinese and Javenese. Bragard furthermore explores the coolie female imaginary or creative memory by looking at similar metaphors, symbols, motifs, themes and transgressions that she particularly finds in female literature of the Caribbean. This imaginary is nourished by the shared experience of displacement. She particularly mentions the ocean as a site of memory and the transoceanic crossings from the Indian village to Caribbean plantation grounds. In constructing a female perspective in relation to coolitude, Bragard diverts from the colonial archive that separated indentured labourers from slaves, and builds a common imaginary that combines Hindi, Afro-Surinamese Hinduism, imposed Christianity and syncretic religious beliefs. The focus on female characters endeavours to examine women's capacity to creolise, their strong fight for survival and at the same time, maintain community cohesion. Thus, the erasure of the female voice in the colonial archives is reclaimed and the female emotions, reimagined.

[3] Bragard, V. (2005). 'Transoceanic echoes: coolitude and the work of the Mauritian poet Khal Torabully', *International Journal of Francophone Studies*, Volume 8, No 2, p. 8. p. 368-369

[4] Carter, Marina & Khal Torabully (2002). *Coolitude An Anthology of the Indian Labour Diaspora*. London, Anthem Publications. Torabully, 2002, 151-152

Additionally, reconstructing narratives from my own photography-based art practice, I aim to explore several questions and interpretations of images in family archives. By reaching back in time and examining photographic representations, I hope to show how, through the insertion of agency, it became possible for the female labour diaspora in the Caribbean to dislocate imposed colonial identities. They did so by forming diverse linkages that have no linear trajectory and are intimate and personal. I start this essay with a series of hidden family photographs from Sita's late husband's Afro-Surinamese ancestors, found by me in her living room in Suriname. Each time I find a new photograph hidden behind cupboards and chairs, sticking out from behind furniture, I place it on empty nails on the walls in the same living room. I describe the family genealogy up to the moment of the marriage of Dennis Stutgard with Sita Gajadien in 1990. I have traced Sita's family's Afro-Surinamese lineage back to the Berg en Dal plantation, which was operated by German Moravian missionaries. The missionaries resided in Suriname since 1735, when they tried to mission indigenous tribes and later focussed on Afro-Surinamese communities that resided in the 'jungles' and interior of Suriname, besides plantations such as Heerendijk, Berg en Dal, Salem and Alkmaar.[5] Besides missioning, Carl Haarnack describes a passage of a missionary named Riemer who departed in 1779 to Suriname. He studied the language of runaway slaves (Maroons, Saramaccaners) but also engaged with other missionaries in purchasing a slave.[6]

In conjunction with family photographs that span from the 1960s up till 1980s, I will briefly examine the genealogy of the Stutgard family in Berg en Dal starting with the birth of Magdalena Stutgard, in 1824. Through this particular family history, I try to understand the position of Afro-Surinamese women in the context of the plantation and the Moravian missionaries whose histories can be found in the diaries of the EBG Archive in Suriname. Besides this, Humprey E. Lamur (1993) and Maria Lenders (1994) describe the Afro-Surinamese community of slaves for the Hernhutter Moravian missionaries. The Afro-Surinameses were Christianised by the missionaries and their gender patterns as well as family structures changed under Western influence. Besides the change that the missionaries strove for, I wish to describe the gender patterns among Afro-Surinamese women that Lamur occasionally points to. This larger context of the Stutgard family is necessary to understand the historical influences on gender and the mixed ethnicities in the family that came to be known as 'Dogla identities'.

As Kobena Mercer (2012) remarks during a project on post-colonial perspectives in her work on the Netherlands, 'When we look at the individual

[5] Killough, M. (1996). Niels Otto Tank (1800-1864) Moravian Missionary to Suriname and Wiscons. *Moravian Historical Society, Transactions of the Moravian Historical Society,* Vol. 29, pp. 85-102.

[6] Haarnack, Carl (2016) *Missions-Reise nach Suriname. Riemer (1801).* Online publication by Buku Suriname. Retrieved at: bukubooks.wordpress.com/2016/05/21/riemer-2/

frame we are ready to accept that the camera fixes a passing moment in time, but when we consider the multiple sites through which photographs circulate socially we recognise that all photographs are open to a process of decontextualisation.'[7] I wonder if this process in which the photographs are placed in hidden positions in the Stutgard living room is a comparative process. Mercer points to the drift from the 'Western archive' to cross-cultural modernity, '… by showing us how colonial subjects appropriated its picture making technology to depict their own experiences of modern life.' Mercer further argues that photography serving colonial domination and later becoming a tool of self-representation is more complex and multi-layered than one linear history. In the photographs I selected of the Stutgard family, the narrative is one of self-representation, although it is the religious, celebratory moments of Christian faith that are captured by the family. As we have seen, the missionaries on the Berg en Dal plantation in the above genealogy and colonial Western Christian thought dominated the faith of the family.

While the Stutgard family was formerly enslaved at the Berg en Dal plantation, Sita's maternal family line derives from indentured labourers. There is a clear colonial influence on the family traditions of the Bissumbhar, which is a family lineage from my maternal grandmother's side. The oldest photographs of this side of the family are placed on graves—the family tradition of burning bodies being resumed in 1969 after the period of indentured labour ceased in 1920, and cultural negotiations could be made. For both ethnicities that confluence in Sita's family as the Gajadien and Stutgard lineages, the indentured and enslaved labour saw traditions and gender patterns undergo transformation. I analysed Sita's marriage photographs to be able to have an in-depth understanding of gender and cultural mixing in Suriname at the turn of the twentieth century and thereafter.

Recovering Hidden Photographs of the Stutgard Family

Near the Brokopondolaan in Paramaribo is the family home of the Stutgards, where I resided during fieldwork with my aunt Sita Gajadien, her two sons and her husband's sister, Sandra. The home is a typical Surinamese house constructed in the 1960s, consisting of two floors. A gate downstairs leads to a parking lot and an open space with two sets of stairs leads to the upper floor. My aunt lives downstairs in one room and on the second floor, there are separate rooms for her sons as well as their aunt Sandra, along with a living room, a bathroom and kitchen.

As I mentioned earlier, I found many photographs in old boxes and some hidden behind furniture in the living room of the house. The encounters with these photographs were mostly accidental and here, I would like to point to their placement within the household (Figures 2, 3).

---

[7] Blokland, Sara and Pelupessy, Asmara ed. (2010) *Unfixed: Photography and postcolonial perspectives in Contemporary Art.* Jap Sam Books. p.72-73

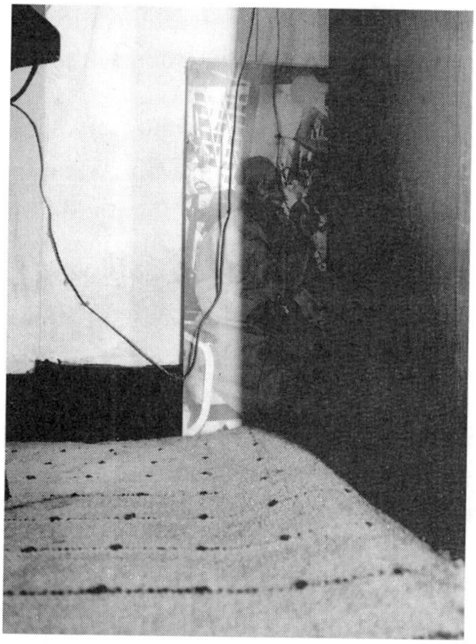

Figure 2. Grandfather Stutgard, photographer unknown. Stutgard living room, c.1980–1990.

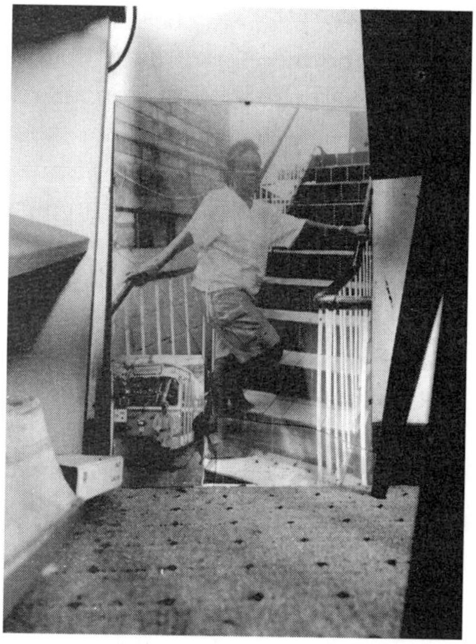

Figure 3. Aunt Sandra in Suriname; photographer unknown. Stutgard living room, c. 1980–1990.

In Figure 2, we can see Grandfather Stutgard's photograph sticking out from behind a cupboard. It is almost like he sank into the carpet on the floor; his full image is hidden behind the cupboard and covered with the electric wiring of a sound system. The carpet seems to have supported the glass frame, merging with the same interior depicted in the photograph, taken inside the family house many years ago. I recognised the interior by the stairs in this house that are in the same position as visible in the photograph. The image carries the memory that the family has of grandfather Stutgard, a memory that appears half-hidden, sunken into the carpet, forgotten but still present. Nevertheless, grandfather is still sitting on his garden chair surrounded by family members visible in the background of the picture; he has not disappeared entirely.

Similarly, Figure 3 is a photograph that was recovered from a space behind a blue cupboard. It is of Aunt Sandra when she was young, standing on the stairs of our family house with the neighbour's wooden house visible behind her. She is wearing a loose striped shirt and short pants—comfortable clothes—while she holds the banisters of the stairs. Her posture is as if she just turned around while walking up the stairs, with someone instantly taking her photograph. I recognise the tiles of the stairs that I use now to go upstairs or downstairs in the house. In the corner is another photograph that appears to be taken in the Netherlands, including an old-fashioned tram that she is posing in front of. By her thick winter clothes and scarf, one can understand that the location is not in Suriname, where the tropical climate keeps it warm throughout the year. Since Sandra still resides in the house, it is strange that the picture has been hidden or stuffed away behind a cupboard. The glass of the picture frame has cracked and therefore it might have been put away to reframe later, but since Figure 2 had also been hidden, there seems to be another motive.

Figure 4 has been taken in an earlier timeframe, during the childhoods of the three children of Grandfather Stutgard, who probably took this photograph. Aunt Sandra (born in 1963) is in the picture with her two elder bothers, Ricky (born in 1960) and Dennis (born in 1961) standing in front of a Christmas tree at a local photo studio. The children are dressed up for this Christian event at a different venue, as families in Suriname would usually not have a Christmas tree in their living room.

Grandfather Stutgard became a pastor of the Evangelic community (the Evangelische Broeder Gemeente) in Suriname after he retired. Religious days were thus celebrated like Christians, as seen in the image of the children dressed up for Christmas. The photograph sticks out of a pile of newspapers and although half-hidden, is placed in a central position in the living room.

After rescuing the hidden photographs from the living room, I decided to rearrange them in a small curatorial gesture. I made a second set of images of the photographs placed in their original positions, gaining insight into a hidden perspective on my aunt's family life. By acting out small gestures bit by bit over a stretch of four months, I wanted to reclaim the familial memory that seemed to be lingering in an obscure zone. Why were these photographs hidden?

I placed the photographs in Figure 4 and Figure 6a, 6b and 6c in visible places (Figure 5), such as an empty wall next to the television and above the bananas and the bread box. These are tiny prints in a standard photographic format of 15 cm x 10 cm. In a wedding photograph, we can see Grandmother and Grandfather Stutgard getting married on 6 April 1960. On the back of Figure 6a, we can see Figure 6c mentioning a few names: Carlien Wolf, Margo Blanker, John Stutgard, Annie Isselt, Anneke, brideswife, Strooisberkje Pater.

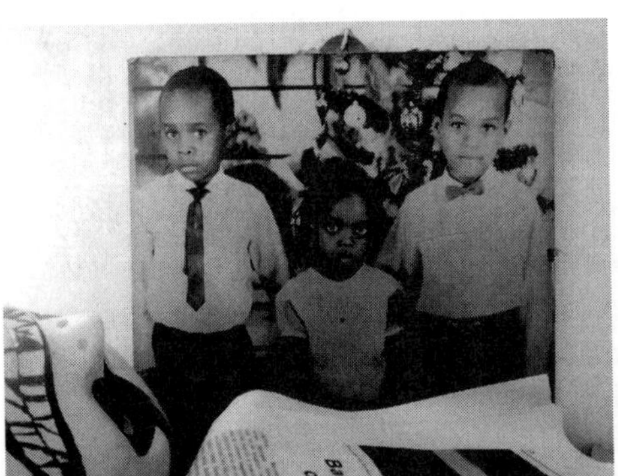

Figure 4. Ricky, Sandra and Dennis Stutgard; photographer unknown. Stutgard living room, c. 1960–1970.

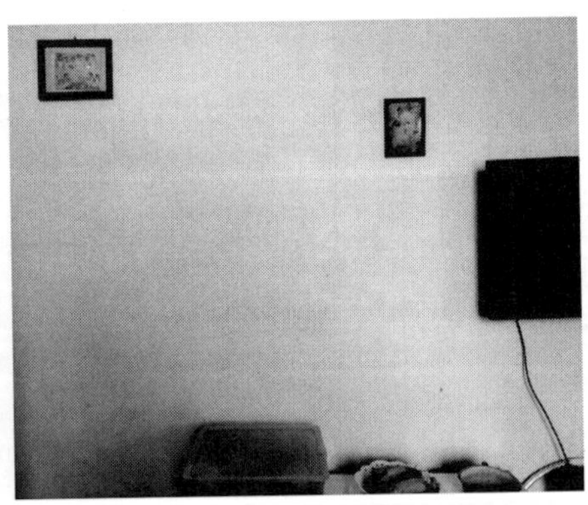

Figure 5. Stutgard Marriage in Suriname; photographer unknown. Stutgard living room, c. 1960.

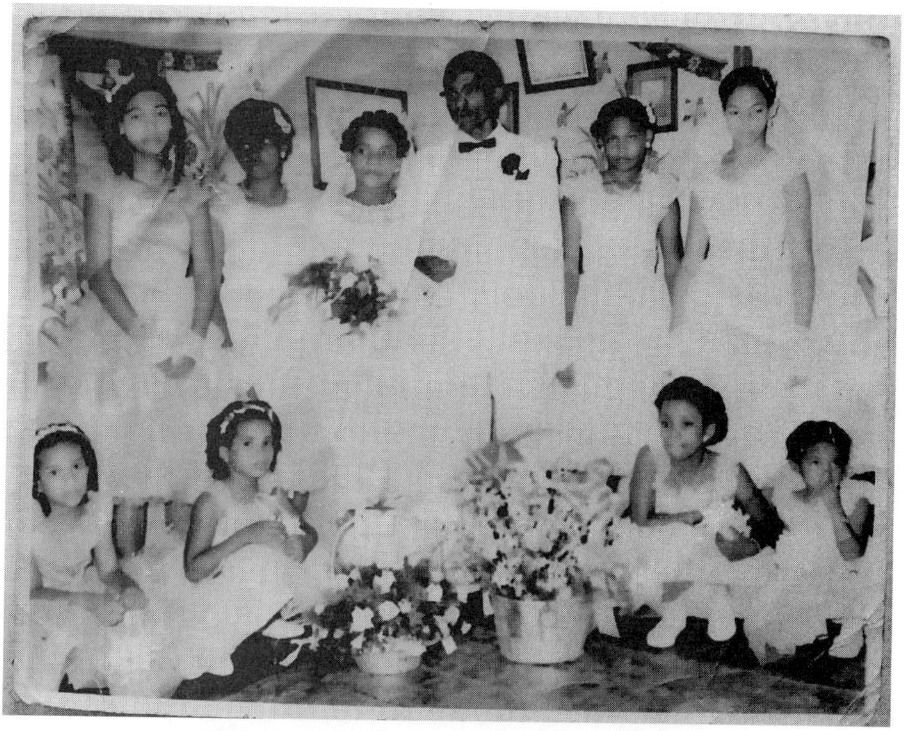

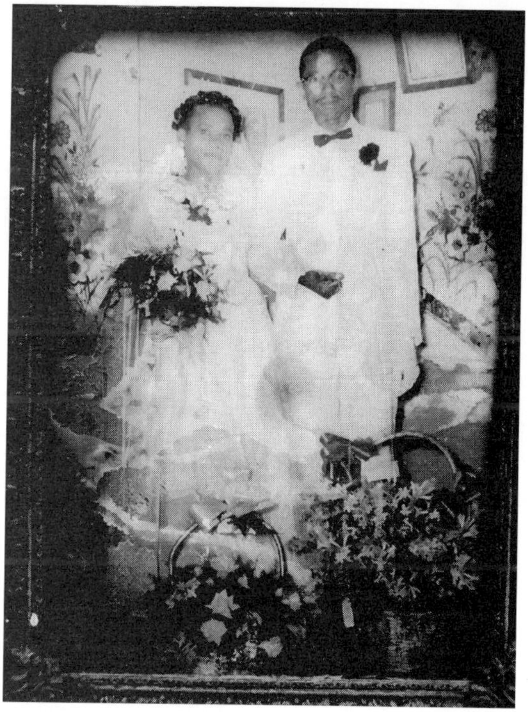

Figure 6a & 6b. Stutgard Marriage in Suriname; photographer unknown. Stutgard living room, c. 1960.

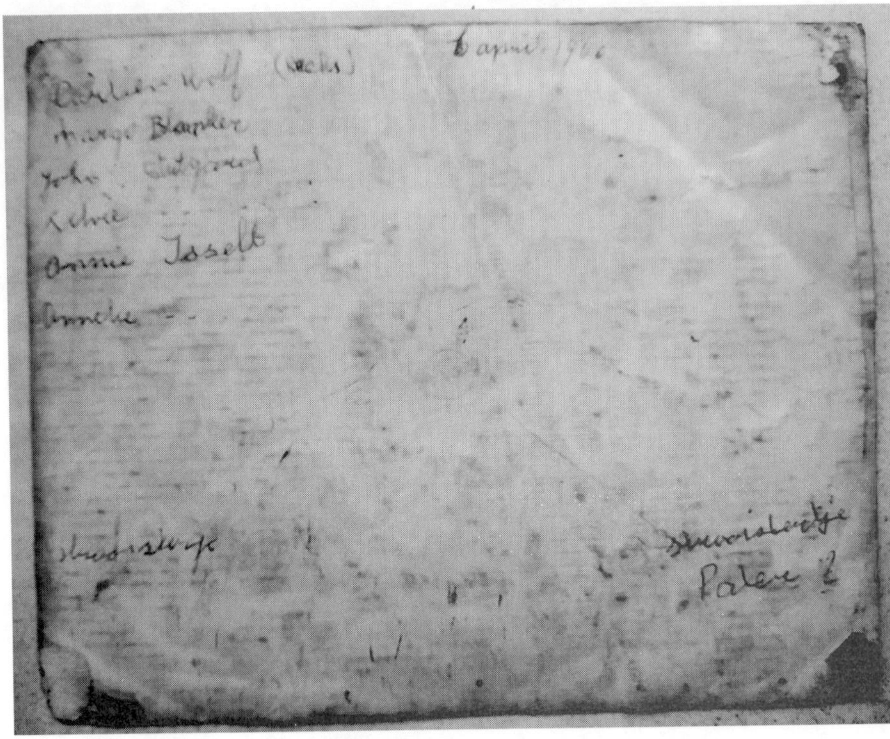

Figure 6c. Back of 'Stutgard Marriage in Suriname'. Photographer unknown. Stutgard living room, c. 1960.

John Stutgard, born in 1935, was the grandfather of Sita Gajadien's sons, and her father-in-law. Sylvia Elisabeth Slijngaart was born in 1937, and is John's bride. The other names belong to the other females dressed up to be bridesmaids or attendees. Since they were all going to the church of the Evangelic community, they had worn appropriate white attire for the marriage.

The Genealogy of the Stutgard Family

This family got its name from Adriaantje Magdalena Stutgard (b. 1824), who, according to the emancipation register of 1863,[8] was declared a free slave on the Berg en Dal plantation. Although the name Stutgart was given to her during the year 1863, there has been no clarity whether she was named so by the plantation owner or the municipality. She was then thirty-nine years old and was designated the task of carrying goods, such as wood, on the plantation. According to the Hernhutters' diaries,[9] the name Stutgard also appears in the

[8] 'Suriname en de Nederlandse Antillen vrijverklaarden slaven (Emancipatie 1863)', National Archives of The Netherlands. Available at: www.nationaalarchief.nl/onderzoeken/index/nt00341?activeTab=nt

[9] 513–517 named (Specialiën) from the EGB Archives in Paramaribo.

late 1870s. Adriaantje Magdalena Stutgart married in 1875 and her children were baptised by the Moravian Church. According to archival sources, she had daughters, of which one was Lydia Apollonia Stutgart, who had four children from four different men (Figure 7).

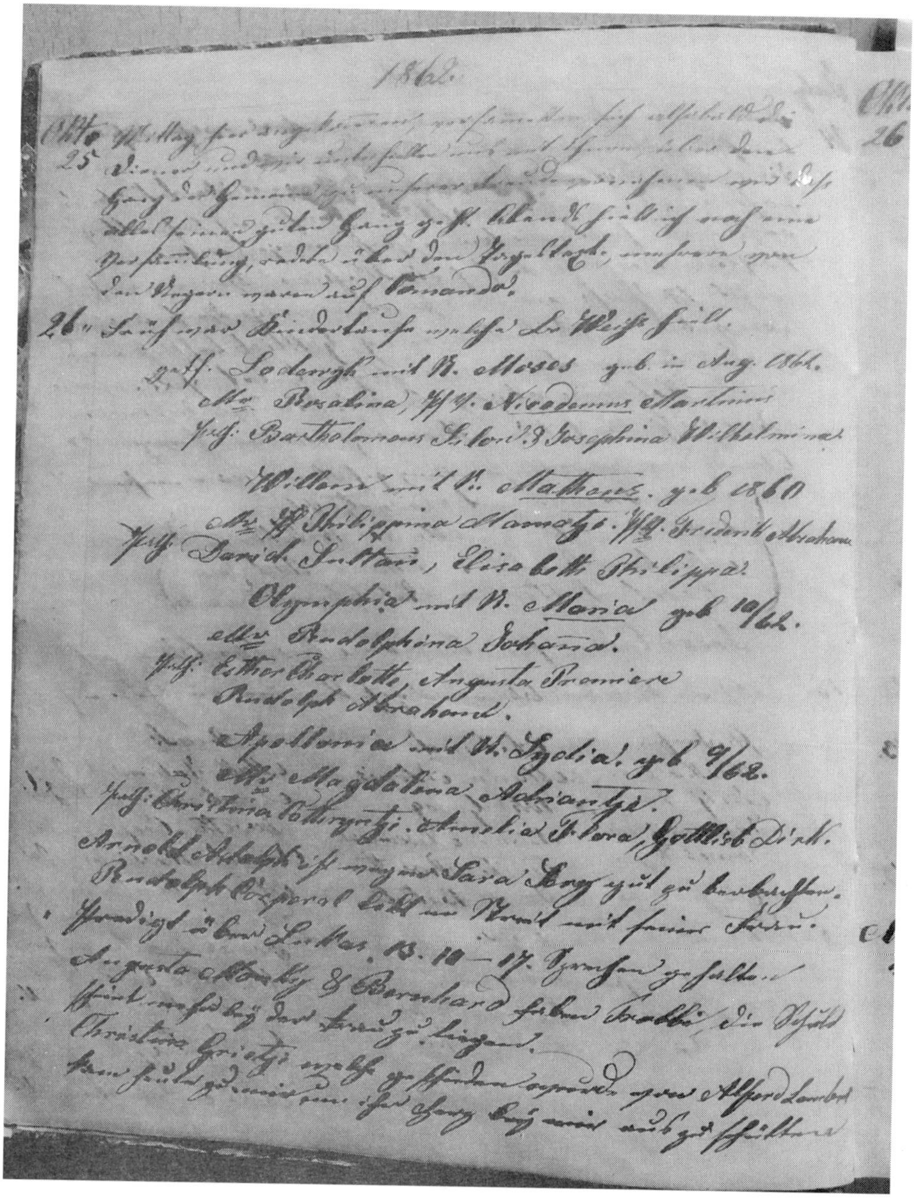

Figure 7. Diaries of Herrnhut Missionaries Specialiën 513 Berg en Dal by unknown missionary. c.1862. Source: Evangelische Broeder Gemeente Suriname. Paramaribo Suriname.

Antionette Adolphine was born to Lydia Stutgart in 1887 by an unknown father—a question mark is left in the place where her father's name should be in the Herrnhut Missionaries Specialiën. To make the family genealogy of the Stutgards visible, I have added a family tree with six generations of the family (Figure 8).

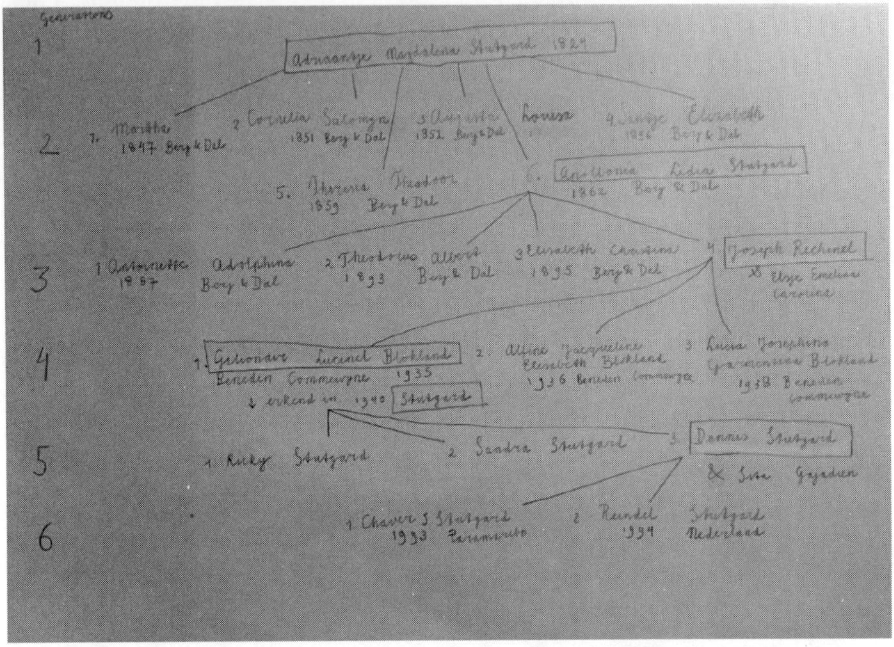

Figure 8. Stutgard Family Tree. Family in Paramaribo Suriname. Sketch with pencil. © Sarojini Lewis, 2022

Theodorus Albert Stutgart, born to Lydia in 1893, by the father Varang Sing, could indicate that the latter was an Indian indentured labourer who worked on the sugar plantations nearby. When I tried to find the contract bearing this name, I found that his details are missing from the accessible archives online. Nevertheless, his contract may have been damaged as not all the contracts were preserved in the emigration register due to humidity. Another option could be that he had enough savings from an earlier contract period and was now a free man.

Elisabeth Christina was born to Lydia in 1985 by the father Jocobus Redroef, and the family's lineage was passed through Lydia's youngest, Gillionair Joseph Richinel Stutgart, who was born in 1899 by the father Eduard Joseph Palem. It is thus remarkable that Lydia had multiple husbands, for besides the occurrence of polygamous relationships, the common law was that marriage among slaves was forbidden and was later introduced into the church.[10]

[10] Blokland, Sara and Pelupessy, Asmara ed. (2010) *Unfixed: Photography and postcolonial perspectives in Contemporary Art.* Jap Sam Books. p.120

Besides this law, the plantation owners had the right to decide whom the slaves had relationships with. Other than the notes in the Specialiën, we have no more information about the family and what happened to them in Berg en Dal on a day-to-day basis.

Joseph Stutgart, who was born in Beneden Commewijne on 22 July 1903, had three children with Elsje Emelina Carolina of the Blokland family. Their first son was Gilionair Lucionel Blokland, who was born in 1935 and was also named Joseph. He acknowledged all his children in 1940, passing down the Stutgart name to them. During this formal process, the city councils made a mistake and misspelled the name as Stutgard. Gilionair L. Stutgard was the grandfather of my cousins, and his nickname was John, as is written on the backside of the photograph in Figure 6c. Grandfather G.L. Stutgard lived in Paramaribo and after marrying his wife, moved to live on the Wanicastraat, in a small house. His elderly family members and his mother lived in Berg en Dal until they passed away.

The grounds that belonged to the Stutgard family have never been divided because of sustained quarrels between family members. The evidence that the ground belonged to the family has been lost and proof needs to be found.

Sandra Stutgard, daughter to Gillionair J.R. Stutgart and my aunt, visited the plantation in 2013. On the day, a historical tour was being organised by Berg en Dal resort, that was initiated by Kersten & Co., a store set up by the Herrnhuter missionaries. When I asked her to recall the landscape of the plantation, she dived into her memories.

The living conditions at the plantation consisted of wooden houses that were six metres by five metres in area. The community of Afro-Surinamese people who work and live there have maintained the houses so that they represent the history of Berg en Dal. There is an old cemetery of people who remained in Berg en Dal, and the former Afro-Surinamese community who passed away during emancipation and slavery. Graveyards are believed to have spiritual presences, therefore people have left this land in peace, uncultivated.

Gender Patterns on Berg en Dal Plantation

Besides the oral narratives of Sandra Stutgard's memories and the former genealogical research of Ricky Stutgard, it is worthwhile to understand the larger context of the plantation and certain historical developments in gender patterns among slaves in this environment.

In 1735, the first Herrnhut missionary brothers, Berwig, Larisch and Piesh, arrived at the Berg en Dal plantation that had existed since 1667.[11] It was located at Blue Mountain and mainly yielded sugar. In 1730, the slaves on the

[11] Lenders, Maria (1996) *Strijders voor het Lam: leven en werk van Herrnhutter Broeders en -Zusters in Suriname, 1735-1900.* KITLV publishers Amsterdam.

plantation were serving colonial masters by fighting against Maroons[12] who had attacked the plantation, and were rewarded with guns and cattle. The relations between the slaves and the missionaries and plantation owners remained cordial, and the slaves were allowed to attend church service, which was held in the house of the plantation owner, until the first church was established in 1928. The Evangelic Brotherhood Community officially owned the plantation since 1870, possibly purchased by the company of the missionaries, C. Kersten & Co. According to the Hernhutters, their archives give a more accurate account in comparison to the colonial archives about Suriname. They claim in their statement that indigenous tribes, the Maroons as well as slaves, were regarded as equals, unlike the colonial plantation holders, who regarded slaves as their commodities. However, it is important to note that the missionaries owned the slaves of the plantation as well when they purchased the land. The archives contain immediate observations about the slaves on their own plantations, therefore the missionaries claiming to be of equal social status seems out of place. Besides the ownership of their slaves, the missionaries were not innocent, and punished slaves when they were disobedient. Besides using physical violence such as hitting or using iron neck shackles, some slaves were even sent to the public place of punishment *het piket* in Paramaribo, where the court would receive payment to punish the slaves.[13]

Missionaries had diaries named 'Specialiën' bearing pastoral notes on the daily lives of baptised slaves. Only these 'type of slaves' were regarded as equals, noteworthy of writing about. The other slaves who did not want to be Christianised, were thus not described. Nevertheless, the missionaries did learn early forms of Sranan Tongo language, and had letters and diaries from a few *granmans* (Maroon village leaders) which are the oldest scriptural cultural documents of Suriname itself.[14]

Prof. H.E. Lamur recounts his findings in a telephonic interview with me,[15] specifically about daily life on the plantation grounds. He mentions that while

---

[12] The Maroons are descendants of Africans who fled the colonial Dutch forced labour plantations in Suriname and established independent communities in the interior rainforests. They have retained a distinctive identity based on their West African origins. Groot, S.W. de. 1963. 'Oudere Marrons willen een stem.' *Parbode*. 5:55. pp. 46-47.; Groot, S.W. de. 1997. Van isolatie naar integratie; De Surinaamse Marrons en hun afstammelingen; Officiële documenten betreffende de Djoeka's (1845–1863). Den Haag: Martinus Nijhoff. [Verhandelingen van het KITLV, 41.]; Hansen, H. and G. de Wagt. 1967. 'Marrons aan de Djukakreek in de achttiende eeuw.' *Oso, Tijdschrift voor Surinaamse Taalkunde, Letterkunde en Geschiedenis*. 16:2. pp. 186–206.

[13] Lenders, Maria (1996) *Strijders voor het Lam: leven en werk van Herrnhutter Broeders en -Zusters in Suriname, 1735-1900.* KITLV publishers Amsterdam. P.191

[14] C. Dekker en H.L.P. Leeuwenberg (1978) *Verslag van een oriënterend en adviserend bezoek aan de archieven van de provincie Suriname van de Unitas Fratum.* Rijksarchief in Utrecht. 33 p. (excl. p. inventaris): 29 cm. - Als bijlage II : Inventaris van het gedeelte van het archief van de Evangelische Broedergemeente in Suriname vanaf 1754, berustende in het Rijksarchief in Utrecht PK: ZZG F-19

[15] Lamur, H.E. (2020) Several Interviews during Sep–Dec. Researcher on Slavery and Indentured Labour in Suriname.

observing day-to-day tasks in the pastoral notebooks of the missionaries, one can observe that female slaves were not in subordinate positions as compared to the men. Interestingly, Lamur points to several occasions of females contacting members of Maroon villages. These incidents appear in several passages in the Specialiën and the pages that I selected reveal some of these incidents alongside the genealogy of the Stutgard family. This is seen, for example, in Para district for several issues such as sickness or partnership. The women acted independently and did not stick to the authority of the Herrnhut missionaries.[16]

In Figure 9, we can see a page from the Specialiën 517 from Suriname, recounting an occasion involving a woman named Bertha and a *wintiman* (an Afro-Surinamese medicine man) in Saramacca.

The below (Figure 9) page of Specialiën 517 from Suriname demonstrates a similar narrative as Lamur narrated about the Maroon intervention of a medicine man. The translation points to a journey made on 21 December 1901 by the missionaries from Berg en Dal. They travelled to attend a ceremony on another plantation, Koffykamp. This is followed by the baptism of two children on 22 December. The diary description ends with the death and the burial of a woman named Bertha. She died with an unborn child in her womb and in the diary fragment, it is stated that the heathens don't bury their bodies this way; this incident would be treated as an unfortunate case by the *Djocka* (a negative reference for Maroon people). The diary also describes an incident in which the body was claimed by the Maroons ('They came to the Christians and said if you are not willing to give the body to us, then we must all die, the Christians being weak enough, left the body to them'). A *wintiman* was summoned from Saramacca to remove the child from the corpse through idolatry; only after this ceremony was she buried.

Lamur declares that enslaved women made decisions independently from the missionaries. The Maroons and the emancipated Afro-Surinamese women could, on some occasions, make these independent choices, as seen in the case of the pressure exerted by the Maroon community to have a funeral for Bertha with a *wintiman*.

The intervention could take place because of the location of the Berg en Dal plantation, which was near Maroon villages located in the south of Suriname, which also resulted in love affairs between the slaves of the plantation and the Maroons. In these relationships, affiliation with Maroon traditions were prohibited by the missionaries. This caused problems because the headmen

[16] Lamur describes an incident when a female slave decided to travel from Berg en Dal to another plantation with her daughter. The latter got sick on the way and was taken to the local community of Maroons, who healed her according to their own cultural traditions and medicine men. The fact that the woman consulted the Maroon community rather than a missionary caused a lot of commotion. Another occasion in 1862 occurred where different villagers went for *Dressi* (ailments and healing) to the Maroons. The missionaries obliged the sinners to pray for forgiveness (Lamur, Berg en Dal Specialiën, 1848–1862).

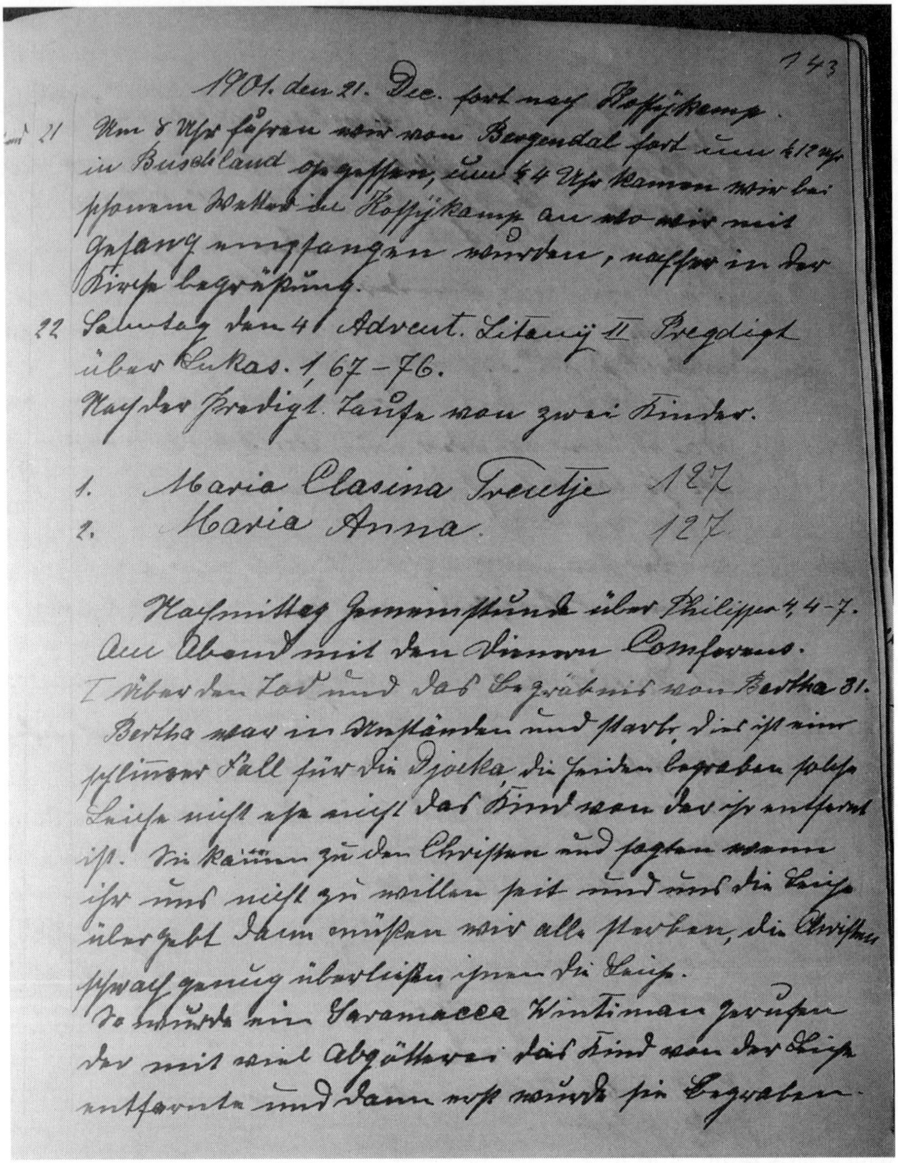

143

1901. den 21. Dec. fort nach Koffijkamp.

21 Um 8 Uhr fuhren wir von Bergendal fort um 12 Uhr im Buschland gegessen; um 4 Uhr kamen wir bei schönem Wetter in Koffijkamp an wo wir mit Gesang empfangen wurden, nachher in der Kirche Begrüßung.

22 Sonntag den 4. Advent. Litaney II Predigt über Lukas. 1,67–76.

Nach der Predigt Taufe von zwei Kinder.

1. Maria Clasina Treutje 127
2. Maria Anna 127

Nachmittag Gemeinstunde über Philipper 4, 4–7.

Am Abend mit den Dienern Conferenz.

I über den Tod und das Begräbnis von Bertha 31.

Bertha war in Umständen und starb, dies ist ein schlimmer Fall für die Djuka die Heiden begraben solche Leiche nicht eher nicht das Kind von der ihr entfernt ist. Sie kamen zu den Christen und sagten wenn ihr uns nicht zu willen seit und uns die Leiche übergebt dann müssen wir alle sterben, die Christen schwach genug überließen ihnen die Leiche.

Da wurde ein Saramacca Wintiman gerufen der mit viel Abgötterei das Kind von der Leiche entfernte und dann erst wurde sie begraben.

Figure 9. Diaries of Herrnhut Missionaries Specialiën 517 Berg en Dal, by unknown missionary. c.1901. Source: Evangelische Broeder Gemeente Suriname. Paramaribo Suriname.

of the Maroon villages wanted the female slaves to practise the same cultural traditions as in their village. The missionaries of Berg en Dal would oppose this behaviour, as can be observed in the Specialiën, in which the performance of the *wintiman* is described as 'a bad case' (Figure 9).

During slavery, living together as if married was encouraged by the missionaries, however it was not tolerated after abolition, and the slaves were then obliged to legalise marriages.[17] These formalities applied to Berg en Dal as well and would have been similarly imposed on slaves there. Nevertheless, Lamur declares that despite the restrictions that were imposed, the slaves created their own family relations and social norms. Polygamy (that included emotional ties with several partners) was present on the plantation; nevertheless, the missionary accounts show quite clearly that two-parent households were more common.[18]

Lamur raises the question of the extent to which slave women were dependent on their husbands. As he emphasises, the divorces in his case studies were initiated as independent acts by women. The more or less independent position of female slaves in Vossenburg was partly associated with the distribution of clothes and food, that they received directly from the slave owner, unmediated by their male partners. Therefore, in providing for basic needs of their children and themselves, females were not dependent on an income from male partners. An important deduction from these facts is that the dependency of Afro-Surinamese women on the men of their society may have occurred only after the abolition of slavery in 1863.[19]

Furthermore, while relations across plantations appeared to prevent incest or intermarriage between relatives, the planters did not permit slaves to move permanently to the plantation where their partners were living, and this resulted in matriarchal households.[20] Besides this, when slaves got married through the Evangelic church, it was possible that they were separated later on because one of the slaves was sold and sent off to another plantation. All these factors contributed to the dominance of female slaves, and their independent everyday lives in the domestic and professional spheres.

In contemplating the Stutgard family lineage, I want to historicise the position of women at the Berg en Dal plantation and connect this history to aunt Sita's maternal Hindustani family lineage. The first known intermixing of ethnicity occurred in the maternal lineage of the Stutgard family with Lydia's son Theodorus being born through a Hindustani father in 1893 (Figure 10).

Besides Lamur's contentious declaration that female slaves were more dependent on their husband after abolition, I argue that there was a significant difference in the social lives of Hindustani women in later generations, when compared to the polygamous relations that occurred in the first generation. Due to the uneven gender ratio created by fewer females compared to males,

[17] Lamur, H. E. (1993). The Slave Family in Colonial 19th-Century Suriname. *Journal of Black Studies*, 23(3), 371–381. p.372. p 374.

[18] Lamur, H. E. (1993). The Slave Family in Colonial 19th-Century Suriname. *Journal of Black Studies*, 23(3), 371–381. p.372. p 375, 376.

[19] Lamur, H. E. (1993). The Slave Family in Colonial 19th-Century Suriname. *Journal of Black Studies*, 23(3), 371–381. p.372. p 380

[20] Lamur, H. E. (1993). The Slave Family in Colonial 19th-Century Suriname. *Journal of Black Studies*, 23(3), 371–381. p.372. p 381

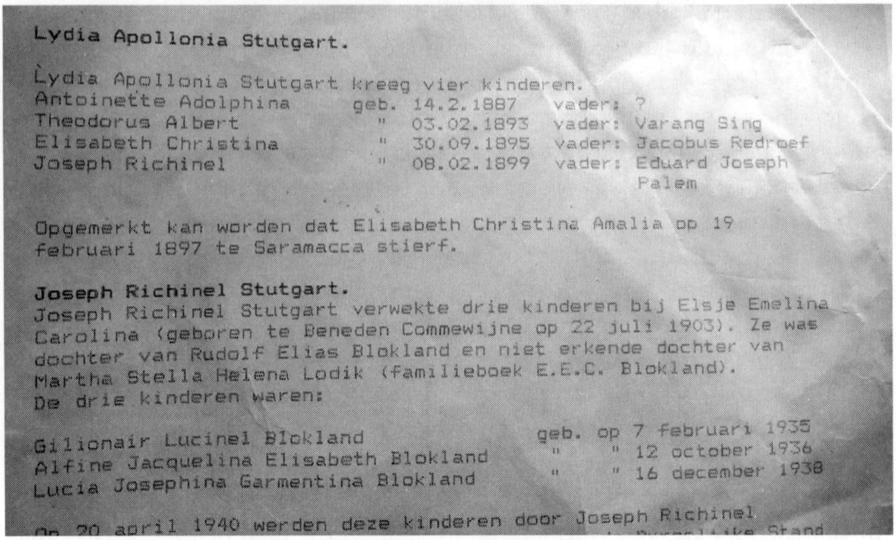

Lydia Apollonia Stutgart.

Lydia Apollonia Stutgart kreeg vier kinderen.

Antoinette Adolphina	geb. 14.2.1887	vader:	?
Theodorus Albert	" 03.02.1893	vader:	Varang Sing
Elisabeth Christina	" 30.09.1895	vader:	Jacobus Redroef
Joseph Richinel	" 08.02.1899	vader:	Eduard Joseph Palem

Opgemerkt kan worden dat Elisabeth Christina Amalia op 19 februari 1897 te Saramacca stierf.

Joseph Richinel Stutgart.
Joseph Richinel Stutgart verwekte drie kinderen bij Elsje Emelina Carolina (geboren te Beneden Commewijne op 22 juli 1903). Ze was dochter van Rudolf Elias Blokland en niet erkende dochter van Martha Stella Helena Lodik (Familieboek E.E.C. Blokland).
De drie kinderen waren:

Gilionair Lucinel Blokland	geb. op 7 februari 1935
Alfine Jacquelina Elisabeth Blokland	" " 12 october 1936
Lucia Josephina Garmentina Blokland	" " 16 december 1938

Op 20 april 1940 werden deze kinderen door Joseph Richinel

Figure 10. Family Tree of the Stutgards. Paramaribo Suriname, c. 2005. © Ricky Stuttgard.

polyandry occurred among the first-generation of migrants.[21] Nevertheless, in the first generations, it was rarer for ethnic mixing to occur in the Hindustani family; for example, in the Bissumbhar family lineage, which was the maternal side of Sita Gajadien. We understand that female independence was related to financial positions as well as cultural affiliations.

I will now revert to discussing the act of replacing photographs in my aunt's living room, treating them as objects coming to life, moving through spaces in time as indicators of family traditions and contemporary developments.

I took the image in Figure 11 out of a garbage bag and placed it on top of the unused computer that was standing in between a pile of objects belonging to my cousins. The photograph had been severely damaged by its exposure to sunlight and therefore, the figures had a ghostly appearance. In the photograph, we can see a scenario captured before the act of confession in church by Ricky and Sandra Stutgard. The trio in the photograph are surrounded by plants in the family garden. The sharp contrasts of light and shade indicate that the photograph was taken during daytime. One can see a tree in the left of the frame and Dennis Stutgard can be seen leaning against its trunk, looking confidently at the photographer. Both brothers are standing in front of their sister. Nevertheless, the body language of both is significantly different, as Ricky Stutgard's straight posture conveys his observance of his day of confession, while his younger brother, informally dressed, leans against the tree. The Christian 'confession' had been practised by slaves as early as the

[21] Reddock, Rhoda (2008). Indian Women and Indentureship in Trinidad and Tobago 1845-1917: Freedom Denied. *Caribbean Quarterly, December, Vol. 54, No. 4,* pp. 41-68.

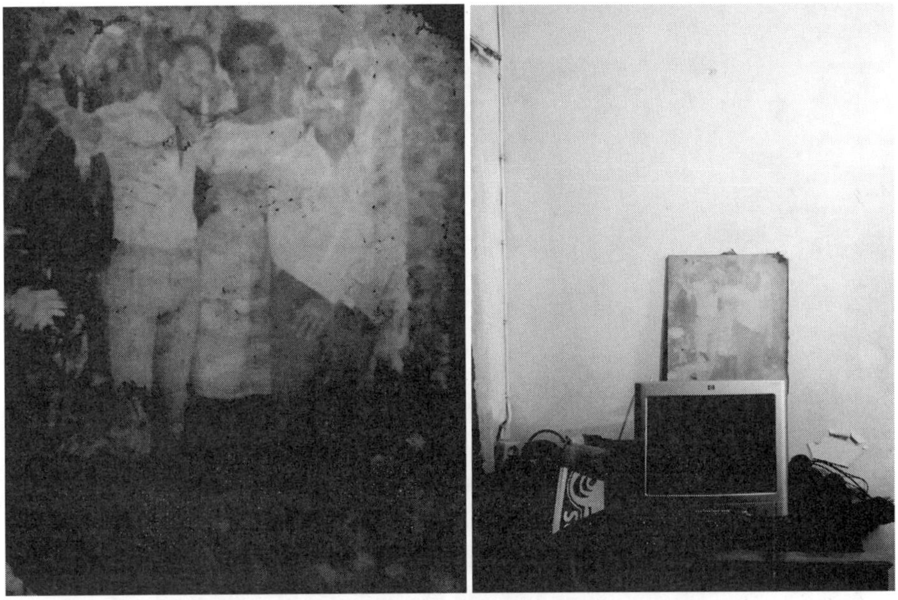

Figure 11. Ricky, Sandra and Dennis Stutgard; photographer unknown. Stutgard living room, c. 1960–1970.

eighteenth century, as is clear from the Specialiën. From Ricky's perspective, it would have been a way to follow the tradition practised by his parents and ancestors from Berg en Dal. In the photograph, he is seen with his hands crossed while holding the holy book in one hand. Ricky is formally attired and wears a pair of glasses, looking directly at the camera. The sister has a stern gaze and wears a white dress and neat shoes. The formality of her pose is akin to her elder brother's.

The Stutgards, it seems, had decided to follow the confession according to the Evangelic Brother Gemeente in Suriname as most Afro-Surinamese families who lived in the capital Paramaribo in this timeframe. Although the family was Christian, they did not force their children to study the Bible and come to church every Sunday. Dennis Stutgard chose not to do his Bible studies and confession, and was amongst the three, not as occupied with religion. He was not interested in dressing up like his elder brother and sister, and remained in his own informal clothing. Despite his father John Stutgard becoming a pastor after his retirement, Dennis did not conform to family traditions. His father too never wanted to force his children to go to church on Sundays. Sandra narrated that confession is made when you reach a certain age, and you have to wear white clothes while going to church (Figure 11, 12). Although she shared her religious conviction with her brothers, she never shared her personal problems with them. She was convinced that one needed to sort out one's own problems and wanted to have an independent position while doing so.

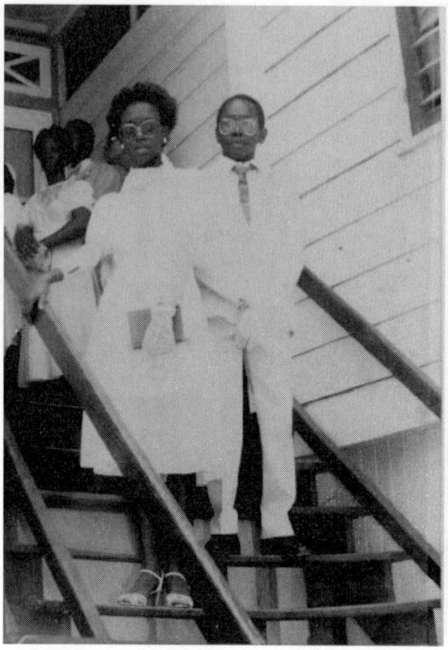

Figure 12. Ricky, Sandra and other Stutgards; photographer unknown. Stutgard photo album, c. 1960-1970.

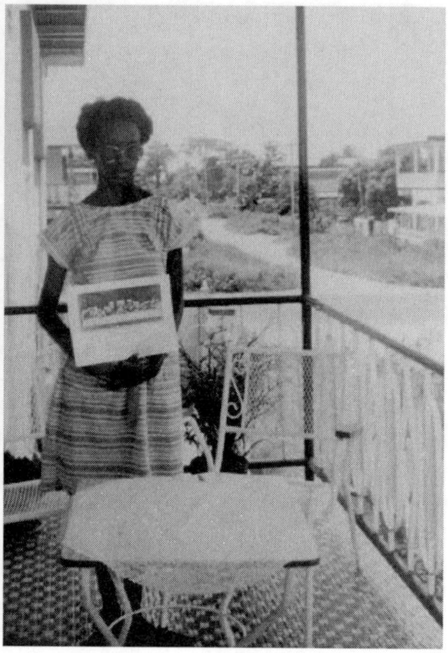

Figure 13. Sandra Stutgard; photographer unknown. Stutgard photo album, c. 1960–1970.

In between the pages of the family albums, I found a remarkable image of Sandra's journey with her mother to Colombia in 1979. She received a certificate that she included in this photo album containing several photos of their journey. They were able to go on holiday, and this presents a certain status of the family, indicating that by 1979, they had sufficient funds to spend on leisure. Everything was organised from Suriname and they travelled as part of the group visible in Figure 14. They were freely travelling together and her father paid for the trip, indicating a liberal attitude towards women within the family. Coming from Suriname, they of course, faced a language barrier, and because they spoke Dutch rather than Spanish, they needed a translator to communicate. Sandra often travelled alone with her mother and lived with her throughout her life.

Although oral memory consists of an uncertain reliance on the memory of its narrator, the unfixed layer described by Kobena Mercer[22] remains in the visual narrative of the post-migrant photographic medium.

---

[22] Mercer, Kobena. 2010. 'Photographs and the Global Conditions of Cross-cultural Modernity'. In Blokland, Sara and Asmara Pelupessy. eds. 2010. *Unfixed: Photography and postcolonial perspectives in Contemporary Art.* Jap Sam Books. p. 73

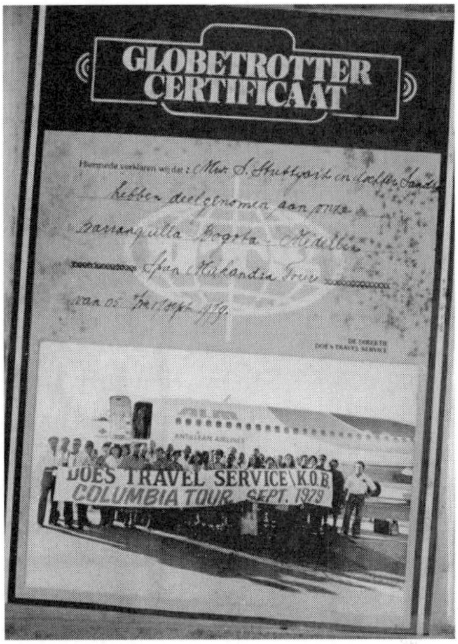

Figure 14. Sandra Stutgard and her mother; photographer unknown. Stutgard family album, c. 1979.

In the photographs I selected of the Stutgard family, the narrative is one of self-representation, while the religious celebratory moments of their Christian faith are captured by the family. The colonial Western Christian influence of the missionaries on the Berg en Dal plantation in the genealogy of the family described earlier dominated their convictions.

Aunt Sandra is visible in the centre of the photograph (Figure 13). The photograph she is holding in her hands probably represents her conducting a Bible study session and the formalities for confession. This colonial history of religious domination and the disappearance of Afro-Surinamese ancestral knowledge influenced self-representation in these pictures. Apparent in this presentation of the self in 1960–70 is somehow the merged affiliation with the Christian religion. Other photographs (Figure 11, 12) seem to be taken on the day of confession similar to Figure 13. There is a difference in the context of how one encounters these images. While Figure 12, 13 are small photographic prints pasted in a family album, Figure 11 is an enlarged faded print hung on the wall, surrounded by household detritus.

The photographs functioned as a hidden archive, not directly accessible due to its invisibility in the living room. Throughout a certain time-engaged process, I retrieved this family material from its original position and repositioned them as 'works of art', functioning as a family archive. I wonder if the photographs, by being kept in a hidden place temporarily, are 'decontextualised' and only when I make a conscious act of re-hanging them in new positions, do they retrieve their connection with the original context. In the examples that Mercer points to, he contemplates the state of decontextualisation by their representation in the galleries and museums, whereas the photographs in my intervention are circulated within the social environment of a family and contextualisation in this chapter happens through archival research. The photographs consist of different timeframes, that include different modes of self-representation and furthermore, their temporary invisibility due to the act of them being concealed. Therefore 'decontext' is not an adequate term to describe temporary marginalisation and family secrets. Mercer points to fiction as an alternative to 'the photography's unfixed potentials',[23] to further investigate diasporic and post-migrant photography.

Rather than fictive thoughts on 'unknowable' aspects of images, I have investigated orality of the photographs. Although oral memory consists of an uncertain aspect that relies on the memory of its narrator, the unfixed layer that is described by Mercer will remain in the photographic medium. Moreover, oral memories can sketch scenarios of emancipation through cultural mixing, which is visible in some of the photographs I present.

Hindustani and Afro-Surinamese Emancipation

I interviewed Sandra Stutgard and her Hindustani neighbour Ursula, in Suriname in 2020, to understand more about the gender relations in her family and her freedom to choose her religious direction, as well as her motivation for further education. Sandra recounts her relationship with Ursula, who is also living on Andrichem street, where the family property was built and the discussed photographs remain. She lived a few houses further down the street, so Sandra asked her to join in the conversation we were having.

Ursula recalls memories of going to primary school together. The friendship that they had since they went to the same primary school has remained till date. They share memories of stealing mangoes together, bothering the neighbours and playing *jogu futoe*, a Surinamese game. Ursula did not study further and remained unemployed, and is therefore dependent on her four children, who provide for her.

Sandra had a different education in which her parents encouraged her to be independent and earn her own living by working. This has been absent from the life of Ursula, since marriage at a young age was obligatory; her parents arranged a marriage for her and did not grant her independence. This is an example of a different education, chosen according to different traditions adopted by Afro-Surinamese and Hindustani families.

Bea Lalmohamed (1992) has researched six generations of Hindustani women notifying a change of identity, starting from the traditional Indian joint family, up until they migrated to the Netherlands and assimilated Western values. She notes that the first three generations of Hindustani women had to give their earnings to their husbands. Their financial independence continued until the fourth generation, and then started to change to more independent positions of women, who could make individual choices. From oral narratives, Lalmohamed starts to trace change and dissatisfaction amongst Hindustani women about their husbands' financial decisions.[24]According to Lalmohamed,

[23] Mercer, Kobena. 2010. 'Photographs and the Global Conditions of Cross-cultural Modernity'. In Blokland, Sara and Asmara Pelupessy. eds. 2010. *Unfixed: Photography and postcolonial perspectives in Contemporary Art.* Jap Sam Books.p.82

[24] Lalmohammed, Bea (1992) *Hindostaanse Vrouwen, de geschiedenis van zes generaties.* Uitgeverij Jan van Arkel. Utrecht p.31

only the fifth-generation Hindustani women were able to improve their situation through jobs in education, hospitals and through office work.

Hindustani families lived traditionally in the joint system, consisting of different generations residing in one house. This resulted in married women living with their parents-in-law, like in India. It was a patriarchal system in which the elderly had the final word, besides the eldest son.[25] Sandra recounts that she dislikes arranged marriages because when the marriage fails, the parents do not accept their daughters back into their homes.

While Sandra had the liberty to have boyfriends, her Hindustani friends were not allowed to do so. When Ursula reached the age of seventeen years, her parents arranged a marriage for her, but she never agreed to it. Her uncle found a man for her and convinced her father that he was a suitable partner. The prospective parents-in-law were not that eager about the match because they were aware of the poor conditions of the family.

After her marriage, she was not allowed to leave her home alone and was not allowed to stay longer than an hour outside of the house, even at the entrance of their home. When she went to a shop, she had to tell her husband the exact details of her experience and he would interrogate her. Eventually, she stayed with him for six years, and was physically abused whenever he got jealous. She was not allowed to talk to any other men and his jealousy imprisoned her. She left for her parents' but her parents would eventually send her back because she was married to him.

After the birth of her first son, when she was nineteen years old, her husband started hitting her, but she can't recall the specific reason why. She was obedient and the thought of hitting back never occurred to her—until one time, when he threw a piece of iron that pierced her body and he tried to strangle her. She tried to run away and her clothes were stained with mud. This time, her parents realised the extent of the physical violence, evident on her body. Believing that he had gone too far, they called the police. As her husband was a Guyanese citizen, they could withhold his passport, deport him and thereafter, the border police stamped it to make Suriname inaccessible to him.

Eventually, she stayed alone for ten years with two children. Then she met a new partner, with whom she had three children. This partner was not violent but he did nothing at all to contribute to the well-being of the family. Then, she chose to be single like many other Hindustani women in Suriname.

The tradition of arranged marriages and patriarchal control over women is evident in the villages of origin in India and therefore was integrated in the life patterns of Bhojpuri female migrants and later generations of Hindustani women. Nevertheless, women reformed their traditions by becoming active agents in reinventing these cultural patterns. According to Sandra, arranged marriages are greatly reducing in the present generation. If parents force the

---

[25] Lalmohammed, Bea (1992) *Hindostaanse Vrouwen, de geschiedenis van zes generaties.* Uitgeverij Jan van Arkel. Utrecht p.38

children to marry or are too strict with them, in some cases, they commit suicide, such as in the district that is commonly known as Nickerie.[26] In Suriname, currently, women and men need signatures of their parents if they wish to marry before turning thirty. Parentage is then verified by the city councils.

Besides Sandra's life, I examined the marriage of her brother Dennis Stutgard and Sita Gajadien, and how this was experienced by the Afro-Surinamese family, as Sita came from a Hindustani family. The marriage ceremony was not regular because of the different religions of the couple. Besides this, Sita Gajadien's father had already passed away and only her mother was alive and present for the occasion. Sita Gajadien had decided to marry an Afro-Surinamese partner, Dennis Stutgard, whom she had met in school. She had a traditional Hindustani upbringing, and some of the Hindustani family members would reject Sita's Afro-Surinamese husband. Some of her brothers were angry about this choice and the siblings never really mended the rift. Sandra recalls that as a result, the relationship between the two families was not good and both families were not represented equally during the wedding. The Stutgard family respected their son's choice, despite the dissatisfied sentiments between the two families. The couple had decided independently to get married and were of the required age. Sandra explains that the family expressed their consent by their presence at the wedding.

During the marriage ceremony, a pandit (Indian priest) and a Christian pastor were present. This was not common but over the years, people did try different methods within their marriage ceremonies. And in this case, since the families belonged to different religions, the couple wanted both the *pandit* and the pastor to perform the rituals for their marriage (Figure 13, 14, 15).

Civil marriage in Suriname was not necessary because of the Asian Marriage Act of 1940, that came into being because there was a strong need for the Indo-Caribbean community to be recognised in the social and political policies of Suriname.[27] With this amendment, all Surinamese citizens could enter into marriage in the presence of a civil servant who specialised in marriages, and who would conduct religious ceremonies and register the marriage. This resulted in the authorisation of some pandits registering legal marriages, as is visible in the aforementioned photographs.

[26] Marchand, I. (2014). *Being Dogla: Hybridity and Ethnicity in Post-Colonial Suriname.* PhD in Social Anthopology University of Edinburgh. p. 137

[27] In 1940, the marriages of Hindus and Muslims were recognised under a separate law; the Asian Marriage law that was valid until 1973. The Act permitted religious leaders who were registered with the city councils to legalise the marriage ceremony. Other civilians were requested to register the marriage with the city councils and afterwards in the church. An article in *The Vrije Stem* in 22 May 1973 describes the abolition of this Asian Marriage Act in 1973, claiming that Hindus and Muslims married at a younger age than was the norm at the Surinamese city councils; the new Act would require men to be of the minimum age of seventeen years old, and women had to be at least fifteen years old.

Sita Gajadien[28] remembers the struggles that were present among both families when she got married in 1990. Despite this, she acknowledges that her mother supported her by being present and cooking food for the wedding. The photographs were taken on the day of celebrations. The marriage rituals did not contain a complete *puja*[29] but the pandit[30] read several *mantras*[31] (Figure 15). There was one ritual in which the *sindur*[32] was applied by Dennis Stutgard underneath a yellow cloth that an aunt from the paternal side held in place to keep their heads covered (Figure 16). After the pandit was ready for the ritual, the pastor Polane started to deliver his sermon and there was some singing and praying (Figure 17, 18). He had to formally ask the question of taking each other as their partner and sing 'Our Father', after which they received a Bible. After this, they all prayed together—the pandit and the pastor, along with both families. This type of marriage was not recognised in the Netherlands, where these ethnic religious functionaries had no legal or civil status, resulting in a very different social bracket as compared to Suriname.

In retrospect to the marriage, Sandra remembers that her parents never suggested that it was better to marry inside of the Afro-Surinamese society in Suriname. Her parents gave her the freedom to decide by herself. Sandra specifically points out that the parents did not want to take the blame for misfortunes in the marriage afterwards and therefore did not decide upon partners for their children. According to Sandra, her brother Dennis Stutgard had some issues during his childhood causing him to have tensions with his siblings. She tried to improve the relationship with him on several occasions. In later conversations with Sita, I understood that he never felt accepted in the family, the parents favoured the other siblings which is why he might have felt left out. He resisted an identification with their Afro-Surinamese family traditions. He might have consciously chosen to look beyond his own community and therefore engaged in a relationship with a Hindustani female.

The couple migrated to the Netherlands after their first son was born in 1993, the reason for their migration was to find a peaceful life. In this

[28] In another interview on 30 March 2022 with Sita Gajadien, we discussed the photographs again.

[29] Rituals associated with Hindu marriage differ from region to region and caste. However, there are some rituals which are common to most marriages. Hindu wedding rituals can be broadly classified into pre-marriage rituals, wedding rituals and post-marriage rituals. The rituals in Suriname derive from North Indian marriage rituals, commonly practised in the Bhojpuri region.

[30] A Hindu scholar learned in Sanskrit and Hindu philosophy and religion, typically also a practising priest.

[31] (Sanskrit) a 'sacred utterance' in Vedism; one of a collection of orally transmitted poetic hymns. A type of religious text, religious writing, sacred text, sacred writing that is venerated for the worship of a deity and is commonly repeated in word or phrase.

[32] It is a vermillion powder applied on the wife's forehead by the husband during wedding rituals to mark his presence in her everyday life. In everyday life, it is considered to be the symbol of matrimony in Indian households and an essential part of a woman's marriage.

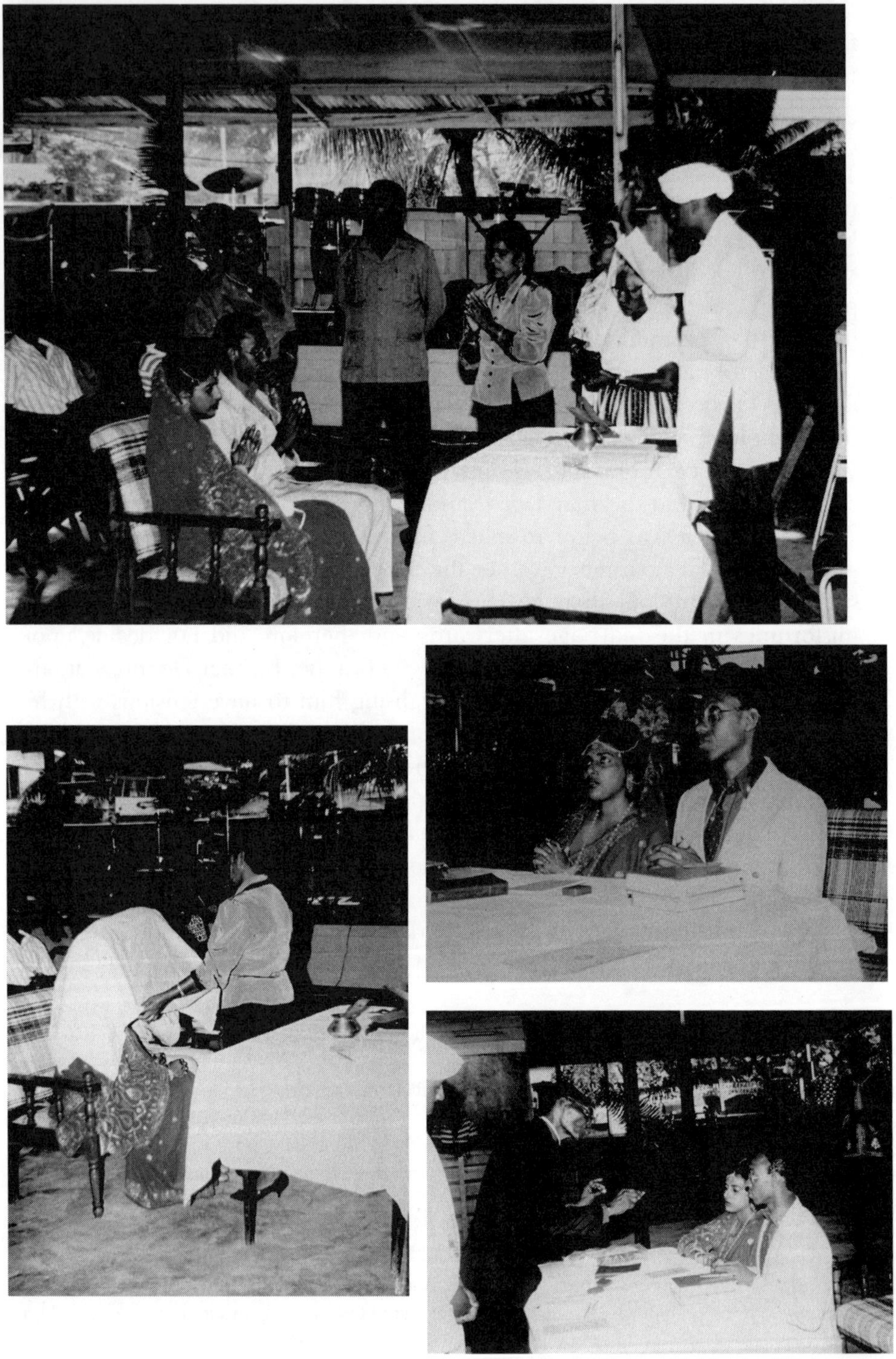

Figures 15, 16, 17, 18. Marriage of Dennis Stutgard and Sita Gajadien; photographer unknown. Source: Sita Gajadien family album, c. 1990.

timeframe in Suriname the community did not accept the inter-religious marriage. Examples of their struggles were not finding housing of their own nearby Paramaribo due to discriminatory reactions.

During their residence in The Netherlands, they didn't have much social support. Financially it was hard to get by because the immigration services did not co-operate with their residence permit. They constantly tried to interfere with their lives. After spending almost a decade in the Netherlands moving from one rental apartment to the other, they were evicted from their house.

Their second son was born in 1994 and both children grew up in Rotterdam where they attended school. I remember the memories of my aunt and cousin vaguely, we saw them some times; when they grew older, we lost touch. I remember my aunt coming to our house and drawing with me during my primary school.

After twelve years, they failed to get a residence permit. Suddenly the immigration authorities commanded their departure. The family was deported back to Suriname. They returned to Paramaribo to live in the Stutgard family home. During this period in their marriage, they lived together in the same house as Sandra until the sudden death of Dennis Stutgard due to a heart attack when their eldest son was about nineteen years old in 2012. While talking about these situations it is remarkable that both parents by birth were Dutch citizens in Suriname during the period of Dutch colonisation. Before Suriname's independence, Sita obtained a Dutch passport for schooling however this was never fully recognised during the immigration policies of the Netherlands in the 90s.[33]

One can question if the cultural mixture of their marriage in Suriname was a form of emancipation from traditional cultural practices that were performed in India. Piet Emmer remarks upon the sexual exploitation of Indian women by white and Afro-Surinamese plantation staff. In trying to understand the survival strategies of Indian women, Emmer points to the sexual exploitation of female slaves that led to the birth of children of mixed ethnicity. For Emmer, the connection between mixed parentage and their children is the immediate result of sexual exploitation.[34] The speculation by Emmer neglects the specificity of certain case studies that could better analyse the social narrative between relations of Afro-Surinameses and Indo-Caribbean women on plantation grounds. Although sexual exploitation is described in female testimonies and recounted by several scholars, the relationship Emmer describes between emancipation and mixed parentages seems only exploitive. I argue that mixed parentages besides other cultural exchanges led female Indo-Caribbeans to emancipate themselves from patriarchal cultural gender constructions.

---

[33] In another interview on January 28, 2024 with Sita Gajadien, we discussed their multiple migrations.

[34] Emmer, P.C. (1987). The position of Indian women in Suriname. A rejoinder. *Boletin de estudios Latinoamericanos y del Caribe* 43, p. 115-120. p. 118.

Chan Choenni describes some oral memories of people of mixed ethnic backgrounds who were shunned by Afro-Surinamese and Hindustani communities in general. One oral memory describes a Bhojpuri migrant woman giving birth to a son with black skin and frizzy hair, who had to leave the plantation because of the *panchayat.* Some lighter-skinned Afro-Surinamese women did not want their daughters to have a darker shade because that would match the skin tone of male indentured labourers.[35] These oral narratives contradict Emmers' observation on mixed offspring. Another narrative is given by Miss Shrimaansingh, about her great-grandmother who was a widowed indentured labourer between 1879–1883 and who started a relationship with a man whose father was still a slave. 'They were allowed to go to church together and were known as lovers publicly. In a black-and-white photograph, you can see that my grandmother and my great-grandmother are wearing headscarves known as 'anisja'. In the time of indentured labourers, a good way of Afro-Surinamese ex-slaves and Bhojpuri migrants was evident and consisted in the family.'

We can understand that examples of ethnic mixing existed for generations in the Bhojpuri community, as we have seen in the second generation in the Stutgard family's descriptions of Berg en Dal.

According to Lalmohamed, in the oral research she executed, only 10 per cent of the Hindustani community accepted Afro-Surinamese or white partners for their daughters and 20 per cent of their daughters were open to other cultures in general.[36]

However, Iris Marchand declares that ethnic and hybrid identification were not about the difference in ethnicity but about redefinitions of spatial belonging, forms of power, culture and personhood, that were built on diverging memories of immigrants and reconfigured in a newly shared locality with colonial baggage that was not easily left behind.[37] As an example, Marchand narrates the narrative of Cynthia McLouds, *Hoe Duur was the Suiker?,* in which the 'embodiment of mixed and mulatto women that the system of racial control of empire "fell"; mixed race concubine women attached to the planters' families in colonial Suriname increasingly disturbed hierarchical distinctions of colour that the colonial administration tried to maintain'. Similarly, Homi Bhabha understands hybridity as a self-empowering means to resist colonial domination, by creating what he called 'cultures in between'.[38] Specifically, the term '*dogla*' has been used in the Caribbean as a marker of racial difference for the offspring of Indian and

[35] Choenni, Chan E.S. (2016). *Hindoestaanse Contractarbeiders (1873-1920) van India naar de plantages in Suriname.* L.M. Publishers. p.646, 645, 644.

[36] Lalmohammed, Bea (1992) *Hindostaanse Vrouwen, de geschiedenis van zes generaties.* Uitgeverij Jan van Arkel. Utrecht p. 77.

[37] Marchand, I. (2014). *Being Dogla: Hybridity and Ethnicity in Post-Colonial Suriname.* PhD in Social Anthopology University of Edinburgh. p.14-30

[38] Bhabha, H. K. (2004). *The location of culture.* London: Routledge.

African sexual union. They were categorised as ethnic bastards or outcasts, so this group has been subjected to silencing in the past and locally, people have been rather negative about this term, whether in Trinidad, Guiana or Suriname.[39] Rhoda Reddock declares that the voice of the dougla[40] or those projecting 'dougla identities' of mixed African and Indian ancestry, is largely missing.[41] Reddock navigates these identities through performance and artistic production, and the concept of 'dougla poetics' that was conceptualised by Shalini Puri in 2004.[42] Puri understands 'the hybrid' as a critical discourse in the Caribbean, as well as a perspective for nation-building. She furthermore argues that the concept of hybridity finds a positive expression in the arts. She points to the Calypso king from Trinidad, Mighty Dougla (Cletus Ali), who imagines the following: '...if a law were passed mandating persons to return to the country of origin, they would have to split me in two'. Reddock further remarks that the voice of the dougla received no public echo up until the 1990s, which was the timeframe when the first child of Sita Gajadien and Dennis Stutgard was born.

A sexual song sung by Bhojpuri women during the tradition of *matikor* (pre-wedding), moved from the private to all-women spaces and was named 'Chutney', the more hybrid form being 'Chutney Soca' in Trinidad and Tabago.[43] Indian women were thus criticised for 'sensuous behaviour' that was associated with Afro-Trinidadian women. With these hybrid categories in music, hybrid identities were also associated and included. Besides hybridity that created new cultural patterns for the female Bhojpuri migrant's social domination, colonial rule with laws concerning family life influenced the ritual structures of marriage and death ceremonies.

Within all these biographies and oral memories that are represented in family photographs, I would like to argue that there was female emancipation from traditional cultural patterns rooted in patriarchal dominance, based on norms and values brought by Bhojpuri migrants. It was possible to shift gender patterns by cultural mixing. Through this process of six generations, Bhojpuri migrant status changed to a non-migratory status and finally a Bhojpuri identity is integrated into the idea of Indo-Caribbean Surinamese females. New associations through 'dougla identity' as well as other cultural mixing and

---

[39] Mehta, Brinda (2003) Addressing Marginality Through the "Coolie/Dougla" Stereotype in CLR James's "Minty Alley". *The CLR James Journal*, Winter 2002/2003,Vol. 9, No.1 p.39

[40] According to Reddock the term Dougla comes from the Bhojpuri language in which it signifies 'bastard'. The common position of the Indian indentured community would not be positive towards the mixture of their kin with people of Afro-Surinamese origins, as this would be against their strong identification with religious ideas of purity.

[41] Rhoda Reddock (1999) Jahaji Bhai: The emergence of a Dougla poetics in Trinidad and Tobago, *Identities*, 5:4, 569-601 p. 569, 573, 577

[42] Puri, S. (2004). *The Caribbean Postcolonial*. Palgrave Macmillan, New York.

[43] Rhoda Reddock (1999) Jahaji Bhai: The emergence of a Dougla poetics in Trinidad and Tobago, *Identities*, 5:4, 569-601 p. 577

hybrid identities at present, mean that in Suriname, the Bhojpuri identity is not rooted in one nationality any longer.

As Bragard and Bhabha argue, cultural mixing and hybridity in the current timeframe in Suriname and the larger Caribbean, in the end, destabilise national and ethnic narratives. However, the inner lives of Indo-Caribbean females still hide complexities that we are sporadically able to trace in the self-representation in photographs.

Over time, photographs circulated in family albums and were installed on walls. At certain moments, they were forgotten; thus, the memories of expired loved ones became confrontational. Dust gathered on some of the frames that were taken off the walls years ago, and insects and mice damaged the albums in the cupboards. All the moments of family gatherings slipped from the minds of living family members, who were not part of these gatherings. The oldest black-and-white photographs contain faces that nobody presently remembers—who were these people?

Only a shelf containing the albums full of photographs remains, evidence of these warm gatherings and a much more social family life than in the present, when a more individual way of life seems to be prevalent. By intervening in the family house and rearranging the photographs of the grandparents of the Stutgard family, I tried to make a statement.

I had hoped that forgotten family members that had once lived with them and surrounded them could be remembered, as well as the value of the photographic presence and quality that this material contained. The empty wall filled with some of the found photographic prints of themselves would now speak to them, possibly through raising awareness of their own rich family history and survival through the colonial era, as well as their own unique mode of self-representation. In making this small gesture of replacing photographs on the wall, my ideas and conceptual approach fall in line with the mode of the creator. I wanted to give back something that already belonged to them but was forgotten. An act repeated in different timeframes, but in the same location. An act that dwells in time as I am a distanced family member and not integrated in its process of creation; a visiting family member from abroad who is not part of their household. The effect on family members encountering the old photographs in new positions remains unknown—an act that could be repeated again and again as time passes.

3

Identities (re)gendered: Sexuality and the family

What Would My Father Think?

Charan Singh

Father's presence was everywhere.

I began to see him all around me. The more I have tried to escape him, the more I have been confronted with the notion that he is, certainly, present in every choice that I have made since childhood. Questions of which neighbourhood to live in, which school to go to, who could be our favourite aunt, whom we must visit, what to play in our idle time, which friends to play with, what to be and how to be. Indeed, he has the ability to govern every possible thought I could have. Or should I say, I have just been acting on the choices he made for us, all along. And, as they say, 'like father, like son', therefore, *what* he would be thinking comes as second nature to my view of the world; something that reflects in the patterns of my own thinking process.

Father indeed, is present everywhere; though this is nothing new and it seems nothing can be done about it!

Stay at Home! Or even better still, *Stay Home and Save Lives*!

Until this point, we had learned to assemble in solidarity, shoulder to shoulder, hand in hand, in human chains, weaving a tapestry of struggles and triumphs on the streets of cities and villages. Chanting slogans and humming the songs of freedom. In sweat, in blood, in love, in despair, in rage to fight for lives and to live with dignity. But now, the act of speaking, breathing in and breathing out could put others' lives in danger, hence we had been told to stay put, locked-down. The responsibility of a global public health crisis becomes the duty of each individual. Overnight, we all became expert virologists and psychologists, and we certainly knew how to handle international laws and security around the pandemic. As I began thinking about this piece in 2020–21, home was the only place one could be, and I remained locked up in its apparent safety. At the same time, I also witnessed many who generally were the most tamed by the system, not able to stay at home; who were not able to do what was being asked of them anymore; who were ignoring, disobeying, crossing borders and leaving one home for another.[1]

[1] Historian Mario Da Penha draws our attention to the mass exodus that occurred between the seventeenth to nineteenth century, and how different administrations have dealt with such crises. See Penha, Mario Da. June 2020. 'The Peshwa's tax holiday: How the Mughals and Marathas dealt with distress migration'. *The Hindu*. www.thehindu.com/society/history-and-culture/the-peshwas-tax-holiday-how-the-mughals-and-marathas-dealt-with-distress-migration/article31875853.ece (Last accessed 12 July 2022).

In the much-circulated article, 'The Pandemic is a Portal', Arundhati Roy penned down not only her rage but also expressed her *hope* that this halt in capitalist society could give us an opportunity to reconfigure a way out of the clutches of the biggest patriarchs of all—the State and Capital. But both of these have a failsafe operating system; they will ultimately resume their power. Commenting on the migrant labourers' exodus from urban to rural areas, Roy writes how 'India revealed herself in all her shame—her brutal, structural, social and economic inequality, her callous indifference to suffering.'[2] To not see the obvious, one needed to be sitting in an echo chamber, where the ability to see or hear are annulled. Or one could be an uncaring patriarch who unsees and unhears the never-ending sufferings of their victim—the family. Both were possible in the precincts of one's home.

As we witnessed the unfolding of events, a year later, still in the midst of the pandemic, hope itself drowned in the depths of the holy river Ganges, when hundreds of thousands of people, *sadhus*—mostly men—took a dip,[3] along with those who were being coaxed to or accustomed to participate in the political rallies elsewhere in the country. Some of them may have watched on their televisions and mobile phones—the mass exodus of the migrant workers, or perhaps walked amongst them, who have survived the first wave of the pandemic, yet they are exposed again by the other patriarch—this time, the system.

These forms of patriarchy are a pernicious virus, that has been uninterruptedly spreading among men, contaminating one after another. How can one survive such a pandemic of mutating patriarchy? This question has become more important because this patriarchal virus is continuing to erode the system that is supposed to favour the masses, and has been oblivious to their basic needs. Some of us grew up with the understanding that access to running water is a luxury, and every summer, we witness the headlines of newspapers reporting on drought-ridden, cracked fields upon which a farmer waits for the monsoon to come, as in the city too, lower class people struggle to get a bucket of water from the municipal water tanker. Yet, we must wash our hands thoroughly, until we finish singing 'happy birthday' at a normal pace, as suggested by most health practitioners and celebrity activists in a few 'viral' videos on social media, assuming equal access to water, publicised by the very same newspapers.

Still, something is deeply troubling here.

Amongst all this, where is mother?

Like in Roy's article, where an unmasked woman struggling to board her masked child onto a bus, while a masked man, presumably her husband, is

---

[2] Roy, Arundhati. April 2020. 'The Pandemic is a Portal'. *Financial Times*. www.ft.com/content/10d8f5e8-74eb-11ea-95fe-fcd274e920ca (Last accessed July 2022).

[3] A few months later the same river returned the dead. See 'The Ganges Is Returning the Dead. It Does Not Lie', 17 June 2021. www.nytimes.com/2021/06/17/opinion/india-covid-ganges.html, June 2021. (Last accessed July 2022).

adjusting his mask. Why is she not wearing a mask? Must we all not protect ourselves, cover our faces and wash our hands?

But would *her* washing of clothes and cleaning of dishes during the years and years of marriage count as the washing of her hands? She has already begun to lose the sense of touch as the grip of her fingertips loosens. Every day after her household work, she religiously uses her fingertips to mark her own duress—the sindur[4] in the middle parting of her hair; she must wear it 'as a symbol of her fidelity towards her husband', she was told. For a married woman like her, there is no escape from it. This also keeps her nail a translucent red for the rest of the day. Although her fingertips are wearing out and her wrists are not so agile, yet she continues to create magic in the kitchen with a mere pinch of salt and cumin. Hesitantly, but often, she says, 'I just hope that this excessive washing of my hands dissolves the lines of my palm, which could possibly change my fate too …' Would these faded lines on her palm have the ability to conjure a new life for *her*?

This making it more apparent.

Father. [5]

He who remains untameable. But the walls that he has created for her, to keep her in the house, get taller and taller by the day. This way, it becomes inevitable to say that the future of *Mother*, and *India* are at *his* mercy.

Before diving deeper into the picture of the family, we must return to the task we set out to do. How might we approach the question that I invoked in my title? One way is through academic pedagogy, borrowing quotations to theorise this space called home and who it belongs to, questioning anything that seems alien to the concept of home. The other is by deploying stories as tools to explore everyday narratives, which can help grasp not only the complex lives that the home tends to generate, but also what issues it hides, when we say home–family–home. My interests lie in the latter. In this experimental essay, I propose to investigate these notions through *writing the image*.[6] Even though these utterances often are about a temporal gesture, however, they have a radical potentiality which demands to be read aloud, henceforth forming a *listening encounter*.[7] While occupying a conceptually created space, these unfolding articulations are intended to be heard and not buried by the growing normativity about margin again.

In recent decades, we have seen how notions of 'home' and 'homecoming' tend to reproduce normativity around religion, caste and other forms of societal embeddedness within a wider range of politicised discourses. And yet,

---

[4] Red vermillion marking married Hindu women.

[5] By Father, in this context, I intend to invoke and speak with the notions of obligatory and sometimes self-imposed forms of patriarchy, which sometimes takes the shape of society, system, state and thus potentially can become the Law.

[6] Lomax, Yve. 2000. *Writing the Image: An Adventure with Art and Theory* (London: IB Tauris).

[7] Golding, Johnny. 2018. 'Friendship'. in *The Edinburgh Companion to Animal Studies*. Turner, Lynn, Undine Sellbach and Ron Broglio. eds. (Edinburgh, UK: Edinburgh University Press).

it seems almost necessary to have a happy home or at least aspire to have one, whether in conformity or defiance of dominant forces. The notion of 'home' gives stability, especially when everything else is in flux. So it is still imagined as a place of intimate relations, providing a sense of security, privacy, a place to nurture oneself and a place where one does not have to pretend, but just be. So the question becomes—how do we create this home and when does a place become home?

Another crucially layered provocation this title makes is to *name* the modes of governing apparatus of the supposed home and those who live within it. Due to its vast scope, a more relevant definition to consider here could be, 'The rule of the father applies not only over all women in the family, but also over younger and socially or economically subordinate males.'[8] It is because 'What would father think?' has been the question for many queer people, that the notion of patriarchy has continued to extend to other forms of governing systems. Feminism has taught us how to be critical of patriarchal structures, but what would a home be when imagined through a queer lens? Therefore, in this work, my intention is to create an immersive photographic experience by offering a range of examples. Whether it is slowly setting up the scene to a

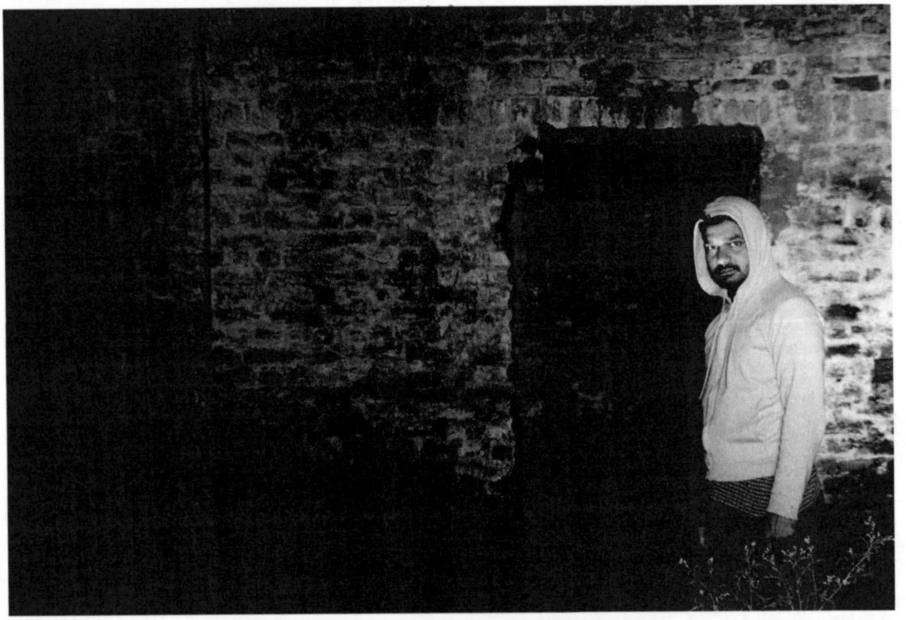

Figure 1. Untitled, 2014. From the series Not at Home. Courtesy the artist and SepiaEye. New York © Charan Singh, 2022.
('Where I stand, I can see that my choices are very clear.
But the only dichotomy I face is what I want him to be—dictator or dynast.
There are no other ways to cohabit.')

[8] Geetha, V. 2007. *Patriarchy* (Kolkata: Stree).

mundane question that unsettles the patriarch or minor defeats in our everyday lives, I imply that queerness can be found in a variety of gestures which could challenge these narratives of home and the patriarchy. It could also be a form of resistance to the hegemony that has been produced by such patriarchal interventions. The first-person voice of these narratives brings a new form of biography, although that does not necessarily belong to a single person, but functions as a biography of the community and strikes a relation with the reader. Thus, the politics of this work is anchored in the place where one stands, rather than opting for a parachuting vision. With this caveat, I begin my meditation of the photograph, the father and the family.

1

morning assembly at the school,
end of the summer vacations

July 1994

I am not sure why it is called a summer holiday. Is it meant to be a break from school or from hot weather? I thought our school had spacious classrooms, ceiling fans and an open ground. In contrast, the heat doesn't leave us in peace at home, and air does not pass through the tangled lanes of my neighbourhood. Besides, I have spent my entire summer break stretching over two months, pretty much at home. I am sure that most of my classmates would give the same answer, if they were asked. So it must be a break from school. But why?

No answer yet. Waiting in an uncomfortable silence that persisted for longer than he anticipated, Amit continued fidgeting with the drawer in search for the second of his pair of socks.

'Umm … where has it gone?' He asked himself.

Then, after a while Amit found the sock.

Still no answer, but then he realised that he has not even asked these questions of anyone. He was, in fact, grumbling to himself as he was getting ready for the first day of school after the summer holidays.

He gently whacked his forehead and smiled.

'Now I have also started talking to myself, just like you …' he tells his mother.

'Why wouldn't you? You enjoy imitating all my bad habits, instead of following in the footsteps of your father,' his mother replies.

Both giggled without making too much noise, as it was still very early in the morning. They wanted to have their shared time without anyone else.

'Shhh …' his mother put a finger on her lips and whispered, 'You stay quiet and quickly get ready, or you will be late for school.'

Amit finally pushed himself out of the house, and began walking towards his school.

It is a quieter time of the day, not much is happening on the streets, therefore, I can take many different routes to my school. Today, I first walked past the Punjabi *mohalla*. Mother says they were all refugees, and only came here after Partition—unlike my grandmother, who also hailed from the other side of the Indo-Pakistan border. She came much earlier, relocating to Delhi after marriage. But I have been told that like my grandmother, they all worked very hard and changed the city in many ways through their culture and cuisine. Imagine, what would Delhi be without pindi chole?[9]

Next en route is an open ground. We call it a *chauraha*,[10] literally means a crossing of four lanes, although this particular juncture is a crossing of only three streets, where most functions, ceremonies and community gatherings take place. It is followed by the vegetable market. Shops receive their supplies at dawn, so a few people sleep on slightly raised platforms to guard their places and be in time for their deliveries. Soon after the market, there is a small community of florists. I prefer to walk here rather than in the other mohallas. After all, who doesn't like the nice colours and fragrances of different kinds of flowers to start their day?

Also, the other street has many sleeping dogs and they do not like to be disturbed so early in the morning. It is their time to rest, after they have stayed awake all night guarding their territory from dogs of other localities. I can understand that. And then comes a very long street of merchandisers, strange and emotionless—I suppose because they sell raw materials for bags, suitcases and some electrical parts. No women or children ever come to these shops—men sell, men buy. To me, this is precisely what makes this street very cold, emotionless and detached, although not dull, as so many transactions are made during each day. Though there are houses on top of these shops, they somehow don't seem to have a presence of their own, nor do they contribute to the coldness of this street in any way. Towards the end, or perhaps at the beginning of the street, there is a slither of a temple, inhabited by the god Shiva at the centre and surrounded by small idols of many other gods and goddesses, including Sai Baba. A temple for all. There is a peepal tree (sacred fig) emerging from the cracks in the wall, where people offer water with rose petals. Intriguing as it sounds, a few feet away from the tree is a wall niche. It looks dark and old, but you can still see the green paint beneath the smoke of candles and lamps. On each side of the niche, there are green satin curtains with golden fringes. I have never seen these curtains closed, which makes this a place of worship that is always open. Every Thursday, I see people gather to light lamps and candles, and also offer sweetened pitted rice.

Tomorrow, I could take a different route with so many other stories, perhaps the *Patli Gali* (the narrow lane) that has more shade. And now I am almost at

---

[9] A spicy chickpea preparation, usually eaten with fried bread.

[10] Crossing.

school, already soaked in sweat. Although summer has officially ended, the stubborn heat doesn't go away so easily.

* * *

In the morning assembly welcome speech, our headmaster narrates anecdotes from the freedom movement and how much we owe to those who fought for the nation's freedom. He also talks about the importance of good character and reminds us that smoking and tobacco products aren't allowed on the school premises. And then, unexpectedly, he mentions Sushmita Sen, who had just won a Miss Universe title. He began by saying 'Does anyone know that she is only eighteen? The same age as some of the students here. They should have been at university, but instead they are still in the tenth class. I am sure that many of you have already passed that age limit and would never be able to reach where people like her have reached, her confidence is extraordinary. But all I hope is that you will pass your board exams. Success doesn't come easy.'

Then, he concluded his speech by emphasising that we needed to 'Work harder'. But why are so many men in powerful positions oblivious to their own privileges, especially those who come from a comfortable background? They often criticise other people as lazy or fatalistic. Does the headmaster not know the demographic of his students, where their school is located and what social and economic gaps the students must overcome to attend classes? Why is no other member of staff able to challenge his stereotypical and reductive remarks? Surely, teachers know about us more than he does.

Half a day has passed, but his piercing comments have had a prolonged effect; they are still lingering in Amit's ears, he looks upset. He is turning into his mother, mulling over something that has been said. On many previous occasions, the headmaster has used this expression: '*Tum log kabhi bhi nahi sudhar sakte*' ('You people can never improve, ever').

'I am not sure if that speech was meant to encourage the students to work hard,' Amit says to his friend.

'Their scolding is medicinal, like a bitter pill; it is all for our good,' his friend replies.

'Or was it just out of bitterness, aiming to put everyone down? Perhaps it doesn't matter what he meant as no one else is bothered by it, maybe I shouldn't be either,' Amit reluctantly tries to make his peace with it.

Another classmate said, 'It is their duty to tell us, and it is our job to listen from one ear and let it go out of the other.'

'But then what is the purpose of this exercise?' Amit asked.

'You ... think so much, just like girls. No wonder other boys bully you and force you to dance for them,' the friend replied, raising his brows and tilting his head, his eyes closed.

It is a good thing that the boys are distracted, this way they stay off my back. They couldn't stop talking about Sushmita, about how pretty the new

Miss Universe is; for them, it is one more woman to talk about, to fantasise over. In their fantasies, they are all those people that they cannot be in real life. Perhaps, the fiction that my classmates have created for themselves is the place for emancipation for people like us, to imagine our own possibilities on our own terms. And then the bell rings for recess.

That same afternoon, when the heat is at its peak, the air from the ceiling fan makes one even more dry and thirsty. A water bottle is not a thing that one carries here; everyone goes down to the compound where the water tank is located. Amit is waiting for the period to change so that he can go quickly to have some water and come back before the next teacher arrives. But he is also worried that he might get stopped by other boys on the staircase. Will the boys force him to dance again? Will they touch him again, inappropriately, until he screams? Will he be able to scream at all? What would he say to the others if he screamed?

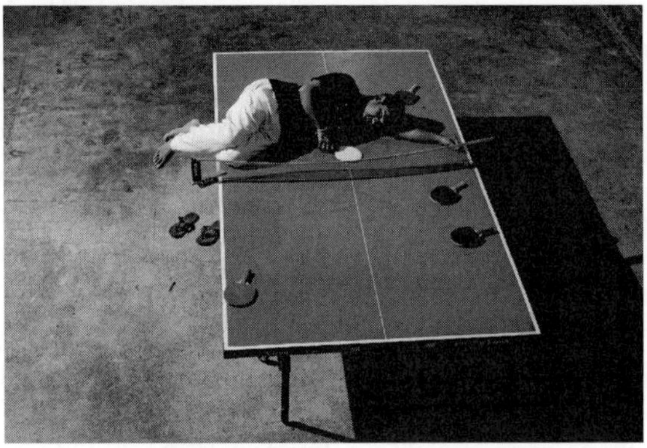

Figure 2. Untitled, 2014. From the series *Not at Home*. Courtesy the artist and SepiaEye. New York © Charan Singh, 2022.

> ('it is almost becoming a cliché but still, where do you disappear in the sport hour,
> why don't you participate in games that normal boys of your age are supposed to play?')

2

in the living room, with my mother,
after a workday

December 1997.

'This is All India Radio, the news read by ...' and then she would switch the radio station to listen to filmy songs while continuing with her day. This was the beginning and end of spoken English language in the household. Other than this, in my limited socioeconomic milieu, the word 'India'occurred mostly on paper—on currency notes or in books, that one could choose not to read. In books, sometimes it would appear in the form of a historical terminology such as 'East India Company', 'Quit India' and 'Indochina'. But India often made its presence felt more strongly when I was among friends. These were strange utterances, like when they talked about cricket matches with particular reference to Pakistan or England. Although I had no interest in cricket as such, I would exclaim regularly, both in shock and awe, just so that I would look appropriately curious during the conversation. After a while, I began to drop names of famous cricketers of the time. Other than Tendulkar, all of a sudden Shane Warne became my favourite, I knew that Akram could not be the one. I thought this was something that would sustain my membership in the boy gang; just to play the part, so to speak. It was all very boyish. But thankfully, school was over for the day and I did not have to participate in those kinds of conversations anymore.

Evenings have generally meant television time with the family. But what we should watch is not something we could ask in the house. The consensus had always already been reached, since we were little. Until the mid-1990s, we used to only watch *dharmic* and *pariwarik* [11] feature films and drama series. Television shows such as *Ramayana* and *Hum Log* have taught us to obey the patriarch of the house.[12] Apart from the mythologies, there were melodramas of suffering and intricate relationships of joint families situated in the cities—fledgling youth in search of jobs, young women fighting for their freedom and autonomy, while the man of the house often finds a way to escape his responsibilities by disappearing behind a newspaper. Through these programmes, an image of family and domesticity was created and televised into people's homes; people entrapped in the cycle of poverty, passively participated in perpetuating multiple forms of patriarchy.

Sometimes, I used to wonder if it was because there was an absence or lack of access to a wider range of programmes. But one thing remains troublesome to me: what if we had changed the channel? What would have happened? Could mother have chosen to see other channels, the same way she used to switch stations to listen to her favourite music on the radio? Perhaps it does not matter anymore, for now we have infinite options to watch or scroll through, on our phones. However, let us return to the 1990s, to the room this family inhabits, where only the father decides what they all watch on TV.

It is wedding season but the new year is also round the corner, so father is trying to be good to everyone. Thus, everyone's mood has been uplifted. There will be several occasions of get-togethers with extended families. But for now, they are all earnestly sitting in front of the TV to watch their favourite

---

[11] Religious and Family genres.

[12] While *Ramayana* was based on a religious text, *Hum Log*—which literally means 'We people' was a modern family drama. Both are classic examples of the 1980s television programmes to which people were deeply attached.

director's new film—*Pardes*, the first of a diasporic trilogy.[13] Invoking the figure of a 'good' patriarch who lives abroad but reminisces about his motherland, the paternal character in the film was raised with *sanskar*,[14] which he still holds dear. Now, to rejuvenate his great admiration for the motherland, he returns to his childhood friend, whose help he enlists to fulfil his wish to find a bride for his son. He wants his Indian values to be instilled in his son, who is a lost, Westernised young man. Ganga, who happens to be his friend's daughter, is portrayed by the lead female actor as someone who is homely and embraces traditional beliefs.[15] The film displays an overtly patriotic and virtuous father figure who stands for truth and integrity, even if that means sacrificing his dream to have Ganga as his daughter-in-law.

In the film, the patriarch is besotted with Ganga and sees her as someone who could be the saviour of his drifting son. He is plausibly happy and sings '*Yeh Duniya Ek Dulhan, Dulhan ke Mathe ki Bindiya / Yeh Mera India, I love my India* …'[16] Ganga also sings and later she dutifully begins her journey to a new life abroad.

It was then that mother asked, 'Why is she calling out for *bindiya*?'[17]

No, Mother.

'Then what is it she keeps calling for?'

The dot on the forehead of the world is India, the country. 'Hindustan!' I exclaimed.

And then, she makes an attempt to repeat after me, 'Ohh Endiya?'

I secretly wished that my mother talked to me about the famous *Made in India* (1995) video and song by Alisha Chinai. At that time, I was much younger and reticent about talking to her about things myself. In the video for this song, a disenchanted princess, played by Chinai herself, rejects all the princes of the world as she is looking for a sweetheart 'made in India'. Her search ends only when the half-naked, popular actor and model, Milind Soman, appears through a magic mirror, exposing his muscular body, luring the princess with his gaze, ultimately carrying her away in his arms. My mother was only interested in the many dresses that the princess changed in the video, saying '*Aisi bahu lani chahiye tere liye* ('We should find you a bride like her') and then you can both dance in your room'. Reluctantly, indirectly, my mother accepted that I liked dancing, something that was otherwise not welcome in our heteronormative household.

---

[13] *Pardes* was directed by Subhash Ghai, Mukta Arts, India, 1997.

[14] Traditional values often refer to Hindu scriptures.

[15] Ganga, the name of the holy river, has often been instrumentalised in cinema as a symbol of purity for the Hindus.

[16] This world is a bride, and India is the dot on this bride's forehead. Such is my India, I love my India.

[17] An ornamental, coloured dot worn between the eyebrows on the forehead.

3

at the bus stop,
spring evening

Late February 2004.

The terrace of my office is abloom with jasmine, which keeps me calm and gets me through stressful days at work. Unexpected rain last night had washed the dust off all the leaves, making the fragrance of the flowers more pungent. It also made the weather nippier. Hopefully, this untimely rain will wash away the winter smog. Luckily, I manage to finish work in time, so I risk ridiculing myself in public by running on the wet streets to catch an early bus. However, I miss my bus, Route 502 for Old Delhi Railway Station. The next one won't be coming for a while, by which time there will be rush-hour traffic.

Yusuf Sarai is a peculiar stop. Neither here nor there. A space in between two proper places, AIIMS (All India Institute of Medical Sciences) and Green Park. Many times, they don't even stop the bus here and autorickshaws huddle in front of you as you gather yourself to catch the bus, often jumping onto a moving one. So even if I had made it in time, I might not have been able to catch it due to the general chaos at the stop. This is the same as when I catch the bus on time to come to work but still get delayed as the bus makes unexpected, longer halts. When you try to survive on the margins, you encounter many disappointments, sometimes they are endless and unbearable. Thus, I must make up some rationale, otherwise, how else could I possibly concede this minor, everyday defeat to myself?

In that moment of despair, a man combing his hair at the bus stop caught my eye. He is not very tall, nor fair-skinned; a rather ordinary man. But his bright turquoise sweater is illuminated in the evening sun, giving a pleasant hue to his cheeks. As most men stare, I do too. But it felt different, and it was just that moment longer which changed the intention of this kind of casual staring. I felt the expansion of time. As if those few seconds had stretched into hours of looking at his deliciously handsome face before my eyes. It is becoming something of a dreamscape, but in reality, I am standing at the bus stop eyeing this charming-looking man.

The next day, I miss my bus again. I am not sure if it is unintentional.

Another delay, another minor defeat against the economic use of time.

The days are passing quickly, one after another, and now February is almost gone. I purposely begin to squander time at office. For in these minor defeats, there seemed to be small chances to win his glances as he arrives at the bus stop. Perhaps, lovers' defeats eventually turn into a victory. Although we have not even said a word to each other, I feel an unspoken temptation between us. We look into each other's eyes before he takes his bus. Looking alone seems to create sweet memories of him for the rest of my journey. Something nicer to think about on the way back home. I wish I could have his photograph, so I could see him more often.

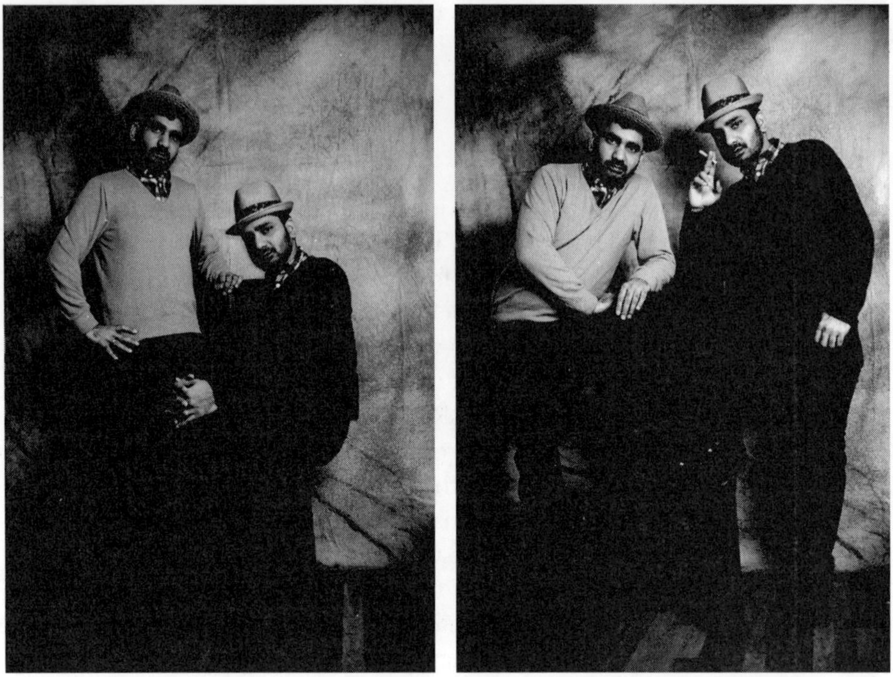

Figure 3. Untitled 5 and 6, 2013. From the series *What Would My Father Think?* Courtesy the artist and SepiaEye. New York © Charan Singh, 2022.

Looking and looking again. Looking for what makes a picture, so a fair amount of looking has to come before a photograph. Looking at the surroundings. Looking out for what you want to photograph. Looking through the lens. And in the end, looking at what you have photographed.

There has always been a photograph, a memory to hold on to, between you and me.

4

at the doorway, whilst
almost kissing
and getting ready to say goodbyes…

August 2005.[18]

Monsoon is a space where lovers meet,
between the sweltering earth and the melting sky.

It rained all weekend. Rain seems to be a marker of changing seasons. After an exhausting summer, it is particularly important to have the sky pour its

[18] A version of this section has been published in *PROVA4*, an art and humanities research journal by Royal College of Art, London, in 2018.

heart out over Dilli, so that lovers can fill their hearts with love after the sultry summer, all over again.[19] All the dirt and smog gets washed away. Now the air feels fresher. The rain also leaves so many skies behind, one could look at them for hours. After hours of pouring water, they seem to be going home, the clouds. But why have they been disguising themselves as shapes and patterns? As if they are hiding something; as if they don't want to be seen as clouds, just like us. We too, try not to be seen as lovers whenever we spend a weekend together.

'It has been so nice spending time with you,' the lover exhaled heavily and continued crawling out of bed, 'but as all good things must come to an end, this too has come to an end. And so, for now, we must say our goodbyes.'

'Well, yes, or do you want me to sing a song for you? What was that song, ah … "*Aaj ki mulaqat bas itni, kar lena baatein kal chahe jitni* …" (today's meeting must end here, tomorrow you can talk however much you desire …)'

'No, no, actually, I should sing for you, "*Abhi na jao chhod kar, ke dil abhi bhara nahi.*" (Don't leave me yet, my heart is still unfulfilled.)'

'Aww, I want this to continue and have you in my life, so that we can sing these songs forever.'

'Yes, I would like that too.'

'Then, let me stay.'

'I wish I could.'

* * *

'What is stopping you?'

'No one and everyone. Besides, you are married. So what would the future be of it all?'

'Yes, but we both are here, this is about *us*.'

'How can this be about *us*, *w*hen there are other lives involved in this that get suspended, and remain waiting somewhere else?'

'That's the point, they are all somewhere else and not here. Here, it is only us.'

'But is it fair?'

'I can't tell, only they can. But I am going to see them next week. I am sure they are doing fine.'

'That's what I am saying. You don't know how they are?'

'Perhaps, we can move to another city so that we can live together *and* remain friends. It would suit everyone.'

'I believe you!'

'And … and I hope this is all true and possible. But what do you think I would be doing on those weekends when you go away? When that *us* would no longer be an *us*? And I would be a mere *them*. Just an abandoned *me*.'

With their stammering tongues, they continued.

---

[19] Dilli is a Hindustani term for Delhi, the capital city of India; it derives from '*Dil*' which means heart, and by this logic, Dilli is the heart of the nation.

'Babu, don't say such things.'

'What do you want me to say?'

***

'Well … as I have been telling you for a while, you should get married too. This way, both of us will be married. We will be able to fulfil our duties of having families and maybe children. Then, nobody will be able to point fingers at us. Perhaps then we will be free. And more importantly, we will have you and me to ourselves for eternity,' the lover explained further, this time in a more hopeful manner.

'How can we be free *then* if we are not free now? Is that your idea of freedom?'

'That's what everyone told me when I was younger.'

'Err … They also said that *this* is a phase, but it is clearly not.'

'Yes, but I thought that's what others have done, all along, everywhere.'

'They might have. But do we have to do the same?'

'No. But how can we change society?'

'Maybe we can't. Perhaps our desires are dangerous for society, that's why everything around us bears a guise of respect. Our desires repeatedly get buried in the darkness of shame and sorrow, and get portrayed as consequences for not listening, not following norms. Something that rarely gets talked about is that beyond these norms, there can be other ways of living, other ways of being, and that there can be other ways of seeking love.'

Looking at each other, their eyes were searching for answers. But no one could say much at this point. Both were quiet, looking at each other for a while. Then faintly, someone uttered,

'But … you know that I love you.'

'I know, but it would be a tragedy to become another example for lovers who resist norms.'

***

The lovers are unable to speak for themselves as lovers. It seems, they now require a proper name for their relationship, to make sense of it. Maybe we have come too far from them or perhaps we just don't want to hear their plea anymore. Is it because they do not conform like the rest of us? Is this why they appear to be seeking sanction for their relationship? What the lovers want, is it permissible at all? Could this be reconsidered? Could they have a second chance? What it might cost them to breaking the norms?

That is a different matter.

This ghost of marriage haunts us all. In a culture where all questions end at marriage, the lovers find themselves returning to it too, after escaping for the entire weekend in the monsoon. And why wouldn't they? It has been a significant institution and an almost inescapable destiny for most in our society.

That is precisely why marriage is often termed as a responsibility, a way of living and a way of being, a settling down of things. It is a system where desire does not matter. And father has successfully managed to create a fear of marriage since the beginning, in the form of *Ramayana* and *Hum Log*, in his discursive production of an unquestionable requirement of society; the only way to belong and exist.

Both lovers seem to be struggling with the question of marriage, from either side of the door. Most of 'us' are born into it and feel the moral burden that demands our hearts to die first, then the mind, and later, only the soulless bodies remain, hanging in between the two worlds. Now, we must go back to the lovers.

'I just wanted to say that there is a photograph between us, a memory to hold, which will remain mine, no matter where we are, no matter what our destiny will be.'

Postscript: *we/us*

This term 'we/us' always mystifies me—how is it being used, in what context and by whom? Who is included in this 'us' and who is being excluded? It seems to be holding a place of power and at the same time, it also occupies a void where vulnerabilities lie. Often, it gets difficult to separate the isolation of an 'I' from a meaningless 'us'. How has this 'us' been produced and reproduced repeatedly? How does a new 'us' get made from within the debris of un-used 'us'? How can one sell and buy these currencies of we/us? And who benefits from all this 'us'? And even though one would like to be critical of this political framework, it is a frightening thought to be left behind by the 'us'. What would we *be* without the 'us'?

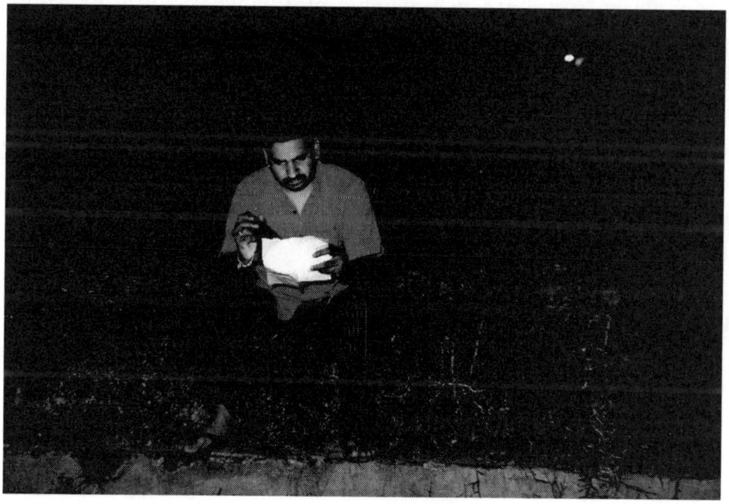

Figure 4. Untitled, 2014. From the series *Not at Home*. Courtesy the artist and SepiaEye. New York © Charan Singh, 2022.

Oh well, never mind, we were talking about these lovers, somehow, we have left behind. Let's get back to them. So the 'us' between them was an ambiguous trajectory. An assumed, yet unspoken and blurry 'us'. Perhaps this strange ambiguity had brought them together in a queer togetherness. Could love transpire from this strangeness? In fact, sometimes, I yearn for this strangeness to be love itself, although I despise the fact that it often lingers between the *care*—control, the fidelity—betrayal, and the *us*—*them*. But this might be true for all of us.

> (On 2 July 2009, in an historically important verdict on Section 377 of the Indian Penal Code, 'private space' became an important hinge to which our fundamental rights were tied. We can only avail them if we have access to privacy. My image was aimed at portraying this dichotomy between lived realities of queer people, and the language of law and human rights. We did not have privacy to read our letters, let alone to express our intimate love to lovers.)

5

In the bedroom,
In search of a lost photograph …

November 2009.

Family albums are everywhere—they occupy walls, TV trollies, refrigerators, cupboards, grandmother's trunks, and they fill drawers; all of them. And yet, the photograph I was looking for over the past few days was found in the pages of an unread book, unseen by anyone else in the family.

The hidden photograph of lovers should not be seen by anyone. I could not locate it easily, and that was my exact motive when I hid the photograph.

The photograph of lovers in between the pages of the unread book, was meant not be seen by anyone else and thus can be called a hidden photograph. A secret that I wanted to preserve and consume only by myself. And since I could not locate it easily, that was the precise reason why I hid the photograph, years ago. The decision was made on a poor assumption that no one else would read the book in the house. But as we know, a book can keep many secrets, and in a matter of no time, they can be revealed. Secrets are always waiting to be discovered.

Thus, it is time that I destroy this amorous archive of my past, in the same way as I have had to burn all my letters, due to a lack of privacy. They live with me as memories, as unmet desires, and I spent time with them. But in their absence, one learns how to remember. The process of remembrance is not always easy; memories can conjure a past, or refer to a reality that you may or may not want to remember. Thus, if understood differently, a misunderstanding remains in our memories, forever. However, in a time when the future is so uncertain, through tools (photographs, memories and photographic memories), we can certainly say that at least the past is safe in some form.[20] Even if this was a made-up past, a fiction, or a dream. Perhaps, these dreams are the missing archives, a sort of unrealised reality of a life inside the walls of patriarchy.

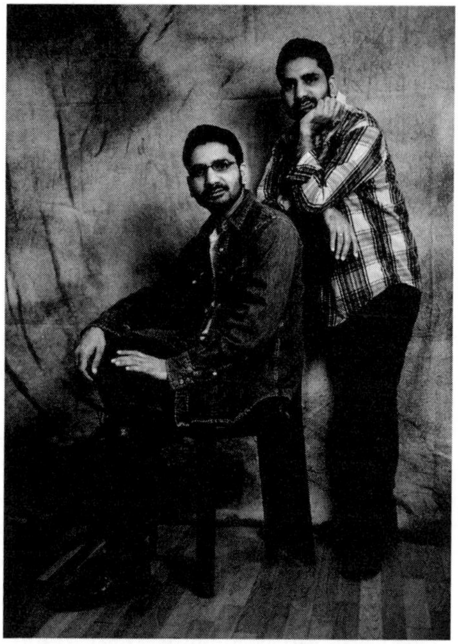

Figure 5. Untitled 2, 2013. From the series *What Would My Father Think?* Courtesy the artist and SepiaEye. New York © Charan Singh, 2022.

Very early on, we learnt how to imitate masculinity of a particular kind, even though we all knew there are other temperaments of men who lived in the neighbourhood, which meant there must be other forms of masculinities that exist in the world. Our already-bruised patriarch has been left with no other choice but to enforce his vivid dreams onto his sons. Thus, they want a masculine 'ideal of chiselled features and gym-crafted bodies suggesting armour, not flesh; imagined as if in cybernetic resistance to ageing or [the] plague'[21] and in the current scenario, they want us to aspire towards invincibility, to fight for our pride with impunity. This mimicry also meant that we rejected other ways to be men, different iterations of human beings. But does this insistence on being a man or a woman come before being human?

Without succumbing to imitation, could the question of masculinity be asked differently?

The Lost Photographs of a Family Album

There is nothing new about the urgency to say something to the question of the family and its photograph; generations of thinkers have struggled to define its meaning. As it is clear, the 'images' that I have presented in this work are not necessarily a tangible thing, they are immersive. I have also alluded to a more ephemeral nature of home in this writing. Nonetheless, we have seen tropes such as 'there is no place like home' unfolding before our eyes numerous times, discursively produced through a range of media in art, literature, cinema and popular culture. So, what can be said about it?

[20] Sontag, Susan. (1973) repr. in I, *Etcetera* (1978). 'Debriefing'. *American Review* (New York).

[21] Deitcher, David. 2001. *Dear Friends: American Photographs of Men Together, 1840–1918* (New York: Harry N. Abrams, Inc.).

Photography has been practised in India since its invention in the 1840s. The original purpose of those early archives has been contested from many different points of departure, therefore, since the beginning, photographic practices and images have carried an enormous burden for both makers and viewers. A broader genealogy of these photographic practices could be 'viewed as an ethnographic document or a family portrait, collected as a souvenir, or held as an image on a postcard, (since) the colonial photograph occupies multiple registers of representation.'[22] After India's independence, photography continued to play a crucial role as it was deployed to provide the visual records of nation-building activities, but also to capture evidence of war and crime, documenting social inequalities, the poor, the marginalised and their families. And yet, this provocation that comes with a family photograph, somehow seems to be divorced from its quintessential politics. A politics that resides in the gendered nature of home and how that has been reproduced so that it is contained as an opaque site within which the family lives. From an inside-out perspective, in a caste- and class-ridden society such as ours, gender norms form an impenetrable barrier to critical engagements by a variety of participants.

So how do we agitate these notions and whose family it is that we see? As stated earlier, within documentary work, we see images of homes on the margins that have overly saturated our visible premises, undermining 'ways of extending bodies into spaces that create new folds, or new contours of what we could call liveable or inhabitable space.'[23]

Years later, as the consumption of images grew, photo theorists started to make claims that the access to a camera had been liberating for people, including people in former colonies. Their work 'outlines the liberatory possibilities of photography for postcolonial Indians who use the camera to fashion representations of themselves as modern subjects and as national citizens.'[24] Such claims impair, if not erase the complexities of this supposedly 'liberated postcolonial subject'. What is intriguing is how we can separate social and emotional economies from the images that we see, without making a spectacle of the subject. We also know—and it has been demonstrated sufficiently—that not only the consumption, but our imagination situates our desire for the picturesque within 'the colonial genealogy of mimesis'.[25]

Thus far, visual discourse takes the photographic corpus as given to make claims to draw upon, but what about those people whose archive simply does not exist—people without a history, as it were. What does it mean 'to

[22] Mani, Bakirathi. 2020. *Unseeing Empire: Photography, Representation, South Asian American* (Duke University Press).

[23] Ahmed, Sara. 2006. *Queer Phenomenology: Orientations, Objects, Others* (London: Duke Press).

[24] Ibid.

[25] Chaudhary, Zahid K. 2012. *Afterimage of Empire: photography in nineteenth-century India* (University of Minnesota Press).

be deprived of the reality that comes from being seen and heard by others'? How one can comprehend this loss of history?[26] Even if the archive survives, it relies on interpretation and intellectualisation, which makes impossible 'how we imagine ways of knowing the past'.[27] In other words, the 'subaltern' cannot appear without the thought of the 'elite'.[28]

How can we make use of the tension arising from the socio-political ruptures that we find ourselves in today's India? Since these are locations that are not necessarily at the centre, do they allow us to make space for different voices and bring forward those issues which have gone unnoticed? Moreover, to me, 'language' has the ability to break open such an 'abridged discourse' of representation. For this, I propose an artistic refusal to conform to the colonial grammar of gender and desire, for which the language has been instrumentalised in order to make the many folds of one's identity visible, dwelling on an 'ethical necessity of historical fiction'.[29] Furthermore, using such tactics makes us witness to possibly 'a conflict at the margins of modern life, visible only in speech'.[30] Through these methods, we will be able to integrate diverse voices by creating resistance between forms and shapes that embody their despair, dissent and dreams.

An example of this can be seen in a written work, 'Among Four Friends' (2018), in which I am musing over an image through language that eventually creates an immersive photographic experience.[31] In my art practice, I try to make images without a 'fixed' vantage point. Shapes and boundaries spill out of the frame, into the text, sound and atmosphere, which creates discursive portraits of the underclass, queer people of Delhi.

We are only beginning to come to terms with the knowledge and the aesthetic norms of revelation that were produced by colonial photographs and still dominate contemporary image-making practices. I would also like to suggest that the language associated with photography often reflects these tensions of power—load, frame, point and shoot, capture, cut and grab—and as such, suggest the intrinsic quality of enslaving the photographic subject.[32] This is especially relevant to India, where even art photography practices have emerged from documentary and photojournalism which, as illustrated earlier, have deep-rooted colonial ties. Perhaps, here, the camera remains an instrument of exercising power by showing things and by photography's

---

[26] Arendt, Hannah. 1998. *The Human Condition* (University of Chicago Press).

[27] Sharpe, Christina. 2016. *In the Wake* (New York: Duke University Press).

[28] Spivak, Gayatri. 'Subaltern Studies: Deconstructing Historiography'. In Spivak, Gayatri and Ranajit Guha. eds. *Subaltern Studies*, Oxford University Press, 1988.

[29] Hartman, Saidiya V. 1997. *Senses of Subjugation* (New York: Oxford University Press).

[30] Cole, Teju. 2011. *The Open City* (Random House).

[31] Singh, Charan. 2018. 'Among Four Friends'. *On-Curating*. Issue 42.

[32] Singh, Charan. 2021. 'Photographic Rehearsal: A Still-Unfolding Narrative'. *TAP Review* (Canada).

inherent subjugation of them; but at the same time, an image can also be equally compelling. Putting it differently, 'photography is an apparatus of power that cannot be reduced to any of its components: a camera, a photographer, a photographed environment, object, person, or spectator.'[33]

We must therefore consider that holding a camera to aim at the subject can be ethically challenging, requiring one to discern the continuing structural and power imbalance between the photographer and the photographed. Photographers, even if they make gestures of collaboration by giving the camera to their 'subjects', or calling them 'friends', or claiming 'we are equals', cannot help but make them even more 'exotic and scenic or picturesque'. This is true especially when exploring delicate relationships within homes, families, lovers, whilst also confronting notions of masculinity and patriarchy. To overcome this ethical dilemma, and as an interlocutor of these two parallel worlds—the image maker and the subject, I often deploy self-portraiture as a method, as seen in the examples that I use in this essay.[34] As someone who inhabits a location on the other side of the camera, this choice is with awareness of the ethical boundaries, vulnerabilities, as well as anxieties of 'being seen', which has persistently informed my visual practice, even if at times, this knowledge appears to be a burden. Albert Camus once said that 'fiction is the lie through which we tell the truth'. This is why my methodologies are queer, muddied and evolving every time I use them. It is one way to maintain the distance from the centre. In other words, I improvise with the usage of images, while writing of an image. For example, the photographic series *Not at Home* (2014) along with the illustrative commentary underneath the images, is an experiment for this particular essay which blurs the inside–outside split of the artist as an ethnographic subject. This also exposes the complicit nature of image-making, for the ethical questions that I ask myself when I am encountering the work of others are the same. To amplify this muddiness, I have deployed a constructed documentary approach to the work, creating a fictional narrative.

Through the stories and the series of images I cite in this work, my quest is to find the lost photographs and minor stories that get buried in the grand narratives of a family album, that need to be found by the patriarch of the house. It will also be his chance to come to terms with the ignored and hence unseen realities that the photographs reference. In the photographic series *Not at Home*, I am revisiting my memories by enacting the roles of the people involved in an event. But the reconstruction of the event in this version may or may not be the 'truth' as remembered. The intention is to complicate this

---

[33] Azoulay, Ariella. 2008. *The Civil Contract of Photography* (New York: Zone Books).

[34] Self-portraiture has been considered a genre of its own to express a range of life, such as gender identity, desires, sexualities, intimacies, political positionalities and other vulnerabilities by the technologies of control and coercion, and in this regards, the *self* is possibly the most ethical and easily accessible model for making photographs.

visual version or memory by questioning the action of storytelling. For the underlying idea behind the second project, *What would my father think?* (2013) is to forge a photographic archive of same-sex desire. In defense of doubling myself into a *self-portrait* — I would also say: after a while, I felt too alone, too lonely in my own portraits, but the urgency, to be and to see myself with someone was excruciatingly difficult. I was trying very hard not to feel like that, but through a rather discursive method we all have been taught that we are incomplete without a partner. We learn this, thus, I always dreamt of living with another, even in these self-portraits I was trying to carve a space for lives that have [*sic*] been overshadowed by various discourses.

In these photographs, instead of spectacularising my subject, I tend to document a quotidian but queer life. Restaging and photographing their *remembered* gay experiences was to consolidate not only an individual's memories but to add to the creation of the collective memory of a community that is still underrepresented in parts of the world.

My critical reflection on this photographic work also provides insight into how people negotiate law and language, and what forms of representational politics they offer to queer discourse in India. My aim is to expose the danger of speaking for the subjugated and the consequences for the communities who are affected, so as to lay bare the conditions that systematically deprive subjects to access self-representation; their inability to speak for themselves, the imposed silence which then becomes the norm and therefore unquestioned by people in India. Through this analysis, I attempt to bring to light to a complex societal structure, where ideals have been compromised by prolonged caste and class struggles, and wherein processes of translation have established the framework in which sexuality comes to be seen and unseen.

To conclude this meditation, I evoke the memory of the expert of loss, absence, separation, exiled in her own home—the mother. Along with her, all the others, who for multiple reasons, could not call a place 'home' and therefore could not be included in a family album. Thus, thinking of home in its ephemeral sense allowed me to imagine gestures when home really comes alive; an early morning whispered conversation between mother and son, while the father is still sleeping, for example. I learn how to be empathetic with her. And even though my mother is already dead and I am still alive, I am growing old with her within me. So in these unfathomable and strange times, the cooking, care, compassion and courage, henceforth and forever, make me my own mother.[35] In other words, the rule of the father in my mother tongue that excludes her and me, is not a rule at all for us.

[35] For this remark I am indebted to Friedrich Nietzsche and Roland Barthes in particular, to remind us of a mother's place in one's life and thinking.

Epilogue: Are You Comfortable with Me?[36] Or 'How to Slowly Dismantle Patriarchy' … Or 'Taming the Patriarch?'

> *MIND blwing f'bdy relaxation by Qlfd h'sme, Eng. spkn, modal lking Pnjb, Jat, Kshmri, Russn, Swdsh hunk 4 Bjs & more in 45 min, satisfaction grntd. ONLY 4 high status clients*

on the terrace with tea,
and the invitation for an adventure in the Sunday newspaper …

The early 2000s.

I would often come across such advertisements in newspapers, typically in the English language, and particularly from metropolitan cities such as Delhi and Mumbai. We could talk at length as to whether what such adverts were implying was desirable, but what struck me was that they were very visible and at the same time, hidden, as they were targeting a specific group of people. These big, bold but cryptic messages have given away mobile numbers. These 'discreet and trusted' male-to-male services offered paid intimate encounters, working from a 'beauty parlour' or spa-like establishment to attract clientele with a high economic status. I used to find them amusing and if they had been in multimedia advertising, one can almost imagine that they would have had flashing signs saying, 'BJ Now', along with a salacious video of those English-speaking, model-looking hunks running on a loop, all pointing to a flourescent pink arrow for you to 'click'.

So whenever I saw these advertisements in the newspapers, they reminded me of Dilbagh, who once told me that he had approached one such parlour for work, but they refused him. 'We are looking for something else,' he was told. Dilbagh knew he would not get the job. But the reason, as their advert suggested, perhaps was his slender, almost frail-bodied frame plus his soft mannerisms, which would not have suited their requirements. He said, very proudly, 'Never mind, *unke kehne se main badalne wala nahi hoon. Mujhe apne aap par aur apni tehzeeb par naz hai.*'[37] And we agreed that all of us do not have to conform to what others wanted us to look like. We don't have to be 'rough and tough', an unbuttoned body in an advert that was beginning to propagate a certain type of heteronormative masculinity. Thus, at that time, he didn't manage to become part of those establishments due to his tehzeeb, or maybe because of his language skills. He remained independent, although not by choice. It is perhaps the high-status clients of newspapers who were the ones with phobic tendencies, 'The paanwaalah in my neighbourhood is more tolerant or rather accepting of feminine men like me!'

---

[36] An earlier version of this section has been presented at the Royal College of Art, London in 2018.

[37] 'Never mind, I am not going to change because of them, I am proud of myself and my mannerisms.'

Dilbagh lived up to his name, a man with compassion and love—the happy-hearted. He always maintained pleasant mannerisms whenever we met. He was also a chatterbox and I was not sure whether to believe his stories or not. Were they true stories or was he making them up? Stories are amusing, as one tells them, but they could go either way, couldn't they? One of the stories he told me was about a gentleman caller of his.

Dilbagh lived in multi-storey Janata flats, tucked away from the main road, surrounded by a busy neighbourhood social housing project for lower-income groups in Northeast Delhi. The flats were small, so everybody was accustomed to living in close proximity. A lot of domestic chores used to spread out into the corridors—sometimes washing, cleaning and even bathing would happen in the corridors, which made them the busiest places in the building. All these bustling activities created a strange urban symphony within their everyday lives. Even though it was an architecturally planned building, I would not use the word 'encroachment' to describe this modification. But the inhabitants of this place have adapted and improvised its shape to suit their own needs and purposes, which has extended the usefulness of the space to its maximum potential—a queer use, indeed. However, from below, the staircase seems like a game of snakes and ladders; you don't know where they go until you reach.

On a regular Wednesday morning, Dilbagh appears on his balcony, speaking on his mobile to a man outside his house, who was waiting on the road to be guided to the entrance of the building. Dilbagh has the ability to change his name and gender in most of his stories; in this, he said he was Ayesha. Dilbagh waved to the man from his balcony, and while directing him towards the staircase, said, 'Come straight up, it's the blue door on third floor, okay?' The man's eyes followed Dilbagh's hands, pointing to a narrow passage. Then he reluctantly agreed to come up and said to Dilbagh, '*Accha, aata hoon*'.[38] They hung up. The man looked anxious and stood there for a moment before he walked towards the stairs.

'*Uff, iska toh abhi se dum nikal raha hai, baad mein kya hoga?*[39] In the photos, he looked very strong and randy in a uniform, I hope my morning does not go to waste. Well, let's see,' Dilbagh thought to himself. He then quickly rushed to the bathroom, to touch up his make-up.

As the man climbed the stairs, he looked uneasy, but continued to move ahead. A middle-aged woman was hanging freshly washed clothes to dry in their corridor. Water was dripping from the clothes, which was making the corridor's floor slippery. The man had to be careful not to slip on the wet floor. He was cautiously walking ahead and began to look more and more anxious. What could be the reason for his anxiety? He was a man, and not only that, he

---

[38] 'Okay, I am coming.'

[39] Literal translation is "Sigh, he is already dying, what will happen after?" but the implication is that the manliness of the officer who looked so commanding in his uniform is destabilised by Dilbagh's overpowering femininity.

was a man in a uniform, who, if he was 'at work', would hold exorbitant power and control in such neighbourhoods. Perhaps he felt that he was being exposed to other people due to the complicated access to Dilbagh's home. Perhaps, this is a strategic choice to be safe when Dilbagh invites gentleman callers home. Perhaps, this is how one undoes the patriarchy.

As the woman was putting clothes on the rope, she was also talking to her neighbour, right across her balcony, 'Listen, watch out for my clothes. If there is a gust of wind, they get blown away.'

'Haan Amma, I am not leaving before I finish my crochet cover,' the neighbour replied. But in addition, she also asked for her chilli pickle recipes that she was being offered last week. On the floor above, a young boy was feeding corn to his parrots, while a few steps away, an old cat, after a busy night of prowling, finally dozed off in the window, getting a little bit of sun. It was the third floor that the man had to reach. Finally, he arrived at the blue door.

'Hello, welcome to my humble abode!' Dilbagh said with his hearty smile. By this time, Dilbagh had applied a fine line of kohl to his eyes and a shimmering peachy lip gloss.

An awkward silence.

'Ah … are you comfortable with me?' Dilbagh asked.

After a long pause, with a stammer the man nervously replied, 'Ya … Yes.'

Acts of Presentation

Women and Incongruous Impasses in Family Albums

Hardik Brata Biswas

'And in some archive of paper or stone, on some roll of microfilm, we could read a sentence. I read it here, let it be the opening sentence of this introductory address, for example this:—One might say that we represent something ***(nous somme en representation).***

Are we sure we know what this means, today? Let us not be too quick to believe it.'

— Jacques Derrida[1]

The family, *as if and already*, has emerged in the context of family photography. Since the end of the nineteenth century, coeval with the arrangements of a broad social reality, the space of the family album has worked towards the cultural reception of a family form based on heteronormativity, causally organised women's visibility, and the exchange of women in marriage. Beyond such dissemination and reception of photography in the context of the family, as a representational method and strategy, the photographic image can effect a puncturing of essentialised tropes of gendered structures. Here, in haste but cautiously, I am positing two such profound formulations already discussed in critical thinking around visual representation. The scope of this essay lies at the intersection of these two, in a shared, negotiated space. On the one hand, I will do a survey of the larger questions of representation and the archive in the context of representing women, and will move on to moments of cross-dressing and death photographs in family albums to think them as possible moments where the rational-essential nature of women's representation falls apart. On the other hand, this will not be a reaching-out to a programme of radical overthrow and seemingly unproblematic rendering of the liberatory, in the visual spaces of the photograph in the context of the woman and the family. At this point, one should be cautious so as not to propose any quickly derived structure from the genre of family albums and especially in the excitement of encountering something 'new'.

In view of the photographic examples through which I will be moving here, one is confronting a threshold, a borderland of photographic representations. In a way, such photographs evidently represent what is to be represented;

[1] Derrida, Jacques. 1982. *'Sending: On Representation'. Caws, Peter and Mary Ann Caws. trans. Social Research. Vol. 49:2 (Summer). Current French Philosophy. pp. 294–326.*

performing the prima facie task expected of the photographic image. In another way, the same photographic images of cross-dressing and death approach a horizon of meaning and reception that moves beyond the manifest nature of representation. The reception, at this point, of such images proposes an affiliation with the incalculable, an excess impossible to define or represent in finite terms. This might be an enabling (not as something which one can *do* right now) move in approaching the other, not as separate from the self, rather emanating from the self but not yet familiar, catalogued, documented or named. It is like a trace, barely in proportion to the social.

It indexes but moves further towards acknowledging the possibilities of the photographs in realising its *representedness*—an aspect which has been broadly overlooked in readings of family albums and domestic photography. Accepting these photographs of cross-dressing and death in terms of an unquestioned new idea, might be problematic since one is looking into remediation of the acts of cross-dressing and death in photographic prints. However, there seems to be something new happening here, apparently unseen and without any ordinary possibility of a simple return. An altogether unproblematic acknowledgement of *newness* might forego questions of return and repeat in the economy of representation. Acts of cross-dressing, poignant moment of passing on of the loved one, come across as facts, singular in its enunciations and problematising the neat translatability between the general and the particular.

Generally speaking, it was the democratisation of photographic image-making that set forth a process that would ring the death knell for the hegemony of traditions of representations in the hands of elite. Bourdieu (1990) argues that the relationship between individuals and photographic practice is essentially a mediated one. Although surveys of photography as a critical category are available, there are fewer critical insights on family photography. The contours of analogue photography that I have traced, more often than not, try to posit the figure of the woman as well as the man in definite generic social moulds. With the interiorisation of photography from the late nineteenth and early twentieth centuries, simultaneous to the emergence of women in the nationalist pictorial imagination, a different, unnoticed trend of family albums began to develop among middle-class families in Bengal. In a way, the subjective nature of photographic albums, each with their distinctive 'narrative' do not allow a closure of the possibilities of the visual but vastly open up the scope for reading patterns in social gendering. The non-public or the limited public access of family albums gives them the chance to preserve the moments which otherwise could attract prejudice in spaces beyond the limits of kinship, within which such images of women are subject to discursive exchanges.

In order to separate the universal and the hegemonic from the fragments of daily experience, it is necessary to contextualise and access other 'intimate' information, thus turning the observer into a privileged reader. In family albums, a combination of professional photos, amateur and spontaneous ones, immediate snapshots (these are rare to find in early albums because of the expensive and cumbersome nature of photographic apparatus in late nineteenth and early twentieth century) that lack overt symbolic intent but reflect the desire to arrest movement and time in a precise instant, are common. Probing into lives through photos can also be problematic. Despite their documentary power, their status as historical evidence has been the subject of intense debate. The notion that a photo can summon up the past in any unmediated, transparent way is now generally regarded as a form of naïve realism. According to Hall, 'The evidence that the photographic text may be assumed to represent is already overendowed, overdetermined by other, often contradictory meanings, which arise within the intertextuality of all photographic representation.'[2] However, before that, one can begin by looking into the meaning of the word 'representation'.

I

Representation and its other formations such as 'representative' and 'representing' will inform the scope of the essay not merely as incidental-pragmatic usage but in its critical enunciations. Representation is a word which has wide and common currency in the English language. In fourteenth-century English usage, 'a crucial extension' was noticed when the word 'represent', apart from meaning corporeally presenting oneself 'often to some person of authority', also began to mean 'standing for something that is not present'.[3] Although following a trajectory of evolution of meanings and usages from the realm of political democracy in England, it is from the nineteenth and twentieth centuries that the word was 'widely used as an identifying element of realism or naturalism'. Much later and probably not before the twentieth century, the word became a standard utterance for exactitude in reproductions, especially in the category of representational art.[4] The prefix 're' enunciates more than one possibility of meaning of the 'present'. I am, in the context of this review, keeping afloat two such possibilities. First is the representation of A (in absence) by B (in presence) where B is taken to be wholly or mostly standing in for A. The second is when A (in absence) is represented by B (in presence) where B is presenting A, not in terms of exactitude, but communicated through sensory experience.

I go back to the epigraph by Derrida (1982) cited in the beginning of this essay. In 'Sending: On Representation', a 1982 lecture, Derrida reviews the scope of representation. He cites the much-used arena of representatives as

---

[2] Hall, Stuart. 1991. 'Reconstruction Work: Images of Post-war Black Settlement' in Spence, Jo Spence and Patricia Holland. eds. *Family Snaps: The Meanings of Domestic Photography* (London: Virago). p. 155.

[3] *The Complete Edition of the Oxford English Dictionary: Complete Text Reproduced Micrographically* (1971). Vol. II, P–Z. (Oxford University Press).

[4] Williams, Raymond. 1988 [1976]. *Keywords: A Vocabulary of Culture and Society* (London: Fontana Press). pp. 267–69.

in government, to language (and its translatability) and then to the Hegelian and Heideggerian schema of representation and being. Hanna Pitkin (1967) provides, perhaps, one of the most straightforward definitions—to represent is simply to 'make present again'.[5] Derrida, in his argument, would not accept the structure of representation in such a transparent and unproblematic manner: 'We do not "represent something" only as representatives, as delegates and office holders sent to an assembly which is to discuss representation; the problem of translatability that we shall not be able to avoid will also be a problem of representation.'[6]

He says that in the 'philosphic use of so-called natural language', the French word 'representation' does not carry the 'same semantic field' as its English, German or other translated variants, therefore problematising the very specific use of the word representation itself across borders and thresholds of usage. Derrida calls for a presupposition of the meaning of representation in its shared discursive fields and *franca lingua*, and thus attempts a sending of 'representation', avoiding all possible misunderstanding of the content and destination of the message. He pushes the argument towards contextualisation of the word 'represent' and warns the reader of the general trend of 'bad philosophy', where the word will be pushed to its extreme. In doing so, the word will scale off all specific connotations, contexts and use value towards the destination of where the word will be abstract and independent of any 'contextualised function'. If it happens so, then what will become of the inquiry into the meaning of Being, of which we all have a vague idea, at the least? It is here that Derrida says that philosophical 'common usage always tries to stop the philosphic vertigo' and it is of the form of philosophy against philosophy. The move is, at the same time, of a 'prephilosophical' nature, where 'as if one knew what "representation" meant and as if one had only to adjust this knowledge to a present historical situation, to distribute the articles [*as in the seminar where Derrida was delivering the opening address*], the types of the problems of representation in different regions but belonging to the same space [*of the seminar*].'[7] Derrida argues against a quick closure of 'representation is [*as*] bad' without the rigour of placing the evaluation of the argument in terms of specificities of disciplines and structures. In tracing the Being of representation, he brings in the example of, in an oversimplifying way, the teaching apparatus where acts like seminars and publications attest to the representation of the being. The objective purpose of representation for the subject will be necessary in the process of 'institutionalising of knowledge'.

---

[5] Pitkin, Hanna Fenichel, The Concept of Representation, Berkeley: University of California, 1967.

[6] Derrida. 1982. 'Sending'. p. 297.

[7] Derrida. 1982. 'Sending'. pp. 300–01. Derrida invokes Greek thought and tries to pose the question: 'What is representation in itself and in general? What makes all these representations called by the same name? What is the eidos of representation, the being-representation of representation?' Derrida. 1982. 'Sending'. p. 302.

As one of the many genres of photographic types seen in the family album in the regional context, portraits of cross-dressing invoke the work of memory while attesting to family history. Consequently, while such photographs find their way into albums or displays within households, they act both as history as a *res gestae*—of things that happened—and as *historicum rerum gestarum*, or the commemoration and recording of these things themselves. The ideas of playfulness, romance and conjugality being on the rise since the nineteenth century via various popular forms like poems, the novel form, etc., had their impact on the visual world of photography. The attempt to represent what was private and what could not be 'practised' in an otherwise censoring public, was a curious process.

Performances of the self before the camera can make representation go beyond the grasp of the normative structural economy of framing. Representational spaces, studios and photographs opened up possibilities of identity formation and performance by the subject in a changed historical context. Economic, social and political events in the region and related forms of knowledge in turn produced new sensibilities for the people within the parameters of social spaces. It is where inter-subjective communication and negotiation is made possible for subjective refashioning and invention of the modern self. Rational or imaginative emotional histories also shape perceptions of the people through the way photography works in social spaces.

A conscious self-presentation of an ideal nature in the performance space of the studio not only represents internal aspirations, but also an aspiration to be recognised as a distinctive social subject (Parayil 2003, 284).[8] The objectivity of the photographic process lends it mass credibility within structures of visual modernity.[9] At the same time, photographic performance acted as agent mediating history through the meaning of 'signifying properties', where the subjects become 'social actors'. The couple in studio photographs represent a distinct case when they are constructed within the realm of imagination, which is interconnected with the disposition of habitus. Further, considering the 'reality' in these photographs, neither the subject nor the object simply remains s/he since, as the portrait changes identities for posterity. Similarly, the couple in the photo are not the way they appear in everyday life but on the contrary,

---

[8] Parayil, Sujith Kumar. 2003. 'Photography and Colonial Modernity in Kerala'. in Ray, Manas. ed. *Space, Sexuality and Postcolonial Studies* (Kolkata: Centre for Studies in Social Sciences). p. 284.

[9] To quote Bazin (1992 [1964]):'Only a photographic lens can give us the kind of image of the object that is capable of satisfying the deep need man has to substitute for it something more than a mere approximation, a kind of decal or transfer. The photographic image is the object itself, the object freed from the conditions of time and space that govern it. No matter how fuzzy, distorted or discoloured, no matter how lacking in documentary value the image may be, it shares, by virtue of the very process of its becoming, the being of the model of which it is reproduction; it *is* the model' (Bazin, André. *What is Cinema?* Trans. H. Gray, California: University of California Press, 1992, p. 14).

they reproduce the cultural notions of the desired image of oneself. Here, photographs are not functioning as a reliable natural sign, but accentuate—through the multiplication of appearances—a problem of reliability inherent in natural appearance itself.[10]

Although Judith Butler's formulations on performance and performativity are not specific to the area of photographic representation, her critique can be used in this context, with obvious reservations, as she deals largely with the problem of identity politics and processes of gendering. Here, I will use Gill Jagger's (2008) reading of Judith Butler.[11] Butler shows that identity categories are fictional products, in the sense that they do not predate the regimes of power/knowledge but are performative products of them.[12] They become performative in the sense that the categories themselves produce the identity they are deemed to be simply representing. Identity becomes a matter of social and political regulation rather than any sort of innate property of the individual.[13] The cross-dressing photographs of women that I have used here, such as figures 114 and 115 of Chinmayee Bandyopadhyay, further problematise the reversal of gender. Here, one is not simply donning a man's attire. Chinmayee Bandyopadhyay *performs* in terms of religion and caste. In Figure 114, she and Rama Mukherjee (left) play the roles of the rural upcountry women performing the gendered task of fetching water. In Figure 115, Chinmayee Bandyopadhyay is dressed up as a Muslim woman. One is now looking at the crossroads of gender, caste and religion in the broad social context of India.

As one experiences the realm of family photography in India, it is not enough look into how genders play out. The grounding of the gendered look is often *essentially* performed through the accentuations of caste and religious identities. One might observe a violent continuation of early colonial photographic trends of frontally marking castes, trades and religion. In case of family albums, it has changed and diffused into the habitus of the family and its associated affects. Here, to peek into the sociology of the camera, the differences between 'performance' and the 'performative' should be taken into account. Performance of gender, according to Butler, produces a sense of an essence, which is nothing but a repetition of sustained social performances which create the reality of gender, but which, as Jagger (2008) points out, are not separable from agents or actors preceding the performances, as in a theatrical model. What is important is that what seems to be an apparent free choice to 'choose' the role one wishes to play, like in theatre, is not so much of

---

[10] Kumar, Udaya. 2002. 'Seeing and Reading: The Early Malayalam Novel and Some Questions of Visibilities'. in Mukherjee, Meenakshi. ed. *Early Novels in India* (New Delhi: Sahitya Akademi). pp.161–92.

[11] Jagger, Gill. 2008. *Judith Butler: Sexual Politics, Social Change and the Power of the Performative* (New York: Routledge).

[12] Ibid. p. 17.

[13] Ibid. p. 20.

a choice. The 'doer' is produced in and by the act.[14] She does not stand outside the act itself, or before it, or in a position to reflect. A phenomenology of the body of the subject is necessary to such an understanding of identity and performance, which are not matters of naïve volition.

Butler (2002, 2011, 1997, 1988) has argued that the ways of gendering (practices) that construct ourselves as gendered subjects simultaneously provide the ways for resistance and agency.[15] Butler (1988) argues that according to Merleau-Ponty, the body is not only an historical idea but a set of promises to be incessantly understood.[16]

II

The camera, in the form we have received it in contemporary times, especially in the age of emulsion-based photography, has a long history of development. The camera sought to develop 'itself' as part of the 'human' desire for correct and exact likeness. The move toward perfecting the machine which could capture moments in exact and have a natural tactile quality, was a thing achieved in nineteenth century. Walter Benjamin's 1935 essay 'The Work of Art in the Age of Mechanical Reproduction'[17] discusses the change in the domain of perception and reception as one meets the camera and the photograph. Benjamin, while doing away with the aura of an artwork in the case of technical reproducibility in his 'Work of Art' treatise, mentions the traces of the aura[18] in art forms in ways differing from notions of ownership or the singular-original. The auratic, in case of the photograph, is discussed in Benjamin's *Little History of Photography* in terms of the optical unconscious, where he writes:

---

[14] Most of the images of women and groups inside family albums are conditioned by durations of time exposure whose aesthetic structure was initially practised in the nineteenth century portrait tradition and which relied on having the sitters face the camera and remain immobile for long durations of time. Benjamin concluded that the direct look of sitters encapsulated them in their cocoon while the stillness that was required of them for long exposures was felt in the general impression of silence that they exuded. 'The procedure itself', wrote Benjamin, 'caused the models to lie, not out of the instant, but into it; during the long exposure they grew, as it were, into the image.'

[15] Ibid. p. 89.

[16] 'The body is not a self-identical or merely factic materiality; it is a materiality that bears meaning, if nothing else, and the manner of this bearing is fundamentally dramatic. By dramatic I mean only that the body is not merely matter but a continual and incessant materialising of possibilities. One is not simply a body, but, in some very key sense, one does one's body and, indeed, one does one's body differently from one's contemporaries and from one's embodied predecessors and successors as well.' Butler, Judith. 1988. 'Performative acts and gender constitution: An essay in phenomenology and feminist theory'. *Theatre Journal*. p. 521.

[17] Benjamin, Walter. 1992 [1973]. 'The Work of Art in the Age of Mechanical Reproduction'. in Arendt, Hannah. ed. *Illuminations*. Zohn, Harry. trans. (London: Fontana Press).

[18] Benjamin, Walter. 1991. 'Little history of photography'. *Selected writings*. Part 2. pp. 1931–1934.

> The camera is getting smaller and smaller, ever readier to capture fleeting and secret images whose shock effect paralyses the associative mechanisms in the beholder. This is where inscription must come into play, which includes the photography of the literarisation of the conditions of life, and without which all photographic construction must remain arrested in the approximate.[19]

While acknowledging the proliferation of stereotypes universally and in specific histories of representation of women, the puncture of the aura opens up space for thinking about otherness. This is a move through which I see ruptures in the continuum of family photographs and albums, within the boundaries of photographic form, placing them in contexts of history, sociality and the criticality of the other in forming ideas about women.

The re-entry of aura provides one with a tool for the future of photography, especially while looking into possibilities of negotiations and challenges that the medium posits to already-evolved structures of photographic cultures—the modern family being a primary one among them. However, one is not trying to locate a radical reversal of gendered roles assigned and exhibited through photographic conventions of women in the context of the family. It has been such that the history of the modern subject has also had simultaneous histories of erasure, of violation of rights and privileges, and the birth of new technologies of control. I will come back to this point at a later stage, while reading the photographs and conventions of the Bengali upper-caste, middle-class woman. At this juncture, and in spite of being charged of reifying the bourgeoisie and their subjecthood in case of nineteenth-century India, the photographic medium presents itself as a new insight into realism. Broadly speaking, the novelty of the form and technique did epistemologically stir up the effects and affects in the domain of representational arts for the human condition. The early work of Jean Baudrillard details some of the conditions of this new terrain in which a nineteenth-century observer was situated. For Baudrillard, one of the crucial consequences of the bourgeois political revolutions at the end of 1700s was the ideological force that animated myths of the rights of man to equality and happiness. In the nineteenth century, for the first time, observable proof became necessary in order to demonstrate that happiness and equality had in fact been attained after watershed struggles that gave birth to the possibility of an essentially non-elite culture. On one hand, 'Happiness' had to be measurable in terms of objects and signs.[20] On the other hand, the calculus of such happiness structurally kept women out of its purview in terms of agency and choice. Hereon is scheming in terms of community and nation, where women appeared to be the given pivot on which the movements happened.

---

[19] Ibid. p. 527.

[20] Baudrillard, Jean. 1970. *La societe de consummation* (Paris: Denoel). p. 60.

III

Photographic representations of colonised Indian women, segregated by the double burden of being colonised and of womanhood, faced further representational violence in the canons of colonial photography. Colonial photographic albums contained pictures of high-caste respectable ladies or rural, vulnerable, malnourished women from the famine years. The albums also had a distinctive liking for 'nautch girls', 'bazar women' and courtesans. The albums generally illustrated categories of Indian women divided into the exotic, the respectable and the vulnerable. Gradually, the late nineteenth and early twentieth century pictorial/photographic representations of the stereotypes of Indian womanhood began to be distributed through popular picture postcards. Here, many more typified representations of women engaged in various kinds of work were published. Always, like the early representations in colonial albums, picture postcards relied on social difference. The more plebeian and unwelcome sisters of the Brahmin lady, such as the ayah and the sweeper (Figure 1, 2), nautch girls and the 'Hindoo' lady became subjects of picture postcards.

Early Indian photography became a dominant tool for representing regional identities in India, framing the 'other'. These were areas of target, where a justification for the imperial drive needed to be settled and the

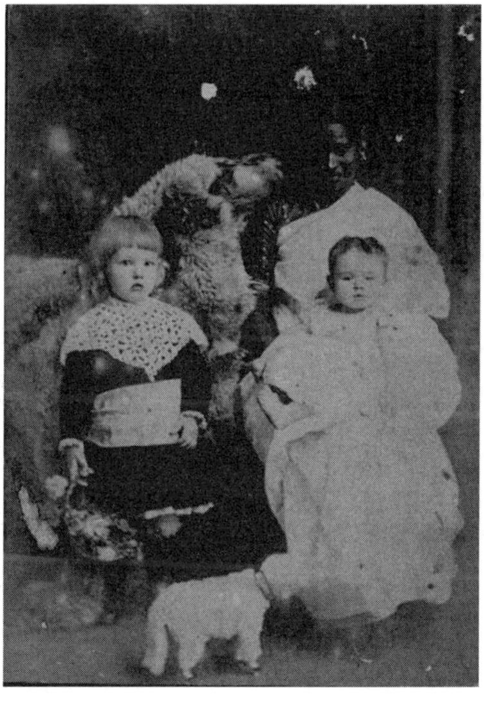

Figure 1. Indian nanny, white children, toy poodle dog. Cabinet Photo.

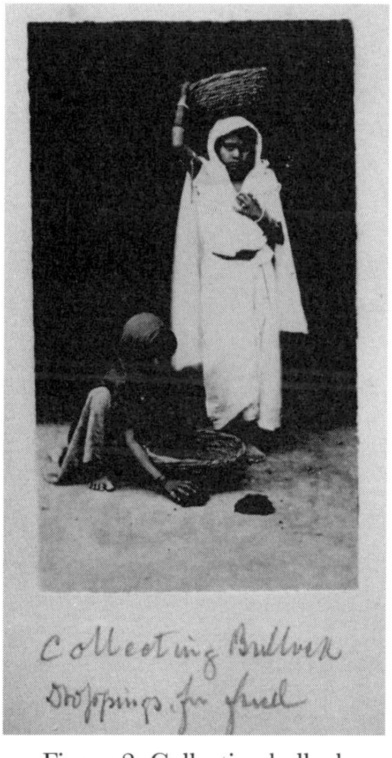

Figure 2. Collecting bullock droppings. c. 1880s.

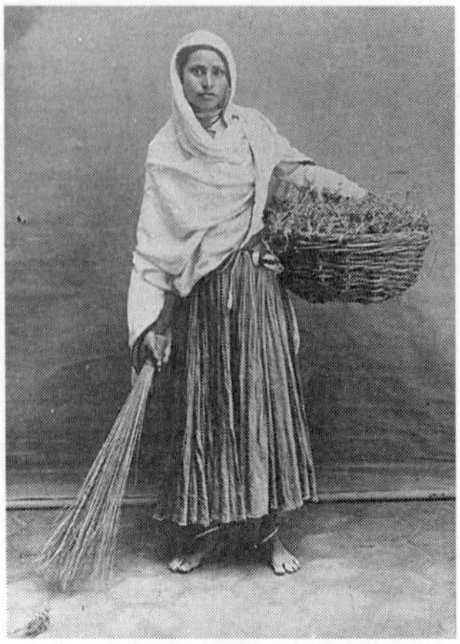

Figure 3. Studio portrait of young woman with basket and broom. India, c. 1921.

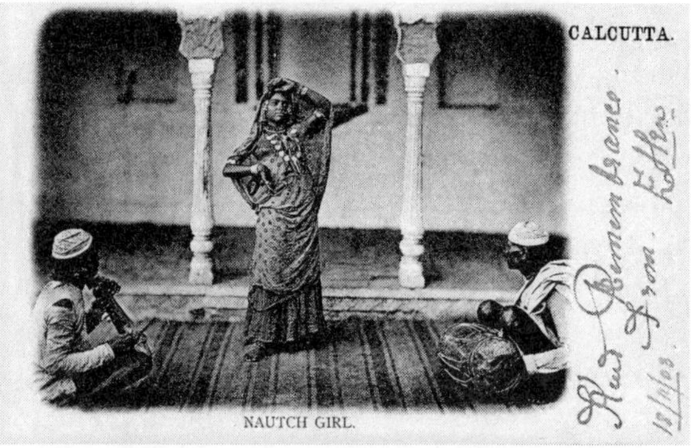

Figure 4. Nautch girl. Picture postcard from Roessler & Co., Calcutta. This picture probably derives from a photograph by Samuel Bourne taken in 1860.

civilising drive of European colonisers needed to be argued. Indians, especially females in India, faced a process of double othering, while the Indian male was reproduced generally as effeminate, in finite sections of the workforce, as trader, criminal, lawbreaker, or member of a superstitious mass without the capacity of reason. As a consequence, women were deferred another step back vis-á-vis their already veiled representations inside Indian societies. Broadly speaking, early Indian photography attested the stereotyping and gendering of women inherent in various Indian traditions of representation.

Malavika Karlekar (2005), in her pioneering survey of photography in Bengal, argues that to add a visual element to a history, context, or even relationship that may have been written about, discussed and analysed, is not merely to slip in 'pretty or telling' images. Rather, she argues, 'reading' photographs is to introduce another dimension to the experience of colonialism in Bengal. With the advent of colonial modernity and its institutions of education, professionalism and commerce, it led to a 'controlled fuzzing of the limits of the racial divide'.[21] Photography studios emerged as one among the few shared public spaces after the 1860s. Karlekar argues that studios emerged as a democratic space where the 'porousness' of colonialism was acted out.[22]

From the 1870s to the early decades of the twentieth century, photography played a significant role in the construction of the social and family history

[21] Karlekar, Malavika. 2005. *Re-visioning the Past: Early Photography in Bengal 1875–1915.* (New Delhi: Oxford University Press). p. 4.

[22] To quote: 'Where control over access to physical space was a marker of racial and colour difference, the studio acquired a curiously powerful status. The white rulers and their subjects shared the same physical ambience sequentially in a social regime where access to clubs, railway compartments and even benches was determined strictly on the basis of colour and racial origin.' Karlekar. 2005. *Re-visioning the Past.* pp. 4–5.

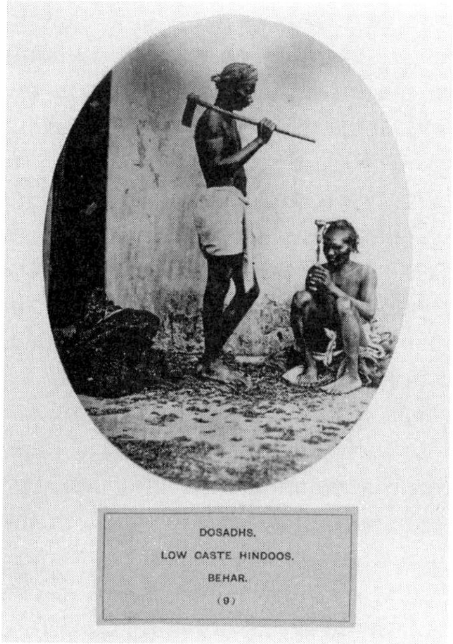

Figure 5: From *The People of India.* Watson and Kaye, 1868–1875.*

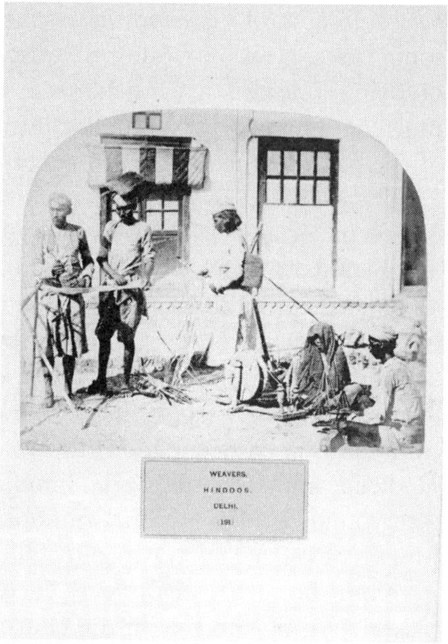

Figure 6: From *The People of India.* Watson and Kaye, 1868–1875.**

* Watson, J. Forbes & Kaye, John William. Eds. 1868. The People of India. *A Series Of Photographic Illustrations. With Descriptive Letterpress Of, The Races and Tribes of Hindustan, Originally Prepared Under The Authority Of The Government of India And Reproduced By The Order Of The Secretary Of State For India In Council.* Volume One. (London: W. H. Allen & Co.)

** Watson, J. Forbes & Kaye, John William. Eds. 1868. *The People of India. A Series Of Photographic Illustrations. With Descriptive Letterpress Of, The Races and Tribes of Hindustan, Originally Prepared Under The Authority Of The Government of India And Reproduced By The Order Of The Secretary Of State For India In Council.* Volume Four. (London: W. H. Allen & Co.)

of the region. The *bhadra samaj* in Bengal accepted photography as a useful innovation that fractured the public/private dichotomy without too much dislocation. The varied degree of exposure of the public in the private and the private in the public through photography also helped, to some extent, the project of the reformers,[23] the English-educated middle class and

[23] The social reform movement began in Bengal around 1860s with sections of indigenous communities coming out of Hindu orthodoxy, especially in terms of the position of the woman in Bengali society. The coming into being of the *nabina* (new woman), follows from the history of social reform movements since the middle decades of the nineteenth century mainly with respect to education and marriage. The heterogenous community of bhadralok, which consisted of the members of the Brahmo Samaj and men from the Kayastha, Brahmin and the Baidya castes, and who were by no means unanimously decided on any single agenda, devised plans to educate the women of their community. The colonial state and the indigenous intelligentsia sought to create new social spaces and purge old ones in order to 're-claim' the civilsation lost, obviously with differing goals. The coming together of these was centred primarily on the

babus[24] to control the exposure of their women (mostly wives, relatives and in some cases, even mistresses). It was necessary to prove the teleological point of being a *bhadralok*, who shares a social space with the *bhadramahila* in the nineteenth and early twentieth century with some differences from the figure of the babu[25]—the nineteenth-century figure of the Bengali dandy.

The evolution of the modern family, progress in girls' education, women's emergent socially visible roles and other similar/dissimilar discourses were, to a large extent, helped by the dynamics of the new visual space. The debut of photographs into Bengali middle-class homes from the 1870s onwards can be seen as proof of the affiliation between the coloniser and the colonised, as the technology of photography went inside Bengali homes in a spirit of assimilation. Sections of bhadra samaj which were increasingly moving away from land-based occupations to professions such as government service, law, medicine and teaching, were simultaneously redefining their lifestyles. The foregrounding of a rational outlook was important to such changes in the process of refiguring in which women emerged as primary exhibits.

From the 1870s to the early decades of twentieth century, photography played a significant role in the construction of the social and familial history of the region. For Karlekar, a 'reading' of images is to introduce another dimension to the experience of colonialism in Bengal.[26] For the bhadra samaj, photography was useful in depicting family life and the professional roles that they had newly acquired.

---

concept of the woman. As we shall see, Western and Indian class-bound positions produced discourses in union that deepened already-existing asymmetries, including the extremely touchy question of sexuality. Srivastava, Sanjay. 2007. *Passionate Modernity: Sexuality, Class, and Consumption in India* (New Delhi: Routledge). p. 43.

[24] Earlier used in the sense of the city-bred dandy but later more generally used to refer to the respectable middle-class man. The word is generally used after the proper name of the man.

[25] I am quoting from an anonymously written, cheap-print Bengali farce from 1881, showing Hindu revivalist tendencies. The educated women, showing signs of choice, however ordinary, in going out of the bounds of the domestic were a figure of attack:

> In the same way a Bengali babu copies his master by writing in English, the Bengali wife is doing ditto. Whoever imitates the English woman's behaviour, we shall call them bibi. ...The babu wears the boot, the bibi puts on a pair of slippers or shoes ...The babu wears an open neck coat with the dhoti, the bibi wears a jacket over the saree ... The babu plays the harmony flute, the bibi plays the piano. The babu drinks brandy while the bibi prefers port ... refusing to cook as it will make the hands dirty with soot is not bibiana, refusing to pick up the child so as to avoid getting the clothes stained is not bibiana, whistling away time by reading plays or playing cards is not bibiana ... nowadays our wives are getting increasingly attracted towards the bibiana way of life, it is high time we become alert otherwise some great danger will befall us.' [Sri... (Anon) 1881]

Anonymous popular farce in Bangla cited in Biswas, Hardik Brata. Ed. 2011. *Prahashane Kolikāler Bangamahila 1860-1908*. (Kolkata: Charchāpada)

[26] Ibid. p. 4.

Structures like the evolution of the family, progress of girls' education and women's emergent roles were, to some extent, helped by the dynamics of the new space of the studio and the camera. In a formerly *purdah*[27] society, the visibility of woman became a metaphor of their changing status, and 'as Calcutta increasingly afforded the opportunity for new definitions of the household, family, conjugality, parenting and childhood, the camera was available to record them.'[28] In most formal or informal couple's photographs from the late nineteenth and early twentieth centuries, the couple was seen blissfully separated from the complex and restrictive formation of the undivided family structure. Newlywed couples made best use of photography and the studio space 'to create public and formal representations of the bourgeois couple from among themselves.'[29] Performances of the self before the camera can make representation go beyond the grasp of a normative economy of visual framing. Representational spaces, studios and photographs opened up possibilities of identity formation and the performance of subjectivity in the changed historical context.

Re-figurations of women in dichotomised private and public spaces found in the late nineteenth and early twentieth centuries saw a change in their iconography. The unyielding look in formal wedding portraits and couple's photography gave way to acknowledging the mundane. Facilitated by the fact that the camera was getting more mobile with the years and the growing number of amateur photographers among family members and friends, photographic representations of women began to take note of the profane moments of daily lives without leaving out formal occasions.

IV

Photographs, especially from the decades of the early twentieth century, can question the apparent transparency of daily lives. Photographic representations might render them as problematic and contested, given the highly gendered implications of the socio-historical contexts from which the visuals emerged. The archive—here, the family albums or the depositaries of domestic photography—has long occupied a privileged space in affirmative culture, and as a result, the archive has been revered from afar and aestheticised, but not always understood as a potential object of critical practice. The birth of the disciplinary self, modernity, the family, the woman in the family and outside the physical boundaries of the domestic, the surveilling camera, and in stereotypical poses before the camera, reminiscent of emerging popular cinema cultures in India, are a few elements that contributed towards a somewhat different type

[27] I have generally used the term purdah in the sense of veiling associated with orthodox Hindu Bengali societies.

[28] Ibid. p. 94.

[29] Majumdar, Rochona. 2009. *Marriage and Modernity: Family Values in Colonial Bengal* (New Delhi: Oxford University Press). p. 127.

of historical narrative. In that sense, as Ben Highmore (2002) argues that the everyday presents us with a recalcitrant object that does not give up its secrets too readily.[30] The archive, on the other hand, provides the time and space to think things through. The complex relationship between photography and the formation of subjectivities, between gender and cultural milieus, can be gleaned from the images themselves. Can it be done without the problems of signification? Conventional uses of photographic archives regard images as illustrative in character, subordinate or add-ons to writing.

The reconstruction of the past, ostensibly the main task of archives, more often than not severs intricate associations with sociopolitical anchorage, to become the archivist's and the historian's choice to put forward their own projects of historical reconstruction. In doing this, we are risking a naïve move of particularly extracted representations that are used as tools of the project of history along preconceived structures of control.

However, the regime of strict subjection, even if operational at the level of imagination, did not hold ground for describing and reproducing the 'woman'. High-caste women in Bengal were considered to be proper subjects of reform movements, 'newness' and obedience, even though they formed only a part of the whole spectrum of women in Bengali society. Critiques of cultural nationalism in Bengal and in other parts of India have already established through literature, history and other disciplinary means that women, in spite of attempts at social upliftment, remained unevenly visible and invisible in multiple registers of the social. If this is already part of the accepted post-colonial, historical re-reading of Bengali women, then why does one not question the methods of archival reading when it comes to corresponding photographs? Representations of women and their contextual uses in various phases of Indian history, in popular canons of Indian art such as calendar art, the sculptural traditions or the re-awakening of the ideal Indian woman in the Bengal school of art have been studied and critiqued as bearing essentialising, eroticising or exoticising trends and tropes.[31] The work of the scholars range from the curious histories of female temple sculptures in terms of the moral and the obscene, metaphoric relationships with maps of India and the body of the idealised Indian woman, and the popular realm of calendar arts and its

[30] Highmore, Ben. 2002. *The Everyday Life Reader* (Psychology Press).

[31] Guha-Thakurta, Tapati. 2004. *Monuments, Objects, Histories: Institutions of Art in Colonial and Post-Colonial India* (Columbia: Columbia University Press); Guha-Thakurta. 2007. *The Making of a New 'Indian' Art: Artists, Aesthetics and Nationalism in Bengal, c.1850-1920* (Cambridge University Press).

Ramaswamy, Sumathi. 2009. *The Goddess and the Nation: Mapping Mother India* (Duke University Press).

Chatterjee, Ratnabali. 1990. *From the Karkhana to the Studio: A Study in the Changing Social Rules [i.e. Roles] of Patron and Artist in Bengal* (New Delhi: Books and Books).

Jain, Kajri. 2007. *Gods in the Bazaar: The Economies of Indian Calendar Art* (Duke University Press).

Uberoi, Patricia. 2006. *Freedom and Destiny: Gender, Family, and Popular Culture in India* (New Delhi: Oxford University Press).

various uses of women's corporeal presentations, throughout a large part of the twentieth century.

If other spheres of representing women, however well-documented and accepted, have been subject to feminist critiques, can the photographic archive hold its ground for long? Anxieties are already pouring in—will it be possible to represent the woman, given the apprehensions regarding the works of representation, literary or visual? Where 'exactly' can we place the 'histories' of women in the archive, when the density of the 'experience' of being a woman remains un-enunciated through most of modern historiography? An archive of the woman, pertaining to her representations, is a strategic and important step for feminist ways of history-making. It produces information and history, and looking at the archive also can provide a moment of solace for the things and times lost, especially when we turn to women in classifiable categories of demography, census, history, ethnography or the family album. But the production of knowledge in the archive might look as if it is an essentialising move—a thing which most feminisms have avoided.

Following formulations by Judith Butler, to whom the category of gender is problematic and endowed with performance, one can draw links with photography. If gender is performance, photography as a form of representation can work to both dramatise and naturalise this performance. It can be stated that such dynamics are particularly evident in late nineteenth- and early twentieth-century India, when the newly imported camera had to negotiate existing representation systems, such as painting and lithography. While briefly commenting on the possibilities of photography, it can be tentatively argued that Bengali women, who had minimum or no publicly visible sociopolitical agency otherwise, forged a cult of the self through photographs. Photographs, unlike other forms of performance, can be seen not only by others but also by oneself, and photography suggests a will to empower in terms of presenting one's body and identity according to one's wishes.

Photography that calls attention to the body's performance echoes both traditional aesthetics and a new commodification of the female figure. Roland Barthes[32] has argued that photography's ability to capture reality gives its representation two contradictory features: its closeness to reality makes representations extremely polysemous, which Barthes has described as 'madness'. Photography also tends to hide its mediation process, mythologising representation as natural instead of constructed; connotations become denotations. Therefore, while photography seems to destabilise gender meanings, photographs can also be easily manipulated by dominating gender ideologies—a process that explains why women's photographs in family albums are organised by the gaze of heteronormativity. In other words, photography is polysemous but its polysemous nature can be easily subdued in a definite web of politics and usage.

[32] Roland Barthes, Camera Lucida: Reflections on Photography, London: Macmillan, 1981.

New meanings arise through the placing of photos in various contexts and in dialogue with different narratives. Photography has a dual ability of setting free and disciplining femininity in the context of family albums. It is ostensibly the direct and honest representation of reality inscribed within a mechanical reproductive system that always implies a network of reception beyond the producer's control.[33] I want to argue that images of women do not always conform to stereotypes which they are continually cast into.

At this point, one can think of at least two ways in which this claim can be substantiated in the case of the middle-class Bengali woman. First, on a documentary–evidential level of particular genres of image-making, it is conventional knowledge that photographs do present one with a kind of truth. For example, we can take journalistic photography, which has been stretched to its extremes, affecting the corroboration of 'truth' and 'event' in spite of the knowledge of the political and visual choices that photographers make to suit their perspectives and purposes. Second, on a more conceptual ground, the desire of the image itself is summed up by Mitchell, when he states, 'What pictures want in the last instance, then, is simply to be asked what they want, with the understanding that the answer may well be, nothing at all.'[34] This might be the other end of the spectrum of analysis of the image in recent art history and visual culture, where the historicity of the interpretation of images is argued as a challenged territory. The recent interest in family photographs as a way to the narrative of the family and history, lies somewhere between the two mentioned positions. Affective histories, the looking at family albums and photographs and getting on with the work of nostalgic remembrance, the spread of intergenerational family knowledge, and the process of knowing persons through images, are all possible moves in constructing a history but this is not to say that all such evidence-based constructions will work on the 'true'/'false' binary. I will, with specific examples of family photographs, discuss the problematising of true/false polarisations and the possible or impossible spaces of representation within them. My point here, before progressing further, is that visual histories of women, such as by Karlekar, from a particular time of the modern, forms an analogy of the written and documented histories within contemporary trends of feminist historiography and emerging research. Albeit naming such histories as visual histories, what is the specific visual knowledge about women that the spectator/viewer gets from them that are different from written forms? Will it be possible to attempt such a reading from the specificities of the photographic image? Or will it be another essentialising move to find the quintessential woman in the family album, reducing her to terms that have already been described and produced as an object of knowledge?

---

[33] Pang, Laikwan. 2005. 'Photography, Performance and the Making of Female Images in Modern China'. *Journal of Women's History*. Vol. 17.No. 4. pp. 56□85.

[34] Mitchell, W.J.T. 1996. 'What do Pictures "Really" Want?'. *October*. Vol. 77 (Summer). p. 82.

Scott's (2011) reading of Foucault's theorisation in the context of a feminist theory archive, is one way in which the specificity of the woman in the representative image, i.e. the photograph, can be thought of.[35] Dwelling upon Foucault's theory of the archive as a heterogeneous, dense space of discursive practices that pronounce statements as events and things, Scott argues that an archive of feminist theory can be built on this conceptual substratum. Such a construction will only expose as evidence 'that there are contests about what counts as knowledge, that knowledge is no surely or commonly agreed upon thing, even within what might be called as cultural or discursive "systems".'[36] Scott does not stop her argument at this permeated presence of the archive. She further iterates the necessity of a feminist archive of theory which will build on the critical work for dissemination among generations of feminists to come. She is trying to think of the archive as a 'living heritage' in the contemporary 'fashionable' thinking of a post-feminist situation, and names it as a post-post institution, continuing the vitality of feminist theory.[37] Her stress is on the activities of reading and reception and not exactly on the classificatory process of the archive. It is not my task here to do away with history. One is aware of the importance of historical reverberations in the spread of feminist movements, methods and thinking. Scott's (2011) work is an attestation of this importance. Even if there are chances of producing historical knowledge from the uses of the archive, it can possibly be done through thinking about the space of the archive, in its Derridian (1996) reading as a space that has suffered an *irreplaceable loss* in its conceptual inception.[38] It is not just in the act of remembering that physical objects in the archive appear as fragmentary, the work of the memory produced by it depends largely upon the conditions of the receiver/spectator/reader.

Annette Kuhn (1995) links family with broader social categories in a lucid theorisation that helps in understanding the positioning of women in family albums.[39] The family is taken to be a place of safety, closeness and intimacy. According to Kuhn, if the family ties are given and not chosen, then they have that much in common with other attachments of nation, race, class and gender. It is rare, if not impossible, to find in family albums, women of any age dressed in nonconformist ways or 'exposing themselves' beyond accepted norms of civility of the middle-class milieu. The photographs of women in family albums can be read as testimonies, not only to the development of family at various stages, but also to the development of women to a point of normalising where the 'self' of the woman is lost.

---

[35] Scott, Joan Wallach. 2011. *The Fantasy of Feminist History* (Durham and London: Duke University Press).

[36] Ibid. pp. 142–43.

[37] Ibid. p. 143.

[38] Archive Fever: A Freudian Impression, Chicago & London: The University of Chicago Press, 1996.

[39] Kuhn, Annette. 1995. *Family Secrets: Acts of Memory and Imagination* (London: Verso Books). p. 1.

Deriving from Kuhn, on a theoretical level, the possibility of multiple interpretations is never exhausted. The point is that, when reduced to the specific contents of family photographs, all possibilities of multifarious interpretations of women's live and '*punctums*' are in ways erased by the dominant narrative of the family and role-playing, when evidently, the male members control the language (signifier) which builds the woman (subject), through an intricate mesh of hegemonic apparatuses. Family photographs are quite often deployed, shown, talked about in series, where the figure of the man/boy takes centre-stage and the figure of the woman is relegated to a place of companionate or appendage reading. Pictures get displayed one after another, their selection and ordering in the meaningful construction of a family story like a classical narrative: linear, chronological, through cyclical repetitions of climactic moments—births, men's initiation rites, holidays. In the process of using, producing, selecting, ordering and displaying photographs, the family is actually in the process of making and archiving itself.

V

In true fact, the family album appears as one moment in the cultural construction of the family. The apparent pessimism and finitude affecting its experience of discontinuity and distance can be thought of as a power 'as the very difference, indeed of ontological difference (ontic-onticological: between Beings and beings, between the presence of the present and the present itself).'[40] The memory of the photograph and the woman in the photograph, read through Derrida, becomes a tricky one, turning the impossibility of the untraced/unidentified photograph into a qualifying point of memory. I have discussed earlier, and I am repeating again, that the family album as a material site for historical reconstruction of women's history can be a disappointment to the extent of searching for 'exact data' to construct a specific history of the woman. On one hand, the materiality of history, as in the tangibility or tactility of the photograph, will always be limited, cut off from the figure of the woman whom one is attempting to decipher. On the other, the climate of history (here mostly working as a disciplinary methodology) around the photographic image potentially reduces its traces to only as past, which it is not. If one is not cautious about this overtly phenomenological urge to read the photography *only* as what it appears to be, then one might approach the photograph as an object which has already emerged; an object of study that has given up all its possible enunciations that might come to play in the future of reception.

The family album is one of the places/spaces where such images can be found to reside and risk its stability of identity formation. The family

---

[40] Derrida. 1986 [1989]. *MEMOIRES for Paul de Man*. (Columbia University Press). pp. 57–58.

album in particular, in its reception, invokes both the ideological and the personal at the same time. It is ideological in the sense that it concedes to the genre of familial-looking and the personal at the same time, as it triggers the memory-work of privileged onlookers related to the photograph. In the case of family photographs I have seen and identified with members of the family, there are many such examples of either a blurry photo or a blurry memory about a well-focused and easily readable photograph. Both the insufficiency of the photograph and the insufficiency of the memory might act at the same instant.

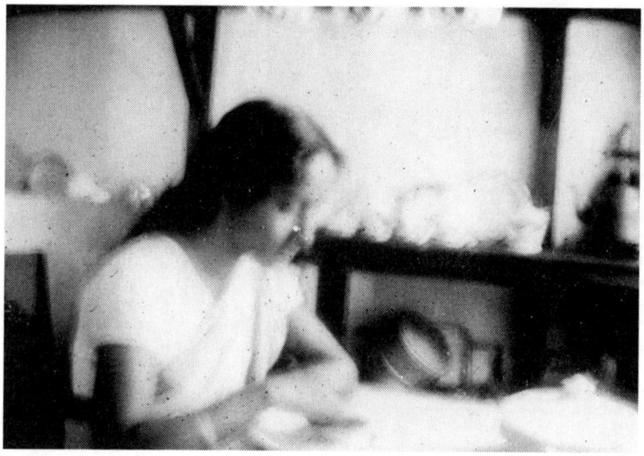

Figure 7. Unidentified/undated. [ADC]

The blurry image in a way invokes the kind of cipher writing that Derrida instances in his argument on the communicability of communication. It takes away the specific history of the woman in the photograph, only to give it back to the image through a trace. The idiosyncratic visual is there, beyond comprehensibility, but it is part of the family album and the family keeps it. The subject, here a woman, probably eating (Fig. 7), however forgotten in the instant of recognition, can be thought of coming back through iterability. As Das (2006) argues:

> The mutual interaction of the 'user' and the 'language' has to give an account of the structuration *and* a radical undecidability in language—where every utterance is singular in its eventness—and an account of a similar constitution and singularity of the 'user'. The notion of *iterability* is one such 'name' which describes the 'event' of language in this manner[41]—of course, setting the correspondence of the name to an event problematic in its very enunciation.[42]

[41] Notions on language in later Wittgenstein may very well be compared to this thinking. *[Footnote by Das, 2006]*.

[42] Das, Anirban. 2006. 'Embodied Knowledges: The Limits and Possibilities of Knowing the Body'. PhD diss., Jadavpur University. p. 79.

It is here that the consideration of the difference between that which is present (in the photograph) and the presence of the thing (the subject along with the backdrop) can take one to the work of the memory which again will generally think about the presence of the present and try to think through it.

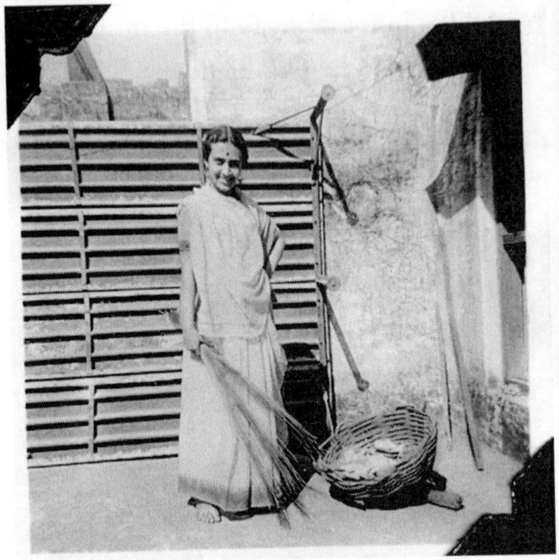

Figure 8: Bijoylakshmi Mitra, 1964 [Ashok Roy Collection]

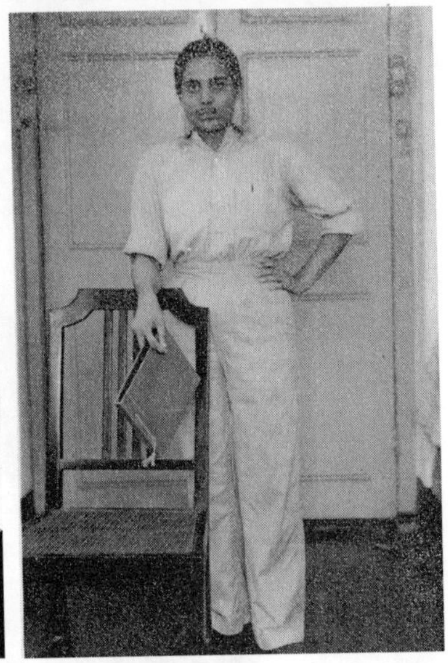

Figure 9: Minati Sengupta, 1948 [Gita Dasgupta Collection]

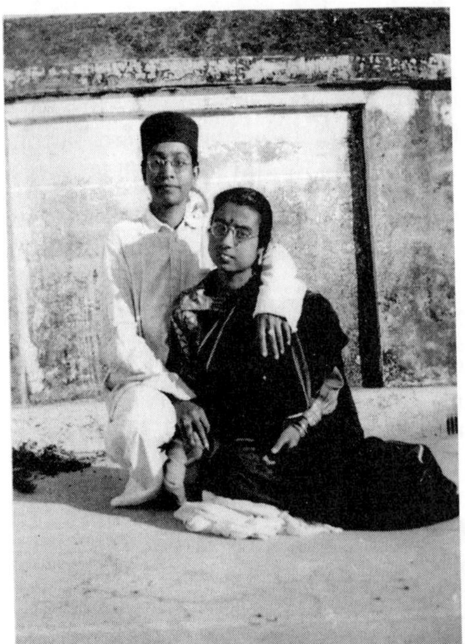

Figure 10: Unidentified & undated. [Esha Chatterjee Collection]

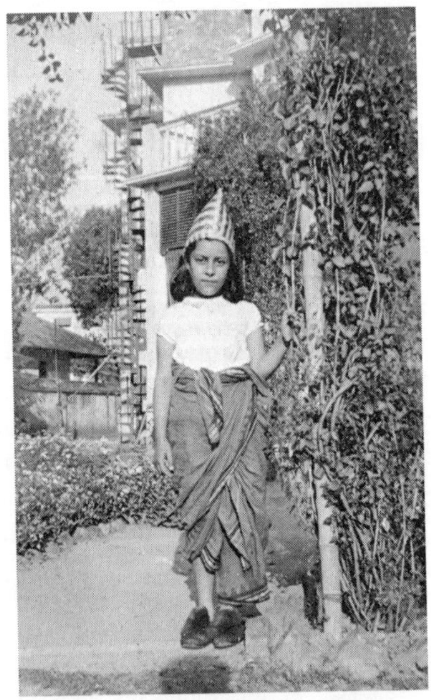

Figure 11: Tutu Lahiri, 1944 [Bijoya Goswami Collection]

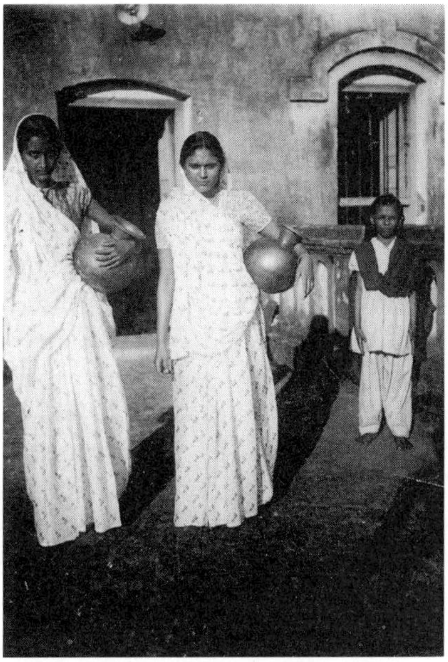

Figure 12: [from left] Rama Mukherjee, Chinmayee Bandyopadhyay and her youngest sister Arati, 1951. [Sibaji Bandyopadhyay Collection]

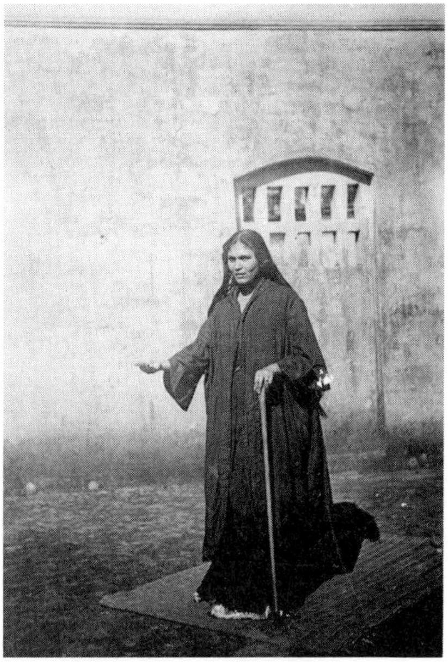

Figure 13: Chinmayee Bandyopadhyay, 1951. [Sibaji Bandyopadhyay Collection]

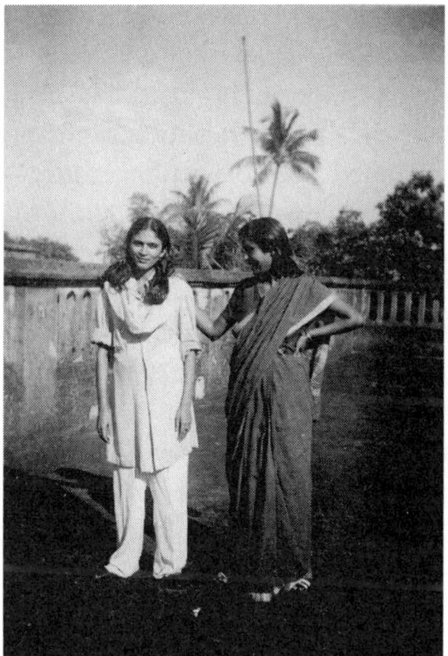

Figure 14: Chinmayee Bandyopadhyay [right] and her cousin, 1951. [Sibaji Bandyopadhyay Collection]

VI

Let me discuss this through a few photographs. Figure 9, a 1948 photograph of Minati Sengupta, shows her dressed up in men's clothing and a pencilled moustache. She is holding a photographic album in her right hand. This is an indoor photograph, taken inside a room. Given the general trends of photographic representations we have witnessed in this essay, this seems like an impossible performance of the Bengali bhadramahila. The exact reason(s) for putting on this attire and make-up remains unknown. The primary concern that informs my argument here is whether one certainly needs to know the reason behind it. We can only conjecture. It might have been done for acting in a play or perhaps Ms. Sengupta wished to see herself as a man without any 'specific reasons'. In Figure 13, a 1951 photograph of Chinmayee Bandyopadhyay shows her in a burqa with a stick in her left hand and her right hand extended as if asking for alms. She, a Brahmin woman, is masquerading as a Muslim beggar. Similar to Figure 9 the photograph is taken on the roof of the Bandyopadhyay household at Hooghly in West Bengal. This particular photograph is one amongst a series of photographs of Chinmayee Bandyopadhyay (Figures 12 and 14) taken on the same day at the same location in different costumes, representing different roles played by them. Also Figure 8, a 1964 photograph of Bijoylaskmi Mitra, dressed up as an upcountry woman, *methrani*, has something in common with Fig. 12, which shows Rama Mukherjee and Chinmayee Bandyopadhyay posing as rural North Indian women going to fetch water. Both these photographs mimic the labouring body of the woman in her activities and occupations. Such occupations, as of the *methrani* or the sweeper, are marked by caste. People from specific castes, lowly marked in the caste hierarchy in India, usually perform such services/ professions in India. Can these two photographs be accepted as masquerades that break the entrenched play of gender and caste inscribing bodies on a register of violent difference? Also, one is confronting an urgent question at this point: who can play the role of the others without having the necessity of bearing ethical responsibilities towards the otherised bodies represented? While one is not looking for a quick answer (also the answer seems evident if one looks at the social position of the 'types' masqueraded) but at the same time it opens up ways for receiving the photographic image. Or does it re-establish the epistemic violence on the body of the other woman (here the rural upcountry woman), who is the other of the Brahmo/Hindu, educated, upper-caste woman? Does it entail a different drag act in representing the other of the self by making it visible in photography, or is it the visual play of caste-based usurpation of the Other in postcolonial India? These may be the result of an unsure mixture of the multiple reasons that I have just flagged exhaustively.

With Figures 10, 11 and 13, one possibly enters the world of citation but not fully. The photographs point towards a performative playfulness, entering into perceived notions of dressing up as someone else. In case of Figure 10, it is dressing up as a *non-Bengali*[43] couple. The objective is evidently achieved by positioning themselves as a heterosexual couple. Figure 11 is more than what meets the eyes. It shows Tutu Lahiri, a young girl dressed out of convention yet she does not belong to the stereotypes of such photographic conventions found in family albums in Bengal. Almost pointing towards a representational singularity, a singularity that cannot be easily usurped by what goes on with regards to character role playing in the field of family photography; such photographs/images open up the possibilities of representational spaces. However, with Figure 13, one is again back into the realm of posing as a Muslim woman asking for alms. It is the general feature of all signs that there is the citing of the performative through iterability. It necessitates, as Nakassis (2013) shows by reading Derrida that the sign must conform to some common codes which makes iteration of the Other as the 'same'.[44] But even when it is repeatable, every sign has its context-specific meaning carrying a force that breaks with its contexts toward a re-contextualisation of the meaning. We arrive through Derrida (1988) that the sign simultaneously becomes a type and a token.[45] The citationality, as the core of the explitive performative, in case of the man and the female Muslim beggar here, is possible through the reanimating of the 'grammatical structure of the citational act, interdiscursively bringing into play multiple events that it sutures together through the very event of its utterance. In doing so it balances the tension of iterability—the duality of the sign as token and type—that Derrida identifies (also see Derrida 2002).[46] But more than balancing this tension, the performance effaces, or conflates it such that this token event of utterance here and now is the type which it invokes. It evaporates that duality and tension, bringing the events which it calibrates into alignment, if only in that act and for that moment' (Nakassis 2013, 68).

This Derridian move gives the act of dressing up as the Other a possibly creative enunciation. The exactitude that is promised in the act of the photographed women masquerading as someone else, remains an act of citation in its obvious cognisability as citation. As Nakassis (2013) argues that the act will remain as the act in its failure and falseness. If the act of citation is not too explicative, it might be bordering on plagiarism. It should be taken note of that the possibility of a citation not seen as citation is built within its structure. In its contextual failing (the hand-drawn moustache), in bringing out and displaying its impossibilities, the citation comes through. It renders

---

[43] Non-Bengali is a widely and commonly used expression amongst Bengali people to denote anything and everything that is *not* Bengali. However, this is a general expression, without specific connotations and popularly used in essentialising terms to denote communities who are not culturally or linguistically Bengali. Also, beyond communities and individuals, non-Bengali often denotes food practices, dressing habits and parlance.

[44] Nakassis, Constantine.V., 2013. Citation and citationality. *Signs and Society*, *1*(1), pp. 51-77.

[45] Derrida, Jacques, 1993 [1988]. *Limited Inc*. Evanston, IL: Northwestern University Press.

[46] Derrida, Jacques. Typewriter Ribbon, Limited Ink (2). *Without Alibi*, Stanford, CA: Stanford University Press, 2002.

itself possible (Nakassis 2013, 70). The Bengali middle-class bhadramahila, in the momentary act which is otherwise an impossibility, turns herself into a Bengali middle-class gentleman (or any man). It creates the sign, with its obvious failures, not by replacing the meaning but by displacing it. The being-present of the middle-class bhadramahila is rendered possible through the act of call to recognition or interpellation, which at the same time, through the act of dressing up, is displaced. This displacement, at the level of the photographic representation is again, carefully recognised as displacement in the meaning—a possible displacement of the familial look of the woman in the family album.

As Das (2012) observes, the specific cannot be interpreted in terms of the universal as a difference-deferral informs the iteration of the universal norm in the particular.[47] In the realm of the representation, this can be a potentially liberating moment for the woman, who can, through the camera, relocate herself into what she is not. Let us be watchful here. The dislocation/relocation/displacement of the sexed body of the woman in family photography is not something that one arrives at with any sense of finality. This can be a move, to re-locate the representation of women, with all its downsides and lacks in place. It is the nature of representation to try to locate a different body for the woman through finding the place of a representational agency. As Jagger (2008) argues, agency might become the reworking of certain detrimental interpellations of woman. It also partially unsettles the passionate attachment to subjection that is an active part of subjectivation. The subject and the subjectivation can be found in the combined operations 'of social power and psychic regulation and in the possibility of resistance and resignification'.[48]

The woman, as part of the heteronormative marital romantic couple, as the dressed-up figure, possibly can think of herself as going beyond the nodal modes of signification. The place (Crasswell 2004)—more in the sense of a surely known space than the immanent thinking of space itself—of the family album assumes the role of the substratum to archive such relocations[49]. The ideologically presumed album also, in a way, such as the figure of the woman in it, interrupts the general flow of woman's visual representation in it. Even if not emancipatory in the collective political sense, the album and such moments of representation archived in it, can be a way to read agency in two ways. Firstly, through iteration of the figure of the woman, as new (not in the sense of the originally new, but contextually new) in certain fantastic photographic representations. Secondly, through agency leading to resistance and resignification simultaneously being aware of the fact that it 'does not

[47] Das, Anirban. 2012. *Toward a Politics of the (Im)Possible: The Body in Third World Feminisms* (London: Anthem Press). p. 65.

[48] Ibid. p. 104.

[49] Crasswell, Tim, 2004, *Place: A Short Introduction*. Malden and Oxford: Blackwell Publishing.

necessarily mean that resistance will be successful'.[50] Now, I move on to the last section of the essay, to see the location of photographs of death and women in the Bengali middle-class family albums, another moment which might open up thinking around women's visual representation.

VII

It seems that I am trying to make an exceptional case of the existence in an otherwise happy motif: of the family album and women's representation in it. Choosing the most microscopic of sources and reading it closely is a way of doing history. My purpose here is somewhat different. I will only cite two photographs of death where there is the 'presence' of the 'corporeal' woman and with her is the presence of the bodily man.

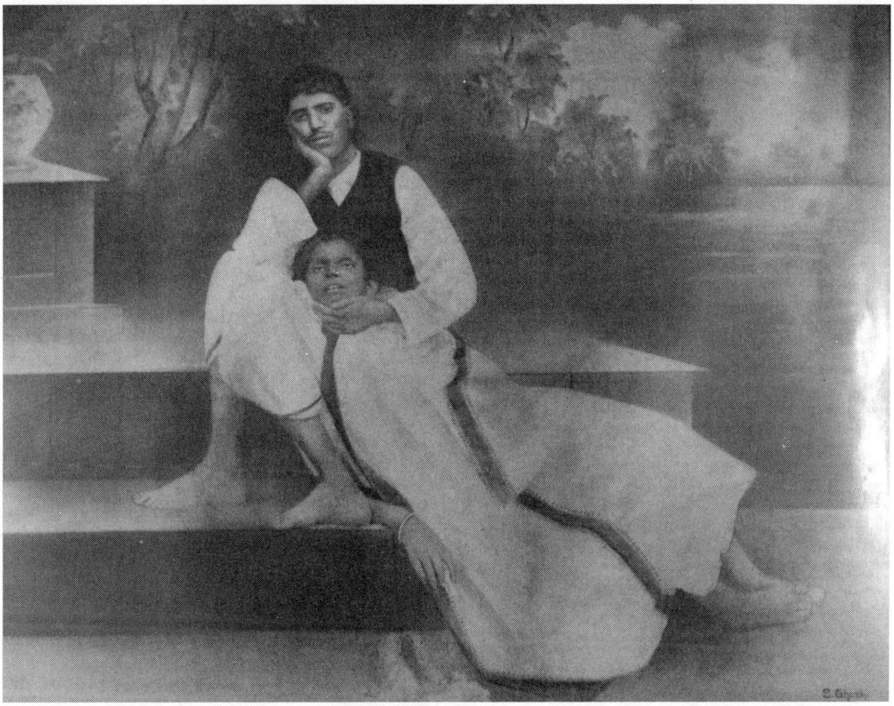

Figure 15: Sris Mukherjee with his deceased wife photographed at the Hooghly burning ghat, 1930s. [Sibaji Bandyopadhyay Collection]

Figure 15 is a photograph of Sris Mukherjee with his deceased wife. The print is heavily hand-retouched, almost giving it a graphic image quality. The purported naturalness of the photographic image is lost here, at least in the copy of the image I am looking at now. In all probabilities, the *original*

[50] Das, Anirban. 2012. *Toward a Politics of the (Im)Possible: The Body in Third World Feminisms* (London: Anthem Press).p. 104.

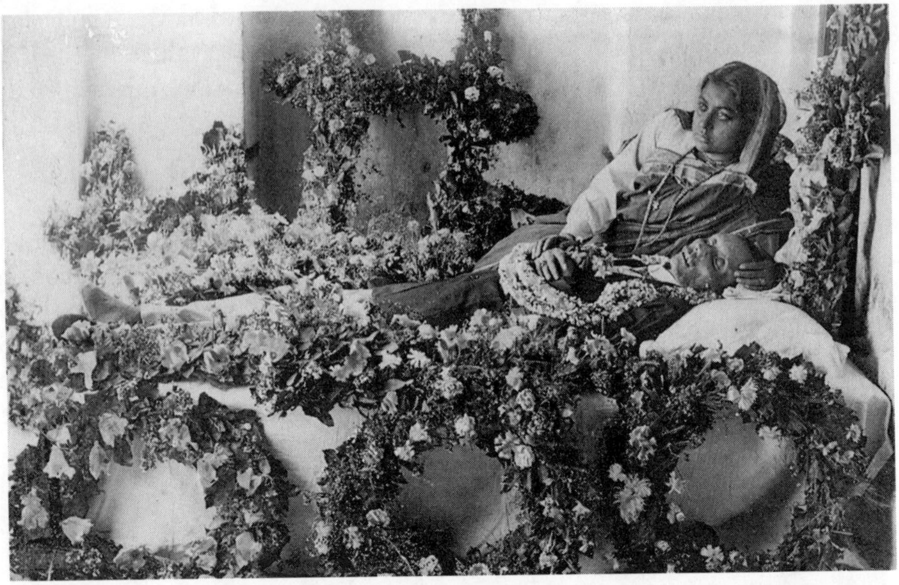

Figure 16: Unidentified wife and deceased husband, 1925. [Amitabh Ghosh Collection]

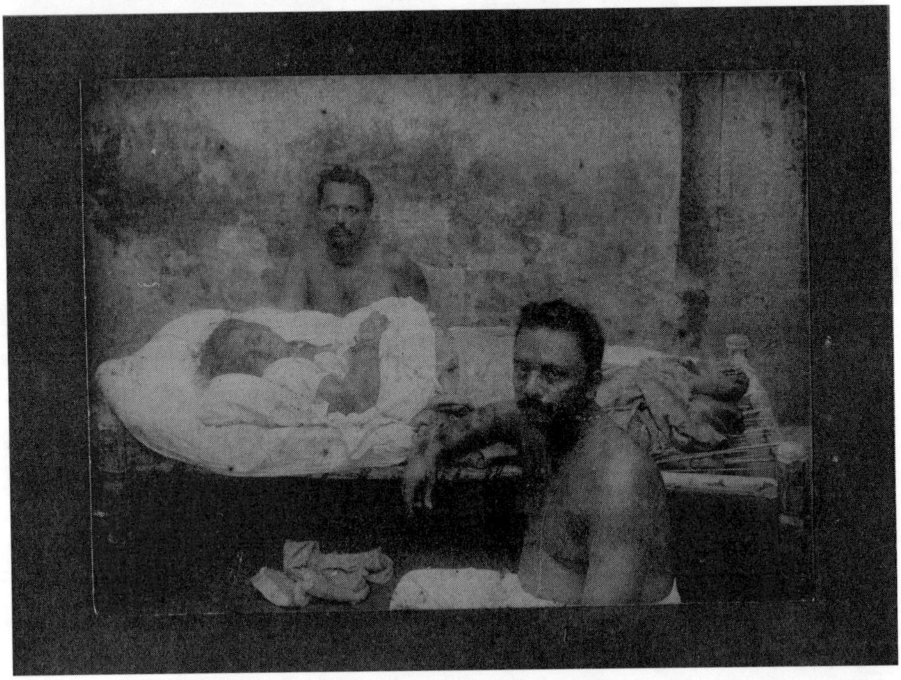

Figure 17: Unidentified and undated photograph of two sons with deceased mother, 1940s (approximately), Studio mark: B Dutta & Bros, Calcutta. [Author's collection]

photograph went through a series of graphic retouchings, enlargements, and printing on newer kinds of photographic paper in order that it survives and serves its altered function now. By *altered function,* I mean that in more than ninety years of the photograph's life, it has changed its place and space from being a testimony of death and personal loss to a photographic object arousing a morbid wonder. A slightly discomforting cohabitation of the dead and the alive, which is a seeming impossibility yet provokes one towards a horizon of the incalculable and the singular. A singularity, in terms of Derridian reading, which becomes a responsibility, coevally a chance and a risk, towards the other, also a simultaneous responsibility towards the future involving a struggle to think of a future in terms of openings 'within which the other can appear beyond any of our programs and predictions', and 'can come to transform what we know or think we know' (Derrida & Attridge 1992).[51] What I am proposing is to locate the literary here. One can think of this as the *work of the photo*. However, this cannot be thought of as methodology. An object-photograph that is available mnemonically, yet cannot be subsumed wholly within its apparently liberal rubric of reception because the mnemonical entry points dissolve/fail/vanish without trace after a passage of time and networked history. Yet, one has to continue beyond the networks of kinship and genealogy towards an ethical relationship with the photographic image. In this move to address well the photograph, one is cautiously thinking of an ethico-politics beyond the assumptions of nostalgia, or for example the simple assertion of a recovery of the past as *how it was*, and on the farthest side resisting the urge to posit an archive while in all practicality museamising the photographic object. The photo was taken at the Hooghly burning *ghat*. The body of the wife was arranged at the crematorium before the photograph was taken. The painted backdrop and the stairs were probably added later. The husband, with his left arm, lifts up the face of his deceased wife and with the other hand, rests his own face in a pensive mood. Possibly, the wife, on her last journey, is carrying all the insignias of the married Hindu woman on her body. In popular regional belief, the married woman who dies before her husband goes to heaven and is considered as lucky compared to the figure of the Hindu widow.

Figure 16 is a hand-coloured photograph of an unidentified dead man with his wife. The photo is from 1925. It shows the elaborate arrangement of the dead body being laid to rest before the funeral, among wreaths of flowers, hand-coloured in the print. The wife is posing with the husband, caressing the man's head. She is looking out into the distance, as if at an eternity of grief. From the Western dress and the style of arranging of the body, this can also be a postmortem photograph of a Bengali Christian couple, but it is known to come from the family album of a Hindu family. The third photograph, figure 17, documents a deceased mother with her two sons, probably from a Hindu

[51] Derrida, Jacques, & Attridge, Derek ed., 1992, Acts of Literature (New York: Routledge). p. 5.

Brahmin family evident in the presence of sacred insignia pertaining to Brahmin males. Compared to Figures 15 and 16, this is stripped of the sophistications in representing death. Somewhat bordering on the phenomenological rawness in its graphic depiction of the dead and the alive sharing photographic space, it exhibits the coming-to-terms with death almost as fact. The irreversible facticity of death as if captured visually in terms of the one who is *sleeping* and the other(s) who are *awake*. An incongruity that cannot be otherwise (in terms of technique, material) made to perform. Moments that reserve the anxieties of not being able to reach out properly to the one who died. At this point, the work of representation, in non-empirical ways, in addressing the incongruous, proposes a going towards the future, a reworking of the economies of reception.

There are known instances of similar photographs arriving and leaving the pages of the album arbitrarily. The present owners of such albums are not capable of rightly accounting for the appearance and disappearance of such photographs. The practice of taking photographs of deceased persons began in the nineteenth century in Europe and in the United States of America. Dead children were often dressed up in their best, made to appear as living and in the company of their siblings, parents or family members in photographs. The bodies were made to look as close as possible to the living. The mnemonic act producing a frame for eternity in a time when photography—especially organising it in one's home—was neither easy nor cheap, exhibits the moral and emotional involvement users had with photography. It was a technology but beyond that, it went far to capture in 'exactitude' what would not have been possible otherwise.

One is faced with an aporia when thinking about death. The feeling of the aporia or its structure is not of a failure or that of simple paralysis. One is experiencing death in the sense it has no boundary as found in any constant concept, as an unquestionable experience with no fixity of a 'thing'. The referent of the noun cannot be definitively fixed or identified in overflowing all limits. Taking aporia as an object of knowledge is also seemingly impossible. Dialectical sophistication or sensible analysis will always fail at this point.[52]

In 1928, Heidegger implicitly claimed that Dasein, by virtue of its ability to be, projects itself ahead of itself in its relation to possibility. By doing so, it opens up the temporal horizons of futurity, where one can understand oneself futurally.[53] Das (2012) argues that taking death as the future anterior to presence is a source for futurity as such, which is also beyond the possibility

[52] 'To endure the 'impossibility' of an aporia is thus to risk the chance of an 'other' possibility, an impossible possibility that is perhaps the only one worth its name. (An entirely 'possible' possibility would surely operate within an already existent field of 'potentials', and would thus open up no possibility beyond what may already be established, predicted or prescribed.)' (Wortham 2010, 15).

[53] Thomson, Ian. 1999. 'Can I die? Derrida on Heidegger and Death'. *Philosophy Today* (Spring). p. 32–33.

that flows from the present.[54] Through the photographs, in their differences of the presentation of death, the couples also face in the photographic moment, an aporia in feeling the structure of death and the death-that-happened. If the ritual—if at all—of photographing the dead exists in case of the family album, it is through the working of this futurity in death and impassable aporia.

In the case of the dead photographed mortally for the persons around her, nothing will remain as such. The two photographs cited here, signify in prosaic ways, this occurrence as familial responsibility which will look beyond the body of the deceased. The photograph here instantiates the memory of the body. The instantiation of death remains an impossibility through the photograph. The pictorial depiction of the dead in the family albums is not only as death represented in the body that is dead, or perpetuation of the family that remains, but also about a kind of love. The families in the structural framework of being, cannot be reduced to the question of heteronormative violence only, but in them, love remains a notion which binds them together.

This also takes one back, however idealistically, to some extent to an assertion of love in our represented spaces inhabited by women. The space of the album and the technology of the camera provide the chance of capturing death in its entire aporetic stance. The representational place of the album can potentially be the field where approaching this futurity of the Being is rendered imaginable. The family album, as a site, can be thought of a place-space where the woman, however ideologically enmeshed in the gendered and castiest representative thrusts, can enter, challenge and keep alive the possibilities of a singularity. However, this is not a quick and resolved moment of redemption but a cautious process of looking into the work of representation itself. The processes of gendered signification remains through the family album's/family photography's own history and the history of the woman, where one has generally witnessed different kinds of bodies, as if different from the seduction of the stereotypes in images, but succumbing to structures of domination. The Brahmo[55]/Hindu Bengali middle-class women, as represented in family

---

[54] Ibid. p. 92.

[55] The phrase 'brahmo samaj' literally means the society of the worshippers of the One True God. 'Brahmo' means one who worships Brahma, or the Supreme Spirit of the universe, and 'samaj' means a community of men. The brahmo samaj, therefore, represents a body of men who are struggling to establish the worship of the Supreme Being in spirit as opposed to the prevailing idolatry. The movement was started on 20 August 1828 by Raja Ram Mohan Roy and his friends, by opening a place for public worship on Chitpore Road in Calcutta. This was duly and publicly inagurated in January 1830, by the consecration of the first house of prayer, now known as Adi Brahmo Samaj.

The Sadharan Brahmo Samaj was formed in a public meeting of Brahmos held in the Town Hall of Calcutta on 15 May 1878, 2 Jaishta 1284 of the Bengali calendar. A letter from the venerable Maharshi Devendranath Tagore communicating his blessings and prayer for the success of the new samaj was read at the meeting. At the time of its foundation, the Sadharan Brahmo Samaj was headed by three men universally esteemed in Brahmo society for their high moral character. They were Ananda Mohan Bose, Shibchandra Deb and Umeshchandra Datta.

albums and in visual histories based on their factic materiality might end up in the photograph as subjects mirroring the social while at the same time provoking us to look beyond the obvious and the evidential.

As I have already mentioned, the purpose here is not doing away with history, either of the family or the notion of woman—which in itself is an important tool of feminism—but a move toward being notionally responsible for the expositions. Women's photographs amidst family and their interpretations and ways of seeing, should be a responsibility for the future to come in the sense of delivering critical feminist thinking and politics. A typical anticipation of the visual representations of middle-class women as *what is seen* in the albums might push one to further elucidate the larger questions of image-based representations of women in Bengali middle-class societies.

Further reading:

Bourdieu, Pierre. *Photography: A Middle-brow Art*, California: Stanford University Press, 1990.

Hall, Stuart. 'Cultural Identity and Diaspora.' *Identity, Community, Culture, Difference* edited by Jonathan Rudeford, London: Lawrence and Wishart, 1990.

Hall, Stuart. 'Reconstruction Work: Images of Post-war Black Settlement.' *Family Snaps: The Meanings of Domestic Photography*, edited by Jo Spence and Patricia Holland, London: Virago, 1991.

Hall, Stuart. 'Cultural Identity and Diaspora.' *Identity, Community, Culture, Difference*, edited by Jonathan Rutherford, London: Lawrence and Wishart, 1990.

Williams, Raymond. *Keywords: A Vocabulary of Culture and Society*, London: Fontana Press, 1988[1976].

Derrida, Jacques. 'Sending: On Representation.' Peter Caws and Mary Ann Caws Trans. *Social Research*, Vol. 49, No.2, Current French Philosophy (SUMMER 1982): 294–326.

———*Archive Fever: A Freudian Impression*, Chicago & London: The University of Chicago Press, 1996.

———*MEMOIRES for Paul de Man*. Columbia University Press, 1986 [1989].

———*Limited Inc*. Evanston, IL: Northwestern University Press. 1993 [1988].

Benjamin, Walter. *The Work of Art in the Age of its Technical Reproducibility and Other Writings on Media*, eds, Michael W. Jennings, Brigid Doherty and Thomas Y. Levin, Cambridge: The Belknap Press of Harvard University Press, 2008.

———'The Work of Art in the Age of Mechanical Reproduction.' In *Illuminations*, ed. Hannah Arendt, Translated by Harry Zohn, London: Fontana Press, 1992 [1973].

Baudrillard, Jean. *L'échangesymboliqueet la mort.* Paris: Gallimard, 1976.

——— *La societe de consummation*, Paris: Denoel, 1970.

Of the three, Ananda Mohan Bose was the youngest, scarcely more than thirty-one years at the time, yet he was placed at the head of affairs. Thus the Sadharan Brahmo Samaj was launched into existence with these three distinguished men as its leaders.' (thesadharanbrahmosamaj.org). See also Kopf, David. 1979. *The Brahmo Samaj and the Shaping of the Modern Indian Mind* (Princeton: Princeton University Press).

Karlekar, Malavika. 'Kadambini and the Bhadralok: Early Debates over Women's Education in Bengal.' *Economic and Political Weekly* XXI, 17 (April 1986): WS-25-WS 31.

Karlekar, Malavika. Re-visioning the Past: Early Photography in Bengal 1875-1915, New Delhi, Oxford, 2005.

——— *Visual Histories: Photography in the Popular Imagination*. New Delhi: Oxford University Press, 2013.

Majumdar, Rochona. *Marriage and Modernity: Family Values in Colonial Bengal*. New Delhi: Oxford University Press, 2009.

Highmore, Ben. *The Everyday Life Reader*, Psychology Press, 2002.

Guha-Thakurta, Tapati. *Monuments, Objects, Histories: Institutions of Art in Colonial and Post-Colonial India*, Columbia: Columbia University Press, 2004.

——— *The Making of a New 'Indian' Art: Artists, Aesthetics and Nationalism in Bengal, c.1850-1920*, Cambridge University Press, 2007.

Ramaswamy, Sumathi. *The Goddess and the Nation: Mapping Mother India*, Duke University Press, 2009.

Chatterjee, Ratnabali. *From the Karkhana to the Studio: A Study in the Changing Social Rules [i.e. Roles] of Patron and Artist in Bengal*, New Delhi: Books and Books, 1990.

Jain, Kajri. *Gods in the Bazaar: The Economies of Indian Calendar Art*, Duke University Press, 2007.

Uberoi, Patricia. *Freedom and Destiny: Gender, Family, and Popular Culture in India*, New Delhi: Oxford University Press, 2006.

Barthes, Roland. *Rhetoric of the Image in Image, Music Text*, New York: Hill and Wang, 1977.

——— 'The Photographic Message.' *Theorizing Communication: Readings Across Traditions*, 2000: 191-199.

——— *Camera Lucida: Reflections on Photography*. London: Macmillan, 1981.

Pang, Laikwan."Photography, Performance and the Making of Female Images in Modern China." *Journal of Women's History*.Vol. 17.No. 4. (2005): 56□85.

Mitchell, W. J. T. "What do Pictures "Really" Want?." *October*. Vol. 77 (Summer, 1996): 71-82

Scott, Joan Wallach. *The Fantasy of Feminist History*. Durham and London: Duke University Press, 2011.

Kuhn, Annette. *Family Secrets: Acts of Memory and Imagination*, London: Verso, 1995.

——— "Photography and Cultural Memory: A Methodological Exploration." *Visual Studies*, Vol. 22, No. 3, December 2007.

Das, Anirban. "Embodied Knowledges: The Limits and Possibilities of Knowing the Body." PhD diss., Jadavpur University, 2006.

——— "In Search of the Third World Woman: The (in) corporeality of Body□ metaphors." *Margins*, Vol. 2, No. 1. (February 2002): 102□123.

——— *Toward a Politics of the (Im)Possible: The Body in Third World Feminisms*, London: Anthem Press, 2012.

Parayil, Sujith Kumar. "Photography and Colonial Modernity in Keralam." In *Space, Sexuality and Postcolonial Studies* edited by Manas Ray, Kolkata: Centre for Studies in Social Sciences, Calcutta, 2003.

Kumar, Udaya. "Seeing and Reading: The Early Malayalam Novel and Some Questions of Visibilities." in *Early Novels in India*, edited by Meenakshi Mukherjee, New Delhi: Sahitya Akademi, 2002.

Jagger, Gill. Judith Butler: Sexual Politics, Social Change and the Power of the Performative, New York: Routledge, 2008.

Butler, Judith. "Performative acts and gender constitution: An essay in phenomenology and feminist theory." *Theatre journal* (1988): 519-531.

——— *Bodies that matter: On the discursive limits of sex*, Taylor & Francis, 2011.

——— *Excitable speech: A politics of the performative*, Psychology Press, 1997.

——— *Gender trouble*, London: Routledge, 2002.

Thomson, Ian. "Can I die? Derrida on Heidegger and Death." *Philosophy Today*. (Spring 1999): 29-42

Wortham, Simon Morgan. *The Derrida Dictionary*, London and New York: Continuum, 2010.

4

Ties (re)invoked:
Archives imagined, borrowed and lost:

Ghosts in the Mirror

Unearthing the Family Archive, Renegotiating Collective Memory

Nadia Nooreyezdan

In the winter of 1960, my grandfather, Sheriar, visits his family home in Nasrabad, a village in the central Iranian province of Yazd. He is twenty-nine years old and although he has given up his dream of becoming a documentary filmmaker, his Zeiss camera continues to be strapped around his neck the entire trip. This is his first trip back home after he and his mother were forced to leave Iran in 1938. His father, Faredoon, had fled four years earlier, settling in Bombay before arranging for his wife and son to join him. When the news of Sheriar's grandfather's death reaches them, both father and son make the trip back to their family.

His grandmother, Morvarid, now lives with her daughter and son-in-law in Nasrabad but Sheriar hopes to bring her back to Bombay with them when they leave. He and his father jump through bureaucratic hoops in Tehran to have a passport made for her, but in the end, she refuses. She does not want to

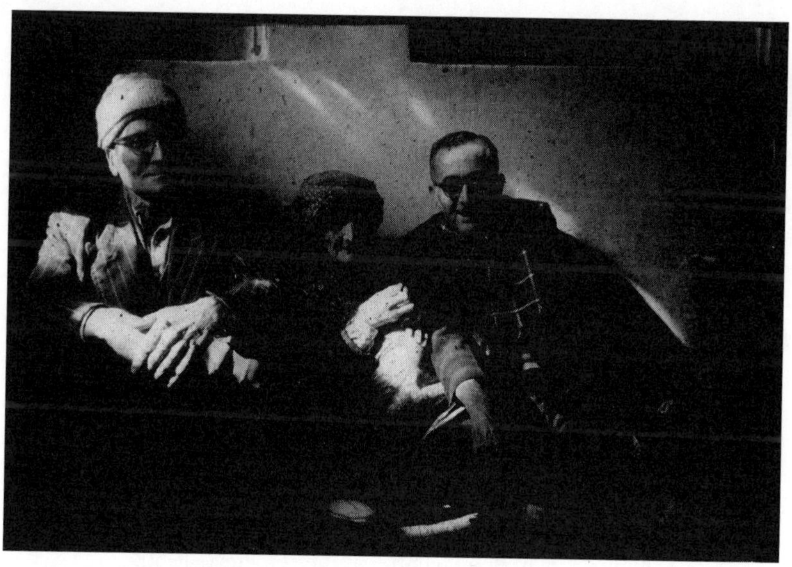

Figure 1: From left - Bahram, Morvarid and Faredoon. Yazd, 1960.
[Author's personal collection]

leave her home. Sheriar takes a picture, the only photograph he will ever have of her, sitting on the ground next to her son. She has on a cloth turban and smiles gummily, with Faredoon's arm around her. She has piercing blue eyes and complains about the flash of my grandfather's camera. A few months after they leave, she passes away.

Three years later, in the summer of 1963, Sheriar returns with his wife to his childhood home and to the family that they had left behind. Over these two trips, he documents everything he can. He takes pictures of the family, sitting together around a table, squinting in the sunny courtyard, and standing next to each other in the pomegranate orchards behind the house. My grandmother, Ruhi, has her head uncovered and holds the hands of the children, a small smile on her face. My great grandfather Faredoon is photographed looking solemn, wearing a white linen suit and tie with his hands clasped behind his back.

Sheriar takes photos of the streets, buildings in the neighbourhood, trees heavy with fruit, intricate tapestries inside Yazd's famous Amir Chakhmaq Mosque, and the monument of the fourteenth-century poet, Hafez. Here are three children standing in the sunshine wearing striped pyjamas with only a hint of a smile. Their father, my great-granduncle Rustom, in his signature black hat, is standing in the background. Here are the students of the all-girls school that Sheriar's maternal grandfather set up in the village. Here is Faredoon in the distance, head bowed in the cemetery, visiting the graves of his relatives.

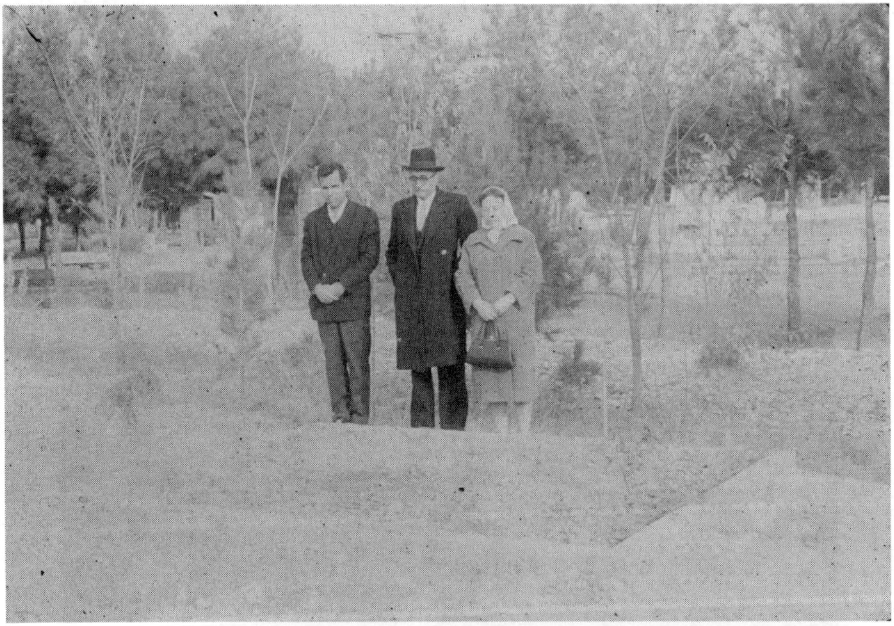

Figure 2: Faredoon (centre) at the cemetery, 1960.
[Author's personal collection]

When Sheriar takes a trip south to the city of Shiraz with his wife and cousin, he photographs the neighbourhood near the House of the Báb, a central figure in the Bahá'í Faith. My grandfather tells me he was furtive in his movements so as to not raise suspicion that he was a Bahá'í and that this street, this neighbourhood, and this house held spiritual importance to him. He takes a picture of the orange tree growing in the courtyard of the house and plucks a few oranges to take home. And then he kneels at the threshold of this house, a place of pilgrimage for Bahá'ís. At this moment, his cousin takes a photo. It is the only image from either trip in which Sheriar is the photographed subject rather than the photographer. He kneels near the carpet by the door, his arms folded in deference. My grandmother stands behind him with a hand on his shoulder. Sheriar's cousin's wife, Monira, is next to them. The photo is framed by the branches of the orange tree.

My grandfather returns to Bombay and stores the collection of 35 mm Kodachrome slides from these two trips back home in a yellow Kodak box. The box is compact and the two large piles of slides don't allow the top to fit as snugly as it was intended. On the top of the box, he writes 'FAMILY'. And he does not look at them for another fifty-eight years.

In her book, *Suspended Conversations*, Martha Langford suggests that the photo album provides families with a way to perform oral tradition, to pass down stories that educate younger generations about their identity, history, and family values. 'The structure and content of oral tradition – the fabric of memory in oral consciousness – are met in the photographic condition. ... Our photographic memories are nestled in a performative oral tradition.' The selection and sequence of photographs in the album provides a framework, 'a horizontal narrative shot through with lines of both epic and anecdotal dimension,'[1] says Langford. But what happens when there is an absence in the family album, a void in the history? What happens when the horizontal narrative is fractured and memories go missing?

When I ask my grandparents, almost sixty years after they had made that trip, whether they have any photos of our family in Iran, they say no. 'No, I don't think so'; 'Maybe, but I can't remember'; 'Perhaps if you look in the cupboard, there might be one or two photos.' I spend weeks going through albums and boxes of loose photographs, pictures spanning years of family picnics, birthdays, weddings. My eyes scan each image for the unfamiliar—unrecognisable landscapes, women wearing *chadors*, strangers in the pictures. Is this unknown enough to me to be Iran? But that is a simplified version of the question I was really asking myself—is there some part of me that recognises what home could have been, had my grandparents never left? If I search each photograph, can I identify some small piece of my grandfather—the way he stands, his aquiline nose, the look of his hands—reflected back at me through

[1] Langford, Martha. 2001. *Suspended Conversations: The Afterlife of Memory in Photographic Albums* (Montreal: McGill-Queen's UP). p. viii.

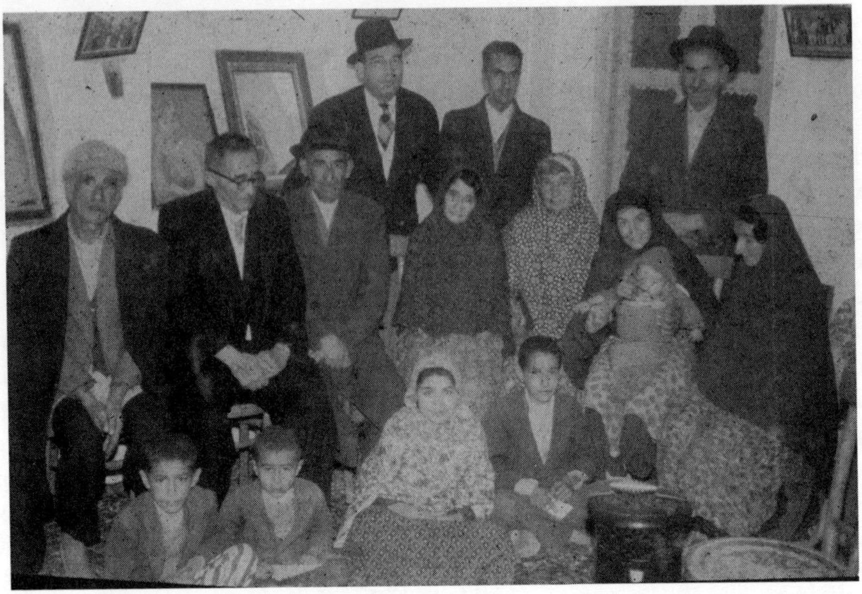

Figure 3: Family in Yazd, 1960. [Author's personal collection]

the image of a stranger? I was looking for the familiar in the unfamiliar, a far more complex task.

In the bottom shelf of the steel Godrej cupboard in my grandfather's bedroom, hidden behind piles of old, yellowing documents, cut-glass vases and bric-a-brac gathering dust, I finally find the Kodak box with the slides. The places, people, and moments in time that my grandfather diligently documented had been buried for so long that the colour dye layers have stained the images. Each photograph is tinged with a magenta hue when I hold them up to the light. They feel precious in my hands as if they exist in defiance of memory.

My paternal and maternal grandparents left Iran during the 1930s, when Reza Shah Pahlavi ruled Iran and the persecution of Bahá'ís was gaining steam. The Bahá'í Faith, an independent world religion, was established in nineteenth-century Persia, by Bahá'u'lláh, a prophet who preached the oneness of God, man, and all religions. There is no clergy or priest class and Bahá'í teachings espouse racial unity, gender equality, universal education and the value of science as well as religion. But in Iran and many other Muslim-majority countries, it is seen as apostasy from Islam.

Bahá'ís are currently the largest religious minority in Iran (estimated at 350,000), but unlike other minorities in the country—Zoroastrians, Christians and Jews—the state explicitly denies them recognition.[2] During my great

[2] DaBell, Bijan. 3 September 2013. 'Iran Minorities 1: Diverse Religions', The Iran Primer, United States Institute of Peace. iranprimer.usip.org/blog/2013/sep/03/iran-minorities-1-diverse-religions. Last viewed 23 March 2021.

grandparents' lifetime, massacres were taking place across the country. In 1903, 100 Bahá'ís in Yazd were killed and by 1930, Bahá'í schools—set up because Bahá'í children were not permitted to study with Muslim children—were forced to shut down.[3] Mohammad Reza Pahlavi, the last Shah of Iran, came to power in 1941 and during his reign, he appeased the Islamic clergy by condoning and often supporting anti-Bahá'í campaigns, including propaganda and incendiary sermons broadcast on national radio and published in leading newspapers. Mob violence, arson, and murder were normalised and anti-Bahá'í organisations like the Hojjatiyeh[4] gained social and political prominence.

With the Islamic Revolution in 1979, the persecution of Bahá'ís took on a different, more systematic approach. Bahá'ís holding positions of power in government offices or private companies were let go. The new constitution excluded the religion amongst its recognised minorities. The Islamic Republic Penal Code denied rights to Bahá'ís since they were unprotected citizens or 'apostates', and the courts denied Bahá'ís any rights to redressal. Ayatollah Khomeni, the founder of the Islamic Republic, decreed that the punishment for apostasy is death and any Muslim who kills an apostate shall not be punished.[5] Government ministries, organisations, and factories established 'purging' committees'[6] to compile lists of Bahá'ís in their employment. Any Bahá'í who refused to embrace Islam was fired and their pensions annulled. A government decree in 1981, published in the newspaper Keyhan,[7] made the dismissal of all Bahá'ís employed in the public sector official government policy.

In addition to the mob violence and attacks, the state started targeting community leaders. Their homes were ransacked and property seized, their families were interrogated, and they were arrested and executed without trial. By 1983, all Bahá'í activities were banned,[8] including memorial services and community gatherings. The Islamic Republic maintained that the arrests and executions were because the Bahá'í community had links to foreign powers, including and especially Israel, and were therefore a threat to Iran.

In 1993, a confidential government memorandum titled 'The Bahá'í Question' was made public by the UN Human Rights Commission. It serves as concrete evidence that it was government policy to discriminate against Bahá'ís. Prepared at the request of Ayatollah Khomeni as well as the then President of Iran, the document stated that 'The Government's dealings with

---

[3] Bahá'í International Community Report (2008). *The* Bahá'í *Question: Cultural Cleansing in Iran.* (New York: Bahá'í International Community). p. 42.

[4] Ibid. p. 50.

[5] 'Mona Mahmudnizhad'. Memorial. Abdorrahman Boroumand Center for Human Rights in Iran. www.iranrights.org/memorial/story/-2990/mona-mahmudnizhad. Last viewed 12 March 2021.

[6] Vahman, Fereydun. 2019. *175 Years of Persecution: A History of the Babis and Bahá'ís of Iran.* (London: Oneworld Publications). p. 204.

[7] Vahman. 2019. *175 Years*. p. 205.

[8] Bahá'í International Community Report. p. 26.

them [Bahá'ís] must be in such a way that their progress and development are blocked'.[9] To this end, it lists measures to curb Bahá'ís' educational, economic and religious freedoms, including expelling members from higher educational institutions and denying them employment. These policies continue to be in place today.

Since the revolution, over 200 Bahá'ís have been executed or killed and hundreds more have been imprisoned. From 2005 onwards, the arrests and attacks on the community have intensified. National and state budgets have allocations to 'confront' the Bahá'í faith. Bahá'ís are currently denied work permits and licenses for twenty-five kinds of 'high-earning businesses'. Trade unions and businesses must compile lists of Bahá'ís registered with them. University authorities have been instructed by the state that students 'must be expelled from universities, either in the admissions process or during the course of their studies, once it becomes known that they are Bahá'ís'. Community members have reported receiving threatening phone calls, texts and letters; anti-Bahá'í pamphlets are published and distributed in public places; and graffiti denouncing Bahá'ís as heretics and infidels mark their gravestones, shops, houses and vehicles.[10] On 26 March 2018, a fatwa was put out by the Supreme Leader Ali Khamenei against 'association and dealing with Bahá'ís.'[11] As Supreme Leader, Khamenei's word is tantamount to divine directive.

Meanwhile, the Iranian government is relentless. In early April 2021, more than twenty-five arrests were made and Bahá'í families' homes raided by security forces, despite the wave of COVID-19 cases and cities in Iran put on high alert.[12] My grandparents are often the ones to inform me of these incidents. They send me forwards on WhatsApp about the stories of the martyrs and news of prisoners being released after serving decade-long sentences. On 8 April, my grandmother sends me an audio file of a prayer being chanted in Persian. It is the voice of Soroush Abadi, a Bahá'í who was arrested for the second time in Shiraz. His voice is low and soothing. My grandmother texts, 'Pls offer prayers for his release.'

What my family keeps silent about is our own link to this trauma, to the lives of the Bahá'ís suffering in Iran. But once I find the buried photographs that my grandparents had forgotten about, other memories are easier to uncover. On a trip back home when she was nineteen years old, my maternal grandmother, Mahvash, remembers walking down the streets of Yazd with her family on a hot summer's day and craving Shirazi faloodeh. 'We went in one shop but when they saw us, they said, "Oh we've run out of faloodeh" because

[9] Ibid. p. 23.

[10] 'Situation of Bahá'ís in Iran' (January 2023). Bahá'í International Community. www.bic.org/focus-areas/situation-iranian-bahais/current-situation. Last viewed on 22 April 2021.

[11] Ibid.

[12] Kian Sabeti. 16 April 2021.'Iran Steps up Tactics to Eliminate the Country's Bahá'ís'. Iranwire. iranwire.com/en/features/9360. Last viewed on 15 April 2021.

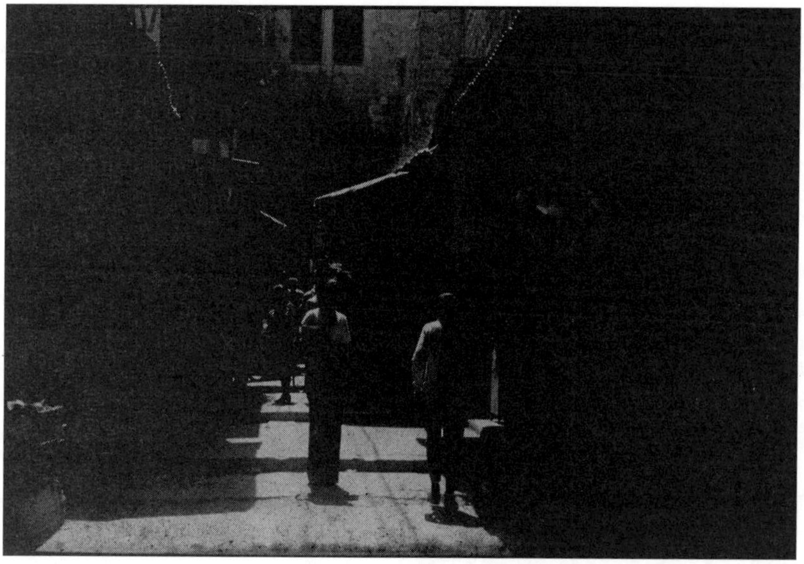

Figure 4. Street scene. Yazd, 1963. [Author's personal collection]

they saw that we were not wearing the black chador that Muslim women wear,' she says. 'At the next shop, they told us don't touch, "Dast nazaan, najasthi".' She does not translate the last word, 'najes', for me.

Sheriar also knows the weight of the term 'najes'. He describes a memory of his mother sending him to buy a box of matches from the village shop when he was eight years old. The shopkeeper had a bowl of water on the counter. He instructed him to drop the coin in the water so that he did not have to take it directly from the little Bahá'í boy's hands. It was unclean coming from him. 'Najes' means untouchable, unclean. Bahá'ís and leftists were regarded as najes and were seen to contaminate Muslims if they shared anything that touched them.

But these memories were not available to me growing up. What I knew of Iran was through the history of community persecution and trauma, and what I saw of Iran were the photographs—of destruction, state-sanctioned violence and the faces of the martyrs. One of the fastest-growing religions in the world, the Bahá'í faith has spread to 235 countries with 8.5 million adherents worldwide, out of which 2 million reside in India. In Mumbai, the community includes a few families from Iran who were able to leave before the revolution. At regularly held community gatherings every fifteen days, Bahá'ís from all over the city meet to pray and socialise.

It was at these meetings that I'd slowly learn about what was happening to the Bahá'ís in Iran. Their stories were told, their names remembered and photographs of them—with their families, smiling brightly at the camera—were shared, as if in death, their family albums became our own. Unlike a photograph in an album, their faces were blown up, projected onto screens

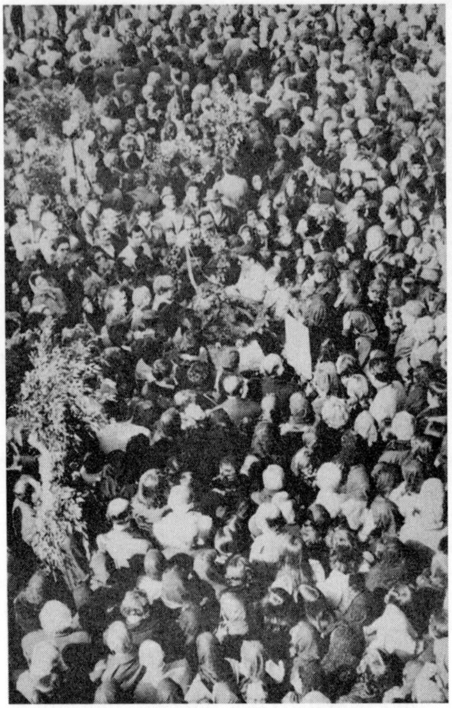

Figure 5: Dr Hakim's Funeral, from *A Cry from the Heart: The Bahá'ís in Iran.*

Disclaimer: This photo has been sourced from Sears, William. 1982. A Cry From the Heart. Oxford: George Ronald Publishers. Despite multiple attempts to trace the original copyright owner, we have not been successful. Should any reader be aware of any information that can help us trace the copyright owner, we would be grateful to receive it.

or printed in pamphlets, reproduced over and over. The photographs became evidence of persecution and proof of their sacrifice, but also a way to mourn, to demand visibility and to commemorate and remember the people who were killed because of their faith. But these images that I grew up with, also become a source of unspoken, unacknowledged guilt. Nowadays, Iranian Bahá'ís' photographs are shared on social media. Poetry written by Bahá'ís in prison are forwarded online. Photographs of families holding flowers, seeing their wives or mothers after a decade in Tehran's Evin Prison are uploaded onto Facebook. An article about the forty-four Iranian Bahá'ís who were arrested in July 2022 is shared on WhatsApp groups. It is followed by a sign-up sheet for a prayer chain 'for our dearest Bahá'ís in Iran who are in prison to remain steadfast in their faith'. In some ways, I am glad of the silence of my family about their connection to Iran because it means I do not have to unpack my own privilege in escaping what so many did not.

Amongst the titles on my grandparents' bookshelf is William Sears's *A Cry From the Heart: The Bahá'ís in Iran.*[13] Sears was an American Bahá'í and a prolific writer. In 1982, he wrote this book which detailed individual stories of Bahá'ís who had been killed in Iran, and outlined some of the tactics used by the state and religious authorities to persecute Bahá'ís. Alongside the text, the book includes family photographs of the dead, pictures of the rubble from demolished holy sites, and a facsimile of a letter from a school in Yazd expelling a child for being a Bahá'í. A full page is occupied by a photograph of the funeral of Dr Manuchehr Hakim, a well-known doctor in Tehran who

[13] Sears, William. 1982. *A Cry from the Heart: The Bahá'ís in Iran* (Oxford: George Ronald). p. 78.

served as the Director for the Bahá'í Hospital and the Home for the Aged, an institution run by Bahá'í donations providing medical care to all. He had received anonymous threats against his life, which increased after he refused to provide the state authorities with a list of Bahá'í physicians practising in Iran. He was shot to death in his clinic on 12 January 1981. Although the Revolutionary Guardsmen warned the community that any demonstration would be dealt with violently, the funeral saw 4,000 people gather on the streets and accompany the hearse to the Bahá'í cemetery. In the photograph, it is difficult to make out the shape of the hearse transporting Dr Hakim's body—the frame is filled with people thronging together, with bursts of flowers between them. At the end of the book, Sears lists out the names of Bahá'ís who have been killed, imprisoned or have 'disappeared' since 1978. He mentions how they were killed—burned to death, mobbed, tortured and hanged, stoned, executed. And he notes the places they came from—Ahram, Shiraz, Tehran, Tabriz, Isfahan, Rasht, Karaj, and the home of my grandparents, Yazd.

A year after Sears's book was published, on 18 June 1983, ten Bahá'í women were executed. They had been arrested and imprisoned in Shiraz for teaching Bahá'í children's classes. They had been through repeated interrogations and torture where they were given the option to recant their faith and go free. In an interview published by an Iranian newspaper, *Khabar-e Jonub*, the head of the Islamic Revolutionary Tribunal in charge of their cases confirmed that he warned the women to 'embrace dear Islam and recant Bahá'ísm, which is rationally and logically doomed, before it is too late'.[14] After each one of them refused to sign a document which stated that they were not Bahá'ís, they were sentenced to death.

The women executed that day were[15]:

1. Mahshid Nirumand, 28 years
2. Simin Saberi, 24 years
3. Akhtar Sabet, 21 years
4. Shirin Dalvand, 25 years
5. Zarrin Muqimi, 29 years
6. Tahereh Siyavashi, 32 years (her husband was executed three months earlier)
7. Nusrat Yaldai, 56 years (her son was executed two days earlier)
8. Ezzat Janami Eshraqi, 57 years (her husband was executed two days earlier)
9. Roya Eshraqi, 23 years
10. Mona Mahmudnizhad, 17 years (her father was executed three months earlier)

[14] 'Mona Mahmudnizhad'. Memorial.

[15] Vahman. 2019. *175 Years*. p. 193.

A specific set of photographs of these ten women—small, passport-sized pictures placed next to each other—began to be circulated. They were used in pamphlets, newsletters, websites, books and videos memorialising their sacrifice. Slowly, these images and the stories of the ten women reached Bahá'í communities all over the world. Shirin's photograph is from her graduation, the square academic cap on her head; Ezzat's photo is cropped as if it may have been part of a group picture. She is laughing in it, and so is Tahereh in the photo to the right of hers. This grid of women's faces becomes an image in its own right, shared and reproduced over and over again in the same structure and order. Two rows, five photos in each row.

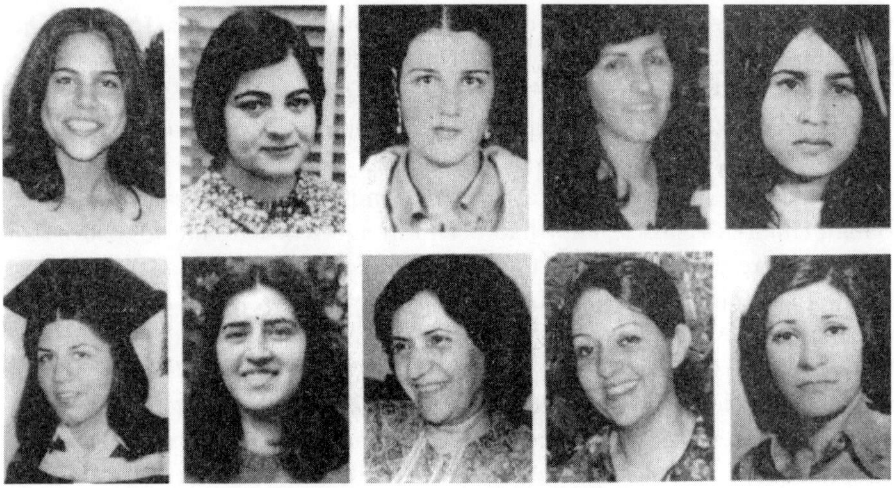

Figure 6: The ten women martyrs of Shiraz. 1983.
Courtesy of Bahá'í World News Service.

Stories were shared by inmates who had been with them, family members who were able to visit them in prison, even the bus driver who had taken the women to Abdullah Mesgar Base (Chougan Square), where they were hanged. Similar to family histories passed down through generations, these stories take on a reverence and become almost lore. That the women being driven to their execution were singing, happy to give their lives up for their beliefs, that each woman was given four chances to recant and each refused, and that Mona, who was sixteen when she was arrested, asked if she could be hanged last so that she could pray for the souls of the women being executed before her. That she kissed the noose before placing it around her neck. In her neighbourhood, Mona Mahmudnizhad was lovingly called the 'Angel of Shiraz'. In death, that moniker became known to Bahá'ís everywhere. Photographs of Mona were shared by her family and friends—of her sitting next to her father, who was arrested on the same day as her; of her doing a split in a traditional Shirazi outfit, laughing at the camera; of her at the beach hiking up a green skirt, standing knee-deep in the Caspian Sea. The images seem to confirm people's descriptions of her as warm, friendly, always happy. In 1985, a Canadian musician, Doug Cameron, wrote a song titled 'Mona with the Children' which made it to the Canadian pop charts. The music video opens with the guards who had buried the women, spitting on their graves, and stages a reenactment of days leading up to Mona's execution. At the end of the video, the face of the woman who plays Mona in the reenactment morphs into a black-and-white photo of her, with text explaining her story and the persecution of the Bahá'ís in Iran.

My mother remembers watching that music video when she was twenty years old and being moved to tears. The photographs of Mona seem to have stayed with her the same way that they have stayed with me. 'I remember her face so clearly,' she tells me. She recalls the visit of an Iranian Bahá'í to Bombay, a woman who had been in prison with Mona, and was eventually released. My mother remembers her description of the kind of torture and interrogation that they had to go through and how Mona told them to be cheerful. They would pray because they never knew who would be taken to be executed next. It was like a lottery system, she says.

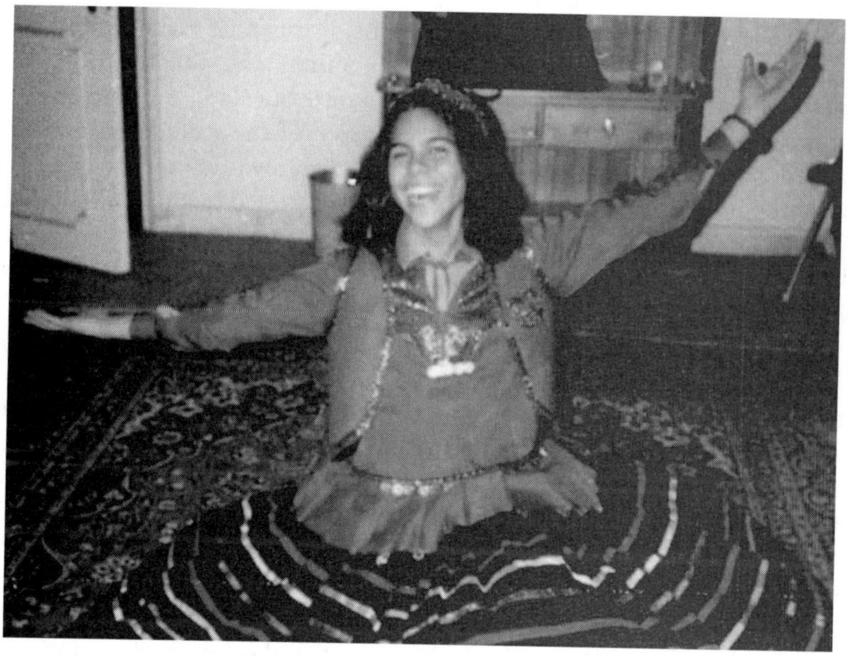

Figure 7: Mona Mahmudnizhad.
[Published by Iran Press Watch: iranpresswatch.org/post/19322/narrative-execution-17-year-old-mona/ Accessed last - 26 April, 2024]

Disclaimer: This photo is widely available on various platforms on the internet. Despite multiple attempts to trace the original copyright owner, we have not been successful. Should any reader be aware of information that can help us trace the copyright owner, we would be grateful to receive it.

'We were born in the same year, Mona and I,' my mother tells me. 'We were the same age. And I always wondered whether I would have had the strength to do what she had done if I was in her place. I don't remember exactly when I saw pictures of her or what they were, but her face is so clear in my mind.'[16] Like my mother, I can conjure up Mona's face instantly. It's almost as if she has become so familiar to me that I can recall her green eyes and the way the angles of her face change when she smiles, divorced from any singular photo of her. I feel like I could recognise her, that I would know her anywhere.

In 1987, in the midst of the trial of Klaus Barbie, a Nazi war criminal known as the 'Butcher of Lyon', Lorie Novak, a Jewish-American artist, created a work titled 'Past Lives'. Novak's piece is a projection of three different photographs onto a single wall. Centred in the work is the image of a group of Jewish children hiding in an orphanage in Izieu, France, who would soon be sent to their deaths in Auschwitz by Barbie—a photograph that was widely distributed and published at the time as a symbol of Barbie's war crimes. Projected onto it are two other photographs—a picture of Ethel Rosenburg, a Jewish mother of two who was convicted for atomic espionage and executed in the United States, and Novak's own family photograph of herself and her mother. In the photo, she is clutching at her mother's blouse, terrified. Novak's childhood is literally overshadowed by images of other mothers and children who loom large in the collective memory of a community. Speaking about her work, Novak says, 'I wanted to expand my investigation of the relationship between personal and collective memory by looking at my own documented history against the backdrop of public images. … I was haunted by the smiling image of the children; "Past Lives" is dedicated to their memory. In my projected collage, images of Ethel Rosenberg, the children from Izieu, and me clutching my mother, merge. I become the recipient of the weight of my cultural past.'[17]

Marianne Hirsch also mentions being haunted, but by Novak's piece itself. In her book, *The Generation of Postmemory*,[18] she points out that Novak is only connected to the Holocaust and the children who did not survive it through a transgenerational act of adoption and identification. Hirsch also echoes the kind of identification as well as the questions that my mother has about Mona. She writes, 'I have been haunted by "Past Lives" since the first time I saw it. Where would I have been, then? How would I have acted? The doorbell rings in the middle of the night, the Gestapo is at the door, what do I do? The imbalance of Novak's image speaks to me forcefully: in remembering my childhood, I too feel as though I were crouching in the corner of a bare room populated by larger-than-life ghosts: my parents' younger selves during the war

---

[16] Nooreyezdan, Nohid. 3 January 2021. Interview. Conducted by Nadia Nooreyezdan.

[17] Novak, Lorie. 2005. 'Fragments and Past Lives'. *Gender and Culture in the 1950s. WSQ* (Fall/Winter).

[18] Hirsch, Marianne. 2012. *The Generation of Postmemory: Writing and Visual Culture After the Holocaust.* (New York: Columbia University Press). p. 160.

and children who had to face dangers that I, a child born after, tried hard to imagine.'

I worry about projecting memory in this way. Mona has become a symbol, a stand-in for what could have happened to my mother or to me but simultaneously what never could have been because we can never know it. In my mind, Mona's face begins morphing, like in Cameron's music video, into other faces, blurry like so many ghosts in the mirror.

As I switch back and forth between this collective history of trauma and my family's own entanglement with it, memories get hazy and details mixed-up. My mother remembers the woman who was with Mona in prison as Roya. She tells me yes, Roya came to Bombay and told us about what happened. But it couldn't have been her. Roya was executed on the same day as Mona, I remind her. A similar correction, a readjustment of memory, happens with the story of my maternal great-grandfather's death. He was murdered by a mob near his home in Taft, a village in Yazd, in 1951. My mother's version of the story, which was told to her by her uncle in Persian, is that her grandfather, Bahram, was on his way to the market. He was a well-known Bahá'í in the area, which had seen increasing tension and anti-Bahá'í sentiments. He was attacked on his way, stoned to death by a mob from the village. His body was left under a nearby tree as the attackers scattered. In the days that followed, his wife was inconsolable, particularly because of how painful she thought his death must have been. But in her dream, her husband visited her. He said, 'The first stone that struck me hurt. But after that, it was as if I was a bird. I was sitting on the branch of that tree watching below as they were attacking my body. I felt no pain.'

Although I hear this story only once and only briefly, it becomes a memory that I hold inside of me, an unearthly photograph of my great-grandfather sitting in this tree, looking down at his own murder. I think of his wife, I think of the rocks red with his blood and how it mixed with the dust on the road. The story of Bahram's death feels like a secret and so I carry that image with me, in tandem with the other photographs I have seen of desecrated cemeteries, the barbed wire-topped walls of prisons, and the faces of the other martyrs in Iran.

The story gets buried, like so much in my family. But what is also buried, kept away like a secret, are two objects—a candle from the funeral that took place in Taft all those years ago and a piece of bloodied cloth from the shirt Bahram was wearing when he died. When my maternal grandfather came back to Bombay from Yazd, he had brought these talismans of his father's death with him. My grandmother only reveals that she still has these two objects, tucked away in her cupboard, decades after his death. She corrects the story now. 'No, it was knives. They knifed him to death. It was those *kebabis*, we used to call them kebabis because they would sell their kebabs near this tunnel on the way to the market. There was a stream nearby, and the tree. But it was knives, they had knives with them. After they struck him, things calmed down in the village for the other Bahá'ís for some time. He gave his life and others were spared.'[19] I ask her why we haven't spoken about it, ever; why this story and the keepsakes that were carefully preserved and passed down to her, were shrouded in silence. She shrugs and says, 'Maybe we weren't ready to talk about it openly before. It was a wound. But we should be proud of his sacrifice.'

The image I have carried in my head shifts, the photograph must be readjusted, reframed. The detail in my grandmother's story somehow makes his death all the more gruesome, the hatred for this father of three, this amicable man in the village, all the more inexplicable. But as I start asking more questions about who he was, the image of him grows beyond the story of his death. I find a family in Bombay who knew him from the village of Taft, who remember him as a peacemaker, a figure who people would turn to when there was trouble. One evening, my grandmother points to a small picture on the wall, above the cupboard in her bedroom. It has always been there—I remember days spent at my grandmother's house, lazy afternoons laying her bed and laughing at the toothbrush moustache that the man in the picture had. Now when my eyes are drawn to it again, I go numb. In black and white, my great-grandfather's eyes stare back into mine. My grandmother had never identified who the man in the photo was until now and I had never thought to ask.

Ariella Azoulay, a curator and theorist, writes about the kinds of photos that we carry in our mind in *The Civil Contract of Photography*.

> Each one of us carries with her an album of these planted pictures. In some cases, the violence needed for their insertion in the album is evident – as happens when the image is engraved through trauma. … What distinguishes such pictures from regular photographs is the mode of their transmission. They are planted in the body, the consciousness, the memory, and their adoption is instantaneous, ruling out any opportunity for negotiations as regards what they show or their genealogy, their ownership or belonging.[20]

In the absence of a family archive, these planted photographs become how I connect the communal memory of Bahá'ís in Iran with my own family's history. They are how I negotiate an idea of home, albeit one that is marked by trauma and loss. I see Faredoon jumping across neighbours' terraces in the dark of the night, fleeing from Yazd. I see Bahram sitting on the branch of the tree, looking down at his corpse. I see Mahvash squeezing her mother's hand in a crowded truck, being smuggled through Afghanistan by Baluchis. I see Sheriar reaching the port in Bombay, his shirt in tatters. It is the only thing he was able to bring with him. And among these images, I see others, hazier in detail. The faces of family members who I have never met, whose names are mentioned aloud only when they pass away. I imagine their homes, their

[19] Rowhani, Mahvash. 19 December 2020. Interview. Conducted by Nadia Nooreyezdan.

[20] Azoulay. 2008. *The Civil Contract.* p. 13.

lives, what they eat for lunch, what birds they can hear from their windows. Meena, Seema, Keku and his brother Daryush, Khalleh Homayun, Maman Bonu. I know they are family because of the familiarity in how their names are spoken, the prefixes to their names—Khalleh meaning aunt, Maman meaning mother. But on the few occasions that I ask about them, I am told, 'You don't know them. They were in Iran. They are not there anymore.' I try and fail to draw a family tree, getting caught up in each individual's stories, snippets of lives touched to different degrees by the same kind of trauma. In my mind, our family album is crowded with these bodies, outlines of people whose faces I do not recognise and cannot imagine. Other faces of the dead, like Mona's, swim to the surface, clearer than any family member of mine. For Azoulay, the way to rid oneself of these 'phantom pictures' is through photography which allows for civic negotiations. If we look at photographs, if we see them correctly, we may be able to intervene, to 'reopen the image and renegotiate what it shows, possibly even completely overturning what was seen in it before'.[21] Photographs offer opportunities to renegotiate the civil contract between the spectator and the subject.

In Mehraeen Mavaddat-Mottahedin's memoir, *Flame of Tests: The Story of Farhang Mavaddat*, she details the persecution that her family and many others faced in Iran. She describes the repeated raids and confiscation of Bahá'í homes, and the arrests, torture and execution of loved ones. Her book also includes, among other family photographs, two images of her husband's body after he was executed at Tehran's Evin Prison in 1981. Farhang, Mehraeen's husband, was a chemical engineer and well-known Bahá'í in Karaj, a city close to Tehran. After nine months in prison, he was executed by a firing squad.

Reported in the newspaper, *Ettela'at*, the Revolutionary Court found evidence that he was a 'mofsed-e fel arz' meaning a 'corruptor on earth'. When Mehraeen went to collect his body from the prison, she found that the guards had written the inmates' names on their chests and the crimes they were charged with on their legs. On Farhang's leg, the phrase they had written was simple—'anti-religion'. Blood still coated his body from the bullet wounds in his shoulder. Without specifying her motivation, Mehraeen took photographs. The two that are shared in the book divide his body into two halves. The first photo shows Farhang's torso, layed on a plastic sheet with a blood-stained cloth wrapped around his right arm, his name scrawled across his chest in black. The second shows his legs with his crime written neatly, occupying a small area below his right knee.

The markings on Farhang's body serve as a further warning, beyond his execution, to Bahá'ís and those who sympathise with them. The hypothetical spectator is assumed to be his family and friends, to whom this would cause pain and would further confirm to them that Bahá'í bodies were to be stamped with the disapproval of the State, even in death. But the photographs now

[21] Ibid.

seem to be doing something different. The images become a document of the State's purposeful violence, the bullet wounds in his shoulder confirming Mehraeen's claim that the firing squad aimed for less lethal parts of the body to ensure the most suffering.[22] The viewers of these photographs occupy a space outside of the subject's immediate context, they transcend any one religion or nationality. So the negotiations between the viewer and the photograph take on new meaning. The accusation of the crime seems to be pointing not to the body on which it is written, but to the executioners. Who is anti-religion in this context—Farhang Mavaddat or the men who ordered his death because of his faith?

A third photo, published in an interview with Iranian Press Watch[23] serves as a family photograph of sorts. A group of six people standing around Farhang's body, now washed and shrouded in a white cloth so that only his face is visible. Mehraeen stands in the centre of the group. While the others look away or down at Farhang's body, she stares directly into the camera. Her head is lowered, making her gaze all the more troubling, almost like a Kubrick stare, and her lips are upturned but she is not smiling. She seems to be looking directly at the viewer in the same way that Azoulay describes the gaze of photographed subjects, as though the photograph may offer 'an alternative—weak though it may be—to the institutional structures that have abandoned and injured them'.[24] Her gaze seems to be a challenge, to demand the civil contract of photography that Azoulay mentions in the context of her own viewing of photographs of the Occupied Territories during the second intifada. She writes, 'When the photographed persons address me, claiming their citizenship in photography, they cease to appear as stateless or as enemies, the manners in which the sovereign regime strives to construct them. They call on me to restore their citizenship through my viewing.'[25]

But even as photographs offer ways to resist the regime, the family album is often lost, seized, destroyed, or remains unopened. When the Revolutionary Guards raided Mehraeen's home, she describes how they began seizing and tearing up all of their books, papers and photographs while screaming abuses at her. They tore Bahá'í books as well as scientific journals and legal books that belonged to them, the children's school books, report cards, academic awards and certificates. Their passports, chequebooks, bank documents and a few photo albums were seized to be confiscated as evidence. She describes how she offered to help them, tearing up photos and papers so that they would finish

---

[22] Mavaddat-Mottahedin, Mehraeen. 2017. *Flame of Tests : The Story of Farhang Mavaddat.* (Toronto). p. 158.

[23] Almasi, Nasreen. 2 March 2018. 'Memories of the Bahá'ís of Iran, a Tear-filled Tale: A Conversation with Mehraeen Mavaddat'. Iran Press Watch. iranpresswatch.org/post/18799/memories-of-the-bahais-of-iran-a-tear-filled-tale-a-conversation-with-mehraeen-mavaddat/. Last viewed on 3 April 2021.

[24] Ibid. p. 18.

[25] Ibid. p. 17.

their task quicker and leave. Mehraeen was able to send her children out of Iran before her husband's arrest, but she writes movingly of the loss of those memories. Her memoir includes a photograph of their home after one of the raids. There are so many papers and photos torn and scattered on the ground that it is difficult to see the floor.

In Tehran, about an hour's drive from Mehraeen's home in Karaj, my aunt's sister-in-law, Bahareh Sabet's home was also in disarray. It was December 1980 and her family had twenty hours to pack their things and flee the country. In the months before, her husband was let go from his job heading the criminal forensics department in Tehran, when the state was ridding itself of any Bahá'ís employed in positions of power. They knew they had to escape the country before the situation got worse but there were no flights or visas being issued because of the Iran–Iraq war. A friend at a travel agency told Bahereh there was a flight leaving for Egypt the next day, if they could make it. 'We had twenty hours to leave. Twenty hours to pack our lives. I just kept going through our things, I didn't know what to take. I didn't think of our albums, of our valuable things. Just our passports, documents, diplomas,'[26] she says. She describes the harrowing hours at the airport, hoping the authorities wouldn't withhold their passports or detain them for being Bahá'ís. When I ask her how she decided what to leave or take with them, her eyes fill with tears. 'There were missiles going over the house, food was rationed, we were just living minute by minute, hour by hour. I had two young girls—three and eight years old—and my husband was unwell. I could only think of them and how to get them out of this place. I wasn't thinking about the future. Now I wonder "Why did I bring this? Why did I bring cutlery and not our albums?"'

Bahareh had hoped that she might return home someday, or that her husband's family could send the photos—pictures of her daughters growing up and their childhood, her husband and their friends, their home and community—but it was never safe for either of those hopes to come true. 'My husband's family didn't have the courage to respond to authorities' questions about whose photos they are and why they were sending them. They were scared that they would get into trouble and the photos would be confiscated.'

Over several months, I find myself returning to the faded yellow Kodak box with 'FAMILY' written on the top, holding the slides up to the light, feeling the weight of each image in my hand. Of all the images burnt, lost, destroyed and confiscated, of photographs imagined and blurry, of pictures of the dead smiling back at us, these slides are finally a concrete visual language in which to tell my family history. But even as this collection of memories fills a gap in the personal archive, the outlines of other absences, shadows, and ghosts become clearer.

When I ask about figures in the photographs, the answers as to who they are and what happened to them are hazy and uncertain. My grandmother Ruhi

[26] Sabet, Bahareh. 12 March 2021. Interview. Conducted by Nadia Nooreyezdan.

names people I've never heard before. 'Gol aunty passed away, then Rustom Kaiyani died in a car accident. Gustasp … we don't know. He must be in Iran. Merwhan died recently, his family went to Spain. Mary went to Pakistan but we don't know where she is now. Homanyun and her children went to Austria. They stayed in a refugee camp there and then went to America, but we have no news of them. They just had to leave everything and go, you know? They've all gone away, they've all left.'

These family photographs seem to confirm the extent of loss. But if we 'watch' photographs in the way that Azoulay suggests, they mark not just a past but a continuing presence. 'The verb "to watch" is usually used for regarding phenomena or moving pictures. It entails dimensions of time and movement that need to be reinscribed in the interpretation of the still photographic image.'[27] She goes on to note that,

> in contradiction to the famous statement by Roland Barthes, which sought to capture the essence of photography as testimony to the fact that this something 'was there,' when these photographs are watched, not looked at, when they are read both out of and into the space of the political relations instated by photography, they seem—conversely—to testify to the fact that the photographed people were there. When the assumption is that not only were the photographed people there, but that, in addition, they are still present there at the time I'm watching them, my viewing of these photographs is freed from the risk of becoming immoral.[28]

It seems useful to think of photographs in this way, not just as markers of what 'has been', but as objects both in and out of time. That the people and places still exist inside of the frame, inside of a kind of reality constructed between the image and the viewer, if we just watch them closely enough.

In my grandfather's box of slides, there is one photograph in particular that triggers this feeling of time outside of time or of an alternate timeline itself. It is the picture of my grandparents at the House of the Báb in Shiraz in 1963. One of the most important places for Bahá'í pilgrimage; the site was targeted several times by anti-Bahá'í groups and the Revolutionary Guards. In 1942, parts of the building were damaged in an arson attempt; in 1955, it was vandalised and looted, and finally in the first week of September 1979, the house was razed to the ground. Kurush Tala'i, a Bahá'í engineer, was able to document the demolition as it was happening. In the photographs that he took, the demolition looks haphazard and poorly planned. The revolutionary students of Shiraz University, young boys holding hammers and pickaxes, came to assist around 150 armed men from the local Komiteh (Islamic Revolutionary Committee). It took them ten days to finish the job. A road and public square was built on the land, extending the area in front of the

[27] Ibid. p. 14.

[28] Ibid. p. 16.

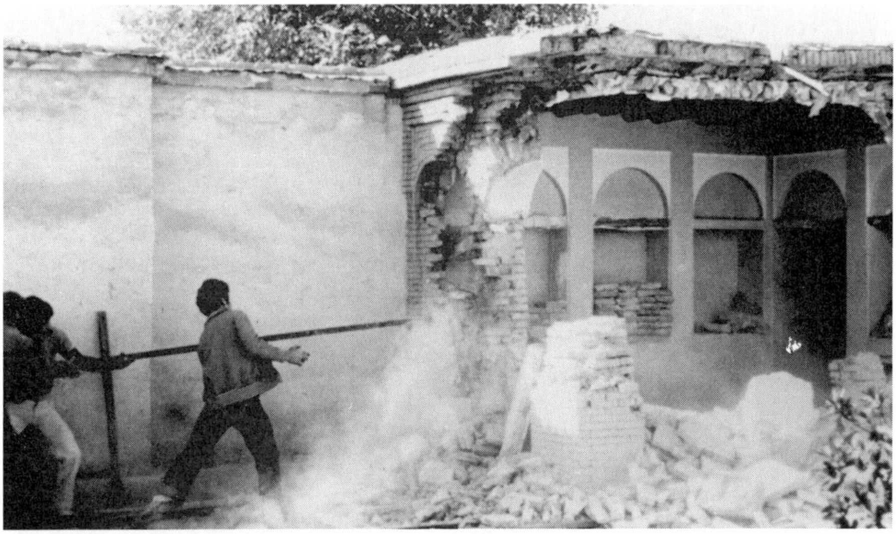

Figure 8: The demolition of the House of the Báb, 1979.
Courtesy of Bahá'í World News Service.

Mahdi Mosque. Three years after they demolished the structure, Tala'i—who had meticulously documented the destruction—was arrested and executed by firing squad.

In one of Tala'i's photographs, you can still make out the arches in the entrance way, as a figure on the left of the frame backs away from the falling rubble. The image seems to move, the bricks tumbling down and the dust rising through the air in the sunlight. Behind the structure that is being torn apart, brick by brick, is the top of the orange tree in the courtyard. It is the same orange tree in my grandfather's picture. When my grandfather identifies his photograph to me, it is as if I am watching this demolition happen in reverse, the bricks moving of their own accord back to slowly rebuild the walls and arched doorways, the courtyard becoming clearer and the shards of the stained glass windows putting themselves back into place. Suddenly, I am watching my grandparents there. I see the roses in the courtyard and my grandfather plucking an orange from the tree. Finding this photograph after the memory of those images of its destruction and holding the two in my mind at the same time feels like they offer different realities, both plausible and both simultaneously real. The building was destroyed in 1979 but it still stands unharmed in this photograph that has been living in our home, amongst my grandfather's possessions, buried in his memories for over fifty years. The discovery of this forgotten archive of family photographs offers an alternative to the erasure of Bahá'ís in Iran, a way to reorient memory itself.

The aim of the state's persecution of Bahá'ís in Iran is to systematically erase them. They do this by striking their names off school and university

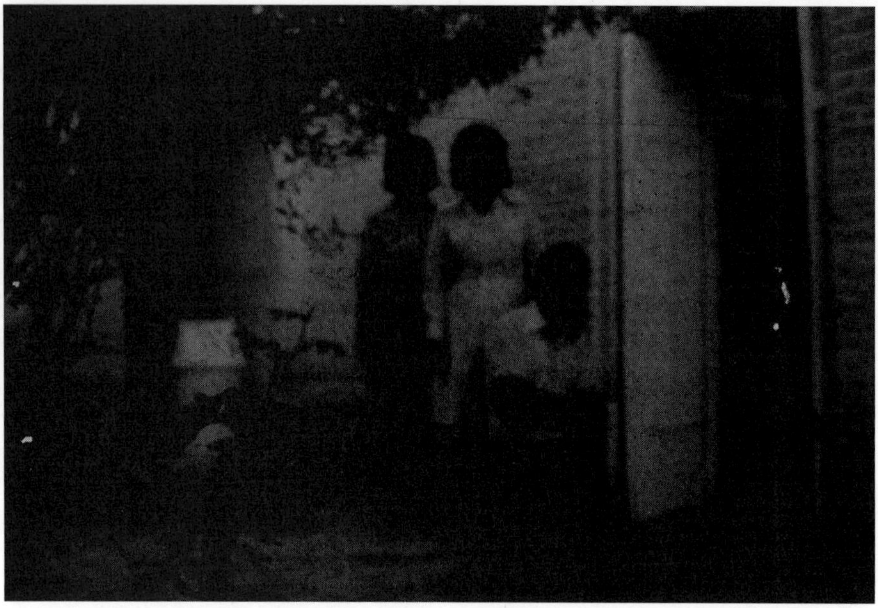

Figure 9: Sheriar, Ruhi, and Monira at the House of the Báb, 1963.
[Author's personal collection]

lists, denying them employment, not recognising their marriages as legitimate, forcing them to halt any community gatherings or activities, destroying Bahá'í books, burning their homes, demolishing holy sites, arresting them, executing them, 'disappearing' their bodies, and desecrating their graves. Those who manage to escape, experience a different kind of erasure, marked by silence and absences. Photographs then function as a tool, a technology against erasure even as it offers up a glimpse of the scale of loss. In a way, my grandfather's photographs offer an alternative visual memory where Bahá'í monuments still stand, houses untouched by fire, and Bahá'ís looking back at the camera. They create a space, not for mourning or nostalgia, but one that is marked by a kind of resistance against erasure.

In 1979, after the Iranian clergy had completed their goal of demolishing the House of the Báb, they cut down the orange tree, sliced the tree trunk in two, and burned both halves. In *A Cry From the Heart*, Sears writes about this tree, and how Bahá'í pilgrims, including himself, used to sit together in the shaded garden with the caretaker and his wife, drinking tea and eating oranges from that tree. He writes,

> I can't help but wonder at the foolishness of such enemies. Don't they know that they really haven't cut down that orange tree at all? Pilgrims from everywhere have taken home oranges and planted seeds from that tree. Don't the authorities in Iran know that tomorrow, if access to Iran were permitted, Bahá'ís could fly in from all over the world, and plant a whole row of orange trees all round the

> city of Shiraz? From the trees grown from the seeds of the tree they thought they had cut down.[29]

Outside our home in Bombay, the proof of this stands—a physical representation of both the personal and collective archive—an orange tree grown from the fruit my grandfather brought back with him in 1963.

Further Reading

news.bahai.org/legal/

[29] Sears. 1982. *A Cry from the Heart*. p. 78.

Between Silences and Erasures

In Absence of the Family Archive

Shilpi Goswami

'My city is like a long debate.
Its roads like pointless arguments lead to blind alleys
its contentious streets thrust aggressively,
in myriad directions

Every house is like a clenched fist,
with its walls gritting their teeth,
as its epileptic drains froth at their mouths.'

—Amrita Pritam[1]

While thinking about one's family's photographic archives, we are presented with memories of innumerable images of family gatherings such as weddings, festivals, birthdays, picnics, outings, etc. In Martha Langford's[2] words, they represent a kind of 'oral consciousness' embedded within the personal and social processes of commemoration. Analogue family photographs carry impressions of time—unintended and accidental. More than just triggers for personal memory, these absences stand as a testimony to the political reworking of classed notions of identity. Family photographs come into public circulation and display, raising the question of how memory endures within this process. Retaining photographic materiality, along with original meanings previously associated with these images, has been presented as one way of defending against loss. But how does one respond to the absence of this imagery and the materiality involved? What happens when there are significant gaps in the visual and tactile photographic archive of a family? A certain anxiety around the loss of meaning develops around the process of appropriation, in cases of archives that are absent. In this essay, I attempt to explore the absent family album/photographs that create a site of struggle.

This essay looks at photographs from two families archives: that of Mr. Birendra Kumar Bhattacharjee (1920–1999), my maternal grandfather, and Mr. Hiranmoy Goswami (1921–1991), my paternal grandfather.

[1] Pritam, Amrita. 2009. *Punjabi Poems of Amrita Pritam*. Khushwant Singh. trans. (New Delhi: Star Publications).

[2] Langford, Martha. 2001. *Suspended Conversations: The Afterlife of Memory in Photographic Albums* (Quebec: McGill-Queen's University Press).

Mr. Bhattacharjee's first family photographs date back to September 1947, travelling through the gullies of Bazar Sitaram and the middle-class government colonies of first Timarpur, and then Kidwai Nagar, before finally stationing in Chittaranjan Park, New Delhi. On the other hand, Mr. H. Goswami's absent family pictures before and after the Partition until 1991, culminate with his death in Benaras, coinciding with the rise of the communal tension in Benaras and other parts of Uttar Pradesh, which eventually led to the demolition of the Babri Masjid. The curfew in a riot-stricken city also led to a complete loss of any and all materiality. Through the family photos of Bhattacharjee and Goswami, I have intended to make inquiries into the formation of the Bengali middle-class in Delhi from the 1950s onwards, arising from displacement and ending in an engulfed diaspora. There has been an intentional inquiry into the realisation of a new national identity within this Bengali community formed in Delhi of the 1950s–60s, added by a later influx of another batch of immigrants in the 1970s, in the wake of the formation of Bangladesh in 1971. I have attempted to look into the microhistories of Delhi's Bengali institutions such as schools, *mandirs* and Durga Puja associations, which are a testament to the establishment and geographical movements of the community in Delhi. I have intentionally spelled out names and other necessary proper nouns as an ode to the first generation of the Bengali middle class in Delhi, who were forced to call a foreign land their home and in spite of the building blocks of their community, whose names would otherwise be lost in time and history.

There has been a conscious intent towards tracing the earliest settlements of the Bengali population in areas including Bazar Sitaram, Karol Bagh, Pahargunj, Mukherjee Nagar and Timarpur in North Delhi, and eventually, Chittaranjan Park in South Delhi. Looking into the microhistories of these institutions established by the earliest Bengali immigrants in Delhi in search of a cultural citizenship; the formation of the Bengali middle class in the new capital[3] of the country has helped place my own family in a larger context of the Bengali community in Delhi.

Another aim of this essay is to draw a relationship between photography, tactility and memory. It also explores the 'fabric of memory' of two middle-class Bengali gentlemen rendering different cultural and geopolitical relationships

[3] During the Delhi Durbar on 12 December 1911, King George V, then Emperor of India, made the announcement that the capital of India would shift from Calcutta to Delhi. The foundation stone of New Delhi was laid by King George V and Queen Mary at the site of the Delhi Durbar, called the Coronation Park, Kingsway Camp, on 15 December 1911. The decision was taken during the tenure of Lord Harding, the Viceroy of India. It was popularly said that this was because Calcutta was located in the extreme east of India, and the capital of India needed to be centralised in terms of geography for better management. However, there were a couple of other factors, such as the fact that Bengal was gradually slipping out of British control and rigorous and extremist movements were giving the administration sleepless nights. They aspired to control as much of the Central Asian region as possible, spreading all the way up to the Middle East.

with the past. With this essay, I have attempted to trace the photographs and the 'absent' photographs—with their multidimensional meanings. There is an organic inclusion of the tenets of 'found photography', where the image provenance is usually unknown. Here, however, despite of the provenance being known, the struggle is to navigate the cultural appropriation of memory and the sociopolitcal events that prompted the associated environment of loss in recognising the complexities of the photograph. This paper is largely based on the oral history of my family, and after much deliberation, I decided to write in first person to ease my conflict with agency.

The Premise

When the sun finally set on the British Empire in this part of the world, it gave rise to 'two sovereign nation states'—Pakistan and India (Sarkar: 2009). What followed was a 'bloody and protracted affair'; an abridged version of this geographical, communal and political divide is referred to as the Partition of India that happened in August 1947. The Radcliffe Line[4] butchered millions of people in North India. The death toll reported on the eastern part of the divided land varied, depending on the agency that was reporting it—ranging from a few hundreds to a few thousands—the actual figure being as obnoxious as that reported in North India. A loss of millions of people was reduced to politically downplayed statistics. More than 10–12 million (*The New Yorker* quotes 15 million)[5] were forcefully displaced, terrorised by murderous riots that broke out all over the region.

> Across the Indian subcontinent, communities that had coexisted for almost a millennium attacked each other in a terrifying outbreak of sectarian violence, with Hindus and Sikhs on one side and Muslims on the other—a mutual genocide as unexpected as it was unprecedented. In Punjab and Bengal—provinces abutting India's borders with West and East Pakistan, respectively—the carnage was especially intense, with massacres, arson, forced conversions, mass abductions, and savage sexual violence. Some seventy-five thousand women were raped, and many of them were then disfigured or dismembered.[6]

As Bhaskar Sarkar so eloquently puts it, 'That India's Independence from colonial occupation in 1947 constitutes a watershed in the annals of global decolonisation is well established, what remained far less acknowledged for

---

[4] The Radcliffe Line was the border demarcated between India and Pakistan (East—which eventually became the separate nation of Bangladesh—and West), drawn by Sir Cyril Radcliffe, the joint chairman of the boundary commissions for the two provinces, comprising of approximately 4,50,000 km^2 with roughly 88 million residents. The whole process was shrouded in secrecy and haste.

[5] Dalrymple, William. 22 June 2015. 'The Great Divide: The Violent Legacy of Indian Partition'. *The New Yorker*. www.newyorker.com/magazine/2015/06/29/the-great-divide-books-dalrymple. Last viewed on 28 September 2023.

[6] Ibid.

decades was the salience of that historic conjuncture as a catastrophe with haunting repercussion for community life in South Asia.'[7] My birth, whether one sees it as a familial lineage or as a citizen of a country, is a direct result of this 'repercussion' in a community and in a country that cradled itself from a communal genesis.

> With the nationhood emerging as the modern form of collective political organisation, the leaders of a nascent nationalism in the subcontinent had worked to splice together a secular national identity that could withstand the centrifugal challenges of a polity marked by dizzying differences of race, class, creed, caste, language and regional lifestyles. The slogan 'unity in diversity' encapsulated the hope for a national *imaginaire* that would transcend all difference. The realisation of the invidious two-nation theory in 1947—one country for Hindus, one for Muslims—rendered a crushing blow to this hope undermining the belief that a united India could exist in the face of confounding diversity. The rancour and violence raised serious questions regarding the very possibility of continuing community life in South Asia. In spite of the widespread disavowal of 1947 and its reduction to a historical anomaly, Partition emerged as a national trauma—an experience whose memory cast its long, disquieting shadow on public consciousness, tinging subsequent national endeavours with an unspeakable sadness.[8]

The practical charge of the previous paragraph for me, an archivist, lies in the fact that for a manufactured disaster of this scale, causing the displacement of a couple of million people, although being deliberated on academically, has led to no comprehensive visual studies projects. The result being an unsurmountable number of individual histories being lost. It is only in the past decade or so that organisations like The Partition Archives and the Partition Museums have drawn focus towards this historical event and are doing commendable work towards its remembrance. But they are relatively new organisations with obvious limitations.

Material culture mediates our relationship with the past and for lack of a better word, roots. 'Objects, images and practices, as well as places and spaces, call to mind or are made to remind us'[9] of the sense of our belonging and its continuity. Whether in the form of personal mementos or public memorials, material objects and embodied social practices associated with the material culture can be viewed from a variety of perspectives, which might be personal, social or political. They highlight myriad social values and cultural meanings that are attributed to our social existence. The current memorialisation of the "Partition" draws attention to the Wagah/Atari military performance. What

---

[7] Sarkar, Bhaskar. 2009. *Mourning the Nation: Indian Cinema in the wake of Partition* (Durham: Duke University Press). p. 1.

[8] Ibid. p. 2.

[9] Hallam, Elizabeth and Jenny Hockey. 2001. *Death, Memory and Material Culture* (Oxford and New York: Berg). p. 2.

gets lost in that political imagery is that the geographical division stretched over thousands of kilometres on the western as well as the eastern part of our country. The eastern belt being much more dense, as Bangladesh (erstwhile East Pakistan/ East Bengal) shares its borders with a majority of the northeastern states of India. The lives of all the people living near these borderlands as well as the ones who crossed them, essentially dissassociated from everything tangible and intangible. What remained with them or what they acquired were primarily survival kits, of sorts.

'The archiving process and the decisions taken in it thus fundamentally determine Memory—and this is not only the case with personal memory but also with archival memory.'[10] My personal journey, that is the academic attempt that I have made to examine my own family's photographic 'archives', has been nothing less than ironic. I have worked as the photo archivist for one of the biggest photographic archives of late nineteenth- to early twentieth-century photographs of South Asia.[11] I was surrounded by photographic images all day, looking at the cultural histories of photographic practices in South Asia and the world, deliberating on the role of photography in changing the systems of the world, information distribution, the altering negotiations of new media, questionable publicity and the proliferation of the global systems of misinformation.[12] My work encompassed intense research on the people present in the pictures, and on the ones who were not present as well—the photographers, studios, photo agencies, printing presses, camera and film manufacturers, and eventually the cultural theorists and photo and visual culture historians. The basis of my work was the materiality and the tactility of the photographs, and not just the visual imagery.

As I delved deeper into my own family archives, especially my grandparent's generation leading up to my parents' childhoods, the sheer absences brought out the silences and conscious and subconscious erasures. The sense of loss—rather, the permanence of this loss—is unfathomable.

Reflecting on my family photographs and albums—whatever is left of them—I find myself in the middle of layers of mental struggle, not as much owing to the photographs which are present, but the ones that are absent. Unfortunately, almost all photographs have been lost with passage of time. The lack of willingness to keep these safe indicates a deeper tragedy that partitioned families went through. 'The familiarity of photographs builds our sense of the present and immediate past. Photographs lay down routes of reference, and serve as totems of causes: sentiment is more likely to crystallise around a photograph than around a verbal slogan. And photographs help—and revise—our sense of a more distant past, with posthumous shocks engineered

---

[10] Helff, Sissy and Stephanie Michels. eds. 2018. *Global Photographies: Memories, History, Archives* (Austria: Transcript Verlag). p. 12.

[11] I worked at the Alkazi Foundation for the Arts as their photo archivist between 2011–2016.

[12] Berger, John. 2013 [1967]. *Understanding a Photograph* (London: Penguin Books).

by the circulation of hitherto unknown photographs.'[13] Furthermore, 'within photography theory and practice, the family album has represented a site of struggle for meaning.'[14] Photographs in general, as everyone now recognises, form a part of 'memories'. Although Sontag refers to these 'memories' as fiction, she critiques, 'strictly speaking, there is no such thing as collective memory—part of the same family of spurious notions as collective guilt. But there is a collective instruction.'[15] The cultural politics revolving around memory and memorialisation is well understood. Nonetheless, one cannot argue that they do constitute the visual consciousness of society at large. The materiality and the tactility that comes with photographs and all sorts of photographic material such as albums and the camera itself, aids this consciousness. But the question is—how does one navigate in absence of this tactility?

Tracing the Earliest Bengali Diaspora in North India: A Brief

If popular narratives can be believed, the first wave of Bengali settlers came between the late eighteenth and early nineteenth centuries. Although, the earliest records of Bengalis visiting North India can be found 'in a number of Bengali *bhadralok* travelogues.'[16] Sandeep Banerjee and Subho Basu, in their paper titled, 'The City as Nation: Delhi as the Indian Nation in Bengali *bhadralok* travelogues 1866-1910' write,

> by discussing Bholanath Chunder's *The Travels of a Hindoo to Various Parts of Bengal and Upper India* (1869; hereafter, *Travels*), one of the first Indian travelogues written in English. Subsequently, it engages with Durgacharan Ray's Debganer Martye Agaman (*The Gods Visit Earth*; hereafter, *Gods*) (1880), a farcical documentation of the travels of Hindu Gods across India. The chapter concludes by discussing Nabin Chandra Sen's Prabasher Patra (*Letters from Distant Lands*; hereafter, *Letters*) (1892) and Dharanikanta Lahiri Chaudhuri's Bharat Bhraman (*Travels across India*; hereafter, *India*) (1910).[17]

These published accounts date between 1869-1910 which indicate the travels made before the dates of the publications by the authors since they are travelogues.

According to the city historian, R.V. Smith, a few Bengali families migrated to Agra and Mathura during the Revolt of 1857. Quoting his own father, Thomas Smith's article in *The Statesman* of 25 July 1987, titled, 'And Agra Gharana—The Bagchis', he writes,

[13] Sontag, Susan. 2003. *Regarding the Pain of Others* (New York: Picador). p. 85.

[14] Cross, Karen. 2015. 'The Lost of Found Photography'. *Photographies* (Taylor and Francis). pp. 43–62

[15] Ibid. p. 85.

[16] Banerjee, Sandeep and Subho Basu. 'The City as Nation: Delhi as the Indian Nation in Bengali *bhadralok* travelogues 1866-1910'. *Cities in South Asia.* London: Routledge, 2015. p. 126.

[17] Ibid.

> Agra has been the home of several Bengali families of note, among whom are the Bagchis. The family traces its ancestry to Rameshwar Bagchi (1789-1863). He was a descendant of Rambhadra Bagchi, who settled down at Jamshedpur, in Nadia district, about 1650 A.D. Later the area came to be known as Bagchi-Jamsherpur. The first of the family to come to Agra was Dr R.P. Bagchi, MD, a physician, who stood first in the MB (now MBBS) examination of Calcutta University in 1885. He was the only candidate who was successful at the MD examination of the university in 1888 and the third student in its history to obtain this degree.

He further quotes,

> Dr R.P. Bagchi, who was nine years old when Ghalib died in 1869, settled down at Agra in 1890, becoming a lecturer in medicine at what then was the Agra Medical School for Licentiates ... He died in July 1931, at the age of 71, leaving behind three sons—Hari Prasad, Kali Prasad and Ajit Prasad, and two daughters, Nirmala and Kamala. The eldest son was a reputed lawyer, who went on to become Professor of Law at Agra College, being closely connected with the Nagri Pracharini Sabha and the Agra Bengali Library. He died in Delhi after a stroke in February 1981, on his 93rd birthday.
>
> Then there was the historian and writer Prof. Nirad C. Chaudhuri, whose photographer-author son, Dhruva, a photographer by profession, lived in Faridabad before he passed a couple of years back. Dr. H.K. Sen and Shyamaldas Seth of Roshanara Gardens were the two with whom Swami Vivekananda stayed when he visited Delhi at the fag end of the 19th century. There were others of note and fame too, among them Swami Gokulananda of the Ramakrishna Mission in Paharganj, the founders of the Bengali Club at Kashmere Gate in 1925 (whose indefatigable past president was S.P. Mitra) and the organizers of the first Durga Pujas in Delhi in the opening decades of the last century. More recently, Neepesh Talukdar and his sister Deepali Nag were among the notables that include Nandan Dasgupta, publisher of the quarterly *Hindol* magazine and the late Shankar's *Weekly*-cum-*Statesman* artist, Reboti Bhushan Ghosh.[18]

One can agree that there were a few Bengalis here and there, but the actual turn of events was marked by the prolific expansion of the East Indian Railway Company (EIR). The Yamuna bridge near Delhi was completed in 1864 and EIR established the Delhi terminus. On 1 August 1864, coaches were ferried across the Yamuna in Allahabad to allow the first through train to travel from Kolkata to Delhi. During 1863–64, work progressed rapidly on the Allahabad (now Prayagraj)–Kanpur–Tundla and Aligarh–Ghaziabad sections. Once the Yamuna bridge in Allahabad opened on 15 August 1865, Kolkata and Delhi were directly linked, in 1866. It will be safe to assume that the big wave of

[18] Smith, R.V. 26 July 2018. 'The Bengali Diaspora in North India'. *The Statesman*. www.thestatesman.com/supplements/section/bengali-diaspora-north-india-1502665386.html. Last viewed on 28 September 2023.

Bengalis began settling in Delhi when Calcutta (the then capital of British India) and Delhi were connected by train.[19]

Family's Oral Narratives: The People and Broken Homes[20]

My grandparents on both sides—maternal and paternal—were amongst those millions who lost it all. But unlike the ones who had to cross the borders and left their homes amidst the rampant bloodbath and commmunal riots, they were stranded in what would unknowingly become their domicile, that is Delhi. Growing up amidst families from similar backgrounds, my grandparents' friends and acquaintances remembered or narrated their past lives—that is, their childhood or ancestral villages and related stories. Of course, they would be filled with nostalgia and a sense of tremendous loss. But I seldom heard anything at all from my own grandparents. Not that they were trying to hide anything or that there was anything secretive about their lives; it's just that nothing was ever discussed on its own. If anyone of us (I mean my cousins) asked any questions, we got an answer. But it was always to the point. There was no conversation regarding the past lives of our elders or our ancestors. None of them—our parents' generation (who were born in the newly independent country) or our grandparents (who migrated just to stay alive)—ever discussed things amongst themselves. Even as a child, I found this strange because all my uncles and aunts were good conversationalists with a great sense of humour and sharp wit. Unknowingly, we had adopted this silence as the norm. It was only when I was coaxed by my co-editor to write about my own family, that I first began asking and talking to my immediate and larger family. It was a very strange mix of narratives that I gathered. Not a single bit of information that I gathered was linear. And that is when the impact of generational silence hit me. I shall try and put it all down as comprehensively as possible.

Let me begin with my maternal grandfather, Mr. Birendra Kumar Bhattacharjee, who was in North India since 1938–39. He was born in Barisal, Undivided Bengal/India in 1920. The fourth of eight children, he lost both his parents by the time he was sixteen years of age. He ran away from his house and joined the British Army. The British did not take kindly to nationalists and freedom fighters. One day, he was made to participate in a firing squad and many amongst the people he was supposed to shoot at were his childhood friends. Fortunately, his turn to fire the gun did not come, as he would not have been able to shoot anyway and would have landed himself in the line of people to be killed for not following a military command. This is one of the very few incidents that he had told me, himself.

[19] This particular paragraph has emerged out of the research the author did from various sources about the connectivity between Calcutta and Delhi. Histories of Railways, waterways through the rivers Ganges and Yamuna and the Grand Trunk Road were looked into.

[20] This entire section is not only based on the oral history of the author's family but also her own memories from her childhood till date.

That very night, he ran away from the British Army and went straight to the camp where they were recruiting for the Indian National Army (INA). He had once very proudly mentioned that he took direct orders from 'Netaji' himself. According to one of my uncles, he was an intelligence officer in the INA, but there is no way to verify this. He followed Subhash Chandra Bose to Gujarat when he was the still with the Indian National Congress (INC), and left with him when Bose resigned from the INC. This, I believe, is true as he had once told me that Gandhiji himself had taught him how to operate the *charkha*. The said *charkha* remains in my possession now. After the INA disintegrated, my grandfather likely went to Meerut for work, from where he would visit his distant relatives in Bazar Sitaram. One of these relatives, incidentally, was the historian Prof. Neeladri Bhattacharya's father.

Bazar Sitaram in Chandni Chowk is where my grandmother, Mrs. Meera Bhattacharjee, resided with her parents and brothers. Her family had also migrated from Faridpur, Undivided Bengal/India, when she was two years of age. She came from a family of Bengali priests. Her maternal uncles were already in Delhi and assured them that they would help her father establish himself in Delhi. They were amongst the founding members of the New Delhi Kali Bari, Mandir Marg, which is also the office of the Joint Puja Committee (JPC), the nodal office that issues permissions for any Durga Puja celebrations in Delhi.

My grandparents were married on 2 September 1947. My grandmother (who also happens to be my last living grandparent) recalls how they got permission for only two hours to complete the marriage ceremony amidst the curfew, imposed due to widespread communal riots that had engulfed the entire city. She shares, 'A new bride took her first steps outside the house into an alley filled with dead bodies and screaming chants of "Allah-hu-Akbar" and "Har Har Mahadev" all around. The city had gone mad.' My grandfather eventually joined the Department of Customs and Excise, Central Revenue Building, Income Tax Office (ITO). They lived in Timarpur briefly before moving to the newly made Kidwai Nagar (East), earlier known as North of Medical Enclave. They stayed in government accommodation there till his retirement, after which they moved to Chittaranjan Park.

When I tried to find out about my grandfather's ancestors, the oral history got very complicated. I was able to establish that his ancestors were founding members of the Brojomohun College (B.M. College) in Barisal (this college still stands in Bangladesh), and taught Sanskrit and Bengali. Unfortunately, I was unable to establish whether they were his uncles or grandfathers. What was funnier was when I tried to find out about his father, that is my great-grandfather, I got different versions of his professions from various cousins of my mother. Some believed he was a professor, some said he worked as a *dewan* in some raja's estate, some said he was in a clerical job. The more glamorous the people's own professions, the fancier his supposed profession became. My mother and a majority of them were of the opinion that he was a teacher in Ranchi. Although none of them could say anything about any other ancestors.

The history of my paternal side becomes even more complicated. Unfortunately, my father is the only living member in his immediate family. My paternal grandfather Mr. Hironmoy Goswami was born in Noapara, Faridpur, Undivided Bengal/India. Incidentally, even he lost his father at a very young age. After his mother became a widow, his extremely wealthy maternal grandfather brought his beloved daughter and her two sons to live with him on his Benaras estate. My father's elder uncle, who was a couple of years older than my grandfather, used to manage their own ancestral estate in Bengal till his younger brother came of age and could help him. My paternal grandfather, too (like my maternal grandfather), ran away from home and joined the British Army. He remained in the British Army and served in the Second World War. According to my father's assessment, based on some childhood recollections, he was posted around the Mediterranean, and then in the Gulf. After the war ended, he came back to a riot-stricken, physically divided country.

My grandmother, Mrs. Hena Goswami, was already in Benaras. Her family hailed from Rajshahi, Undivided Bengal/India. Her father was earlier the dewan of the Nator royal family and then the Tahirpur royal family. After he retired, he settled in Benaras with his family. It was quite a common practice amongst financially comfortable Bengali Brahmin families to settle in Kashi after their worldly responsibilities were fulfilled. Most of the families had smaller, ancestral estates in Benaras as well. My grandmother was the fourth of five children. My grandparents married somewhere around 1948–49. My grandfather came to Delhi in search of work as he refused to go join the Indian Army, and instead joined The Welfare Board. Once he got his government accommodation in Kidwai Nagar as well, he brought his family from Benaras. So my parents knew each other since childhood, growing up in the same colony/neighbourhood.

As a school-going child, I used to often find myself out of place as most of my classmates would talk about their daily experience at their paternal grandparent's houses. And here I was, someone who spent most of her childhood with her maternal side of the family. I saw my paternal grandmother and knew where she stayed, but we did not spend much time together. Not as much as I spent with my Nani. I knew I had a grandfather and that he stayed in Benaras, but I never met him.

My paternal grandparents had separated when my father was thirteen years old. Nothing was spoken about any family member of my father's—immediate or extended. Again, it was not something anyone was trying to keep under wraps, but as a child, I had realised that I might hurt my father if I ever asked him about it. My mother was anyway a woman of very few words, extremely measured when it came to conversations. The first time I dared to ask any questions about it all, was after a telegram came from Benaras in 1991, informing us of my grandfather's demise. It did not mean anything to me as I had never met him. So the ten-year-old me was not able to grasp as to why was there such a commotion at home. There was great communal violence that had engulfed the city and curfew had been imposed, with no trains or buses plying. I had never seen my father in such a frenzy, going to the train station every single day and trying to figure out how he could reach Benaras; if it was possible to get there by changing buses.

Another strange thing that happened was that my grandmother came home crying and stayed with us for a couple of days. Prior to this, she would visit us only on my birthday and on one or two other occasions, but just for a few hours. My Nani is and always was the quintessential Bengali grandmother, who woke up before everyone and cooked for her huge family for most of her life. It is unbelievable for us today to think about how much housework she did all by herself all her life. Contrary to this, my paternal grandmother was well educated, well-spoken and outgoing. She was always well-dressed, wore make-up and carried herself with style. I feel the need to state here that this is not an attempt to draw any rosy pictures or a comparison of any kind between the two ladies.

The first step towards finding out about my ancestors was to look towards my immediate elders—my parents' and my grandparents' generation. And there itself, all consistency and continuity was lost. Generational silence and conscious evasion from engaging with any person or situation in our family's past had erased concrete evidence about who we were. It had never occurred to me earlier why, at a personal level, I did not feel emotionally connected to a place or have any sense of belonging to the particular geographical demarcation to which I apparently 'belonged'. I had never understood why, for me, home was and still is just people. In a nutshell, I could never understand why it never bothered any of my cousins or me that we could not think of ourselves as belonging to the 'Bengali community'. This exercise forced me to think things through and made me realise that we all understood without ever having to discuss it that the two generations before us were just trying to survive each day, so subconsciously, we never felt the need to inquire much about their past.

Negotiating a Cultural Citizenship: Making of the Bengali Middle Class in Delhi

The Geographical Spread

'Spaces are real precisely because they are imagined.'[21] One of the major outcomes of the Partition was 'multifold asymmetry'. It broke the structure of Bengali society with quickly changing social realities and apparent nationalities. The permanent outcome of the Partition was the total disintegration of the cultural trope of societies and our nation. 'Cultural ... flow is the means through

[21] Radhakrishnan, Rajagopalan. 2003. *Theory in an Uneven World* (Malden: Blackwell). p. 27.

which [exclusion] can be understood and—on a more interventionist level',[22] if the nation is an imagined community created through discourse,[23] then an affiliation to the nation state, feeling like a part of the nation, can arise only when this mediated nation discourse is democratic, accessible and susceptible to change.[24] Furthermore, as Lion König explains, 'Cultural citizenship emerges out of the interplay of state, society, culture…' geographically, politically and socially.

It is a popular belief in Delhi that any Bengali roaming the earth here resides in Chittaranjan Park. A whole lot of them do, but the narrative is not as linear as it appears to be—that as part of the rehabilitation process, the small Bengali community (as compared to the large number of people who came from Punjab) was given land and that is what has become Chittaranjan Park now. A big wave of Bengalis came to Delhi when Calcutta and Delhi were first connected by train in 1864; thereafter, with the change of capital to New Delhi in 1911, the shifting of government employees followed logically—all of whom were Bengalis. The next big waves settled in 1947 and 1971 respectively.

The earliest Bengali settlements were in the Chandni Chowk area, a substantial one in Bazar Sitaram, to where both my maternal grandparents can trace back an association. Other major ones were in Paharganj and Karol Bagh. New Delhi did not exist then and Delhi was within the walls of Shahjahanabad, as we understand it today. Apart from a few Bengali businessmen and their workers, there was not a huge population of Bengalis here. The major migration happened with the transfer of the capital from Calcutta to Delhi in 1911. After King George V laid down the foundation stone of New Delhi, for the present Central Secretariat area to be built, government offices began shifting to the newly declared capital. The earliest offices were central government offices, like the Accountant General of Central Revenues (AGCR), Post and Telegraph, Government of India Press and Railways. They had set up their offices in Timarpur. Thereafter in 1924, new government housing came up near Raja Bazar, known as Gole Market today, for employees of the Secretariat. Over time, many employees settled in Karol Bagh and Paharganj after retirement, and much later, in South Delhi.

Chittaranjan Park

Both my grandfathers managed to get a residential plot in this newborn EPDP Colony. As I mentioned earlier, the general notion of the Bengalis in Delhi is that most of them reside in Chittaranjan Park, and it was a refugee colony where a handful of Bengalis were granted land on a 99-year lease by

[22] König, Lion. 2016. *Cultural Citizenship in India: Politics, Power and Media* (New Delhi: Oxford University Press). p. 2.

[23] Anderson, Benedict. *Imagined Communities: Reflections on the Origin and Spread of Nationalism.* United Kingdom: Verso. 2016 [1983].

[24] Ibid.

the Government of India, so they came and settled here. The reality is far from this. A large group of government 'officers', hailing from East Bengal, who had migrated to Delhi as part of the central government offices, lobbied for a residential neighbourhood. In 1954, an association was formed for the inhabitants who were displaced from their homes in East Pakistan during the Partition. In the 1960s, land was assigned in a barren rocky area in the then-distant southern parts of the city, and the colony was named the East Pakistan Displaced Persons (EPDP) Colony. Curiously enough, sometime in the last few years, they have changed the name of the association to East Bengal Displaced Persons! Members were required to provide some documentation as proof of their residential status, and were required to be 'already residing in Delhi and gainfully employed in the capital'; based on this, 2,147 people were given plots of land, initially on lease for 99 years, but subsequently converted into freehold ownership. Many people who could not afford to build a house on their plot of land, got the Delhi Development Authority (DDA) to build houses for them, and they gradually paid off the cost of construction in yearly installments. The original layout had 2,000-odd plots, divided into eleven blocks from A–K, along with a number of markets and cultural spaces.

What doesn't get mentioned normally are a couple of key points which are as follows. The land allocation was for an extremely small population of well-placed officers in the central government. When it did open up for others, not everyone could afford to buy it even at the subsidised rate the government would have given. Even after getting the plot and making a two-room house, many people could not sustain living there. We saw many people selling off their properties and moving away. That is how neighbourhoods of Mahavir Enclave, Palam Village, Vasundhara, Vaishali, Rohini and eventually, Dakshinayan in Dwarka, came up. After 1971, when Bangladesh became an independent country, CR Park acquired new blocks, called M, N, O, P, K-1, K-2, Pocket 40 (referred to as Navapalli), Pocket 52 (referred to as Dakhinpalli) and Pocket K. The main thoroughfare of the colony is Bipin Chandra Pal Marg.

Claiming Culture

There are three pillars on which a Bengali society of *bhadraloks* base their cultural growth—the Bengali school, *barowari*[25] Durga Puja, and Kali Mandir (or a temple of Goddess Kali). The pun is intended ofcourse. For a middle-class Bengali society, the need for a Kali/Durga *Bari* and a *barowari* Durga Puja is a marker of a substantial number of the population attempting a 'territorialisation of history', that is, 'it contends that the Bengali middle class

---

[25] *Barowari* refers to the public organisation of a religious entity. *Barowari* has significance associated with the durga puja festival of the Bengalis, in which the hindu goddess *durga* is worshipped; symbolising the victory of good over evil by the wole community.

constructed a dialectical pairing of the spaces of'[26] Bengal and Delhi. These two institutions, that is, a Kali/Durga Bari and a Durga Puja function are a community catalyst in Bengali society, wherein people interact with each other on a daily basis, contributing to a middle-class cultural ethos.

The first Kali Bari in Delhi is believed to have been established in 1826. But the temple was apparently destroyed during the plunder of 1857. The idol was salvaged and a temple was built in Roshan Pura. As the Bengali population grew, space started to fall short to accommodate the devotees. So a piece of land was bought and a new temple was built in 1917. This temple still stands in Tis Hazari.[27]

It is believed that the first private Durga Puja in Delhi was celebrated in 1842, by one Mr. Majumdar, who came from Rajshahi (presently in Bangladesh), followed by a few more *pujas* that continued for the next few years. The first *barowari* Durga Puja, is that of Kashmere Gate. This started in 1910, and still continues to be celebrated every year.

History of the Kali Baris

New Delhi Kali Bari

The original temple of the New Delhi Kali Bari was situated on Baird Road (today's Bangla Sahib Road) since 1930, where the local Bengali community also gathered for the annual Durga Puja. After the temple came up in 1931, the community shifted here. According to their website, 'After several years of demands by the burgeoning expatriate Bengali population, one acre of land was allotted on the new Mandir Marg (temple road), next to the Laxminarayan Temple (popularly known as Birla Mandir). The small, and if I may say so, unpretentious temple of Goddess Kali came up shortly. The *pratima* (idol) was made with its appearance and aesthetic resembling the one at the Kalighat Kali Temple in Calcutta….The mandir committee was formalised in 1935 with Subhash Chandra Bose as the first president and the first mandir building was inaugurated by Sir Justice Mamatha Nath Mukherjee.'[28] The Durga Puja celebrated at the Kalibari is one of the oldest Durga Pujas in the city, which started in 1925. Till today, it continues to be the nodal point for the hundreds of puja committees in Delhi, and is widely revered among Delhi Bengalis. The only older pujas in Delhi are Kashmere Gate (organised by the Delhi Durga Puja Samiti, which started in 1910), the Timarpur Puja (organised by the Timarpur and Civil Lines Puja Samiti, established in 1914) and the Karol Bagh Baniya Samsad. The tradition of community Durga Pujas in the capital gathered momentum only after 1911. The employees of the Government of

[26] Banerjee, Sandeep and Subho Basu. 2015. 'The City as Nation: Delhi as the Indian nation in Bengali *bhadralok* travelogues 1866-1910'. *Cities in South Asia.* London: Routledge, 2015. p.126

[27] Corroborated from family oral history.

[28] As gathered from personal conversation with the mandir office and family oral history.

India Press, which had shifted from Kolkata to New Delhi, were behind the Minto Road Durga Puja. It is also the office of the Joint Puja Committee (JPC)—the nodal office which grants permission to hold a Durga Puja and the arrangements are made by them. Amongst the founding members of this temple were my maternal grandmother's uncles and her father, Shri. Taraprasanna Shiromani.

Once the Central Secretariat area was functional and government housing came up in Sarojini Nagar, Naoroji Nagar (collectively known as Vinay Nagar, earlier), Ramakrishna Puram (R.K. Puram), Laxmibai Nagar etc. came up too, as did the need for more temples!

Dakshina Dilli Kali Bari

The idea of setting up a Kali Bari was conceived in 1967 at an informal meeting of some members of the Phalguni Sangha Club of Sector 7, R.K. Puram. The club organised a Durga Puja the same year, on an open ground. The puja went off well, but there was little surplus fund to initiate the building of a Kalibari. The members were undaunted and the search for a site continued. One winter morning, one of the pioneers came to the ground at the foot of Swami Malai hillock and felt that the undulating land—a little above ground level, but not too high—could be an ideal place for the abode of Kali. The Welfare Association of Sector 7, R.K. Puram, heartily endorsed the idea. A temporary temple was constructed on Saturday, 13 July 1968, under heavy downpour, and an idol donated by Srimati Purnima Gupta was installed on the same day, which the organisers started worshipping regularly. This small idol is still preserved in the permanent temple as 'Adi Devi'. The first elected executive committee was formed in December 1969. Shri V.V. Giri, President of India, visited Kalibari during the celebration of Durga Puja in 1969. A Development Board was constituted in early 1982 with the President of India, Late Dr. Pranab Mukherjee, then Finance Minister, as Chairman (and eventually the chief patron), for the construction of the temple complex.[29]

Matri Mandir Samity

Matri Mandir Samity was established in 1965 with Late A.K. Sarkar as President and Late S.R. Banerjee as General Secretary. In 1966, it was registered under Societies Act and Late Sachindra Kumar Maitra became its president, while Late Bimal Bhusan Chakraborty, became general secretary. The first construction, a small Kali temple, was taken up in 1969. The foundation stone was laid by Late S.G. Basu Mallik, the then Vice Chairman of the DDA. The temple was inaugurated during the auspicious occasion of Kali Puja in 1969. A small clay deity of Maa Kali was installed and daily puja started after Prof.

---

[29] As gathered from personal conversation with the mandir office and the website: www.dakshindelhikalibari.com/about-history.asp

Debiprasad Chattopadhyay, the then Hon'ble Minister of Commerce, laid the foundation stone on 22 September 1974, in the benign presence of Late (Justice) Nagendra Singh, Late (Dr.) Santosh Kr. Sen and Late (Smt.) Kalyani Kumaramangalam, among many others.[30]

Bengali Schools in Delhi: Humble Beginnings

'To be "modern" in postcolonial India is to align oneself with projects such as developments, science, progress, invention, and discovery; in turn, to be "traditional" means to react to the terms of debate, yet often make alternative claims couched in the very language of modernity.'[31] The role and history of Bengali schools for middle-class Bengali children becomes crucial as the majority of our parents' generation studied in these schools. At one point in time, there were many regional language schools (not only Bengali) that came up all across Delhi, which were and still are run and funded by the Government of India. The location of the schools marks the respective area's population concentration. Naturally, the schools grew from their humble beginnings into fully functional institutions, along with the students, and became an essential backbone for the diaspora, who wanted their children to learn at least basic cultural markers. Language was the most important of these, alongside modern ways of gaining education.

Bengali Senior Secondary School, Shamnath Marg (erstwhile Alipur Road)

Bengali Senior Secondary School on Shamanth Marg, Alipur Road, Civil Lines popularly known as Kashmere Gate Bangla School, was the first Bengali School in Delhi founded on 23 February 1899 (as per the school website). As per the oral history in the school, partly backed by the school records, in its earliest days, the school changed addresses rather frequently. It began its journey in Kara Masrut in Dariba Kalan, Chandni Chowk. Then it shifted to a building adjoining the Satya Narayan Mandir in Esplanade near Chandni Chowk, eventually moving to Hamilton Road. Later, it moved to Church Road near the iconic St. James Church in Kashmere Gate. I believe this is where it got its colloquial name of Kashmere Gate Bangla School having moved from the place. It stayed there for almost the next 40 years. In 1961, the school moved to its present and permanent premises on Alipur road (now Shamnath Marg, opposite Indraprastha College for Women), in Civil Lines, Delhi.

The school began with 40 students and one teacher, Mr. Narayan Das. Mr. Das worked in a company called Karatak & Company in Chandni Chowk. He volunteered for two hours every morning before going to his place of work.

---

[30] As gathered from personal conversation with the mandir office and the website: www.matrimandirdelhi.com/history.html.

[31] Bavisar, Amita and Raka Ray. eds. 2011, 2016. *Elite and Everyman: The cultural politics of the Indian middle classes* (New Delhi: Routledge). p. 251.

He was then joined by one Pandit Net Ram, a year later in 1900. Panditji continued till early 1930s. Apparently, Pandit Net Ram was not a Bengali but was believed to be very well-versed in the language. He was followed by Mr. Pearson, a British gentleman who joined the school a few years later and continued to teach English there till 1933. A particularly cherished name as a teacher was that of a Sanskrit scholar, Pandit Jitendra Mohan Bhattacharya (popularly referred to as Master Moshi). He apparently was a great astrologer as well. Unfortunately, all the teachers were men for a very long time. The first woman teacher came in after fifty years of the school's existence—Ms. Anupama Taran, who was appointed in the year 1952.

In 1901, the school received a grant of ₹50 from the Directorate of Accountant General, Post & Telegraph. Mr. S. Wright and Pandit Shiv Dayal brought the school under the fold of Punjab University. Initially, it was run privately to teach Bengali boys and give them an opportunity to study until matriculation. But by 1913, it ran into serious financial crises. There was then a proposal to demote it to a middle school rather than a senior school. This led to the transfer of management into public hands. Mr. Manav Chandra Bandopadhyay was elected President and Dr. J.K. Sen was chosen to be the secretary of the Managing Committee. The school was brought under the Delhi Education Board in 1936. The year 1949 proved to be a remarkable one in the school's history. It opened to girls as well, and was turned into a co-educational school till class VII. 'During this year a decision was again made by the Education Board to reduce the school to middle level and scrap the co-education system. Anticipating hardship by the "Probasi Bengalis", the then Secretary of the school Late Paresh Chandra Mitra along with Prof. Shaileswar Sen (Principal of the Commercial College, Delhi), Late Baidyanath Sarakar (Kaviraj Moshai) and Late Rashbehari Sen had met and convinced Sir Maurice Gwyer (the then Head of Education Dept.) to allow the school to run as per the existing structure, thus averting the crisis. The school was later converted to a full-fledged co-educational school in the [new] Capital.'[32]

The Union Academy

This traces its origins back to the year 1887, when the 'Bengalee Boys High School' was founded in Shimla. '... on 22nd September 1934 in a public meeting in the Shimla Kali Bari Hall under the chairmanship of Sir Nripendra Nath Sircar, the then law member of the Viceroy's Executive Council, the decision of setting up a new high school for boys was taken which was also implemented the very year.' The peculiar name (as compared to the usual names of schools then) was carefully chosen so as to reflect a 'non-denominational character which is free from all provincial prejudices and religious or communal bias.'[33]

---

[32] As noted from the Bengali Senior Secondary School's website last checked on 27 April 2024.

[33] As noted from the Union Academy's school website last checked on 27 April 2024.

The academy was brought to New Delhi in the year 1939, and was housed in a spacious building in its current address in Raja Bazar, Gole Market area, New Delhi. It was inaugurated in Delhi by Mr E.M. Jenkins GCIE[34], KCSI[35], the then Chief Commissioner of Delhi, on 13 December 1939. It opened its doors in the same year. By 1940, this institution secured a permanent affiliation for its primary, lower and middle schools. By 1941, after securing an affiliation it upgraded itself to a senior secondary school. It moved on to the 10+2 pattern in the year 1977.

Raisina Bengali School

The transfer of the capital from Calcutta to Delhi essentially and practically meant the transfer of the offices of the Deputy Accountant General, Central Revenues; Accountant General, Central Revenues; Deputy Controller of Currency, Northern India; and the Comptroller and Auditor General of India to Delhi. This move brought with it a large number of Bengali employees, all of whom wanted opportunities of proper education for their wards. 'The first groundwork in this direction was laid by a few enterprising Bengali gentlemen whose names will always be remembered with reverence and gratitude by the community. Shri Gokul Chandra Mukherjee was the leading pioneer who, in 1922, moved Mr. J.A. Richie, the then Education Commissioner, Government of India, through Rai Bahadur Manmatha Nath Chakrabarty, Registrar, Department of Education, Health and Lands of Government of India, for opening a school, where education could be imparted through the medium of Bengali. Shri Mukherjee got the willing support and assistance of Sarbasree Madhusudan Chakrabarty, Amrita Lal Banerjee, Khetra Mohan Singh, Phani Bhushan Chakrabarty and Sailendra Nath Sen. Mr. Richie was reluctant to the appeal of opening of a separate Bengali School, but the determination and persuasion of Shri Mukherjee to the noble cause gave him inspiration to send a representative to Sir Frederick Gauntlet, the then Auditor General, requesting him to make arrangements for the education of the children of Bengali Government employees. Sir Frederick took a sympathetic view and through his intervention, the Government agreed to the proposal for a separate Bengali School.'[36]

The Raisina Bengali School was established in 1925. According to the school's website, 'at a meeting of the Bengali residents of Raisina Hill surroundings, held on 28 December, 1925, at 24, Dalhousie Square, it was decided to start the school. A Managing Committee for the proposed school was formed consisting of the following office-bearers and members:

---

[34] GCIE is an abbreviation for Knight Grand Commander of the Order of the Indian Empire

[35] KCSI is an abbreviation for Knight Commander of the Order of the Star of India.

[36] As noted from Raisina Bengali School's website last checked on 27 April 2024

- President: Dr. J.K.Sen
- Vice President: Shri Satish Chandra Gupta
- Secretary: Shri Srish Chandra Mitra
- Members: Rai Bahadur A.L. Banerjee, Shri Khetra Mohan Singh, Capt. A.B. Roy Choudhury, Shri Surendra Nath Bhattacharjee, Shri Gokul Chandra Mukherjee, Shri Radha Ranjan Bose, Shri Madhu Sudan Chakrabarty'

The first head master of the school was Shri Prabhat Chandra Sen, who stayed for a short period. 'He was succeeded by Shri Satish Chandra Ganguly, who joined the school in 1926. The teachers who joined Shri Ganguly at that time were Sarbashri Nani Lal Sen, Hara Prasanna Banerjee, Naresh Chandra Ganguly, Bhutesh Bhattacharjee and Manmatha Nath Mazumdar.' Shri Ramesh Chandra Sengupta became the head master of the school in 1927 and served in the position till 1944. In the following years, the school shifted to a 'rented building in Doctor's lane, as the premises occupied by it was required to house the Willingdon Hospital.' The school was given recognition as a high school on 26 November 1928.The constitution of the school was framed and adopted on 24 February 1929. According to the school's website,

> The school henceforth began to flourish, and the number of scholars continued to mount, raising the problem of accommodation, which was temporarily solved by the occupation of the bungalow at Lady Hardinge Road, now used by the D.A.V. Management. 22 September, 1932, stands as a landmark in the history of the school, when the Govt. allotted the present premises to the school, free of rent, the maintenance of the building being vested in the New Delhi Municipal Committee. The school was registered under the Society Registration Act (XVIII of 1860), on the 21 September, 1939. The scheme of Higher Secondary Education was introduced in Delhi in 1943 and because of the very high standard maintained by our school, it was one of the few institutions to be given recognition as a Higher Secondary School in the very year of its introduction. This was followed by permanent recognition in 1945. R.C. Sengupta left the institution in 1944 and with his departure there was a general fall in the standard of the school. A new and dynamic Managing Committee was formed in 1946, headed by Shri Nishikanta Sen, a distinguished educationist, Dr. S.N. Sen, Vice Chancellor of Delhi University as Vice-President and Dr. A.B. Roy Choudhury as Secretary and Manager.

Shyama Prasad Vidyalaya, Lodhi Estate

The whole area of Raisina Hills, that is the Governor's residence (Rashtrapati Bhawan), the Parliament House, the Secretariats and all the other elaborate structures came up during 1911, upon the transfer of the capital and laying of the foundation stone by King George V himself.

Lodhi Estate and Lodhi Colony were amongst the last settlements to have been built by the British as part of the new capital— Delhi. 1945 saw the end of the Second World War. Many offices related to armaments and other war machinery were shut down in Calcutta. The staff at these offices, mostly Bengalis, were transferred to the new capital. Most of these people who got transferred got their government accommodation in these two colonies. Unfortunately, the infrastructure wasn't like it is now. The whole of Lodhi Road area was completely isolated from the infrastructure of the city as the habitation was centred around North Delhi. Lodhi Road and Lodhi Estate were situated towards the southern most parts of Delhi, far away from the connectivity of the North and the newly developed central Delhi. Proper education for their children became the primary concern of these new residents of the Lodhi area.

> For establishing a school the primary requirement was of a place where students could assemble together for studying. So they decided to approach New Delhi Municipal Committee for help. They wanted to take some accommodation on rent—in one of the two existing Primary Schools in Lodhi Colony. Members thought that it would be easier to proceed further, if the proposed school could become a part of any one of the schools already established. It was decided that the proposed school would be established as a branch of Union Academy School, Raja Bazar. In June 1948, three rooms of the girls' Primary School of New Delhi Municipal Committee at Lodhi Colony were taken on rent and the new school started functioning from there. After almost two months, on 8 August 1948 with the initiative taken by the Chairman of the Co-ordination Committee, Mr. D.L. Majumdar, Dr. Shyama Prasad Mukherjee officially inaugurated the school.[37]

The main school in Raja Bazar took in Bengali as well as Non-Bengali students, so it was decided that the same system will be followed in this branch as well.

> In May 1949 the School got the approval of the Primary Section (I to V) from the Directorate of Education. In November 1952 the Secondary Section (VI to VIII) was approved by the Education Department and finally in 1956 the Education Department gave their approval for the Higher Secondary Section (IX to XI) and subsequently to class XII.

The Managing Committee of this school was very persistent in their efforts to have a permanent residence for the school. In August 1953, the Land Development Office awarded 3.5 acres of land to the school in Lodhi Estate on a 99-year lease. With the growing popularity of the school, there was a lot of pressure on the management to admit a larger number of students. So the committee was forced to shift onto the granted land almost immediately, and the school started 'functioning from its own premises from the year 1954'. The classes were held in tents. Apparently, the management of the Union Academy at Raja Bazar suggested separating this branch, since they had their own land.

---

[37] As noted from Shyama Prasad Vidyalaya's website last checked on 27 April 2024.

So in the two meetings held by the Management Committee in March 1957, it was decided that a new sinstitution will be set up. They also decided to name the school after Dr. Shyama Prasad Mukherjee, who had inaugurated the school in 1948. Shyama Prasad Vidyalaya came to be housed in Lodhi Estate, where it still stands. Dr S. Radhakrishnan, then the Vice President of India laid the foundation stone on 6 March 1960. The double-storey building of the school was completed in the year 1961.

Vinay Nagar Bengali Senior Secondary School

Located in Sarojini Nagar (erstwhile Vinay Nagar, hence the name of the school), its humble beginnings were a small room in the residence of Smt. Monica Sen. A teacher by profession, she started the school with six students on 11 November 1952. The journey of the formal school began with a plot of land in the middle of the central government colony. The classes began in tents, till a three-storey building was erected after a couple of years.

Similarly, Bidhan Chandra Vidyalaya came to be established on 1 July 1962, named after the famous doctor and Bharat Ratna, Dr. Bidhan Chandra Roy. Mr. K.B. Ghosh, who was a teacher, joined in 1963 and fought a long battle to bring the school up to its senior secondary status. Initially it schooled students up to class VIII with not more than 50 students on its roll. Eventually it graduated to only two streams at the secondary levels, that is, Humanities and Commerce. Much later in 1989, the school opened its doors to students interested in the stream of science.

While so much was happening in terms of infrastructural changes, individual families such as mine were struggling to come to terms with the lasting impact that the Partition had left. How does one separate their individual history from that of the community's? The whole trajectory of the Bengali community in the city can be mapped through these geographical movements and expansion, as without the lobby and substantial representation, the government would not be forced to allocate funds to these institutions. While all this was taking place, there were innumerable personal struggles unfolding in people' lives.

Epilogue

While speaking about his 'Winter Garden Photograph', Roland Barthes intended to reveal a few pertinent points to the readers of *Camera Lucida*—including how the image formed for him 'a catastrophe which has already occurred'.[38] He explains the death of his mother—a loss he was doomed to suffer, over and over again, when faced with or even just imagining the photograph. All he could possibly see when looking at it, was that 'she is going to die'. 'It would appear that this is because the photograph provides a stark realisation of the inevitable absence brought about by the passing of human

[38] Barthes, Roland. 1999. *Camera Lucida*. p. 96.

life.'[39] While functioning as a 'trace', the photograph provides some solace. But this image of Barthes' mother is more than that. It sends him to the brink of madness because 'it evokes an earlier infantile experience, also involving the loss of the mother, but which is too painful to bring into consciousness.'[40] The image is what Sarah Kember, using the thinking of Christopher Bollas, terms a 'transformational object' (Cross: 2015), in relation to which the earliest moments of object-relating are being replayed. Cathexis is the investment of energy in the object which is transferred from the mother to other objects; here, the photograph. 'In "the shadow of the object", Barthes perceives loss. Not the loss of his actual mother but, rather, the loss that constitutes what he calls "a secret thing (monster or treasure)"[41]: the unspeakable action, which formed the earliest loss, for which Barthes and his own destructive impulses were responsible.'

About my maternal family: my mother had once asked my grandfather if he had any deep desire that he would like to fulfil. He said, 'When I die, I wish to be cremated in my ancestral home.' This was in Barisal, present-day Bangladesh. My grandfather was born after the first partition of Bengal in 1905. For him and probably for others as well, the partition that had happened in 1947, was similar to the previous one. That was essentially a division of administrative and legislative offices. Of course, there was a huge cultural difference between the East Bengalis and the West Bengalis, but they were from one community in terms of language. In 1947, they witnessed the mass migration from Punjab to Delhi; in spite of that, they waited for things to normalise in Bengal. They all thought it was temporary, since Bengal was already divided and it functioned just fine. But slowly, the permanence of what had happened began to seep in and post 1971, all hope was lost.

As adolescents, my cousin and I discovered a big sack of photographs when we were trying to look through an almirah which we were barred from. We found lots of images of our mothers' childhood and of the larger family. No one had ever kept these pictures properly. In 'the shadow of the object',[42] Barthes, while explaining the 'loss', says it exists only for him and 'would be nothing but an indifferent picture'[43] for us, the readers. Over a period of time, a lot was lost to termite infestation and all that survived was only one album, which I have in my possession. The photographs in this album forms some sort of a collage of the lives of my mother and her siblings. Having a vague idea about my profession, my grandmother handed over my grandfather's *charkha* and the album to me for safekeeping. The strangest part is, no one from my larger family has ever inquired about these things from me.

[39] Cross, Karen. 2015. *Photographies*. p. 45.
[40] Ibid. p. 46.
[41] Ibid.
[42] Barthes, Roland. 1999. *Camera Lucida*. p. 33.
[43] Ibid. p. 73.

About my paternal family: when my paternal grandmother passed, which was a couple of years after my grandfather, I remember asking my father how he could not feel any anger or angst against his parents. He said, 'Your grandfather served in the Second World War and saw so much bloodshed, then he comes back to his country to realise that he cannot go back to his ancestral home and estate. Whatever they as a family owned here [present-day India] was nothing as compared to what was left behind. How does one stay normal after that?' What he was referring to was undiagnosed Post-traumatic Stress Disorder (PTSD) and its prolonged impacts. He further said, 'And your grandmother was a smart, stylish woman with a mind of her own—her decisions might have appeared unwise to society but the reality was she did not want to succumb to domestic misconduct that was otherwise normalised.' This conversation happened in Bangla, and I have taken the liberty to translate it. Whatever my grandfather owned—and that was substantial, still, as compared to innumerable others—he sold off and donated to the Ramakrishna Ashram in Benaras, renouncing his family. One cannot live in this particular ashram unless one renounces all worldly ties. That is where he decided to spend his last years alone.

After a few months, I asked my father about the family pictures, to which he said that he himself had destroyed most of them. The images that you see here are all that remain. That day, I also understood that his silence did not mean he had been able to evade the trauma, which had now become generational.

Writing about your own family is like entering into an arena of war unarmed, but completely aware of the consequences that will ensue. I say this at the risk of it appearing to be a mindless generalisation. And writing

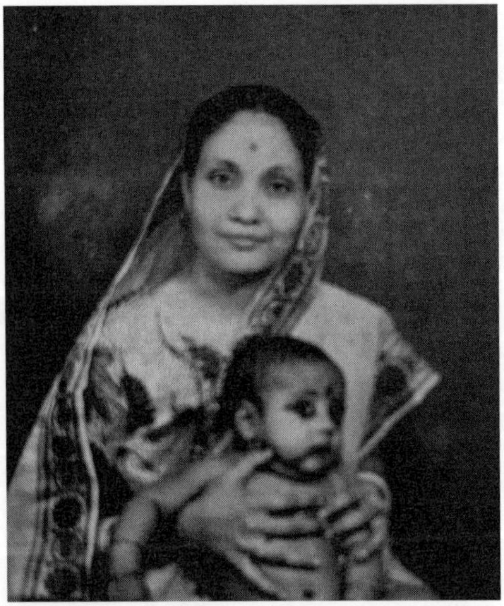

Figure 1: My father with his mother, Mrs. Hena Goswami (CE 1952).

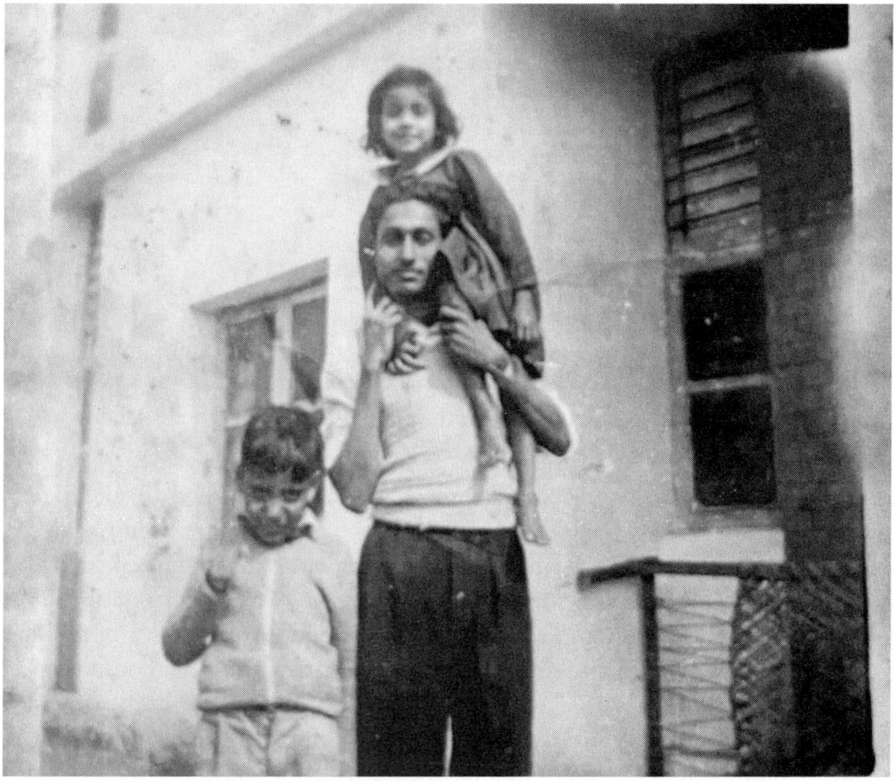

Figure 2: My father (left) and his sister with an older cousin (CE 1958-59).

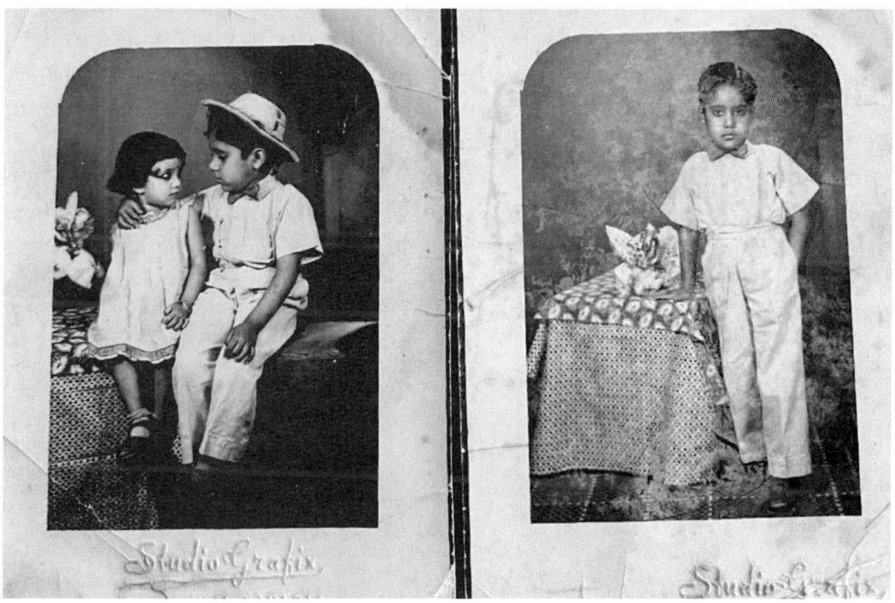

Figure 3: Studio portraits of my father. The one on the left is with his sister, Late Mrs. Rooplekha Das (CE. 1956-57).

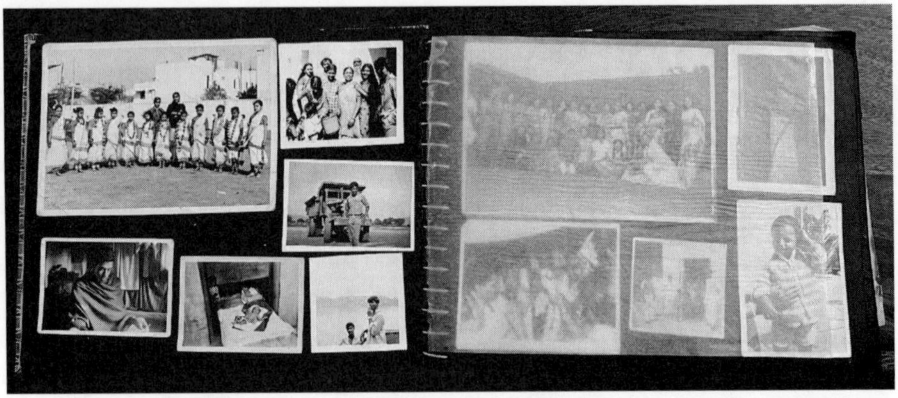

Figure 4: A double spread from Mr. B.K. Bhattacharjee's Family Album.

about your diasporic family turns your academic space into 'an ideological and ontological battleground'.[44] The bloodier the past, the more complicated it becomes to renegotiate the terms of engagement with time that has passed and the individuals stretched between generations. Otherwise linear relationships, all of a sudden turn rhetoric. It places you in the middle of a riot of emotional responses—grief, loss, deprivation and agony—constituting the composite of transgenerational trauma.

'Photographs of the suffering … of a people are more than reminders of death, of failure, of victimisation. They invoke the miracle of survival. To aim at the perpetuation of memories means, inevitably, that one has undertaken the task of continually renewing, of creating, memories—aided, above all, by the impress of iconic photographs. People want to be able to visit—and refresh—their memories.'[45] I cannot help but think the same is true of photographs which are not there anymore. Moreover, 'Memory is a tool and a political project—an honouring of those who are gone, and a reminder to those who will listen …'[46] and I am compelled to reflect on all three generations of my family—the first one (my grandparents') so distraught that they unknowingly resort to silence, the second one (my parents') so caught up in somehow surviving that silence is subconsciously reinforced, the third one (ours), for whom by now the silences have turned into erasures.

---

[44] Lê, Việt. 2021. *Return Engagements: Contemporary Art's Traumas of Modernity and History in Sài Gòn and Phnom Penh* (Durham: Duke University Press). p. 2.

[45] Sontag. 2003. *Regarding the Pain of Others*. p. 87.

[46] Brown, Elspeth and Thy Phu. eds. 2014. *Feeling Photography* (Durham: Duke University Press). p. 248.

5

Families (re)calibrated: Visualising class and caste hierarchies:

Framing Domestic Servitude

The Politics of Visibility in Family Photographs

Divya Gauri

This essay aims to trace the connections between the visibility and invisibility of servants and servitude in Indian family photographs across colonial and post-colonial contexts. Photographs as a visual medium present the social and political order of their time. Family photographs make this order contingent, as their meaning-making depends upon what the family wants to remember and archive, and not all narratives revolve around the family that owns the album. In a lot of the cases, we encounter photographs of people who are not biologically part of the family but are generally addressed as family or distant relatives, or as those who are 'just like family'. These include those who are employed by the family to perform daily chores as part-time household help or live-in domestic workers. It is rare to find photographs that exhibit family members themselves involved in daily chores, making it important to question how much or what reality is being veiled while another is presented for the perfect family photograph. Can there be a way to still reflect upon servitude as part of any household, through this invisibility?

The discourse of master–servant relations might have received limited academic attention, but it has always been and still continues to be an integral part of our society.[1] Domestic labour along gendered lines in a household has an age-old history in India. Uma Chakravarti in 'Lineages of Servitude', mentions texts from Pali literature that reflect upon the presence of serving bodies in households that included both dutiful wives and orderly domestic helpers.[2] This social system continued in colonial-period autobiographies of upper caste-class women, who have written about their households and the servants they were surrounded by.[3] Apart from textual sources, servants and serving bodies have also been registered in visual culture across genres, and for this essay, I will look at family photographs that depict domestic servitude

---

[1] Sinha, Nitin, Nitin Varma and Pankaj Jha. eds. 2019. *Servants' Past: Sixteenth to Eighteenth Century South Asia*. Vol. 1 (Himayatnagar, Hyderabad: Orient BlackSwan Private Limited). pp. 1–87.

[2] Chakravarti, Uma. 2019. 'Lineages of Servitude: Stray Thoughts about Servants in the "Ancient" Past'. *Servants' Pasts*. Vol. 1. pp. 89–101.

[3] S.M. Banerjee. January 2004. 'Down Memory Lane: Representations of Domestic Workers in Middle Class Personal Narratives of Colonial Bengal'. *Journal of Social History*. 37:3. pp. 681–708. doi.org/10.1353/jsh.2004.0001.

and the bodies that are associated with it. From the 1970s–1980s, we find a conscious attempt by academicians and activists to critically theorise the 'unpaid domestic labour' of housewives,[4] adding to studies on domestic servants to expand the overall ambit of subaltern studies. Today, we might address them as household help or domestic workers instead of servants, but this does not change the fact of their existence in a highly stratified society, and the invisibility and inequalities that plague their lives. Indeed, they are the spine of most Indian households, whether serving a joint family or a nuclear one, in rural or urban India, as part-time or full-time live-in help.

The family album generally invites a sentimental approach, recalling memories for the viewer. Many times, these albums have photographs of people who may be extended family members, neighbours, acquaintances or people who are mostly part of the 'household' but not the 'family', explaining their invisibility through the merging of their identities with the precincts of the household. In engaging with one's family album, one does not usually ponder on larger questions around the politics of gender, caste and class. While exploring the photographs of our family, how many times do we find ourselves examining the general structure of our households? In this essay, I evoke the subtext of social hierarchy that is an integral part of any family, and I seek to examine if these inequalities can be observed in photographs.

In the few photographs where domestic workers are included, it is easy to identify those who are part of the household but not family, hired to perform all kinds of chores so that the family can have a comfortable life. There, social, cultural and biological differences between family and the house help, are visualised through tropes of distancing or hierarchical compositions of family montages in photographs. The Victorian ideal of the family as mentioned in Robin Fox's *Kinship and Marriage: An Anthropological Perspective*, is a group in which everyone was loyal to everyone else without question, simply because they were 'of the same blood.'[5] In *Seeing like a Feminist,* family is described as a legally recognised institution. It suggests that it can only be patriarchal and heterosexual i.e. a man, his wife, and 'his' children.[6] Domestic workers have families of their own that reside outside their employer's household, in case of part-timers, while for live-in servants, they either reside on the premises of the employer's house or remain back 'home' in another village or town. While studying master–servant relations, the household becomes an important space to witness rigid differences as well as grey areas between these figures.

---

[4] Menon, Usha. 1982. 'Women and Household Labour'. *Social Scientist.* 10:7. p. 30. doi.org/10.2307/3516936; Sangari, Kumkum. 1993. 'The "Amenities of Domestic Life": Questions on Labour'. *Social Scientist.* 21:9/11. p. 3. doi.org/10.2307/3520425.

[5] Fox, Robin. 1984. 'Kinship, Family and Descent'. *Kinship and Marriage: An Anthropological Perspective* (London: Cambridge University Press). pp. 27–53, 15.

[6] Menon, Nivedita. 2012. 'Family'. *Seeing like a Feminist* (New Delhi: Zubaan Books). pp. 3–50, 5.

In a patriarchal society like India, a woman's primary identity has been limited to nurturing, sacrificing for the family and being a dutiful wife and mother. The unpaid nature of their labour has been largely obscured in the name of duty; their maternal role is glorified, invisibilising the endless nature of their day-to-day work.[7] In contemporary times, when women across classes are career-oriented, house help is no longer a feudal remnant from the past, but a realistic need. If the household help is a woman, she performs double labour, doing similar work multiple times in a day, once for her employer's family and then for her own. While most household helps today are women,[8] if a housewife is engaged in managing her domesticity then it is considered her duty bearing no monetary value. But if the same family hires domestic help, the nature of the work changes from presumably compassionate and voluntary, to professional. In my investigation, I explore whether family photographs can reveal these complexities between different kinds of housework, household help and female labour. I focus on the overlaps between feminine identities of the woman of house and the female household help, as they configure differentially in family photographs. By way of examples, I look at a range of images to develop a comparative perspective, from my own family photographs to those of neighbours and friends, ethnographic portraits to social media images, that address the central theme of this essay.

My Family Albums

My rather traditional, middle-class, nuclear family in Patna mainly photographed festivals and celebrations while I was growing up. All those photographs are now in multiple family albums, occasionally glanced at during family get-togethers. The pandemic of 2020 presented an opportunity for me to revisit my family albums, after nearly ten years. I noticed that none of the photographs had any trace of daily household chores being performed, not even cooking, which was done thrice a day. Domestic workers were the other unregistered figures in those photographs, who were always around but somehow never captured, hence absent from our family albums. The family albums that hold everyone's likeness from our neighbours to our distant relatives, doing all kinds of things, fail to capture the labour that went into running domesticity.

It is not just the domestic workers that failed to get registered but also the labour that was part of my mother's day-to-day life. For a woman in our

[7] Bagchi, Jasodhara. 2017. 'Motherhood and Patriarchy'. *Interrogating Motherhood* (Los Angeles: Stree). pp. 32–48.

[8] According to the International Labour Organization's 2019 figures, of the 75.6 million domestic workers worldwide, 76.2 per cent are women, and only a quarter of the domestic workers are men. In India, its share constitutes 1.3 per cent of total employment, where 3.5 per cent are women and only 0.7 per cent are men. See 'Who Are Domestic Workers (Domestic Workers)'. ILO. www.ilo.org/global/topics/domestic-workers/who/lang--en/index.htm. Last accessed 9 May 2022.

society, even if they have house help, they still they have to supervise them. Also, for a lower middle-class family, cooking is still performed mostly by the mothers. In such cases, when we travel through family photographs and enter into a particular moment, our memory also lingers on the work or preparation behind that particular event. In most of these photographs, people both from family and extended family, and neighbours, are most likely to have a different memory than the one who was managing the event, which in the case of family events, would mostly be the woman of the household; either the mother or the wife. Any celebration or festival meant that they were engaged in preparations beforehand, but that part of the event was never important for the camera. By ignoring the mundane daily activities and labour of our family lives, it is not just the unpaid labour of our mothers that is ignored, but also their memories. Gillian Rose reflects upon this selective representation where domestic labour is never visualised, although most of her interviewees mention it being an important part of their family lives. One of them mentioned how arranging photos in the albums or the boxes was mostly done by the women in families. The initiative taken by women towards the preservation and arrangement of family memories and histories, and the labour that is part of such a task has never been discussed.[9]

As compared to colonial families residing in India during the colonial period, the invisibility of servitude in the family photographs of Indian elite was more visible. With the advent of camera, documentation of the social divide between the two classes became prominent and unfiltered. In case of the Indian elite, the household-serving bodies, that is both the domestic servants and the lady of the household, were either invisible or presented in a more romantic way, separating the labouring part of their daily lives. In the case of colonial families, their servants were not just part of their photographs, but were also presented at their respective job, that is an ayah would typically be seen with the child in the photograph, or a groomer would be seen with the horse. These servants may not have been photographed while they were at work, but there are photographs in which they pose with their object of work; Rebecca Brown argued in 'Colonial Polyrhythm: Imaging Action in the Early 19th Century' that ethnographic images do more than simply represent ethnic or occupational groups; rather, a closer look actually focusses on the action, hence while reading the subject matter, one should interpret its do-ing rather than do-er.[10] Through this as the pivot, one can actually deduce that colonial family photographs or ethnographic photographs didn't just capture the domestic servants, their occupation and ethnicity, but also the entire process of doing their job, even if it was just a posed photograph.

---

[9] Rose, Gillian. 2003. 'Family Photographs and Domestic Spacings: A Case Study'. *Transactions of the Institute of British Geographers*. 28:1. pp. 5–18. doi.org/10.1111/1475-5661.00074.

[10] Rebecca M. Brown, "Colonial Polyrhythm : Imaging Action in the Early 19th Century," *Visual Anthropology* 26, no.4 (2013):1-2, doi: 10.1080/08949468.2013.804368.

To understand this distinction in family photographs, the essay will be divided into four sections. In the first section, I will be looking at conventional, posed family photographs for the presence and absence of labouring bodies. This will include photographs from the late nineteenth and early twentieth centuries. In contrast to family photographs and to trace the labouring body per se, I will discuss ethnographic photographs of domestic servants that were taken for documenting native people under the aegis of the Raj. The second section will focus on the representation of mothers and maids, in their single as well as maternal roles. By comparing a studio photograph of domestic workers with their digital photographs from contemporary times, this section will present multiple narratives of women, both as domestic labourers/workers and the lady of the house, reflecting upon their differences and similarities as they were present within the same household. This section will also engage with photographs from a competition conducted by the International Labour Organization of the United Nations in 2010, as a part of the campaign theme 'Your Work Is Important'. Photographs were submitted from all over the world, reflecting upon different aspects of labour. The third section of the essay will further tease out narratives from the work of contemporary photographers Anay Mann and Jannatul Mawa, who tried to capture the veiled realities of house work through their art. As one of them captures the lady of the house as she performs her 'duties', the other photographs women with their 'extensions' or helping hands within the same frame. The fourth and final section will discuss how things have changed with the coming of social media, digital photography and selfie culture. For this section, images from social media platforms like Instagram or X (formerly Twitter) will be analysed. A major question that the final section of this essay tries to address is how families address their domestic workers as 'just like family'. Women in their written and visual records, have always registered the presence of their household help, and children, while growing up, encounter several caregivers who become part of their childhood memories, so the word 'just' can have several meanings that can be further dissected. Conclusively, I inquire if the pandemic can be credited for the acknowledgment of domestic workers, on the one hand unveiling the dark realities that they face, and on the other, their resilience and social ubiquity. On social media platforms like Instagram, we certainly saw an increase in people sharing photographs of their domestic workers, recognising their importance in their lives. Does that mean that it is in their absence during COVID-19 lockdowns, restrictions on movement and actual sickness, that domestic workers regain visibility among those whom they serve?

Tracing Servitude in Early Photographs

In 1840, Thacker, Spink and Company, a Calcutta-based photography firm, started advertising the sale of daguerreotype cameras, marking the

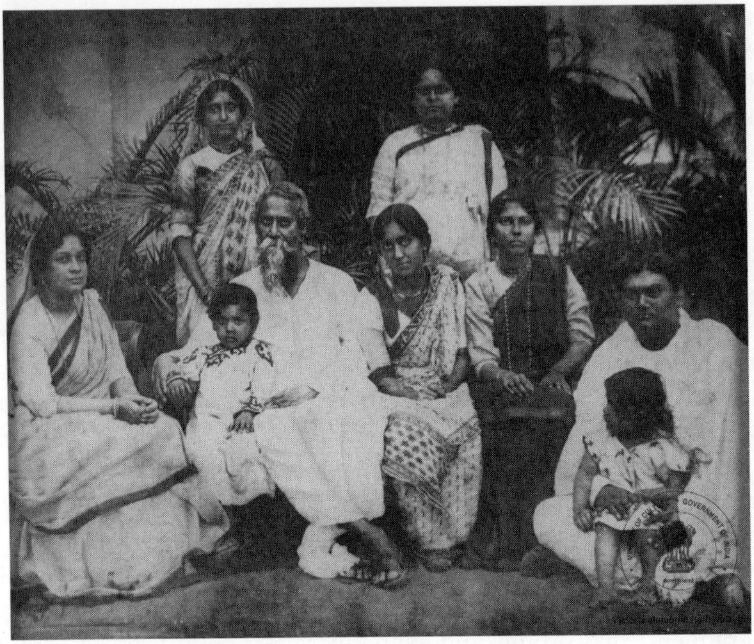

Figure 1. Rabindranath Tagore with his family members; unknown artist. Victoria Memorial Hall Kolkata Collection, nineteenth century. © Victoria Memorial Hall

arrival of photography in India.[11] And by the 1880s and 1890s, photography underwent a double technical revolution, where at one end, there was a mass production of cheaply printed half-tone blocks, and on the other, there was a mass production of simple and convenient photographic equipment like the hand-held Kodak camera.[12]This was the time when photographs were mostly used for ethnographic documentation by the British Raj, providing a likeness of the indigenous population that was to be ruled and controlled. There are photographs of European families with their servants, and of Indian elites engaged in self-representation. Unlike European families, in the photographs of Indians, one can rarely find any domestic helpers along with their masters. European families, while including their domestic workers in family portraits, tried to cater to their fascination with the exotic East, visually representing a microcosm of the social structure they were part of. Such a family portrait represented the state of colonialism at the grassroots. When a domestic helper entered the frame with an Indian master, it was always read in relation to her relative social status within the same racial group. Elite Indian men were shown sitting on a chair with an attendant holding a flying whisk by his side

---

[11] Christopher Pinney, "Camera Indica: the Social Life of Indian Photographs," *Camera Indica: the Social Life of Indian Photographs* (Chicago: University of Chicago Press, 1997), p. 17.

[12] John Tagg, "A Means of Surveillance: The Photograph as Evidence in Law," The Burden of Representation: *Essays on Photographies and Histories* (Basingstoke: Palgrave MacMillan, 2007), pp. 66-102, 66.

indicating class and caste separations. Apart from these rare representations of the domestic worker, plenty of ethnographic photographs portray working class men and women performing their respective jobs, as they were instructed to pose with tools and in their costumes that highlighted their caste-based professions. As per the findings of my ongoing PhD research on 'Servants in the Colonial Household: A Study of their depiction in the visual materials of 18th-19th century India', natives working for colonial households as domestic workers came mostly from the lower caste, the caste that was mostly prohibited to enter the household of any Indian elite in the colonial period.[13]

The first volume of *Servants Past* (2019), encapsulates narratives from the pre-colonial period that reflect on the lives of servants from different perspectives. Pankaj Jha, in his essay 'Securing the Naukar', mentions that servants have been an integral part of the household in India since before the medieval period.[14] Both Jha and Chakraborty draw references from Vedic texts like Puranas and Buddhist *Jataka* stories, stating that servitude was not introduced in the subcontinent by immigrant Muslims, but already had a foundation in Indian culture. The status of domestic work has been a shape-shifting one, changing definitions in different contexts. 'Domestic servant' is often a relational term to refer to a range of relationships based on the hierarchy within households. In the census of 1891, even the sanitation workers who were already absorbed within the corporation workforce from the 1870s, were categorised under domestic servants.[15] I hope to display these differential identities of domestic workers through photographic records among families and other archives, as they remain a fluid category through time.

A photograph from the collection of Victoria Memorial, Kolkata depicting Rabindranath Tagore with his family (Figure 1), represents a conventional family photograph theme. The reason for engaging with this photograph is not that it belongs to a famous leading Indian family, but the fact that a lot of written records are available from the Tagore family reflecting on their daily life, which also mention them being surrounded by several servants. In Rabindranath Tagore's biography, a servant named Shyam was criticised and even blamed for restricting the children's movement so that he could escape

[13] Mary Martha Sherwood, *The Life of Mrs. Sherwood: (Chiefly Autobiographical) with Extracts from Mr. Sherwood's Journal during His Imprisonment in France & Residence in India*, ed. Sophia Kelly (Darton and co., Holborn Hill, 1857), 300; Fanny Parkes and William Dalrymple, *Begums, Thugs and Englishmen: The Journals of Fanny Parkes* (New Delhi: Penguin Books, 2003), 93-94; Emma Roberts, *Scenes and Characteristics of Hindostan, with Sketches of Anglo-Indian Society*, vol. 1 (Leadenhall Street, London: W.H. Allen and Co., 1835), 90.

[14] Jha, Pankaj. 2019. 'Securing the Naukar: Caste and "Domestics" in the Fifteenth Century Mithila'. *Servants' Pasts*. Vol. I (Hyderabad: Orient Blackswan). pp. 134–36.

[15] Sarkar, Tanika. 2019. 'Caste-ing Servants in Colonial Calcutta'. in Sinha, Nitin. ed. *Servants' Past Late-Eighteenth to Twentieth-Century South Asia*. Vol. II. pp. 239–64. (Hyderabad, Telangana: Orient BlackSwan).

his job of looking after them.[16] As photography was a luxury till the second half of the twentieth century, even a well-to-do family heavily populated by servants could not share space in the frame with them. There can be several reasons for this, but the most common was likely that domestic servants were not part of the core family, hence in a family photograph, generally only those related by blood or matrimony were included. Another reason for the invisibility might be the social disparities along caste and class lines,[17] or maybe the nature of their work, mundane household chores, which cannot be pictured in the luxury of photographs till the twentieth century.

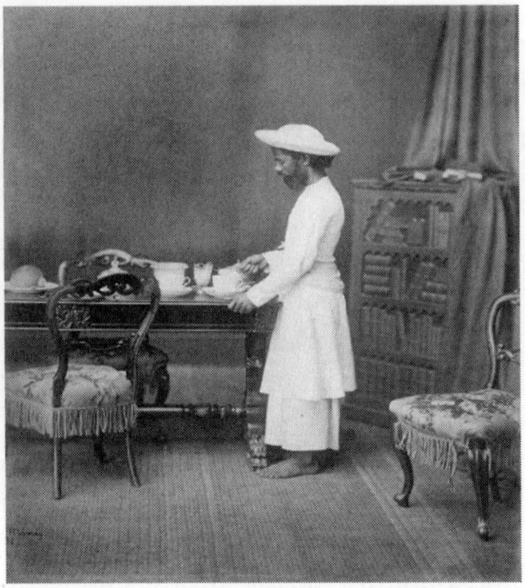

Figure 2. Indian servant arranging teapots; unknown artist. Public domain via Wikimedia Commons, 1869.

The concept of being presentable while getting photographed can also be a reason why working bodies of the household engaged in their respective works were kept outside the frame, and as Roland Barthes explained, the photograph is an object of three practices (or three emotions, or intentions)—to do, to undergo, to look.[18] Through a photograph, one can tap into the time and memory of those captured in the frame. The photograph, since its inception, holds the quality of being a material that captures time in two dimensions—one experiences the presence of past through this medium, hence those getting photographed or those commissioning the photographs had an agency over how they wanted themselves or their subjects to appear in the photograph.

The ladies in this photograph are all well-dressed, very presentable and in denial of, or concealing the labour that they might have been involved in before this frame was composed. This could even include instructing their helper on what clothes they will be wearing, or how the sitting will be arranged. This is not the only photograph that showcases a conventional family setup; there are several in private collections, part of family albums, none of which register labour or labouring bodies. One reason behind the invisibility of labour can be

[16] Roy, Kshitis. 1934. *Rabindranath Tagore: A Life Story*, V (New Delhi: Publication Department, Ministry of Information and Broadcasting, Govt. of India).

[17] Frøystad, Kathinka. 2003. 'Master-Servant Relations and the Domestic Reproduction of Caste in Northern India'. *Ethnos*. 68:1. p. 80-81.

[18] Barthes, Roland and Richard Howard. 1980. *Camera Lucida: Reflections on Photography* (London: Vintage Classics). p. 9.

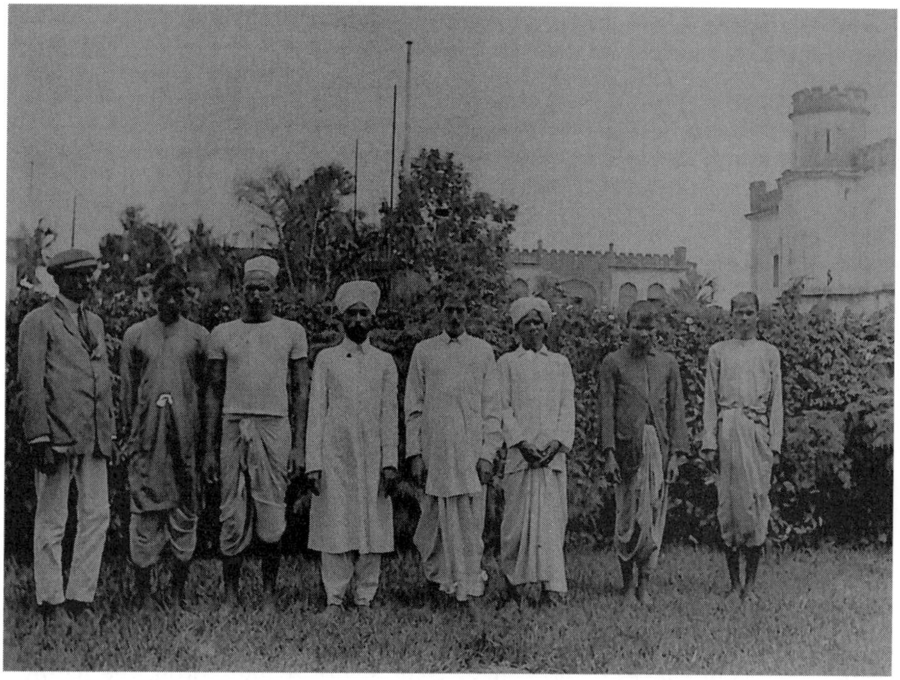

Figure 3. Native Indian servants; unknown artist. Jalan Museum Collection, Patna, nineteenth century. © Aditya Jalan/Jalan Museum

that traditionally feminine tasks, such as nurturing and caregiving are devalued because they are traditionally associated with women. Hence, this could be the reason for low-income jobs conventionally associated with women.[19]

A wide range of ethnographic photographs (Figures 2, 3) from the colonial period fill the blanks in the family albums of the native population, whose households were otherwise full of servants. While exploring digital photographic collections in India,[20] one comes across plenty of ethnographic photographs that capture the likeness of domestic workers from the time. These men and women from the serving class were mostly photographed while performing their respective jobs. In the nineteenth century, as the photographers travelled the globe, they acquired images of exotic lands and the diverse people that

[19] Sengupta, Nilanjana and Samita Sen. 26 October 2013. 'Bargaining over Wages: Part-Time Domestic Workers in Kolkata'. *Economic and Political Weekly*. 48:43. pp. 55–62, 58; Magnusson, C. 2008. 'Gender, Occupational Prestige, and Wages: A Test of Devaluation Theory'. *European Sociological Review*. 25:1. pp. 87–101. doi.org/10.1093/esr/jcn035; Crawford, Charmaine. 2018. 'Decolonizing Reproductive Labor: Caribbean Women, Migration, and Domestic Work in the Global Economy'. *The Global South*. 12:1. p. 33. doi.org/10.2979/globalsouth.12.1.03.

[20] 'Indian servant Khitmatgar during the Raj'. old.harappa.com/hawkshaw/70.html. Last accessed 28 May 2022; 'Old Indian Photos', archive: 01/01/2009–02/01/2009. www.oldindianphotos.in/2009_01_17_archive.html. Last accessed 28 May 2022; Underwood & Underwood, Public domain via Wikimedia Commons.

inhabited them. These photographs, as opposed to textual accounts and sketches, gave an accurate portrayal of their indescribable encounters. Through nineteenth-century ethnographic photographs, it is fascinating to learn about many civilisations, their people, and how they lived, as represented by their particular equipment, clothes and surroundings. To concentrate on the task and tools that were used by indigenous domestic servants in colonial India during the nineteenth century, they were singularised and decontextualised in ethnographic pictures. It was intended to separate one profession from another and one individual from another on the basis of these photographs.

Figure 2 shows an Indian domestic servant arranging teapots; the lower left corner of the photograph has 'Murray 91' inscribed on it. In this 1869 photograph of the native domestic servant, probably the *Khitmutgar* is captured arranging the teapots. Other than him, there are just accent furnishings like a Victorian- style table and chairs, and a bookshelf with books; the curtain hanging behind the bookshelf resting on top of it. Unlike Figure 3, where all the servants are facing the camera, in Figure 2, the Khitmutgar is looking at the work he is engaged with. All the servants in both the photographs must be wearing white, as in the colonial period—generally to erase all the visible trace of domestic work—there was a fetish for clean clothes, which were mostly white. The white gloves of governesses, the maid's white apron, the nanny's white sleeves, were—according to Anne McClintock in *Imperial Leather*—fetish symbols of the conflict between women's paid work and unpaid work.[21] She goes into great depth on the colour white, pointing out an old Pears' soap advertisement, among many others, and explaining how they all highlighted the purity of Imperial White.[22]

Swapna M. Banerjee in her article 'Down the Memory Lane: Representation of Domestic Workers in Middle Class Personal Narratives of Colonial Bengal' (2004), explores middle-class personal narratives reflecting upon how household and family are cultural constructs with power-based dependencies. In households of colonial India, the 'family' was largely recognised as a conjugal kin group living together on the same premises, with shared values. The 'household' is a larger entity engaged in activities necessary for the seamless functioning of the family, including production, consumption and reproduction. In the mentioned article, Banerjee writes on childhood recollections of male writers and the personal accounts of women writers, as both reflect upon employer–servant relationships on the basis of otherness and differences. She includes narratives by the Tagores, as they were one of the most prominent families of the time, both socially and culturally. She mentions the writer of a late nineteenth-century women's journal, Ambikacharan Gupta, who asserted that '[T]here is no way a *bhadralok* can function for a

[21] McClintock, Ann. 1995. *Imperial Leather: Race, Gender and Sexuality in Colonial Context* (New York: Routledge). pp. 163–64.

[22] Ibid. p. 32.

moment without a servant … one needs servants to perform domestic chores; servants are necessary even to travel around; without servants it is impossible to maintain one's dignity.'[23]

While mapping native domestic spaces through the memoirs and autobiographies written by the Bengali bhadralok, she also mentions how the role of the housewife became more elaborate and complicated. Modern Indian women were combining the manifold functions of a nurturing and sacrificing mother and a dutiful wife, along with an educated and professionally qualified woman. There was hence an increase in the employment of domestic servants towards the end of the nineteenth century, marking modernity across women of different classes, of those who were actually becoming domestic workers and those who were employing them for the sake of their own socio-cultural progress. Through the account of Sarala Chaudhurani (1872–1945), daughter of the writer Swarnakumari Debi, Rabindranath Tagore's sister, she notes how children in the Tagore family, like many other wealthy families of Calcutta, were 'entrusted to the care of a suckling midwife.'[24] Her recollection reflected upon the extreme importance of maids in the aristocratic families of Calcutta, who not only protected the children of the family but at times, could also challenge the authority of their employers. Banerjee mentions Premankur Atarthi (1890–1964), a filmmaker and writer, who remembers an old domestic help who was night-blind and never responded to his mother's scolding. Through all these accounts and others, Banerjee's work notes the presence of domestic helps and their importance in families. By juxtaposing these written accounts with family photographs, I propose that a crucial part of personal narratives is missing and can be traced, for instance, by considering the photographs of servants represented in Figures 2 and 3.

Apart from these two separate kinds of photographs focussing on two separate subjects—firstly, photographs that capture the family, and secondly, photographs that represent the domestic help—there is another kind of photograph, wherein elite men of Indian origin are depicted sitting on the chair with servants attending to them, or women pose in front of the camera with or without their partners, accompanied by a helper.

The next photograph of Maharani Sita Devi of Baroda (Figure 4), depicts her in the centre of the frame, while her maids help her wear a necklace. One of the maids in the foreground is shown holding a mirror for the Maharani and the one behind her also holds something, maybe perfume or a refreshment. With these photographs, the presence of domestic servants is registered with evidence. These instances indicate that such photographs exceed themselves to capture things and people that buttress another's desires,

[23] Banerjee, S.M. January 2004. 'Down Memory Lane: Representations of Domestic Workers in Middle Class Personal Narratives of Colonial Bengal'. *Journal of Social History*. 37:3. pp. 681–708. doi.org/10.1353/jsh.2004.0001.

[24] Ibid. p. 691.

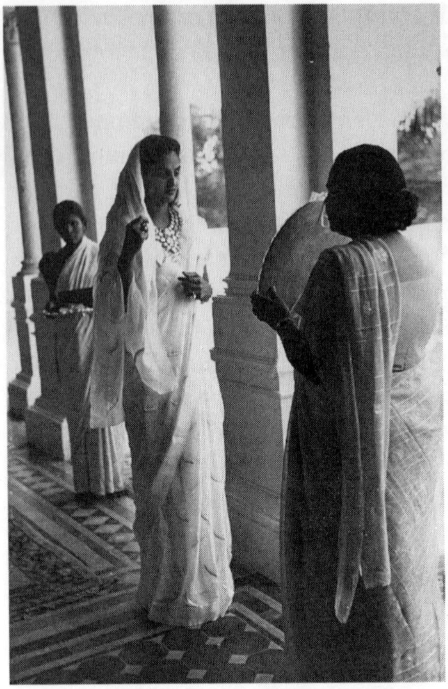

Figure 4. Maharani Sita Devi of Baroda with her maids; photograph by Henri Cartier Bresson. Museum of Art and Photography Bangalore Collection, 1948. ©MAP

or to establish the social standards of the family. I contend that they indirectly also register the presence of labour that has gone into the very making of the montage of a family, including the labour involved in preparing the central subjects of the photographs. For instance, the photograph of Maharani Sita Devi actually reveals the labour of her two maids. The labour of domestic workers is constitutional to family photographs, as it arranges the very space where the family will assemble for their portrait. They may never enter the final family photographic frame, but the polished, shiny surfaces within it, reflect the presence of their labour and labouring bodies. McClintock (1995) mentions the invisibility of labour as she decodes advertisements that created commodity spectacles for Victorian domesticity, where labour was not just blurred but working-class women were also presented as manly and lustful, whereas upper middle-class women were portrayed as nurturing *madonnas*.[25] People often saw women throughout history as motherly and tender caregivers, since that is how they were categorised and depicted in art and society. In her essay, *A Book of Her Own. A Life of Her Own: Autobiography of a Nineteenth-Century Woman*, Tanika Sarkar recalls 'Rashsundari Debi', who, although was an upper-caste Brahmin, taught herself to read and write, and wrote her biography *Amar Jiban*, which was published following her husband's death (it was a common belief that literacy brought widowhood to women, in earlier times).

In the article, Sarkar talks about Rashsundari's *sansar,* that exhausted all her life experience. The term *sansar* here refers to the householder realm, a *grahasthya* stage that is a crucial stage in the four-stage life cycle of a pious Hindu. The sole sacrament accessible to woman through marriage, that entails a never-ending list of daily chores, such as cleaning, serving, and raising children.[26] According to Rashsundari's biography, the name she had in her

[25] McClintock. 1995. *Imperial Leather*. p. 96.

[26] Sarkar, Tanika. 1993. 'A Book of Her Own. A Life of Her Own: Autobiography of a

father's house was forgotten at her in-laws' house because there she was known just as the 'mother'. 'That was the end of my days of playing,' she says while speaking about her life prior to being married, as after marriage, she had to work all the time. She described in her biography how she was cruelly torn from her family as a small child and placed in an unfamiliar household as the daughter in-law, which to her felt like a life sentence, referring to her sansar as a prison house. In a later section of Sarkar's paper, it is asserted that a woman's life is carried out in perpetual homelessness, where she never knows an identity other than being her child's mother.[27]

Mothers and the Maids: Women at Work

Mothers are at the core of almost every Indian household, always regarded as the pivot of the family. The image of a simultaneously nurturing mother, dutiful wife and successful professional have shaped the modern and contemporary woman in urban India. Being a woman myself, growing up in a middle-class family, I witnessed my mother taking care of the household, supervising our female helper and also working as a teacher. I make a distinction here between unpaid and paid housework performed by modern women belonging to different social strata. The modern moment, with the additional demands of urbanisation and professionalisation of services, saw lower-class women working outside their households, including working as household help. The need for domestic work increased with the rise in career-oriented office-going women of the middle and upper middle classes, who had to manage both their households and professional lives. Women of the upper class thus leaned on those from the lower class to support their careers and maintain their homes, generating income in a trickle-

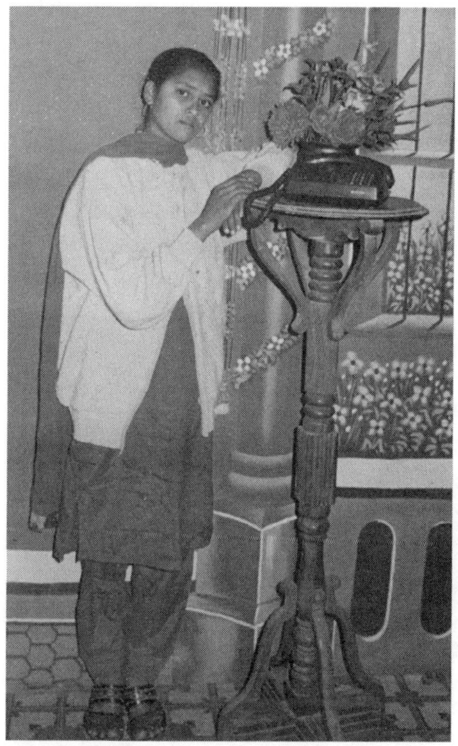

Figure 5. Shanti, a studio portrait of the author's neighbour's maid. Author's family album, Patna, 1998. © Divya Gauri.

Nineteenth-Century Woman'. *History Workshop Journal.* 36:1. pp. 35–65. doi.org/10.1093/hwj/36.1.35, 39.

[27] Ibid. pp. 44–47.

down effect. In a dual mechanism, the women who choose to become domestic workers monetise the otherwise unpaid labour of housework by doing it for another household. In their employer's household, unlike their own, they have to work according to the standards and needs of the family.

As mentioned earlier, the journey of this paper started with me diving into my own family album. While going through the photographs, I found one photograph of a young girl in an orange *salwar suit*, standing in a studio space, posing with a telephone (Figure 5). Her name is Shanti, and she was in her teens when I met her as a child. Shanti was the live-in help of a newly wedded Bengali couple from Kanpur, who were our neighbours in Patna. I recall looking at their wedding album years ago, wondering why Shanti was absent from the photographs, for she had been sent as a companion for the bride from her mother's home. I had asked her this question, to which I received no reply. After a few days, she came to my house and gave my sister and me this photo of hers. She asked us to keep the photograph and it inadvertently became a part of our family album. It is crucial to consider how she saw herself in the photograph and how she wanted to be seen. She might not have had agency in her employer's wedding album, which she was anyway not a part of, but here in this studio photograph, she did. However, in this photograph, posing along with a phone placed on a Victorian pedestal stand-table might not be her choice, but rather something that was suggested by the studio photographer. Typically, studios had props to enhance the *mise en scène* of the photographs, which also included backdrops—a house with a window decorated by plants and creepers in the case of Shanti's photograph. Shanti is not smiling in this photograph; instead, she appears pale. The picture presents her as expressionless, although here, she is not a subordinate or presented as a house help to someone; here, she has agency and can encapsulate her desire to be presented in a more accurate way. However, if we look at Tala (Figure 6), another such live-in house help, the story entirely changes.

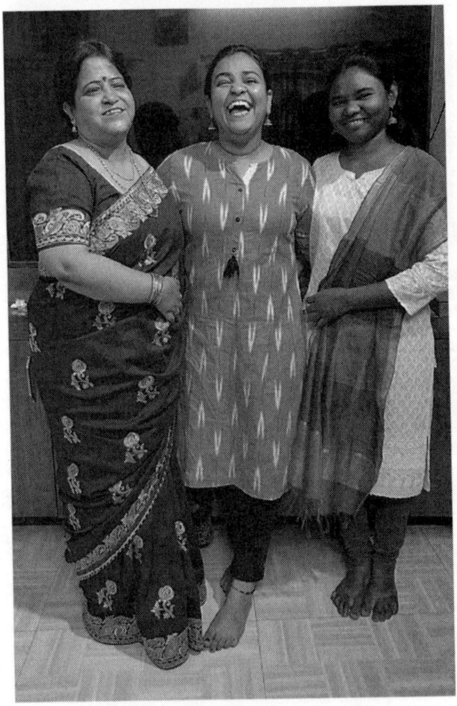

Figure 6. Tala with family; phone photograph. Paul family collection, Patna, 2021. © Ishita Paul.

Tala, a Santhali tribal girl I encountered, is employed at a Christian family's household in Patna (2021). She came to this household when she was very young, probably the reason why the family she is working for is 'like family' to her. Tala, unlike Shanti, does not have to wedge her presence into the family photographs of her employers. From family celebrations to selfies, she is everywhere. Tala's photographs and her relationship with her foster-family might not reflect upon her servitude, as she performs domestic chores for them, but it definitely registers her presence among the several family photographs. In them, Tala is as expressive as the other youngsters of the house. While looking at Tala's photographs, one can figure out her identity as the household help by her distinguishing complexion and facial features, which highlight her tribal identity while differentiating her from everyone else in the family. But she has visual agency despite her role as a domestic worker, in a sense obscuring the latter identity as she is absorbed into family photographs. The family accepts her as one of the children, a member of the family and also someone who takes care of her own finances. Despite the fact that she works for them as a housekeeper, they never treat her with disdain, which is registered well through the smiling faces of Tala and her family in the photograph.

Apart from live-in domestic workers, there are also all-rounder female part-timers, whose time is clearly divided as they work for more than one household, besides their own. While talking to Vimla, a part-timer working as a domestic worker for a family in Patna,[28] I learned that she only started working as a maid during the COVID-19 pandemic lockdown of 2020, as her husband was out of work and she had to manage her own household expenses. The very first household she was employed at was that of a government official, and she thought the lady would be supportive, but it turned out the other way. Her employer questioned her character and they never paid her a full salary, putting the pandemic forward as an excuse. For her, working as domestic help felt demeaning and she would have never opted for it if she had any other way to take care of her family.

The International Labour Organization (ILO) declared in June 2020 that over 55 million domestic workers around the globe—of whom 37 million domestic workers were women—were at risk of losing their jobs and income due to the pandemic. The women who are employed as domestic workers primarily come from places like Jharkhand, Bihar, Bengal and Orissa. They are mostly from the lower caste, belong to an ethnic minority or disadvantaged populations.[29] ILO launched a campaign on domestic work in 2010. The aim of this campaign was to raise public awareness around the importance of the job that domestic workers do, the contribution that these helpers make to the

[28] Vimla. 7 June 2021. Interview. Conducted by Divya Gauri.

[29] Chadh, Neymat. 2020. 'Domestic Workers in India: An Invisible Workforce', Social and Political Research Foundation. p. 7. doi.org/ sprf.in/wp-content/uploads/2021/02/Domestic-Workers-in-India-An-Invisible-Workforce.pdf.; 'About Domestic Work'. 4 June 2010. ILO. www.ilo.org/newdelhi/areasofwork/WCMS_141187/lang--en/index.htm. Accessed April 8, 2024.

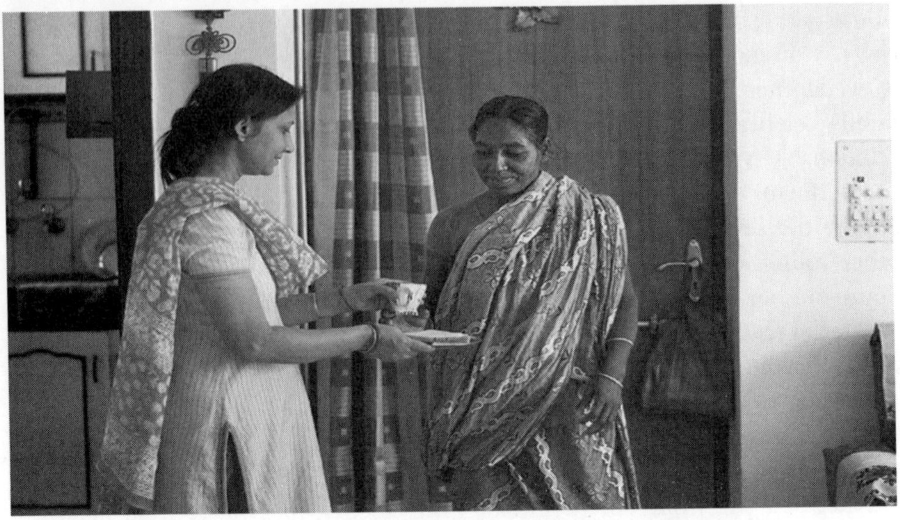

Figure 7. Woman giving tea to her maid, photograph by Shilpa Gavane. ILO competition entry for 'Your Work Is Important', 2010. © Gavane S. / ILO /Flickr (CC BY-NC-ND 2.0)

household they are employed at, and to promote decent work for domestic workers. As Vimla noted in her interview, the general public typically views domestic work as low-status labour performed by underprivileged women and men. As a part of promoting the campaign, a photo competition was organised on the theme 'Your Work Is Important'.[30] The purpose of this competition was to protect and advance domestic worker's rights in their capacity as 'workers'. The ILO chose a photo competition as the medium to increase visibility of the domestic workers and their work in society, providing photographs with the agency to register and archive the category of domestic helpers. The competition encouraged people to click photographs of domestic workers whereby the dignity of their work can be registered. A few of the photographs from the entries are discussed here as an entry point into households and housework.

Among the several entries, the first two photographs that are included here to support the discussion of this paper visualise domestic workers with their employers. In the first photograph (Figure 7), two women are seen standing in front of each other, and one can immediately distinguish between their statuses by just looking at their attire. The mistress is shown offering tea and toast to her household help and neither of them is looking at the other. Their gaze is directed towards the action. Although giving food and other necessities has long been a part of master–servant relationships, there isn't a particularly seamless

[30] "Photo Contest - Promoting Decent Work for Domestic Workers," Photo contest - Promoting Decent Work for Domestic Workers, June 4, 2010, www.ilo.org/newdelhi/info/public/WCMS_141181/lang--en/index.htm. Accessed April 8, 2024.

interaction between the two women presented in this photograph, performing their respective tasks. Even though every element of the photograph appears perfectly placed, the blue bag hanging on the door latch grabs the attention of the spectator. The bag might have belonged to the domestic worker and contained her belongings or other things she might have received from her employer. In a way, there is a lack of genuine expression here. If this same photograph had been taken candidly, one might have caught a glimpse of the relationship these two women shared; their natural interaction is completely missing from this photograph. This photograph is captured solely for the competition and not to add to any family albums. This can also be read as a photograph indicating the reversal of household work and dependency, as usually serving food is one such task that the help does for her mistress.

Servants are the invisible forces behind functional households, while also being extensions of the lady of the house, who holds an agency over all domestic chores. The action captured in the centre of Figure 7 is an interchange that can be performed by both the ladies. Another important thing to highlight here is why the photographer chose to capture this particular moment and not moments where the house help is actually performing their task. What about this photograph makes it appropriate to the theme of the ILO competition, 'Your Work Is Important'? Does the photographer want this particular action to be seen as an appreciation of the labour the domestic worker performs? The placement of cup and the plate also evokes the widespread, still-practised custom of keeping household helpers' cups separate from the family's. Similar to this, another photograph shows a lady preparing tea for her family (Figure

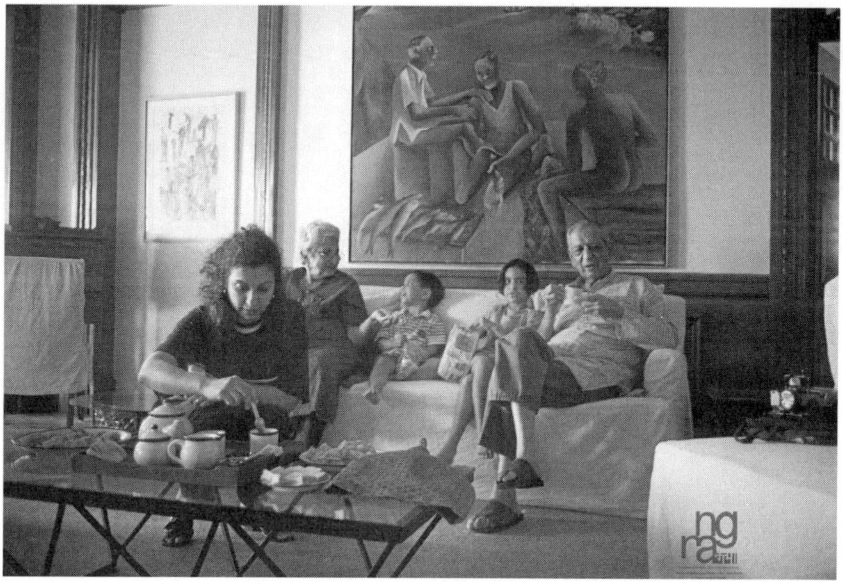

Figure 8. Gandhy Family at Kekee Manzil, Bombay, photograph by Sooni Taraporevala. National Gallery of Modern Arts Collection, 2000. ©NGMA

8). Despite being a well-known individual, the woman in the photograph did not care about herself being captured while she prepared tea for her family, which not only reflects her agency, but also signals her caring side. Everyone in the photograph is much at ease. Also, photographs being two-dimensional, cannot capture things that lie beyond the frame. The helpers who might have arranged the space, made all other arrangements for the photographic moment, including setting up the sitting space, cleaning and dusting things, and even preparing the tea, are not directly part of the photograph, but one can sense their presence in the clean and well-placed objects and other actions that constitute the image.

Now, the second photograph from the ILO competition that will be discussed here is of a woman seen spreading a sari out to dry, along with her son (Figure 9). The subjects are placed at the centre of the visual narrative, surrounded by the colourful saree and the labour being performed has a raw quality. The boy standing on the stool while spreading the sari is not aware of the fact that the help he is offering to his mother is also a silent training in domestic chores for him. Growing up, he might not have to perform these household tasks, even though doing them will come naturally to him. The narrative of the photograph would have changed completely if instead of the boy, there was a girl child in it, for male children do not usually do basic

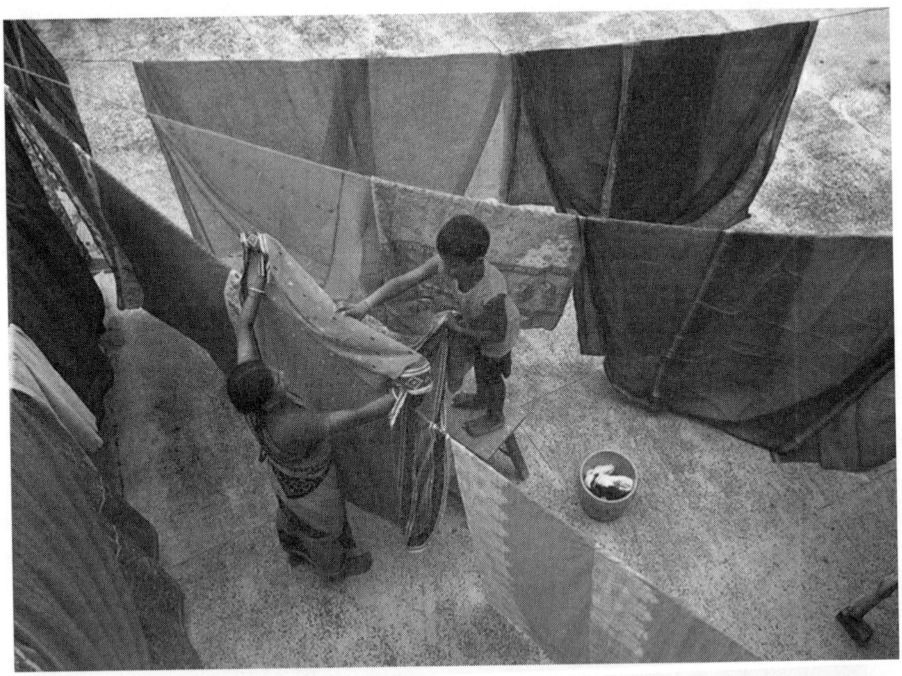

Figure 9. Mother and child drying a sari; photograph by Somenath Mukhopadhyay. ILO competition entry for 'Your Work Is Important', 2010.

household chores, while female children perform these tasks as part of the family or as hired help.

An invisible cycle of household chores and training operates among women living under the same roof, from the lady employer to her employee to the daughters of the household. This invisible transfer of inheritance of a domestic system happens in almost every Indian household, mainly middle and lower class. In 'Masculinity, Femininity, and Servitude: Domestic workers in Calcutta in the late twentieth century', Raka Ray addresses a scene from the 1956 film *Aparajito*, in which Apu's mother Sarbajaya quits her job as a cook after discovering that her son was making a hookah[31] for the master of the household she was employed at, whereas in *Pather Panchali* (1955), the first movie of The Apu trilogy, Apu's elder sister Durga handles all the household chores and, despite being young herself, is incredibly maternal and caring towards her younger brother.[32] In these two movies, it was both the caste and gender of Apu that did not destine him to work as a domestic worker for someone, whereas for Durga and Sarbajaya, domestic work was part of their gender identity.

Similar to this, UNICEF's popular animated series, *Meena*, that pushed social transformation in South Asia in the 1990s, also aimed to teach children about gender, health and social inequalities, and how to deal with them. Knowing that it was broadcast in several languages, including English, Bengali, Hindi, Nepali and Urdu, among others, says a lot about its appeal. Every episode of *Meena* focused on a different issue, such as the value of a girl's education, the need for both male and female children to receive equal share of food. In addition, in episode 12 of the series, Meena also experiences life as a domestic worker after her father leaves her in the city to attend to an emergency. Meena is seen doing daily chores in multiple episodes, whereas her brother is not. In episode 2, to prove that Meena's brother and Meena should get equal amount of food, her brother is challenged to perform her daily domestic duties for a day, including cleaning the floor, bringing water, feeding chickens, etc. in order to demonstrate that Meena's work is not easy and that she deserves better nutrition.[33] Even though it is a cartoon series and does not relate to this article directly, the problems it addresses may have presented the idea of the invisible transfer of inheritance among females, as mentioned above. The series also emphasises the need for explanations as to why certain issues were chosen for this cartoon series to focus on, as well as what else occurred while those issues were being highlighted. For example, Meena performing household work is

[31] A type of pipe that brings smoke through a container of water before it is breathed in (Cambridge Dictionary).

[32] Ray, Raka. 2000. 'Masculinity, Femininity, and Servitude: Domestic Workers in Calcutta in the Late Twentieth Century'. *Feminist Studies*. 26:3. p. 691. doi.org/10.2307/3178646, 691.

[33] McKee, Neil and Rachel Carnegie. 1993. *Meena–Dividing the Mango* (Bangladesh: The Light Box for UNICEF).

not questioned in the series but depicted in it, which may be because girls performing these chores may have been a common practice in the regions this cartoon was broadcast, highlighting the gendered division of labour once more. The middle- and upper middle-class girls are trained knowingly and unknowingly to be ideal women, which also includes managing the home and house help. Girls of lower income groups are similarly trained in housework from a young age. Going back to the photograph, the placement of mother and son opposite each other, separated by a sari, evokes an anomaly; the boy is helping his mother spread a six metre long cloth and his labour is largely invisible to known narratives. His position is usually occupied by the opposite sex, and it is perhaps the uniqueness of his own subjectivity that invites a photograph in the first place.

Among the selected few photographs from the 2010 ILO competition entries that were meeting the criteria for discussion in this article, is this last photograph where the domestic worker is positioned washing utensils on the right and a man, probably her employer, is seated on a chair reading the newspaper on the left (Figure 10). The two subjects of this photograph are placed in such a way that if we fold the image down the centre, each part will be complete without the other. It is simple to see how gender functions in the patriarchal family by contrasting this image with the preceding photograph. Through this photograph, one can read both class and gender disparities that are present in our society, presenting men at leisure, reading newspapers—probably the politics section—while the woman is engaged in cleaning utensils. While reading the photograph, although none of the two subjects are looking

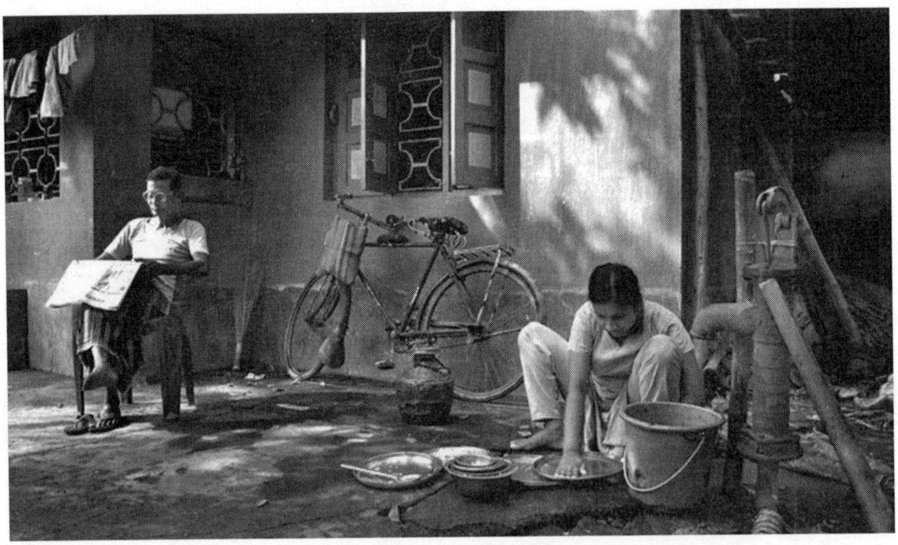

Figure 10. A domestic worker washing utensils; photograph by Sujata Jana. ILO Competition entry for 'Your Work is Important', 2010. © Jana S. / ILO /Flickr (CC BY-NC-ND 2.0).

at camera, the man appears more relaxed as compared to the woman. They are placed completely separately so that their roles are well-defined and just by a look, the social disparities between them are obvious.

Through the Lens of Contemporary Artists

While discussing the framing of domestic servitude in family photographs, the works of two contemporary South Asian photographers, Anay Mann and Jannatul Mawa, offer insight into an age-old domestic reality that has largely been veiled. They look at women engaged in household chores alone, or side by side with their helpers. In these photographs, one can easily witness the alternative narrative that has always been sidelined in mainstream studies. I analyse two photographic series, *About Neetika* (2007) by Anay Mann and *Closed Distance* (2013) by Jannatul Mawa, to unearth parallel narratives. The photographs that are part of these series might not be family photographs in the conventional sense, but rather artworks that reflect on domestic, gendered narratives. These photographs can be read as the interjections in family photographs, filling gaps and highlighting that home is not only a place of comfort but also a workspace. Anay Mann is a Delhi-based photographer who started his career as a model before he became a photographer. The constructed image became the idiom he sought to explore with his camera. In 2001, he started photographing his wife Neetika while she performed her daily household chores. He named this series of portraits that present his everyday domestic reality, *About Neetika*. While he photographs her through windows and doorways, busy with cooking, cleaning or childcare, he not only registers his wife but also thousands of other women whose domestic work never has been visibilised.

In one of the photographs from the series *About Neetika*,[34] a woman is captured standing in front of a glass surface with a spray bottle in one hand and a cloth in the other. She is possibly wiping a glass surface; she has already cleaned it, as it appears clean, and the image centres the enactment of her gesture. This might be a posed photograph, but that cannot deny the preparation for the photograph itself, an act not only of the moment but a culmination of years of nurturing and care by her. In another photograph from the same series, which is beautifully divided into background, middle ground and foreground, he tries to capture his wife as the backbone of his family. Similar to the last image, the artist captures the woman here behind a window; however, this time, the window is partially open. The mother is portrayed in the middle ground, on the right, behind the window, spreading the cloth for drying, while the child is in the foreground, on the left, in front of the window. Additionally, many more clothes are hanging in the background behind the woman, drying

[34] The artist's interpretation of his series differs from the interpretation of the author, hence there is no image included from the series *About Neetika*.

and registering the labour that is invisible. Viewers might have not known the identity of the woman in these photographs if the artist had not made it obvious that the series features his wife. By photographing his wife, and her never-ending household chores, the artist at once reflects upon the lives of tens of thousands of women who are involved in their household chores, day in day out, with no recognition except when their labour is a part of their identity as dutiful and nurturing women.

Jannatul Mawa is a Bangladeshi photographer. Through her work, she has tried to bridge the gap between those who work for a household and those who reap the benefits of their labour. Her 2017 photographic series *Close Distance* portrays the unevenness we have all witnessed but are largely ignorant of. Although Mawa positions her subjects in symmetrical settings (Figure 11), it is hard to not notice the space between two people, separated by class and status, even if they are sitting on the same couch. Mawa as a photographer has largely visualised unseen sections of our society, emphasising on the marginalised. In *Close Distance*, Mawa has tried to portray an intimacy that's rather rare.

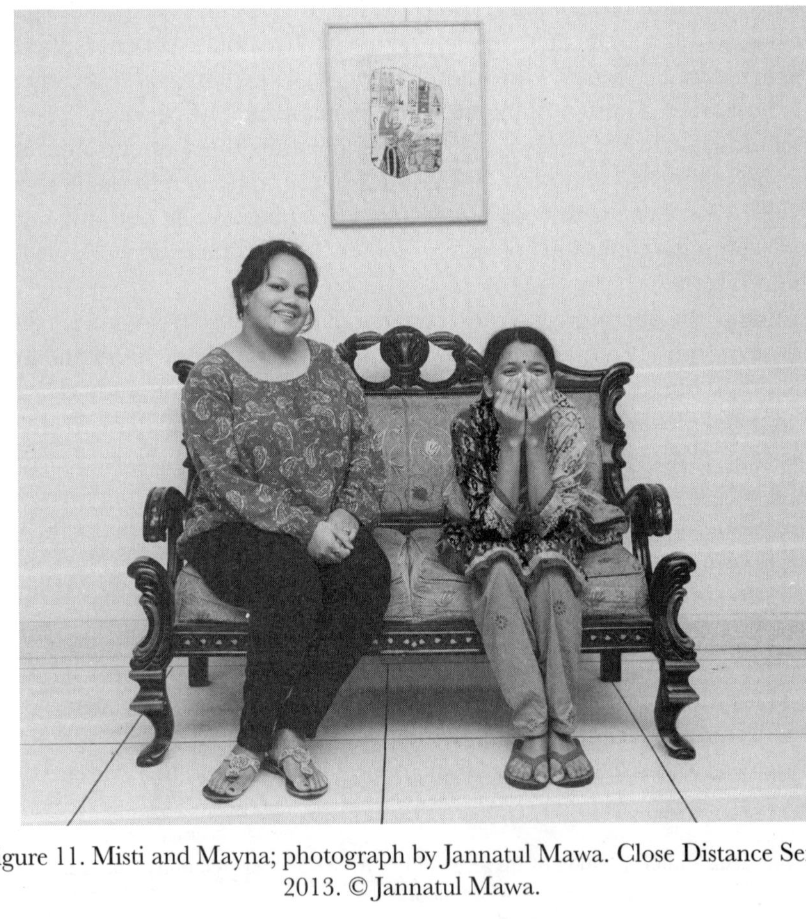

Figure 11. Misti and Mayna; photograph by Jannatul Mawa. Close Distance Series, 2013. ©Jannatul Mawa.

Although she tries to bind socially disparate figures together in the same frame, class inequalities through gestures, clothing and appearances are starkly visible. Of the two women placed under the same roof, as they spend most of their time together, for one it is home and for the other, a place for work.

'#Justlikefamily'

As the smartphone with a camera entered the everyday lives of people in the millennial world, and social media became a popular vehicle for displaying one's life, the veiled reality of our daily lives also started revealing itself. It was more visible as the 2020 COVID-19 lockdown restricted us to our homes. This was also the time when on Instagram, many users started appreciating their domestic workers, recognising how their absence drastically altered their lives, even posting photos of themselves engaged in housework. Domestic chores had blurred the lines between employers and domestic workers, thereby temporarily equalising them. The concept of 'just like family' came into question as a form of address that people have used in relation to domestic workers, long before the pandemic. How were domestic workers reconfigured with regard to the family, with their physiology coming into question due to the fear of contagion during the pandemic? While the family needed to be protected from the virus, housework became a major problem for several Indians who were not used to doing any of it by themselves. Some kept part-timers away, others absorbed them as live-ins, 'just like family', while still others lost them to the village-ward migration of the displaced from urban areas. Just before the lockdown of 2020, I met a vegetable vendor in Greater Kailash Extension in New Delhi. She was earlier a house help in the same locality. While sharing her life story,[35] she mentioned that her employer used to treat her like family. But this cordial environment would sustain only if she did not take leave. Once, when her mother was not well, she had to go home for four days, resulting in her losing her job. Those who addressed her as family could not accommodate her when she went home to look after her own family. As such, this case points to the emptiness of the 'just like family' concept, for underneath the endearment, lie unstated hierarchical conditions of the relationship.[36]

The photographs discussed in this section were shared on Instagram accounts of various people. All these photographs were uploaded with #househelp in appreciation of their effort, stating that they were 'just like family'. Sharmila is a domestic worker from Katihar, Bihar and her story was shared by her employer of thirty-five years.[37] The date of the post was August 2020, the time when most migrant workers went back from cities to

---

[35] Jyoti (vegetable vendor). 2020. Interview. Conducted by Divya Gauri.

[36] Grover, Shalini. 2018. 'English-Speaking and Educated Female Domestic Workers in Contemporary India', *Journal of South Asian Development*, 13: 2. pp. 1-24. doi.org/10.1177/0973174118788008, 16.

[37] Motabhai915, 26 August 2020. *Instagram*, www.instagram.com/p/CEVxt0QFByh/.

smaller towns and villages, due to the pandemic. On reaching his hometown, he met Sharmila and found his and his mother's names tattooed on her arm. Such a gesture reflected a familial relationship, even though Sharmila might have never entered the frame of a family photograph with her employers. In the age of social media, where through selfies, servants can enter the public domain along with their employers on the same platform, they still rarely enter the frame of family photographs, because they aren't family itself. A cordial acknowledgement of their work and gratitude during the pandemic came mainly from women Instagram influencers who regarded their help as extensions of themselves. By extensions, I mean those who shared in the gendered nature of female-oriented domestic work as caregivers of children or other performers of household chores, like cleaning, dusting or cooking that are still considered women's jobs.

Unlike physical family albums where only one side of women's lives are portrayed whereas the other side is invisibilised, in the age of social media, women have greater agency in displaying their side of the story, which includes their engagement with household work and also those who help achieve it.[38] Their Instagram posts not only register the working class and how they are an important part of almost every middle-class Indian family, but have also become records of societal differences. The act of archiving enabled by social media has provided both employers and employees a more democratic space where they can register their lives without needing approval, and the formal inclusions and exclusions of family albums.

Reference/ Further Reading

Agrawal, Ravi. 2020. 'Google's Saathi Women and the Smartphone'. *INDIA Connected: How the Smartphone Is Transforming the World's Largest Democracy* (New York: Oxford University Press). pp. 21–42.

Gurtoo, Anjula. 2019. 'Occupational Prestige and Informal Work: Women Domestic Workers in India'. *Workers and Margins*. pp. 193–213. doi.org/10.1007/978-981-13-7876-8_10.

Haggis, Jane. 1998. "Good Wives and Mothers" Or "Dedicated Workers"? Contradictions of Domesticity in the "Mission Of Sisterhood", Travancore, South India'. *Maternities and Modernities*. pp. 81–113. doi.org/10.1017/cbo9780511621826.005.

Mahanta, Upasana and Indranath Gupta. 2019. *Recognition of the Rights of Domestic Workers in India: Challenges and the Way Forward* (Singapore: Springer).

Ray, Raka and Seemin Qayum. 2020. *Cultures of Servitude: Modernity, Domesticity, and Class in India* (Stanford, CA: Stanford University Press).

[38] 'Arwa Didi and I are like sisters. I've been working at her home for 10 months now. Some days, we exchange recipes, and other days, I teach her to garden and she teaches me make-up tricks. I love make-up so she lends me her make-up and jewellery'. officialhumansofbombay. 19 October 2020. *Instagram*. www.instagram.com/p/CGhmCoWnA3k/.

Sarkar, Tanika. 1992. 'The Hindu Wife and the Hindu Nation: Domesticity and Nationalism in Nineteenth Century Bengal'. *Studies in History*. 8:2. pp. 213–35. doi.org/10.1177/025764309200800204.

Sinha, Aakanksha, Megan Quint, Pritikusum Sinha, Anupama Singh and Pravin Sinha. 2019. 'Undervalued and Overrepresented: Voices of Migrant Domestic Workers in India'. *Global Social Welfare*. 7:3. pp. 285–96. doi.org/10.1007/s40609-019-00149-0.

Sinha, Nitin and Nitin Varma. eds. 2019. *Servants' Past Late-Eighteenth to Twentieth-Century South Asia*. Vol. 2. (Telangana, Hyderabad: Orient BlackSwan).

Sinha, Nitin. 2020. 'Who Is (Not) a Servant, ANYWAY? Domestic Servants and Service in Early Colonial India'. *Modern Asian Studies.* 55:1. pp. 152–206. doi.org/10.1017/s0026749x19000271.

Tagg, John. 2007. 'A Means of Surveillance: The Photograph as Evidence in Law'. *The Burden of Representation: Essays on Photographies and Histories* (Basingstoke: Palgrave MacMillan). pp. 66–102.

When I Start Photography, I Start with My Family

Jaisingh Nageswaran and Rajyashri Goody

Jaisingh Nageswaran and Rajyashri Goody met through their common friend, Sohrab Hura, in 2018 in Kolkata. They have remained close friends and peers since, and so the conversation-based format of this essay, interspersed with images from Nageswaran's work, *I Feel Like A Fish* (2020–ongoing) and Goody's *Eat With Great Delight* (2018), felt like an organic way to put down their thoughts related to themes of family, photography, and representation.

Photography has played a significant role in Nageswaran and Goody's lives. In their individual art practices, they combine their own images and work with their personal archives to explore various themes of identity, culture and the self. They have also been involved in documenting their families' social work activities. Though Nageswaran is Christian and comes from Tamil Nadu and Goody is a Buddhist from Maharashtra, both their families have been working towards the education and empowerment of Dalit communities for decades. As a result of this, they grew up with an awareness of caste from a very young age, as well as a strong sense of dignity and self-respect owing to the hard work and perseverance they have been surrounded by.

In this essay, transcribed from Zoom video calls they had in late 2020 and early 2021, Nageswaran and Goody discuss each other's work and issues of access and visibility in the context of their upbringing, shedding light on their shared responsibility towards building a more complex and nuanced visual narrative of Dalit family life and culture.

JAISINGH NAGESWARAN: I learnt photography in my late teens through my family members, my immediate people—they were my muse. When I left home in Vadipatti after college, I lost that connection. I lived in different places and travelled a lot. For more than fifteen years, I shot many things other than my family. I did think about them often, but I didn't feel comfortable photographing my home. I didn't want to show my lower middle-class Dalit family to outsiders.

Because of the pandemic of 2020, I had to stay home for a long period of time, and once again realised the true importance of documenting my daily life in the place that I grew up. I have spent the lockdown at home with my niece and nephew, swimming in and photographing by the Periyar river.

RAJYASHRI GOODY: I love the photographs you have been taking since the lockdown began. They have a warmth to them that is particular only to family photographs.

My father always carried a camera with him. When he first moved to India from the UK in 1974, he documented the social work he was involved in with the Ambedkarite Buddhist movement in Maharashtra. After my parents got married in Pune in 1984, my mother, my uncles and aunts also began to take many pictures. My mother is especially fond of taking photographs. My father got all of his images scanned in the mid-2000s, including all our family photographs, and I started to spend hours on the computer just clicking through album after album, folder after folder. I still find this process very comforting.

What does your family album look like?

JN: My mother's family is Christian, and her brother had a camera. They lived in Madurai, which is a big city, so they had access to this technology. My father comes from a Hindu background, and from a rural area, a *pakka*[1] village of T. Vadipatti. They didn't have their own camera, but they had access to a photo studio. I remember my mother taking me to a studio when I was a child; I was probably one or two years old. I am standing with a pen in my hand. That was the photograph.

When my brother began studying architecture in 1996, he bought a camera for site visits. A Yashica MF-2 Super DX 35mm. We would photograph ourselves and our family members with it. This was when I was in twelfth grade. I don't remember if we did much documentation before that. We photographed so many things with the Yashica: my sister's coming-of-age celebration, Christmas, the neighbours coming over for dinner, the choir singing at church … We would take the film, go to the lab, see the prints and put them in the family album. When December arrived and we would decorate the house and the Christmas tree, we would go back to the album and reference how it had been done the years before.

I am in the process of scanning our photos, and it is very interesting. I've found pictures I had completely forgotten about. I found one of my grandmother blessing me. My grandmother established a school, the Gandhi Primary School, in Vadipatti, in 1953, which still exists. Fifteen years ago, when I first started taking pictures, I would take group photos of the students, of the children sitting in class, of my parents working and teaching. Without realising it, I was documenting our school and our history. They are so valuable to me now.

RG: In my late teens, I loved taking pictures, and my family was very supportive and bought me an SLR in 2009. Over the years, I began photographing my parents' social projects, particularly Nagaloka in Nagpur, which is an

[1] Hindi term roughly translated to real, strong.

educational institute for young people from minority communities. This helped me understand the significance of the work that was being done, of the students that were studying there, who had travelled from remote areas across India to be there and learn about Buddhism, and about Dr. Ambedkar. Looking back, I think only through the act of photographing did I recognise the significance of what was going on.

JN: My father saw a photograph I had taken of my sister and he appreciated the way I had shot it, a portrait, and he said, 'You have something.' He believed in me and he gave me the money—₹12,000—to buy my first SLR camera. Those first few pictures are now very important. The house we don't have anymore is in them. It has completely changed now. We had a parrot, a dog and a cat. I photographed the house floor, and the first time we laid mosaic on the floor. Only rich people would use mosaic. When I see it in the photograph, I remember how my father and I went to buy the stone, and the shopkeeper gave us some sample stones to choose. We had a tape recorder and cassettes my father had bought. We had a carrom board. We would listen to music and play carrom. When my brother's friends came to the village, we took photographs with them, and took them to the river, sat with the cows. Our faces were so fresh. No beard, no moustache. I keep returning to these photos again and again.

RG: The body of work you are working on at the moment, *I Feel Like A Fish* (2020–ongoing), feels similar to these scenes you are describing in your family photographs. They have a joy and playfulness to them. You use your phone, primarily, to take these images. Does this change the way you shoot?

JN: The phone helps me find moments. My niece and nephew can be playing, for instance, and I can just grab my phone and join them, and take their photographs. They aren't self-conscious around me, especially not when I am holding a phone. My mother and sister, they like to wear a nice sari before I take their pictures, even though I don't want them to dress differently.

I think I have only recently learnt how to shoot people the way I would like to, and this method doesn't require an SLR. Earlier, I used to go to far-off places and shoot large events like the Kumbh Mela, but now, wherever I am, I know I can take intimate photographs. At first, it was a challenge to capture the intimacy and the closeness of my family, but once I stopped shooting like a photographer, it became easier.

RG: There is a stereotypical 'photographer's gaze' that I was trying to replicate in my early twenties, associated with documentary-style images of exotic people and places. I had to unlearn that in order to consider my family photographs as archives of Dalit history and culture. The everyday images of us growing up, eating and travelling, speak to something much larger. There is power in our representations of intimacy, and I feel this resonating in your work.

JN: It's very difficult to document the people you love. The more you love, the harder it is. It was never easy to photograph my parents. Over time, I stopped thinking of myself as a photographer and recognised that I am just a family member here. I am a son. I am an uncle. I have to just go with the flow.

Taking photos of my family also helped me connect with them after so many years of being away from home. In the photographs I take of them now, you might be able to notice either the distance, or the closeness, between us. If I have to photograph someone I don't like, I tend to stay away from them and shoot them from a distance.

But if I like the person, I like the camera to go very close to them. When I take portraits of my father, or my niece, the camera goes right to their faces quite automatically. They do get irritated sometimes, but I can't help myself.

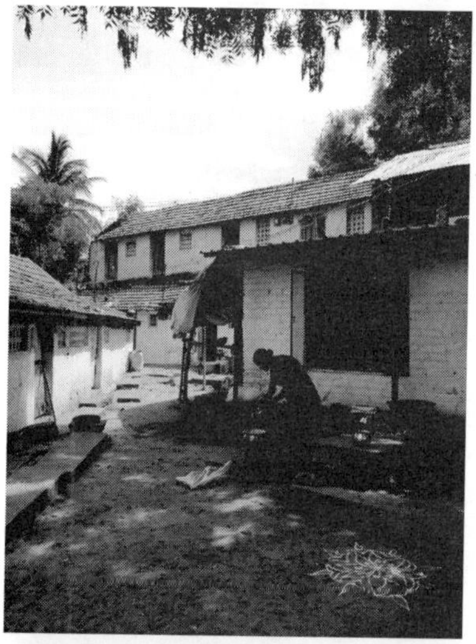

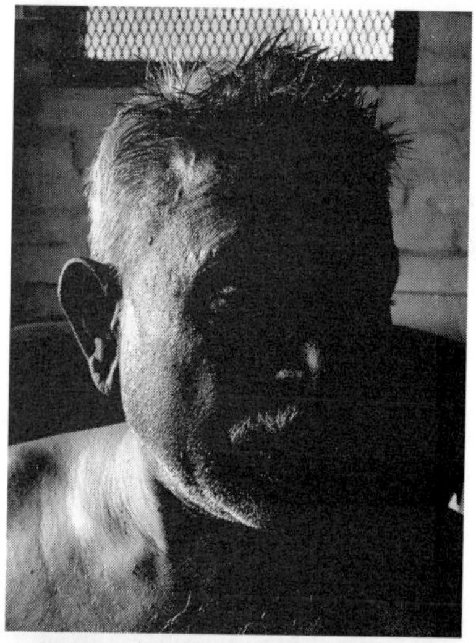

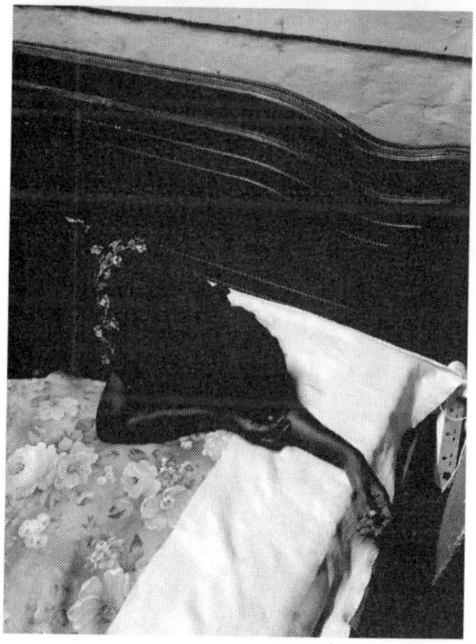

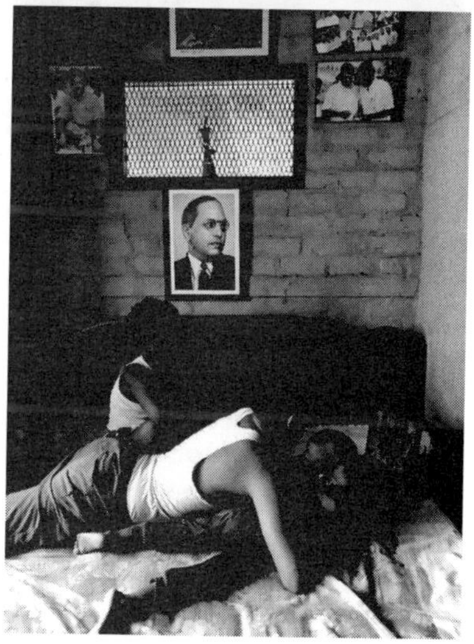

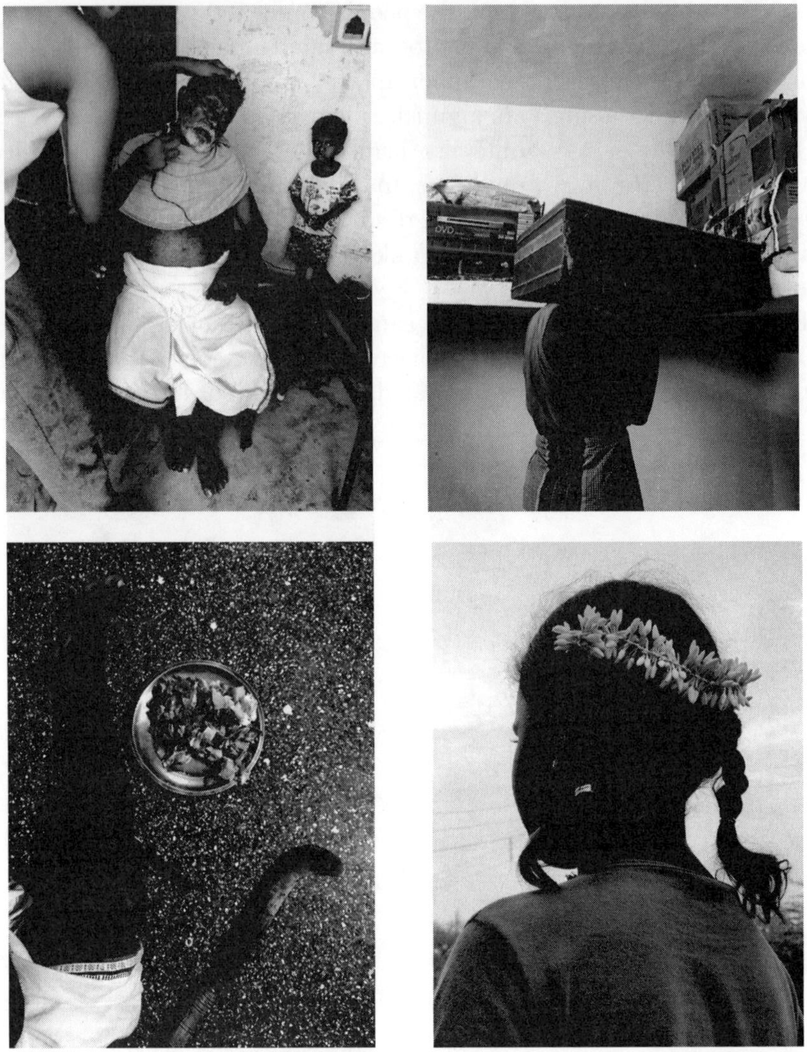

Figure 1: Images from *I Feel Like A Fish* by Jaisingh Nageswaran

RG: It is brave to capture intimacy, because you are also allowing yourself to be open and vulnerable to the person you are photographing. In this case, it's your family, which isn't as easy as one would think. I think I stopped taking many photographs partly due to this reason. I tend to become too shy and too afraid of opening up with a camera in front of my family. I am also nervous of what the outcome will be and how they might open up to me. This hesitance has cost me—I wanted to photograph and record my grandmother Tarabai for years, but I kept putting it off, and now she is gone. We do have many photographs of her, but I feel like I was too afraid to do my part, and I missed out on listening to her life stories as a hardworking, pioneering Dalit woman.

JN: It is important to capture the stories of our families, especially because we belong to Dalit communities. Most photographers in India come from privilege, have access to equipment and wide networks. These photographers are in charge of representing us in the media. When you look at newspapers and see how outsiders portray Dalit life, it is normally only in the context of painful headlines—'Dalit houses demolished', 'Dalit women assaulted' … When they portray Dalit leaders, they deliberately print ugly photographs of them. Photographers from the West have also documented Dalit people, but as manual scavengers.

They don't show the other side of our culture. We push to educate our children. We start schools. My grandmother Ponnuthai started a school, Ponnuthai Amma Gandhiji Primary School, in 1954, and it's so hard for others to believe that because of how our people have been portrayed. In their mind, we don't own nice things. My upper-caste classmates in college were jealous of my clothes. They didn't believe I was Dalit because I wore jeans. They would ask how I claimed to be Dalit when my brother and father rode a Splendour motorbike. They would taunt me. For people like that, it is very difficult to digest that we could have a good life.

Wedding photographers also behave similarly: they often refuse to enter a Dalit colony. If they do, they spend as little time there as possible. They also charge us much more than they would an upper-caste person. The entire documentation of the wedding or function is compromised because they refuse to even listen to what we want them to photograph.

I am a photographer and I have a responsibility to document my life, and my family. As Dalit people, we don't have any proper documentation, or formal archives; it has always been done by others, who see Dalit life as dirty. But when I see your work, which uses the photographs of your home and family, there is so much care.

RG: We are not just victims, despite all the horrific things that have, and continue to, happen to us. And yes, the representation of us simply as victims needs to be made more complex. I do however recognise that the daily violence happening to Dalit people must be documented, whether by people from our community or outsiders. Otherwise, the violence—to which most people turn a blind eye—will be made completely invisible, and that is another kind of violence.

When I first started making art about my community, people questioned my 'motives'. There were, and still are comments from upper-caste peers about me not being 'Dalit' enough, not having done enough work or 'activism' to claim this space as mine. For a long time, this made me anxious, and it was hard to keep making work.

I found a lot of comfort in my family photographs. Looking at them made me relive my happy childhood with my brother Ashok, my parents, my grandparents, my aunts and uncles, and my cousins. I began to recognise how privileged I am to have grown up in a wonderful family that has done so much to break barriers, not just for themselves but for so many others in our community. I would be doing a great disservice to their generations of resistance if I gave up my research and practice around caste.

Eat With Great Delight (2018) emerged from this space of self-confidence in my identity. The images are simple, honest, family photographs of celebrations and day-to-day happy moments centred around food and kitchens. They are accompanied by 'recipes' that I gathered from Dalit autobiographies. They shine a light on the painful memories of leftovers, begging and hunger that have scarred our people. The juxtaposition of these with my family photographs hopefully helps in shattering narratives of victimhood associated with Dalit people.

I don't know if upper-caste people will ever really understand how deeply important these documentations of joy are, and the power they hold within them. Would they even be interested in shooting positive images of us? I doubt it. There's not much in it for them, no juicy story, no hard-hitting violence that evokes shame and disgust, no refuge from their newly recognised *savarna*[2] guilt, and no pat on the back from their fraternity.

JN: Our issues are a seasonal thing to them, like mango season, or a fashion trend. They might think about Dalits and write about Dalits, and even keep a photograph of Ambedkar at home, but how will that change their attitude? They refuse to talk about their own casteist practices openly. Instead, they just want to focus on the plight of the Dalit subject, so they can gain some sort of mileage from it. So many documentary filmmakers have used me as a ladder.

When I was a child, we had a Western toilet at home, but my classmates would not believe me. They would try to explain to me how a Western toilet works. This happened to me recently as well, at a prominent person's home. When I visited him and I noticed that he had images of Ambedkar, and other revolutionary leaders all over his house, he still felt he had to teach me how to use a Western toilet.

In photography circles, I am always introduced as a Dalit photographer. Why? I am simply a photographer. But these terms make them feel very good about themselves, because they feel like they are supporting a Dalit photographer. They don't really care about how we feel, or our sense of dignity. At first, I would want to run away from these mixers and events, but now I don't care. Why should I shame myself for something others are doing?

Many of these people have always had a camera in their homes. Fortunately, because my brother was able to buy a camera, we started documenting ourselves. Now, many Dalit people have a phone. Working-class people are now able to take photographs. I don't know just how many people actively shoot and document their lives, but the number has definitely increased. But

[2] Those that belong to any one of the four dominant Hindu castes.

where do they store them? Do many of us have a computer? What if the memory card gets corrupted? Do they print them?

RG: I was with some colleagues the other day, at a ceramics studio I work from, and they were talking about just that. One of them was advising the other what to do with the photos, to buy a pen drive, take it to a photo studio, and get someone there to save them as well as print them out. It's not very straightforward, and maybe more complicated because of the large number of photographs people take on their phones these days. People just forget the photos they take on their phones.

I see my family taking photos with their smartphones all the time, especially my cousins. I really enjoy it, everyone photographing their new outfits, taking selfies at birthdays and weddings. It seems like a very simple act, but in our context it is a significant one. I don't think many of my cousins even see themselves as Dalit. Perhaps they don't want to be associated with the word. These are the possibilities that open up with more access to resources, to technology—where you can be anyone you want to be. Our old family photographs definitely have the charm and nostalgia of film and print, and they were made when a considerably less number of us were able to own a camera. Today's selfies are just as momentous.

JN: Non-Dalit people have a lot of material culture surrounding them. Their homes have nice rooms, shelves and cupboards. These are all places to put up photographs. We have a nice house now, but not so long ago, we were living in very bad conditions, and I had to consciously store all the family photographs carefully in photo albums. Many of them got damaged, the photographs got stuck to each other. And we lost them. That's also so important, to be able to care for and maintain these photos. Even though I have been a photographer for a long time, I was careless with these documents, and didn't preserve my family's photographs well. Only now am I cleaning them, and getting them all scanned.

Maybe it's a Dalit mentality? We don't give much value to our life and our belongings, not as much as others. People from higher castes seem to value everything they have much more. They document their lives more, and they have space to keep things well and safe. For us, because of external and internal caste issues, we did not have enough room to keep things. We just threw them away. Even when the government gave us land, we sold it to others for just Rs. 1,000. Other people, they keep things for their next generation, but Dalit mentality is not materialistic. Our people are all heart, they are okay letting go of things. Maybe that's why we lost our land and our culture. We don't think about tomorrow, or the new year. We just think about the present. But other people, non-Dalit people, think about keeping things for their descendants.

RG: Do you think this could be because our relationship with pride is quite new? Savarna families have been allowed to be very proud of themselves and of their community, and have fought to protect that honour for thousands of years. They have been able to pass this on, in the form of family wealth or legacy, and along with that, confidence and self-respect too. Our ancestors didn't have much to pass on to us in terms of material wealth, but my family is strong, proud and confident. Social reformers like Babasaheb and Jyotiba Phule urged our people to inculcate these values and look ahead, and because we are so focussed on making a better life for ourselves in the future, this doesn't leave much space for nostalgia.

JN: We have too many painful memories for nostalgia. My family has been able to have a good life because of the church. They are proud to be Christian, and happy to proclaim that. But my father, I don't think he has had much in his life to be proud of, because of his Hindu upbringing. When he married my mother and converted to Christianity, he began to have a better life.

RG: Perhaps what we are doing, through our photographs, is acknowledging the pride and dignity inherent in small instances of everyday life.

To me, conversion to any religion is such a brave statement. We are Buddhist, and in Maharashtra, many Dalits have followed in Babasaheb's footsteps when he converted to the religion in 1956. When I was younger, I always felt like religion in general didn't matter, but over the years, I have begun to understand the transformative power of conversion for people who have been pushed to the bottom of the rung for generations. Could you tell me a little bit more about conversion to Christianity in Tamil Nadu by Dalit people?

JN: In Tamil Nadu, Brahmin Christians are very rare, and very few. Upper-caste Hindus have all the temples, they have a good base, and strong local community allegiance. The majority of Christians are from Dalit communities, and the writings of Periyar and his principles of self-respect have been very influential. The Indian Bible was first printed in Tamil, here in Tamil Nadu, in 1714 by missionaries from Europe. Then, when the British colonised us, many of their staff members were from the *pariah* community, who are Dalits, and they converted to Christianity. They still followed a caste structure, but because they had more access to education, they have been able to get out of their poverty.

RG: In what way do they follow a caste structure? I belong to what was the Mahar subcaste, the same as Babasaheb. They make up the largest number of Buddhists in Maharashtra. Other sub-castes such as the Mang people have been hesitant to convert to Buddhism, because they see it as a Mahar stronghold. I learnt a lot about these issues through Eknath Awadh's autobiography, *Strike A Blow To Change The World* (2018).[3]

[3] Originally published in Marathi as *Jag Badal Ghaluni Ghaav* (2011). Translated into English by Jerry Pinto, it was published in 2018 by Speaking Tiger Publishing Pvt. Ltd.

JN: In our church, even though most of the congregation is from a Dalit background, the front rows, closest to the pew, are reserved for those belonging to what we call 'BC' (acronym for Backward Classes). They are Dalit, but belong to a higher caste than Pariah. My family sits toward the back. I once sat in the front, and people got very agitated. They said, 'Thambi, this is not your place. Why are you sitting here?' Only then did I realise the caste divide in the church.

The Bible says you must love yourself and love your neighbour, but still, caste is very strongly embedded in our belief system. Mixed marriage is still very uncommon. My mother and father are from different religions but from the same caste, Pariah. My uncle, because he is not from a BC background, never got a chance to become church president. He is a very strong person and did a lot of work for the church all his life, but positions on the church board have always been given only to BC people.

But most importantly, Christianity has given us access to education. My mother is a member of the Tamil Nadu Lutheran church. Her side of the family is made up of teachers. They have been able to get good jobs, and have studied a lot. They have a piano in their house, and they all know how to play it.

RG: I think our families are similar in that way. My mother has been a teacher all her life, at Dr Ambedkar College in Pune. Many of my aunts and uncles are also educators. Their commitment to Babasaheb and his values have played a huge role in their social mobility.

My mother once told me that one of the reasons she married my father—a foreigner—was so that her children could get the best possible opportunities in life. She was born in a village on the outskirts of Pune, and her parents moved to the city in search of a better life. My mother was able to attend the local government school, but the quality of education was poor. The teachers never paid much attention to the students, and my mother, at the age of ten or eleven, realised that she didn't know how to read despite attending school for so many years. She had to teach herself how to read and write properly. She didn't have the money to buy books for school, and so had to borrow them from other students or the library. She also had to work while studying to bring in some money. And it was because of her insistence that her younger siblings all studied hard and got good jobs for themselves.

JN: Education is our only weapon. We don't have any other choice. Only through this can we build our future generations, and that is especially important for our community.

RG: It allows us mobility as well, from the entrenched caste structures of village life. Babasaheb talks about leaving rural areas for the cities. When I visit a village, even if it is my ancestral one, I don't feel comfortable. People are always inquisitive about my caste, the caste divides are too visible for me to feel at home.

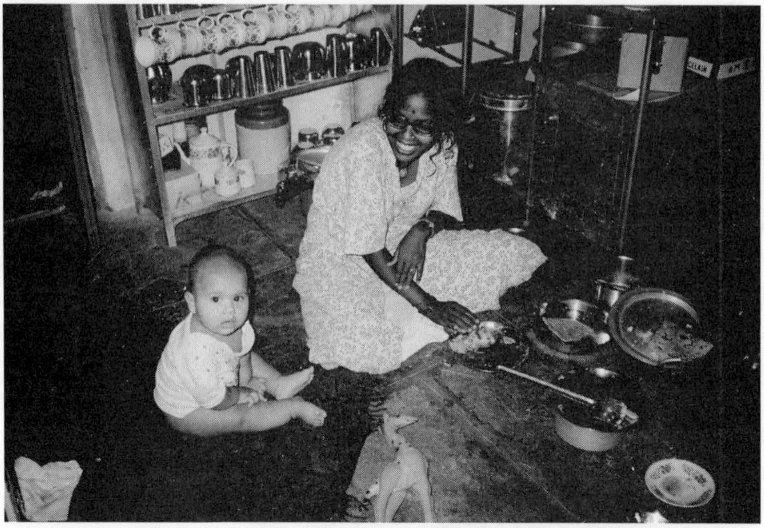

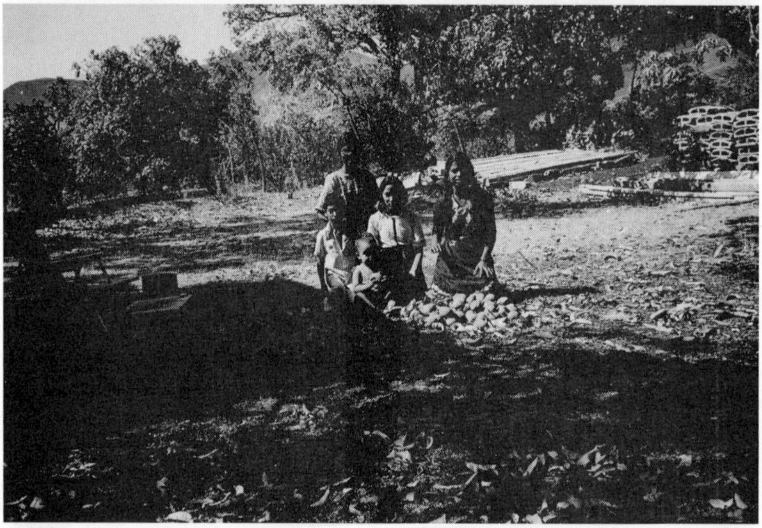

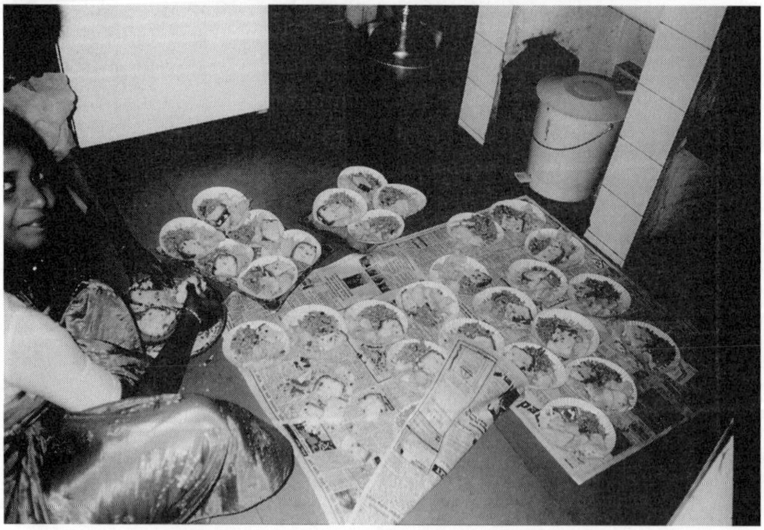

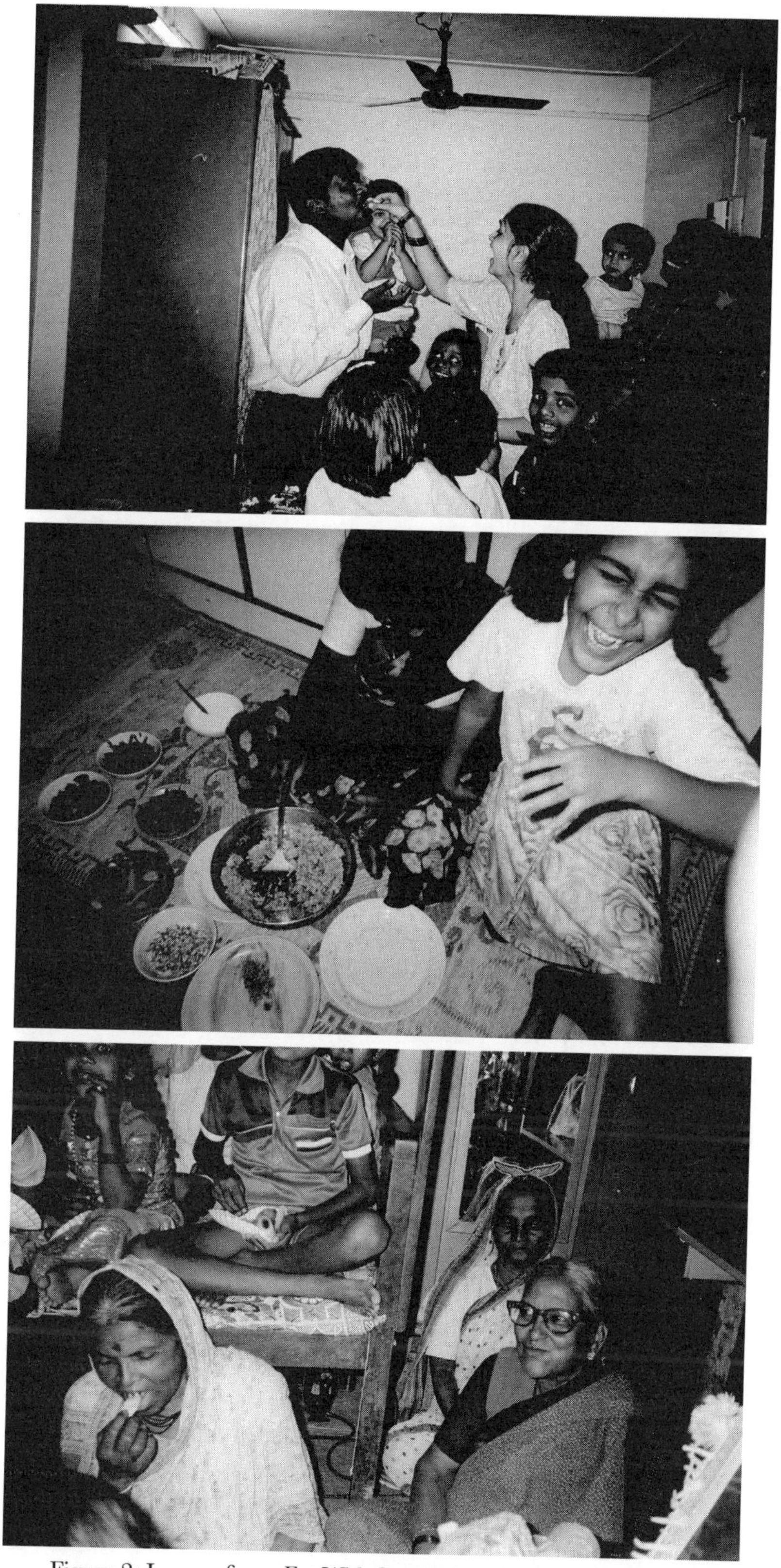

Figure 2: Images from *Eat With Great Delight* by Rajyashri Goody

JN: My grandmother's father had to move to Vadipatti from Usalamatti in Madurai district when higher caste people started threatening his life for wearing shirts and sporting a moustache. He would always encourage his community to reject manual scavenging jobs. People felt like he was trying to look and act like an upper-caste person, and they didn't like it. They got violent, and he had to migrate.

My grandmother grew up in Vadipatti, and also trained as a teacher there. She began teaching at a local school, but she was ill-treated there. When she left, all the students would come to her house to study instead of going to school. Once, the education inspector visited the school, and found the students missing. He saw them all at my grandmother's house, and encouraged her to start a school, which she did.

In the 1980s, upper-caste villagers demolished the school out of anger and jealousy. I was two years old at the time. We rebuilt it from scratch, and the school has been running for seventy years. It currently has ninety-five students, and three teachers. My grandmother has left a strong legacy behind, of her struggle and fight.

RG: You can see this legacy reflected in the wonderful photographs you have taken of the school.

JN: My father wanted me to become a lawyer, because we had to face a lot of legal issues related to land. He even took me to Madurai and enrolled me in coaching classes for law. He hoped that once we had a lawyer in the family, people wouldn't dare to mess with us.

Unfortunately, I was not good at studying, because I have dyslexia. I really wanted to become a pianist, but the dyslexia made this difficult. When I got a camera in my hands, I realised there might be some talent there. My family came to one of my first exhibitions, and even though they didn't really know what I was doing, they were very proud of me. Today, when I get invited by people for workshops, or when I go to Chennai to meet the filmmaker Pa Ranjith, my family feels very good about my work. Even though I am not making much money, they are happy. They don't tell me directly, but through their bodies, I can understand.

RG: I think what we are talking about has so much to do with dignity, not just in what and how we think about photographs but also how we are trying to live our life. I hadn't thought about this much when I was younger, but over the last few years I feel like I have to keep pushing for higher standards and become a better artist and person, because wherever I go, I am carrying the honour and dignity of my community.

JN: I was searching for just that word—dignity. It's essential. Dalit writers like Daya Pawar and Narayan Surve have proved its value with their work. A publisher once told me that the most amount of literature that people in Tamil

Nadu are reading at the moment is Dalit literature. It has the most amount of life in it. Looking into a subject with dignity allows you to explore it in a much more honest way.

I feel the same way about how I try to photograph my subjects. As an artist, your work, the way you look at and think about family; this will change the way others perceive us and our lives. This is our duty. Otherwise, we won't get very far, both individually, and as Dalits. Instead, those who have documented us will get exposure and keep pushing our community down. They are not going to be there to save us. We have to make up our mind not to do degrading jobs, even if it means suffering for these choices. Only then can we stop from passing these down to our children, our nieces and nephews.

RG: That's one of the reasons I am interested in ways of moving forward, even if that means disassociating from our Dalit identities. So many people from our community have adopted higher-caste surnames, or like us, converted to different religions like Buddhism or Christianity. We have left behind those past associations of being considered. My mother, for instance, doesn't even refer to herself as Dalit. She is Buddhist, no longer Dalit. I know many others from our community who absolutely detest the term 'Dalit'. And although I personally think of it as an empowering term which I am proud of, I think it works for the progress of our community as a whole when each of us individually decides how best we want to represent ourselves.

I Feel Like a Fish

Jaisingh Nageswaran

There is a fish tank in my house. Whenever I happen to see the fish, I know I am looking at myself.

How do I know that I am a fishbowl fish? The fish can see that there is a world beyond the bowl. But every time he tries to touch that world, beyond the one deemed appropriate for him to exist within, a wall appears. People think they can see into his reality, seem to believe they have the right to watch him. But they come and go from his life as they please. And for him to leave the bowl alive, miracles have to happen.

The caste system creates many such fishbowls. And the lower your caste, the smaller your bowl.

My grandmother is from Usilampatti, a small village close to Madurai in Tamil Nadu. In Usilampatti, they wouldn't let her break her bowl. So she moved to Vadipatti, where she founded the Ponnuthai Amma Gandhiji Primary School.

She was our first miracle.

When I decided to become a photographer, I thought the only way for me to leave my caste behind, to forget my Dalit-ness, would be to leave for the city. My father warned me that discrimination would follow me.

For a long time, I thought I was the second miracle. I've moved from one cosmopolitan city to another, photographed celebrities and pursued a career in film.

But atrocities also followed me. And the more images I took, the more I realised that Dalits were practically non-existent in the visual consciousness of India.

Suddenly, a severe illness brought me home. And soon, my money disappeared. I was faced yet again with the reality that there was no one to protect me but my family.

After I recovered, I was due to head back to Bombay, to Film City, to make the money I so desperately needed.

But the coronavirus brought me back home yet again.

This time, my health and will are with me. I see the beauty of the place where I have grown up, and feel an intimacy which has eluded me my entire photographic career. I now know that the two things I will lose last in this world are family and home.

I Feel Like A Fish has been exhibited at:

- *Everydayness*, Dalit History Month Photo Exhibition, Chennai, India, 2022.
- *Growing Like A Tree*, curated by Sohrab Hura, Ishara Art Foundation, Dubai, UAE, 2021.

Eat With Great Delight

Rajyashri Goody

Eat With Great Delight is a set of family photographs taken between the 1980s and the early 2000s on point-and-shoot cameras, primarily by my parents. They document gatherings of our family members and friends, special occasions and moments of everyday joy—often around food and the kitchen. The images are accompanied by recipes adapted by me from Dalit literature that bring out the link between food and caste, the stomach and oppression.

Writing and photography are deeply linked to power. They are essential tools for documenting lives and telling stories, but access to them has been only in the hands of a few, and denied to many at the bottom of the caste pyramid. I see Dalit autobiographies as essential texts for learning about my Dalit history and culture, and as more and more people from my community get access to cameras—including my family—I see these as part of a growing archive of Dalit life.

While conducting my research into Dalit food culture and literacy, I became aware of the lack of 'positive' imagery associated with Dalit communities that were in public circulation. Having grown up in a family of social workers, I understand how immensely important it is to extensively document and circulate images of the oppression of the caste system and the deplorable conditions that many Dalit people are forced to survive under. But I think there is something significant—and humanising—in disseminating positive depictions of Dalit people, too. With this in mind, I turned to my family photographs.

The title of this body of work, *Eat with Great Delight* is borrowed from Dalit writer Omprakash Valmiki's autobiography, *Joothan*. In the book, like many other Dalit memoirs, Valmiki embodies seemingly contradictory emotions of shame, hunger, satiation and celebration that surround the Dalit experience, in this case, in relation to the practice of '*joothan*'—gathering leftovers from upper-caste wedding feasts.

Eat With Great Delight has been exhibited at:

- Clark House Initiative, Mumbai, India, 2018.
- Body Building, curated by Nada Raza, Ishara Art Foundation, Dubai, UAE, 2019.
- Breda Photo Festival, Breda, Netherlands, 2022.
- Jogja Fotografis Festival, Yogyakarta, Indonesia, 2023.

Decoding Memories, Writing Histories

The Dalit Family Photo Archive in Mid-twentieth-century UP

Vijay Kumar

Introduction

Photography, since its beginnings in colonial India, has remained an elite business and practice. Dalits, although not entirely absent from the frame, were located in the background of the family photos as servants of European and native elite and middle class families.[1] They were between being invisible and partially visible among these families in social and visual terms.[2] Since the 1920s, Dalits started keeping photos as visual records of their presence as actors and leaders in the history of North India,[3] even though the inter-war decades saw photography attract only a small section of elite Dalit families and a few success stories from poor ones. Thus, the documentation and preservation of family photos have been very rare among Dalits. Despite this, family photos are significant sources of Dalit histories due to a lack of written records attesting to their history. This essay suggests that a Dalit family photo is a socio-visual diary of selective memories, expressed emotions, lived realities, political and gendered assertions, everyday struggles, silent resistance and empowerment. The Dalit family photo is a document of the community's spatial relations with the houses, *bastis*,[4] markets, villages, towns and cities that they have lived in. It is also a record of their spiritual practices, including the moment

---

[1] For the elite and middle-class families in photos, see Karlekar, Malavika. 2013. *Visual Histories: Photography in the Popular Imagination.* (New Delhi: Oxford University Press). pp. 85–90, 101–105; for servants, labourers and working classes, pp. 111–112. For Dalit female servants, see Sinha, Nitin and Nitin Varma. 2019. Introduction. *Servants' Past: Late-Eighteenth to Twentieth-Century South Asia.* Vol. 2 (Hyderabad: Orient Blackswan). p. 27. Pinney, Christopher. 1998. *Camera Indica: The Social Life of Indian Photographs* (Chicago: The University of Chicago Press). Pinney, Christopher. 2008. *The Coming of Photography in India* (London: The British Library).

[2] Tartakov, Gary Michael. ed. 2012. 'Introduction: Invisibles?'. *Dalit Art and Visual Imagery* (New Delhi: Indian Institute of Dalit Studies (IIDS) and OUP). pp. 1–12.

[3] Dr. Bhim Rao Ambedkar started his movement for civil and human rights for Dalits in the 1920s. In UP, Swami Achhutanand and his associates set up the Adi-Hindu Mahasabha and started mobilising Dalits for Ambedkar's movement. During the Simon Commission visit in 1928, they were photographed. For the photos of UP Dalit leaders, see Rawat, Ramnarayan S. 2012. *Reconsidering Untouchability: Chamars and Dalit History in North India* (New Delhi: Permanent Black). pp. 151–154.

[4] *Basti* means a residential locality.

of *darshan*[5] with caste gurus, dead ancestors and heroes; their modernity, as seen with the arrival of radios, televisions, bulbs, tube lights, bicycles, cars; their recent achievements—educational, professional and social—and their everyday practices of clothing, food and leisure. The essay suggests that there is a need to critically study and analyse family photos available in unorganised Dalit archives to understand their everyday lives and histories. I argue that the family photo is a site of negotiation and contestation between memory and history, upper-caste Hindus and Dalits, elite and subaltern, master and servant, masculinity and femininity, as well as visible and invisible.

This essay proposes to study these trajectories through the case of Chaudhari Mulkiram (April 1910–Aug 1954), the first Dalit from the United Provinces (UP), who qualified for the Public Service Commission (PSC) in 1939 (Figure 1). He belonged to Dhangar, a sub-caste of the Khatik caste in Meerut. Between the mid-1930s and mid-1950s, Mulkiram served at many high positions such as Superintendent of Agra Rural Development Department, Deputy Collector, Sub-Division Magistrate (SDM), Additional District Magistrate (ADM), Regional Transport Officer (RTO), Hakim Pargana (head of an administrative unit of some villages within a district), and Head of the UP Harijan Sahayak (Harijan and Social Welfare) Department. He was an Arya Samaji and Gandhian. The essay proposes to study his life and career through his family photos and written memoirs to understand continuity and change in his status in the mid-twentieth century.

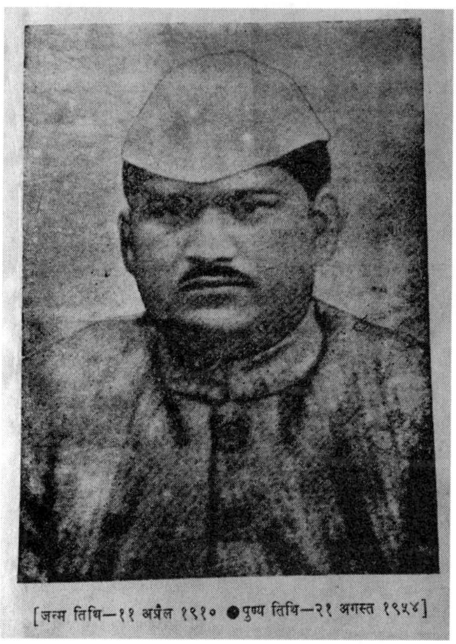

Figure 1: Magistrate Mulkiram

I centrally locate the *Chaudhari Mulkiram Smriti Granth*, a memorial edited by Tarachand Pal Bekal, as my chief source of information, both photographic and textual, published in October 1969 and sold at ₹10. This book has some photos of Mulkiram, his family members, friends and well-wishers, who wrote memoirs on his life. The number of contributors is very high (54), therefore, the paper will discuss some selected memories and photos within their historical context.[6] In analysing these writings, I observe the multiple dispositions of Dalit people as a

[5] *Darshan* means a meeting with/glimpse of caste gurus, dead ancestors and heroes.

[6] Bekal, Tarachand Pal. ed. 1969. *Chaudhari Mulkiram Smriti Granth*. First Edition (Saharanpur: Shanti Prakashan).

non-homogenous group, with different generational and gendered values and aspirations, articulated at a time when the Indian nation, at a large scale, was struggling to define itself.

Mulkiram's Early Life: A Struggle

Mulkiram was the son of Chaudhari Dan Shah, who was an agriculturist and a small moneylender. His father had a high reputation in the Khatik caste and among *zamindars*[7] in Hapur in the Meerut district.[8] But he died when Mulkiram was eight or nine years old.[9] Mulkiram's daughter Vidhya writes that according to her grandmother, Bhuri Devi, after the death of his father, Mulkiram had the responsibility of three family members: his widowed mother (Bhuri), and two young brothers, Tejram and Layakram. Bhuri had about ₹60,000 (her husband's savings), which she hid inside a wall in their home, but it got stolen. Consequently, Mulkiram's childhood saw financial and paternal crises after his father's death.[10] During his high school, Mulkiram used to tutor his juniors in Hapur for a fee to support the everyday survival of his family.[11]

Mulkiram often played football, hockey and kabaddi with village kids in the fields whenever he went there.[12] According to Mohanlal Sharma, Mulkiram looked like a wrestler but was a famous kabaddi player in the schools of his district. Sharma was a classmate and friend of Mukiram at Junior High School, Gulaothi near Hapur, in 1922,[13] and recounts how the latter once went to Balwant Degree College, Agra, to meet the village boys and sons of local zamindars. Later, they played kabaddi and Mulkiram's team won.[14]

Tarachand Pal Bekal, a nationalist Hindi writer and a Khatik by caste, knew Mulkiram since his student days.[15] He says that the colonial period was a period of illiteracy for Dalits, and very few people in the community allowed their children to get higher education. In the first half of the twentieth century, after English, Urdu was the second official language. Therefore, after receiving an Urdu middle-school degree, anyone could be recruited for the positions of

---

[7] Zamindars means landlords.

[8] Bekal. 1969. 'Jivan-Jyoti'. *Chaudhari*. pp. 9–10.

[9] Ibid. p. 13. In his childhood, Mulkiram's mother called him 'Bulli'. See Bhurasingh. 'Abhigyan'. ibid. p. 225.

[10] Sonkar, Vidya. 'Smritiyon ke Punj—Pitaji'. Ibid. pp. 91–92.

[11] Ibid. pp. 93–94.

[12] Nirbhay, Omkar Singh. 'Avismarniya Vyaktitya'. Ibid. p. 196.

[13] Sharma, Mohanlal. 'Vilakshan Vyaktitya'. Ibid. pp. 252–55.

[14] Titauriya, Bhojilal. 'Mere Guru—Mere Pujya'. Ibid. pp. 116–17.

[15] As an editor, Bekal had already published Mulkiram's poems in a small booklet titled *Hridyodgaar* before Mulkiram's memorial text. It was published in 1968 from Saharanpur and Meerut. See Sonkar, Ramdas. 'Sampadak aur Smriti Granth'. Ibid. pp. 5–8; Rivariya, Mamchand. 2009. *Khatik Samaj ke Ratan* (Delhi: Rivariya Sahitya Prakashan).

a *Munshigiri*,[16] *Patwarigiri*[17] and *Mukhtargiri*.[18] For the Dalits, it was difficult to get these positions but Mulkiram had a high school degree, which was highly valued at that time as it was a rare thing for someone who was not from a wealthy or zamindar family.[19]

In the early 1930s, Indian politics witnessed the Civil Disobedience Movement (1930–32), three round table conferences (1930–1933), the Poona Pact (1932), Guruvayur Temple politics (1932), Achhutoddhar movements (1932), communal riots, and elections (1930, 1932, 1937). Gandhi had launched the Harijan Sevak Sangh (1932). At this turning point of Indian politics, Congressmen, Gandhians, Hindi–Hindu writers and newspapers projected Gandhi as the mahatma and leader of the Hindus and the Dalits. The dominant castes considered Ambedkar as a traitor to the nation and the Hindu society, because he demanded civil and human rights for untouchables, advocated conversion to another religion, and dreamt of the annihilation of caste for *Prabuddha Bharat*—an enlightened, egalitarian and inclusive India. His ideas were modern and secular.[20] In this vibrant period of the 1930s, Bekal mentions how it was the Gandhian philosophy attracted Mulkiram, who remained a Gandhi *bhakt*[21] his whole life. A few years after his graduation from Meerut college in 1935, Mulkiram started studying law in the same place. However, due to his Gandhian ideology of supporting the truth, he was unhappy with false representation of facts by lawyers and left his law education midway.[22]

In 1937, Mulkiram was appointed as Superintendent of the Rural Development Department under the Commissioner of Agra during the first Congress government (1937–39) in UP. According to Bekal, Mulkiram had connections with the powerful congressman Pandit Krishandatt Paliwal, who helped him get the job. For Paliwal, Mulkiram was an educated man with a rural, poor Dalit background, who could help spread Gandhian ideas.[23] Before his appointment as the Deputy Collector (1940), Mulkiram went to apply for a Sub-inspector's job at the Meerut Superintendent of Police office. But a police officer asked for a bribe of Rs. 1 with the application and so Mulkiram returned home without submitting it.[24]

---

[16] *Munshigiri* means accountant.

[17] *Patwarigiri* means village accountant.

[18] *Mukhtargiri* means legal advisor.

[19] Bekal, 'Jivan-Jyoti', pp. 13-15.

[20] Kumar, Vijay. 2021. *An Untouchable Caste: Social and Political Histories of Khatiks in United Provinces, 1881-1956*. Unpublished PhD Thesis, University of Delhi, Chapter 4.

[21] *Bhakt* means a devotee.

[22] Bekal, 'Jivan-Jyoti'. Ibid. pp. 15–17.

[23] Bekal, 'Jivan-Jyoti'. Ibid. p. 17.

[24] Singh, Vikram. '*Mast Swabhav*'. Ibid. p. 248. For Dalits and Khatiks as *chaukidars* in the colonial UP police, see Kumar, Vijay. June 2020. 'The Chaukidari Force: Watchmen, Police, and Dalits from the 1860s to the 1920s in United Provinces'. *Studies in People's History*. 7:1. pp. 65–78.

Later in 1939, Mulkiram qualified for the UP Public Service Commission (PSC) and became the Deputy Collector at Hardoi in November 1940. According to Bekal, this was a big achievement for a common man like Mulkiram, because in the British Raj, this was a highly respected position with the master's power (*Sahabiyat*) accruing to the post's bearer. With power and authority, the magistrate position was an essential part of colonial administration and bureaucracy. In a magistrate's court, the laws, punishment and justice often helped and frightened rural people. Hence, now, the magistrate position empowered a Dalit man, bringing happiness to Mulkiram's family and community.[25]

It should be noted that in his text, Bekal used the term '*Pichad/Pichadi*[26] castes', 'villagers' and 'common men' more than terms like Harijan, Achhut, Dalit and Khatik. Besides, Bekal does not mention the Poona Pact of September 1932 and the Scheduled Caste Act of 1936 that granted reserved seats to Dalits in educational institutions, government jobs and local political wards, and which enabled Mulkiram's success. It seems that Bekal did not want to discuss the impact of Ambedkar's Dalit movement which co-existed with Mulkiram's career. However, Bekal portrays Mulkiram as an exceptional figure.

Memory, Photography and Historical Props

In *Mulkiram Smriti Granth*, the editor, contributing authors and family members do not mention where, when and who took the photos of Mulkiram and his family members.[27] However, the montages, postures and gestures of people in these photos subscribe to the overall visual conventions of modern photographic culture. Standing and seated, people being arranged in tiers were very common in twentieth-century official photographs that hoped to communicate a sense of order among officer-class people in formal setups. Usually, photographers took such pictures in lawns, gardens and doorways of offices and educational institutions, fulfilling requirements of space, light and an appropriately genteel background.[28] Their garments reflect their formal and ideological affiliations, and have different degrees of modern and traditional elements. These conventions are reflected in four photos of Mulkiram with his staff and classmates, taken at the court, office and Hapur High School.

For instance, the Hapur High School photo (Figure 2) has four rows of people. The teachers sit on chairs in the second line. The students sit on the floor in the first line before the teachers and stand behind them in the

---

[25] Bekal, 'Jivan-Jyoti'. Ibid. p. 18.

[26] *Pichad* or *Pichadi* means backward.

[27] The photographic studios had arrived in the late nineteenth century in urban UP (Lucknow). See Karlekar. 2013. *Visual Histories*. p. 86.

[28] For the back-to-back lines in the Bengali upper-caste family photos of the 1920s and 1930s, see Guha-Thakurta, Tapati. 2020. 'Chittagong Childhood' and 'A Dacca Childhood'. *Pastconnect: Love, Life and Connected Pasts*. www.pastconnect.net (Last accessed on 31 March 2021).

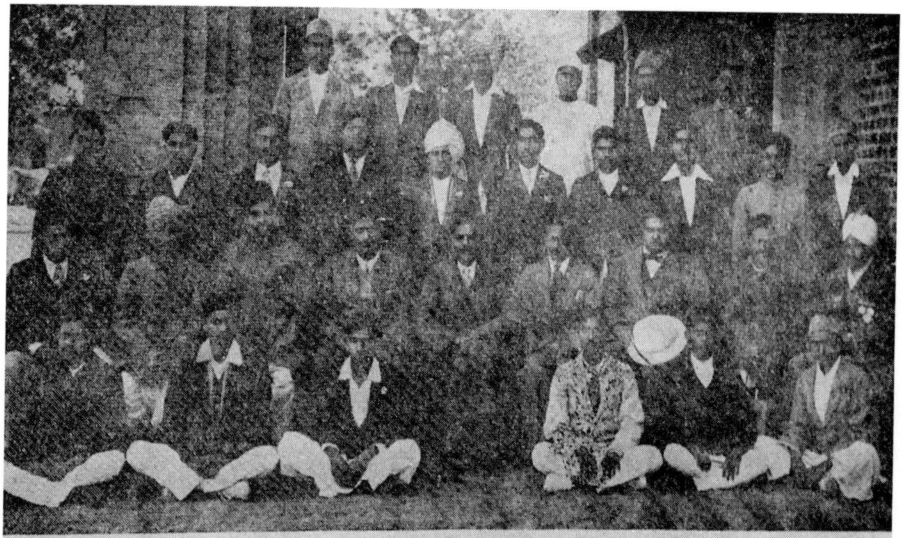

चौधरी मुल्कीराम अंतिम पंक्ति में मध्य में पगड़ी बांधे हुए—राजकीय हाई स्कूल हापुड़, फोटो सन् १९२९

Figure 2: The Hapur High School photo

third and fourth lines. Teachers and students are controlled in their bodily gestures, folding their arms and legs in the first two lines. The students' arms in the last two lines are mostly either straight or behind them. Both teachers and students wear suits and *achkan sherwanis*[29] with *pagaris*[30] and caps, mainly the Kashmiri cap, also known as the Gandhi cap. One teacher holds a *sola topi*, a white English hat/pith helmet, a 'symbol of British imperialism'.[31] In the last row, young Mulkiram wears a white multilayered pagari, covering one ear (Figure 3). Such a pagari was very common and associated with the *Chaudhari* and *Panch*[32] of the caste panchayat, the heads of caste sabha, in North India. This photo was taken at a pavilion of the school, built by colonial architects, with pointed arches and strong pillars. Such a pavilion was a common fixture at the gates of colonial school and college buildings. One can see these pavilions at Agra University and Allahabad University as well.[33]

---

[29] *Achkan sherwani* means a knee-length coat for men.

[30] *Pagari* means turban.

[31] Tarlo says that in the late 1920s, 'Gandhi wore it [Kashmiri Cap] for less than two years'. See Tarlo, Emma. 1996. *Clothing Matters: Dress and Identity in India* (London: Hurst and Co.). pp. 62–94; for sola topi, Kashmiri cap and loincloth, see mainly pp. 68–70, 78–79, 83–85.

[32] *Chaudhari* and *panch* mean traditional heads of caste or village panchayat with hereditary rights.

[33] For more details of colonial pavilion and school and college architecture, see Metcalf, Thomas. 1989. *Imperial Vision: Indian Architecture and British Raj* (New Delhi: OUP).

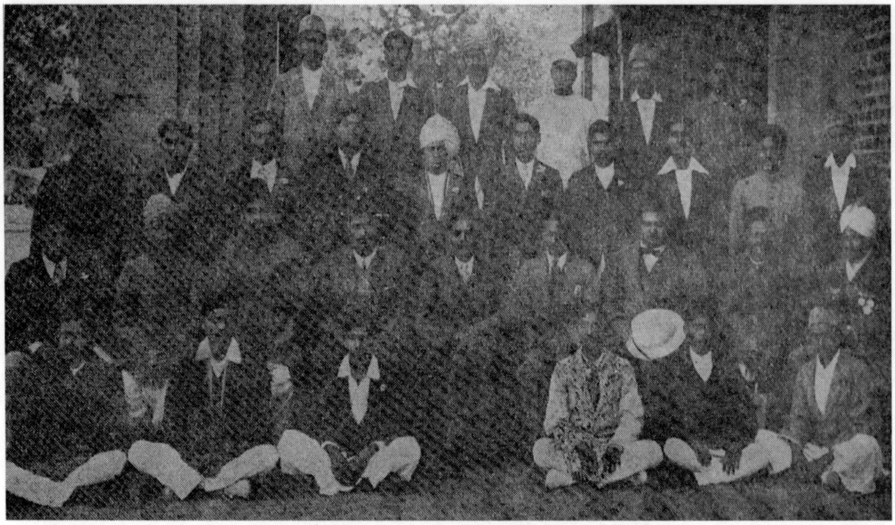

Figure 3: Young Student Mulkiram

The District Magistrate Court photo dated 1948–49 (Figure 4) shows three rows of staff and officers. The first line is of senior officers and the police, sitting on chairs. In this line, Mulkiram appears with a flower garland in the middle of the officers. The second line is of young and junior officers, and the last of *chaprassies*, clerks, gardeners, sweepers, driver, watchmen, etc. Similarly, the Transport Department photo dated 1949 (Figure 5) shows five rows of staff members. The first one has staff members' children. The second row is of senior officers and their wives, who sit on chairs, along with Mulkiram and

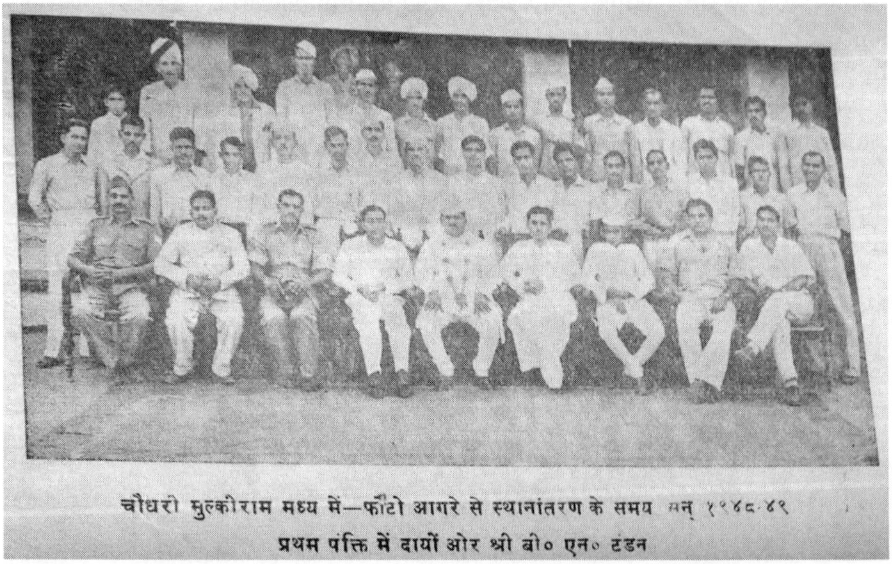

Figure 4: The District Magistrate Court photo. 1948–49

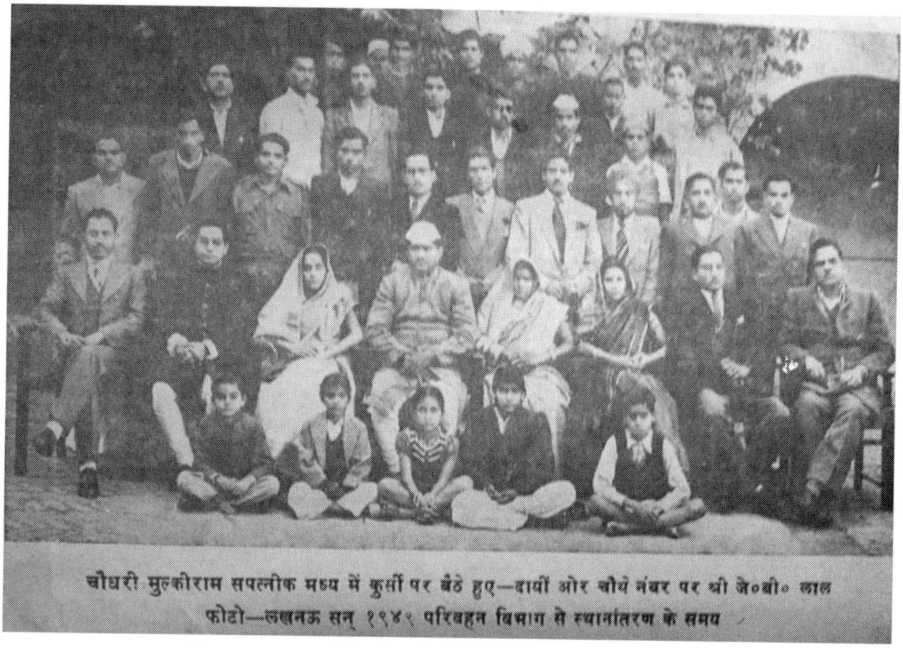

Figure 5: The Transport Department photo. 1949

his wife. The third line is of junior officers. The chairs were hence reserved in the middle row for the highest administrative category in the group concerned, while floor seating was taken by the lowest. The intermediate level of people stood at the back in each frame.

Almost all senior and junior officers are in Western attire, although their wives wear saris, their heads covered with a *pallu*.[34] Among them, Mulkiram and a senior officer are in their native dress. The fourth and fifth rows again comprise chaprassies, clerks, gardeners, sweepers, drivers, watchmen, etc. In both photos, the hands of the low and no-ranked staff are either straight or behind their backs, again a formal gesture adopted for the photograph. It is interesting to note that in both photos, the low and no-ranked servants wear pagaris, Gandhi and Jinnah caps, and Mulkiram wears the Gandhi cap too, indicating a confluence of identities in his figure; affiliations that cut across social and professional hierarchies. Indeed, in the first half of the twentieth century, caps were the symbols of political ideologies. It is essential to mention that in these frames, it is difficult to identify clothes with caste and religious identities, even though political affiliations are in plain sight, as the garments have an eclectic, modernised sensibility, fusing different stylistic elements. The suit-pant and achkan sherwani often signalled the educated and elite people and 'dress codes reflected occupational status'[35] but figures such as Mulkiram,

[34] Pallu means a side of sari.

[35] Karlekar. 2013. *Visual Histories*. p. 86.

who had transcended social hierarchies within a single lifetime, appeared more ambiguous.

Three family photos of Mulkiram's daughters and daughter-in-law and one solo photo of Mulkiram's son (see below, F. No. 6,7,8,9) are taken in photo studios. Married couples with children standing and sitting around them appear in controlled gestures. The subjects wear new saris, wristwatches, sunglasses, jewels, *kajal* in their eyes and make-up, for family photos taken at the studio in an attempt to portray 'happy domesticity'.[36] These are in contrast to Mukiram's ideologically informed sartorial choices, his simplicity in the face of a modernising world, that included the rest of his family.

Gendered Spaces and Photographic Negotiations

In an article, historian Prem Chowdhry says that there are (and were) many masculine spaces in the village: the traditional panchayat,[37] *baithak*, *chaupal*,[38] educational centres, sports, army, places for alcohol consumption, spaces for leisure activities, etc.[39] In this list, one can add photographic space as well, which was also male-dominated. In all these spaces, upper-caste Hindus had a stronger control than Dalits.

Since the pre-colonial period, upper-caste Hindus had a monopoly over the educated elite domain (schools, colleges, universities). The church missionaries had already started the educational programmes for Dalits since the mid-nineteenth century.[40] But Ambedkar's Dalit movement from the 1920s began questioning the monopoly of high-caste Hindus in educational institutions.[41] The demand for equal education for Dalit men and women led to the colonial government's introduction of the UP District Boards Primary Education Acts of 1919 and 1926. Due to these acts, the provincial government started focusing on education for Dalits and granted scholarships to them. Also, the government

[36] Ibid. pp. 88–90.

[37] Panchayat means a council and governing body in a village or a caste.

[38] The terms 'Baithak' and 'Chaupal' are used as popular platforms for men to sit on in North Indian villages.

[39] Chowdhry, Prem. 2009. 'Masculine Spaces: Rural Male Culture in North India'. *Economic and Political Weekly* (hereafter *EPW*). 49:47. pp. 41–49.

[40] For instance, the church missionaries set up a mission school in the Dalit neighbourhood of Agra in 1859. But when Dalit students started opting for higher education, high-caste students submitted a joint petition to remove Dalit students from St. John's College in November 1862. Some 180 high-caste students had withdrawn their admission from St. John's college following the strong decision of Principal Barton in favour of Dalit students. Later, seven Gujarati-Brahmin teachers of the same college also resigned from their posts. Meanwhile, these caste Hindus set up a 'Hindu College' for themselves 'on strict caste principles'. Later, they renamed the Hindu college to Victoria College. See Haythornthwaite, Rev. John Parker. 1932. *St. John's College, Agra 1850-1930* (London: The Highway Press). pp. 48–56.

[41] Rawat. 2012. *Reconsidering Untouchability*; Ambedkar, B.R. 2020. *Dr Babasaheb Ambedkar: Writings and Speeches* (hereafter *BAWS*). Vasant Moon and et. al. eds. Vol. 17:2,3 (New Delhi: Dr Ambedkar Foundation).

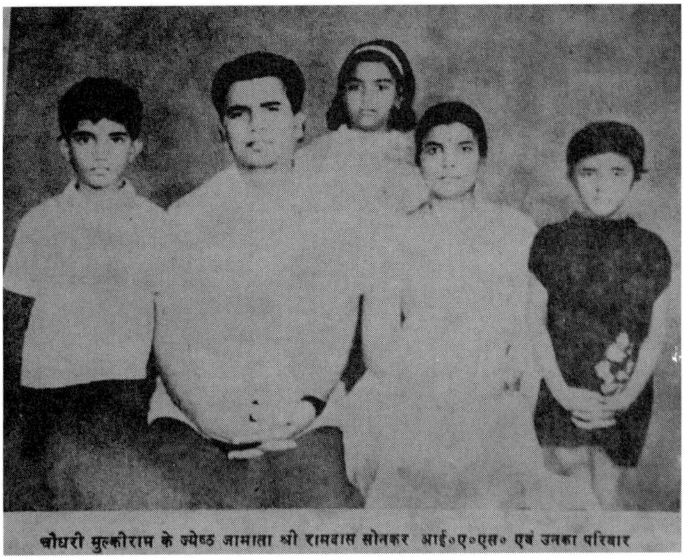

Figure 6: Vidhya, her husband Ramdas Sonkar (IAS) and kids

granted lands to different social, religious and political agencies to spread education among lower sections of society.[42] To prevent the Dalit movement, Gandhi, the Congress and the Hindi-Hindu agencies such as the Arya Samaj and Hindu Mahasabha, started working for Dalit education in the late 1920s and the early 1930s.[43] Consequently, in the 1920s, Mulkiram received primary education and qualified from the Hapur Government High School in 1929–30. However, Mulkiram's mother and wife were not educated because the Khatik caste was not very actively involved with the cause for women's education in the first half of the twentieth century.[44] However, his daughters Vidhya and Prem were highly educated. Vidhya had a BA degree and registered for an MA course. Her husband Ramdas Sonkar was the first Dalit to qualify for Indian Administration Service (IAS) in UP in 1957 (Figure 6). He had BA and MA degrees from Allahabad University. Four years after Mulkiram's death, Ramdas Sonkar married his elder daughter Vidhya, in 1958.[45] Mulkiram's younger

[42] File No. 1020/1925. Box No. 171. List no. 10. Education. Uttar Pradesh State Archive, Lucknow.

[43] For educational activities of the Harijan Sevak Sangh and Arya Samaj for Dalits, see *Sainik* 4 Aug, 1 Sep 1936. Vidhalankar, Satyketu. 1984. *Arya Samaj ka Itihas*. Vol. 1–2 (Delhi: Arya Swadhyay Kendra).

[44] Turner, A.C. 1933. *Census of India, 1931: United Provinces of Agra and Oudh*. Vol. XVIII. Part 2 (Allahabad). p. 481.

[45] Sonkar, Ramdas. '*Pratham aur Antim Bhent*'. Ibid. pp. 75–76. In 2011–12, when I started my research on the Khatik caste in UP, I was told that Ramdas Sonkar is a Khatik writer, thinker and a retired IAS. Therefore, I met him for an interview on Khatik social history on 31 May and 17 June 2012. During his interview, he narrated a few stories of his father-in-law, Chaudhari Mulkiram. He told me that within the Khatik caste, the sub-castes held ideological differences

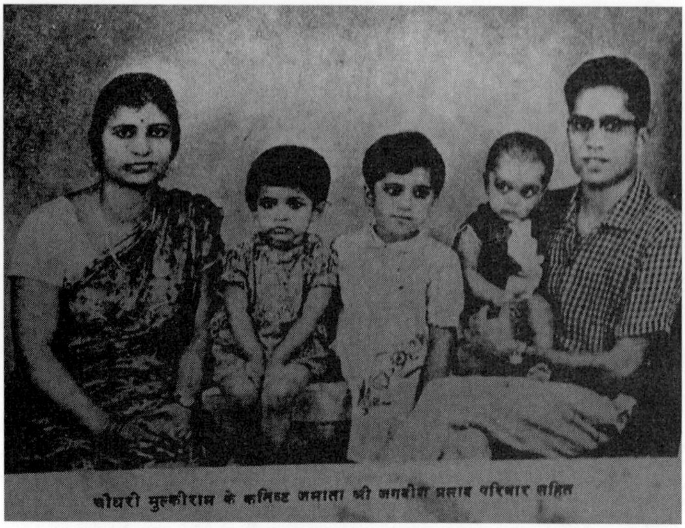

Figure 7: Prem, her husband Jagdish Prasad and kids

daughter Prem married Jagdish Prasad, an assistant engineer in UP (Figure 7). His only son, Satya Prakash 'Pankaj', became a film director (Figure 8) while Satya's wife, Ved Chaudhari, worked in the Delhi Transport Department (Figure 9).[46] After his death, the Chaudhari Mulkiram Smarak Library and Reading Room were established at Mohallah Dhangar Samaj, Hapur. Jagdish Prasad Chaudhari was a childhood friend of Mulkiram and the president of this memorial library. Hence, Dalit men and women were clearly asserting their new power in the male-dominated educated elite domain. And they were spreading education.[47]

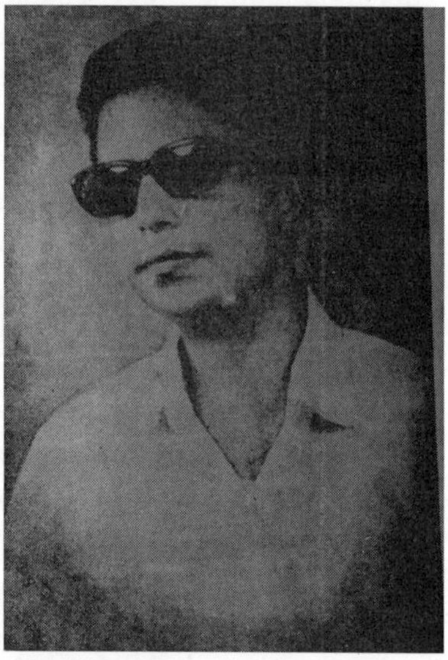

Figure 8: Satya Prakash 'Pankaj'

In professional photography (mainly studio and newspaper), Dalits emerged as the heroes and heroines of early twentieth century India during the Dalit movements. Dalit women also asserted themselves as the centres of focus for the camera in a male-

---

in the colonial period. But when he married Mulkiram's daughter Vidhya in 1958, it built a bridge between their different sub-castes (Sonkar and Dhangar Khatiks). Over three meetings, Ramdas gave me his books and booklets to read about Khatiks. Since then, I wanted to write about Mulkiram and his family. For this, I thank Late Ramdas Sonkar.

[46] Bekal. 'Jivan-Jyoti'. Ibid. p. 56.

[47] Chaudhari, Jagdish Prasad. '*Manav Shreshtha*'. Ibid. pp. 192–94.

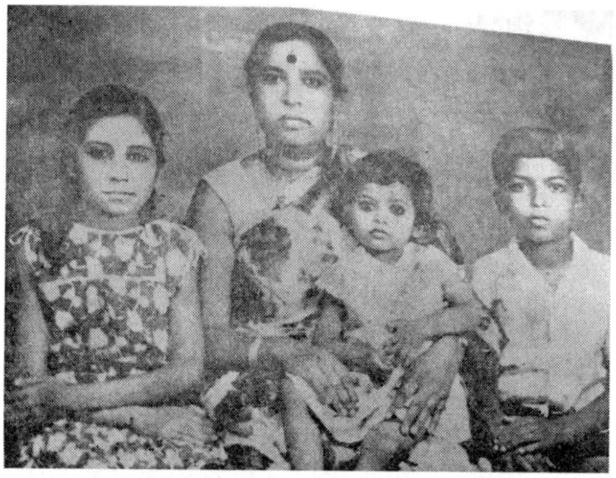

Figure 9: Satya's wife Ved and kids

dominated photo domain.[48] For instance, none of the writers in *Smriti Granth* provides details of Mulkiram's mother, Bhuri Devi and wife, Nattho Devi, making it difficult to write about them. In textual narratives by contributors, Nattho is presented as an illiterate Dalit woman, a housewife, a follower of Mulkiram's ideas and a caretaker of Mulkiram's family members, guests and students (Figure 10).[49] However, it is interesting to see Nattho surrounded by educated elites, mostly male, in their domain. In her photos, it is difficult to identify her sari with *khadi*. Although Nattho had a pallu on her head as a sign of marriage, subservience, simplicity and the local tradition, her daughters, Vidhya, Prem and daughter-in-law Ved do not wear pallus. This is one of the ways in which their changing ideologies, higher education and a semi-modern pattern of thinking is clearly asserted against the stronghold of tradition and patriarchy within their Dalit caste. These photos help to understand the changing life of a Dalit family. Thus, family photos were a site of assertion and contestation for Dalit women.[50] Satya's sunglasses

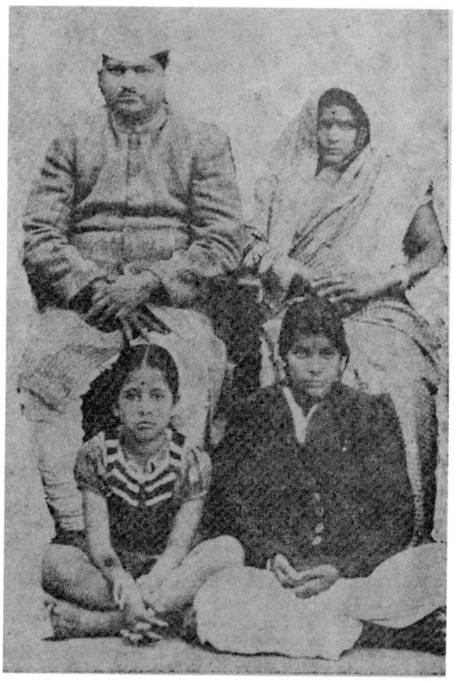

Figure 10: Mulkiram, his wife Nattho Devi and his elder daughter Vidhya with her friend

[48] Chowdhry. 2009. 'Masculine Spaces'.

[49] Bekal. 'Jivan-Jyoti'. Ibid. p. 56. Besides, Gandhi instructed women to follow their husbands' will like Sita and other ideal Hindu women. See Kishwar, Madhu. 1985. 'Gandhi on Women'. *EPW*. 20:41. pp. 1753–58.

[50] It is important to discuss that in December 1938 in *Harijan* (a weekly), Gandhi criticised, 'the dress code of the modern women.' According to Gandhi, modern dresses were not for the self-defence or self-protection of girls, but for Juliet(s), who looked for Romeo(s). Gandhi remarked, 'I have a fear that the modern girl loves to be Juliet to half a dozen Romeos. She loves adventure. My correspondent seems to represent the unusual type. The modern girl dresses not

also assert a new Dalit masculinity, which was inspired by the heroes of cinema in a changing socio-political domain. His new masculinity contested with traditional privileges of the higher castes, and urban, town and village elites.

Clothing for Portraits

By the 1910s, Gandhi started experimenting with clothing by adopting the indentured labourer's/coolie's dress in Durban and the poor natives' and peasants' dress in India to communicate with the different masses and to visualise poverty, sorrow, mourning, unity and Indianness. He worked 'to restore the Indian hand-weaving and hand-spinning industries.' Therefore, by 1919, Gandhi called Indian men and women to wear white khadi clothes, a swadeshi or 'sacred cloth' fashioned as the Gandhi cap, *kurta*,[51] pyjama, *dhoti*,[52] and saris, as part of a moral, national and religious duty. He called to boycott foreign goods, which were presented as 'untouchable', 'impure' and 'our greatest outward pollution'. Wearing khadi was a way to purify the body 'physically and mentally'. 'Gandhi even suggested that people should seek darshan not from himself but from khadi'. The white Kashmiri cap became a famous political symbol, known as 'the Gandhi Cap', 'swadeshi cap', 'a garment of "truth"' and 'a visible mark of swadeshi and swaraj'. Similarly, the white dhoti and half-naked body had become 'a sign of Gandhi's saintliness' and 'voluntary poverty'. However, after Independence, Gandhi was not happy because 'those who had once adopted khadi were now returning to foreign cloth'.[53] One can see the impact of Gandhi's call in the lifestyle of Mulkiram, whose narrators show a contestation between his professional and personal clothes.

For 'sartorial uniformity', the British and Indian civil servants had to strictly follow a professional western dress code.[54] Bekal says that a Western lifestyle and dress had become part of everyday lives of students, teachers and civil officers. However, Chaudhari Mulkiram did not adopt Western dress. In a Hapur high school photo, he wears a dhoti, a kurta and a coat to maintain the simplicity

to protect herself from wind, rain and sun but to attract attention. She improves upon nature by painting herself and looking extraordinary. The non-violent way is not for such girls'. See Guha, Ramachandra. 7 January 2017. 'When Even Women of Bengal Took on Gandhi'. *The Telegraph*. In other words, Gandhi suggested khadi saris and dhotis as the Swadeshi dress for women.

[51] Kurta means a long shirt.

[52] Dhoti means loincloth.

[53] In September 1921, Gandhi proposed to wear a dhoti, 'a temporary "sign of mourning"' for about a month during the Non-Cooperation Movement. However, 'the Indian people were still dressed in foreign cloth'. See Tarlo. 1996. *Clothing Matters*. pp. 68–72, 75–77, 87–91; for foreign cloth and 'the concept of untouchability', see pp. 91–93 for a sola topi, Kashmiri cap and loincloth, see pp. 68–70, 78–79, 83–85. Besides, Debendranath Tagore had introduced the dhoti, '*punjabi* [kurta] and *chador* [shawl] as the official dress of men' (followers) of the Brahma Samaj. See Karlekar. 2013. *Visual Histories*. p. 86.

[54] Karlekar. 2013. *Visual Histories*. p. 86.

and devotion he felt for swadeshi ideals.[55] While studying in the Hapur high school, Mulkiram had married Nattho Devi. After completing his high school education, he went to pick his wife from her parents' house following the practice of *gauna.*[56] According to Bekal, his in-laws and villagers had assumed that after a high school education, he would have become Westernised. But they were shocked to see him in the native dress, wearing a turban and gold earrings. His wife told Bekal that some people mocked Mulkiram, but he countered them.[57] Moreover, after Independence, Mulkiram often participated in religious and cultural gatherings where he appeared in his Gandhi cap, cotton pyjama and achkan sherwani. Therefore, Bekal writes that many times, people believed that he was a big leader or a social reformer, not a magistrate.[58]

As a Gandhi bhakt, Mulkiram loved khadi, says his daughter Vidhya. She also says that from 1939 to 1947, Mulkiram was forced to wear a coat, pant and tie to maintain the civil service tradition and discipline. For Mulkiram, *Angrezi pahnawa*[59] was a sign of slavery. The tie was a *fansi ka fanda.*[60] He often wished for India's independence. Consequently, on the day of India's entry into freedom, he abandoned his coat, pant and tie. He went to court in *churidar pyjama*,[61] sherwani and a Gandhi cap. In this garb, his personality was like a leader's.[62] Interestingly, there is not a single photo of Mulkiram in Western dress except for the school photo in which, as a young man, he wears a coat.

Although his swadeshi dress was a sign of protest against the colonial officer culture, his clothing was not replicated by his family members. Neither his son (Satya), nephew (Rampal Chaudhari), nor his sons-in-law (Ramdas and Jagdish) took to swadeshi dress. In their photos, they all appear in shirts. Also, Satya wears sunglasses, Rampal wears a tie and Ramdas and Jagdish are in pants. None of them donned the Gandhi cap. Similarly, neither his daughters nor his daughter-in-law appear in white khadi saris. Nattho too wore a colourful sari for a family photo taken probably in the 1950s or 1960s.

Here, it is essential to discuss that in colonial UP, as Charu Gupta writes, 'Swadeshi clothing did not make much sense to Dalits as they wished to use dress as a way to transcend their position in systems of inequality.' Due to the conversion to Christianity, the modern Western dress for Dalits 'was a material marker of upward mobility and had an aspirational quality to it. For a section of urban educated, articulate Dalits, it was associated with emancipation and assertion of manhood.'[63] Even if Gandhi's swadeshi clothing mantra made

---

[55] Bekal, 'Jivan-Jyoti'. Ibid. p. 13.

[56] Gauna refers to a common post-marriage practice in North India.

[57] Bekal, 'Jivan-Jyoti'. Ibid. pp. 13–14.

[58] Bekal, 'Jivan-Jyoti'. Ibid. pp. 32–33.

[59] Angrezi Pahnawa means Western dress.

[60] Fansi ka fanda means a noose.

[61] Churidar pyjama means a long tight-fitting trouser.

[62] Titauriya, '*Mere Guru*'. Ibid. p. 100.

[63] Charu Gupta notes anxieties, binaries (a simple swadeshi Hindu woman versus an immoral

sense to Mulkiram in his life, his family members abandoned it and adopted Western dress without converting to Christianity. Indeed, with 'desires and ambitions', Dalit empowerment and education played a significant role in their lives. Hence, some agents, contestants and negotiators in the politics of swadeshi versus western clothing co-existed in the Dalit community. Besides, occasional visits by a suit-clad Dr. Ambedkar in parts of UP and his printed and published images also gave Dalits the sense that westernised clothes were a sign of assertion. In May 1936, in a conference speech in Dadar (Bombay), Ambedkar asked, 'The Law guarantees to the Untouchables the right to wear decent clothes but the Hindus do not allow them to put on these clothes, what is the use of this right?'[64]

Mulkiram, His Houses and Darshan

Mulkiram's house was very simple, says his friend Mahadev Prasad Arya, a *Vaidh* by profession at the Arya dispensary (*Aushadhalay*) in Hardoi. According to Mahadev, the rooms in Mulkiram's home did not have flooring, furniture,

---

Westernised Hindu Memsahib) and contestations (Hindus versus Christians, Muslims and converted Dalits) in the swadeshi campaign for women's clothing. The upper-caste nationalists and reformers, who were mainly urban middle-class, reinterpreted and spread the swadeshi discourse of clothing to revive 'a nostalgic golden past', traditional values, to create a divine image of Hindu women, a Hindu community, 'a mechanism of inclusion and exclusion'. They also wanted to introduce new socio-moral codes, self-discipline and 'a form of social control' on women's bodies and their domestic space. While discussing happiness, economic responsibility and the swadeshi lifestyle in a household, upper-caste writers claimed that a Hindu mother (a simple woman) 'used indigenous items like a handwoven sari, jacket, petticoat, shawl, open-heeled sandals, coconut oil, cloth bag, nut, gram flour and twig of neem to clean teeth, and her monthly expenditure was Rs. 7.70. On the other hand, the Hindu 'Lady' or Memsahib's 'monthly expenditure on [the] sari, blouse, petticoat, wristwatch, fur, fountain pen, handbag with [a] make-up case, scent, gloves, lipstick, soap, socks, toothbrush, powder, hairspray and haircut was a whooping Rs. 120.80.' She often spoke English, used sunglasses, 'played tennis and visited the theatre and was a spendthrift who made a fool of her husband.' Moreover, Gupta notes, 'modern spaces like tennis clubs, parties, cinemas and theatres too came to be seen as threats to the nation and to the swadeshi ideals of simplicity and service.' See Gupta, Charu. 2002. '"Fashioning" Swadeshi: Clothing Women in Colonial North India.' *EPW*. 47:42. pp. 76–84; for Dalits see pp. 81–82.

[64] Ambedkar, *BAWS*, Vol. 17 (3), Part 3, pp. 127. In May 1936, in his conference speech in Dadar (Bombay), Ambedkar said, 'There are several other causes for which atrocities are committed on the Untouchables by the Caste-Hindus which if revealed, will surprise the public outside Hindustan [sic]. The Untouchables are beaten for putting on clothes of superior quality. They have been whipped because they used the utensils made of metal like copper etc. Their houses are burnt because the land has been brought for cultivation. They are beaten for putting on the sacred thread on their body. They are beaten for refusing to carry the dead animals and eat the carrion, or for walking through the village road with socks and shoes on, or for not bowing down before the caste-Hindus, for taking water in the copper pot while going out in the field to ease. Recently, an instance has been noticed, where the Untouchables were beaten for serving chapatis in the dinner party.' Ambedkar, *BAWS*, Vol. 17 (3), Part 3, pp. 117.

decoration, *chilman-o-Parda*,[65] flower pots, a garden, images, calendars, radios, and other modern amenities. However, Mulkiram passionately followed the practice of doing of *havan pooja*[66] every evening and morning.[67] With Vedic rituals, the participation in and practice of *yajna* was one of the duties of an Arya Samaji in this period.

In 1948–49, Mulkiram was transferred from Agra to Lucknow to serve as a regional transport officer. In the Regional Transport Department, Mulkiram controlled and exposed many corrupt transport inspectors. One such inspector filed a complaint of corruption against Mulkiram. According to the complainant, Mulkiram had used his black money to buy an old car and repair his house. However, Chandrabhan Singh, Mulkiram's cousin,[68] says that Mulkiram had bought a Chevrolet car at ₹9,500 and repaired a *kachcha* house in Bhatiyana village, Hapur, only after many requests from his relatives and friends. The house had three rooms made of non-baked bricks and one room with a veranda made of baked bricks. Therefore, the Anti-Corruption Department rejected the case.[69] The Chevrolet was the first car in Mulkiram's house, but his family members did not discuss its arrival because it had the unpleasant memory of corruption charges against him tied to it. It is essential to mention that although Gandhi was against modernity, he used cars, trains and ships to travel in India and overseas. Therefore, perhaps, Mulkiram too did not completely reject the Western idea of owning a vehicle.

In late 1940s, Mulkiram was transferred to Agra as the SDM, and later, he became the RTO there. Vidhya says that he lived in Raja Bardman's *kothi* in Nai Mandi, Agra.[70] Bhojilal Titauriya, a family member and a student of Mulkiram, says that kothi was made of white marble and luxurious. People called Mulkiram the Sant of Bardman's kothi.[71] According to Chandrabhan, Mulkiram's reading room was filled with books and autobiographies of great men and saints, such as Swami Dayanand, Mahatma Gandhi, Arvind Ghosh, Ramkrishna Paramhans, and others. He often purchased them from Arya Samaj rallies, centres and fairs.[72]

Sandal Singh Sandal was a Khatik poet, teacher, social activist and Mulkiram's good friend from Saharanpur.[73] In a photograph, Sandal too wore a Gandhi cap and kurta indicating his own ideological affiliation. In June

---

[65] Chilman-o-Parda means screen curtains.

[66] Havan-pooja means yajna.

[67] Arya, Mahadev Prasad. 'Maharishi Mulkiram'. Ibid. p. 216, 219.

[68] Chandrabhan Singh was in the Law Ministry of the Indian government. He closely observed Mulkiram because he was a son of Mulkiram's *mama*'s (maternal uncle). See Singh, Chandrabhan. '*Nirbhik aur Nishchhal Vyaktitva*'. Ibid. p. 145.

[69] Singh. 'Nirbhik aur Nishchhal'. Ibid. pp. 154–55.

[70] Kothi means house/mansion. Sonkar. 'Smritiyon ke Punj'. Ibid. p. 97.

[71] Sant means saint. Titauriya. 'Mere Guru'. Ibid. p. 109.

[72] Singh, 'Nirbhik aur Nishchhal'. Ibid. p. 159.

[73] Sandal, Sandal Singh. '*Rashtragaurav, Gandhibhakt*—Ch. Mulkiram' . Ibid. pp. 80–81.

1949, he planned to visit the Taj Mahal and to take Mulkiram's darshan.[74] He stayed with Mulkiram between 22 and 29 June 1949. In his account, Sandal added the story of Sudama's meeting with Krishna in this context. Sandal had carried some mangoes in a bucket for Mulkiram, like Sudama had carried *tandul*[75] for Krishna. Sandal went to the kothi where some people sat on a *charpai*[76] in the lawn, and an orderly told Sandal that Mulkiram had gone on an official visit to the prison. Sandal then handed over his mango bucket to the orderly, who carried it to Mulkiram's house. Soon, *Chaudharayan* (Mulkiram's wife Nattho) returned the mangoes because Mulkiram had ordered her not to accept any gifts. Sandal felt proud of Mulkiram because he did not follow the practice of Western people, who readily accepted gifts. In other words, in Sandal's eyes, the practice of accepting gifts was often a cover for taking bribes from people in colonial offices. Thus, he says that Mulkiram had the life of a renouncer.

Later, when Sandal introduced himself to the orderly as Mulkiram's friend, his gift was accepted and he was invited to sit inside. According to Sandal, the simplicity of Mulkiram was reflected in his room and its swadeshi cotton curtains, pillows and chair covers. On the walls, he saw images of Maharishi Dayanand, Yogi Arvind and Mahatma Gandhi. His almirah was full of religious books. According to Sandal, the room seemed like the *ashram*[77] of a rishi or saint. He further says that in the evening, he was happy to see Mulkiram and noticed that his dressing sense revealed the *sahabiyat*[78] of a 'deputy sahab'. Mulkiram wore his *khaddar*[79] and carried a *chhadi*.[80] After their conversation, Mulkiram went for yajna and *bhajan*, which was an everyday practice. Thus, Sandal considered Mulkiram a true saint, and was happy to be at the saint's house.[81]

It is important to note that Ramdas Sonkar, who became Mulkiram's son-in-law in 1958, mentioned an identical description in his memoir. In July 1954, while pursuing his MA from Allahabad University, Ramdas first went to meet Mulkiram for an official certificate at his bungalow at Fatehpur. When he entered the meeting room, he saw that it was very clean, and the floor was decorated with some *mrigchhale* (images or designs of antelopes).[82] The walls of the room had portraits of Swami Dayanand and Maharishi Arvind. Ramdas writes that it seemed that the room belonged to a *Rajshri*,[83] and as he was

[74] Sandal considered Mulkiram a saint or godlike figure. Therefore, he called his meeting a darshan.

[75] Tandul means rice.

[76] Charpai means a type of native, woven wooden bed.

[77] Ashram means a residential place of a saint and his followers.

[78] Sahabiyat refers to the power and status of a master or ruler.

[79] Khaddar means cotton cloth.

[80] Chhadi means handstick.

[81] Sandal. 'Rashtragaurav, Gandhibhakt'. Ibid. pp. 81–83, 85.

[82] Mrigchhale means antelopes.

[83] Rajshri means a wise man.

reflecting on Mulkiram's personality and character, the latter entered the room in a white khaddar pyjama and kurta. He looked like a great man.[84] However, according to another observer, Mulkiram also wore a *baniyan*[85] and *tahmad*[86] in his house.[87] These reflections on Mulkiram's self-fashioning reflect his persona, integrity and political affiliations, sketching a visual portrait for those who never met him. Mulkiram's photographs evidence these characteristics, locating him as a figure who was individuated in his premodern lifestyle even as he worked for a modern bureaucracy.

After his father's death, Chandrabhan recounts how Mulkiram's family back in the village suffered an acute financial crisis. Mulkiram stopped coming to the house and often stayed in the garden with other villagers. He only ate *chane*[88] and never accepted food from anyone. While he was there, he encouraged students to pursue education, as several children from his own and neighbouring villages came to his house for learning.[89] His house was a *dharmshala*[90] for students and needy people; his wife took care of the food and shelter of their guests. Bekal calls her Annapurna, the Hindu goddess of food, because she continued the practice of hosting people at home in Hapur even fourteen years after Mulkiram's death.[91]

Bekal says that Mulkiram's house was a temple of knowledge, truth and love. He wanted his family to have the *sanskar*[92] of Indian culture, philosophy and religion. He wished that his son and daughters should be good citizens, and therefore, named his elder daughter Vidhya (knowledge), younger daughter Prem (love) and his son Satya (truth).[93]

Conclusion

Mulkiram was close to Gandhi, Gandhians, local Congressmen, Arya Samajis and his family members. These people played different roles in the development of Mulkiram's personal and professional images. For instance, many contributors to *Mulkiram Smriti Granth* were nationalist Hindi writers and Arya Samajis. Therefore, they portrayed his life in metaphors of saintly images of Gandhi and Dayanand.[94] However, in the photos, his family members

[84] Sonkar, 'Pratham aur Antim Bhent'. Ibid. pp. 77–78.

[85] Baniyan means undershirt.

[86] Tahmad means a towel-like, long wrap.

[87] Arya, Rajendra. '*Nisprah Vyaktitva*'. Ibid. pp. 229–230.

[88] Chane means gram legumes.

[89] Singh, 'Nirbhik aur Nishchhal'. Ibid. p. 155.

[90] Dharmshala means rest house.

[91] Bekal, 'Jivan-Jyoti'. Ibid. pp. 24–25.

[92] Sanskar means a knowledge of cultural values.

[93] Ibid. p. 33.

[94] To understand memories and imagination of Gorakhpur peasants and local nationalists for their Mahatma Gandhi(s), see Amin, Shahid.1988. 'Gandhi as Mahatma'. *Selected Subaltern Studies*. R. Guha and G. Spivak. eds. (New York and Oxford: OUP). pp. 288–350.

appear contrary to his own sainthood—regular, modern individuals with aspirations of progress different from his own.

Mulkiram followed the ideas of Gandhi and the Arya Samaj. Thus, he promoted Indian cultural, traditional and nationalist identities and ideas. But the essay argues that with the help of higher education, *sahabiyat* and photos, Mulkiram's family asserted new Dalit power, masculinity, equality, semi-modern thinking and lifestyle in the Hindu society, educated elite and the male-dominated photo spaces. Mulkiram's *sahabiyat* and high education provided high status, respect and honour to his family from Dalits and non-Dalits.

As mentioned, record-keeping is a rare process in Dalit families. *Mulkiram Smriti Granth* helps us to see not only the systematic documentation of family photos and the history of a Dalit family, but also allows us to examine the continuity and change in a Dalit family at an important juncture in the history of India, when it was a nation in the making. The essay also suggests that Mulkiram's life presents only one aspect of the Dalit past in colonial and post-colonial India, which is against the grain of the general repression and destitution faced by the community. Indeed, many different aspects of Dalit history need to be explored to get a clear picture of the Dalit history and Khatik history. Indeed, the everyday work, lives, living standards and ideas of many Khatiks were completely different from those of Mulkiram and his family. The colonial ethnographical census and police records show that Khatiks were the unregistered day labourers performing unorganised work, living in unplanned and unauthorised Dalit bastis. They worked as leather dyers, tanners, leather-bristle dealers, fruit sellers, *kabariya* (buyers and store-keepers of rubbish), masons, construction labourers, butchers, goat and pig breeders, pork bacon vendors, *tanga/tonga* drivers, carters, domestic servants, etc. They were and still are the victims of social, political, economic and religious discrimination, illiteracy and untouchability. They are still invisible.[95]

For instance, see below a birthday celebration photo of a Khatik family (Figure 11). It was taken in the Khatik basti in the Ambala Cantonment between the mid- and late 1970s. The Khatik family organised a goat sacrifice in honour of the local goddess, Kaila Devi, whose temple is in Karauli, about 160 kilometres away from Agra. The Chamar *bhagats*[96] displayed the printed images of Kaila Devi and Bhairo, a local god. They came to organise a devotional gathering for singing before the goat was slaughtered. The Dalit men also displayed their masculinity by bearing a sword or big knife. In the

[95] For socio-economic and political conditions of Khatiks, see Kumar, Vijay. 2021. 'Locating Dalit Bastis: The Sites of Everyday Silent Resistance and Works from the late 19th-century to the mid-20th century United Provinces'. *Neighbourhoods in the Urban India: In Between Home and the City*. Sadan Jha, Dev Nath Pathak and Amiya Kumar Das. eds. (New Delhi: Bloomsbury). pp. 119–43. For an ethnographical survey on UP Khatiks in 1961, see Singh, H.N. 1971. 'Khatiks of Uttar Pradesh'. *Census of India 1961*. Vol. 1 (Monograph Series: Ethnographic Study, No. 9), Part V-B (iv) (New Delhi: Ministry of Home Affairs).

[96] Bhagats means devotees of the goddess.

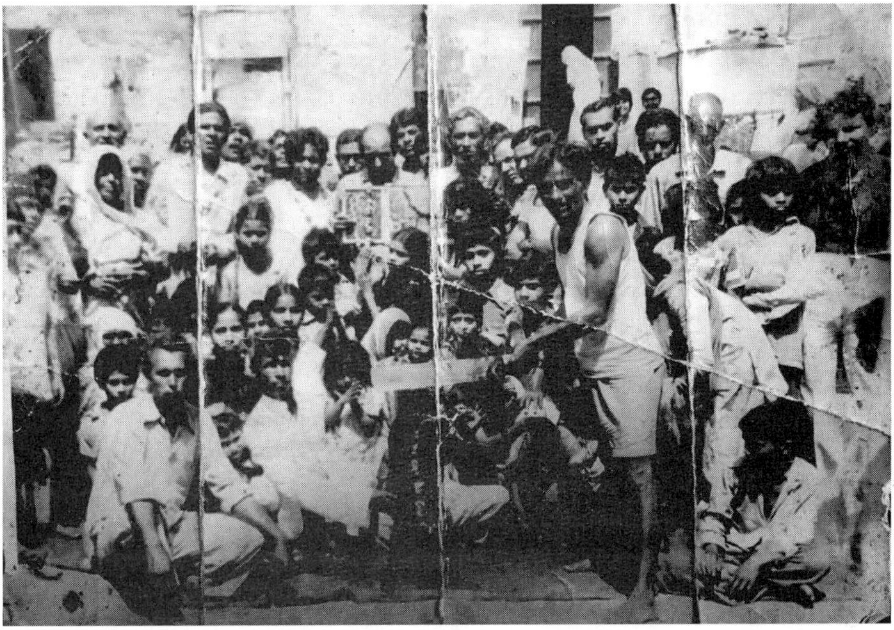

Figure 11: A Birthday Celebration Photo of a Khatik Family in the 1970s

Khatik family, the members worked as horse- and bull-cart drivers, *lifafewalis*, leather workers and rickshaw-pullers. They had marriage ties in Agra and Meerut. None of the Khatik men, women or children in the photo appear in a coat, achkan sherwani, sunglasses, pagaris or the Gandhi cap. Two houses in the photo had a kachcha structure made of mud bricks, wooden doors and a mud floor. The rooftop is also made of mud, straw and wood. There were similar houses on the opposite side, and a big, open *ganda naala*[97] flowed, and still flows, in the middle of the Khatik basti.[98]

It is essential to remind ourselves that according to Gary Tartakov, 'If we want the issue of caste and the destruction of the caste system to become central political issues, we need to bring the situation of Dalits, who are the epitome of the caste system's injustice, into view and to keep them and consideration of the issues of caste hierarchy and discrimination before our eyes, and so in our consciousness.'[99] Dalit family photos help us see the caste issue (a Dalit man Mulkiram at the margin of the school photo)[100] and the assertion of equality and power (in the rest photos of Mulkiram's family) by Dalits, as seen in Mulkiram's biographical account. This essay attempts to visualise the visible and invisible Dalits alike, for their own unique trajectories.

---

[97] Ganda naala means dirty city drainage.

[98] Interview with Jamna, a member of the Khatik family. 14 April 2021. Conducted by Vijay Kumar. Delhi.

[99] Tartakov. 2012. 'Introduction'. *Dalit Art*. p. 7.

[100] Like servants of European and native masters in their family photos.

Further Reading

Gordon, Sophie. 2007. *Photography in India.* IIAS Newsletter. 44. pp. 10–11. Online. www.iias.asia/sites/iias/files/nwl_article/2019-05/IIAS_NL44_1011.pdf

Gupta, Charu. 2016. *The Gender of Caste: Representing Dalits in Print* (Ranikhet: Permanent Black).

Kishwar, Madhu. 1985. 'Gandhi on Women'. *EPW.* 20:41. pp. 1753–58.

Kshirsagar, R. K. 1994. *Dalit Movement in India and its Leaders* (New Delhi: M.D. Publications).

Kumar, Vijay. 2021. 'The Etymological Origin of Caste, Communication and Khatik in the 19th and the early 20th centuries UP'. *Caste, Communication and Power.* Biswjit Das and Debendra Prasad Majhi. eds. (New Delhi and London: Sage Publication and Spectrum). pp. 84–100.

Mulkiram, Chaudhari. 1983 [1968]. *Hridyodgaar.* Tarachand Pal Bekal. ed. Second Edition. (Meerut and Saharanpur: Chaudhari Mulkiram Vichar Manch and Shanti Prakashan).

6

Identities (re)centred: Negotiating ethnic margins

Snapshot of a Modernist Muslim Imagination

The Aligarh Photo Archive

Uzma Mohsin

> 'Photographs offer a prism through which to study the postmodern space of cultural memory composed of leftovers, debris, single items that are left to be collected and assembled in many ways, to tell a variety of stories, from a variety of often competing perspectives.'
>
> — Marianne Hirsch[1]

In the summer of 2018, I returned to Aligarh, a town in the state of Uttar Pradesh in North India, where I grew up, to document it photographically. Historically, Aligarh has been the focal point of a reform movement envisioning a modernist idea with an emphasis on secular education and liberal Muslim culture. The educationist Syed Ahmed Khan (1817–1898) initiated the Aligarh Movement in the late nineteenth century, setting up a college at Aligarh, which evolved into the Aligarh Muslim University (AMU), providing educational opportunities to the Muslim community from across the Indian subcontinent. I arrived in the town amidst widespread civil unrest. A heated row had erupted over a portrait of Muhammad Ali Jinnah hanging in the Students' Union office at AMU. Local right-wing groups opposed Jinnah's portrait being on display. The students challenged this objection, triggering a clash. The university authorities defended the portrait claiming that it had been hanging there along with portraits of many other leaders of the freedom movement for decades. They reiterated that Jinnah, a founder member of the University Court, had been granted a lifetime membership of the student union,[2] just as Mohandas Karamchand Gandhi, whose portrait was also hanging at the Student Union Hall since before Independence. The chaos over the portrait resulted in protests and violence on university campus with a curfew being imposed in the city.

Indian Muslims frequently face doubt and distrust regarding their 'modern and secular' credentials as citizens while attempting to converge identity, history and nationality. More and more, they are being compelled to conform to an

---

[1] Hirsch, Marianne. 1997. *Family Frames: Photography, Narrative and Postmemory* (Harvard University Press). p. 13.

[2] The AMU spokesperson in a statement to Express Web Desk issued a clarification on the portrait of Jinnah. See 'AMU Jinnah portrait row: What has happened so far'. 5 May 2018. *The Indian Express*. indianexpress.com/article/india/amu-jinnah-portrait-row-what-has-happened-so-far-5164394/.

idea of a nation defined by the majority Hindu populace. There is an attempt to erase their history and contribution to India's syncretic culture. Divisive politics and oppressive laws are eroding Muslims' constitutional rights and freedoms. If they resist, they are challenged, marginalised or excluded. Furthermore, with society's growing political and communal polarisation, Muslims increasingly witness intolerance and violence as they find themselves caught in the ever-widening gulf of an impairing binary—the majority's constricting stance against their worsening situation as a minority. The social scientist Seema Kazi argues in a paper presented at a National Seminar at the AMU in 2018, that Indian Muslims 'are bound to a narrative of "national"—and by extension, "universal" modernity—wherein any and all expression of their "difference" is equivalent to disloyalty. This has resulted in self-censorship by the community when it comes to expressing their histories, fearing retribution. They are often forced to use the trope of ahistoricism to fit the majoritarian view of what a modern Indian Muslim citizen is.'[3]

The incident at AMU also illustrates how images increasingly influence our sense of culture and history in today's world. For a visual artist, it poses challenging questions. How could photography with its ever-expanding dissemination, open up conceptual and creative possibilities to examine public history? Do specific images evoke a particular response, or could photographs help look at the past beyond the hegemony of majoritarian rhetoric? Could they operate as a premise for building an alternative understanding? Moreover, could photographs help frame cultural memory in telling the story of Muslim lives associated with Aligarh from their own perspective? These questions prompted me to research visual material around the community and start a digital archiving initiative—the Aligarh Photo Archive—as part of my artistic practice. The archive's raison d'etre is to develop a repository of photographic material to uncover people's life trajectories in the course of defining Muslim identity in relation to the discourse on modernity and nationality. Family photographs are an integral part of the archive, working as real and aspirational cultural motifs that reveal a nuanced portrayal of the community besides affirming kinship and community ties. I first began building the archive by scanning my own extended family's photographic material and then expanding it by approaching others. Access to family photographs entirely depends on trust. My grandfather came to Aligarh in the 1920s to study and then became a teacher there. Three generations of my family have either studied or taught at the university, and this association of my family with the town helped me forge contacts. The digitisation process works through agreed-upon contributions, with photographs being scanned at the premises of the contributor. Rough black-and-white prints are annotated and image details are written alongside

[3] Kazi, Seema. 15 November 2018. 'Minority Women and Marginalization: A Historical Perspective'. Paper Presentation at National Seminar on Women of Marginalized Communities: Concerns About Exclusion. Centre for Women Studies. Aligarh Muslim University, Aligarh.

conversations that are usually audio-recorded. Finally, high-resolution digital scans are shared with the contributor. This method is followed so as to not displace the original material. Since 2017, hundreds of family photographs have been scanned, and the work is still in progress. Whether shot formally at a commercial studio or taken as candid amateur snapshots, these family photographs work as illuminating indices revealing the community's joys and struggles, whether real, imaginary, aspirational, domestic or public. Scenes depicting the household—relatives, friends, occasions, events, pets, beauty and love—all affirm the idea of home and belonging.

My essay draws upon the Aligarh Photo Archive to bring forth untold stories about the Muslim community as they face a changing notion of home today, with a shrinking public presence in a country they have historically played a vital role in shaping. Using a broad definition of family photographs, it examines familial material from a diverse cross-section comprising of families and consanguineous networks associated with Aligarh, to provide crucial insights and readings of the community. The chosen material and families follow a loose, fragmented chronology presenting flashes of time to construct a snapshot of a few moments from the more than 100-year history of the Aligarh Movement. These photographic junctures uncover how diverse Muslim lives are and how rooted they are in the country's historical, political and cultural fabric, and show how family photographs help reframe the discourse around history, representation and photography.

In a series of lectures in the early twentieth century, while addressing the idea of nationalism, Rabindranath Tagore remarked that the real problem in India was not political but social.[4] In his opinion, India needed 'constructive work coming from within herself'.[5] Aligarh became the locus of a similar reckoning because of Syed Ahmed's conviction and efforts to enable educational opportunities to improve the status of the Muslim community after the failure of the Uprising of 1857. Syed Ahmed, immensely affected by the community's plight, started his educational efforts in the United Provinces (now Uttar Pradesh) by first setting up a Persian Madrasah at Moradabad. The Madrasah became a government school by the late 1850s[6] after which he instituted a reformist literary organisation called the Scientific Society in Gazipur in 1963–64.[7] After Syed Ahmed moved to Aligarh in 1864, the Scientific Society relocated there. Aligarh grew into a centre for new educational initiatives. In 1875, Syed Ahmed established a residential school to impart modern education grounded in the community's cultural ethos. The school became the

[4] Tagore, Rabindranath. 2020. *Nationalism* (New Delhi: Fingerprint Classics, Prakash Books India Pvt. Ltd.). Reprint edition. p. 87.

[5] Ibid. p. 101.

[6] Lelyveld, David. 1996. *Aligarh's First Generation: Muslim Solidarity in British India* (Oxford University Press). pp. 71–72.

[7] Ibid. p. 76.

Mohammedan Anglo-Oriental College in 1877, and eventually, the Aligarh Muslim University evolved out of it in 1920.

The failure of the Uprising of 1857 marked the formal end of Mughal rule with the massacre of thousands that intensified racial prejudices and communal hatred. Also, as the British Crown replaced the English East India Company, a need for mapping and surveying the colonised lands and its people for better administrative control arose. In 1868, as part of an ethnographic probe, an eight-volume photographic survey, *The People of India*, was commissioned.[8] The objective of the exercise was to examine the various 'ethnological types'[9] for studying various attributes and aspects of the 'native' life under colonial rule.

In his book *The Coming of Photography in India*, Christopher Pinney quotes from a letter taken from Syed Ahmed's biography *The Life and Work of Syed Ahmed Khan*, by G.F.I. Graham.[10] It gives an account of his visit to London in 1869, where he came across a copy of *The People of India*. The letter, addressed to the secretary of Aligarh Scientific Society, voices his objection to the survey's representation of his people.

> In the India Office is a book in which all the races of India are depicted both in picture and letterpress, giving the manners and customs of each race. Their photographs show that the pictures of the different manners and customs were taken on the spot, and the sight of them shows how savage they are – the equal of animals. The young Englishmen... desirous of knowing something of the land to which they are going... look over this work. What can they think, after perusing this book and looking at its pictures of the power or honour of the natives of India? One day Hamid, Mahmud (Syed's two sons), and I went to the India Office, and Mahmud commenced looking at the work. A young Englishman... came up and after a short time asked Mahmud if he was a Hindustani? Mahmud replied in the affirmative but blushed as he did so, and hastened to explain that he was not one of the aborigines, but that his ancestors were formerly of another country. Reflect therefore, that until Hindustanis remove this blot they shall never be held in the honour by any civilised race.[11]

Zahid R. Chaudhary points out that in spite of being shocked at the publication's representation of 'native' types, Syed Ahmed was persuaded by the civilisation discourse upon which *The People of India* depended. However, his narrative of improvement and self-making was not entirely contiguous with the English civilising mission for India.[12] Syed Ahmed believed that a scientific

[8] Pinney, Christopher. 2008. *The Coming of Photography in India* (London: The British Library). p. 41.

[9] Edwards, Elizabeth. 2001. *Raw Histories: Photographs, Anthropology and Museums* (Berg: Oxford International Publishers Ltd.). p. 134.

[10] Ibid. p. 42.

[11] As quoted in ibid. p. 42.

[12] Chaudhary, Zahid R. 2012. *Afterimage of Empire: Photography in Nineteenth-century India* (University of Minnesota Press). p. 3.

temperament and an 'English' education were vital for the progress of the Muslim community and would help them secure jobs and give the community the ability to influence the British government. Jawaharlal Nehru has argued that 'Sir Syed's decision to concentrate on Western Education for Muslims was undoubtedly a right one. Without that, they could not have played any effective part in the building of Indian nationalism of the new type, and they would have been doomed to play second fiddle to the Hindus with their better education and far stronger economic position.'[13] Despite the varying debates and opinions, Syed Ahmed has left an indelible impression on Muslims of the Indian subcontinent with his reformist ideas. The Aligarh community often eulogises him as a father figure. Much scholarly work about him and the Aligarh Movement is available, but not many photographs. A small selection of reproductions of a few portraits and some group photographs from the early days of the Mohammedan Anglo-Oriental College repeatedly appear in the various books and publications about him. The published photographs are essentially copies from untraceable sources, whether prints or negatives.

One such publication from the 1980s by the late historian Khaliq Ahmad Nizami[14] collates a visual study around Syed Ahmed and the Aligarh Movement exploring the format of an album. Put together like a memento and titled the *Sir Syed Album*,[15] the publication attempts to illustrate his life, interests and achievements photographically. The *Sir Syed Album* has a few pictures of Syed Ahmed's childhood home, family, colleagues, personal belongings, books and travels, along with some portraits formatted like a scrapbook. A section titled 'Sir Syed as Host of Viceroys' shows painted portraits of various viceroys who visited the college. There are some photographs of the early buildings of Mohammedan Anglo-Oriental College and the staff (mainly British), followed by small descriptive texts and portraits of his associates 'who dedicated their lives to his mission.'[16] Many section titles of the publication use words such as 'father', 'guardian', 'leader', 'champion', and 'architect', reiterating Syed Ahmed's position as a benevolent patriarch. The publication ends by commemorating him with two photographs showing the release of a postal stamp with his image and the inauguration of an academy bearing his name. However, there is no mention of the sources for the photographs in the book.

A trouvaille from Midhatullah Khan Sherwani's family photographs[17] shows a popular image of Syed Ahmed from the *Sir Syed Album* publication.[18] The rare silver gelatin print was discovered in a forgotten pile of undisplayed

---

[13] Nehru, Jawaharlal. 1984. *Jawaharlal Nehru: An Autobiography*. Third edition (Jawaharlal Nehru Memorial Fund). p. 462.

[14] Khalil Ahmad Nizami (1925–1997) taught at the Aligarh Muslim University.

[15] It is the first comprehensive photographic study of Syed Ahmed Khan and the Aligarh Movement. Published by Idarah-I Adabiyat-I Delli in 1983.

[16] Nizami, Khalil Ahmad. 1983. *Sir Syed Album* (Idarah-I Adabiyat-I Delli). p. 58.

[17] Now housed at the Muzzammil Ullah Khan Library in Aligarh.

[18] The image is on p. 22 of the *Sir Syed Album*.

framed photographs. The print unfortunately did not reveal any inscriptions or the photographer's name on being removed from its broken frame. The photograph is most likely from the early 1880s and shows Syed Ahmed sitting in the middle, forming a bridge between his friend and associate Nawab Mohsin-ul-Mulk (Syed Mehdi Ali) and his son Syed Mahmud (Figure 1). Both of them played a significant role in the Aligarh Movement's early phase, as his eager supporters. However, what the photograph reveals on a closer look are the competing viewpoints of the two—Syed Mahmud's anglicised manner as he sits upright holding his hat, in contrast to Mohsin-ul-Mulk in a *fez*[19] languidly leaning on the side table. Mohsin-ul-Mulk and Syed Mahmud indicate the two different outlooks prevailing in the Muslim world of the late nineteenth century—the conservative and the modern, both of which Syed Ahmed had to balance to make way for reform. Mohsin-ul-Mulk was a staunch supporter of the Aligarh Movement and had joined Syed Ahmed's efforts from the very start. He was an active member of the Scientific Society from its inception, writing extensively in the society's magazine to support Syed Ahmed's education

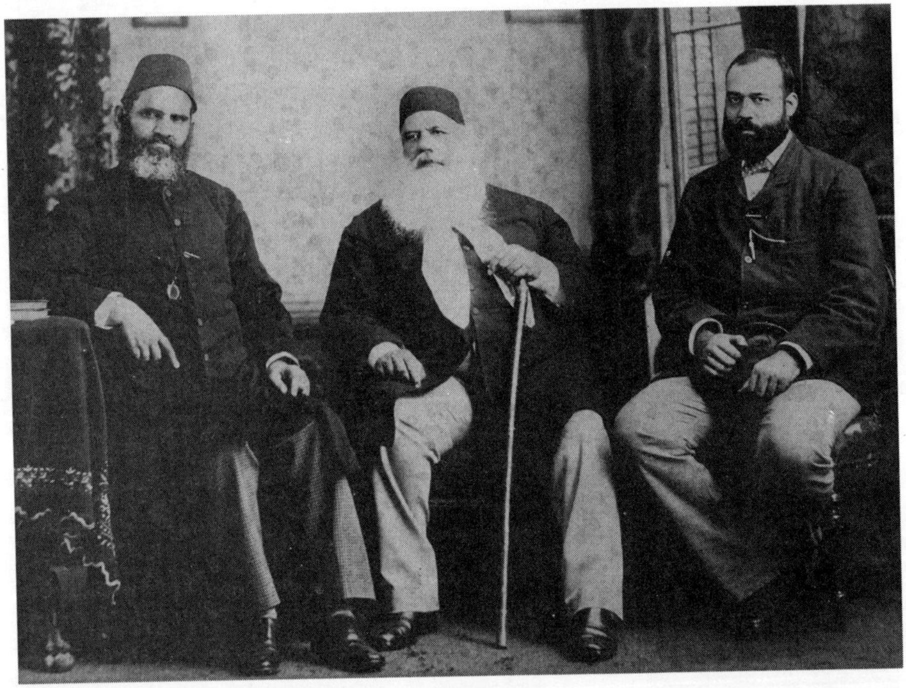

Figure 1. Silver gelatin print of Syed Ahmed Khan (centre) with Nawab Mohsin-ul-Mulk (left) and Syed Mahmud (right). Photographer and date unknown. Archival Photograph from Muzammil Ullah Khan Library, Muzzammil Manzil, Aligarh. Courtesy Midhatullah Khan Sherwani/Aligarh Photo Archive.

[19] Turkish cap.

efforts. However, being a traditionalist, Mohsin-ul-Mulk disapproved of Syed Ahmed's religious views and strongly criticised his writings on it. On the other hand, Syed Mahmud, on returning from England after completing his studies, helped his father put together the Mohammedan Anglo-Oriental College's proposal and introduced a modern curriculum and pedagogy for the college.

The 1880s threw up questions around Muslim representation and their role in British India's polity, accentuated by a new emerging class of educated Muslims and the emergence of the Nationalist Movement under the aegis of the Indian National Congress. Syed Ahmed anchored the various Muslim opinions and energies through a determined focus on education and the authority of a statesman, forming an essential centripetal link between varying Muslim voices. The photograph captures a moment from that decisive period. A different phase of the Aligarh Movement began with Syed Ahmed's death in 1898, with Mohsin-ul-Mulk taking over the college secretaryship and Syed Mahmud leaving Aligarh.

Other photographs shared by Midhatullah Khan show Aligarh in its early formative years. Midhatullah Khan's grandfather late Mohammad Muzzammil Ullah Khan Sherwani, played a prominent role in the Aligarh Movement. He became the vice-chancellor of the university twice in the 1920s. The Sherwani Pathans of Aligarh district, the clan to which Muzzammil Ullah belonged, claimed their descent from a tribe in the Sperwan (corrupted to Sherwani) near Qandahar in Afghanistan. According to the *Sherwani Nama*, which chronicles the family's history, the Sherwanis supposedly settled in Aligarh when Isa Khan Sherwani was made the *haakim*[20] of Kol (modern-day Aligarh) before the coming of the Mughals. Over time, the Sherwanis grew into powerful *taluqdars* and *zamindars*[21] by acquiring land and status across the region.[22] The Aligarh Movement's initial phase was supported and funded by regional rulers and local elite of the area, including the Sherwanis.

Many photographs from the Sherwani family collection show a glimpse of the lives of the landed gentry of Aligarh in the late nineteenth and early twentieth centuries. Photography arrived in India soon after its invention. A Calcutta-based firm, Thacker, Spink & Co., is known to have advertised daguerreotype cameras by January 1840 and by March of the same year, *The Calcutta Courier* reported the first daguerreotypes produced in the city.[23] Photography gained popularity amongst the nobility and the wealthy elite because of their close interaction with the British. The flourishing of Photographic Societies contributed to the expansion of photography across the metropolises of the three presidencies, with Indian photographers sharing

---

[20] Governor/judge.

[21] Aristocratic land-owning ruling class and feudal landlords responsible for collecting taxes.

[22] Siddiqi, Jamal Muhammad. 1981. *Aligarh District: A Historical Survey from Ancient Times to 1803* (Munshiram Manoharlal Publishers Pvt. Ltd.). p. 185.

[23] Pinney. 2008. *The Coming of Photography*. p. 9.

their works at various meetings and exhibitions.[24] By the end of the nineteenth century, the commercial photo studio emerged, further accelerating the interest in photography. The Indian aristocracy and feudal elite used photography to record their stature and prestige in society, often gifting photographs as souvenirs either to show their dominance or as gestures of allegiance. A late nineteenth-century undated cabinet card of Lady Curzon, the Vicereine of India, by the photographer H.A. Mirza (Delhi) or a signed portrait of William Sinclair Marris (29 November 1924), the Governor of the United Provinces, found in the Sherwani family collection, were probably exchanged as gifts between Muzammil Ullah Khan and a touring dignitary or influential bureaucrat. In many group photographs, Muzammil Ullah Khan is seen attending various meetings and functions hosted by the local administration or participating in the university's activities and gatherings. Mostly, he takes centre-stage, mirroring an awareness of both photography's importance and his own clout, surrounded by stylishly dressed provincial upper-class gentry with Englishmen and women amongst them (Figure 2). Racial power structures and gender hierarchies are visible in the sitters' composure and arrangement. Sometimes the Indian men appear in official regalia with medals decorating their lapels while the women, primarily British, are mostly seen in elaborate hats.

Besides the Mohammedan Anglo-Oriental College English staff, Aligarh also had a small community of British and Anglo-Indian residents. Most British

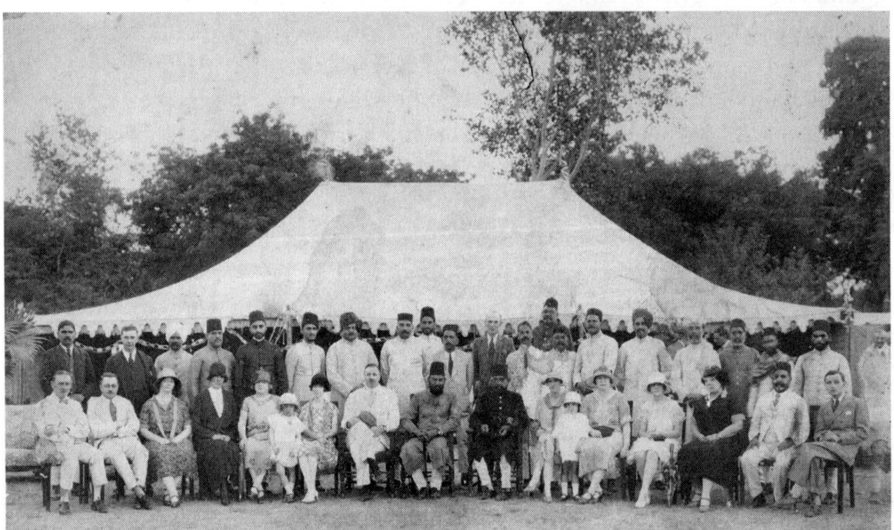

Figure 2. Group with Nawab Muzzammil Ullah Khan Sherwani in the centre (eighth from the right). Photographer and date unknown. Archival Photograph from Muzammil Ullah Khan Library, Muzzammil Manzil, Aligarh. Courtesy Midhatullah Khan Sherwani/Aligarh Photo Archive.

[24] Ibid. p. 12.

families were associated with the civil administration barring some who were employed in trade, mainly of indigo and saltpetre. A few worked in the lock industry set up by the British or in private jobs. A photograph from the early twentieth century with a scribbled message of 'good wishes' from Barbara Donaldrow shows an English lady lovingly holding an infant girl named Lucida May, wrapped in a white shawl. It is a portrait sent to the Sherwani family by their English governess on her return to England. Midhatullah Khan[25] explains that many well-to-do Muslim families employed English private tutors and governesses to help foster the ideals of good etiquette and proper civil behaviour under the care of British tutorship.

The ideas of guardianship, supervision and decorum were also part of the rationale behind the residential framework of the Mohammaden Anglo-Oriental College proposed by Syed Ahmed. He believed that the moral influence of a planned social environment would be more persuasive in raising the new generation than merely books. In his opinion, education was of two kinds. *Ta'līm* prepared a person for a profession, while *tarbiyat* helped develop the innate qualities of character. Each boarding house of the Mohammaden Anglo-Oriental College was envisioned as a world unto itself, with dining rooms, a mosque, a library, a reading room, a debating club, a garden and a playground.[26] Staff, many of whom were British, and other boarding-house workers, were appointed to guide the students. However, attracting students to the new school was not easy, and the earliest students were sons and nephews of Syed Ahmed's colleagues and associates. Concerted efforts were made to entice more students, and admissions were kept open throughout the year.[27] Whether it was the offer of scholarships or the need to be educated to counter the British administration's unfamiliar ways, or the lure of a better livelihood, or the attraction of being tutored by an English staff, many feudal families eventually sent their wards to Aligarh. The boarding house often became a home away from home for the first few generations.

A batch of students from as young as seven to seventeen accompanied by their tutors and a matron named Mrs. Duncan, are seen in a photograph titled 'English House, M.U. Aligarh 1939–40'at the Muzammil Ullah Khan Library. The English House was initiated by Theodore Morison, the principal of the college, as a boarding house for young aristocratic students in 1900. Starting with 13 boys under the care of the housemaster G. Gardner, it doubled up as a finishing school for youngsters who largely came from feudal setups.[28] In his book *Aligarh's First Generation*, David Lelyveld writes that some of the

[25] Conversation with the author. November 2019.

[26] Lelyveld. 1996. *Aligarh's First Generation.* pp. 128–29.

[27] Ibid. p. 167.

[28] Khan, Iftikar Alam. 2001. *Sir Syed Aur Fan-e-Tameer* [Sir Syed and The Story of Building] (Aligarh: Publication Division, Aligarh Muslim University). p. 217.

students with aristocratic backgrounds who came to Mohammedan Anglo-Oriental College were sent there by the British government. They were wards of the State, and the district collectors and deputy commissioners managed their upbringing and property. Syed Ahmed had to often resort to lengthy negotiations with various provincial governments and the viceregal establishment to solicit such students' patronage. In one case, it was agreed that a certain Oudh *taluqdar* would be allowed to come to the college with an entourage of servants, including a groom for his horse and a grass cutter.[29]

The late Nawab of the principality of Chhatari in Bulandshahr district, Mohammad Ahmed Said Khan, joined the Mohammedan Anglo-Oriental College in 1904. Having lost his father at a very young age, he became a boarder at English House under the protection of the Court of Wards. However, Ahmed Said Khan left the college without completing his education and became interested in politics, forming the Agriculturist Party. Later, he became both the governor and chief minister in 1933 and 1937, respectively, of the United Provinces. He served as President of the Executive Council of the last Nizam of Hyderabad (Prime Minister of Hyderabad) from 1941 to 1946, and then in 1947. After retiring from the Nizam's service, he settled in Aligarh, becoming the Chancellor of Aligarh Muslim University from 1965 to 1982.

A diverse collection of pictures with an assortment of ornate monograms capturing his life's course adorn the walls of the family's house in Aligarh. Names of studios like Deen Dayal & Sons and Acharaya & Bhagania (Hyderabad), Sawn Studio (Allahabad), M.M. Beg and Mull & Co. (Lucknow), Begg & Co. and S. Mahmood (Meerut), and Zaki & Sons and City Art Studio (Aligarh) appear on the displayed photographs. A set of photographs from the 1930s decorating the main dining hall shows his vibrant and busy social life as an astute local leader and politician. Amongst them, a beautifully framed large group photograph shows Ahmed Said Khan attending the Round Table Conference in London in 1931. Other images from his days as the Chancellor of Aligarh Muslim University show him escorting visiting dignitaries, interacting with students or enjoying a cultural programme. Through these images, what unravels is Ahmed Said Khan's energetic personality and remarkable presence, engaging in politics, nation-building and generally interacting in the public sphere.

Many of Ahmed Said Khan's photographs are taken from the time he spent in Hyderabad, working for the Nizam. They are shot by the renowned Indian photo studio set up by Raja Deen Dayal who was the Nizam's State photographer. An interesting collaboration occurred between Raja Deen Dayal and Mahboob Ali Khan, the sixth Nizam of Hyderabad, when Deen Dayal became the court photographer in 1885. It not only resulted in an overwhelming visual record of the opulent splendour of India's wealthiest prince, his durbar,

[29] Ibid. p. 174–75.

military exercises and hunts, but also allowed the photographer time and space to set up his commercial establishments in Secunderabad, Indore and later in Bombay.[30] With Raja Deen Dayal's demise, the firm struggled to stay afloat on the account of decreasing patronage, financial difficulties and family misfortunes. It was only under Deen Dayal's grandson Ami Chand Deen Dayal, that the business was revived. Ami Chand extensively chronicled the rule of Mir Osman Ali Khan, the last Nizam of Hyderabad, in the 1940s, when Ahmed Said Khan was employed there and continued to photograph the city of Hyderabad until his demise in 1984.

A carefully composed studio portrait of Ahmad Said Khan from the 1940s shows him sitting on a baroque chair in an opulent setting of potted plants and Persian carpets. The photograph is taken at Raja Deen Dayal studio in Secunderabad. In other photographs taken by Raja Deen Dayal & Sons, Ahmed Said Khan is seen officiating his various duties as chief official of the Nizam: 'A Visit to the Osmania University Annual Convocation 1942', 'Giving A Civic Address at the Town Hall', 'At the Hyderabad Army Training School', or celebrating 'Deepavali 1941' (titles on the photographs). Sometimes, the photographs of Ahmed Said Khan's official visits by the Deen Dayal studio are put together in an album as mementoes. 'Souvenir of the Visit of His Excellency Lt. Col. Sir Mohammad Ahmed Said Khan, The Nawab of Chhatari, President H.E.H., The Nizam's Executive Council, to Gulbarga, November 1941', is one such album with bold gold lettering printed on its cover. The album, which gives an insight into his public life, is full of scenes from numerous tours and activities with type-written captions. Another album is 'Visit to Gulbarga and Bidar'. Interestingly, the album has pictures of Ahmed Said visiting various sites juxtaposed with architectural images and details of the buildings, including a panoramic view of the area's funerary monuments. There is likely a collusion of interests, between Ahmed Said Khan and the photographer, in producing this album. Raja Deen Dayal & Sons were known to specialise in the oeuvre of architectural and landscape photography. At the same time, numerous examples in the family collection, like 'Viewing the Ajanta Caves from the Viewpoint', 'Having Tea at Cave No. 8, Ajanta', or 'Returning from the Ashokan Edict', reflect Ahmed Said Khan's keen interest in historical monuments.

What is striking about the photographs is the presence of Ahmed Said Khan's son, Ibne Said Khan, in most of the images. Ibne Said accompanied his father on most of his tours whenever he visited Hyderabad. The photographs double up as an intimate account of their relationship as father and son, and as mentor and pupil. In many of the photographs, one notices Ibne Said present somewhere in the background, carefully observing his father as he accompanies him. As he emulates his father, a similarity of pose and stance

[30] Karlekar, Malavika. 2013. *Visual Histories: Photography in the Popular Imagination* (Oxford University Press). p. 15.

reflects their close bond. Sons usually succeeded fathers in suzerainty in the Muslim feudal world. The photographs uncover the idea of a father figure in landed families as a predominating patriarch and a role model for his male progeny representing authority, discipline and leadership. Traditionally, fathers set the example of how to navigate the outside world for their sons to inherit their legacy and estate (Figure 3).

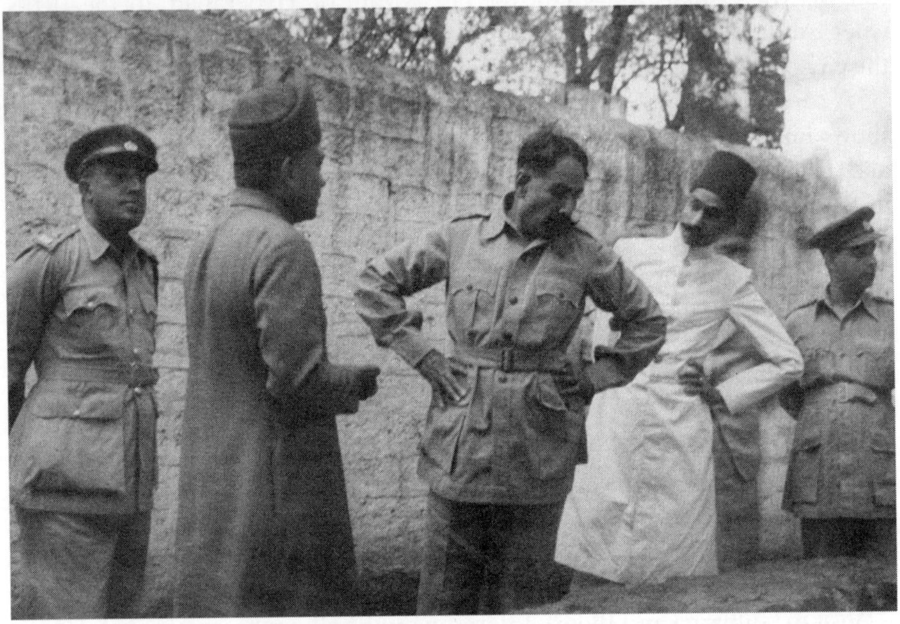

Figure 3. Mohammad Ahmed Said Khan on an official tour along with his son Ibne Said Khan. Bidar, 1940s. Photographer: Unknown. Private collection of Mohammad Ahmed Said Khan; courtesy Nawab Ibne Said Khan/ Aligarh Photo Archive.

Ibne Said Khan[31] carefully maintained his father's photographic collection. All sizes of photographs, unbound pages from albums, letters and other memorabilia made their way into large plastic files, safely stored under his care. Ibne Said Khan enjoyed curating the images, often pasting news clippings and other memorabilia next to the images on the album pages to substantiate his father's story. Interestingly, such interspersion of news clippings with personal photographs gives a broader context to the images, often simulating a documentary feel. Sometimes, it also provides amusing cues and humorous trivia. A news clipping with a picture shows Ahmed Said Khan as a governor, inspecting the Royal Indian Military Academy at Dehradun. It reports he 'was dressed in *achhkan*,[32] pyjamas and *fez*'. The curated images

[31] Ibn Said Khan, who shared his family photographs with the author, was ninety-eight when last interviewed in March 2021. He passed away in June 2021.

[32] Achhkan is a traditional long coat worn with pyjamas.

reflect his impressions of his father. However, Ibne Said Khan believed that the material is of historical importance and deserves to be adequately organised and conserved. He[33] recounted an incident of how after his father's demise in 1982, on a visit to his ancestral home in Chhatari, one winter night, he saw his help lighting the brazier with some old papers. On inquiring where the paper for the fire had been taken from, he discovered that they were abandoned documents and photographs of his father. Many family photographs meet a similar fate and are lost to neglect and termites.

Troupes of power and prestige surface again and again over time in the photographic representation of landed feudal families. What is conspicuously missing from the early images of Muslim lives are women's photographs, because of the stricture of *purdah*. Most women led a screened life, rarely stepping out of their homes, especially women from rich and powerful families. *An Illustrated Historical Album of the Rajas and Taaluqdars of Oudh* of 1880, which contains 344 cartes-de-visite portraits by the Lucknow photographer Abbas Ali, highlights this seclusion of women from the public eye. While discussing the album, Christopher Pinney points out that instead of photographic portraits of women *taluqdars*, a medallion bearing the word '*pardanashin*' is used. *Pardanashin* means 'maintaining the veil', a term adopted in legal parlance when the British enacted special provisions under the Law of Contract Act of 1872, to safeguard the interests and rights of *pardanashin* women in cases of contracts, property and inheritance. The courtesy is extended to both Hindu and Muslim women in the album.[34] The use of the medallion shows that photography often adhered to cultural traditions and local customs, developing hybrid photographic forms, aesthetics and practice.

Shaheen Sherwani, [35] the maternal granddaughter of Muzzammil Ullah Khan, remembers seeing a passport in her family documents with '*pardanashin*' written in place of the passport bearer's photograph. She shares a set of images of an older generation of women from her family who probably faced the camera for the first time when photographed for a passport. A sense of apprehension can be seen on the faces of the women in the images. One of them clasps her hands trying to hold on to her burqa. Her discomfiture comes from her conditioning of space and gender roles. This traditional viewing of women as being linked to the 'interior' or domesticity, led to the introduction of home photography services. Identification images were taken to be used in legal documents or for procuring a passport to travel to Haj by calling a photographer home, reveals Shaheen.

By the end of the nineteenth century, concern about Muslim women's status and education arose in Aligarh. In the late 1890s, the All-India Mohammedan Educational Conference, an organisation founded by Syed Ahmed to promote

[33] In a conversation with the author. August 2019.

[34] Ibid. p. 39.

[35] In a conversation with the author. January 2020.

education amongst Muslims, debated the mandate of women's education in its annual meetings. Shaikh Muhammad Abdullah, an alumnus of Mohammedan Anglo-Oriental College who lived in Aligarh, was the resolution's main advocator. By 1902, Shaikh Abdullah became the secretary of the Women's Education Section at the All-India Mohammedan Educational Conference, and finally, in 1904, during a session at Lucknow, a resolution for setting up a girl's school was passed.[36] Shaikh Abdullah championed the cause of women's empowerment by starting a magazine called 'Khatoon', publishing articles to persuade people to educate their daughters. He also established the Female Education Association to further favourable public opinion on the issue.[37] Shaikh Abdullah faced considerable opposition in the initial years, as many families preferred home tuition and were reluctant to send their *purdah* observing daughters to school.

In 1906, his wife Waheed Jahan and he started a boarding-cum-day *madrasah* for girls at Aligarh with the financial support of Sultan Jahan Begum of Bhopal. The *madrasah* was set up in a small rented house at Mohalla Balai Qila in the city's old parts. In the beginning, only seventeen girls, including his three daughters, enrolled in the *madrasah*, and a carriage was acquired to ferry the girls to and fro. Slowly but steadily the number of students increased. Shaikh Abdullah wanted to convert the *madrasah* into an all-girls residential school to accommodate the expanding numbers and provide stay for students from outside of Aligarh. In 1911, the foundation for a residential Muslim girls' school was laid by Mrs. Porter, the wife of the Lieutenant Governor of the United Province.[38] By the early 1920s, the school grew into an intermediate college that eventually became part of the university as a graduate college in 1937.

Sayera Habib,[39] who taught Economics at the Aligarh Muslim University (from 1963 to 1992), says that the stricture of *purdah* depended primarily on a family's outlook, and the practice had reasonably reduced by the time she was in college. Sayera did her graduation from the Women's College in the late 1940s. She recalls that women rode bicycles to college, like herself, by the time she was studying. After completing her graduation from the Women's College, Sayera joined the university in 1951 for her masters' degree in Economics. There were only three girls in the class, including her. Narrating an incident from her first day at the university, she recounts how, on arriving at

---

[36] Fareed, Sadaf. 2 February 2022. 'How Sheikh Abdullah Brought About A New Era Of Women's Education In Aligarh'. *Outlook*. www.outlookindia.com/national/how-sheikh-abdullah-brought-about-a-new-era-of-female-education-in-aligarh--news-56502. Accessed 2 June 2022.

[37] Alavi, Azra. ed. 2007. *Dreams & Destinations: An Illustrated History of 100 years of Women's Education (1902-2006)*. Roomana N. Siddiqui. Associate ed. (Centenary Publications, Women's College, Aligarh Muslim University). p. 25.

[38] Ibid. pp. 30–31.

[39] In a conversation with the author. July 2019.

the lecture hall, she noticed a screen with three chairs and tables behind it, kept for the female students. Since she and the other women did not observe *purdah*, they decided to set the screen aside, despite a warning by the boys in the class, who thought that the girls would be reprimanded for doing so. However, she says that when the professor arrived, he noticed the missing screen. 'He exclaimed, "Oh, so there will be no screen this year!" To which we girls replied, "Sir, won't it look odd that we come on our bicycles to class and then sit behind a *purdah* screen?" The professor smiled and said it was all right.' Later, Sayera went for further studies to England. A picture shows her as a student with a cycle while on tour in France (Figure 4).

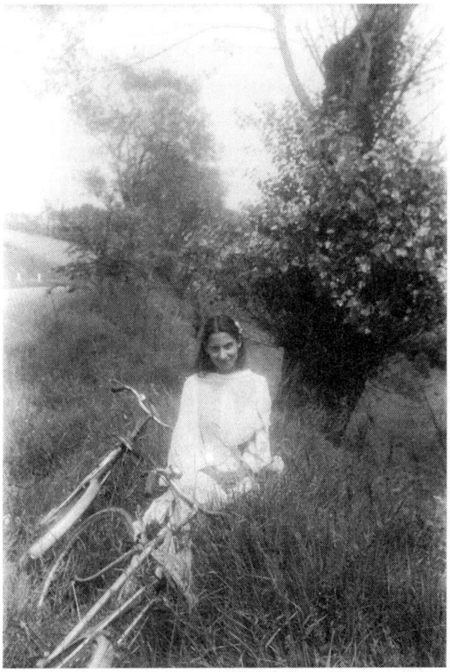

Figure 4. Sayera as a student with a cycle while touring France. Courtesy: Sayera Habib/Aligarh Photo Archive

The American photographer Margaret Bourke-White visited Aligarh Muslim University while travelling through India on an assignment for *Life* magazine in 1946. A photograph[40] taken by her at the time, shows an ongoing zoology class at the university with female students sitting behind a *purdah* screen while, in contrast, their male counterparts sit freely in the open.

'No one could insist on the *purdah* after 1947. The *burka* was prevalent as part of the Women's College's uniform before 1947, but that disappeared after Independence. *Mulk hi badal gaya* 1947 *ke baad* (the country itself changed after 1947). Earlier, there were no women teachers in the university, barring the Women's College teachers. However, after the Radhakrishnan Commission in 1948, women were granted equal rights to appointments in various university teaching posts. This change was brought in even before the Constitution was fully adopted,' says historian Irfan Habib.[41]

The real stirrings of women's engagement with the public domain throughout India began with the Non-Cooperation Movement in 1920,

---

[40] Bourke-White, Margaret. 1946. Silver gelatina print of an ongoing zoology class at Aligarh Muslim University. The *LIFE* Magazine Collection, 2005. ICP. www.icp.org/browse/archive/objects/zoology-classes-divided-with-female-students-sitting-behind-a-purdah-screen. Accessed 4 June 2021.

[41] Irfan Habib, Professor Emeritus at the Aligarh Muslim University in a conversation with the author, December 2017.

when Gandhi mobilised women. As more and more women stepped out to participate in the movement, they started to carve out a niche in the nationalist and gender discourse, a space hitherto dominated by men. A page from one of the family albums of Irfan Habib, shows a young Sohaila Mohammad Habib, his mother, at her home in Baroda (Figure 5). Sohaila relocated to Aligarh after her marriage to Mohammad Habib, a professor of history at the University (from 1922 to 1958). This portrait of Sohaila, taken in 1921, is a portrayal of youthful confidence and an entirely new kind of Muslim woman in 1920s India. Next to it on the page is another image, that of her parents Amina and Abbas Tyabji, and her sister Sharifah and brother Shujauddin (Figure 5). A scribbled caption below says that the image is from 1928. The Tyabjis were a prominent Sulaimani Bohra family from Gujarat. Abbas Tyabji had—like his well-known uncle Badruddin Tyabji, the President of the Indian National Congress in 1887—studied law in England. At first, he led a life influenced by Western thought and culture, but the Jallianwala Bagh incident in Amritsar in 1919 completely changed his outlook. Abbas Tyabji became a devout Gandhian thereafter. Pictures in the family's collection reveal his close association with Gandhi and his active participation in the freedom struggle. One such image from 1930 shows him addressing the Congress's Working Committee before going to jail for taking part in the Dandi March. The picture shows Amina Tyabji and Kasturba Gandhi by his side.

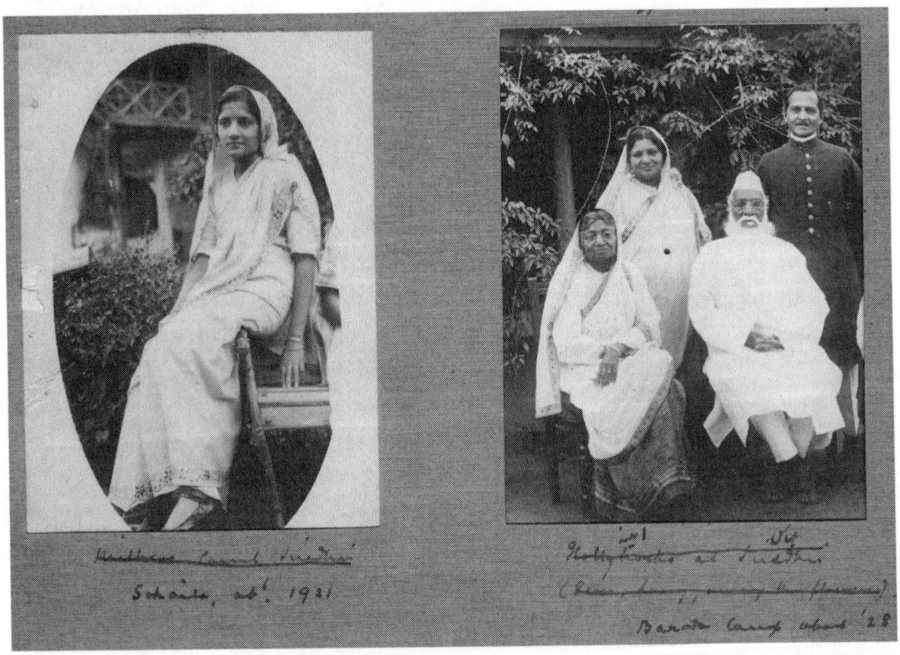

Figure 5. Left: Sohaila Habib, Baroda, 1921. Right: Sharifah and Shujauddin (standing) with Amina and Abbas Tyabji (seated), Baroda, 1928.
Courtesy: Irfan Habib/Aligarh Photo Archive.

Sohaila grew up in an environment which encouraged education for women, enabling independent thinking and self-reliance. The Tyabji family kept an open house in the evenings where family and friends would assemble for sports and amusement. Sohaila was a keen tennis player. 'All of Abbas Tyabji's daughters learnt music. Sohaila's eldest sister Sharifah played the veena while Raihana, the middle sister, and Sohaila trained in Hindustani vocals. Raihana is said to have sung devotional songs at sessions of the Indian National Congress. She also loved conjuring up short theatrical plays to entertain the family, which they lovingly called "tableaus". Parents, cousins, close friends would all be enthusiastic participants,' reminiscences Saman Habib,[42] Sohaila's granddaughter. She points at a picture of one such tableau depicting a scene from the epic *Mahabharata* when the Pandavas lose their kingdom in a game of dice. Raihana appears in the middle of the picture, confidently facing the camera as she plays Lord Krishna's role in the tableau.

Sohaila found herself amidst parochial attitudes and a non-existent social life when she moved to Aligarh in 1927. The only social outlet in Aligarh at that time was a club exclusively for British officers. Along with some friends from the university community, she helped set up the Indian Club in the early 1930s (Figure 6). The Indian Club made its humble beginning from a small bungalow rented from the railway authorities, across from Sohaila's house. Members of the club, including women, would assemble and play tennis, badminton and bridge on most evenings and discuss the country's changing state of affairs. The early decades of the twentieth century had marked the beginning of nationalist leanings and a turning point for Muslim politics. The Mohammedan Anglo-Oriental College had also become a full-fledged university. By the 1930s, it had grown into an eminent centre for scholarship under the tenure of Syed Ahmed's grandson Ross Masood as the vice-chancellor, with many distinguished personalities visiting the campus, including Gandhi, the poet Mohammad Iqbal, the physicist C.V. Raman, the historian Tara Chand and Jawaharlal Nehru, to name a few. Jawaharlal Nehru came to Aligarh several times, but his first visit was in 1933, when he addressed a meeting with students presided by Ross Masood at the Strachey Hall of the university. In later years, he revisited the campus to address the university's convocation in 1948 and to lay the foundation stone for the Maulana Azad Library in 1960.

A letter dated 4 November 1960 from the correspondence between Jawaharlal Nehru and late Jamal Khwaja, a professor of philosophy at the university, states:

> As I expected, Col. Zaidi [the then Vice Chancellor of the university] is pressing me to have lunch with the university authorities... I would prefer to have a quiet lunch with your father... it is important that the lunch I have with your

[42] In a conversation with the author. July 2020.

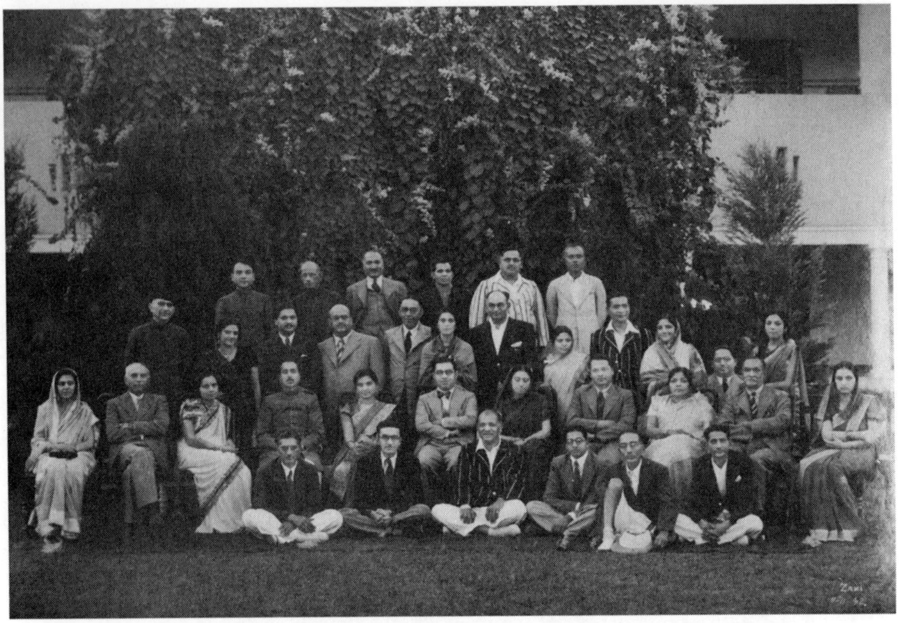

Figure 6. A group of the Indian Club from early 1930s, Aligarh. The picture is taken in front of Prof. Manzur's home, a member of the Indian Club and Sohaila's neighbour. Sohaila is standing (second from right) in the middle row. Courtesy: Irfan Habib/Aligarh Photo Archive.

> father should be a quiet affair and... possibly, the lunch maybe confined to the family. (personal correspondence)[43]

Abdul Majeed Khwaja, Jamal Khwaja's father and Nehru were contemporaries at the Christ College, Cambridge. Nehru would visit Abdul Majeed Khwaja and his wife Begum Khursheed Khwaja at their home, Sami Manzil, whenever he came to Aligarh. A family photograph from 1956 captures one such occasion (Figure 7).

Abdul Majeed Khwaja was born in Aligarh in 1885. His father, Khwaja Mohammad Yusuf, was a prominent lawyer in the city and a fervent supporter of Syed Ahmed and the Aligarh Movement. After informal studies in Arabic and Persian at home, Abdul Majeed Khwaja initially joined the Mohammad Anglo-Oriental College before going to Cambridge to study law. He first saw and heard Gandhi as a student when he visited Cambridge in 1909, while campaigning for the rights of Asian residents in South Africa.[44] Gandhi's ideas and philosophy so influenced Abdul Majeed Khwaja that he gave up practising law on his return to India and joined the freedom struggle.

---

[43] Personal correspondence. Letter in the possession of the Khwaja family.

[44] Khan, Yasmin. 1 February 2018. 'Gandhi in Britain'. *History Extra*. www.historyextra.com/period/20th-century/gandhi-in-britain/. Accessed 2 June 2022.

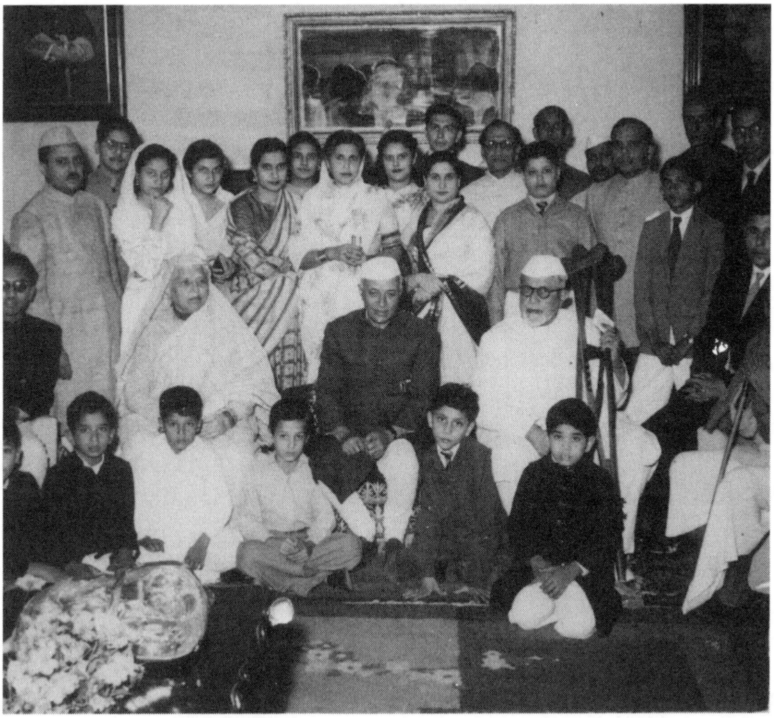

Figure 7. A visit of Nehru (sitting in the centre) to Sami Manzil, the home of Abul Majeed Khwaja (sitting on the right) and Begum Khursheed Khwaja (sitting on the left) from 1956. Photographer: unknown. Jamal Khwaja collection. Courtesy R.H. Khwaja and Nasser Khwaja/ Aligarh Photo Archive.

Along with many other Muslim voices like the Ali Brothers, Hasrat Mohani, Hakim Ajmal Khan, Mukhtar Ahmad Ansari and Maulana Abul Kalam Azad, Abdul Majeed Khwaja supported Gandhi and actively participated in the Non-cooperation Movement. The main concerns of the Non-cooperation Movement were to back the Khilafat cause, attain 'Swaraj' and strengthen Hindu–Muslim unity. In the summer of 1920, after an All-Party Conference at Allahabad, a committee drew up a programme for non-cooperation, which included a call to boycott all educational institutions supported or run by the colonial regime. Nationalist fervour gripped both the country and the AMU campus.

Accompanying Maulana Mohammad Ali, Gandhi visited Aligarh on 12 October 1920. He gave a speech at the Students' Union, appealing to the students 'to pressure the college to refuse aid from such a tyrannical government.'[45] A resolution passed by the Students' Union condemned the British government's attitude towards Turkey.[46] Many students boycotted

[45] Hadi, Syed Mahmud. 1972. *Ali Braderan Aur Unka Zamana* [Ali Brothers and their Time] (Muktabah Jamia Ltd.). pp. 97–98.

[46] Hasan, Tariq. 2006. *The Aligarh Movement and the Making of the Indian Muslim Mind 1857-2002.* (Rupa Publications India Pvt. Ltd.). p. 162.

their classes as a mark of protest. The British supporting administration of The Mohammad Anglo-Oriental College shut the campus and evacuated the hostels. Leaders associated with the Non-cooperation Movement, like Maulana Mohammad Ali, Hasrat Mohani, Hakim Ajmal Khan and Abdul Majeed Khwaja, supported students' defiance. They proposed a new alternative college based on nationalist lines instead of the British-aided education system. After much difference of opinion and heartburn among the university community, finally a separate national university—the Jamia Millia Islamia was born in 1920. A picture in the Khwaja family's collection shows Jamia Milia Islamia's convocation ceremony in Aligarh in 1924, the year before it shifted to Karol Bagh in Delhi. Abdul Majeed Khwaja played a pivotal role in Jamia Milia Islamia's initial years as a founding member, modelling the institution on secular nationalist values.

As a young person, Jamal Khwaja witnessed his father's political journey and his interactions with different national leaders and luminaries. He imbibed his father's secular predilection from an early age. In a photograph from the early 1940s, a young Jamal Khwaja and his two brothers are seen dressed up and role-playing their favourite national icons (Figure 8). In his reflections on his father, Jamal discloses that to honour his father's 'idea of Hindustan', he gave secular names to his children, fusing together names from Hindu and Muslim traditions—Jawahar Kabir, Sundar Habib, Geeta Anjum and Nasser Navin—invoking the syncretism which was so dear to his father.[47] Abdul Majeed Khwaja was a staunch believer in the cause of Hindu–Muslim unity and vehemently opposed the 'two-nation theory'.

Tariq Hasan, Abdul Majeed Khwaja's grandson, writes that though the demand for Pakistan's creation was raised formally in 1940, concerns for safeguarding Muslim political representation started circulating in the early 1930s. However, increased support for the Muslim League among the Aligarh community began only after the elections of 1937, when Jinnah started visiting AMU. Tariq believes that Nehru's contemptuous attitude towards the Muslim League after its disastrous performance at the 1937 polls led to a sympathy wave

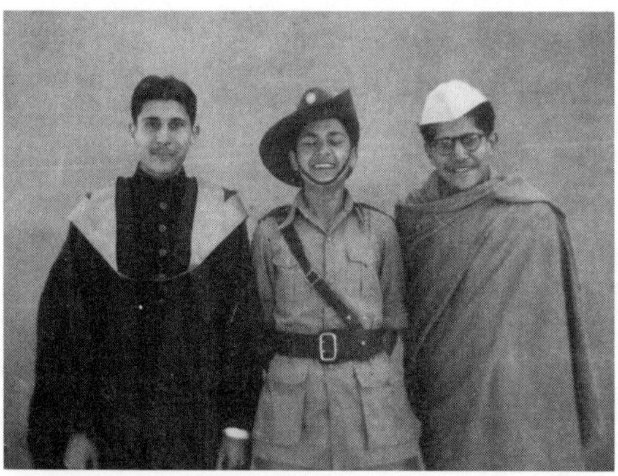

Figure 8. Jamal Khwaja and his brothers Ajmal Khwaja and Raveend Khwaja. 1930s. Jamal Khwaja collection. Courtesy: R.H. Khwaja and Nasser Khwaja/Aligarh Photo Archive.

[47] Qureshi, M.H. (Compiled by). 2015. *Abul Majeed Khwaja: A Biographical Narrative* (A.M. Khwaja Chair, Jamia Millia). p. 123. Unpublished manuscript.

favouring the League.[48] The 1940s saw religious obscurantism and a tremendous rise in the influence of the League in Aligarh, and when Partition happened, it led to many families migrating to Pakistan. 'There were only 850 students left in the university at one time,' says Irfan Habib.[49]

Conversations around Partition are difficult and often draw a silence. Seema Kazi believes that August 1947 has become the new default post-colonial chronological entry point for discussion and analysis on the Muslims of India. In her writings, she argues that in modern India, the liberal narrative of the ahistorical universal citizen has emerged out of an act of amnesia on the part of mainstream historians and political scientists by way of the excision of the tragedy of the 1947 partition. One of the catastrophic outcomes of this self-censorship is the obliteration of Muslim histories and struggles of undivided India.[50] The photographic material's vacuity from the period of the Partition also echoes this erasure with much of the material tragically severed, misplaced, destroyed or lost.

I find a forgotten small black-and-white photograph in my mother's photo album. It is a picture of my aunts in white salwar kameez, sitting together, reading a newspaper (Figure 9). The small print of the headlines on one of the newspaper pages reads 'New Development in Congress – League, Talks for United Bengal'.[51] The headline gives away when the photograph was taken. It is from the year 1947. On showing the photograph to my ninety-two-year-old aunt, who is in the photograph, she recounts,

> We were in Kanpur in 1947. It was the year before we moved to Aligarh. I clearly remember that Abba and all of us children stayed awake to listen to Pandit Nehru's famous speech 'Tryst with Destiny' on the eve of Independence. The next day, all over Kanpur, it was decided that people would do *chiragahs* (lighting of candles). We wanted to draw India's map in the courtyard and light candles around it to celebrate. *Appijaan*, being the quintessential eldest sister, decided to take charge. On picking up the chalk to draw, she became unsure of what kind of map to draw, as Partition had taken place. I remember Abba saying, make the full map, *azadi sabko mili hai* (freedom has come for everyone)...[52]

The immediate years following the Partition were a time of transition for the university and its community, with many people leaving for Pakistan. A new phase of transformation began under Zakir Husain, who restored the

[48] Ibid. pp. 225–27.

[49] In a conversation with the author. July 2018.

[50] Kazi, Seema. 16 June 2016. 'Accommodation, Co-option, Assimilation'. *Kashmir Narrator*. Srinagar. kashmirnarrator.com/accommodation-co-option-assimilation/. Accessed 7 June 2022.

[51] A proposal for an undivided Bengal was initiated by Huseyn Shaheed Suhrawardy in the summer of 1947. He tried to mobilise members of both Congress and the Muslim League against Bengal's division on communal lines. The effort failed and eventually Bengal was partitioned according to the Mountbatten Plan along the Radcliffe Line.

[52] In a conversation with the author. July 2018.

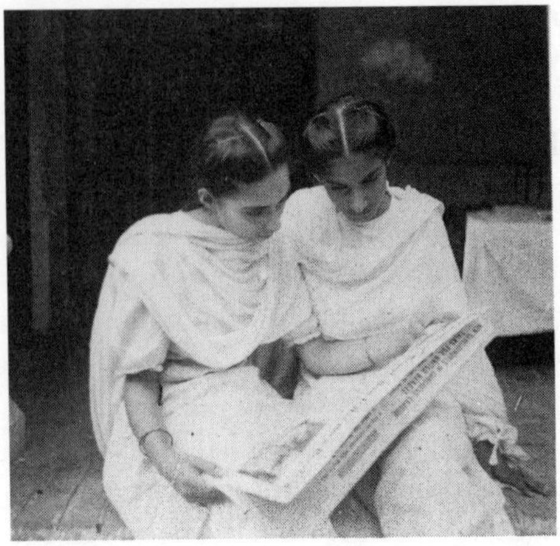

Figure 9: Tahira and Sayera. 1947. Courtesy the author/Aligarh Photo Archive.

community's confidence and rebuilt the institution when he took charge as the university's vice chancellor in 1949. Hopes and aspirations centred around secularism gained prominence, mirroring independent India's socialist, modern vision under its first prime minister, Jawaharlal Nehru. A meteoric rise in family photography marks the changing times. The Kodak Brownie camera had entered the Indian home by the start of the twentieth century and induced much interest in amateur domestic photography. In another few decades, the availability of affordable cameras improved photographic technology, and new social attitudes led to a tremendous increase in the consumption of photography and the mushrooming of local commercial photo studios everywhere. Family photographs of that time seem to celebrate the everyday. Images of *dulhans*, happy couples, graduation portraits, birthday parties and family holidays reappear in different forms to commemorate daily moments of life. At times, there is a triteness to the captured shots. Sometimes, the images project a conformist narrative or frame archetypal social roles and values. Moreover, most importantly, they reflect a rising middle class's desires, aspirations and cultural ideals. The local city photo studio played a crucial role in popularising the latest styles and trends. The charm of being reinvented in a photograph through lighting, framing and posing captivated an entire generation.

'As young women studying at the Women's College in the 1950s, we were fascinated with getting our pictures taken. We would often sneak out of the hostel to get ourselves photographed at a Shamshad Market photo studio adjoining the university,' recalls Yasmeen Tahir.[53] She shares beautifully composed black-and-white portraits showing different poses, personas and hairdos that reveal individual expression and self-exploration as a young college-going woman. Shot by the studio 'Cameracraft', the images also uncover the prevailing standards of beauty and fashion. 'Cameracraft' at Shamshad Market was the only photo studio near the university in those days. Run by Laxmi Narayan Sharma, it specialised in studio portraiture. Laxmi Narayan left his hometown Chharra, near Aligarh, in 1940s, at the young age of sixteen, to learn the craft by apprenticing at various studios. He first opened a shop in Mussoorie and later moved it to Aligarh. He carefully crafted photographic images, often spending long hours retouching the negatives, manually spot-correcting the

[53] In a conversation with the author. October 2019.

prints and sometimes even hand-colouring the pictures. The studio was very popular with the students, says his son Suresh Chandra Sharma.[54] Cameracraft was tragically burnt down during riots in the city in the 1961, and had to relocate to the old city area of Aligarh.

Radhe Shyam, the owner of City Art Studio, has been taking pictures of the university community for more than five decades. He specialises in taking formal group portraits of students, the teaching and technical staff and other employees of the university, using a large format camera. Many of his prints decorate the walls of various departments, hostels and halls to date. By the 1980s, numerous small photo studios had cropped up in the city to cater to a growing demand for an expanding university town. The development also attracted the migrant workforce from adjoining areas, and Shazia Saleem's family came in search of work to Aligarh from Bihar. Shazia completed her studies at AMU to become the first postgraduate in her family. Shazia regrets not having a graduation portrait taken at a studio. She says, 'My family followed the customary ritual of visiting a photo studio every Eid (Figure 10). An extra photo session with the props and a graduation outfit would have meant an additional expense, unlike today, when anyone can take a photograph anytime.'[55] Many Muslim families still visit a studio to get themselves photographed to celebrate the end of the month of Ramzan or Muharram.

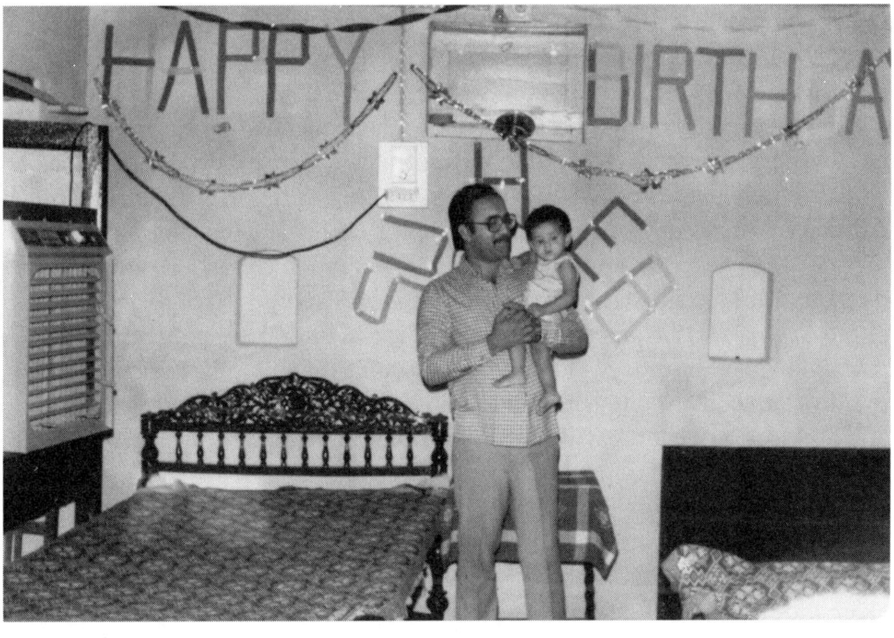

Figure 10. Parvez with his son Suheb. 1990s. Photographer unknown. From the collection of Parvez Akhtar Alvi. Courtesy Anas Ahmad Alvi/Aligarh Photo Archive.

[54] In a conversation with the author. December 2019.

[55] In a conversation with the author. February 2021.

There are plenty of fine examples of amateur photography in various family collections. Family images taken by S. Azmat Shah, who taught at the Department of Fine Arts at the university (from 1956 to 1992), are of the straight documentary style popular in the 1950s and 1960s. His younger brother Tahir M. Syed, a trained sculptor, would often spend time in Aligarh creating sculptural portrait busts of poets, writers, academicians and other prominent personalities. Tahir created his sculptural work based on live models. He often got Azmat Shah or a friend to photograph his works to capture the resemblance of the sculptural pieces to the subjects. The outcome is a series of idiosyncratic images showing him as the artist, the subject and the finished sculpture, all together in a single frame. The series includes images of the Progressive Writers' Association's members, including writers and poets like Qurratulain Hyder, Sardar Jafri, among many others.

A set of colour images shot on a point-and-shoot camera by late Parvez Akhtar Alvi depicts small-town family life in the early 1990s. Parvez, who otherwise had a job at a bank, was fascinated with photography and enjoyed documenting his home and family. Domestic spaces and events are captured in muted colours as the family moves, because of his transferrable job, from one small town to another, before settling in Aligarh. Parvez appears to be the model father photographer, incessantly photographing his two children, Suheb and Anas. Jennifer Orpana points out that the image of the 'father-photographer' created by Kodak in the 1950s to promote its products, embodied nuclear 'middle-class' family values and paternal domestic responsibility, unlike the 'Kodak Girl' of the 1920s, which represented freedom and femininity. The later Kodak advertisements mainly centred on the 'father-photographer' using the camera to capture his family at home. This strategy was devised to incorporate local cultural values and helped Kodak entrench its association with 'snapshots in a family album' for the Indian customer.[56] Anas Ahmad Alvi, Parvez's son, feels his father's focus on home in the photographs stems from the absence of a carefree childhood. Parvez had a difficult early life, taking care of a father who had Parkinson's disease. Anas[57] says photography became an escape for his father. Memorable moments—children celebrating their birthdays, climbing a giant stone dinosaur in a park, pretending to ride a red scooter—project a 'happy' life not only far removed from inner strife and everyday struggles, but also from the political turmoil of the early 1990s on account of the demolition of the Babri Masjid (Figure 11).

My own family collection reflects keen interest and engagement with photography. One can find boxes of Ektachrome colour slides taken by my father and 4x5 negatives shot by a great uncle. Obaid Siddiqui, my mother's elder brother, was an avid photography enthusiast. He would print many of

---

[56] Orpana, Jennifer. 2018. 'Finding Family in *The Times of India's* Mid-Century Kodak Ads'. Guest Edited by Deepali Dewan. Vol. 9. Issue 1. Fall. *Trans Asia Photography Review*, hdl.handle.net/2027/spo.7977573.0009.107. Accessed 7 June 2022.

[57] In a conversation with the author. November 2019.

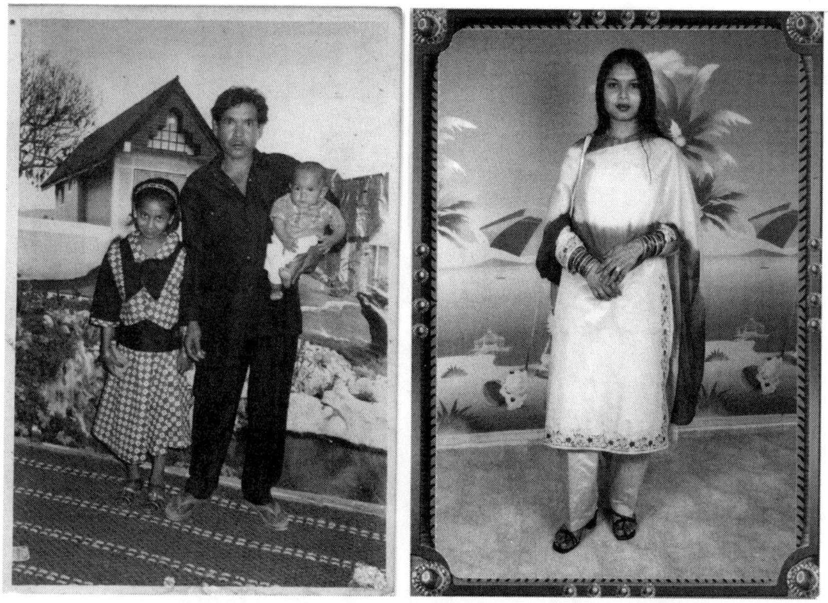

Figure 11. Shazia Saleem with her father and brother, 1997, unknown studio (left). Shazia, 2007, FotoFast Studio (right). Courtesy: Shazia Saleem/Aligarh Photo Archive.

his black-and-white images by maintaining a darkroom at home. Simple visual compositions and collages formed by cutting up the leftover tiny contact prints from the darkroom by my mother adorn her albums. She and my aunts loved to dress up and have their photographs taken by Obaid. One of the earliest family portraits in my mother's collection is shot by him. It shows my mother and her siblings with their parents before the family moved to Aligarh in the late 1940s (Figure 12). With its educational opportunities, Aligarh was not only my grandfather's favoured choice, but attracted many Muslims from North India as well. Family photographs from across space and time populate the various personal collections found in the homes of Aligarh. They unravel the diverse historical characteristics and trajectories of Muslim lives in the Indian subcontinent. The heterogeneity of the Muslim persona—from its role in education to playing a significant part in India's freedom struggle; from sectarian politics to secularist leanings; from leftist activism to present-day marginalisation—traces the immense change the university and the community around it have gone through.

Family photographs never tell a single story. At times, they divulge detail and description, while at other times, they initiate interpretations, while sometimes, they remain silent. Often, their material presence prompts conversations, turning them into 'instruments of remembrance' (Hirsch 22).[58] Frames turn into mnemonic devices for retrieving the absent and remembering the forgotten. The telling of personal histories and alternate accounts provides an

[58] Hirsch, Marianne. 1997. *Family Frames.* p. 22.

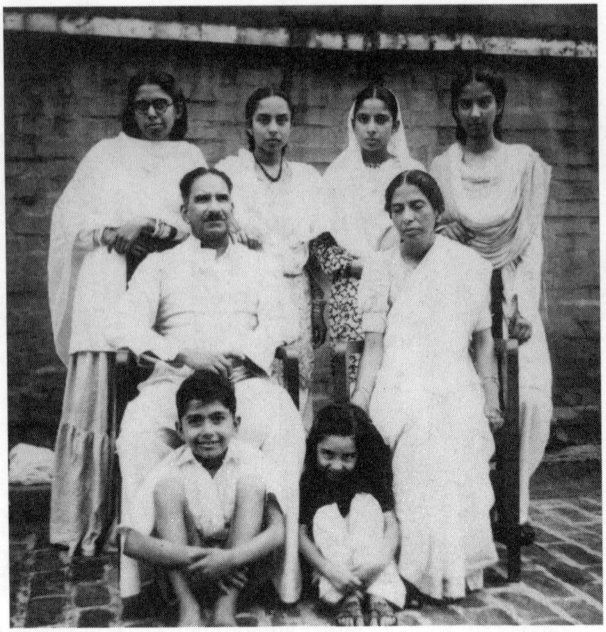

Figure 12. My mother Sahista (second from right) with her siblings and her father Abdul Qadeer and mother Umme Kulsum. 1940s. Photographer: Obaid Siddiqi. Courtesy the author/Aligarh Photo Archive.

opportunity for engaging with people, providing insights into their experiences and aspirations. Family photographs open space for an intimate look at the past, going beyond the paradigm of nostalgia. They transcend the grand narrative and dry facts of conventional historical reconstruction presenting a people's version of history with nuanced ideas, diverse voices and plural views. In these turbulent times, as the story of the community and the nation gets rewritten, the myriad picture of Muslim lives that emerges in the Aligarh Photo Archive exposes an alternate narrative challenging the negative unidimensional typecast of Muslims propagated in mainstream media and popular culture today. In her essay, the 'Archive', Ariella Azoulay says an archive helps us hold on to 'items of our shared world, it preserves that which enables us to shape it differently, anew, in common.'[59] The Aligarh Photo Archive helps us envision that collective experience of a polyphonous reality. It can be read and used in multiple ways: as a counter site for self-representation and artistic intervention; as a keepsake of the Muslim community's forgotten identities by preventing their erasure from the collective consciousness and getting written out of history; or as a tool for research and discourse to shed light on the converging trajectories of the Aligarh Muslim University, the city of Aligarh, and its tryst with a modernist imagination.

---

[59] Azoulay, Ariella. 'Archive'. *Political Concepts: A Critical Lexicon*. Translated by Tal Haran. issue 1, www.politicalconcepts.org/issue1/archive/. Accessed 20 May 2022.

'Ake nde nai tadno?'

A Naga Perspective on Collective Forgetting and Remembering: The Great June Uprising of 2001

Anna Sireiliu Charenamei

Introduction

Hungry pigs squealing from three nooks of the house, the stench of the great Nagaram *nala* (drain) rushing in as the windows are opened; it is impossible to sleep past 5 a.m. in this little but boisterous *leikai* (locality) called Fairyland. The infamous nala of Nagaram behind my house (Figure 1) acts as the divider between Nagaram and Fairyland, two leikais that are situated in the heart of Imphal East and predominantly populated by Tangkhul Nagas and other smaller Naga tribes. My family, belonging to one of the smaller Naga tribes, Liangmai, have been living in Imphal since the 1960s when my grandfather, Phousabou Charenamei (Figure 2), in search of better education and healthcare for his eight children and the village, bought a plot of land in an area of the capital that was covered in paddy fields. As the daughter of Phousabou's sixth

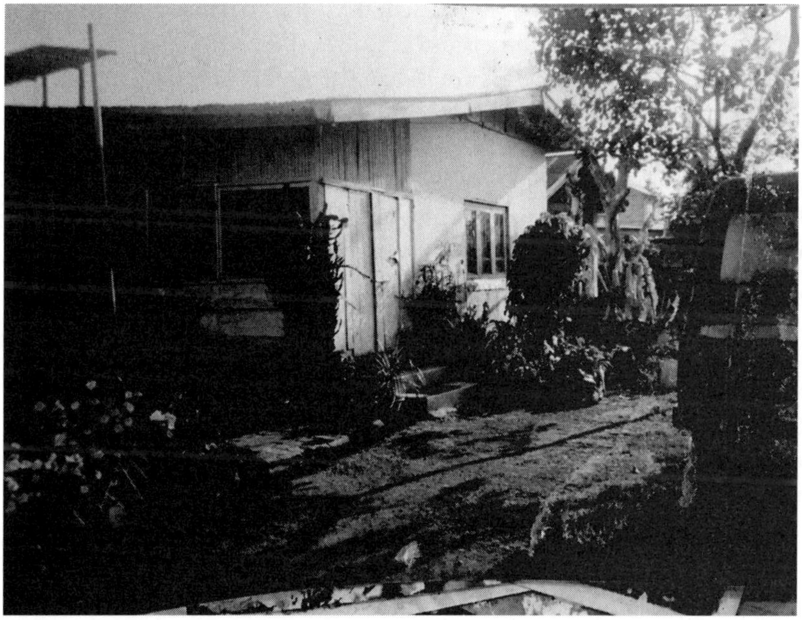

Figure 1. Our house in Fairyland, 1999.

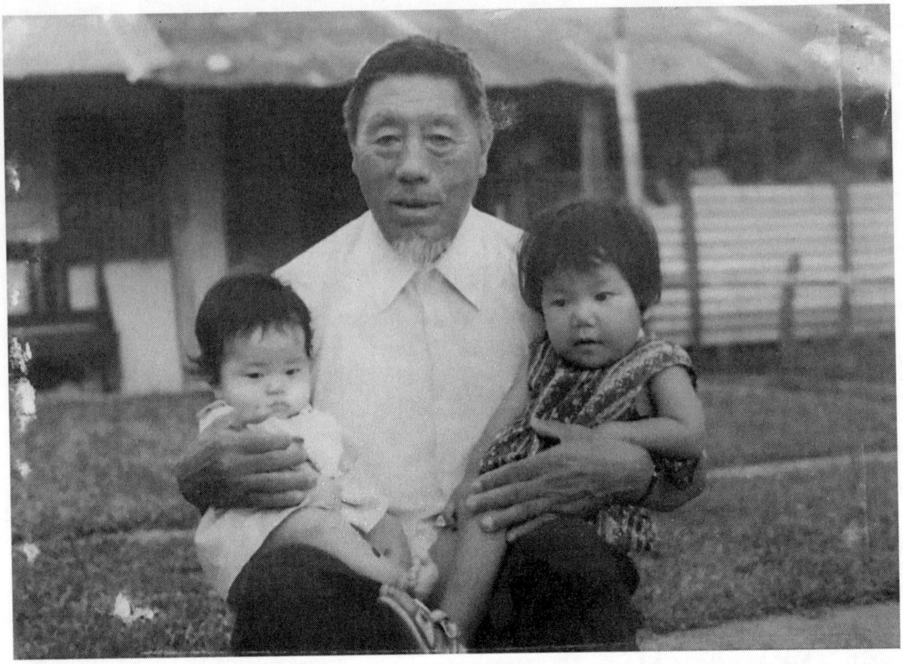

Figure 2. Phousabou Charenamei with his granddaughters Agimanailiu on his right and Sireiliu on his left. Imphal, 1997.

child, along with his many other grandchildren, Fairyland is the first space that I called home. Having lived in this house for more than twenty-five years, I sometimes threaten, to no one in particular, to shift permanently to Lamphel, where my maternal grandmother and aunt live (Figure 3).

My mother, Lois Panmei (Figure 4) like the quintessential 'Lamphel *Macha* (kid)', grew up among a diverse multi-ethnic demography, owing to the peculiar fact that Lamphel was where residential quarters of the members of the Manipur Legislative Assembly, state bureaucrats, other government officials, medical officers and staffs, as well as Regional Institute of Medical Sciences (RIMS) and Central Agricultural University (CAU) were located. Belonging to the Rongmei community and having grown up with more friends from the Kuki Zomi and Meitei community, she had not prepared herself for the culture shock she would experience when she moved to a leikai that was only a fifteen minute-drive from her natal home after marrying my father. Fairyland, a Naga leikai, is surrounded by four Rongmei/Kabui villages and four other dominantly Naga leikais. My mother suddenly found herself in this cocoon of urban Naga villages, discovering that the Tangkhul language is the unofficial second lingua franca after Meitei Lon,[1] which my father and his entire family speak with so much ease and fluency as though they grew up in the hills of Ukhrul town. On the other hand, my mother needed time to accustom herself

[1] The language of the Meitei community.

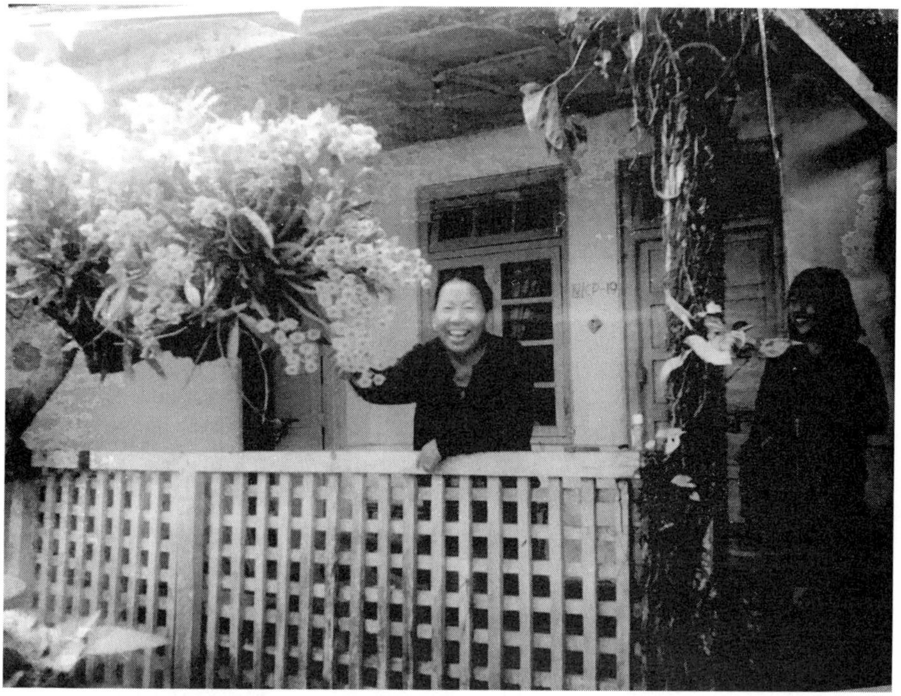

Figure 3. My maternal grandmother Areng and my aunt Mary in Areng's old quarter. Lamphel, 1999.

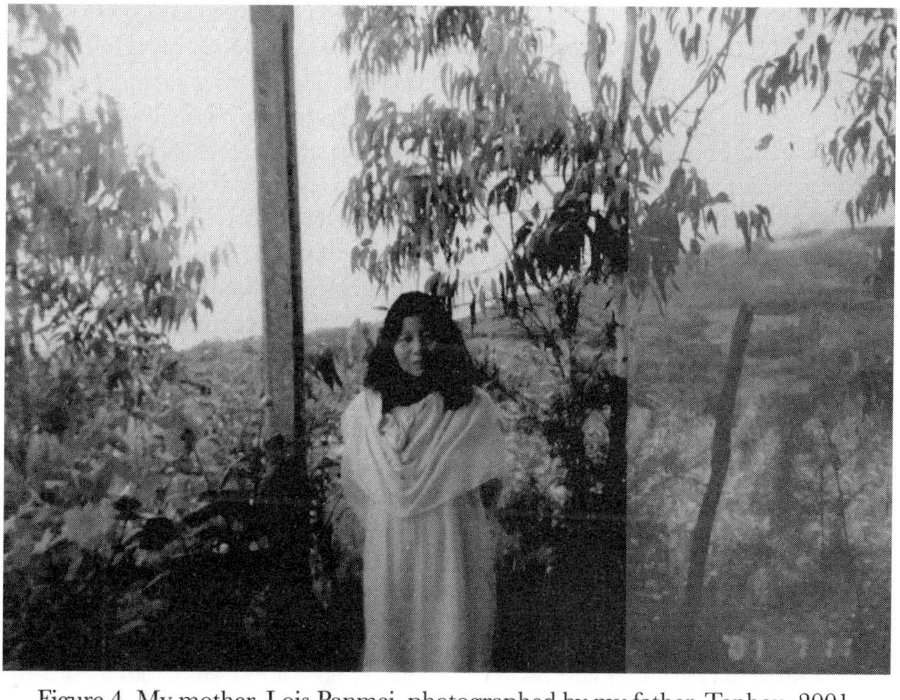

Figure 4. My mother, Lois Panmei, photographed by my father. Taphou. 2001.

to this simulation of a Naga country inside the capital valley, Imphal. Manipur is geographically divided into two parts; the valley and the hills. The hills are inhabited by various tribal groups, whereas the valley is primarily occupied by the Meiteis.[2]

Although a cacophony of disdain and affection for this leikai and the house that we inhabit has been vocalised ever since I could make sense of my surroundings, none of us actually have the heart to leave this ostensible safe haven we have created for ourselves. The year 2001 was the first time my family and almost every family of Naga association fled our Imphal homes. While this incident produced both a temporary and lasting outcome—some relocated permanently, while many returned to what they had left behind. This enforced exodus was instigated by the Great June Uprising of 2001 ensued by the joint statement put forth by the Naga Socialist Council of Nagaland—Isak and Muivah (NSCN-IM) and the Indian government to impose a 'ceasefire in disturbed Naga areas "without any territorial limits"'.[3] Whereas, it has been clearly emphasised that 'this stipulation will not in any way affect the territorial integrity of any North Eastern States' (2001); putting in perspective the intentions of the 'ceasefire' to not affect or undermine any territorial boundaries vis-à-vis Manipur.

Unfortunately and regrettably, this joint statement caused unprecedented anxieties and hysteria, charged with organised anger mobilised by civil societies. Fear emanating from the possible shrinkage of the Manipur territory into a small valley, that is, Imphal, foregrounded the turmoil that followed. A sense of betrayal enveloped the valley, as a sizeable Naga population demonstrated their affinity towards the call made by the NSCN-IM. This betrayal felt by the Meiteis escalated into various protest rallies, burning of effigies and torching of the residents of the members of Legislative Assembly. The culmination of their fear and anger manifested in a blaze set upon the Legislative Assembly buildings, wherein numerous individuals sustained injuries. It is to be impressed upon that this whole uprising resulted in many lives lost—in the frenzy of torching government buildings alone, at least thirteen people were killed.[4] To make sense of the misplaced betrayal felt by the dominant community of Imphal, the joint statement of the NSCN-IM and the Indian government concretised the tacit hostility between the Nagas and the Meiteis. This hostility emanates from the long-standing collective desire for a separate Naga sovereign nation from the Naga tribes, while the Meiteis have always expressed their

[2] Parratt, Saroj and Arambam, Nalini. 2005. *The Court Chronicle Of The Kings Of Manipur The Cheitharol Kumpapa*. (London). p. 2. Also see Devi, Khwairakpam Renu. 2001. 'Representation of the Pre-Vaishnavite Culture of the Meiteis: 'Cheitharol Kumpapa' of Manipur'. Proceedings of the Indian History Congress. Vol. 72. Indian History Congress. p. 501.

[3] Press Information Bureau of the Government of India 2001. peacemaker.un.org/sites/peacemaker.un.org/files/IN_010614_ExtensionCeasefireNSCN-IM.pdf.

[4] '13 Killed In Firing As Protestors Go On Rampage'. Imphal Free Press. 2001. e-pao.net/GP.asp?src=8..190601.jun01. Accessed 10 August 2021.

anxiety over the possible delimitation of the state if Greater Nagalim were to crystallise.

The Naga Movement can be considered to have started since the inception of Naga Club in 1918 and carried forward by the likes of national leaders like Phizo after the creation of Naga National Club (NNC) in 1946. Owing to varied internal turmoils and disagreements, there has been an eventual break-up of the movement, creating multiple factions in the process. However, among the factions, NSCN-IM, led by Thuingaleng Muivah and Isak Swu, emerged as the torchbearer with popular support, taking the Naga National Movement forward. The desire for the unification of all Naga territories into one sovereign state is echoed by a major population of the Naga tribes in Manipur, more strongly than anywhere else. An opinion piece in *India Today* stressed that 'the naga insurgency problem lay not in Nagaland but in the hill districts of Manipur.'[5] The alienation from the other Naga areas and the bitterness around sharing resources and power with other ethnic communities seem to have led to a greater longing and urgency for a separate nationhood.[6]

The bloodied history between the Government of India (hereafter GOI) and Naga National groups started after the transference of power from the colonial Raj to the newly formed Indian state. The Shillong Peace Accord of 1975 signed between the 'representatives of the underground organisations' and L.P. Singh, the erstwhile Governor of Nagaland, was an agreement that the said organisations and the liaison committee of Nagaland Peace Council would accept the Constitution of India and submit their arms and weapons. This subsequently led to an even more violent fight for self-determination from the Indian state by various factions, ushering in the first ceasefire agreement in 1997, signed between GOI and NSCN-IM. The extension of this prior ceasefire on 14 June 2001 sparked unrest in all states with Naga inhabitants, primarily Manipur, Assam and Arunachal Pradesh.

The bone of contention emanates from a particular sub clause in the official notice *Extension of Cease-Fire with the NSCN-IM* put forth by the Press Information Bureau of the Government of India on 14 June 2001, wherein it underscores that the Nagas should extend truce by one year without any territorial limits. This sparked agitation and uprising,[7] especially in Manipur, as it came in direct conflict with the state's own 'Manipuri identity'.[8] It is important to note that many other non-Manipuri tribes, along with the Nagas, ascribe to this notion of 'Manipuri identity' out of convenience for easier assimilation, notably the smaller minor tribes. It would be pertinent to also highlight the sentiments of a

---

5 Iyer, Lakshmi. 13 August 2001. 'Government goes back on ceasefire agreement with NSCN, angers ultra group'. *India Today*. www.indiatoday.in/magazine/nation/story/20010813-govt-angers-nscn-as-it-reneges-cease-fire-agreement-once-again-774001-2001-08-13. Accessed 10 August 2021.

6 Kikon, Dolly. 2015. 'What is unique about Naga History?'. *Economic and Politic Weekly*. p. 12.

7 Oinam, Bhagat. 2008. 'State of the states: mapping India's northeast'. p. 1.

8 Akoijam, A. Bimol. 2001. 'How History Repeats Itself.' *Economic and Political Weekly*. p. 2810.

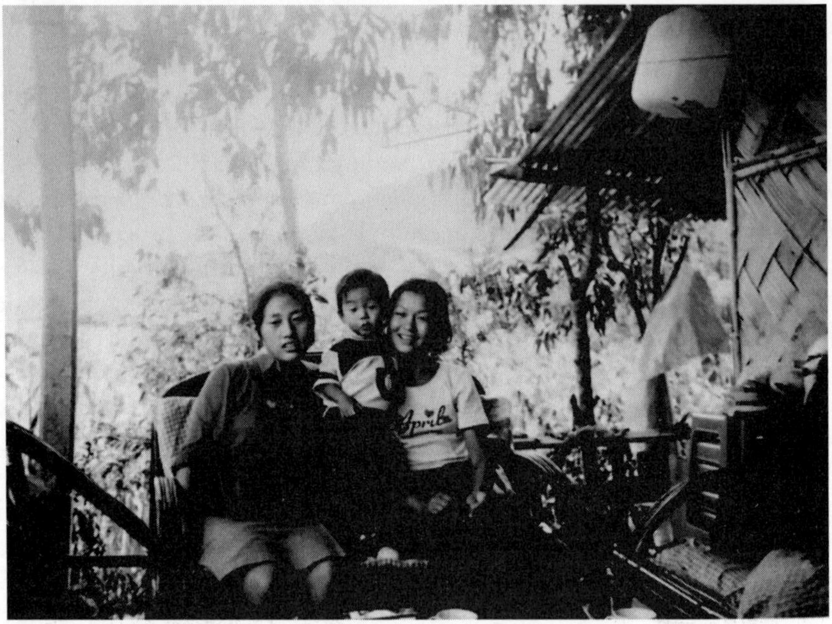

Figure 5. Dinpiliu, Marannang and Simpe. Taphou, 2001.

few Meitei scholars, who espouse that such 'political designs of vested interest' should not allow Manipur to become a sacrificial lamb for establishing political legitimacy of the Indian 'nation state'.[9]

The impetus to reference an anecdote from my childhood stems from photographs found in our family albums, of the time we had fled to Taphou village in Senapati district for refuge. These images present an alternative narrative to the more iconic journalistic visuals of the protests. A recent return to family photographs from this time opened conversations with my family and friends present in the photographs. These conversations were an effort to recollect anything from that moment of our lives that were lost in time. Our family photographs, unsurprisingly, reveal nothing of the violence or the communal tensions. Almost as if belonging to another reality, my cousins and I are seen enjoying an idyllic village life. This kind of parallel visual evidence from the same moment in history has led me to question the role of family photographs in recalling and erasing events from the past, and the deliberate gravitation of the personal camera towards happy moments instead of scenes of disturbance. This essay is a study in the dissonance between family photographs and watershed political events such as the Great June Uprising of Manipur, which changed the course of several lives pictured within them. I inquire whether family photographs are made with a deliberate attempt towards creating amnesia, obscuring violence and pain with scenes of joy, and

[9] Ibid. p. 2807.

whether this could be a significant social function of family albums per se. The alternative is to regard family photographs as triggers for memories that often lie beyond the frame.

I use photo elicitation as a method to recount the forgotten events and narratives of 2001, through my family photographs, which reveal narratives that are far more diverse and personal as compared to the texts provided by mainstream journalistic images. My family photographs provide a stark contrast to the visuals that were available on news channels and newspapers of 2001. I was struck by how these two sets of images, as outcomes of the same political moment, seemed to exist in parallel universes. Twenty years hence, while researching for this essay, my family photographs helped create a network of collective remembering amongst relatives and friends who grew up under the same circumstances.[10] Our telephonic conversations in recent months have spanned hours, recollecting, reminding and recognising so many things that we had learned to forget. According to the American Psychiatric Association's different clusters of trauma, my generation's response to the trauma of 2001 and the transmission of 'postmemory'[11] seem to belong to the second cluster of symptoms, which is the persistent avoidance of stimuli associated with the trauma, an avoidance of thoughts or feelings related to the event, often used to the total absence of recall of the significant event. Going against the grain of our habitual forgetting, this essay highlights the importance of personal family albums in challenging the mainstream state narratives and the authority of apex bodies that claim to speak for an entire community. I inquire whether our experience weighs less without photographs of violence and moments of fear. Even in the frozen moments of happy events, there is much to say about what we choose to forget and remember. How do family photographs obscure or reveal such memories, even though they do not portray scenes of disturbance? I dwell on the fact that the same event can present many contrasting childhood experiences, hence knowledge-gathering through narrativisation is significantly varied. This essay is an attempt to look at family albums/photographs as vital memorabilia, having the power to shift focus from narratives circulated in the public by political stakeholders and state-sponsored media through which biased perspectives are made manifest in political decisions.

The Authority of Some Images

On 18 June 2001, the people of Manipur were glued to the television in complete disbelief as they saw their capital being set ablaze. Before this, the oppositional political groups, All Manipur United Clubs Organisation (AMUCO) and NSCN-IM, in anticipation of the official release of the

[10] The names of the interviewees have been changed for this publication keeping in mind the sensitive nature of the topic.

11 Hirsch, Marianne. 1997. *Family Frames: Photography, Narrative, and Postmemory*. (Harvard University Press).

ceasefire, had published statements emphasising the need for peace, mutually accusing the other of being ignorant of the facts of a troubled history.[12, 13] Both asked the other to take responsibility for the violence that might occur. AMUCO, which was largely a Meitei organisation, reflected the emotions of the general Meitei populace, who felt blindsided and betrayed that no state representative nor any of the other communities had involved them in 'peace talks', while on the other hand, the Naga groups couldn't fathom why the Meiteis wouldn't let them have their own state like they had their own. Manipur was already established, in the eyes of many, as a Meitei state. The ceasefire was feared by the Meitei as a step closer to the creation of 'Greater Nagalim', which would leave only the Imphal Valley as the remnant of an erstwhile Manipur. AMUCO and United Committee Manipur (UCM) with the support of the general populace were not going down without a fight. They pointed out that the 16 Point Agreement[14] between the GOI and Naga People's Convention (NPC) in 1960 and then 1964, did not include the Naga areas of Manipur, hence the ceasefire agreement between them was null and void—the Meitei people of Manipur had never been consulted during this process. Although there are multiple truths and narratives of the experiences felt and seen during this period of political turmoil, the common reference remains the set of visuals released officially by the press. Whether vivid or blurry, it is these official visuals one looks to for pinning the authenticity of the experience of violence displacement.

I now begin to take a look at the journalistic visuals that were screened on TV in June 2001; an angry large mob shouting slogans, thronging to challenge the political leadership of the state legislative assembly, along with the Indian flag—a symbol of the Indian Constitution—being burnt to embers,[15] the sky engulfed in black smoke, troops of the Central Reserve Police Force (CRPF) deployed on the streets, firing at civilians. These visuals created fear and panic amongst all viewers—especially amongst the non-Meitei communities—of falling victim to collateral damage due to their close proximity to the chaos and of the possible targeting of these communities by the Meitei protesters, owing to the fact that they are tribals. Fearing the prospective loss of land inhabited by the Nagas, violence erupted in and around Imphal very spontaneously. Soon after the order of extension of ceasefire to all Naga-inhabited areas, there was an immediate call for a 66-hour state-wide general strike. Joint committees were formed in the interest of keeping Manipur's territorial integrity in check,

---

[12] 'AMUCO Warns Against Challenging History'. 8 June 2001. The Imphal Free Press. e-pao.net/GP.asp?src=2..090601.jun01. Accessed 10 August 2021.

[13] 'AMUCO Ignorant of Own History Says NSCN (IM). 7 June 2001. The Imphal Free Press. e-pao.net/GP.asp?src=2..070601.jun01. Accessed 10 August 2021.

+ The 16 Point Agreement between the Government of India and the Naga People's Convention, 26 July, 1960. peacemaker.un.org/sites/peacemaker.un.org/files/IN_600726_The%20sixteen%20point%20Agreement_0.pdf Accessed 8 April 2024

[15] Ibid. p. 2810.

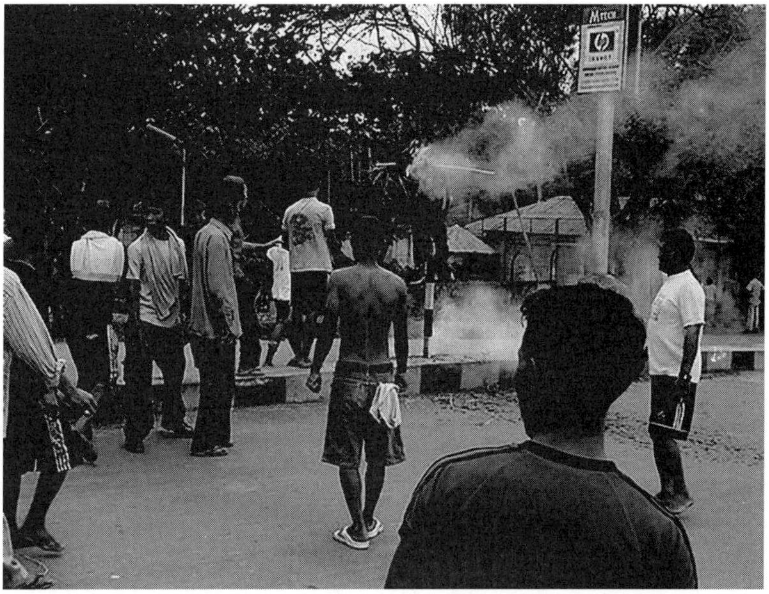

Figure 6. Protestors burning the effigy of Th. Muivah, leader of the National Socialist Council of Nagaland (IM). Photographer: M. Dilip.

already anticipating violent protests. There was a call for participation against the ceasefire given out to schools, localities and other institutions, encouraging mass sit-ins and rallies. The television screened numerous burning of effigies (Figure 6) of Prime Minister Atal Bihari Vajpayee, Minister of Home Affairs L.K. Advani and the two IM leaders, Th. Muivah and Isak Swu, for passing the ceasefire. There were young men burning the Indian flag, copies of the Indian Constitution and simultaneously hoisting the Manipuri seven-colour flag that seemed to be a resurrection of Manipur's old national pride.[16] A strong visual memory that is common to all, was of Imphal enveloped completely by grey smoke, and glass shards and sandals littering its streets.[17]

The Manipur police and army squad called Manipur Rifles, were deployed everywhere. On 18 June, the Manipur Legislative Assembly was set ablaze by a mob that then proceeded to set fire to the MLA residential quarters. Security personnel fired over 200 rounds in the air from the Palace gate to Sanjenthong, which was a distance of less than 1 kilometre, and lobbed more than 50 tear-gas shells. Three protesters were found dead inside the chief minister's office complex. An indefinite curfew was imposed in Imphal and Greater Imphal areas by the end of the day.[18] 18 protesters in total lost their lives, amongst

[16] Oinam, Bhagat. 2008. 'State of the States: Mapping India's Northeast'. p. 2.

[17] 'Effigies, Tear Gas Smoke Envelope Imphal Skyline'. 17 June 2001. *The Sangai Express*. e-pao.net/GP.asp?src=1..180601.jun01. Accessed 10 August 2021.

[18] '13 killed in firing as protestors go on rampage'. 18 June 2001. *The Imphal Free Press*. e-pao.net/GP.asp?src=8..190601.jun01. Accessed 10 August 2021.

whom were some unlucky civilians who happened to be at the scene of the protest. Many volunteer organisations including Naga ones, paid homage to the departed souls and condemned the unjustified firing by the CRPF. The Manipur Olympic Association decided to boycott the 6th National Games and celebrated personalities like M.K. Binodini Devi, the novelist, and the playwright Ratan Thiyam, renounced their awards in protest if the ceasefire was not withdrawn.[19]

The horrifying visuals finally prompted the Centre to review the ceasefire agreement, confining it to the Nagaland state on 27 July.[20] It is pertinent to note that beyond what was telecast by national and regional media, the Meitei population of Imphal witnessed the frantic packing and shifting by their Naga neighbours during ungodly hours, and leaving for their respective villages in the hills. This central decision was welcomed by the Kuki, Meitei and Kabui groups, while statements of shock and disappointment came to light from all Naga groups. The Centre's resolution to restrict the area affected normal life in the hills, which led to another round of strikes and protests in Naga areas. Markets stayed closed and human chains were formed in Ukhrul district. Mass casual leaves were exercised in Tamenglong and Chandel districts. 2,000 people took part in sit-ins and government offices remained closed in the Senapati district.[21]

> 'However, not a single instance of interethnic violence was reported. The protests remained invariably disciplined. Civil society groups in the hills where NSCN - IM has its stronghold (sic) came out sharply against Meitei chauvinism and dominance. They criticised the GOI for succumbing to the pressure by the Meiteis. The divide of the peoples on ethnic lines came out openly.'[22]

Although Oinam writes that there were no reports of inter-ethnic violence that we know of, the protest was not disciplined in its nature and one cannot deny the fear that overtook the hearts of the tribal population; more so the Nagas, resulting from the breakdown of law and order, ensuing from the actions of the protestors. How then do we conceptualise and process the events leading to the mass exodus of Nagas from the valley if the rhetoric of the absence of inter-ethnic violence was to be sustained? With casualties on the Meitei end and the memorialisation of their deaths as martyrs by the Manipur state, the coerced guilt manufactured from the Nagas upon return, wholly undermined the Naga experience of the Uprising. This fabricated an acute consciousness of one's ethnicity everywhere with the complicit blaming of the Nagas by the

---

[19] 'Binodini, Ratan Thiyam to disown Padmashree titles'. 3 July 2001. *The Sangai Express*. e-pao.net/GP.asp?src=3..040701.jul01. Accessed 10 August 2021.

[20] 'Truce to be restricted to Nagaland state'. 27 July 2001. *The Sangai Express*. e-pao.net/GP.asp?src=1..280701.jul01. Accessed 10 August 2021.

[21] 'Protests in hill against truce reversal intensify'. 8 August 2001. *The Imphal Free Press*. e-pao.net/GP.asp?src=4..090801.aug01. Accessed 10 August 2021.

[22] Ibid. p. 3.

Meiteis, producing the quintessential victims through martyrdom.

The compelling images from the TV engaged the viewer's personal and social identities as witnesses, who consumed the graphic visuals of the ongoing mob violence. The spectators became hypervigilant of their own ethnic identities and social locations and feared possible repercussions were they to come in direct or indirect opposition with the antagonised communities. Thus, the subsequent media coverage of events excluded many narratives[23] and public attention was steered by a biased media towards a singular account that catered to the dominant community. The visuals of the State Assembly burning and protesters taking to the streets, are propellent images circulated in multiples on TV and in the print media.[24] I contest the predominance of these images by critiquing the authority, based on the authenticity of the myriad experiences and lived realities of those people present and affected. The exposé of the Uprising through the techniques of dominant documentation clearly envisages the invisibilisation of alternative narratives; a recurring phenomenon in the exclusivist politics of remembering and forgetting. Jangkhomang Guite puts this in perspective in his essay 'Monuments, Memory and Forgetting in Postcolonial North-East India',[25] where he stressed that the act of remembering is political in nature as collective memory is usually a constructed one.

The idea of Manipur is encapsulated in the hearts and minds of the Meitei community, who have a generational sense of ownership of their own identity, language and habitat, that has been passed down through the handing over of power by colonial authorities to the Meitei kingdom in 1947. Thus, the official memory of Manipur is filled with events that are Meitei-centric in nature, for example, there are several monuments commemorating the Anglo-Manipur War of 1891, and the rebels are cast as patriots after statehood was attained in 1972. The Manipur State Museum and Kangla Museum are filled with visuals that narrate the mythical powers of Manipuri kings, their legendary origins and the imagined sacred geographical maps of Manipur. These visualisations represent the Meitei idea of Manipur, which tells us where the nexus of power really lies; this could also be because the Meitei-governed state had successfully indigenised its pre-colonial past in public spaces.[26] Their visual predominance in the archives and public spaces gave them legitimacy as the true claimants of the land and of Manipuri identity. In continuation with this tradition of visual commemoration, the Meitei populace was able to officially legitimise the mourning of the 'martyrs' of June 18, 2001 (Figure 7), by declaring it a State Holiday on 2005 with a public memorial. The official memorial

---

[23] Sontag, Susan. 2004. 'Regarding The Torture of Others'. *New York Times Magazine*. Issue 23. no. 5. p. 4.

[24] Azoulay. 2008. *The Civil Contract of Photography*.

[25] Guite, Jangkhomang. 2011. 'Monuments, Memory and Forgetting in Postcolonial North-East India'. *Economic and Political Weekly*. pp. 56–64.

[26] Savage, Kirk. 2011. *Monument Wars: Washington, D.C., the National Mall, and the Transformation of the Memorial Landscape* (Berkeley, CA: University of California Press).

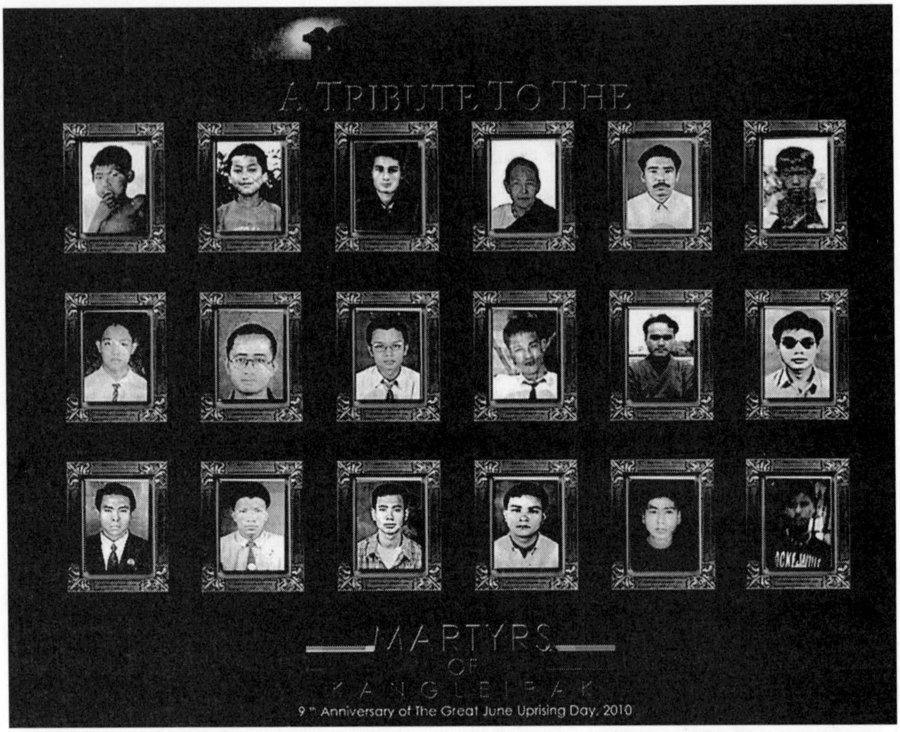

Figure 7. A poster of a tribute to the Martyrs of the great June Uprising, 2001.

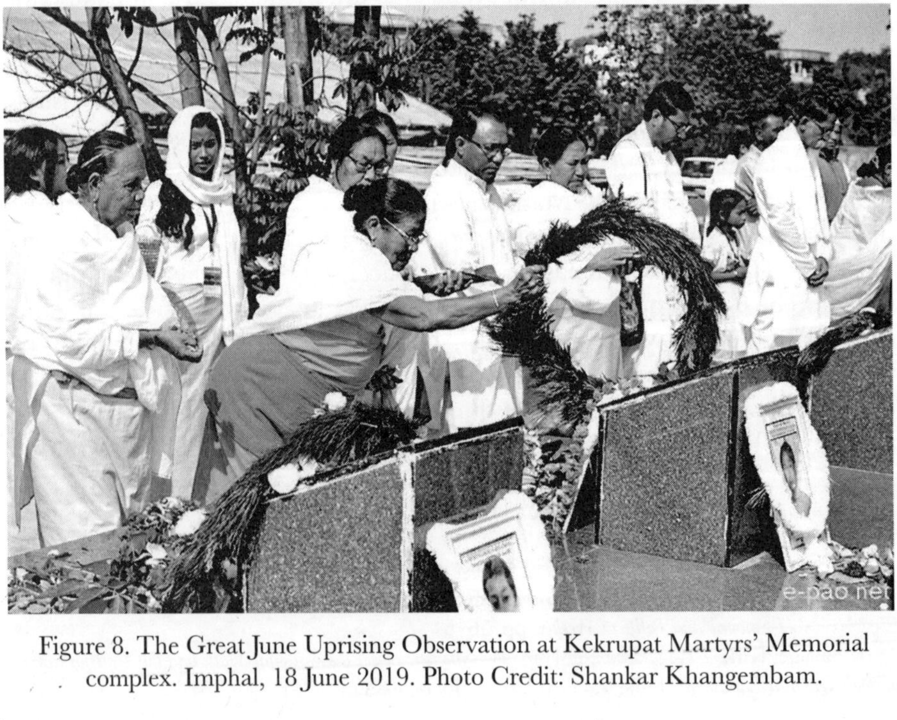

Figure 8. The Great June Uprising Observation at Kekrupat Martyrs' Memorial complex. Imphal, 18 June 2019. Photo Credit: Shankar Khangembam.

(Figure 8) commemorated the actions of what was then seen as a mob, as now a selfless and courageous group of heroes. It was built for the purpose of grieving. For the tribal communities in Imphal, the mob never represented selfless saviours of the land; instead, it represented Meitei chauvinism whose authority could never be questioned and a demonstration of what they were capable of if their idea of Manipur was ever compromised. As non-Meitei communities have never uniformly had a public space for mourning, their tragedies and struggles have always been rendered less genuine in front of events that have been legitimised as historical, and thus there is a need for their own site of memory. The declaration of 18 June as 'State Integrity Day' by the state government was met with agitation by the All Naga Students' Association Manipur (ANSAM). They demanded that it be revoked as they felt that it was a 'coercive and belligerent attitude towards a peaceful assertion of the Naga people's democratic will'[27] and announced an economic blockade, shutting off the districts within Manipur from the rest of the country. This left hundreds of trucks carrying essential supplies stranded on the highway, and it is the common public from the valley and the hills who suffer the most during such blockades, rendered helpless by the lack of essential ration. ANSAM had organised Remembrance Day in memory of nine Naga people who were killed fighting for the protection of their rights, amongst whom Neli Chakho and Dikho Loshou, were killed by state forces on 6 May 2010 at Mao Gate, when there was a protest against the ban of Th. Muivah from visiting Somdal, his native village, by the state government. This was during a time when there was already an economic blockade on National Highway 39 held by ANSAM in protest against the elections for six autonomous district councils, which they felt was a tactic being used by the state government to dismantle the Naga unification process. This led to the economic blockade being extended, and it was lifted on 14 June after 68 days.

An Absence of Photographs: The Collective Memory of Forgetting

Not all moments of life are photographed, especially moments of fear felt in private and the constant anxieties of marginalised groups. These moments without visual evidence in the age of photography, TV and digital media—where the memory of particular events become closely associated with their visual images[28]—should act as a precursor to understanding the experiences not covered by the media. As personal narratives such as these fall outside the scope of official documentation of events, the authentic experiences of those directly impacted by the troubling events are invisibilised. During the early 2000s, owning a camera was a rare privilege that could only be exercised by

[27] economictimes.indiatimes.com/news/politics-and-nation/naga-students-call-off-manipur-blockade-finally/articleshow/6067062.cms Accessed July 1 , 2023

[28] Burke, Peter. 2008. *Eyewitnessing: The uses of images as historical evidence* (Cornell University Press). p. 124.

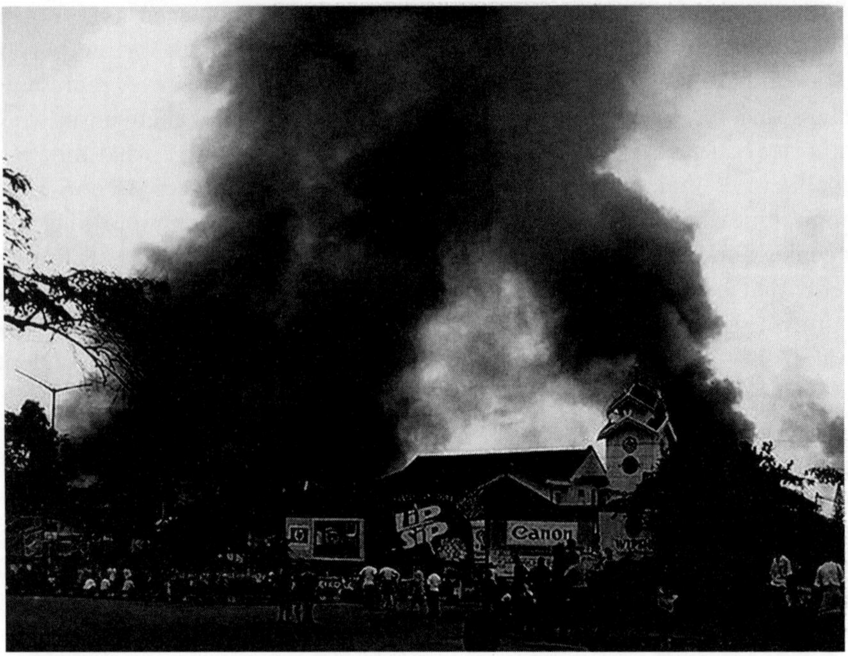

Figure 9. Smoke from the burning Manipur Legislative Assembly building and Office of the Manipur Pradesh Congress Commmittee (I) in Imphal. Photographer: M. Dilip.

the middle class. Between the violent spectacles of destruction and the idyllic family album, the moments when fear really gripped our hearts have been left unphotographed. The absence of photographs of everyday life from tribal families thus reveal a lot about the conscious enactment of memory-making and deliberate amnesia.

Our memory, that is so vulnerable to manipulation,[29] entails that the same event can be felt and narrated differently by members of the same locality. There is a need to bring out vernacular memories, that is, everyday memory, even in the absence of photographs, enabling a decentralised and democratised telling of history.[30] Our vernacular memory is also disrupted and subsumed by mainstream media, that only shows us the distant suffering of a particular community's narrative, instead of our own.[31] The Manipur Nagas carried the difficult identity of being Nagas, the Meitei community were scared of losing geography and the other communities desired peace, but in all this, we knew we did not want to lose home. Whatever it was, in whichever imagined nation,

[29] Nora, Pierre. 1989. 'Between memory and history: Les lieux de mémoire'. *representations*. 26. pp. 7–24.

+ Ibid. p. 14.

[31] Anden-Papadopoulus, Kari. 2003. 'The Trauma of Representation, Visual Culture, Photojournalism and the September 11 Terrorist Attack'. *Nordicom Review*. 24:2. pp. 89–104.

for us as children, we wanted to go back home to the ones we had left behind. The ones who stayed back were also anticipating a homecoming.

The people that have been interviewed for this essay were all very young, the eldest interviewee being eighteen at that time. Similar memories of sights, sounds and smells were felt across all their families; they overheard elders in muffled discussions, seeing the visuals on the TV, our eyes red from the smoke and the sound of poles being struck. It is imperative to keep in mind while reading the narratives of the respondents that these are personal experiences and opinions.

From the accounts of David, John, Dani and Richard (all names changed) who are all from the Meitei community, they were assured that the anger felt by the elders in their families was clearly aimed towards the State, and it was never communal hatred against the Naga population.

David remembers participating in the rally without any idea of what was going on, and all John remembers are the visuals of people lying on the road when he walked out of his house. People were shouting 'Go back inside if you are not going to join us.' Dani remembers her mother going out to the protests held by the Meira Paibi[32] and heaving huge sighs of relief that her sons were far away from the city whenever there was a call for all the male members of the family to come out and participate in the protests. Slowly, in our telephonic conversation, Dani begins to wonder why her memory of significant events such as this are so faint but memories of her exciting school life, sharing tiffin with friends, are so vivid.

Rahul, who lived close to one of the oldest Kabui[33] villages called Muji Khul, and had generational ties to the Kabui community, was able to pinpoint the moment when the Naga identity started entering the folds of the Kabui village. It was through a group of young nationalist men who had asked the announcers of the 'Lai Haraoba'[34] ceremony to add 'Naga' after 'Kabui' during the announcement.

---

[32] Meira Peibi is a women's social movement in the Indian state of Manipur. Referred to as the 'guardians of the civil society', it derives its name from the flaming torches which women carry while marching through city streets, often at night.

[33] A section of the Rongmei people from the hill districts of Tamenglong and Noney were employed by the Maharajas of the erstwhile Manipur kingdom since the eighteenth century, in warfare and other forms of labour. These people have since then settled in and around for Imphal for centuries and a majority of them wish to be identified as 'Kabui'—a term used by the Meitei people for the Rongmei community. Majority of the Kabui population follow the indigenous religion Tingkao Raguang Chapriak (TRC). Due to the difference of religion, geographical distance from the hill people and close association for centuries with the Meitei Kingdom, most of the Kabui apex bodies do not subscribe to the Naga identity. A comprehensive history of the settlement of the Kabui people in Imphal can be found in Prof. Gangmumei Kamei's *History of Zeliangrong Nagas: From Makhel to Rani Gaidinliu*, published in 2004.

[34] Lai Haraoba is a festival associated with the Meitei people, celebrated to please the Umang Lai, the traditional deities of Sanamahism. Lai Haraoba means 'merry-making of the Gods' in Meitei.

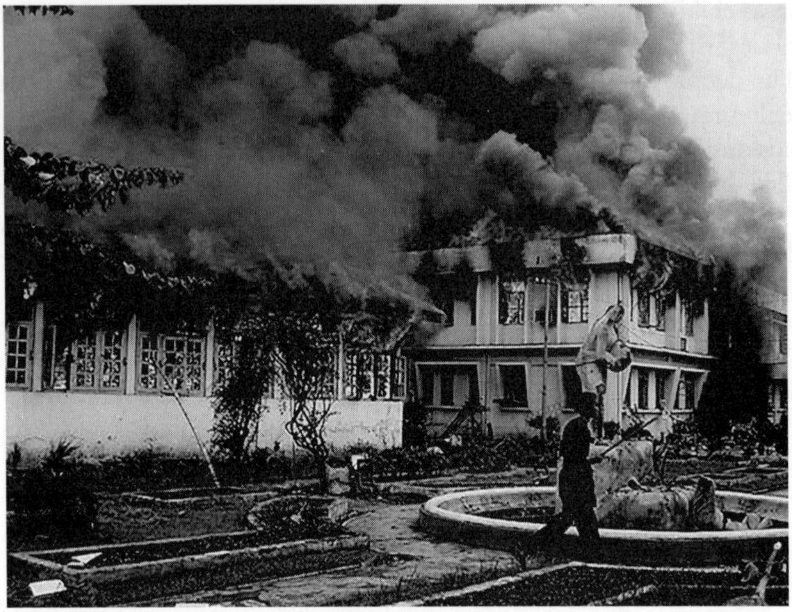

Figure 10. Building of the Manipur Legislative Assembly on fire.
Photographer: M. Dilip.

There was a great deal of fear inside every Meitei household, perhaps to the same measure that the tribal families felt, but the cause of fear and the reaction towards it was starkly different for the tribal and more specifically, Naga families. Like most Naga families, my grandfather arrived in Imphal in the 1960s in search of better education for his own and other children from a small village called Bena Tababang in the indigenous Liangmai language, and known officially as Thonglang Akutpa, a name christened by the Meiteis. It is crucial to understand the social, political and economic position of smaller communities such as my family's Liangmai identity; a community that only received tribe recognition in the year of 2011 (along with five other communities)[35] after a lifetime of being documented as 'Kacha Naga' in the Constitution of India. The economically backward status of the smaller community meant that their cultural and political capital was abysmal and they are often at the mercy of the decisions made in favour of dominant communities, whether it is from bills passed in the Meitei-dominated State Legislative Assembly or from the office of Tangkhul Naga hegemonised NSCN-IM. This was the social position of my family and the reason my grandfather was adamant that no harm comes upon his family.

Perhaps my grandfather was exhausted and wished to cling to some strand of hope because as carriers of the Naga identity, my family—like most Naga

[35] The Constitution (Scheduled Tribes) Order (Amendment) Bill, 2011. prsindia.org/files/bills_acts/bills_parliament/2011/Constitution_(Scheduled_Tribe)_Order_(Amendment)_Bill,_2011.pdf. Accessed 10 August 2021.

families in perennially war-infested Manipur—had suffered so much collateral damage at the hands of draconian central laws, ethnic clashes, and then through violent combing operations, my family had lost so many members to extrajudicial killings over the decades. My cousin Dinpiliu recalls my grandfather assuring her that it was only a fight between the two big communities who were at stake; the Meiteis and the Tangkhul Nagas, but this, instead of placating, made the younger members of the family even more restless, leading them to plead with heavy tears to leave, lest the worst came upon them. It was only after hearing slogans of communal intent like 'Muivah, huichaba' (Muivah, dog eater) 'Ching chatlo' (go to the hills, go to the hills), the burning of the State Assembly and our rusty gate almost dismantled after constant stone-pelting by the mob, that my grandfather finally agreed to leave for the village. We were the last in our leikai to flee. We were hiding under our beds everyday whenever gunshots were heard, and my school-going teenager cousin brothers would come back beaten black and blue in their uniforms, stopped and harassed in the streets by both the state and central forces under suspicion of having ties with underground outfits; finally, my parents who always presented themselves unfazed amidst the ongoing chaos, took us to Taphou Senapati and my grandfather to our ancestral village. In Lamphel, at the heart of the Uprising, my aunt who owned a general store was threatened by police commandos, like so many other Naga shop owners and traders, to close her shop; so my grandmother and she left for the safety of the hill district of Tamenglong.

Peter, who belongs to the Vaiphei tribe, a non-Naga community, lived in Lamphel, right next to the lane of the MLA's quarters, and remembers not having any clue about the political situation except for the exact feeling of fear that gripped his heart and his family's as they watched the chaos unfold on TV. He was ten years old at that time but he can still distinctly recollect the nauseating smell of tyres burning, running out into the garden and seeing the mob inching closer and closer to his house, and the sky covered in smoke (Figure 9). His parents were terrified that the mob would not be able to differentiate between a Naga and a non-Naga tribal. Preparing for the worst, they told Peter and his siblings to pack their bags and they kept shifting from one house to the next as the mob swarmed closer and closer.

Although Agui from Keishamthong—one of the oldest Kabui village in the heart of Imphal—was only five in 2001, she still remembers everything like it happened yesterday, the spine-chilling sonic memory of the clangs of electric poles and cutlery—a calling signal used by the Meira Paibis to gather for protest. She would run upstairs and look out from the roof to see hordes of women and men with torches in their hands, moving from their leikais to the chief minister's bungalow in the dead of the night. The members of civil society organisations gathering in rows with torches ablaze has never been a comforting sight for the tribal population in Imphal, but an image of fear and enforced participation to protect an idea of Manipur. She remembers the sounds of bullets being fired.

While most Naga families whose native villages were situated in Naga-dominated districts found it easier to leave Imphal to seek immediate security and refuge amongst their own people, it was not the same for Kabui/Rongmei families, who had lived in Imphal for generations, some dating back to the late nineteenth century. Most families, having disassociated from their ancestral villages in the hills (Tamenglong and Noney districts), had built their native homes and their indigenous tribal identities in the capital city. While most of the Kabui/Rongmei population ran to seek shelter with their relatives in Tamenglong and Noney, a sizeable population ran to the district headquarter of Senapati and even after the violence died down, decided to permanently situate themselves there, founding a Kabui/Rongmei village at the outskirts of the headquarter. There were also some like Agui's family, who ran to wherever their nearest relative away from Imphal was located. After 18 June, Agui and her family also finally decided to leave Imphal for Cachar, Assam, by bus, a journey that was traumatic in itself. Her family feared stepping down at army checkpoints, and she would hide in the arms of her mother and grandmother. The Indian Army troops would rip their luggage apart with a knife.

After hardly a month's stay in Cachar, Agui had to go back to Imphal to appear for her final examination. She recalls sitting on her uncle's motorbike between her uncle and father till Jiribam and then taking a bus to Imphal from a longer route through the Dimapur–Shillong road. Finally, she fondly remembers her neighbourhood coming together and sharing stories from the places they fled to. Agui also recalls the sharp difference in the school atmosphere upon returning to Imphal, in a class where the majority were Meiteis; everyone became exponentially aware of their ethnic identities and the communal tensions. She, along with many other Naga children who went back to school in Imphal after the violence ended, were met with both implicit and blatant gaslighting regarding how her community (Naga) was the cause of the violence and the lives lost. Agui understands in hindsight that these were words and sentiments echoed from the mouths of the elders in their homes.

Reading My Family Album

Does a tribal scholar have the privilege to be suspicious?

There were many personal, intellectual and ethical concerns that surfaced once I decided to undertake an auto-ethnographic journey into my own past that I had tucked away for a decade. This project unlocked layers of meanings which were not necessarily apparent in the beginning. I had hoped to find in my family album what Walter Benjamin had called in his essay, 'A Short History of Photography' (1931),[36] 'the tiny spark of chance, of the here and now, to

[36] Benjamin, Walter. 1985 (1979). 'A Short History of Photography'. *One-Way Street and Other Writings* (London: Verso).

rediscover something to piece me.'[37] Oral memory has always been thought of as a dangerous tool to read and construct history by many scholars, and while there is no disagreeing that photographs and memories might be 'unreliable',[38] my research indicates that they are crucial in making visible the narratives of marginalised communities. There is a need to take advantage of domestic photographs, as they function as relics and storytelling tools that transcend generations, and as narratives that reflect the past, not always the way it was, but the way we remember it. In my case, I neither remembered nor associated the photographs with the politics of the Uprising, but as a separate, parallel collective memory in themselves. Pierre Bourdieu calls a collective interest in the photograph that overrules the individual, a 'tribal ritual',[39] and although he writes of the 'tribal' in an anachronistic tone, my photographs of tribal families indeed invite a long chain of collective memory, a phenomenon Marianne Hirsch says is inherent to all domestic photographs.[40]

As Patricia Holland[41] writes, my family album portrayed to the world a perfect family, even though we belonged to a conflict-ridden area. However, the 'tribal' family album contradicts her statement that 'family albums overvalue the nuclear family'[42] as most albums of middle-class tribal families bear numerous unrecognisable faces belonging to relatives who many members of my family are likely to have never met. It has been imperative for us to look at our personal albums to refashion our indigenous identity beyond the colonial imagination and contemporary nation-building projects. The conversations that were sparked by the photographs made us laugh, cry, reinterpret and remap our childhood memories into more developed personal narratives, challenging mainstream interpretations. The fragmented collective memory of my family is triggered by the photographs we share, when juxtaposed against mainstream media images. The sets of images do not perfectly encapsulate what we felt, experienced or remembered, but act as catalysts that opened doors to narratives that lay outside the frame.

Essentially, my family photographs do not reflect disturbing events of 2001 but in their context, generated through conversations, one realises the myriad personal experiences that came out of our small valley during the Uprising. The photographs in my family album show a moment of escape that was created by my parents, directed and frozen by my father as the photographer

---

[37] Ibid. p. 7.

[38] Moerman, Theresa. 2012. 'The Magic Mirror: Reflections on Photography as Memory'. Year 4 dissertation, Glasgow School of Art.

[39] Bourdieu, Pierre and Shaun Whiteside. 1996. *Photography: A Middle-Brow Art* (Stanford University Press).

[40] Hirsch, Marianne. 1997. *Family Frames.*

[41] Spence, Jo and Patricia Holland. 1991. *Family Snaps: The Meanings of Domestic Photography* (Virago).

[42] Ibid. p. 7.

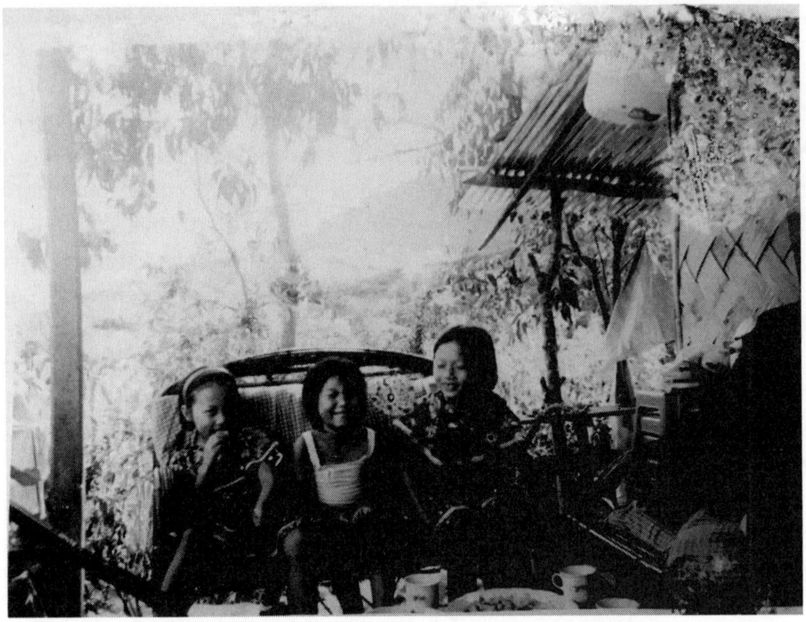

Figure 11. Pitang, Judi and I in Taphou. 2001.

and compiler.[43] Martha Langford insists that family albums can serve as our 'mnemonic framework' [44] that is, a pictorial aid to storytelling. She delineates it further by saying 'the fabric of memory in oral consciousness is met in the photographic condition'.[45] The conversations with my father and those captured in the photographs allowed me to gauge the compiler's intent, for this album was my father's personal anthology of our family. Additionally, it opened the space for alternative narrativisation and the re-inscription of meaning of a significant point in time in our individual and collective histories.[46]

In Taphou

Our trauma disrupts our memory[47] and therefore hazes the context of the photographs in family albums. This could be the reason why so many of us forget and remember only the little things of great banality from 2001. These little things are recounted and pieced together for a collective narrative in

[43] Goldstein, Barry M. 'All Photos Lie: Images as Data.' *Visual Research Methods: Image, Society, and Representation* (2007): 61-81.

[44] Langford, Martha. *Suspended Conversations: The Afterlife of Memory in Photographic Albums* Second Edition. McGill-Queen's Press-MQUP, 2001 : 21

[45] Langford, Martha. *Suspended Conversations: The Afterlife of Memory in Photographic Albums* Second Edition. McGill-Queen's Press-MQUP, 2001: viii

[46] Langford, Martha. *Suspended Conversations: The Afterlife of Memory in Photographic Albums* Second Edition. McGill-Queen's Press-MQUP, 2001

[47] Luckhurst, Roger. The trauma question. Routledge, 2013: 1

this essay with the photographs as an aid to retrieve suppressed memory. The photographs, much like our memory, had been left unopened for more than a decade; mold had formed on a few of the photographs and they could not be salvaged, and the knowledge of unrecoverable evidence leaves a heavy feeling of something being amiss. My father is absent in all of the photographs from Taphou as he is the photographer and the compiler of our family albums. Nevertheless, I begin with the things I remember immediately when I recount 2001.

In a small car, my family and I went up to the district of Senapati. My parents had decided it was safer for us to go to Taphou, a Maram Naga village; we own a plot of land there, where a small makeshift accommodation stood and we had relatives who were willing to look after us. This house eventually became a place of refuge as my family would scurry back here whenever an occasion of conflict arose in the valley. My family relocated again to Taphou for safety when two students were killed by security personnels during a protest against the ban on NSCN-IM's General Secretary Thuingaleng Muivah visiting his native village on 6 May in Mao Gate (the Manipur–Nagaland border).[48] My parents would drop us and leave my two older cousin sisters, Dinpiliu and Simpeliu, my one-year-old brother and myself by ourselves in the house in Taphou. Since we were a group of young children, the locals thought it fun to scare us with stories of ghosts and paranormal activities that happened in the house. The house itself was a rickety one; the tin roofs thundered even when there was little rainfall and sometimes, the neighbours would throw stones to scare us. These things never led to a good night's sleep but when morning came, we would forget everything that had happened at night and spend almost all of our time outdoors rolling down the hills—a rare privilege for city kids apart from their visits to the village during vacations.

In one of the photographs in my family album, we are gathered for a group picture at the house in Taphou; it is my brother Marannang's second birthday (Figure 12) and he stands behind his cake with two candles on it. The cake, my mother recalls, was bought in a hurry from Senapati town bazaar. Upon showing Dinpiliu the photographs, she fondly remembers the time we spent, 'It did feel like a short moment in paradise,' she reminisces. We were more than content with the small cake that barely fed all of us; the birthday candle's flame that was extinguished by everyone else but the birthday boy himself, produced vibrant laughter. My father, an enthusiastic documenter, photographed each and every moment with a mission that would only become known to us when we grew up and understood the times that we had lived through. Pitang, Judi and Chundei, our cousins, had also come up to Taphou from their village called Tagaramphung (Yaikongpao) that was only 30 minutes away. Pitang remembers

[48] 'Two dead in Mao violence: Reinforcement rushed ; security tightened at Senapati HQ'. 6 May 2010. Hueiyen News Service. e-pao.net/epRelatedNews.asp?heading=1&src=070510. Accessed 10 August 2021.

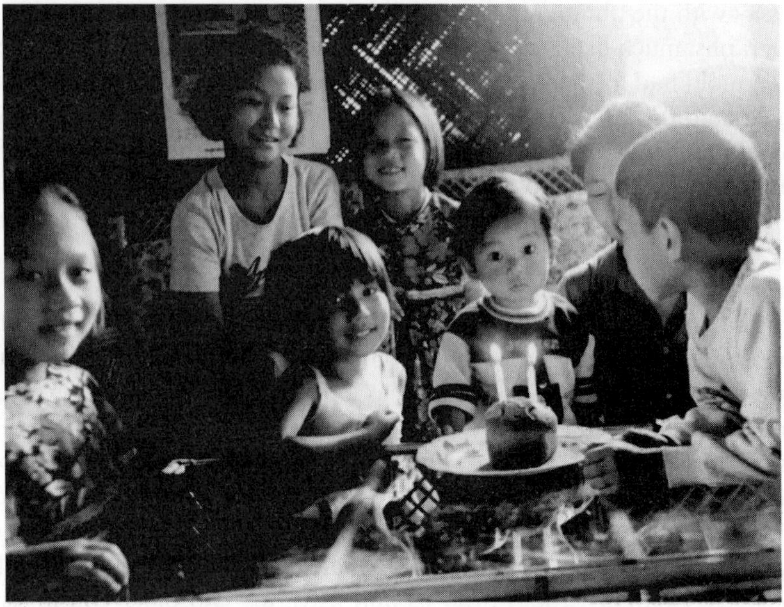

Figure 12. The cousins gathered for Marannang's birthday. 21 August 2001.

all of us snatching the camera from our father to capture each other one by one, and both of us wonder whatever happened to those photos; whether my father ever developed them. Unlike our current selves, we were always eager and ready to be photographed and our favourite spot was the small frontyard space where my father kept some chairs in case of any unannounced guests in 'uniforms'.

The only anxieties I carried with me during that period in Taphou village pertained to not being able to watch TV for months, and only ever having dal and tin fish for every meal, as these were the only food items distributed as ration for Naga families who had fled. We received rations from the Poumai Church or the Assam Rifles canteen; the visits to the latter were always cautious ones, as the infamous and omnipresent camouflage print uniform of the troops that roamed the streets put so many of us at unease. We were afraid they might pull their guns on us if we appeared even a little unfriendly, and I remember as children we smiled unceasingly and let them pinch our cheeks to be left alive. One of my most vivid memories of Taphou, which is now a popular story to laugh over during family dinners, is of the time I climbed down a hill to retrieve a doll that had fallen into a pit of dung and mud. As soon as I picked up the doll, I was stuck and started getting sucked into the mud, deeper and deeper. I held on for a few minutes and screamed for dear life when I saw two buffaloes approaching me. To my great relief, I was quickly pulled out by the father of a friend, who, upon seeing my helpless situation, had gone to call for help. It was also in Taphou that I learnt to pray by myself. My mother taught me to pray in her native Rongmei language and till today, that is the only way I pray, much to the dismay of my father's Liangmai family.

I now realise that moments that felt like neglect at being left alone in a new space, were actually of great sacrifice our parents made for us. My mother and father were denied leave from work, even when they submitted letters containing legitimate requests. As Nagas, they faced harassment from their Meitei colleagues and seniors, and risked their lives driving back and forth across the volatile highway from Imphal to Taphou, only to ensure that amidst all of this, we had only happy memories, as seen in our photographs.

Yet my family photographs reveal so much more than just an idyllic time spent in the village. They have retrospectively encouraged us to bring to surface the painful memories of 2001, for a cathartic re-engagement. My first questions lay in trying to unearth my father's intentions in putting together the album. What story did he want to tell? Martha Langford stresses that the compiler's expression of autobiographical and collective memory, which is intrinsic to the meaning of the object,[49] is seen in the image-selection, annotation and organisation for presentation in discursive spirit—a conversation held by the album in suspense;[50] an oral photographic framework to break down the codes of the member of my family's lore and secret.[51] My family, like every family in Manipur, faced trauma at the hands of state-sponsored violence and communal discord, but we buried it and carried on with life, only to recount these incidents in any abrupt moment as humorous anecdotes. This nature of collective memories and historical references in the tribal family are reflected in the way in which our family albums are orally narrativised. Only happy interludes during periods of long conflict are selected for memorialisation and kept with other photographs from joyous events. Showing these photographs to my father this year, he exclaims at what a lovely time we all had, and how he wishes we could go back. It was an absurd statement, but this way of subsuming all violent events into one good memory has been the community's coping mechanism. Visiting the photographs after a long time revealed previously hidden fears of displacement, the confusion of belonging, identity crises and trauma, from the violence we faced as children. It also converged with mundane anxieties and the constant question of '*Ake nde nai tadno?*' meaning 'When are we going home?' in my native tongue, Lianglad (the language spoken by the Liangmai tribe). In our conversations from the time of political unrest and thereafter, our parents taught us to envision and desire a greater homeland, our very own nation state as it had been imagined by our forefathers. We did try our best, but as alluded to in the beginning, our hearts knew no other home apart from Imphal. The initial excitement of leaving arson-filled Imphal and shifting to a new place was soon replaced by terrible homesickness.

---

[49] Langford, Martha. 2001. *Suspended Conversations: The Afterlife of Memory in Photographic Albums*. Second Edition (McGill-Queen's Press [MQUP]). p. 203.

[50] Ibid. p. 199.

[51] Ibid. p. 199.

As generational trauma converges with mundane anxieties, it becomes difficult to recognise and compartmentalise trauma. Trying to remind someone of a specific experience might need prompting, with graphic details of the things that happened. The memories of 2001 were not necessarily remembered as scarred events immediately; it took hours and sometimes days for recollection. In Taphou, we were out having picnics (Figure 13), but this was also the time that this other, distant, political disturbance was taking place. Although there are two very divergent sets of images, mainstream/political/news and the familial, it also reveals to us that these two sets of images can coexist and show the multiple sides of the same historical moment. Through their contradiction, they are filling out a larger view of the same temporality, and hence are both equally important. What finally matters to people who are aware of both the public and personal sides of their histories, of trauma as well as continuity that ironically coexist in the same moment, is peace albeit different imaginations of peace.

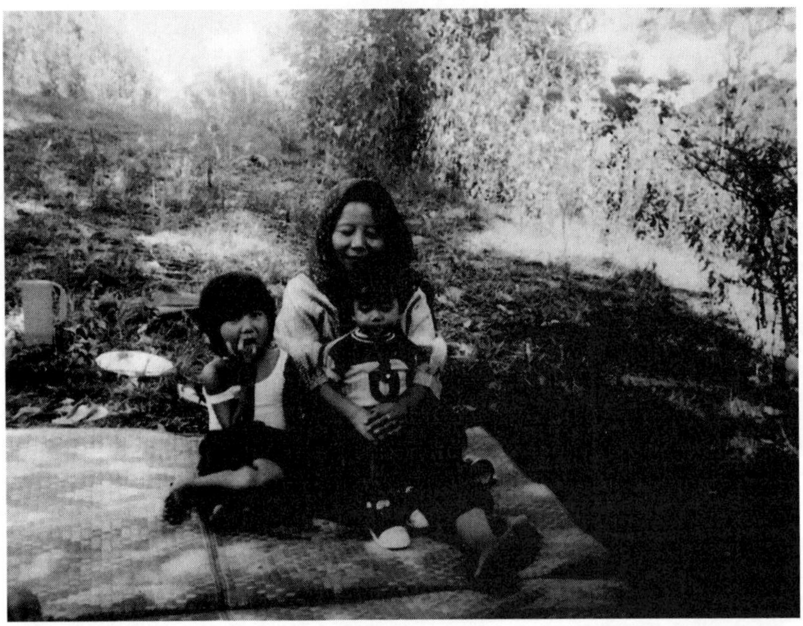

Figure 13. Picnic in one of the fields in Taphou, photographed by my father. 21 August 2001.

Conclusion

For communities ill-equipped with the vocabulary for self-expression and frameworks to articulate, the authenticity of our experiences are always put to question. This was an attempt at reclaiming our narrative by looking at how family photographs/albums can act as 'affective avenger(s) of history'.[52] They

[52] Pachuau, Joy L.K. and Willem Van Schendel. 2015. *The Camera as Witness* (Cambridge University Press).

act as a step forward in writing from our personal experiences, to challenge state-owned, institutionalised histories and the authority of our patriarchal apex bodies and their nation-building interests. The purpose of writing this essay has never been to discount the collective trauma of a particular community, but instead it asks for an equal amount of space and attention for communities that have been misunderstood and misinterpreted for generations. It offers caveats to historical writing, official memory and its claims of supreme authority and legitimacy.

Note of Acknowledgement

This paper would not have seen the light of day without the Grace of God, my father who took the photographs in 2001, my family who helped me remember each and every funny and piercing detail, my friends and respondents who wish to remain anonymous but endured long telephonic conversations. I am indebted to Kinriwiliu and Surya ma'am for their invaluable comments which helped the paper take shape with more substance and sense that I had imagined.

The Art of Belonging in *Imagined Homeland*

Ranu Roychoudhuri[1]

'We belong here, they say, quietly.'

— De, 2018

What does it mean to belong—belong to a space, landscape, community, or perhaps to a pre-given home, family, kinship and state, or to modernity and history? Where must we locate the liminality of these categories, and how must we understand the porous boundaries that shape ideas of belongingness? And how is one to visualise this fluidity when the medium of representation thrives on a promise of realism and fixity of meaning? These layered questions mediate the historical and the 'magical' in *Imagined Homeland* (2013–2019) by contemporary Indian photographer Sharbendu De (b. 1978). Ethnographic in approach, it is a long-term, conceptual photo-documentary project depicting the lives of the indigenous Lisu (Yobin) people in the remotest areas of the Namdapha National Park and Tiger Reserve and other highland forest areas along the Indo-Burma (Myanmar) international border in the Indian state of Arunachal Pradesh (Figure 1). Employing varied styles and genres, the duration of De's project was from 2013 through 2019. I will focus on selected photographs from between 2018 and 2019 in this essay. My choice is guided by increased technical, conceptual and narrative layering in De's later works as compared to his early oevre, his emphasis on the spaces devoid of human presence, and his active engagement with Lisu orality from their pre-colonial, pre-Christian past.

While De's portfolio and artist statement devote substantial space to the lived realities of the Lisu and their location in trajectories of socio-political belonging/s in the recent past, this paper offers observations primarily related to the nature of photographic reality and its dialogic relationship with the extra-photographic. While realism conditions social expectations and analytical thinking about belonging, home, family and photography, this essay aims to act as a meditation on non-realist strategies in contemporary lens-based practices to address belongingness. My analyses emphasise how magical

[1] My gratitude to Sharbendu De for generously sharing his works, experiences, stories, thoughts and responses to an early version of this article. I thank Arvind Elangovan and Rochona Majumdar for their insightful comments on previous drafts. I also thank Tapati Guha-Thakurta and my co-contributors to this volume, Uzma Mohsin and Sireiliu (Anna) Charenamei, for their questions and comments during initial presentations of this essay.

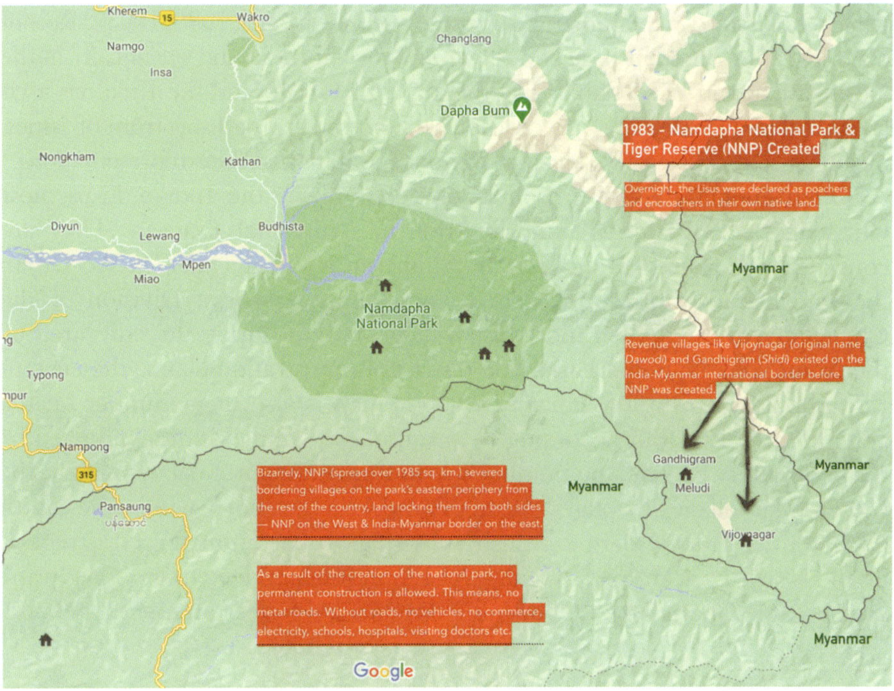

Figure 1. Map of Lisu villages (For illustrative purposes only; not to scale). Courtesy: Sharbendu De.

realism as a visual form complicates the dominant ways of representing ideas of home/homelands and reflects on the role of family photographs as affective–performative spaces to memorialise social bonds. Thus, this article is neither a historical nor an ethnographic account of the Lisu 'tactics'[2] of belonging to a specific tribal identity, statist category, religious faith, territorial boundary, or temporality. Instead, I begin with a brief historical overview of the Lisu's marginal location to argue how surfaces of *Imagined Homeland* craft conceptually provocative, fluid and transient spaces of belonging beyond material particularities.

Precarious Lives

Known as Yobin in India, the Lisu is a collective identity for multiple clans of a Tibeto-Burman ethnolinguistic group spread across hill areas of Arunachal Pradesh, Burma (Myanmar), Southwest China, and northern Thailand. Scholarly research on the Lisu is primarily focused on their communities in China, Burma and Thailand (Arrington 2019; Yu 2007; Hutheesing 1990),[3]

[2] de Certeau, Michel. 1984. *The Practice of Everyday Life*. Trans. Steven F. Rendal (Berkeley, University of California Press). pp. 34–39.

[3] Scott, James C. 2009. *The Art of Not Being Governed: An Anarchist History of Upland Southeast Asia* (Yale Agrarian Studies, New Haven & London: Yale University Press); van Schendel,

while scholarship on the Indian Lisu remains scarce (Maitra 1988, 1993).[4] Recent historiography on other indigenous communities in India and specifically in the Northeast Indian borderlands, like the Naga, the Mizo and the Kuki, vis-à-vis layered ideas of belonging, have variously discussed a broad spectrum of issues, including state, citizenship, kinship, identity, mobility and their representations.[5]

Often euphemised as 'prisoners of geography',[6] the Indian Lisus, now Christian by faith, are a minority tribe in Arunachal Pradesh. They are concentrated around Gandhigram (Shidi) and Vijoynagar (Da-Wo-Di) in the Vijoynagar administrative circle and Nampong Forest Division of the Changlang district, while most Lisu villages remain inside the core area of the Namdapha National Park. The district administration claims the current Lisu population as approximately 2,000, which is also their number on the voter identity list.[7] But according to an unofficial enumeration conducted by the community leaders, the number was around 4,300 in 2019.[8] Formerly, the Indian Lisu villages belonged to the Trirap Frontier Tract within the North East Frontier Tract under the British, subsequently becoming the Tirap district of the North East Frontier Agency (NEFA) in independent India. Finally, the area became Changlang in 1987, after Arunachal Pradesh attained statehood.

Willem. December 2002. 'Geographies of Knowing, Geographies of Ignorance: Jumping Scale in Southeast Asia.' *Environment and Planning D: Society and Space*. 20:6. pp. 647–68. doi.org/10.1068/d16s; Aminta Arrington, Songs of the Lisu Hills : practicing Christianity in southwest China, University Park, Pennsylvania : The Pennsylvania State University Press, [2019]; Zack Michele, *The Lisu: Far from the Ruler* (University Press of Colorado, 2017); Otome Klein Hutheesing, *Emerging Sexual Inequality Among the Lisu of Northern Thailand: The Waning of Elephant and Dog Repute* (E.J. Brill, New York and Leiden, 1990); D Yu, "Gender and Language Use in Lisu Traditional Religion," in *Language and Religious Identity: Women in Discourse,* edited by A. Jule (London: Palgrave, 2007), 172–95.

[4] Maitra, Asim. 1993. *Profile of a Little-Known Tribe*, and Maitra, Asim. 1998. A Guide Book to Lisu Language, Delhi, India, (Mittal Publications).

[5] Longkumer, Arkotong (2010), *Reform, Identity and Narratives of Belonging: The Heraka Movement in Northeast India*, London, Continuum.

Rycroft, Daniel J. and Sangeeta Dasgupta. eds. 2011. *The Politics of Belonging in India: Becoming Adivasi* (Oxford and New York, Routledge).

Sadan, Mandy. 2013. *Being and Becoming Kachin: Histories beyond the State in the Borderlands of Burma* (London: Oxford University Press).

Pachuau, Joy L.K. 2014. *Being Mizo: Identity and Belonging in Northeast India* (New Delhi: Oxford University Press).

Pachuau, Joy L.K. and Willem van Schendel. 2015. *The Camera as Witness: A Social History of Mizoram, Northeast India* (Cambridge University Press).

Bhattacharya, Neeladri and Joy L.K. Pachuau. 2019. *Landscape, Culture, and Belonging: Writing the History of Northeast India* (Cambridge: Cambridge University Press).

[6] Talukdar, Sushanta. 2021. 'Prisoners of Geography'. *Frontline*. frontline.thehindu.com/other/travel/article30188563.ece. Accessed 20 July 2021.

[7] See Vijoynagar, Changlang District. Government of Arunachal Pradesh. changlang.nic.in/tourist-place/vijoynagar/. Accessed 20 July 2021.

[8] See Lisu—Yobin Dreams. yobindreams.wordpress.com/?s=population&submit= Search. Accessed 20 July 2021.

British colonial surveys and documents mention the Yawyin (Lisaw) (Figure 2) as being part of Burma. They appear in the Census of Burma[9] rather than that of Assam till 1937, when Burma became a separately administered colony of Great Britain. However, it is unclear if the Lisus of the Namdapha area were enumerated till later. Given their much larger population in Burma and Lisu linguistic similarities with Burmese, the Indian Lisu's identification with Burma continued in the post-colonial period, resulting in the Lisus' complex relationship with state machinery. For example, the Indian government considered them Burmese refugees from 1980 to the early 1990s. This was despite their earlier tribal status in India since the 1950s and long-standing demands for formal recognition by Yobin civil society organisations like Yobin Tribe Fundamental Rights Forum (YTFRF), Yobin Welfare Society (YWS), and All-Yobin Student Union (AYSU) as well as sometimes the All-Arunachal Pradesh Students' Union (AAPSU), notwithstanding occasional conflict between the Yobin/Lisu and AAPSU leaderships.[10]

Meanwhile, the declaration of Namdapha as a wildlife reserve in 1972 and the creation of the Namdapha National Park and Tiger Reserve in 1983 overwrote the Lisu claim to their ancestral land. Part of the Lisu ancestral homeland became the national park, similar to other instances where national parks were created out of indigenous lands, fuelling prologued land rights debates.[11] The formal creation of the national park pushed the Lisu further away from their traditional homeland and made them encroachers in their ancestral territory, as had been the case for other indigenous and tribal communities' land rights and forest rights across India and beyond (All India Forum of Forest Movements 2021).[12]

Indian Lisu or Yobin were formally granted Indian citizenship in 1994 and Notified Scheduled Tribe status in 2018, after several previous stints of administrative acceptance and refusal of their indigenous tribal identity, confusion over where they belong on the map of tribal rights in India, and their residential status as Indian citizens.[13] Even in the 2018 notification,

---

[9] Bennison, J.J. 1933. *Census of India 1931.* Vol XI. Burma Part I—Report (Rangoon, Burma: Office of the Supdt. Govt. Printing and Stationery). p. vi.

[10] 'Yobins deserve ST status'. 22 February 2015. *The Sentinel.* www.sentinelassam.com/news/yobins-deserve-st-status/. Accessed 20 July 2021.

[11] Brockington, Daniel and James Igoe. 2006. 'Eviction for Conservation: A Global Overview'. *Conservation & Society.* 4:3. pp. 424–470.

Poirier, Robert and David Ostergren. 2002. 'Evicting People from Nature: Indigenous Land Rights and National Parks in Australia, Russia, and the United States'. *Natural Resources Journal.* 42:2. pp. 331–351.

[12] All India Forum of Forest Movements. 2021. *Struggles for the Right to Live in Forests Declared Protected Areas in India: Experiences of Communities in Maharashtra, Madhya Pradesh and Chhattisgarh.* www.wrm.org.uy. Accessed 17 December 2021.

[13] Letter No. YT/1/2017/STGAR/DEOTH/RU-II. 30 May 2018. From National Commission of Scheduled Tribes, Government of India to the Chief Secretary, Arunachal Pradesh.

the Lisu right to affirmative action is guaranteed only under the generalised clause 'all tribes of the territory', and at the time of writing this article, they are yet to be included in the 'individual notified ST list of the state.'[14] Yobins are still awaiting what they call 'constitutional identity by name.'[15] The Lisu civil society organisations continue to mount public protests demanding their constitutional rights, including their rights to traditional lands, denouncing the governmental proposal of extending Permanent Resident Certificates (PRC) to non-Arunachal Pradesh Schedule Tribe (non-APST) and the latter's inclusion in the Panchayati Raj.

The 2018 notification issued by the National Commission of Scheduled Tribes, Government of India, also instructed the state government to 'take immediate action to provide infrastructure like roads, electricity, water supply, medical facilities, education, etc., in the tribal area.'[16] These civic amenities are yet to materialise where the Lisu live, given much of it is within the national park with its own set of prohibitions on infrastructural expansion. The nearest town Miao, 157 kilometres from Vijoynagar and a three to five days' walk through challenging terrain, is where the Lisu could procure essential supplies like salt and cooking oil. In the absence of roads or any form of transportation, the active presence of the Assam Rifles in Vijoynagar since the 1960s provided the Lisu with some form of rudimentary, restricted and monitored connectivity with the world by intermittently bringing them limited essential supplies via choppers.

Contacts, conflicts and negotiations with the armed forces, the Forest Department, a sizeable population of non-indigenous settlers comprising of former army servicemen and immigrants from Nepal and Bihar ensure a substantial presence of Hindi, even if broken, as a medium of communication for the Lisu speakers to interact with others. Ironically, the Assam Rifles credit themselves and their veterans for pacifying the Lisu discontents regarding administrative neglect by extending essential goods and services to the community, despite community members often feeling otherwise.[17] Additionally, many Lisus routinely use English as a communication medium, including in their protests and negotiations with the state and central governments. They also use Lisu with the help of the Lisu–English interpreters

[14] Rina, Tongam. 6 January 2019. 'Yobins resent exclusion from ST bill,' *The Arunachal Times*. arunachaltimes.in/index.php/2019/01/06/yobins-resent-exclusion-from-st-bill/. Accessed 20 July 2021.

Readers' Forum: 'Where do Yobins fit in the proposed APST Amendment Bill?'. 19 July 2021. *The Arunachal Times*. arunachaltimes.in/index.php/2021/07/19/where-do-yobins-fit-in-the-proposed-apst-amendment-bill/. Accessed 20 July 2021.

[15] Readers' Forum. 2021.

[16] Ibid.

[17] See *STORY(Six) Vijaynagar End of The Road* [video] by The Assam Rifles Sentinels of Northeast. 2018. 17:31 minutes. www.youtube.com/watch?v=511YA_SzkRA&t=12s. Accessed 21 July 2021.

for official purposes, as they did for a landmark press conference in Itanagar on 15 February 2019. It demanded constitutional protection, initiating a peaceful, democratic and powerful movement, with stray deviations, like the incident when several governmental establishments in Vijoynagar were set to fire by a 300–400-strong Yobin mob in December 2020, for which All Yobin Students' Union claimed responsibility.[18]

Location of Belonging

Against this backdrop of long-standing administrative and political volatilities and narratives of marginalisation as part of general histories of postcolonial unrests, insurgencies and suppressions in Northeast India, De's *Imagined Homeland* takes place in an administratively and infrastructurally remote, isolated and disconnected but not entirely unconnected tropical rainforest on the highlands of the Indo-Burma (Myanmar) international border. This location also makes De's work grounded in the Zomia, conceptualised by historian Willem van Schendel to characterise the margins of Area Studies divisions of South Asia, Southeast Asia, Central Asia and East Asia as 'an area of no concern'[19] for specialists. According to van Schendel, Zomia is

> derived from *zomi*, a term for highlander in a number of Chin-Mizo-Kuki languages spoken in Burma, India, and Bangladesh. Linguists classify these languages as belonging to the very large family of Tibeto-Burman languages spoken all over Zomia [Kashmir, North India, Nepal, Tibet, Sikkim, Bhutan, Northeast India, the Chittagong Hill Tracts (Bangladesh), Burma, Yunnan, and Sichuan (China), Thailand, Laos, and Vietnam] (van Schendel 2002, p. 653).

Van Schendel and political scientist-anthropologist James C. Scott extensively theorised the immense socio-political and disciplinary-area studies implications of Zomia (van Schendel 2002; Scott 2009). In terms of its material location, Zomia coincides with Southeast Asian mainland massif (or a section of it depending on specific scholarly position), a geographical category marking South-Southeast Asian highlands with an altitude of 300 meters above the sea level. Although Zomia's location is not precisely the same for Van Schendel and Scott, the site of the Lisu habitation is common to both positions. De's portfolio of *Imagined Homeland* mentions Zomia as merely an 'anthropological context' for his ethnographic project. In my analysis, Zomia's socio-political import as an 'area of no concern' and 'shatter zones or zones of refuge'[20] lends itself to how photographic realities produced through a language of magical realism create spaces of mythical refuge for

[18] 'Mob Torches Govt Offices in in Arunachal Border Town,' *Northeast Today: Redefining Northeast* (Dec 12, 2020) www.northeasttoday.in/2020/12/12/mob-torches-govt-offices-in-in-arunachal-border-town/ accessed July 29, 2021.

[19] van Schendel. 2002. 'Geographies'. p. 653.

[20] Scott. 2009. *The Art of Not Being Governed*. p. x.

Lisu desires. This makes *Imagined Homeland* an art of belonging for the people 'not being governed.'[21]

De reflects, 'they [Lisu] live alone and die alone,' highlighting how the Lisu live by themselves without much assistance from the Indian federal or Arunachal state government. The statement also foregrounds De's admiration for the Lisu's 'grace' and grit in their refusal to take up arms despite deprivation, suffering and loss. De chooses two points of departure in what he describes as a 'research-based approach' to represent the Indian Lisu in Namdapha.[22] First, he wants to move away from colonial visual surveys like the *People of India* (Watson and Kaye 1868–75)[23] that generalised, exoticised and decontextualised tribal identities. In other words, De's ethnography wants to dismantle colonial anthropology's objectifying gaze and its widespread positivist practice of fixing tribal identity on the photographic surface, often dehumanising their human referents. Visual anthropologist and art historian Christopher Pinney described 'stern fidelity' and 'penetrating certainty' (Pinney 1998) as the dominant approach of colonial anthropological photographs exemplified in Figure 2, while De's photographs move away from any search for either fidelity or certainty. On the contrary, his works accommodate illusory and fleeting possibilities and fluid identities. Second, De is inspired by literary critic A.K. Ramanujan's phrase 'mythic entities called self-sufficient village communities',[24] despite missing Ramanujan's irony of using 'mythic' to denote a wide spared belief about self-sufficiency that is unreal. De's reading of the 'mythic' leads him to explore the Lisu myths and to represent the forced self-sufficiency of the Lisu in a 'mythical' visual space of refuge. In doing so, De's project resonates with postcolonial critics like Partha Chatterjee, who demonstrate how the dominant state failed to 'represent' the aspirations of its 'people-nation' like the Lisu.[25] A move away from the colonial gaze and an emphasis on the Lisus' mythical refuge equip De to forward a critique of the postcolonial Indian state that kept the Lisu at the margins.

However, the space he creates is not entirely premised on any pre-existing cultural narrative as a myth. Instead, De resorts to his imagination in

---

[21] Ibid.

[22] Growing up in an upper caste professional Bengali family in the Andaman Islands, De was intrigued by the relative obscurity of the Lisu (Yobin) in popular discourses compared to more widely discussed tribal groups like the Naga, the Mizo, and the Jarawa. The artist's social position vis-à-vis the possibility of an exoticising, romanticising, infantilising, and patronising gaze in his work is beyond the scope of this article.

[23] Watson, J. Forbes and John William Kaye. eds. 1868–75. *The People of India: A Series of Photographic Illustrations, with Descriptive letterpress, of the Races and Tribes of Hindustan*. Originally prepared under the authority of the Government of India, and reproduced by order of the Secretary of state for India in council, London, India Museum.

[24] Ramanujan, A.K. 1990. *Who Needs Folklore? The Relevance of Oral Traditions to South Asian Studies*. South Asia Occasional Paper Series No. 1 (Honolulu: Center for South Asian Studies, University of Hawaii Manoa). p. 6.

[25] Chatterjee, Partha. 2019. *I am the People: Reflections on Popular Sovereignty Today* (New York: Columbia University Press). p. 31. And passim.

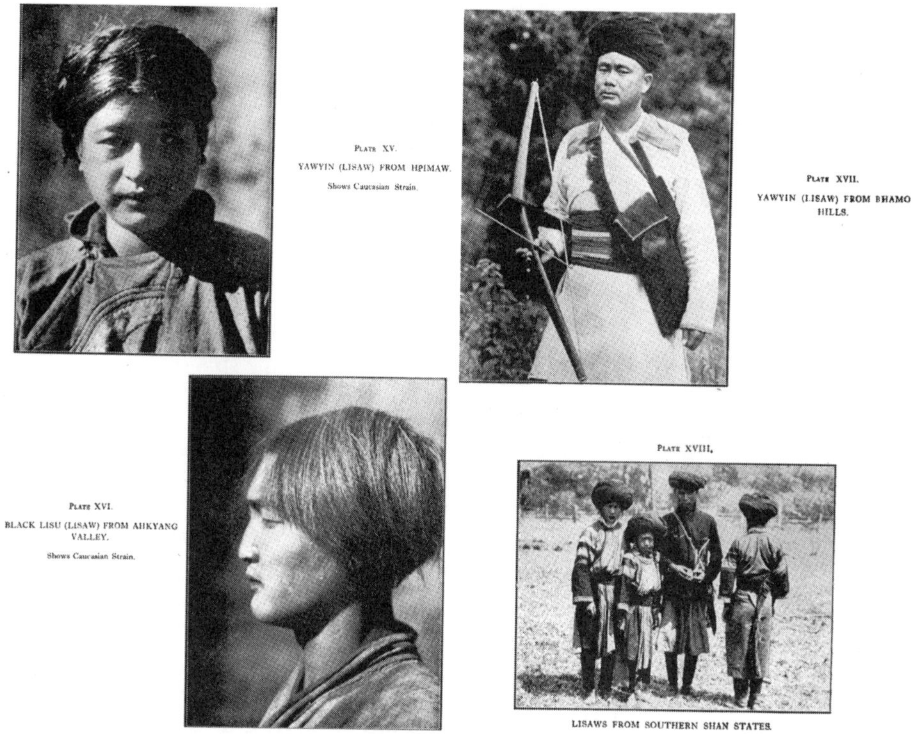

Figure 2. Halftone printed plates from *Census of India 1931, Vol XI, Burma Part I—Report* (Rangoon: Office of the Supdt. Govt. Printing and Stationery, Burma, 1933).

interpreting the word 'mythical' as he documents 'Lisu way of life—philosophy, and magnanimity of spirit'. It makes him 'realise that they epitomise the true essence of being magical.'[26] Inspired by the Lisu folk traditions and oral narratives, he devises a form of magical realism towards this twin impulse to address, on the one hand, a specific history of visualising Indian tribes and, on the other hand, imagination as an operative category to address borderland tribal identity. Without any claim to realism or semiotic fidelity to material realities, *Imagined Homeland* creates photographic realities that can accommodate competing notions of a historically specific borderland tribe and an ahistorical representation of their belongingness to the geography they inhabit. It muddles dominant understandings of home, family, domesticity and citizenship by weaving a layered narrative of how human and non-human subjects coexist in seemingly contradictory worlds of everyday modern objects and supposedly ahistorical wilderness of a tropical rainforest where 'politics collide with fantasy.'[27] With its visual economy and complex narrative, the genre-bending

[26] The portfolio, dated 2021, De shared with me and his artist statement on www.desharbendu.com/imagined-homeland accessed October 30, 2020.

[27] Zamora, Lois P. and Wendy B. Faris. eds. 1995. *Magical Realism: Theory, History, Communities* (Durham: Duke University Press). p. 1.

Imagined Homeland pushes the limits of easy categorisation and encourages looking beyond the critical lenses available within photographic discourses.

After Franz Roh coined the term in 1925 in the context of post-expressionist art, 'magical realism' as a representational genre had a diverse life, most prominently in Latin American literature in the twentieth century. While Roh's understanding of the style in art was flipped on its head when adopting it in Latin America, the flip incorporated more thoroughly Roh's claim that 'with the word 'magic,' as opposed to 'mystic,' [he] wished to indicate that the mystery does not descend to the represented world, but rather hides and palpitates behind it…' (Roh 1925/27).[28] The literary practice of magical realism subsequently manifested in postcolonial literary spaces, where 'magic is often given as a cultural corrective, requiring readers to scrutinise accepted realistic conventions of causality, materiality, motivation.'[29] It is 'closely linked with a perception of "living on the margins".'[30] The possibility of incorporating the magical and the apparently impossible within banal spaces of the everyday makes magical realism a productive lens to interrogate belonging in the margins depicted in *Imagined Homeland*. But how might looking closely at the photographs from the series help us think about belongingness?

In Magical Realism

Seated on wooden benches, an adult man and three children stare at a television set accompanied by a flower vase, both placed on a table covered in patterned fabric, and human faces are illuminated by the screen's neon hue (Figure 3). This description can fit a whole range of family snapshots encoding forms of twentieth-century leisure from across spaces; the reader is transported immediately to a stereotypical modern urban home embodying a sense of comfort. However, 'Waiting in the Forest' (Figure 3) includes two ducks next to the seated man and unfolds in a dense tropical rainforest illuminated by artificial light. Given the limited solar-powered electricity and wireless network in Lisu villages, the television set in Figure 3 signals its limited function, mimicking the limit set by the forest to access modern goods and services. Simultaneously, it signifies the Lisu desire for connectivity with the world beyond their immediate surroundings. Some of these motifs are shared by 'Untitled' (Figure 4), including the little boy glued to the television, the flower vase and the pony. Additionally, Figure 4 has an Airtel dish antenna, a set-top box and a plate of white rice. Unlike 'Waiting in the Forest', the story in 'Untitled' unfolds in a paddy field in what appears to be a valley. Likewise, 'Three Tea Mugs, Father

[28] Franz Roh, "Magic Realism: Post-Expressionism," quoted in Faris, Wendy B., and Lois Parkinson Zamora. *Magical Realism: Theory, History, Community.* 1 ed., Durham: Duke University Press, 1995.

[29] Zamora and Faris. 1995. *Magical Realism*. p. 3.

[30] Slemon, Stephen. 1995. 'Magic Realism as Postcolonial Discourse'. Zamora and Faris. *Magical Realism* (Durham: Duke University Press). Pp. 407–426.

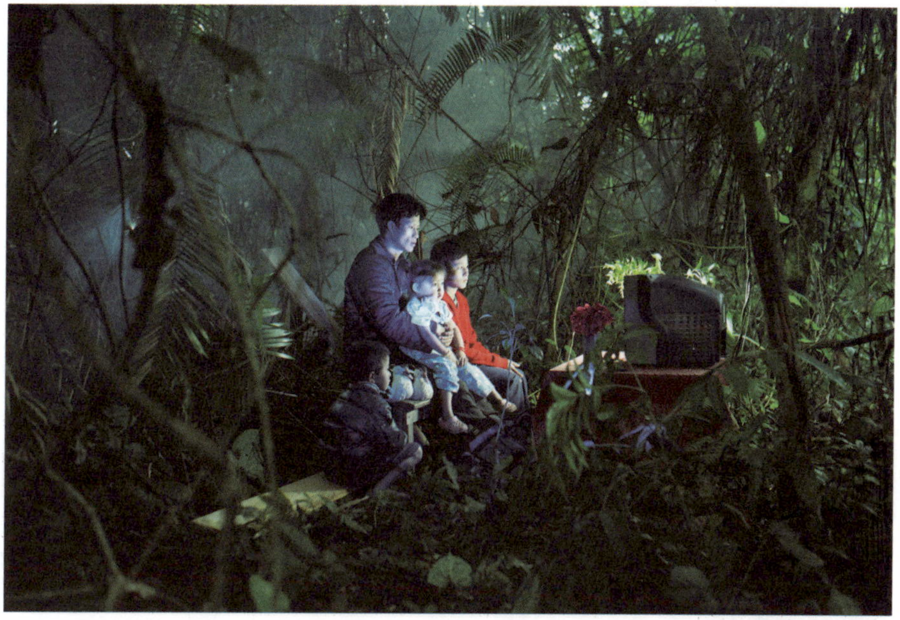

Figure 3. Sharbendu De, *Waiting in the Forest*, 2018, Inkjet print on archival paper. Copyright & Courtesy: Sharbendu De.

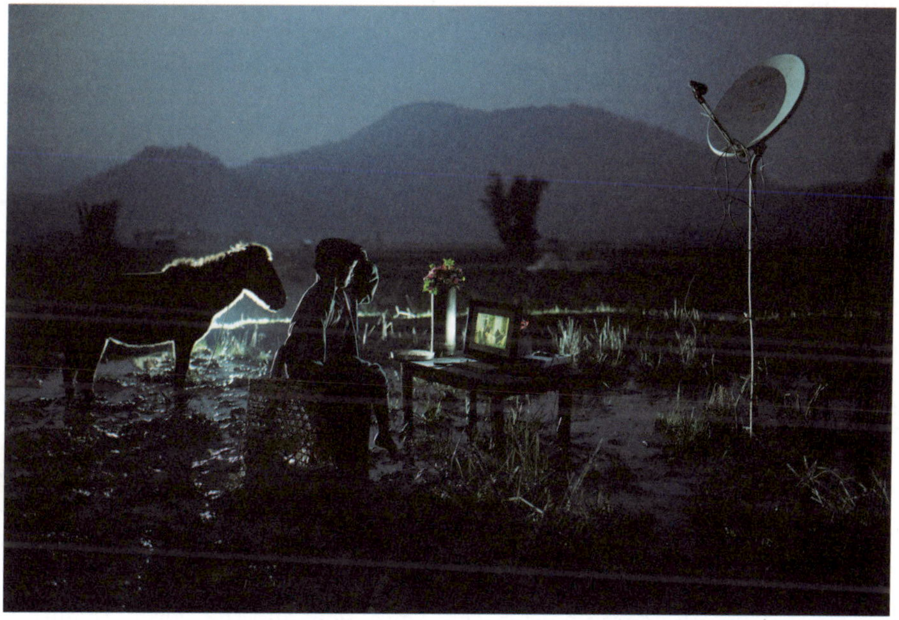

Figure 4. Sharbendu De, *Untitled*, 2018, Inkjet print on archival paper. Copyright & Courtesy: Sharbendu De.

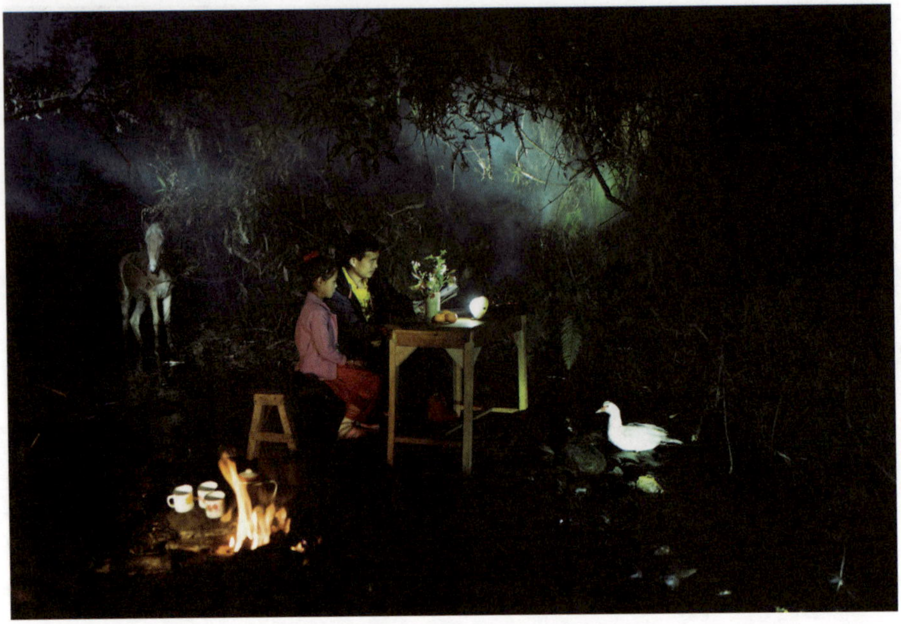

Figure 5. Sharbendu De, *Waiting in the Forest*, 2018, Inkjet print on archival paper. Copyright & Courtesy: Sharbendu De.

and the Child' (Figure 5) has a domestic setup amid the forest. The father reads what appears to be a magazine. The language is uncertain, but the object forges a connection with the world outside. The magazine also locates these human actors in the global contemporary mass culture like the television does. There's a pony and a duck in the frame, but unlike the ducks in Figure 3, it is unclear if the animals in Figure 5 form a part of human domesticity or if they mark its boundaries.

Like many others from the *Imagined Homeland*, these photographs offer staged scenes that are impossible otherwise but are made possible by the 'magic' created by the photographic event. They emerge simultaneously as celebrations of the Lisu's cohabitation with nature, a critique of the colonial discourse of tribes as forest-dwelling primitives, and postcolonial governmental neglect, forcing the community to build a self-sufficient life amid adversities. Forest, animal, human and modern gadgets exist seamlessly in De's magical world. Their simultaneity challenges conventional expectations regarding mass culture, urban comfort, domesticity and leisure. De's human subjects like Ngwalidew Yobin '[search] for a portal to a place where there is a balance between the mythical and the modern' (Figure 6) in the 'magical forest' created on the photographic surface. 'Ngwalidew and the Portal' (Figure 6) directly point to the imbalance between what appears to be the mythic and the modern in the photographic present and thereby emerge as a critique of the extra-photographic reality. In other words, the 'portal' as a channel of

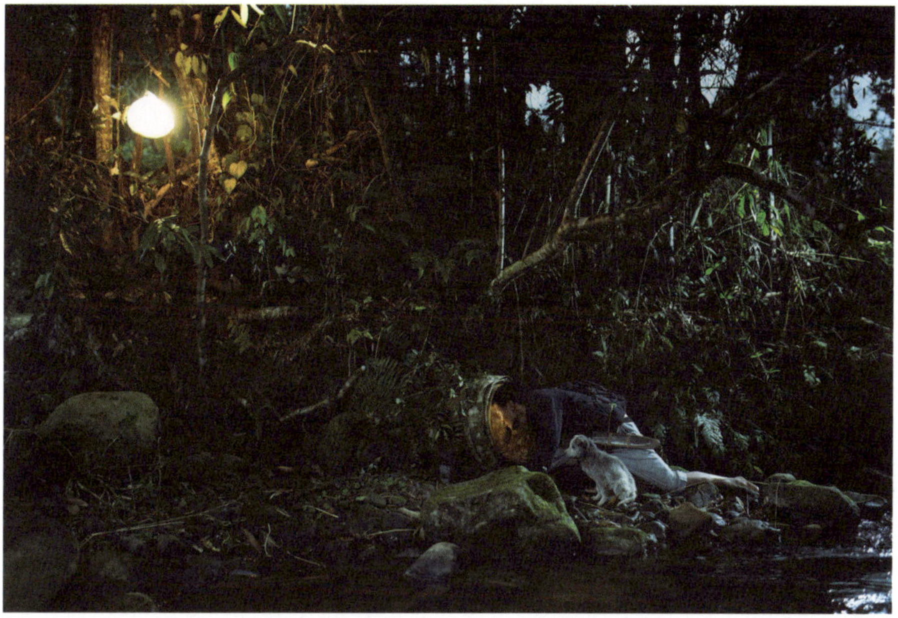

Figure 6. Sharbendu De, *Ngwalidew and the Portal*, 2018, Inkjet print on archival paper. Copyright & Courtesy: Sharbendu De.

communication promises the Lisu a possibility of embracing 'modern' services without having to leave their myths, self-sufficiency, and attachment to their ancestral land. This dual pull of staying grounded in their ancestral homeland and their desire to go beyond those ties mark one of the characteristics of De's work, as they interpret Lisu imaginations and experiences.

According to De, he tried portraying the sensory experiences felt by the Lisus as a result of living amidst nature (away from an urban monetised economy). 'I borrowed from their folklores, journalistic accounts shared with me, dream symbolism etc. to evoke an aura of their world (which included encounters with the spirit-world "*Maamimu*" and "Musi") and explored archetypal interconnections between "man, animal and nature"[31] instead of resorting to spectacle. All efforts were aimed at alluding to their state of mind and feelings, including despair, anguish, relationship with nature, togetherness, family, gentle stewardship of their animals and their rare ability to collectively search for light despite the hardships.'[32]

De's narrative style employs psychoanalyst Carl Jung's notion of the archetype[33] to access the Lisu 'collective unconscious' through their traditions, oral histories, lived experiences and collective dreams. However, he creates

[31] Jung, Carl G. 1981. *The Archetypes and The Collective Unconscious*. Translated by R.F.C. Hull. *Collected Works of C.G. Jung*. Vol. 9. Part 1. (Princeton: Princeton University Press).

[32] Sharbendu De's portfolio for *Imagined Homeland* dated 2021.

[33] Ibid.

archetypical symbols rather than borrowing from Jung's original twelve archetypes. 'Golden light,' duck and water are recurrent motifs as manifestations of the archetype of 'man, animal and nature' in De's visualisation of the Lisu 'collective unconscious'.

De emphasises, '[t]he recurrent usage of this "golden light" is symbolic of something warm, alluring and prosperous, everything that gold as a metal signifies (and partly even fire). I also had in mind paintings, for example, Francisco de Goya's The Third of May 1808.'[34] Spanish Romantic painter Francisco Goya's 'The Third of May 1808' (1814), also known as the 'Execution of the Defenders of Madrid', depicts the execution of Spanish civilians by the French army during the Peninsular War and commemorates the Spanish resistance to Napoleonic aggression. It inspired generations of European painters in their attempt to bear witness to statist violence and atrocities perpetrated on innocent and unarmed individuals. 'The Third of May 1808' has attracted scholarly attention, among other things, for its tonal value and how Goya created contrasting light and dark on the canvas highlighting the figures of the to-be martyred individuals facing the French firing squad. De's reference to Goya is reminiscent of photo-theorist Susan Sontag's exposition on 'regarding the pain of others' concerning Goya's prints and paintings immediately preceding 'The Third of May 1808'. Sontag claimed, '[w]ith Goya, a new standard for responsiveness to suffering enters art. (And new subjects for fellow-feeling …)'[35] (Sontag 2003, p. 45). Shall we interpret De's 'golden light' as bearing witness to the sufferings of the Lisu and their resistance to statist indifference by solidifying their belonging to the warmth of the 'mythical forest?'

The frequent appearance of the motif of the duck in *Imagined Homeland* aligns with De's attempts to 'look beyond the human' in grasping the Lisu lives.[36] These efforts are prominent in De's inclusion of other animals, like the pony in Figure 4. However, De's most notable statement on 'beyond the human' comes in the form of spaces devoid of human beings (Figure 7) or spaces embodying only human cultural objects (Figure 8). Likewise, water in De's work appears repeatedly to assimilate the non-human, even though for De, water signifies human 'life in motion.'[37]

He explains,

> I use water as symbolic of transiting time but also reference dream symbolism where "crossing a water body is symbolic of an impending transition in life, either about to happen, or at least the aspiration." Such tropes entered my lens when years later the Lisus opened up, revealing their belief in dreams and motifs they see in their sleep state, but they also apologetically saying, "They

---

[34] Email correspondence with Sharbendu De (29 July 2021).

[35] Susan Sontag, *Regarding the Pain of Others*, Penguin Books, 2003

[36] Email correspondence with Sharbendu De. 28 July 2021.

[37] Email correspondence with Sharbendu De. 29 July 2021.

Figure 7. Sharbendu De, *Untitled*, 2019, Inkjet print on archival paper. Copyright & Courtesy: Sharbendu De.

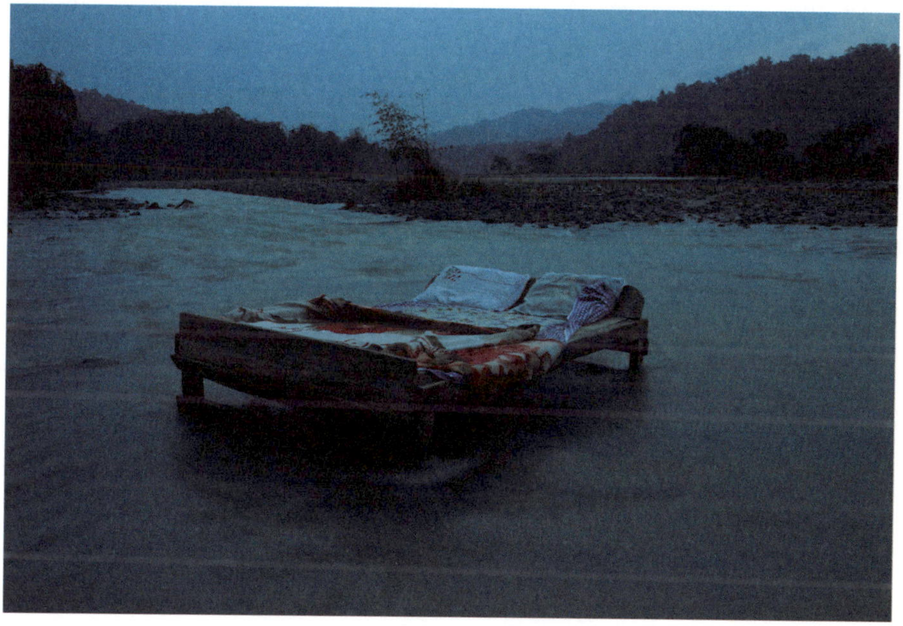

Figure 8. Sharbendu De, *Untitled*, 2019, Inkjet print on archival paper. Copyright & Courtesy: Sharbendu De.

do not believe or practice animism anymore as they are no longer *junglees*, but Christians."[38]

In my analyses, the motif of water in De's work is as much about the non-human and the motion of life, as it is about the fluidity of Lisu belonging in the visual space of the *Imagined Homeland*. Further, thinking 'beyond the human' entails rethinking the idea of humans belonging to the planet Earth; it involves 'decentering the human in our narratives of the world' (Chakrabarty 2021, p. 203).[39] This makes one aware that humans are one of many species inhabiting the planet where human narratives are somewhat 'incidental' (Chakrabarty 2021, p. 67). However, De's quote of the Lisu statement of how they 'are no longer *junglees*, but Christians' grounds the chronicle of Lisu belonging to an anthropocentric world. Indeed, the visual space of the *Imagined Homeland* focusses on the non-human as long as that attention contributes to an unfolding human story of fluid belonging.

The three motifs, namely the 'golden light', duck and water, are instrumental in assimilating seemingly incongruent ways of belonging simultaneously to the specific and the eternal domains of Lisu existence, giving viewers access to magical possibilities. According to De, '[m]agic when explained, deconstructed, analysed, articulated and its origin traced, loses its charm.' So he wishes 'to leave this [magic] unexplained' to keep alive the element of mystery associated with the idea of magic.[40] He further explained that even when faced with adversities and difficulties in life, the Lisu 'grace, gentleness and warmth in their hearts, is what [he feels] is magical.'[41] De describes their grace and grit in the following terms:

> Refusing to protest or take to arms, the Lisus simply focus on finding solutions. They grow their rice and vegetables, sustainably extract forest produce, build each other's homes, bury their dead, pray and feast together. In the absence of an external economy they mostly barter, living symbiotically with nature as a self-sufficient community. These gentle people call the forests 'home' and consider the idea of life outside the forest as inconceivable. We belong here, they say, quietly.[42]

Even though De would refrain from explaining 'magic', his follow-up elaborations intend to use 'magic' as a trope to critique the Lisus' bleak present resulting from the prolonged denial of citizenship rights and access to state resources. Thus, 'magic' is a critical tool for De to comment on the 'impaired

---

[38] Email correspondence with Sharbendu De. 28 July 2021.

[39] Dipesh Chakrabarty, *The Climate of History in a Planetary Age*, Chicago ; London : University of Chicago Press, 2021

[40] Email correspondence with Sharbendu De. 29 July 2021.

[41] Ibid.

[42] De, Sharbendu. 2018. 'Imagined Homeland'. *IQ: The Indian Quarterly*. Jan–Mar. indianquarterly.com/?p=4469 accessed 20 July 2021.

citizenship'[43] of the Lisu. In the process, De employs what I would call a lens of magical realism to understand the complexity of the Lisu belonging. The magic in De's work doesn't happen outside reality in some otherworldly fantasy space; it doesn't provide an escape from lived realities. On the contrary, magical elements are located within the spaces of the ordinary and the everyday; they happen in the forest the Lisu live in or the lands they cultivate. Everyday objects acquire new meanings in the De's 'golden light'. This focus on the ordinary and the everyday is further enhanced by how De did not use any prop that the Lisu did not use in their daily lives, except his photographic equipment and artificial light. By making the apparently impossible unfold through the ordinary, De's articulation of the everyday magic in the Lisu lives in the Namdapha affiliates his work with the broader tenets of magical realism in postcolonial literature, where he doesn't essentialise the unexplainability of magic as the only way of accessing the non-Western tribal consciousness and/or their cultural milieu. Indeed, De employs magical realism with an impulse of a documentarian as he weaves an album of Lisu lives.

Album of (Be)longing in Zomia

While the idea of family albums and family photographs are commonplace, conveying fixed meanings in specific social arrangements and/or communities of photographs—like the bourgeois family or the genre of portrait/group portrait and snapshot—the ideas could be completely foreign and protean in other social, political and visual contexts. In other words, the idea of family photographs and family albums are not seamless across contexts and they are marked by conceptual fissures. Indeed, historians of gender have compellingly discussed the disconnect even between bourgeois imaginings of the family photograph and actual family values, and how the photographic reality and lived reality were not necessarily aligned.[44] This caveat creates room to think that not all families are the same, and not all of them would have family photographs/albums as sites of affect, memory and nostalgia. Consequently, how must we think of the idea of family photo albums as a socio-linguistic space for producing the social and the political when those albums come from socially and politically marginal spaces? Is the concept of a family album an a priori for the Lisu in their *Imagined Homeland*? The conceptual and material location of the Lisu in De's representation of belonging might serve as an entry point to rethink both ideas: of family and album.

The album, the folio and the scrapbook as genres have a long and diverse genealogy in the histories of visual arts in India. They come in all shapes and

[43] Azoulay. 2008. *The Civil Contract of Photography*. p. 15.

[44] Srinivas, Mytheli. 2008. *Wives, Widows, and Concubines: The Conjugal Family Ideal in Colonial India*. (Bloomington and Indianapolis: Indiana University Press).

Majumdar, Rochona. 2009. *Marriage and Modernity in Colonial India* (Durham: Duke University Press).

forms from different periods with diverse patronage and ownership structures. In its variegated public, private and domestic forms, even the modern genre of the photographic album is rich in its diversity. Family albums in this context have mostly remained part of the private and the domestic, despite family photographs often making it to public discourses and acquiring public lives in specific political contexts. The vast personal archives of family photographs and family albums from India, and the existing scholarship on some of them appear to foster several assumptions regarding the social positions of families who would have objects called family albums. They signal social and economic privilege and/or social capital at the elementary level. Simultaneously, they point to how family photo albums embody traces of historically specific photographic practices, including genres and individuals associated with them.

Scholars like Don Slater and Jessica Evans describe family photographs as 'a great wasteland of trite and banal self-representation'[45] and as a 'stultified and stereotyped repertoire of composition, subject-matter and style',[46] while others like Gillian Rose draw attention to how family photographs' association with domesticity and women make them invisible and/or repudiable in critical discourses on photographic aesthetic.[47] Either way, the broader body of scholarship on family photographs from across cultures routinely demonstrated the diversity of uses and afterlives of family photographs and albums. Often, photographs from family albums have made their way into theorising the ontology of photography, for which, undoubtedly, the prime example is the famous 'Winter Garden Photograph' depicting cultural critic Roland Barthes' mother[48] that nevertheless remains unreproduced in his book. Marianne Hirsch argued, 'Barthes cannot *show* us the photograph because we stand outside the familial network … because he claims it is a very private kind of self-portrait'[49] that would not have the same significance for the viewers. Barthes and Hirsch were two of the many scholars, including Julia Hirsch, who emphasise familial and kinship ties as the foundation on which family photographs thrive.[50]

De's ethnography alerts his viewers to the precarity of Lisu families and kinship ties at the margins of statist governance and national narratives. Yet, *Imagined Homeland* demonstrates how '[t]heir sense of identity and feelings

[45] Slater, Don. 1995. 'Domestic photography and digital culture'. Lister, M. ed. *The Photographic Image in Digital Culture* (London: Routledge) pp. 134.

[46] Evans, Jessica. 2000. 'Photography'. Carson, F. and C. Pajaczkowska. eds. *Feminist Visual Culture* (Edinburgh: Edinburgh University Press), pp. 112.

[47] Rose, Gillian. 2010. *Doing Family Photography the Domestic, the Public and the Politics of Sentiment* (Surrey, UK: Ashgate). p. 5.

[48] Barthes, Roland. 1981. *Camera Lucida: Reflections on Photography*. First American edition (New York: Hill and Wang). p. 67. And passim.

[49] Hirsch, Marianne. 1997. *Family Frames: Photography, Narrative, and Post-Memory* (Harvard: Harvard University Press). p. 2.

[50] Hirsch, Julia. 1981. *Family Photographs: Content, Meaning and Effect* (Oxford: Oxford University Press).

of belonging are never entirely shaped by the practices of the state'.[51] De's project highlights how ideas of home, family and domesticity are not exclusive to human bonds and how they incorporate the wilderness and the spirit world of *Maamimu*. As De explains,

> The Lisu believe that a parallel invisible world coexists in the same time-space. They call it *Maamimu*, and the invisible humans living there as *Musi*. For each Lisu, there is a similar looking *Musi* in *Maamimu*, and should one suffer or die, the same fate meets the other … Invisible portals connect both worlds and stories of interactions with the *Musi* exist in the Lisu world. They usually do not share these stories with outsiders, or for that matter, their belief in dreams and symbolic elements from nature. Their relationship with the forest and its innumerable elements is influenced by similar belief systems making them more respectful of nature and its cohabitants.[52]

Consequently, De uses multiple exposures to accommodate the Lisu and their Musi (Figure 9).

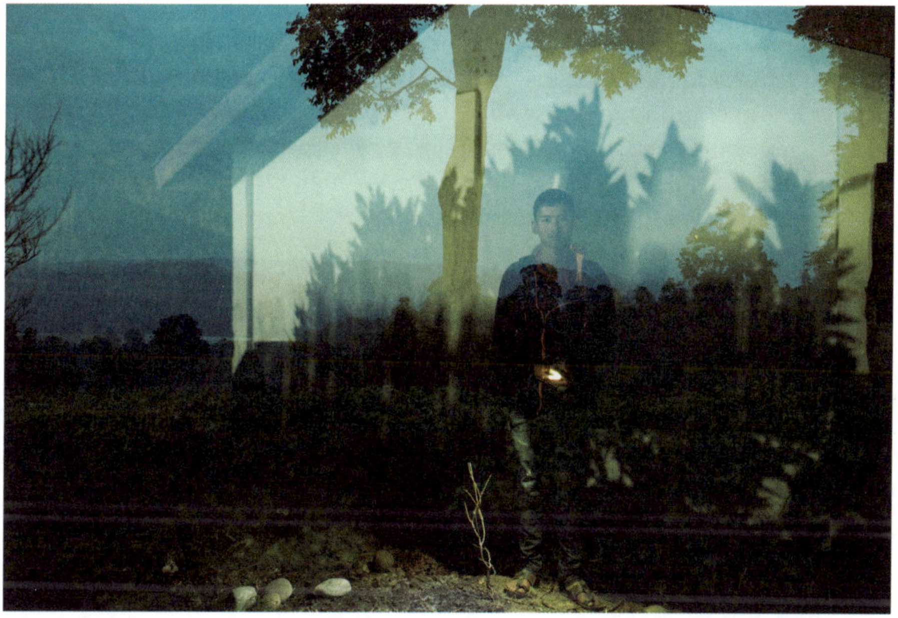

Figure 9. Sharbendu De, *Noyu Yobin*, 2018, Inkjet print on archival paper. Copyright & Courtesy: Sharbendu De.

Likewise, the idea of domesticity in its most comprehensive scope makes it possible for De to position a bed in the middle of a flowing water body (Figure 8) or have the wilderness overpower human presence, signalled by the hint of

[51] Bhattacharya and Pachuau. 2019. *Landscape, Culture, and Belonging*.
[52] Sharbendu De's portfolio dated 2021.

fire (Figure 7). How might one tell stories of material hardship simultaneously with a parallel world devoid of any material existence per se, without resorting to the techniques of magical realism, radically redefining dominant ideas of home, domesticity and family! De's work provides a novel visual language of human belonging in liminal zones, including home/world, domestic/public, family/nature and human/non-human.

The wooden bed frame, printed linens, two pillows and patterned blanket in Figure 8 tell a story of human domesticity devoid of any active human presence. At first glance, the non-human elements seem to be the protagonists of the photograph. But a closer look reveals traces of human habitation. The pillows seem to have been used and the folds on the printed bedsheet and the patterned blanket bear marks of usage. They bear impressions of corporeal presence as if someone just got out the blanket and left the bed, making the absent user of the bed the real protagonist of the narrative. This is congruent with De's understanding of flowing water as a metaphor for flowing human lives. Poignantly, this domesticity unfolds in the most unlikely of scenarios—in the middle of a river flowing through a valley. The absence of the human only reinforces the centrality of anthropocentrism in *Imagined Homeland*. As much as the photograph highlights the conjoined lives of the human and the natural worlds, it also crafts a non-normative form of domesticity, privacy, home and family against the backdrop of mountains, vegetation and a river.

This fluid, liminal and non-normative belonging on the surface of the photographs allows the magical realism of *Imagined Homeland* and the concept of Zomia in its most comprehensive possible scope to co-constitute each other. On the one hand, the material location of the Lisu in the margins, in zones remaining ungoverned by the political power in the valleys and the 'heartlands' provoked De's visual narrative. On the other hand, De's work expands the scope of Zomia by including the 'magic' and the spirit world of Maamimu as zones of refuge from material hardship and the complex engagement with the governmental machinery. While it is uncertain if the Lisu of the Namdapha can be linked in terms of life choices to the Lisu elsewhere, Scott's argument about the deliberate absence of history or clan genealogy among Thai Lisu[53] is illuminating in thinking about belonging to Maamimu as a way to escape the history and the present, without severing material ties. This begs the question if the Lisus in De's works are meant to be the people who inhabit the human world or if they are the Musi from the parallel world who stand in for the Lisus of the extra-photographic material world. What if Musi from the *Imagined Homeland* promise a zone of freedom that is materially unattainable and creates affective and performative sites of belonging that only exist in photographs, pretty much like family albums?

[53] Scott. 2009. *The Art of Not Being Governed*. p. 235.

In Conclusion

In concluding this article, let me briefly reflect on the exhibitionary life of *Imagined Homeland* to think about the kind of family album it would make and the stories of belonging it would tell within and outside the Lisu social sphere. De would carry back in his subsequent trips multiple prints of photographs made during his previous trips to the Lisu villages. He would also carry numerous copies of his published photo stories. However, the postcard-sized prints he would take back as a gesture of gratitude are the ones that depicted their material reality and portraits of individuals. He would not take any print of his conceptual works, which the people could see only in copies of published photo essays. In other words, prints from *Imagined Homeland* would not make it back to the community due to the challenging logistics of carrying them to the villages.

This practice of taking back images locates De in the long lineage of globally practised socially committed documentary ethics, where photographers organised community exhibitions and handed prints over to the people featured in specific photographs. They often emphasised collaboration and trust as foundational to long-term documentary projects that depicted victims of 'slow violence', especially when they belonged to marginalised communities. For example, Magnum photojournalist Eugene Smith took back photographs of victims of the Minamata Event—the prolonged industrial mercury poisoning in Japan between 1908 and 1968 with enduring effects till date—during his subsequent trips to the Japanese coastal town of Minamata. Similar is the case for numerous Indian photographers who conducted long-term documentation on urban poverty or other forms of violence.

Further, these victimised communities at the margins often lack the means to afford photographic prints, both in terms of money and access. Even in the smartphone age, access to photography and digital technology is not universal, particularly in the Global South. Prints brought by photographers often become precious objects and prized possessions. Conventional and dominant styles of family photography are not essential for some of these photographs to enter the discourse of family and domesticity. The genre doesn't matter because, in most cases, these prints are about belonging in photography, owning the prints, celebrating and memorialising the individual/s depicted. De's prints would have similar currency for many Lisu, for many of whom photographs are a luxury in the face of the 'slow violence' that conditions their material reality. As De narrates, some of them have a smartphone and even digital cameras, but for the majority, photographs are certainly not part of their everyday. As he further confirms, many of his portraits of people or candid shots of village weddings become Lisu family possessions for their commemorative value. This is a narrative on the one hand of how the Lisu belong to photographs and on the other hand, how the photographs might belong to Lisu families. However, the series *Imagined Homeland* is not the site of this dialogue between the artist, his works and the community. The series exists somewhat independently of its affective ties with the community.

Outside the community, *Imagined Homeland* is an award-winning body of work that circulated widely through galleries, photo festivals, biennales and print publications, with a very different set of publics than the Lisu. The publics of the gallery would encounter a very different set of photographs printed in larger dimensions than the prints the Lisu would see in their villages. The location and format condition their reception and continued life in the art market. De remains conscious of the exotic value the series might hold for most viewers because of popular discourses about tribal communities, especially from Northeast India. In the artist's talks, he tries to reach out to his audience on how to look at the Lisu lives beyond the exotica. His efforts to make the audience sensitive to the material realities of the Lisu are indicative of his interpretation of belongingness in the Lisu lives within and beyond the frame.

For De, the prints on the gallery walls are only intermediaries between the Lisu and the world beyond their villages. His approach to his audience is similar to what film theorist Fr. Gaston Roberge SJ wrote on a 1970s–80s long-term documentary project on the urban poor that he helped organise. According to Roberge, those photographs were meant to sensitise the middle class about the precarity and resilience of the poor. He wrote, '[w]e do not offer these images to arouse pity. We offer them as one would open a family album with trust in [the] onlooker's readiness to understand others.'[54] Despite the absence of the rhetoric of the 'family album', De's sentiments echo the objectives of social documentary practices.

However, there is a fundamental difference between the visual styles of documentation employed by De in *Imagined Homeland* and social documentary photographers like Eugene Smith or Roberge's team. The former worked with conceptual photography, while the latter practised documentary realism. Unlike realism, conceptual photography is at liberty to not allude to material specificities, provoking the audience to see them independently of the artistic intentionality about the material world of the referents outside the photograph. This stylistic difference accounts for how De's work expands the scope of family photographs/albums beyond the verisimilitude offered by either snapshots in family albums or documentary realism within discourses of social change. As a result, the surface of the prints doesn't simply remain an intermediary between the audience and the referents, as De had asserted. The surface itself becomes the space where the referents belong. It is the economy of the image that creates the possibilities of novel ways of human and non-human belongings. In doing so, *Imagined Homeland* helps introspect the accepted categories of family, kinship, domesticity and competing claims about them by making the idea of belonging an operative thread. *Imagined Homeland* emerges as an art of that belonging.

---

[54] Roberge, Gaston. 1980. 'Shaheed Minar'. *Quarterly Journal of National Centre for Performing Arts*. Vol. IX. No. 2. June.

The Art of Belonging in Imagined Homeland *By Ranu Roychoudhuri: A Response*

Sharbendu De

I am on a break. Finally. Sitting beside a colonial window opening onto a misty mountainscape, I stare at the contour lines gently running along the hillside only to get caught in the window pane while the Teesta's omnipresent rumbling reminds me of my momentary geographic specificity. I contemplate over a question with which Ranu Roychoudhuri opened her essay 'The Art of Belonging *in Imagined Homeland*'—'What does it mean to belong?' It is an evocative question, indeed. Caught in the crosswinds of her seemingly straightforward but layered question, I helplessly waft along, repeating my age-old question, 'Where do I belong?' if anywhere. Always lost, adrift, an erstwhile islander, now neither an islander nor a mainlander, I reckon being in an endless pursuit to locate my axis. The Tibeto-Burman Lisu community portrayed through my series *Imagined Homeland* (2013–19) (the focal point of Roychoudhuri's essay), does not, however, suffer from this existential dilemma. Contrary to the State's position, they know where they belong. And to what, and whom. But is there a singular land they can claim to be undisputedly theirs? The migratory history of the Lisus began from eastern Tibet and moving through southern China, then Myanmar, eventually some of them made home in the contiguous forests of Namdapha (which extend over 20,000 sq. km. from India to Myanmar) in North Eastern Frontier Agency (NEFA), now Arunachal Pradesh, India's remotest northeastern state. At that time, there was no international border demarcation between India and Myanmar.

The history of tribes has been one of migration, land, rivers and myriad elements of nature as resources, but this history transcends beyond valuing nature as just a 'resource'. It has also been shaped by land-based conflicts, at times with neighbouring tribes, but mainly contesting and eventually evading State oppression formerly in the hands of autocrats and monarchs, and later governments following the nation-state theory, zealously determined to bring far-flung communities into the fold of state-making projects in the valleys through slavery, conscription, taxes, unpaid labour, epidemics and warfare.[55] James C. Scott offers valuable insights to understanding indigenous communities that especially reside within the Southeast Asian massif, 'Ethnicity and "tribe" begin exactly where taxes and sovereignty end.'[56] These and more historico-political factors have shaped their identity, including that of the Lisus.

But where do artists, authors, philosophers, art historians and their scholarship belong, and to what purpose? Can there be an axis where our

---

[55] Scott. 2009. *The Art of Not Being Governed.*

[56] Ibid. p. xi.

scholarships can return to? I dive deep into this much contested question of where do indigenous communities belong, but more importantly, how do we associate with and represent them?

In her essay, Roychoudhuri cites, 'Several government establishments in Vijoynagar were set to fire by a 300–400-strong Yobin mob in December 2020, for which All Yobin Students' Union claimed responsibility,' but offers no further context, including that five Lisu youths (with no prior history of violence) were booked under the National Security Act.[57] An unfortunate event, but also a lone exception. While I do not (and cannot) contest the fidelity of this incident and admit this to be a fact, I find myself compelled to attempt to present a context to the cited event in the hope that it helps create a fair and a balanced portrait of the community. Knowing the historical context is vital to understanding as to how a peaceful community slipped into such a violent flashpoint.[58]

Close to eight decades[59] of peaceful existence despite extreme deprivation, neglect and abuse by State and non-State forces in independent India of the Lisu community went largely unnoticed by scholars, journalists and members of the intellectual community who perform a vital representational and image-building/shaping role. And yet, a lone incident is now cited and referenced. This piques me. Since this incident has now entered written records through government and media reports, future scholars and authors will conveniently cite this ad nauseam, thus acting as architects, at best unintentionally, of building a skewed and an unfairly biased portrait, even a violent one, of an otherwise peaceful community. Their decades of gentleness, resilience and peaceful conduct (in the face of loss and suffering), and a firm refusal to give in to the decades of coercions and monetary temptations by the various insurgent groups mushrooming in these wild jungles, barely merited a first-hand investigation[60] and certainly no appreciation. When the Lisus were unconstitutionally deprived of their Scheduled Tribe (ST) status (from 1978 until 2018) with periods of intermittent and random reinstatements and cancellations over the years, local politicians advised them to claim themselves to be 'Any Naga' belonging to the Naga tribe, so as to be able to enjoy benefits of existing tribal welfare policies. The Lisu leaders declined. They said, 'We are not Nagas, and so cannot principally take benefits by claiming to be members of another tribe.

57 Further reading: Sangno, Amar. 15 December 2020. 'Vijaynagar violence: Shooting two birds with one stone?'. *The Arunachal Times*. arunachaltimes.in/index.php/2020/12/15/vijaynagar-violence-shooting-two-birds-with-one-stone/.

58 Further reading: Rina, Tongam. 10 January 2021. 'The Assam Rifles ex-servicemen of Vijaynagar' *The Arunachal Times*. arunachaltimes.in/index.php/2021/01/10/the-assam-rifles-ex-servicemen-of-vijaynagar/.

59 Choudhury, S. Dutta. ed. 1980. *Gazetteer of India, Arunachal Pradesh: Tirap District*. Government of Arunachal Pradesh. p. 90.

60 Based on personal observations and interactions with community members in the field, 2013–19.

We are Lisus.' Off the record, several of these leaders had also shared with me that 'Had they claimed benefits as "Any Naga" they would have had to align with the Nagalim (Greater Nagaland) separatist cause—financially, as well as providing foot soldiers.'[61] The foresight of these elders might have saved the Lisu youth from getting waylaid towards a violent direction. Had those impressionable youths, fuming in anger over decades of the State neglecting their constitutional rights, been successfully lured to pick up arms, it is safe to say beyond doubt that the State apparatuses would have had a huge problem at their hands. That, however, is not the case, for the Lisus staunchly take pride in calling themselves 'Indian' and have unwaveringly followed the path of peace, despite the State barely deserving their patriotism.

Earlier, I had spoken of 'land' being a key factor in influencing tribal identity as well as conflicts. Verrier Elwin (1957) writes, 'To the tribal mind, our attitude about land and forests is as important as any scheme of development or education. The Kol insurrection of 1833 was caused by encroachment on tribal land. The Tamar rebellions, repeated seven times between 1789 and 1832, were primarily due to the illegal deprivation of their rights in land which Has, Mundas and Oraons had suffered.'[62] Enumerating examples from the Santal tribe, Elwin cites Rev. W.J. Culshaw:[63] 'The most powerful motive in Santal life is possession of the land which they till. Land belongs to those by whom the original clearings in the forest were made … No motive is so strong in a tribal people as the preservation of the life of the tribe and its mores, albeit the motive works for the most part at the unconscious level; and a Santal's land not only provides economic security, but is a powerful link with his ancestors. The land is a part of his spiritual as well as his economic heritage.' Alienation of tribes from their land has been a key reason for many violent uprisings in the past. Similar is the case with other indigenous communities, including the Lisus.

The State has, over the decades, taken away land from the Lisus, slowly driving them to frustration. Until May 1961, when Assam Rifles (AR) made its first reconnaissance mission under Operation Srijitga[64] to Dawodi (now Vijoynagar) led by Major Sumer Singh of 7th AR, the Indian government was largely unaware of the presence of Lisus in this region. At that time, the Indian government had no presence here and the India–Myanmar international border was yet to be demarcated, thus leaving the region completely ungoverned, porous and assumedly a no man's land. Following the government's policy of settling ex-servicemen in the border areas, between 1967 and 1971, 200 families of the Assam Rifles were settled in four batches across Dawodi and

[61] Personal conversations with several Lisu community leaders in March 2018.

[62] Elwin, Verrier. 1957. Reprinted 2016. *A Philosophy for NEFA*. Isha Books.

[63] Ibid. p. 15.

[64] arunachaltimes.in/index.php/2021/01/10/the-assam-rifles-ex-servicemen-of-vijoynagar/

several other villages. Each were given 11 acres land or lesser, but by removing the natives off their land. Friendly in nature, the Lisus assisted the Assam Rifles survey the area for international boundary demarcation in 1972, gave land for, and even assisted in the construction of the Advanced Landing Ground (ALG). The ALG till date remains the sole mode of transportation from here to the rest of India. Three such members of the Yobin community, including Akhi Yeliyeh Yobin, were honoured with gold medal citations on 20 February 2019 for their services in the international border demarcation. But as reward for their services, the Lisus were removed from their land and pushed further west. Later, General A.S. Guraya rechristened Dawodi as Vijoynagar, after his son Vijoy, and another village Pritnagar after his daughter, which in itself was a colonial act.

Much later in 1983, the Indian government declared 1,985 sq. km. of the jungles as Namdapha National Park & Tiger Reserve (NNP) without consulting or seeking the consent of the Lisus. Their voices never mattered. This land falls to the west of Shidi (now Gandhigram). This singular act turned the domicile status of the Lisu villages (that now fell within the park area) as illegal, stripping them of their right to stake claim to their native land. Overnight, those Lisus were called 'encroachers and poachers' on their own land, and those who lived outside the park's eastern periphery across villages like Gandhigram, Hazolo, Vijoynagar etc. were landlocked from both sides—park on the west and the international border on the east—pinning them down from all fronts. This is a bizarrely unique situation. It must be understood that NNP's existence meant that no permanent roads could be constructed to connect these outlying villages to the nearest town and administrative subdivision Miao, as well as to the rest of India. This led to the genesis of a great degree of suffering for especially the Lisus, but also the Nepali ex-servicemen settlers, though the latter enjoyed pensions and ration supplies. To illustrate the bizarreness of the situation, it is worth noting that the price of 1 kilogram salt generally worth Rs 25, costs anything between Rs 80–150 in this region, a three–five-fold increment. The same goes for the price of almost every other commodity in this region. Most cannot afford these exorbitant costs. Thus, they trek all the way down to Miao, purchase essential daily provisions and carry them back on head load, usually trekking for anywhere between two to five days with the 30–50 kilogram weight. A noticeable impact of this can be witnessed in their food—as one moves further towards Dawodi, salt and oil content in their food reduces.

Subsistence farmers, the Lisus earlier practised *jhum* cultivation (slash and burn) but have now largely settled for wet rice cultivation on the banks of the Noa-Dihing river. The hilly terrain gives poor returns and the rice fields beside the river get swept away as the river changes course annually. In an opinion piece titled 'Fading fauna, forgotten people' for *Down To Earth* in 2005, Aparajita Dutta of the Nature Conservation Foundation wrote, 'Based on recent mapping, the average landholding for rice farming in Gandhigram is 1.4 hectare; this is simply not enough.'[65] As of 2018–19, the Lisus have complained of a significant drop in annual rice yields.[66] As a result, they now find themselves greatly reluctant to part with their rice stocks for frequenting passers-by.

Over the decades, the Lisus continuously found their land taken away from them, at first by State coercive measures and later, allegedly, by the Nepali settlers expanding their grasp over more land in the Vijoynagar area. The hilly terrain and lately, the river's course changing has led to the loss of land, thus adding to their food security woes. Lisus allege that the non-indigenous settlers with the help of local administrative officials have made permanent address proofs that help them stake claim to permanent domicile status, thus contesting the Lisu ancestral claims to these lands. Liahey Ngwazah, the founder of Yobindreams,[67] in an article titled 'Yobin youths don't deserve prolonged detention' for *Arunachal Times* in 2021, writes,

> In Arunachal Pradesh, panchayat nomination is possible only by the local indigenous residents as per the existing rules (ref: extraordinary gazette notification of GoAP, No 261, Vol XXVI, Naharlagun, 25 June, 2019, amendment of Form 4. 9. iii). However, in Vijoynagar circle, the same panchayat raj has been wrongly extended to the non-indigenous settlers comprising retired Assam Rifles families, comprising five communities, and mostly of Nepali-speaking pensioner families.[68]

He further writes,

> To correct this anomaly, the Yobin tribe of Vijoynagar has been appealing to the authorities concerned for several years. Numerous representations were submitted, five peaceful rallies were held, and a record six-day hunger strike was held at Itanagar in December of 2019. The fasting was ended as the panchayat minister promised to correct what was wrong with the PR affairs.[69]

In 2020, not only did the administration and local politicians fail to take ameliorative measures to stub the inflating tensions between the two communities, but they also gave the lone ticket for Zilla Parishad Member (a position of influence in the local panchayati raj level) from Vijoynagar Circle to a settler named Sujatha Rai, in contravention of the aforecited extraordinary gazette

---

[65] Dutta, Aparajita. 15 September 2005. 'Fading fauna, forgotten people'. DownToEarth. www.downtoearth.org.in/coverage/fading-fauna-forgotten-people-10103. Accessed on 13 April 2022.

[66] Personal conversations with members of the Lisu community across Agohomu, Shidi, Shidi-kha, Hazolo and Dawodi villages, Jan-March' 2018.

[67] Yobindreams is a blog run by Liahey Ngwazah reporting on the life of the Lisus and their struggles in the Vijoynagar Circle. AP. yobindreams.wordpress.com.

[68] Ngwazah, Liahey. 28 June 2021. 'Yobin youths don't deserve prolonged detention'. *The Arunachal Times*. arunachaltimes.in/index.php/2021/06/28/yobin-youths-dont-deserve-prolonged-detention/. Accessed on 13 March 2022.

[69] Ibid.

notification that clearly states that only 'ordinary indigenous local residents'[70] can contest Panchayati Raj elections. The intent was clearly read as mala fide, meant to suppress the Lisus' right to self-determination even at the grassroots level.

The non-indigenous Nepali settlers perhaps feel the need to expand to be able to sustain their growing populations, amplifying the pressure on the land as a resource. The Lisus allege that the settlers have been encroaching on their traditional lands.[71] Further, existing laws state that non-tribals cannot be extended permanent domicile status in tribal areas of Arunachal Pradesh, nor can they be permitted to participate in local governance, including voting. Today, the population explosion of the Nepalis residing in Vijoynagar area very well contests the entire population of the Lisus spread across Vijoynagar administrative circle. These have added further stress on the land and access to resources for a community that was already living in these 'shatter zones or zones of refuge'[72] in a region that Roychowdhury aptly cites as 'prisoners of geography'. It is admittedly true that even the Nepali settlers here endure hardships akin to the Lisus, and both the communities must receive relief through Central and state development schemes, like the construction of a permanent 157 kilometre Miao–Vijoynagar Road.[73] However, the Lisus feel very threatened, and are literally sandwiched between NNP on the western flank and the ingression of Nepali settlers from the eastern edge of India–Myanmar international border, not to mention the presence of insurgent rebels. For decades now, the Lisus lament being caught in a bind from both ends, each allegedly attempting to remove the Lisus off their ancestral lands, perhaps validly raising within them the same question: 'Where do I belong?'. Elwin, in his book, cites Dr J.H. Hutton, 'The excellent original intentions of Government to protect the people were eroded by the tide of civilisation, so that gradually all the best land passed into the hands of the outsiders.'[74]

The continuous and sustained repression of Lisu voices, annexation of their lands, and the deprivation of their constitutional rights brought this peaceful community to this violent flashpoint (December 2020), an event cited in Roychodhury's essay. How did their decades of peaceful cohabitation get outweighed under the burden of a lone anomalous incident? The primary problem perhaps exists in the weightage urban societies accord to written accounts over centuries of oral knowledge transfer.

---

[70] The Arunachal Pradesh Gazette Extraordinary No. 261. Vol. XXVI. Naharlagun. 25 June 2019. Government of Arunachal Pradesh. Department of Panchayati Raj, Itanagar.

[71] Ngwayeti Yobin of Meludi village vide a letter dated 10 January 2017 addressed to the Circle Officer Vijoynagar had complained of the violation of the status quo order (dated 30 March 2016) issued against encroachment of his land made by residents of Ramnagar village. I am in possession of a copy of this letter and related proceedings.

[72] Scott. 2009. *The Art of Not Being Governed*. p. 7.

[73] The 157 kilometre long Miao–Vijoynagar Road is currently witnessing some construction work under the leadership of the present Chief Minister of AP, Pema Khandu.

[74] Ibid. p. 15.

Evidence of similar colonial misadventures are rife throughout India's post-Independent history. It is pivotal to acknowledge 'internal colonialism', including a paternalistic gaze in governance, but also in artistic and art historical scholarships dealing with such communities living on the fringes. Asim Maitra, the author of *Profile of a Little-Known Tribe*, was the lone anthropologist to have taken the pain of going and living amongst the Lisus for a considerable amount of time, resulting in the first and only book on them till date, besides the environmentalists and conservationists for whom botany, ornithology and zoology were of primary importance.

India's first Prime Minister Jawaharlal Nehru wrote,

> I am alarmed where I see—not only in this country but in other great countries too—how anxious people are to shape others according to their own image or likeness, and to impose on them their particular way of living. We are welcome to our way of living, but why impose it on others? This applies equally to national and international fields. In fact, there would be more peace in the world if people were to desist from imposing their way of living on other people and countries. I am not at all sure which is the better way of living, the tribal or our own. In some respects I am quite certain theirs is better. Therefore, it is grossly presumptuous on our part to approach them with an air of superiority, to tell them how to behave or what to do and what not to do. There is no point trying to make them a second-rate copy of ourselves.[75]

If a contemporary history has to be written, especially about communities that have gone largely under-represented, misrepresented or unrepresented, do we artists and historians bear the responsibility of devising new strategies to aid reimagination so as to correct historical wrongs that risk becoming staple narratives? Though in the context of climate change, Amitav Ghosh raises a pertinent question:

> When future generations look back upon the Great Derangement they will certainly blame the leaders and politicians of this time for their failure to address the climate crisis. But they may well hold artists and writers equally culpable—for the imagining of possibilities is not, after all, the job of politicians and bureaucrats.[76]

Though largely subsistence farmers, the Lisus do negotiate today's monetised ecosystem with a modest degree of material and economic aspirations, especially the youth. However, they also hold onto their ancient beliefs. Their creation tales and folklores, just like that of many other indigenous communities, bear similar motifs alluding to their entwined connections with nature and its myriad elements, which can be witnessed in their daily life. For example, a

---

[75] Ibid.

[76] Ghosh, Amitav. 2016. *The Great Derangement*. (Gurgaon: Penguin Random House India). p. 181.

patient reflection on their belief in the existence of *Maamimu* might reveal to us that their connection with nature certainly transcends anthropocentrism. They believe that 'a parallel invisible world' called Maamimu coexists in the same 'time-space continuum' and the invisible human-like living beings there are called *Musi*.[77] For each Lisu, they believe, there is a similar looking Musi in Maamimu, and should one suffer or die, the same fate meets the other, alluding to the 'bush soul' concept—interconnectedness with nature and its myriad nonhuman living and non-living elements. Invisible portals connect both worlds and stories of interactions with the Musi exists in the Lisu world, though not commonly so. Their relationship with the forest and its innumerable elements are influenced by similar belief systems, making them more respectful of nature and its cohabitants. They straddle between the modern as well as the mythical worlds. Cohabiting symbiotically with nature as a self-sufficient community and as 'mythical entities',[78] the Lisus are harbingers of hope. Their gentle stewardship of life amidst the darkness of the forest is illuminating. Here, I must point out that I have never noticed superstitious practices amongst the Lisus; perhaps curbed by the presence of the Church.

In many classic familial visual representations, including the 'Migrant Mother' (1936) by Dorothea Lange (the documentary photograph bears similarities and thus references the iconic painting of the 'Madonna and Child'), the maternal figure has often been portrayed as the key parental figure, even holy. In the case of the 'Migrant Mother', the absence of a paternal figure is believed to have influenced American men to step in with their support for Florence Owens Thompson. In 'Waiting in the Forest' (2018), referencing the Lisu family units, the maternal figure is missing and the adult male emerges as the sole caregiver of the children in the photograph. In the material reality of their lives, it is not uncommon to lose loved ones to unforeseen tragedies, including diseases, fatal accidents caused during treks or foraging activities in the wild. Another commonly witnessed reality is the tender and gentle nature of male parental figures, not just towards their own biological children but towards others as well. After all, the ability to love, protect and care for their children is not endemic to mothers.

Whilst the set of images dealing with family as a unit in *Imagined Homeland* perhaps act as vessels bearing testimonies to filial qualities as well as tenderness, resilience and vulnerabilities, is it possible that they also encourage an ecocentric[79] viewpoint? Going beyond recording a mere physical likeness, and hinting towards their state of mind, feelings and at times, aspirations,

[77] The pronunciation in Lisu language will be different than how it phonetically reads here. It sounds like '*myiss*'.

[78] Ramanujan, A.K. 2009. *Folktales from India* (New Delhi: Penguin Books India). p. xx.

[79] Ecocentrism intrinsically values nature, taking a much wider view of the world than anthropocentrism, which sees the human race as the most valuable than all other organisms. Further reading: mahb.stanford.edu/blog/statement-ecocentrism/

they also allude to their relationship with nature and animals (coexisting, not mollycoddling) as well as the modern times. 'Waiting in the Forest' (2018), 'Three Tea Cups, Father and the Child' (2018), 'Children explore the mythical forest' (2018), 'Exodus- II' (2019) and 'Jemana Yobin, Yuleba and his tortoise in their Pineapple Garden' (2019) are few such examples. Many of these images are mimetic of the human position before the might of a dense forest that is not only wild and powerful, but also one that also provides for most of their needs. The sitters are thus modestly sized, cohabiting in these spaces.

Posthumanities scholar Eduardo Kohn writes, 'How other kinds of beings see us matters. That other kinds of beings see us changes things.'[80] Indigenous communities living closer to nature have always been aware of this interdependent relationship between themselves, nonhuman living beings and other elements of nature. Kohn argues that, 'Anthropology cannot limit itself just to exploring how people from different societies might happen to represent them as doing so. Such encounters with other kinds of beings force us to recognise the fact that seeing, representing, and perhaps knowing, even thinking, are not exclusively human affairs.'[81] I have avoided sharing this on formal platforms until now, but during my years of stay inside the forest, I have had mystical encounters that made me distinctly aware of the presence of elements otherwise invisible to the bare eyes. It also made me aware that I was being watched. One such evening was when a young girl had passed on. I saw nothing, but distinctly heard and felt *their* presence. I have not been able to cease wondering if this was a way for the forest and its invisible residents to communicate with me and assert themselves in the making of *Imagined Homeland*. It was a communication, for sure, except that I lack competency in completely understanding this language. Vivid dreams followed, once fear had subsided. And it was in these dreams that many of the scenes for *Imagined Homeland* were revealed to me, including 'Eliza at the Gate' (2019) and 'Ngwalidew and the Poral' (2018).

Roychowdhury very generously writes in her essay, 'Forest, animal, human and modern gadgets exist seamlessly in De's magical world.' I, on the other hand, perceive it as 'their magical world', one I was allowed to witness. Each of these elements cited above that have entered my photographic frames exist in the Lisu world, and should perhaps be considered as the 'Lisu's magical world' instead of mine. My role was limited to being a keen observer (and partaker) of their world, whilst searching for an appropriate vocabulary to tell the story of their 'belongingness'.

---

[80] Kohn, Eduardo. 2013. *How Forests Think* (USA: University of California Press).

[81] Ibid.

Acknowledgements

I am grateful to Ranu Roychowdhury for her critical inputs to this essay. I remain particularly indebted to my Lisu friends, Avia Ngwazah and Liahey Ngwazah, for reviewing this essay and supporting me with additional relevant documents, as well as to Phuyosa Yobin for an in-person oral feedback.

7

Belongings and albums (re)visited: Visualising materiality:

Images as Digital Objects

Chinar Shah

In the second month of 2016, my parents bought their first new car. All of our extended family members owned at least one car by then, so this was considered a rather late decision on our part. Before this, whenever we needed a car, we would borrow it from a close relative. Often, if a relative was going on a day-long trip because they had the luxury of a car, they would ask my parents to tag along. When my brother got married in 2001, an occasion on which the bridegroom must travel in a well-decorated car, we borrowed a white Honda City from my grandmother's brother. 2016 was finally the year when, according to my father, a family crisis required us to buy a car. He insisted that we buy a Maruti Alto—a true middle-class car, as he would say—as the older staple Maruti 800 was no longer available in the market. A Maruti Alto was considered an appropriate upgrade to his Bajaj scooter. To my father's great disappointment, us kids unanimously vetoed the true middle-class car, and we bought a Hyundai i10 Grand instead. On a coldish Ahmedabad winter night, my brother and I went to the showroom to pick up our car. As we were getting ready to drive it home, we were asked to pose in front of the new car that had been bedecked with a pink ribbon. The car dealer fired a flash and within minutes, we not only had our car keys, but also a framed photograph of us bearing ghostly smiles in front of the car. We took this souvenir home, and my father put away this photograph in his personal drawer. Maybe he looked at it every now and then while he was alive, I don't know. I found it in his drawer a few years after his death in 2016—a car he briefly enjoyed and a photograph he kept close to himself. This personal story is not why I am writing this essay, but it did set me on a curious journey of thinking about this image that acquired a rather lonely, liminal space in a corner drawer, as an outsider to our family albums.

Overview

The primary focus of this essay is the 'public' life of family photographs taken by car dealers commemorating new purchases, and the context of their production and circulation, which form a framework within which our daily experiences are mediated. In car dealership showrooms, the car owners and the salespeople pose in front of the newly purchased vehicle as they hold a giant car key—a pose similar to when trophies or awards are being given out. These images are then circulated through multiple channels in private and public domains—very commonly via WhatsApp or the car dealers' social media profiles. I identify this phenomenon of photographs taken at the dealer's showroom as a rare instance where family images are not only stored and viewed privately but are part of a wider circulation and viewership over which the 'family' has no control.

To examine this idea further, the essay also looks at product review images from the online retailer Amazon, where users regularly upload family photographs and selfies. This instance of family photographs circulating digitally through an e-commerce website is juxtaposed against some of the more personal experiences of the circulation of such images. The breadth of these examples shows that the production of images is not a singular event that occurs in a camera. It shifts the line of inquiry to a broader understanding of production as a continuous event that is intrinsically linked to the circulation of images. Central to this essay's arguments are the dimensions of consumer behaviour that pertain to the sharing of images, the digital context of their circulation, the content of these shared visuals, the platform via which they are shared and the implications of circulating images.

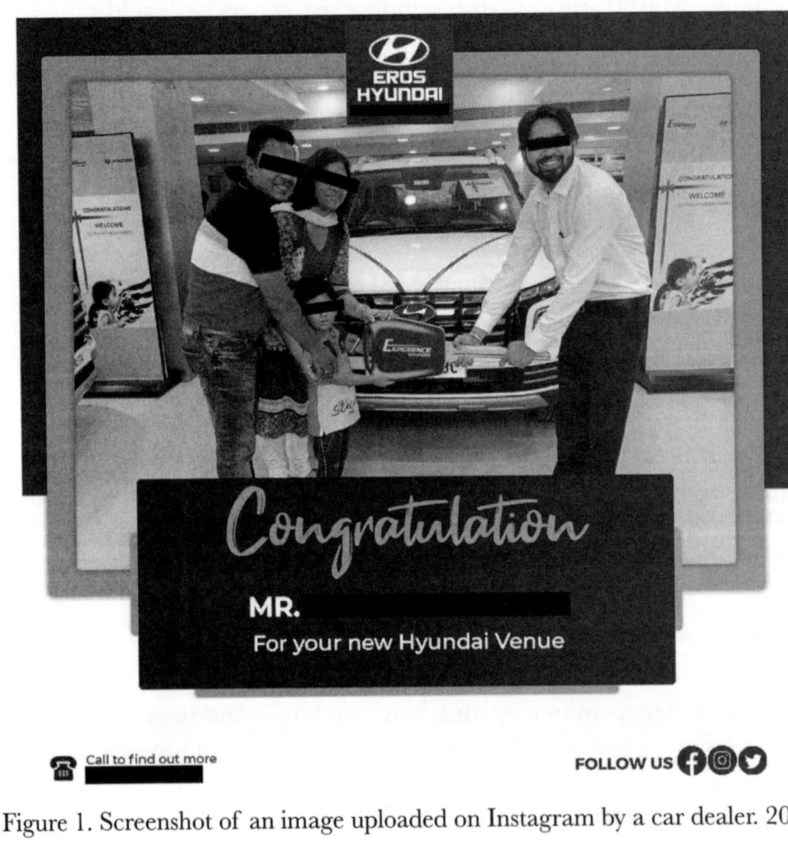

Figure 1. Screenshot of an image uploaded on Instagram by a car dealer. 2022.

For the last three years, I have been collecting photographs of the moment commemorating the purchase of a new car, shot and mostly circulated by car dealers through their social media accounts. Car companies, aware of the consumers' latent desires of owning a car, turn these images into unique vehicles for advertising by imbuing the family portrait with public meaning. The family photograph shot at the car showroom—a space that becomes a temporary photo studio—is a multipurpose image that eulogises both the family that has acquired a new consumer product and the car dealer. The family members become brand ambassadors suited to advertise for the car. In turn, the car as a part of the family portrait, becomes a trope for the family to present itself as successful and happy. Thus, besides being personal in nature, these images are media images that enter domestic life through the backdoor, without requiring any prime real estate or billboard space. They articulate the juxtaposition of family photographs on a consumer economy.

#newcar: Key to Success?

It is important at this juncture to spend some time describing these dealer-orchestrated family photographs of a new car purchase, particular to their narrow time and context of production and circulation. The theatrics of these images are well-planned, even if they are mostly poorly photographed. Sometimes, the car is placed in front of a printed flex banner that carries the logo of the brand and of the dealership, and perhaps a message saying 'Congratulations!' in a celebratory type. The car is decked up with ribbons or flowers, ready to begin its new life in the family. Covering the entire car with a shiny cloth and then unveiling it for the benefit of the camera is also a popular ritual. The family arranges itself perfectly in front of the car and an agent presents them with a giant car key made of foam board. Apart from this giant, phallic car key that appears in almost all such images, other props such as balloons, a cake, flowers or *pooja thalis* also feature in them. Sometimes, a certain regional flavour and local aesthetic are added to the photograph.[1] The event itself is often a family affair, where most of the family members go to pick up the car and get themselves photographed. My informal conversations with a few friends who went to pick up their cars alone revealed that in these instances, the car agents enquired about missing family members or spouses, making assumptions about their marital status and/or other familial relations.

Once the photographs are taken, they circulate through multiple channels. It is common practice for the dealers to frames these images and present them as gifts to the new car owners. The photo frames often bear the logos of the car company and of the dealership. Many car companies use digital backgrounds onto which these images are superimposed. These digital backgrounds vary in

---

[1] For instance, I noticed car dealers handing out turbans (the local headgear) to men in Rajasthan before taking photographs.

nature, but often carry similar symbols, colours or typeface. The ornamental type and the colours of these digital backgrounds loudly proclaim a 'happy' theme, as if to confirm the joy felt by the owners of the new car as they smile from ear to ear.

Today, most car dealers share these images on their social media handles. The family thus circulates on social media without having much control over this. Ben Burbridge in *Photography After Capitalism* notes, 'Social media platforms have not only allowed for, but have expressly encouraged, the public display of what, not long ago, were perceived to be private moments.'[2] Consent to circulate these images across the internet is casually taken and often assumed. Of late, along with the images, short videos are also created and circulated, with the intention of exemplifying customer satisfaction both with the company and with the agent. Knowingly and/or unknowingly, through these visuals, the family becomes a promoter of the brand of their car, coaxing others to trust and choose the same.

Figure 2 was accompanied by following text on Instagram:

> This is just the beginning...
> Always grateful for the love and blessings of my parents.
> #tuchwood #xuv700 #xuv #mahindra #car #mahindraxuv700
> #newcar #koncept #vehicle
> @kuunaal_chopra

These images resemble those typically taken at award ceremonies in terms of their visual aesthetics that foreground the moment when the trophies are received and photographs are posed for. However, unlike contestants who receive an award in an individual capacity or as part of a group not necessarily biologically related to each other, the reception of a car is a family affair. The car is an extension of the household, owned, used and looked after by the family at large as a collective asset. But quite like the photographs taken at award ceremonies, these images too are traditionally not part of a family album. Instead, they end up on a showcase or achieve a rather complex status as they get circulated on various digital platforms by the car dealers. The occasion is regarded as a moment of having

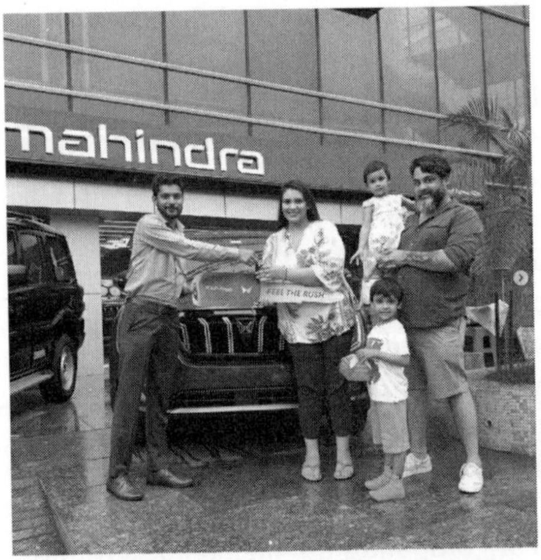

Figure 2. Medhavini Rai Chopra and her family buying a new car. Uploaded on personal Instagram, 2022.

[2] Burbridge, Ben. 2012. *Photography After Capitalism* (MIT Press). p. 52.

achieved something, quite like winning a race or an art competition, where the image is deemed worthy of public consumption.

The symbolic role of the exaggerated giant key reminds us of popular phrases like 'the key to success'. In India, buying a car is directly connected to social mobility, with undertones of caste and class hierarchies. One of the reasons why the Tata Nano didn't succeed, for example, was because it was advertised as the true middle-class car.[3] The 'cheapest' car did not entice the Indian consumer, who aspired to move up the social ladder; the low-priced Tata Nano hindered these aspirations and did not quite feel like a 'key to success'. The giant key made of cheap foam board is a metaphor for having achieved something big, similar to the big cheque handed to the winners of the popular quiz show *Kaun Banega Crorepati* (Who Wants to Be a Millionaire?).[4] The size of the key thus has symbolic value, however unwieldy it may be to hold in the photograph. Many awkward poses often result within the frame, with no Amitabh Bachchan at the dealer's showroom to direct the family members to pose with the giant key and show them where the camera is. The long key with one pointed end creates confusion as to how and where to hold it, resulting in awkward poses where people end up holding the two ends of the key as a prop. Ironically enough, the failed theatrics 'enhance' the overall imperfection of the photograph. The visual relationship established between the buyers and the car dealer/agent is separated by the company logo and the giant key, on one side of which stands the official-looking dealer and on the other, stand the buyers. If a large family comes to purchase the car, this results in a massive imbalance in the frame, with too many people trying to fit on one side of the key and the frame. The dealer/agent has to tactfully enter the frame of the family photograph for the exaggeration to be successful. The key and other props, such as a cake, ribbons, scissors to cut the ribbon, etc., play an important role in aiding this montage, since they frame the entry of an outsider—the car agent who embodies and completes this spectacle.

Car Showrooms as Photo Studios

Car dealership showrooms thus turn into temporary studio spaces, where the moment of buying of a car is visually exaggerated and 'performed' for the benefit of the camera. Props are used to aid this performance, quite like in a

[3] Tata Nano was a car launched in 2009 and advertised heavily as the cheapest car in India. The targeted consumer segment for this car was the urban middle-class that did not own a car and relied on scooters. This was seen as an entry-level car in the most affordable segment. However, the difference in cost between the Tata Nano and some of the other cars in the same segment was not as high as advertised. This, combined with technical problems with the car, eventually led to reduced demand. However, right from the beginning, the car did not attract a huge consumer base, owing to its being advertised as the cheapest car, something that did not appeal to those who aspired for social upward mobility with their consumer behaviour.

[4] The Indian spin-off of the original American reality TV show, hosted by the famous Bollywood actor Amitabh Bachchan.

studio setting. While the exaggeration and performance in a photo studio often transport the subject to another location like Paris or Dubai with backdrops of the Eiffel Tower or the Burj Khalifa, this temporary studio at the car showroom does not aim to transport its subjects anywhere. The scene is an exaggeration of itself, transporting people into a self-referential symbolic order, rather than a physical location.

These advert-ready images are mostly shot by one of the car dealership agents. They are low-resolution images with dubious framing and clashing light sources, given that car showrooms typically have very bright lights to highlight the cars on display. While camera technology is quite ubiquitous, taking images in difficult lighting conditions takes a good deal of skill. However, the stylistic aspects of the image do not matter in this case, as long as the content of the frame achieves its use value. While many professionally shot stock images of families buying a new car appear in high resolution, the images of real families, even though lacking the visual quality of stock photography, become a way for potential buyers to form aspirational relationships with the subjects. The people in the images are not hired actors who can successfully demonstrate the exhilaration of the moment with their bodies, groomed to meet the demands of the media or fashion industries. The amateur quality of the images, with their imperfections in terms of framing, lighting, awkward poses, facial expressions and families huddled together, become part of an advertising strategy as they portray a certain authenticity. The people in these images are not like the doctors in a Colgate toothpaste advertisement where the performance is shot so expertly that the viewers cannot distinguish between the actor and the real doctor. The imperfections of a car showroom photo separate the so-called 'reality' from acting, which is a framework of advertising that has gained great popularity on social media sites today.[5]

All family images retain their privacy to different degrees, holding the potential to become public in specific contexts. Making an image public is not always a very conscious decision and is often driven by where and how it enters the outside world. While family albums remain tucked away in cupboards, the image of buying a car often finds its way into a display case along with other images, ornaments or showpieces, open to viewing by visitors, extended family and the inhabitants of the home. Many such images are also showcased on individual social media accounts. However, the moment car dealers circulate images on their social media accounts, these seemingly private images acquire

[5] Online clothing brands, especially those that advertise primarily through Instagram and Facebook, often post images of their customers wearing their products. Even if the brands use social media influencers to advertise on these platforms, the visual language has shifted to home-style, casual aesthetics. I cannot delve into this within the scope of this essay; however, it is worth looking through the social media accounts of celebrities such as Kareena Kapoor and the use of home-style videos in advertisements that also use the celebrity's personal life (marriage, pregnancy, children) as a way to collapse the fantasy of the product with the reality of the celebrity's life.

a very different kind of public status. They are no longer images to be flaunted in a showcase in a domestic space, but become one of the ways in which advertising functions within consumer culture. As Burbridge says, 'Capitalist realism demands we make commodities of ourselves; that we treat ourselves and others as an image.'[6] The 'family' becomes an active contributor to a digital economy, a bearer of multiple public meanings, along with becoming a different kind of data to be monetised. Before I unpack some of these thoughts, I want to talk about the public nature of something supposedly private.

Family Albums: An Extended Practice

Family albums mostly refer to a book-like object filled with images of various members of the family, sometimes organised around a specific event. Though it is mostly thought of as a physical object, family albums also move onto digital platforms where they tend to mimic the album in its physicality.[7] Family albums are intimate and private, filled with memories of many said/unsaid things. Here, privacy does not mean secrecy, but something that remains in the family. The album is neither thought of as having monetary value nor as something that an outsider to the family would necessarily have an interest in. In that sense, it is an object of affect and memory between friends, family and loved ones. However, family images have been part of the public domain for a very long time, much before the internet and various social media platforms came into existence, so to assume that all family images are private and only belong in family albums would be a mistake. Family photographs have often found a home outside of the family and it is not a new thing for images to circulate outside without the family's consent. We have to begin to think about family albums as extended practice, not as objects sitting in the dark cupboards of our homes.

Traditional albums in their physical form continue to disappear with passing time, since more and more images are stored on the Cloud and in other digital spaces. Rather than having albums that occupy a physical space, especially in small houses, people prefer to store images digitally. This is not to say that albums have disappeared completely. Images from weddings and other important events still condense into albums, though the form of such albums has changed significantly with digital editing, which gives more space to create a book-like form, where the foreground and the background tend to merge into each other. However, images of holidays and other everyday moments find less and less space in a physical album. With our constantly evolving social

---

[6] Ibid. p. 63.

[7] For example, on Facebook, it is possible to create an 'album' which borrows the term from what was once a physical object and continues to perform the same purpose. While sharing images over Google Drive or other such platforms, people often say, 'I have shared the album with you'. So the album has moved to the digital space almost seamlessly, even though there are many new terms that one may use to share images online.

behaviour on the internet, the notion of family images and family albums also gets redefined. The 'family' has grown beyond merely kinship bonds to include communities based on consumer interests and categories that predetermine the audience for the family images. With this, family albums have become extended sites for new relationships, contributions, community and surveillance, all existing within the networked culture of global neoliberal societies. These contemporary photo histories also hold affective memories in their production and circulation, with the possibility of sharing ratings, comments and reviews. It is therefore important to see family albums as an extended photographic practice that encompasses much more than the album or the photograph as a two-dimensional visual object.

Two instances come to mind that illustrate this. In February 2021, I was practising my new camera mount flash on the beach in Pondicherry, when I encountered a family trying to fit into a selfie directed by the youngest family member. The grandfather gestured to me to take a picture of them as soon as he noticed my big camera and even bigger flash. Unsure of my portraiture skills, especially since I had just acquired the flash that very day, I clicked a few images. It was a good opportunity for me to practise with people willing to come in front of my camera. The entire family gathered to see the images quickly and thanked me profusely. No one asked me to send them the images that I took, nor did they try to take the image from me then and there. They just wanted me to take a picture of them as a family without even wanting a copy of it. I'm still unsure about why it was important for them to be photographed by me when they were already taking images of themselves on a mobile phone

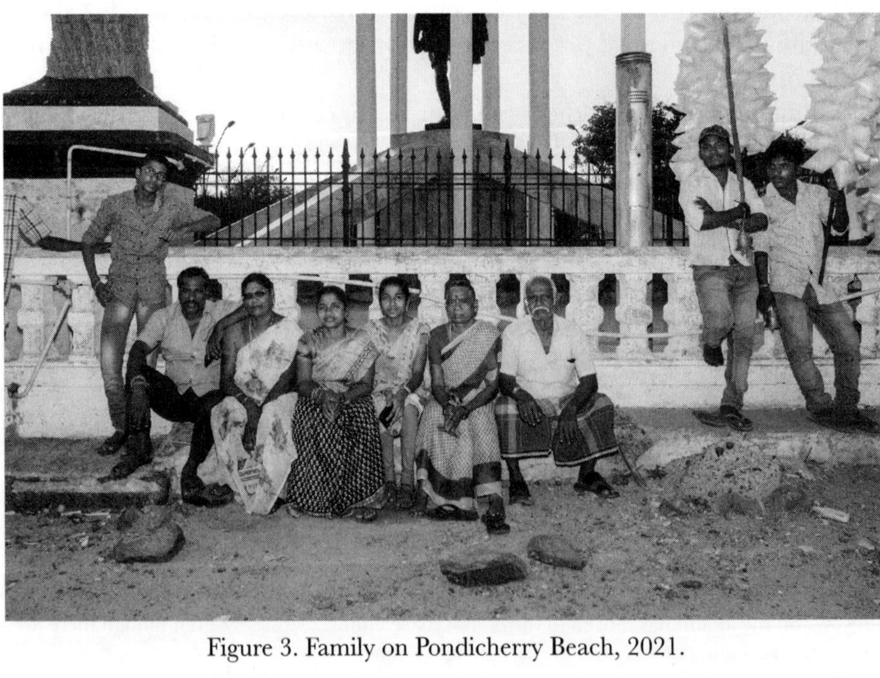

Figure 3. Family on Pondicherry Beach, 2021.

camera. Maybe it was because they thought I had a better camera. But then why not ask for the photograph? Maybe the idea of being photographed is more gratifying than the photograph itself. I can only speculate about this. However, one thing is certain—if you are a photographer in India, this may not be a novel experience for you. In this instance, a family moment on the beach was recorded and stored on a stranger's hard drive. Thus, the impulsive link between privacy and photography becomes rather tenuous, as family albums extend beyond the family more often than we imagine.

I counter this story with one where a family photograph was reclaimed from the photographer several years after its making. Sometime in the 1980s, on a vacation to Matheran, Maharashtra, my parents hired a local photographer to take a few images of them. The photographer promised to deliver the prints at the train station on the day of their departure. To their chagrin, the photographer never showed up. A few years later, when my uncle was travelling to Matheran, my father entrusted him with the task of visiting the studio and claiming the images from them. To my uncle's surprise, he found my parents' pictures in the display showcase up front in the studio. Since then, it has been a joke in the family that '*Satishbhai ane Pannaben to Matheran ma tagata hata*' ('Satishbhai and Pannaben have been hanging in Matheran'). The breach of privacy and trust by the photographer was eventually met with humour, acceptance and the satisfaction at receiving the images after all those years. I am recounting some of these instances to reify how family images have found themselves in the archives of non-family members, and sometimes have been used as commodities.

A more recent example of family images finding their way into the public domain is that of images uploaded as a part of product reviews on the website of the online retailer Amazon, and on other such commercial websites. Amazon

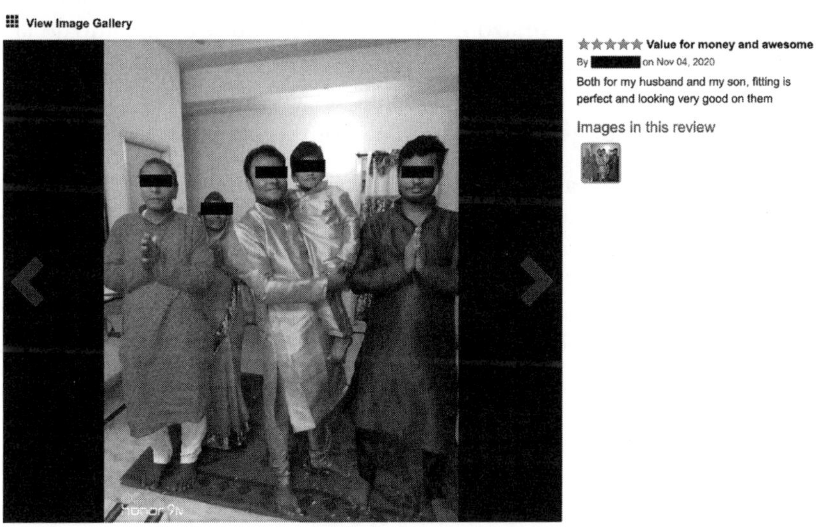

Figure 4. Screenshot of Amazon product review.

offers its clients the feature of uploading images and videos along with written reviews of the product(s) they have purchased. Upon closely looking through images uploaded by Amazon users, one finds many examples of domestic and supposedly private environments being photographed and shared by users. Consumers photograph products as used in their own domestic spaces, such as in the bedroom, the living room or the bathroom, and upload them on Amazon. Thus, a viewer has access to not only visuals of the product, its packaging, its unboxing and its operation, but also of someone's bed, dirty laundry, clean laundry, choice of furniture and much more.

A curious set of images I found among these reviews were selfies or self-portraits. Many people post pictures of themselves with the product, often wearing it—in the case of clothing or jewellery. In a rare case, a wedding portrait was uploaded with other family members in the frame as well, as the user wore a garment bought on Amazon. These are not images uploaded on social networking sites such as Facebook or Instagram, which have in any case become extended digital spaces to the home and personal archives to share family photographs. Nor are these images generated for a personal blog, a website or a YouTube channel. Though all these platforms are owned by a few multinational companies that monetise data in a similar fashion, the family images that become a part of product reviews directly acquire an exchange value as an image. Here, the subjectivity mediated by a network society is the consumer who is self-consuming the product and the platform, and in turn becoming consumable data. Fredrick Jameson, in a 2013 lecture titled 'The Aesthetics of Singularity' says that the ways in which we once consumed the automobile for its libidinal, symbolic and practical use value, has changed to us now consuming both the form and the content of communication. He says, 'We not only use technology, we consume it. We consume its exchange value along with its more symbolic essence.'[8]

Amazon claims ownership of all the data on their website. Thus, these reviews and images are owned by Amazon, which are all products of the unpaid labour of its millions of users. Each review with an image adds value to Amazon itself as a product, irrespective of how many stars the review offers to the saleable object. Talking about harvesting information online, Burbridge says,

> More fundamentally, advertisers pay to access the attention we devote to photographs and, particularly, the ability to manipulate desires facilitated by harvesting user data. Every time a photograph is uploaded, tagged, shared, viewed, liked, geo-tagged and commented on, our preferences, relationships, and social networks become clearer. When algorithms survey what we do, what we like, who we like to do it with, they get better at encouraging us to want stuff, whether sports shoes or presidential candidates.[9]

---

[8] Jameson, Fredric. 9 May 2013. 'The Aesthetics of Singularity: Time and Event in Postmodernity' [video]. *Youtube*. Uploaded by SoCuMUniMainz. www.youtube.com/watch?v=qh79_zwNI_s&t=3097s. Accessed 11 July 2022.

[9] Burbridge. 2012. *Photography After Capitalism*. p. 89.

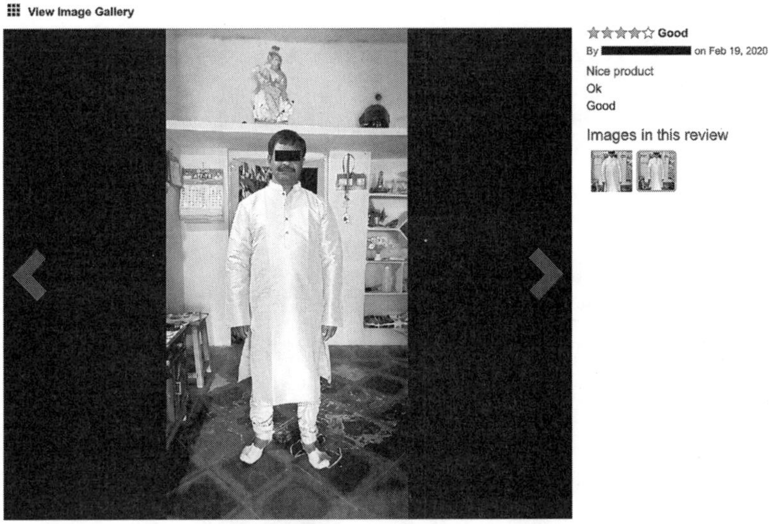

Figure 5. Screenshot of Amazon product review.

The more data online users generate, the more the platform attracts customers who will also participate in furthering the data drive. Jodi Dean in her lecture, 'The Limits of the Web in an Age of Communicative Capitalism' talks about 'the change in the form of our utterances from messages to contributions', where communication is no longer about being a message to 'elicit responses'. All communication is a form of contribution to a data flow where the 'use value' of a message shifts to an 'exchange value'. Burbridge notes, 'Even when the online world is understood to be inherently performative, it is the consistency of individuals' performances in particular contexts or situations that allows sociological patterns to be identified, specific demographics exposed and common desires to be exploited.'[10]

Thus, the family photographs on Amazon or those taken with new cars are not just portraitures, selfies or wedding images, but part of communicative capitalism destined to fulfil neoliberal agendas. Everyday images and activity on the internet become raw data to be stored, analysed, accumulated and monetised without the knowledge or agency of those who produced the data about their lives. This form of separation is very close to Marx's theory of alienation. The producers of the images or the subjects within the images are alienated from the product of their labour. As soon as the image becomes data, it transforms into an alien form and comes back as a product with the potential to oppress and manipulate consumer behaviour in unexpected ways. This is the case even though there is no way to comprehend or trace how the image metamorphises into data and how wide its reach is.

[10] Ibid. p. 100.

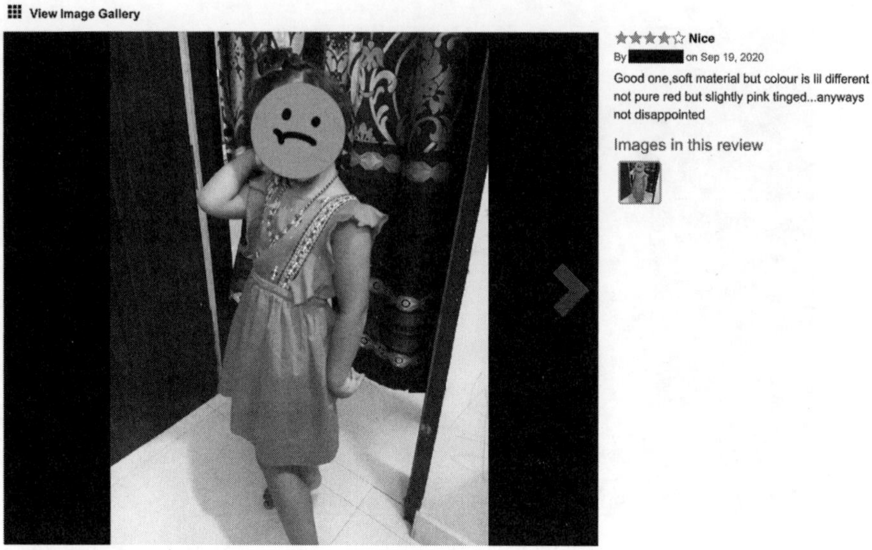

Figure 6. Screenshot of Amazon product review. Identity masked by the reviewer.

Concluding Remarks

Social inequalities prevail all over the world, not just in India, and aspirations of greater social integration have often found expression through consumer culture which helps people renegotiate their 'ancient bonds of dependence' or 'bring about the desire for a better position within existing local hierarchies'.[11] It is often not a privilege to have access to camera technology today, as most people have phones with an inbuilt camera. But the record of a slice of life that gets shared has increasingly gained significant symbolic value. Buying a car might not be enough to move up the social ladder; that moment has to be photographed and shared to achieve the desired 'upgrade'. The purchase of a car achieves its full potential in the production of a photograph that transcends personal circulation and display, by sharing it via social media. Thus, photography has intrinsically shifted from shooting to sharing. Almost all social media platforms that are primarily meant for the sharing of images are embedded with a camera and editing tools. An image taken by the camera feature inbuilt in a social media app automatically becomes a shareable object. The image is no longer the sole object of memories; we 'commit images to memory' with each instance of sharing online where 'visibility is increasingly managed, produced, handled and harvested'.[12]

---

[11] Guérin, Isabelle. 2014. 'Juggling with Debt, Social Ties, and Values: The Everyday Use of Microcredit in Rural South India'. *Current Anthropology*. 55:S9. pp. S40–50. *JSTOR*. doi.org/10.1086/675929. Accessed 11 July 2022.

12 Bridle, James. 6 July 2012. 'A New Aesthetic for the Digital Age' [video]. *Youtube.* Uploaded by Ted Talent Search. www.youtube.com/watch?v=z84EDsnpb4U. Accessed 11 July 2022.

In 1988, John Tagg in *The Burden of Representation* wrote about the meaning and value of portraiture, since certain social exchanges and rituals were impossible to think of without the mediation of photography. In the digital age, there are more and more everyday experiences that cannot be decoupled from photography, both in terms of production and circulation. As Tagg pointed out, to be photographed is far from being a privilege, becoming the 'burden of a new class to be surveilled.'[13] Tagg links the emergence of photography with 'the restructuring of the local and national state in industrialised societies' which advanced 'the network of disciplinary institutions' such as the police, the healthcare system or the asylum.[14] Today, these institutions of control are more invisible as we leave our footprints across digital platforms and their implications are completely obscured since data continues to be extrapolated in unimaginable ways. The family photograph exists within this historicity of class-based social structures where many 'claimed their presence through representation in photography'[15] and its contemporary existence in a networked society in an age of communicative capitalism. Photography is seen as a democratising medium, quite like the internet. On the internet, everyone can have a voice and imaging technology provides the tools to be heard and seen. Jodi Dean says, '… throughout the periods of neoliberal consolidation, participatory media has offered quick, easy and universal democracy.'[16] She calls democracy a 'marketing slogan' in a networked society where conditions of inequality get further solidified, since communication's primary component is the production and circulation of capital. Both product reviews on Amazon and family images of new car purchases are not only an intrinsic part of this structure where images do not stand on their own, but they also produce and reify that structure. With this, I am not attempting to reject a new visual culture, but merely wish to point out its differences from its predecessors, rethink the meaning of photography and lay bare the contemporary conditions within which we make and share photographs.

Szendy, Peter. 9 August 2019. 'The Image in the Age of its General Exchangeability'. *The European Graduate School.* .edu/lecture/the-image-in-the-age-of-its-general-exchangeability-2019-08-09/. Accessed 11 July 2022.

[13] Tagg, John. 2021. *The Burden of Representation: Essays on Photographies and Histories* (University of Minnesota Press). p. 59.

[14] Ibid.

[15] Ibid. p. 37.

[16] Dean, Jodi. 2018. 'Jodi Dean: The Limits of the Web in an Age of Communicative Capitalism – Classroom'. *Art & Education.* www.artandeducation.net/classroom/video/174211/jodi-dean-the-limits-of-the-web-in-an-age-of-communicative-capitalism. Accessed 11 July 2022.

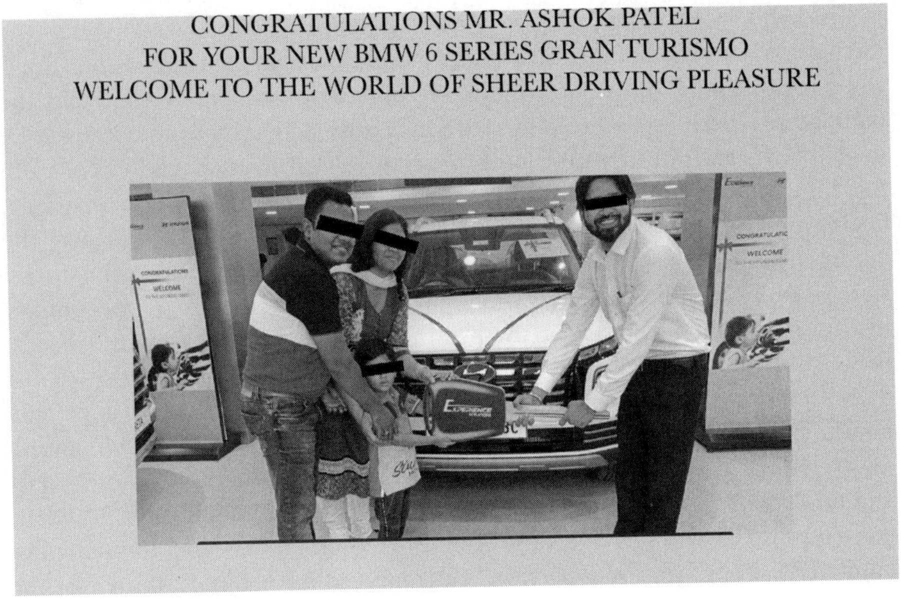
CONGRATULATIONS MR. ASHOK PATEL
FOR YOUR NEW BMW 6 SERIES GRAN TURISMO
WELCOME TO THE WORLD OF SHEER DRIVING PLEASURE

Amateurism, or the Strange and Radical Kinship of the Camera

Mallika Leuzinger

In 1931, the German Jewish philosopher and essayist Walter Benjamin, who was living between the bustling metropoles of Paris and Berlin, published his now canonical *Little History of Photography*. As noted by a recent translator, it was a treatise on how 'photography weaves into lives that are changing and that would change more.'[1] Benjamin had himself been 'born into a world in which photography was becoming commonplace', but as Esther Leslie notes, it compelled him because

> [i]t had transported moments into the future, and so bent time. It had made faraway spaces – the other side of the world, the moon, the stars, the sun – recordable and transportable into every bourgeois parlour and, later, through magazines and postcards, into every home and circumstance. It had altered the meaning and function of memory. It had made its mark on the body, calling poses and postures into being. It had produced new sensations, such as the shock of the moment of exposure, and new gestures, such as the photographer bent over his machine and unleashing his act with a crook of the finger …[2]

Benjamin's reflections have since spawned hundreds of other little histories, and this attempt to grapple with the photographic lives of the Bengali twin sisters Debalina Mazumder and Manobina Roy is no exception: his words burst onto the scene just as they began to wield a camera in and around the apparently provincial North Indian town of Ramnagar. They had turned twelve, and to mark the occasion, their father Binod Bihari Sen Roy, a teacher in the employ of the Maharaja of Benares and a member of the Royal Photographic Society in London, had gifted them an Agfa Brownie.

This camera, a spin-off of the wildly popular Kodak Brownie deemed 'so simple that it can easily be operated by any school boy or girl', was a card and wood box with a rotary shutter and instantaneous exposures. It had V lines at the top to assist with aiming, and a clip-on reflecting finder so that one could aim the camera from hip-level at the subject.[3] One could choose between two

---

[1] Leslie, Esther. 2015. 'Introduction: Walter Benjamin and the Birth of Photography'. Leslie, Esther and Walter Benjamin. eds. *On Photography* (London: Reaktion Books). p. 30.

[2] Ibid.

[3] Coe, Brian. 1989. 'The Rollfilm Revolution'. Ford, Colin. ed. *The Story of Popular Photography* (London: Century in Association with the National Museum of Photography Film and Television). p. 65.

windows to shoot either a landscape or portrait, press down on the shutter to take the image, and then wind it to the next one.[4] With this unassuming machine in hand, Manobina and Debalina were soon photographing prolifically, and yet always with deliberation, becoming proficient in a variety of genres; taking meticulous notes and keeping albums; developing black-and-white photographs in the darkroom; transitioning to their own dual lens, medium-format cameras and sharing their work via the transregional and national amateur photography circles that were springing up around them.

The twins were also literary enthusiasts conversant in English, Sanskrit, Hindi, Persian and Bengali. They read poetry, fiction and nonfiction and wrote profusely, authoring letters to pen pals around the world, columns for newspapers, and in Manobina's case, an unfinished memoir.[5] Towards the ends of their lives, the twins' photography, along with this writing, moved into the realm of their children's memories, homes and custodian projects, with Debalina's grandson Rajsaday Dutt setting up the family blog 'Lives less forgotten', [6] and Manobina's son Joy Roy organising 'A Woman and Her Camera: A Centenary Exhibition' as an homage to his mother.[7] It has lived on, too, in institutional efforts to foreground women in India's modern history.

Debalina's photographs, for instance, were part of the exhibition 'Re-Presenting Indian Women' curated by Malavika Karlekar and the New Delhi-based Centre for Women's Development Studies (CWDS) from formal archives

---

[4] See Forbes, Ted. 21 April 2013. 'Medium Format Photography' [video]. www.youtube.com/watch?v=glI-NGw1O4I. Last viewed on 18 June 2018.

[5] The manuscript of this memoir is with Manobina's daughter Aparajita Sinha in Hyderabad, though I have been unable to access them. Certain glimpses of these memoirs are provided by her children's correspondence with me, and a newspaper article which references them, presumably through the journalist being shown these manuscripts by Aparajita. See Devi, Sangeetha K. 1 September 2006. 'In Black and White'. *The Hindu*. www.thehindu.com/features/metroplus/fashion/in-black-and-white/article2928355.ece. Last viewed on 1 June 2018.

[6] As Rajsaday states: 'This site is a project. It is by its very nature unfinished. If you happen to have other anecdotes, information, materials, suggestions or corrections, please leave a comment or email … and we'll endeavour to add it to the site.' See Dutt, Rajsaday. 'Lives less forgotten'. rajsaday.com/. Last viewed on 30 April 2018.

[7] See Ghosh, Devarsi. 5 November 2019. 'Images: Slice-of-life works by pioneering amateur woman photographer Manobina Roy'. *Scroll.in*. scroll.in/reel/942516/images-slice-of-life-works-by-pioneering-amateur-woman-photographer-manobina-roy. Last viewed on 28 June 2022. As stated in the press coverage: 'The exhibition has been 17 years in the making for Joy Roy. As he wrote in the programme notes, he took the decision to organise an exhibition of his mother's photographs back in 2000, when an exhibition of photographs taken by his father, Bimal Roy, was held at the Nehru Centre gallery in Mumbai. While the press wanted interviews, Joy Roy thought it would be best for his mother to speak to them. "I finally found her seated alone in the far corner of the gallery," Joy Roy wrote. "She was expressionless. Not like ma at all. I asked her what was wrong. Without looking at me she said almost under her breath: no one has ever done this for my photos. My heart gave a lurch and I had tears in my eyes. Then and there, I decided that come what may I would make an exhibition of her photographs happen."' The exhibition was curated by M.C. Mohan and inaugurated in Hyderabad on 16 September 2019, Mumbai on 27 November 2019 and Kolkata on 31 January 2020.

such as the Nehru Memorial Museum and private family collections. It was held at the India International Centre in 2001, whereupon it travelled across the country to Kolkata, Goa, Ajmer, Mussoorie, Dehradun, Bhopal, Panipat, Mumbai, Hyderabad, Mysore, Madurai, Pondicherry, Chennai, Lucknow, Shillong, Guwahati, Bhubaneswar and Jaipur.[8]

In fact, Debalina's 1938 portrait of a fresh-faced young woman gathering wheat outside of Ramnagar and captioned 'Gleaner' (Figure 1) was viewed by international audiences as well: it graced the cover of the accompanying catalogue and coffee-table book *Visualizing Indian Women, 1875-1947*.[9] Perhaps it was chosen for being representative of the spirited character of a photography that emerged out of an affluent upper-caste home but could connect with other Indians, other visions, other labours.[10] After all, 'Gleaner' not only shares the deeply respectful and sympathetic, if romanticised, gaze of 'From Day In to Day Out' (Figures 2a, 2b), Debalina's contemporaneous

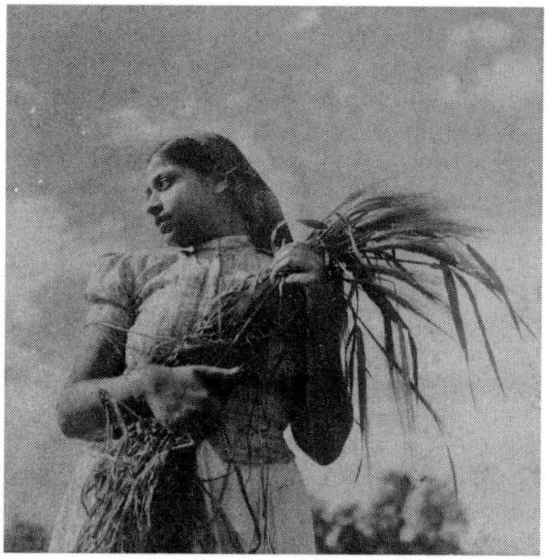

Figure 1. Debalina Mazumder, 'Gleaner', Ramnagar, 1937-38. Courtesy the Centre for Studies in the Social Sciences, Kolkata.

[8] Centre for Women's Development Studies. 'Visual Documentary'. www.cwds.ac.in/activities/visual-documentary/. Last viewed on 18 June 2018. For press coverage of the exhibition and its legacies, see for instance Sen, Titash. 28 December 2016. 'Calendar Girls from a Bygone Era'. *The Wire*. thewire.in/culture/calendar-girls-bygone-era. Last viewed on 18 June 2018.

[9] Karlekar, Malavika (ed.). *Visualizing Indian Women, 1875-1947*. New Delhi: Oxford University Press, 2006. Print.

[10] 'Gleaner' had already caught the eye of the selection panel at The Lucknow University Writers' Associations' First Photographic Exhibition and Portfolio Circles Exibition of Photography in 1941. As I have since learnt from research by Sabeena Gadihoke and conversations with Debalina's daughter Kamalini Mazumder over the course of curating the first exhibition dedicated to the twins' photography, that the woman Debalina photographed was her cousin Arati. In her inaugural lecture, Gadihoke drew out the simultaneously playful and determined energy that inflected this photographic event: Debalina had actually not wanted Arati 'to look like an Indian girl', and had thus asked her to pose in her blouse and petticoat rather than sari, keeping 'one eye on sun and the other [searching] for any signs of an intruder on the horizon that may have disturbed her frame before she clicked her photograph'. For a version of this lecture, see Gadihoke, Sabeena. 8 March 2022. 'Sisters, Cameras and Amateur Photography: Debalina Mazumder and Manobina Roy'. *AJK Mass Communication Research Centre*. www.youtube.com/watch?v=4cgdA_7B9Rc. Last viewed on 30 May 2022.

Ensuing interpretations and circulations of the image as a record of labour speak to the interactive and unsettled nature of photography, in this case by emphasising the role of the spectator as another participant in the photographic event, alongside the photographer, the photographed and the camera. See Azoulay, Ariella. 2008. *The Civil Contract of Photography*.

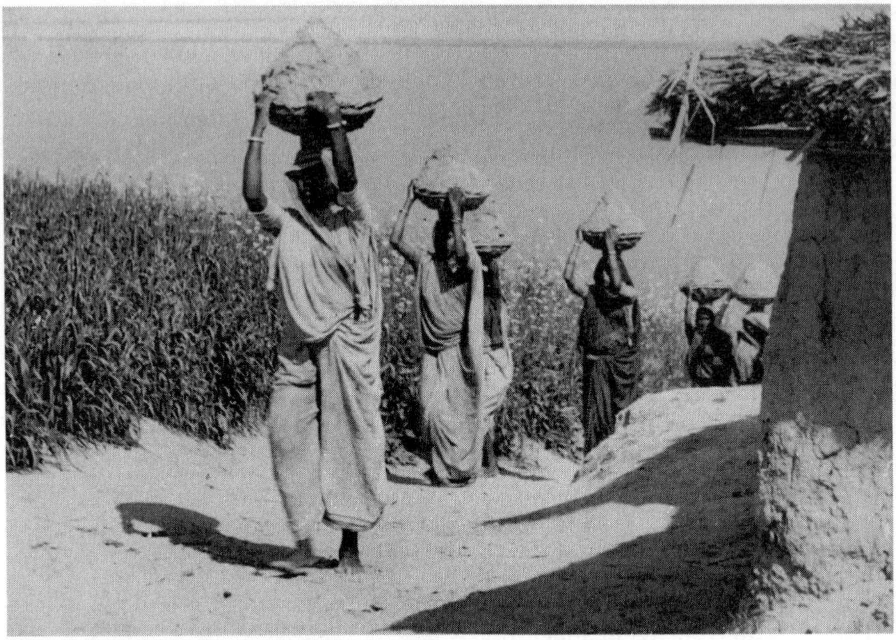

Figure 2A. Debalina Mazumder, 'From Day In to Day Out', c.1940s. Courtesy Kamalini Mazumder.

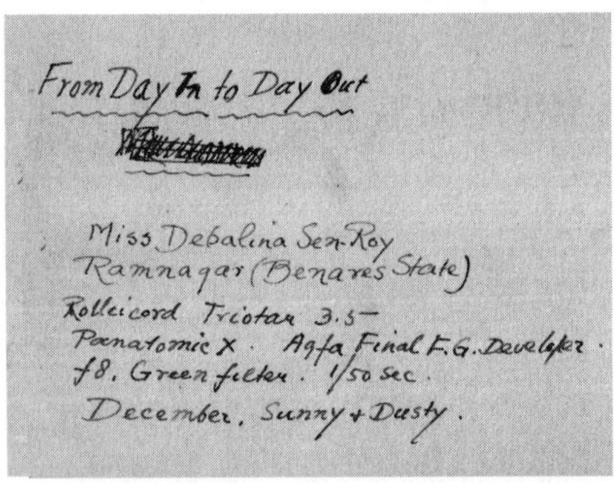

Figure 2B. Debalina Mazumder, 'From Day In to Day Out', c.1940s. Courtesy Kamalini Mazumder.

photograph of a line of women labourers carrying pails of sand on their heads; and of Manobina's cropped portrait of a young tribal women whose smile is beatific. It also resonates with the images of rural women across ten Indian states taken by the photojournalist P. Sainath between 1993 and 2002, and seen in the exhibition 'Visible Work, Invisible Women' by '700,000 viewers in India alone' before they were digitised and made freely available through the People's Archive of Rural India.[11] As such, it is fitting that Debalina lent 'Gleaner' and over a hundred other photographs in her possession to the Kolkata-based Centre for Studies in the Social Sciences (CSSS) to be scanned, such that they also exist as digital files, merging with the other images and

[11] Sainath, P. 'Visible Work, Invisible Women: an online photo exhibition'. ruralindiaonline.org/articles/sainath-womens-work-exhibition. Last viewed on 21 March 2019.

micro and macro-histories the Centre archives and, as in the 2002 show 'Visual Worlds of Modern Bengal', occasionally displays.[12]

The twins have also come to the attention of the press, with their distinctive and subtle ways of talking about, or indeed, talking *down* their practices, often waylaying journalists.[13] An article in *The Telegraph Kolkata* identified Debalina as

> one of our first women photographers, though she herself would be the last person to lay any claims to any pioneering effort. Photography was not for her the means of breaking what may be perceived as the shackles of domesticity. On the contrary, she nurtured her talent within the safe environment of her home. Exposing herself to the world outside would have been unthinkable for one as conservative as she.[14]

Alongside the mistaken claim that Debalina was 'the only one' amongst the Sen Roy children 'to take to photography', the article is notable for its insistence on placing Debalina on the side of tradition rather than modernity, as someone seeking containment rather than exposure—dichotomous characterisations which are undone by Debalina being profiled in the region's most prominent English newspaper.

This slippage, when read alongside the scattered and sporadic exposition of the twins' images over the decades and across geographies, attests to just how difficult it is to find an adequate vocabulary, or framing, for their photography.[15] One that can, in the spirit of Benjamin's whirlwind essay on

---

[12] These images are filed under 'Transparencies of Photographs taken by Debolina Majumdar, 597 Block – O, New Alipore, Calcutta 53' and numbered O1-O142 at CSSS. They comprise images of Durga Puja celebrations between 1962–65 in Calcutta; portraits of family members; landscapes of Benares, Ramnagar and the Kumayun (sic) Hills; street scenes in London and Paris; landscapes of the Lake District. For an archival note on the CSSS exhibition 'Visual Worlds of Modern Bengal', held from 1 March–3 April 2002, see 'Archive'. Centre for Studies in Social Sciences Calcutta. www.cssscal.org/archive.php. Last viewed on 5 May 2021.

During the publication process of this edited volume, the CSSS, supported by the MurthyNAYAK Foundation, held the first joint exhibition of the twins' work at the Jadunath Bhavan Museum and Resource Centre in Kolkata from 24 February to 21 March 2022, based on images from its archive as well as prints, materials and cameras lent by Joy Roy and Kamalini Mazumder. 'Twin Sisters with Cameras' was curated by Tapati Guha-Thakurta, Sabeena Gadihoke and myself, and designed and produced by Anuja Mukherjee and Kamalika Mukherjee. The exhibition travelled to Delhi in August 2022 and resulted in a printed catalogue.

[13] For examples of this press coverage, see Das, Soumitra. 31 March 2002. 'Pioneering Woman Photographer Chose Never to Turn a Pro'. *The Telegraph India*. Calcutta. www.telegraphindia.com/1020401/the_east.htm; Sengupta, Ratnottama. 13 May 2012. 'Portraits of 2 indomitable mothers'. *Times of India*, Kolkata. timesofindia.indiatimes.com/city/kolkata/portraits-of-3-indomitable-mothers/articleshow/13115976.cms; Devi, Sangeetha K. 1 September 2006. 'In Black and White'. *The Hindu*. www.thehindu.com/todays-paper/tp-features/tp-fridayreview/in-black-and-white/article3230558.ece. All links last viewed on 1 June 2018.

[14] Das. 2002. 'Pioneering Woman'.

[15] The recent 'Twin Sisters with Cameras' exhibition seems to have prompted a shift in conversation from biographical understandings of the twins' practices towards viewing them as part of a wider history of photography, and in particular, amateur photography, in India. See,

the revolutionary use-value of photography, reckon with the strange politics of the camera, its inability to adhere or cohere to a set of spaces and relations, its capacity to be both acutely intimate and radically cosmopolitan, its tendency to simultaneously preserve and transform, efface and illuminate, concentrate and disperse, alienate and inspire.

The Home and Beyond

The most capacious understanding of the twins' photography is offered by the media scholar Sabeena Gadihoke, who first grappled with the dynamism of 'amateur and domestic photography by women in India' for a special issue on 'Shaping Technologies' commissioned by the South Asian research platform *Sarai*.[16] Gadihoke had sought out six women from middle- to upper-class backgrounds who were active between 1930 and 1960, including Debalina and Manobina. She interviewed them at length and pored over their images, teasing out how they practised photography within the home (often an expansive, comfortable one with multiple indoor and outdoor spaces), and through postal portfolio clubs, such that those who followed purdah—the practice of women's seclusion—could nonetheless participate in a critical exchange and exhibition culture. She noted how '[p]hotography allowed women to do things that they normally did not do. It allowed them to wander, to look and to stare,'[17] as their movement was in relation to a respectable activity—a view that Kodak promoted in advertisements featuring a smiling, sari-clad Kodak girl with a camera in hand, presiding over a quaint street scene.[18] Moreover, it was an activity that could be adjusted around their schedules and duties as daughters, and later, wives and mothers, such that it complemented rather than compromised these.

A written reflection Kamalini provided me with in 2015 corroborates this view, outlining how the twins' photography was (made) compatible with the family's *bhadralok* existence—'bhadralok' being the Bengali term for 'well-

for instance, Dasgupta, Priyanka. 28 February 2022. 'Exhibition Focus On Twin Sisters' Life Of Photography'. *The Times of India*. timesofindia.indiatimes.com/city/kolkata/exhibition-focus-on-twin-sisters-life-of-photography/articleshow/89859664.cms. Last viewed on 30 May 2022.

[16] Gadihoke, Sabeena. 2003. 'The Home and Beyond – Domestic and Amateur Photography by Women in India (1930-1960)'. *Sarai Reader 2003: Shaping Technologies* (Delhi/Amsterdam: The Centre for the Study of Developing Societies). pp. 61–69, p. 64. Online. Last viewed on 31 July 2021. While this essay was in publication, Gadihoke also published a beautiful and sustained consideration of Manobina Roy's practice that specifically reflects on amateurism: see Gadihoke, Sabeena. Spring 2020. 'The Creative Distractions of Manobina Roy'. *Trans Asia Photography Review*. 10:2. 'Ten Years of the Trans Asia Photography Review/Notes from the Field'. hdl.handle.net/2027/spo.7977573.0010.209. Last viewed on 28 June 2022.

[17] Gadihok. 2003. p. 64.

[18] For an example, see www.gettyimages.co.uk/license/90743110 , which is labelled as 'India May 21: Brochure advertising Kodak cameras to the growing Indian middle classes. A woman in a sari is carrying a camera and watching a snake charmer, while a small girl stands nearby'. Last viewed on 31 July 2021.

mannered', and denoting the respectable, educated, professional and mostly Hindu upper-caste section of Indian society in colonial times:[19]

> Since Ramnagar was a princely state, the movement of women was restricted. The girls could not venture out of the confines of their sprawling bungalow and garden in order to find subjects for their photography. Thus, initially the subject for photographs were their various pets, flowers and butterflies, in short anything that was within reach. Later, my grandfather would send the girls off in his car to the outskirts where they would try their hand at landscapes, or photograph the local villagers.[20]

Gadihoke's own argument was informed by the suspension and divergence of certain aspects of the twins' photography after their marriages. Manobina married the socialist realist Bengali filmmaker Bimal Roy in 1937 and settled, after a brief stint in Calcutta, in Bombay. Debalina accompanied her father to Benares and obtained a degree from Benares Hindu University as a private candidate, marrying the businessman Nitish Chandra Mazumder in 1946 and thereupon moving to Calcutta.[21] The demands of setting up and running their own households, having children, and supporting their husbands' professional lives marginalised their photography, or concentrated it in the family.

Manobina, whose favourite genre was portraiture, did manage to persuade several distinguished personalities, including actors, producers and writers who came to visit her husband, to sit for her. She also photographed the Bengali poet Rabindranath Tagore who was bestowed with the Puri Pagdi while honeymooning in Puri, the politician and diplomat Vijayalakshmi Pandit, her brother (and first Prime Minister of India) Jawaharlal Nehru at a Congress Session in Ooty in 1959, and his daughter (and eventual successor) Indira Gandhi.[22] Manobina told the journalist Sangeeta Devi that her portrait of

---

[19] Roy, Parama. 'Bhadralok/Bhadramahila'. Dharampal-Frick, Gita, Monika Kirloskar-Steinbach, Rachel Dwyer, Jahnavi Phalkey. eds. 2015. *Key Concepts in Modern Indian Studies* (New Delhi: Oxford University Press). pp. 21–23.

[20] Mazumder, Kamalini. 4 December 2015. Personal correspondence with author.

[21] Debalina's daughter Kamalini provided me with more insight into this period. In a biographical sketch she made for me, Kamalini wrote: 'Post his retirement, my grandfather moved to Varanasi. My grandmother died shortly after this. My mother had now taken on the mantle of running the house. My grandfather started losing his eyesight due to glaucoma. For my mother, now, more than ever before, photography became an escape from the mundane routine of daily life. Her father urged her to continue her passion for photography, saying that he would continue to see the world through his daughter's eyes. Being in Varanasi also meant that my mother had much more freedom to move about. Some of her photographs from that period reflect this new-found freedom. By this time, the rolls of film were processed and printed at professional studios since maintaining a dark room was no longer viable.' Mazumder, Kamalini. 12 April 2014. Personal correspondence with author.

[22] Roy, Rinki. 21 October 2016. Personal correspondence with author. Siddhartha Ghosh notes that: 'In 1951, the series "25 Portraits of Rabindranath Tagore" included the work of a lone woman photographer, Manobina, who had taken the picture of the poet at Puri.' See Ghosh, Siddhartha. Spring 2014. 'Zenana Studio: Early Women Photographers of Bengal'.

Nehru, which was published in Devi's write-up for *The Hindu*, was greatly admired by the subject himself. It is a close, soft-lit side profile that engages Nehru's charismatic features, right down to the wisps of white hair at the top of his head and the lines of his face and paints him so affably without actually having him smile.[23]

Debalina, meanwhile, was asked to make portraits of elderly relatives which could be used to commemorate them after their deaths, in accordance with the Bengali ritual of *Shraddha*. It was a task she undertook with mixed feelings. Her relocation to the big city meant that she had few opportunities to keep up the landscape photography she had so enjoyed as a college student, although she made sure to surround herself with other people's photographic works.[24] Rajsaday recalled that her house 'was filled with books … she was a huge fan of Henri Cartier-Bresson and had several of his books. She also liked Ansel Adams and had his, but Cartier-Bresson was her favourite.'[25]

Debalina intended to publish her own photobook based on a project on the famous Durga Puja celebrations in Calcutta, which she pursued between 1962 and 1965. Its street character and intimate framing correspond with Cartier-Bresson's work, but its attention to the arching movements of human bodies engaged in idol-making and worship and materiality of erected façades is also on par with the less famous documentation of Benares made by the American photographer William Gedes between 1969 and 1971.[26] Yet in so far as her series did materialise, taking the form of a dedicated 'Durga Puja' album now in her daughter Kamalini's care, it had to contend with her children's scribbles and attentions (Figure 3).

Photography only resumed its centrality when Debalina was in her sixties

---

Trans Asia Photography Review. 4:2. In Translation. quod.lib.umich.edu/t/tap/7977573.0004.202. Last viewed on 31 July 2021.

[23] Devi. 'In Black and White'. Manobina photographed many of the same people as her contemporary Mira Chaudhuri, whom Gadihoke also profiles, suggesting the close-knit nature of elite metropolitan circles in mid-twentieth century India. See Gadihoke. 'The Home and Beyond'. p. 64.

[24] Kamalini's description of this period in her mother's life corresponds with Gadihoke's argument, with Kamalini writing that after marriage, 'She started taking photographs of various members of her husband's family … a lot of whom were elderly people. The norm in those days was for people to go to a professional studio where they would pose in front of larger than life backdrops and get photographed. There weren't very many candid shots because people didn't own cameras. Anyway, most of the elderly people had never been photographed in their lives. My mother stepped in with her camera and fulfilled many a dream! As a matter of fact, there was a certain period in her life when she assumed the role of provider of photographs to be used at funerals. This role upset her and she almost swore against photographing another human in her lifetime!' Mazumder, Kamalini. 12 April 2014. Personal correspondence with author.

[25] Dutt, Rajsaday. 22 October 2015. Personal correspondence with author.

[26] See 'William Gedney Photographs and Writings'. *Duke University Libraries Digital Repository.* repository.duke.edu/dc/gedney?f%5Bseries_facet_sim%5D%5B%5D=Benares. Last viewed on 20 June 2018. I am grateful to Alisha Sett for alerting me to Gedney's work.

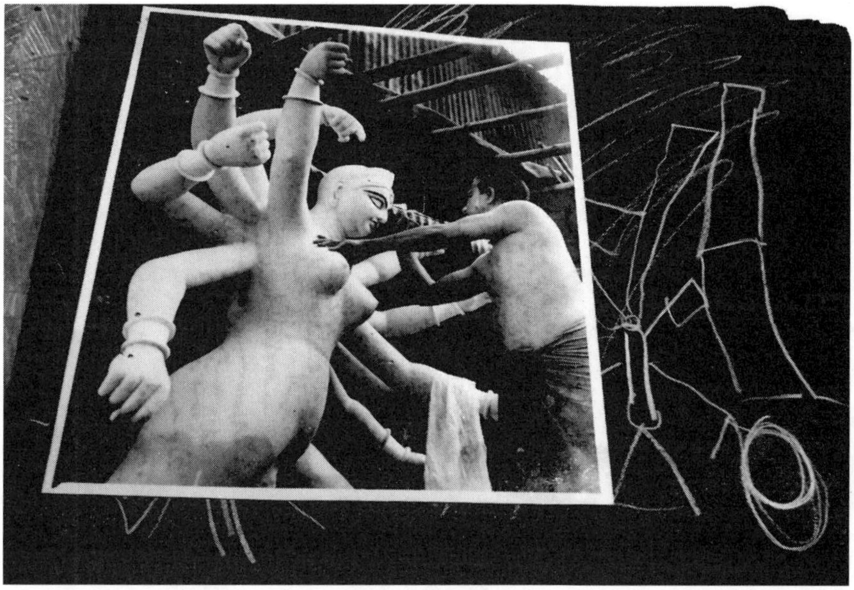

Figure 3. Page from album assembled by Debalina Mazumder, c.1968. Courtesy Kamalini Mazumder.

and decided to subscribe to *Viewfinder*, a journal published by the Federation of Indian Photography, whereupon she discovered that its founders were known to her from the United Provinces Portfolio Club she had been part of as a teenager. The renewal of these friendships resulted in Debalina joining the Photography Association of Bengal, of which she was eventually unanimously elected president.[27]

That said, a burst of photographic activity marked the period in which the twins themselves were reunited. Manobina joined Debalina in a rented house in London for three months, after accompanying her husband to the Moscow Film Festival in 1959. Though they were in charge of a total of eight children, with Debalina's youngest son receiving medical treatment at the Great Ormond Street Hospital, they spent every free moment in parks, streets, theatres and shops, their cameras hanging ever-ready over their saris, delighting in developing their practice around new scenes and subjects. Upon their return to India—via Paris and Geneva—Manobina published some of

[27] Kamalini elaborates that: 'Two of the founding members, Dr. G. Thomas and Mr. S.H.H. Razavi had been members of the Postal Portfolio when my mother had been in her teens. My mother had been extremely excited to have been able to, albeit accidentally, track down two of her old acquaintances. When she contacted Dr. Thomas, he insisted on her joining the PAB (Photography Association of Bengal) without delay. That was the beginning of a very long association with one of the foremost photography clubs of this country .... an association that would lead to her one day being unanimously elected the President of PAB.' Mazumder, Kamalini. 12 April 2014. Personal correspondence with author.

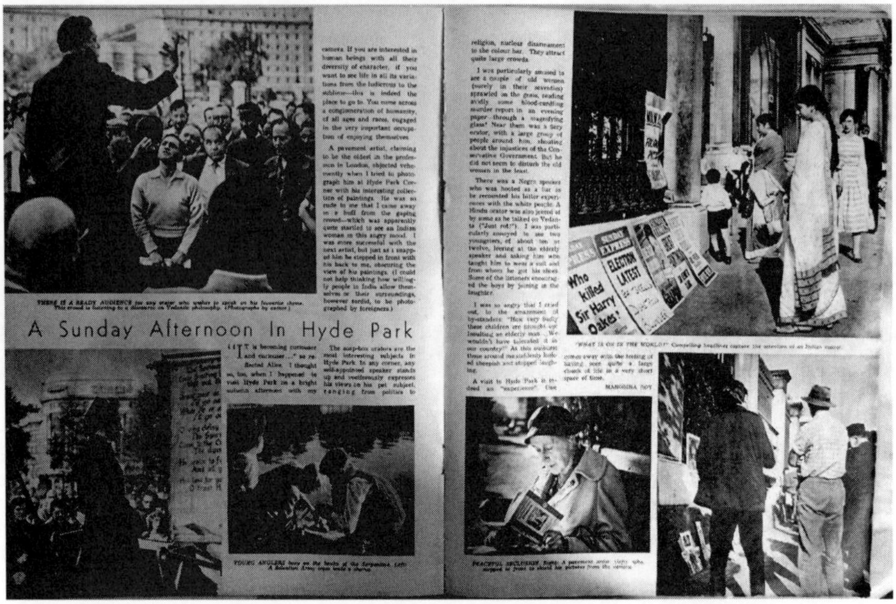

A Sunday Afternoon In Hyde Park

Figure 4. Manobina Roy, "A Sunday Afternoon in Hyde Park", The Illustrated Weekly of India, March 1960. Courtesy Joy Roy.

these photographs with accompanying texts in *The Illustrated Weekly of India*, which counted amongst most-read and respected English magazines (Figures 4 and 5).[28]

In 'A Sunday Afternoon in Hyde Park', Manobina confidently took to task the racism and desolation she witnessed in the former imperial metropole, blending references from literature, personal experiences and political realities.[29] 'Impressions of Moscow', on the other hand, was punctuated by diplomatic observations, or rather, insistences, such as these: 'I should make it quite clear here that I am not politically inclined to like or dislike the land of the Soviets. I went there as a visitor with an open mind.'[30] Both these articles had been scanned, and stored amidst the envelopes, albums and loose prints in a trunk at the Bombay home of her children Joy and Yashodara.

The ebb and flow of the twins' camerawork, its careful movement through 'the home and beyond' and across the decades lead Gadihoke to conclude

[28] *The Illustrated Weekly* is best understood as follows: 'Roughly one half of its contents deals with weekly events and matters of topical interest; the rest is devoted to contemporary Indian literature in translation, and foreign literature; also includes regular features on books, Hindi writing, and special numbers dealing with specific contemporary arts, crafts, fiction, individual writers and artists.' See 'A List of English Language Journals from India and Pakistan'. 1964. *Mahfil*. 1:3. p. 60.

[29] Roy, Manobina. 13 March 1960. 'A Sunday Afternoon in Hyde Park'. *The Illustrated Weekly of India*. LXXXI: 11. pp. 38–39.

[30] Roy, Manobina. 31 July 1960. 'Impressions of Moscow'. *The Illustrated Weekly of India*. LXXXI: 31. pp. 21–23.

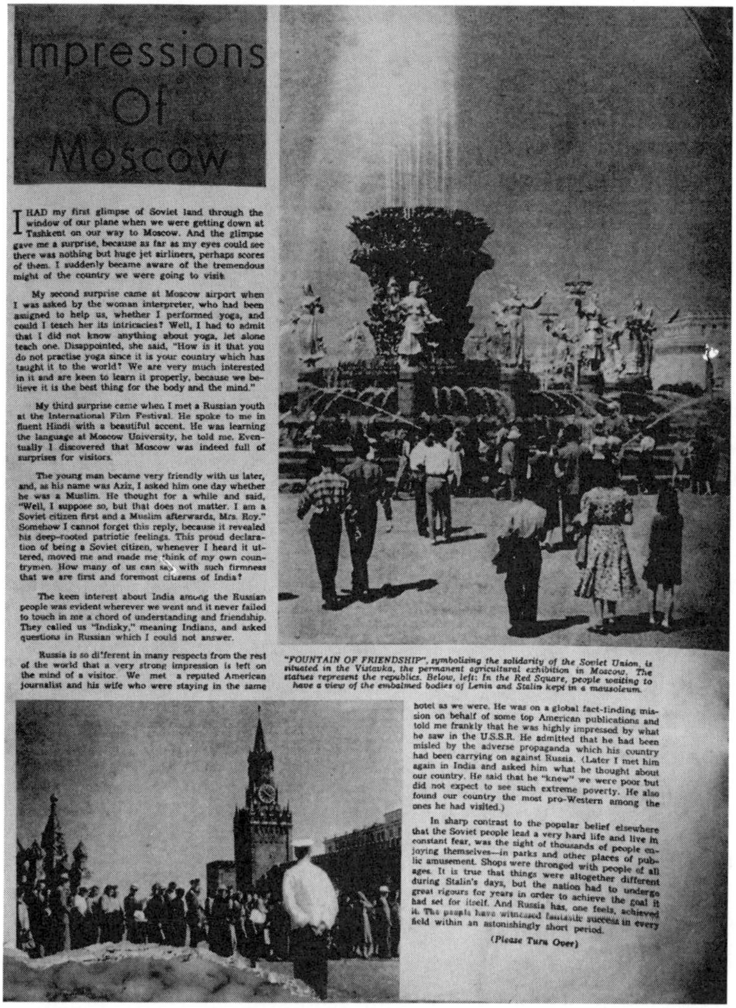

Impressions Of Moscow

I HAD my first glimpse of Soviet land through the window of our plane when we were getting down at Tashkent on our way to Moscow. And the glimpse gave me a surprise, because as far as my eyes could see there was nothing but huge jet airliners, perhaps scores of them. I suddenly became aware of the tremendous might of the country we were going to visit.

My second surprise came at Moscow airport when I was asked by the woman interpreter, who had been assigned to help us, whether I performed yoga, and could I teach her its intricacies? Well, I had to admit that I did not know anything about yoga, let alone teach one. Disappointed, she said, "How is it that you do not practise yoga since it is your country which has taught it to the world? We are very much interested in it and are keen to learn it properly, because we believe it is the best thing for the body and the mind."

My third surprise came when I met a Russian youth at the International Film Festival. He spoke to me in fluent Hindi with a beautiful accent. He was learning the language at Moscow University, he told me. Eventually I discovered that Moscow was indeed full of surprises for visitors.

The young man became very friendly with us later, and, as his name was Aziz, I asked him one day whether he was a Muslim. He thought for a while and said, "Well, I suppose so, but that does not matter. I am a Soviet citizen first and a Muslim afterwards, Mrs. Roy." Somehow I cannot forget this reply, because it revealed his deep-rooted patriotic feelings. This proud declaration of being a Soviet citizen, whenever I heard it uttered, moved me and made me think of my own countrymen. How many of us can say with such firmness that we are first and foremost citizens of India?

The keen interest about India among the Russian people was evident wherever we went and it never failed to touch in me a chord of understanding and friendship. They called us "Indisky," meaning Indians, and asked questions in Russian which I could not answer.

Russia is so different in many respects from the rest of the world that a very strong impression is left on the mind of a visitor. We met a reputed American journalist and his wife who were staying in the same hotel as we were. He was on a global fact-finding mission on behalf of some top American publications and told me frankly that he was highly impressed by what he saw in the U.S.S.R. He admitted that he had been misled by the adverse propaganda which his country had been carrying on against Russia. (Later I met him again in India and asked him what he thought about our country. He said that he "knew" we were poor but did not expect to see such extreme poverty. He also found our country the most pro-Western among the ones he had visited.)

In sharp contrast to the popular belief elsewhere that the Soviet people lead a very hard life and live in constant fear, was the sight of thousands of people enjoying themselves—in parks and other places of public amusement. Shops were thronged with people of all ages. It is true that things were altogether different during Stalin's days, but the nation had to undergo great rigours for years in order to achieve the goal it had set for itself. And Russia has, one feels, achieved it. The people have witnessed fantastic success in every field within an astonishingly short period.

(Please Turn Over)

"FOUNTAIN OF FRIENDSHIP", symbolising the solidarity of the Soviet Union, is situated in the Vistavka, the permanent agricultural exhibition in Moscow. The statues represent the republics. Below, left: In the Red Square, people waiting to have a view of the embalmed bodies of Lenin and Stalin kept in a mausoleum.

Figure 5. Manobina Roy, "Impressions of Moscow", The Illustrated Weekly of India, July 1960. Courtesy Joy Roy.

that photography 'served as a temporary escape from a situation that left women with no time for themselves or for a fantasy world', and 'provided a significant space for self-expression.'[31] This essay builds on Gadihoke's insights to continue tracing how Debalina and Manobina, as photographing women—and after 1947, citizens of a newly independent and non-aligned nation—became producers, critics and representatives of an ambitious, pragmatic and problematic (post)colonial modernity. At the same time, it seeks to move from the idea of photography as 'providing', 'serving', 'allowing' outcomes, as a neat/coherent 'space' of its own and to account instead for its disruptive

[31] Gadihoke. p. 65–66.

and distributive force.[32] Where previous engagements centred on individual biographies, clubs, exhibitions, and the assumption of women's self expression and empowerment (whether in its fulfilment or denial), the sparks of this little history of photography are a set of gendered, classed, generational and cosmopolitan relations that I re-chart as amateur.

Amateur Trappings

'Amateurism' is, of course, a term with existing currency in the histories of photography. Where it appears in the discourse, practice and circulation of photography from the very beginning, it became tied to the global availability of hand-held cameras from the nineteenth century onwards, when increasing numbers of people in places from Moscow to London to Paris to Ramnagar began to take, or make, their photographs.[33] It is a term that the twins' father, Binod Bihari Sen Roy, who is remembered by his descendants as 'an enthusiastic lensman whose B&W photographs were sent to London in a magazine of the time',[34] will likely have used to distinguish his photographic activity from that of 'snapshooters' who simply 'took' photographs whilst on holiday or at a family gathering and had no interest in learning about the technical aspects of the medium, and that of professionals for whom it was a means of income, and/or the result of institutional training.

Debalina, for instance, emphasised the pure and unaffected character of Sen Roy's photographic activity which so shaped her own, recounting to Rajsaday how he had always loved art, and despite not having learnt it through any course or tutor, was a skilled watercolourist. When, in the face of opposition from his father, he had been forced to decline an invitation to accompany an artist friend to France, his inability to pursue art as a career became 'one of the greatest regrets in Binod Bihari's life'. He thereupon decided to 'channel his talent for art into photography', which he viewed as 'painting with light', and pursued with a particular emphasis on composition and background, all whilst establishing himself as a renowned educator whom the Maharaja had not only

---

[32] For this notion of photography as 'disturbance', see Barthes, Roland. 2009. *Camera Lucida*. translated by Richard Howard (London: Vintage). Barthes writes: 'To see oneself (differently from in a mirror): on the scale of History, this action is recent, the painted, drawn, or miniaturized portrait having been, until the spread of Photography, a limited possession, intended moreover to advertise a social and financial status – and in any case, a painted portrait, however close to the resemblance (this is what I am trying to prove) is not a photograph. Odd that no one has thought of the *disturbance* (to civilisation) which this new action causes'. p. 12. While Barthes advocated for a 'History of Looking', of 'the Photograph', the orientation of this essay is towards a 'History of Photograph*ing*'.

[33] Kenyon, Dave. *Inside Amateur Photography*. London: Batsford, 1992. Print. p. 12. For regional iterations, see for instance Reischl, Katherine M. H., *Photographic Literacy: Cameras in the Hands of Russian Authors*. Ithaca: Cornell University Press, 2018. Print.

[34] As told to me by his granddaughter. Roy, Rinki. Personal correspondence with author, 1 February 2016.

appointed Headmaster of the Meeston High School but also entrusted with the education of his heir.[35]

The characterisation of Sen Roy as an 'amateur photographer' continued in Kamalini's descriptions of how 'one room in their sprawling bungalow had been converted into a dark room where my grandfather developed the films and also printed them himself. Being an avid reader, he continuously subscribed to magazines and journals, some of which were journals of photography.'[36] Kamalini further explained how her

> grandfather would lead the twins into his dark room where they sat enthralled as the images magically appeared on the negatives and later, on the prints. It was this sense of 'magic' that first drew the twins towards photography. My mother, while talking about her childhood in later years, would tell us about the excitement of watching images appear on a seemingly blank sheet of paper as the prints were washed and put through a fixer. Their father would leaf through the journals and make the girls look at the pictures printed there. He'd sometimes point to a particular picture and ask them to critically evaluate it. Later, he would tell them about aesthetics, composition, lighting, the use of filters etc. So, in a way, even before the sisters wielded a camera, they had been thoroughly schooled in the art of photography.[37]

Kamalini's words summon the immersive nature of amateur photography, where time and space are suspended, and upended; questions are asked and answered; discoveries are made and unmade. Sen Roy taught the twins to follow his example of maintaining meticulous records, and so, in notebooks and on the backs of prints, they would write down 'the details of the photographs … time of day, place, the aperture and exposure used, etc.'. Kamalini claimed that they 'would often experiment with a permutation and combination of the aperture and exposure, using the same subject' and that the practice of recording 'helped them figure out what worked best under certain conditions', because they could then compare different prints.[38] It is why the back of Debalina's print entitled 'From Day In to Day Out' is rife with annotations. Its title has been decoratively underlined and is followed by a word which has been scratched out, and her name and address: 'Miss Debalina Sen Roy, Ramnagar (Benares State)'. Then come technically precise and simultaneously atmospheric references: 'Rolleicord Tristar 3.5; Panaromic x Agfa Final F.G. Developer; f8, Green filter. 1/50 sec; December, Sunny + Dusty'.

The twins, in turn, sought to inculcate this amateurism in their children and grandchildren. Kamalini remembered how Debalina had wanted her to

---

[35] The nine-minute long video recording, mostly in Bengali, is on *Lives Less Forgotten*. See "Debalina Mazumdar talking about how her father, Binod Behari Sen-Roy, had wanted to be an artist – 2011", 17 February 2013, rajsaday.com/?p=3486 , last viewed on 20 June 2018.

[36] Mazumder, Kamalini. Personal correspondence with author, 12 April 2014.

[37] Mazumder, Kamalini. Personal correspondence with author, 4 December 2015.

[38] Ibid.

keep a little notebook in which to write down 'at least' the time of day and exposure used for every photograph she made, citing the fact that she did not do it as the reason her own photography never progressed beyond a certain point. Rajsaday noted how Debalina

> loved walking me through the photographs of famous photographers explaining how they used the light, used leading lines or why they framed it the way they did and then showing me how she would do it differently. She'd cover up the photo and show me what the better crop might have been. She was spot on of course.[39]

These reflections show how, over the course of four generations, photography became inseparable from certain moral and social qualities: alertness to the tiniest details, deep familiarity with other people's practices, care with regard to the materials at one's disposal, and a willingness to continuously improve.

This sensibility may not have amounted to an occupation, but it had formal trappings. It was undoubtedly Sen Roy's bhadralok background and close relationship with the Benaras royal family which formed and sustained the material conditions of his amateurism by giving him access to the latest information and equipment. The relationship between Indian royalty and photography is well-established, with Indian rulers being amongst the first prolific (native) consumers and practitioners of photography, and setting in motion the careers of well-known photographers such as Raja Deen Dayal.[40] Siddhartha Ghosh's 1988 *Chobi Tola: Bangalir Photography-Chorcha* (*Taking Pictures: The Practice of Photography by Bengalis*), meanwhile, has painstakingly documented how enthusiastically and enterprisingly upper-caste, upper-class Bengali men and women from, or married to those in, bureaucratic, intellectual and professional occupations, took to photography.[41]

This relationship has subsequently been historicised in fascinating detail by Ranu Roychoudhuri in her doctoral dissertation. She argues that 'the introduction of halftone printing in the Bangla language press in 1895/96 by the Calcutta-based photographer-printer-writer Upendrakishore Raychowdhury (1863-1915)' was revolutionary. For, '[a]s photographs started circulating through the press, the reach of photo images expanded and created

---

[39] Dutt, Rajsaday. 22 October 2015. Personal correspondence with author.

[40] See Dewan, Deepali and Deborah Sutton. 2013. *Raja Deen Dayal: Artist-Photographer in 19th-Century India* (New Delhi: Mapin Publishing and The Alkazi Collection of Photography).

[41] For a discussion of how it was predominantly elite subjects who frequented photo studios, availed of the services of professional photographers and experimented with photography themselves, see Siddhartha Ghosh, "Taking Pictures: The Early Days of Photography in Bengal", trans. Debjani Sengupta, *Sarai Reader 2003: Shaping Technologies* (New Delhi: Centre for the Study of Development, 2003), 58-60, archive.sarai.net/files/original/87231087d7d4e58f4d5043cc618dcab9.pdf (accessed 20 June 2018) and for a discussion of the slightly more varied social backgrounds of early photographers, including women studio operators and owners, see Ghosh, "Zenana Studio".

an inclusive space where potentially all members of the reading subscriber-audience were entitled to see photographs.'[42]

Roychoudhuri excavates, for instance, the circulation of photographic journals like the English-language *British Journal of Photography* and the *Journal of the Photographic Society of India*, as well as the vernacular manual *Photography Shiksha* (Training in Photography) and Bangla periodicals such as *Prabashi*, *Pradipa*, *Bharati*, *Bharatbarsha* and *Bhandar*, which began to feature and discuss photography.[43] This co-mingling of hyperlocal as well as global trends in photography was possible because Calcutta was 'the viceregal second city of the British Empire', giving the bhadralok 'access to all the major publications that came out of Europe. They continuously exchanged ideas with photographic artists from Europe and especially from England.'[44] Though Roy was not based in Calcutta, he was named a Fellow of the Royal Photographic Society in London (henceforth RPS). I was able to verify his membership through an entry in the RPS's 1913 annual magazine, recently digitised and made available by the National Media Museum in Bradford, which lists his name (Roy, Binod B. Sen), address (N.A.S., High School, Meerut City, U.P. India) and date of election (1908).[45]

The RPS was established in London in 1853 with the aim of 'promoting the art and science of photography', through the 'the interchange of thought and experience among Photographers'.[46] Details of this interchange can be gleaned from the contents of the 1913 issue, which ranges from articles on photographic techniques and processes, advertisements for photographic equipment, and predominantly pictorial work selected from the annual exhibition. They also emerge through documents discussing the membership application process; its connections, and its royal patronage.[47] Taken together, they conjure a world in which metropole and colony, coloniser and colonised, exist on the same page. Indeed, as photographers the RPS members were not so much identified as coloniser/colonised, but rather as part of a more or less elite global community invested in certain forms of imperial/colonial aesthetic production; and intrigued and inspired by technological developments and cross-cultural networks of modernity to invest further.

---

[42] Roychoudhuri, "The Public Lives", 11.

[43] Ibid., 63.

[44] Ibid.

[45] See entry 'ROY, Binod B. Sen, N.A.S., High School, Meerut City, U.P., India' in *The Royal Photographic Society Archive*, Volume 53 [January 1913], Page 28 (Start date 1/1/1913 End date 31/12/1913), archive.rps.org/archive/volume-53/727300?q=sen, last viewed on 12 November 2017.

[46] Pritchard, Michael. 'Our History', www.rps.org/about/history/history-of-the-rps, last viewed on 6 December 2017.

[47] For more on the class politics of amateur photography, which was elitist until about 1950s, see Kenyon. *Inside Amateur Photography*. 12. See also Lesko, Scott Christopher. 2012. 'Aesthetics of Soft Focus: Art Photography, Masculinity and the Re-Imagining of Modernity in Late Victorian Britain, 1885-1914' (PhD dissertation, Stony Brook University).

Postcolonial Orientations

In the twins' case, this interchange was no longer so imperially/royally oriented, but acquired nationalist, and then federal and secular leanings. Their entry into an 'official' culture of amateur photography was spurred on by their involvement in the 'portfolio club' of the United Provinces Amateur Photographic Association (UPAPA). This was, as Kamalini explained,

> a unique system whereby members sent in one photograph per person, along with a comment sheet. The relevant details about the photograph had to be provided by the photographer. After that, all the photographs collected were put into a folder and circulated amongst the members. Each member had to pen comments about the other photographs before returning the folder. A nominal fee was charged for postage. After doing a complete round, the photographs were returned to the people they belonged to. [48]

Indeed, by the 1960s, the twins' photographs had become affixed with stamps and stickers, and in the officious (English) language of these, 'accepted and exhibited' through networks of feedback and exhibition that had in some ways shrunk from, and in other ways, expanded on their father's. The northern reach of these networks was curtailed by the creation of Pakistan and the re-organisation of the United Provinces, yet they now extended to southern India. The subject matter of the images was also notably diverse, with the twins' photographs comprising religious and historic monuments, natural features, household objects and spaces, and portraits of young and old people from a mixture of social backgrounds and engaged in a variety of professional and leisure activities.

Thus, a print of Debalina's photograph of Delhi's Diwan-i-Khas taken in 1936 travelled under the title 'The Splendour that was India' from the UP Amateur Photographic Association Lucknow in 1939 to the photographic exhibition held under the patronage of the Governor of Bengal, 1940 and organised by the Lens Club Calcutta in 1940, and then on to the 3rd Benares All-India Salon organised by Photographic Society of Bangalore later that same year. Manobina's print of a naked toddler picking flowers in a garden featured in the 1965 All India Photographic Association hosted by the Vishakha Camera Club and the 1966 Andhra Pradesh Salon of Photography hosted by the Mahbubnagar Camera Club; Andhra Pradesh was the unexpected first state formed on linguistic grounds after a constitutional crisis prompted by the death of the hunger-striking Telugu activist Potti Sreeramulu in 1952.[49]

The postcolonial bent of the twins' amateurism was not only manifested in and on their prints, but also in their attitudes to photographic technologies, where thrift as well as manual and analogue self-reliance in the face of

---

[48] Mazumder, Kamalini. Personal correspondence with author.

[49] For a short summary of the creation of Andhra Pradesh, see Guha, Ramachandra. 2007. *India After Gandhi: The History of the World's Largest Democracy* (New Delhi: Pan Macmillan). p. 187.

discombobulating abundance or rapid change were important. For Rajsaday, his grandmother was 'the very antithesis of the modern digital photographer who discards hundreds of shots to find just the right one'. She was loathe to waste film, and 'would plan the shots, almost see them in her mind before shooting and agonise over them'.[50] Kamalini similarly characterised her mother as a simple and self-reliant person unfazed by quickly changing trends and automation offered by the latest gadgets. In the 1970s, she recalls that Debalina bought a Nikon F, 'the first really sophisticated SLR camera she had'.[51] Where the dual lens reflex cameras required the photographer to judge the aperture and exposure and set them accordingly, used 120 mm films, and meant that the negatives were in a square format, the SLR had a built-in exposure meter and a different film format.[52] Kamalini noted with tremendous admiration that her mother 'adapted to the new camera without so much as blinking an eye!' yet that she 'rarely consulted the exposure meter, relying instead on her instincts and experience. [...] She firmly believed that anything completely mechanical or computerised could not be foolproof.'[53] Manobina also maintained that she was not enamoured by technological advancements, even if she, unlike her twin sister, was 'guilty' of having succumbed to them. In her memoirs, she wrote: 'I now cannot do without an exposure metre. The more we depend on machines, our own power of deduction, analysis and decision making become non-existent or weak'.[54]

In this regard, I would suggest that the amateurism of Debalina Majumdar and Manobina Roy is of consequence for historians concerned with the politics of the everyday; and of a South Asian state in a time of rapid change. Between the 1930s and 1960s, the British withdrew from and partitioned the subcontinent into India and Pakistan with violent results; while WWII gave way to a Cold War between those states allied with the capitalist United States and the communist Soviet Union. Nehru, as head of the nationalist Congress party, took charge as India's Prime Minister and B.R. Ambedkar chaired the Constituent Assembly, which on 26 January 1950 declared India to be a sovereign, socialist, secular, democratic republic and guaranteed its citizens universal suffrage, justice, equality and liberty. Alongside domestic Five Year Plans that saw the implementation of big dams and heavy industry, and state-funded and directed cultural productions, Nehru also steered India along a course of non-alignment. This was, as Srinath Raghavan puts it, a foreign policy comprising 'first, the importance of retaining the capacity for independent judgement and action on the international stage; second, the avoidance of military alliances and arms races; third, working towards a more

[50] Dutt. 'Lives less forgotten'.

[51] Mazumder, Kamalini. 4 December 2015. Personal correspondence with author.

[52] Ibid.

[53] Ibid.

[54] Devi. 'In Black and White'.

just and equitable international order', in pursuit of which Nehru espoused 'anti-colonialism, anti-racism, a concerted move away from economic under-development, and the building of ever-widening areas of peace'.[55] This righteous postcolonial ambition—which Nehru articulated succinctly in a 1947 speech by stating '[w]e do not intend to be the playthings of others'[56]—is increasingly being acknowledged as having been broadcast into being, as argued by Srirupa Roy, for millions of Indians.[57]

Roy's focus is on the continuous consolidation of this ambition via the annual Republic Day parade, the documentary films produced by the Films Division of India, and the techno-scientific schemes introduced by the five-year plans such as the steel towns built to house the workers of nationalised steel plants.[58] Other scholars have focussed more on how this ambition was remade through the 'small but decisive acts of agency by countless ordinary people firmly convinced of the justice of their claims', or the ideology and pragmatism of their (own) visions.[59]

Such acts, amongst which the twins' photography might also be counted, are what lead Taylor C. Sherman, Sarah Ansari and William Gould to refer to the post-1947 decades as 'a formative period in South Asian history in terms of citizenship, the politics of development and the secular state', in which 'the nature of the state and the content of citizenship were keenly contested'.[60] In the introduction to *Subjects to Citizens* (2014), they describe how '[m]embers of the population frequently voiced their disappointment with the failures of their new government servants to live up to the expectations that citizens be given fair access to good and services'; noting with interest that 'these expectations were often coupled with a quiet willingness of the part of citizens to use their own guile to circumvent or manipulate the services that the state did provide.'[61]

Joya Chatterji has further argued that following the announcement of Partition, the steps taken by 'local constables, non-commissioned soldiers, spies,

---

[55] See Raghavan, Srinath. 'Nonalignment', in Dharampal-Frick, Gita, Monika Kirloskar-Steinbach, Rachel Dwyer, Jahnavi Phalkey. eds. 2015. *Key Concepts in Modern Indian Studies* (New York: NYU Press). pp. 193–195, 194–195.

[56] Ibid. p. 195.

[57] See Roy, Srirupa. 2007. *Beyond Belief: India and the Politics of Postcolonial Nationalism* (Durham: Duke University Press).

[58] Ibid. Roy interrogates the aesthetic formations of and exhortations by the postcolonial Indian nation-state, but this still leaves much room to address the uptake/(re)production of these aesthetics by ordinary citizens. See especially the chapter 'Moving Pictures: The Films Division of India and the Visual Practices of the Nation-State'. pp. 36–65.

[59] Chatterji, Joya. 2012. 'South Asian Histories of Citizenship, 1946–1970'. *The Historical Journal.* 55: 4. p. 1049.

[60] Sherman, Taylor C., William Gould and Sarah Ansari. 'Introduction'. Sherman, Taylor C., William Gould and Sarah Ansari. eds. 2014. *From Subjects to Citizens: Society and the Everyday State in India and Pakistan, 1947-1970* (New Delhi: Cambridge University Press). p. 6.

[61] Ibid. p. 9.

railways guards and ship captains who handled the flow of migrants without any sanction from above or regard for the tenets of law were as productive as, if not counter-productive to, the policies instituted by the Constituent Assembly of India.[62] She also notes 'the ways in which South Asian citizenship practices travelled beyond the subcontinent, affecting the status of overseas Indians and having an impact upon the citizenship norms of the countries where they lived'. [63] Chatterji thus suggests 'the diffusion of ideas and practices regarding citizenship have flowed in more than one direction' and that the 'history of citizenships [...] may be far more multi-sited, entangled, and intertwined than historians have previously assumed'.[64]

While I am not insisting that the process of turning from subjects to citizens, and of the forging and disruption of policy from unexpected realities and quarters necessarily constitutes amateurism, the strategies, performances and confrontations they entail help us to contextualise the twins' activity. I cannot help but think of the twins and their father when Roy identifies how 'the practice of citizenship was depicted in tutelary and pedagogical terms as a learning activity or an ongoing process of acquiring skills and attributes rather than an already-possessed right or claim that could be exercised in the present';[65] of when, and why photography was, for them, such a serious undertaking.

Amateurism in Other Words

If using the term amateurism in relation to the twins' photography summons a clear set of photographic, and even political, lineages and cultures, it is also methodologically generative because it *doesn't*. After all, its etymology of doing something for the 'love of' invokes fondness, curiosity, rivalry, innovativeness, and assemblage not limited to a specific type or site of production; a littleness and slightness that is hugely capable. It involves, too, a shift away from a politics of identity and subjectivity towards a politics of activity and encounter. For although amateurism might involve a subject, it is an amorphous one at best: a lover, a rogue agent, a bricoleur, an apprentice. Moreover, it is a subject likely to get utterly carried away, dissolved into, or transformed in the pursuit of their passion.

Admittedly, amateurism also comes with baggage: in the twins' times, it was often not a desire but the only recourse against long-established and formal legal and social exclusions. Marilyn Ogilvie, for instance, refers to women in the arts and sciences (she specifically considers astronomy in late nineteenth, early-twentieth century Britain) who were barred from professional status as

[62] Chatterji's work mainly draws attention to how violent these 'small-scale' acts and visions could be. Chatterji. 'South Asian Histories'. p. 1051.

[63] Ibid. p. 1071.

[64] Ibid.

[65] Roy. *Beyond Belief*. p. 44.

'obligatory amateurs'.[66] Proceeding with the term 'amateurism' is not to deny the structural oppressions that produced and sustained amateurism, nor to endorse a related misogynistic and/or elitist tradition of dismissing or deriding the aesthetic engagements of women and/or people of colour as 'amateur'.

Rather, it is to run with new conceptions of it, or to draw on models and iterations of amateurism that are deliberately imaginative. We might, for instance, borrow from the Palestinian critic Edward Said's 1993 Reith Lectures, which offer an understanding of amateurism as 'a stubborn force', a spirit that, while neither totally rebellious nor totally acquiescent, 'can enter and transform' the routine, the everyday, the most personal of projects 'into something much more lively and radical'.[67] There is also a still germinating literary endeavour that, like Said's lectures, apparently has nothing to with photography.

Some years after winning the Pulitzer Prize for Fiction, the Bengali-American author Jhumpa Lahiri moved from writing novels in English, to reading, speaking and writing in Italian. She begins *In Other Words*, a book she wrote in Italian, by admitting, 'I don't have a real need to know this language ... I have only the desire.'[68] Yet, as she qualifies, 'ultimately a desire is nothing but a crazy need. As in many passionate relationships, my infatuation will become a devotion, an obsession. There will always be something unbalanced, unrequited...'[69] Lahiri's embrace of Italian is, consequently, a painstaking process in which she 'grope[s]' her 'way, like a child, like a semi-literate'[70] and remains acutely aware of the obstacles in her path: 'I know that I lack true mastery. I know that my writing in Italian is something premature, reckless, always approximate.'[71] It is, however, precisely through this lack of a solid footing, a rigid framework, that she finds 'the freedom to be imperfect':[72]

> When I read in Italian, I'm a more active reader, more involved, even if less skilled. I like the effort, I prefer the limitations. I know that in some way my ignorance is useful to me. I realise that in spite of the limitations the horizon is boundless. Reading in another language implies a perpetual state of growth, of possibility. I know that, since I'm an apprentice, my work will never end.[73]

Such words point, among other things, to amateurism as a protective impulse, an unexpected legitimising framework. Lahiri is a non-Italian, non-European,

---

[66] Ogilvie, Marilyn Bailey. March 2000. 'Obligatory Amateurs: Annie Maunder (1868–1947) and British Women Astronomers at the Dawn of Professional Astronomy'. *The British Journal for the History of Science*. 33: 1. pp. 67–84.

[67] Said, Edward W. 1996. 'Professionals and Amateurs'. *Representations of the Intellectual: The 1993 Reith Lectures* (New York: Vintage Books). pp. 65–84.

[68] Lahiri, Jhumpa. 2016. *In Other Words*. translated by Ann Goldstein (New York: Alfred A. Knopf). p. 17.

[69] Ibid.

[70] Ibid. p. 55.

[71] Ibid. p. 85.

[72] Ibid. p. 83.

[73] Ibid. p. 43.

brown woman neither expected nor encouraged to have an interest in, let alone know, this quintessential Romance language. She is liable to be called an imposter or censured for trespassing and overreaching. Yet she is able to persevere by cloaking herself in the armour of apprenticeship and imperfection, by feigning and certainly claiming ignorance, by disavowing mastery.

This pedagogical orientation, in turn, evokes the 'proletarian amateurism' espoused by Jo Spence and Terry Dennett in Photography Workshop (based on 'open-ended collaborative practice' and 'deskilling');[74] and contemporary artist Risa Horowitz's recognition of amateurism as 'a critical method of art making'.[75] Horowitz joined the Royal Astronomical Society of Canada and became an amateur astronomer to pursue a technically demanding and long-running project based around capturing images of Saturn as it orbits the sun, thereby setting off a process of 'networking and knowledge-sharing' that productively 'expands and blurs the boundaries between practices and disciplinary domains'.[76] The twins' photographic activity was just as contingent. It developed not just through their father's guidance and the photographic literature and associations they accessed, but also in close connection to marital and maternal responsibilities, reading novels, poetry and magazines; in Manobina's case to extensive and varied forms of writing; in Debalina's case to her university studies, love for gardening and botany, and philanthropic interests and concerns.[77] These connections shaped the range of subjects and styles they knew to photograph, and produced the rich language that sheltered—sometimes by downplaying—their photography in their own and others' memories.

In underscoring the combination of craftiness *and* craftfulness behind the twins' photography, and making it possible to connect it to other art practices by other women, Lahiri's words help render it political.[78] That is, they demonstrate

---

[74] Wilson, Siona. 2015. *Art Labour, Sex Politics: Feminist Effects in 1970s British Art and Performance* (Minneapolis: University of Minnesota Press). While the Photography Workshop gestures to the kinds of futures and politics of photography dismissed as 'apolitical' for its domesticity or amateurism, it is important to note that the specific strategies and clear battle with patriarchal and elitist structures is very different to the quiet and often conservative politics claimed by the twins. Additionally, its deliberately 'crude' aesthetics were very different to the twins' understanding of photography as a practice requiring skill and practice; and of their obvious delight in producing and viewing photographs acknowledged as masterful.

[75] Horowitz, Risa. 2014. 'Imaging Saturn – Amateurism as a Critical Method of Art Making'. *RACAR: Revue d'art canadienne*. 39: 1. p. 39.

[76] Ibid.

[77] Roy, Rinki. 1 February 2016. Personal correspondence with author.

[78] Such craftiness is akin to how Tariq Jazeel describes the 'canny yet decidedly non-subversive re-working of colonial rationality' by elite Sri Lankan women living in post-imperial London and active in the Sri Lankan Women's Association. See Jazeel, Tariq. 2006. 'Postcolonial geographies of privilege: diaspora space, the politics of personhood and the "Sri Lankan Women's Association in the UK"'. *Transactions of the Institute of British Geographers*. 31: 1. pp. 19–33.

how amateur engagements are saturated with transformative power even when their makers and doers themselves shy away from any clear politics, and are not considered political agents in any traditional or disciplinary sense.

Growing Up in Photography

When I met Kamalini in a Kolkata café a few years ago, she had brought with her a selection of photograph albums. We spent the whole morning looking and talking over two of these, both containing slightly dog-eared black-and-white photographs in square and circular format, whose layout on the pages of black card adhered roughly to categories of subject or genre. One bore the charmingly handwritten title 'Sweet Memories 1935' and signature 'LinaBina', a moniker the twins derived by conjoining their names. Kamalini notified me that this was the oldest album in her possession, and thus possibly the first relating to their photographic activity.

Grouped together on a page of 'LinaBina' were four portraits of their father, Binod Bihari Sen, lighting a cigarette; smoking a hookah pipe, and writing at his desk in daylight and at night, though wrapped in a shawl at both times. Another page bore a variety of outdoor shots, including a view of the Taj Mahal, the impressive entrance of their Ramnagar bungalow, a cat bathed in sunlight, and clouds and trees reflected in waterbodies. The second album, enfolded within a brown-and-white checkered cloth cover, more of the same. There were groupings of silhouettes (Figure 6), men at work on the house and in the garden, including a snake charmer, a carpenter, a builder and a painter (Kamalini suggested that some may have been household servants dressed in costume), studio-style portraits of their mother Kironmoyee and older sister Anusuya, united by their adoption of a coy side profile, and a more eclectic spread featuring these women gazing out into the distance from the balcony, the window, the shore; their sari-clad bodies again turned to the side.

Silverfish-eaten and barely held together anymore, these albums were, as it turned out, not all sweetness and light, nor really about representing family life, but rather, akin to Jhumpa Lahiri's ascent/descent into Italian. It was around 1935, after all, that the twins were under the tutelage of their father, and had just become acquainted with Bimal Roy, who was then a camera assistant with New Theatres in Calcutta. As Debalina told the journalist Ratnottama Sengupta,

> When Bimalda saw photography was a serious interest with us, he advised us to see good photographs. He gave us a Kodak magazine, full of information about camera, lenses, rolls and also filled with images. That was a big education for us. We'd already acquired a sense about images, about subjects and lighting but his suggestions honed our senses and we learnt to train our cameras for better results.[79]

[79] Sengupta, 'Portraits'.

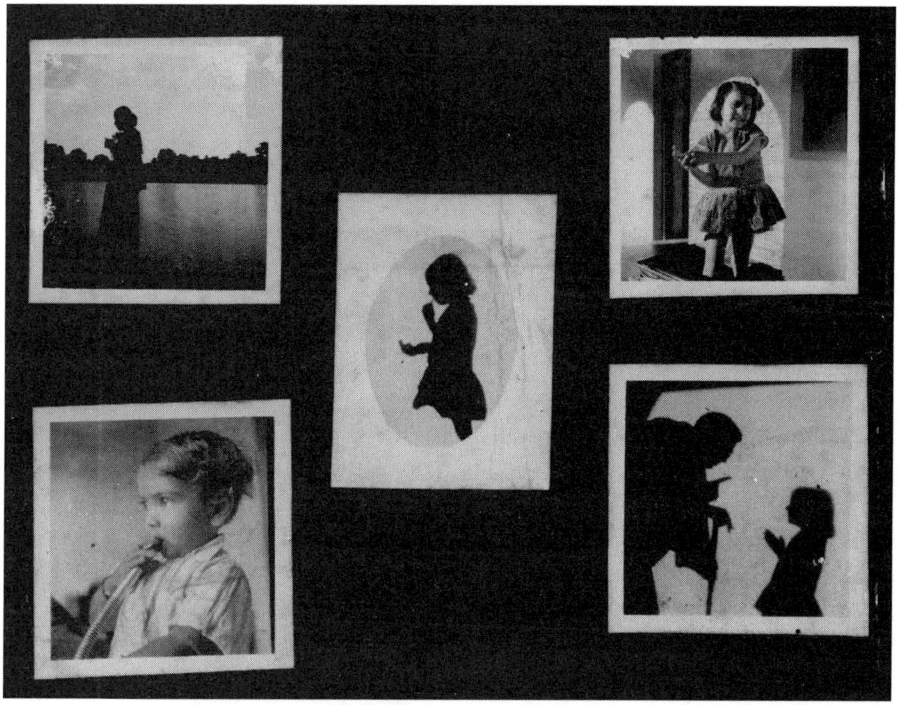

Figure 6. Page from album assembled by Manobina Roy and Debalina Majumdar, c.1935 Courtesy Kamalini Mazumder.

Debalina's recollection graphically evinces how she came to understand photography as an activity involving all the 'senses' even as it sets out a practical, no-nonsense formula for learning photography rooted in prosaic materials. It marks how photography spilled out from the pages of this magazine and into the twins' everyday movements and visions, as well as their interactions with others; how it consumed them and transformed them.

Each of the images in these albums and their layouts attest to an obsessive identification of the elements which would make (up) each photograph and of how this would manifest on paper once their 100 ASA kodachrome film, known for its high resolution and which Rajsaday said Debalina was loathe to waste, was developed and processed.[80] Their landscape techniques were similar to those employed by Bengali photographers such as Mahim Chandra Thakur, with Ranu Roychoudhuri singling out how the 'compositional balance together with prominent vanishing points play[ed] an important role not only in enhancing their pictorial quality but also guiding the viewers' gaze on the photographic plane'.[81] She cites Thakur's description of his practice:

[80] Dutt, Rajsaday. 22 October 2015. Personal correspondence with author.

[81] Roychoudhuri, Ranu. 2015. 'The Public Lives of Photographs: Aesthetic Conventions and Socio-Cultural Change in Twentieth-Century India (Unpublished doctoral dissertation, University of Chicago). pp. 79–80.

> I got out with my camera in the morning after the previous night's rain and that is the most favorable time for introducing pictorial effect in the photographs ... on the very day the sunlight was not harsh and sky was cloudy causing the frame to have a nice and soft effect because the light and dark contrast was not high. This kind of light condition is important otherwise under exposure takes away the details in the frames and over exposure make the image flat.[82]

These words resonate with the experiential and meticulous texture of so many of Debalina's and Manobina's photographs of clouds gathered over water, and light beams through the forest clearings. The twins' photographs of people and animals, meanwhile, entailed being creative with more man-made materials, such as pulling curtains together or apart, opening or closing doors and windows, placing or removing a carpet. They demanded proficiency in judging the most appropriate distance from which to stand or crouch with a camera to get the appropriate focus, and in being ever-ready to press down on the camera shutter at that precise moment when their living and breathing subject was ideally aligned against the light, or had dropped their self-consciousness and relaxed into the act of posing.

The varying degrees of involvement in the photographic encounter by their subjects, on the other hand, suggest how this obsession both infected and alienated. In the case of men, it is unclear whether their consent was given or demanded, but either way, they appear generally unbothered. Some are too busy applying themselves to the tasks at hand (transporting building materials, constructing wooden frames, balancing on scaffolding) to notice the presence of one or two photographing girls, and others are bemused but alert in their body language. In comparison to the manual labour and drudgery of carrying out domestic employment, they might have found it pleasurable to sit down and simply pose for a camera. Or to dress up and immerse themselves in a theatrical performance for the children of the house.

Looking at their mother Kironmoyee and sister Anusuya, however, I cannot help thinking that their cooperation was tempered by a degree of aloofness. Both are slight figures in the memorialisations around the twins' photography, with Kironmoyee noted for her strict adherence to purdah and other traditions of elite Hindu Bengali femininity, and Anusuya for having been married at an early age. While their orthodox lifestyles could explain why they appear so demurely in these 1930s albums, and not at all in later photographs, their tendency to face away from rather than into the camera might also be a response to their exclusion from Sen Roy's and the twins' amateurism, in which they never called the shots.

The inverse of this is how Sen Roy, who was so used to wielding a camera, is an enigmatic yet also blank presence throughout. Swathed in whirls of smoke, or in his signature shawl, his expressions are unreadable not due to shyness, but rather because of his awareness and acceptance

82 Ibid. p. 74.

of being called on as a photographic subject. He features in those images which Kamalini identified as the result of her mother wanting to try her hand at photographic effects, or light 'tricks' that she had seen or heard about. The silhouette series, which features both Sen Roy and Manobina in a gestural exchange that plays on their relation to each other as teacher/student, master/apprentice, father/daughter, and as single apparitions, was thus a photographic translation Debalina made of a puppet shadow play, which had 'been playing in her mind' for several days after she had watched it.[83] In them, the qualities of the silhouette merge with the texture and feel of the photograph as a physical print, an intermingling which continues into the morphing of the photographs against ageing black album paper. A portrait of Sen Roy digitised by CSSS but attributed with a question mark to Manobina, offers another intense engagement with the silhouette, this time enhanced by the white wisps of smoke emanating from his cigarette, and the bright glint of his spectacles.

Getting Lost in Photography

This close reading of the twins' early albums demonstrates that amateurism was as much about clear-headed pragmatism and modesty as about getting absorbed, getting too close, getting carried away, to the point of getting lost in photography. This double movement is equally prevalent in the images they made many decades later in Europe, and which I had initially assumed to be the most straightforwardly and determinedly photojournalistic moments of their practice, attempting as they do to communicate sights (truths) to their families and fellow Indians back home, especially given their appearance in the pages of *The Illustrated Weekly of India*.

Both Manobina and Debalina, for instance, photographed a solitary female figure reading in Hyde Park on an autumnal day. Manobina's photograph functions as a vertical portrait, featuring the woman's upper body as she reads, the novel—a Penguin edition of Monica Dickens' *Mariana*—clearly in focus.[84] According to her daughter Rinki, eighteen at the time of this trip and the eldest of the eight 'children' in the twins' entourage, Manobina simply *had to* photograph this woman as she reminded her of Miss Marple, the elderly protagonist from the Agatha Christie crime series she so adored.[85] She is so closely framed that the wrinkles on her face and the brooch pinned to her coat are visible, emphasising that Manobina must have moved with utmost grace in order to have not disturbed her with the sound of the camera shutter, or the crunch of dried leaves under her feet. Debalina's photograph, meanwhile, is horizontal and verging on the scenic, her attention caught as much by the

[83] Mazumder, Kamalini. 15 November 2016. Personal correspondence with author.

[84] For an image of the 1958 Penguin edition, see www.pinterest.co.uk/pin/376543218835873799/, last viewed on 7 June 2022.

[85] Roy, Rinki. Personal correspondence with author. 21 October 2016.

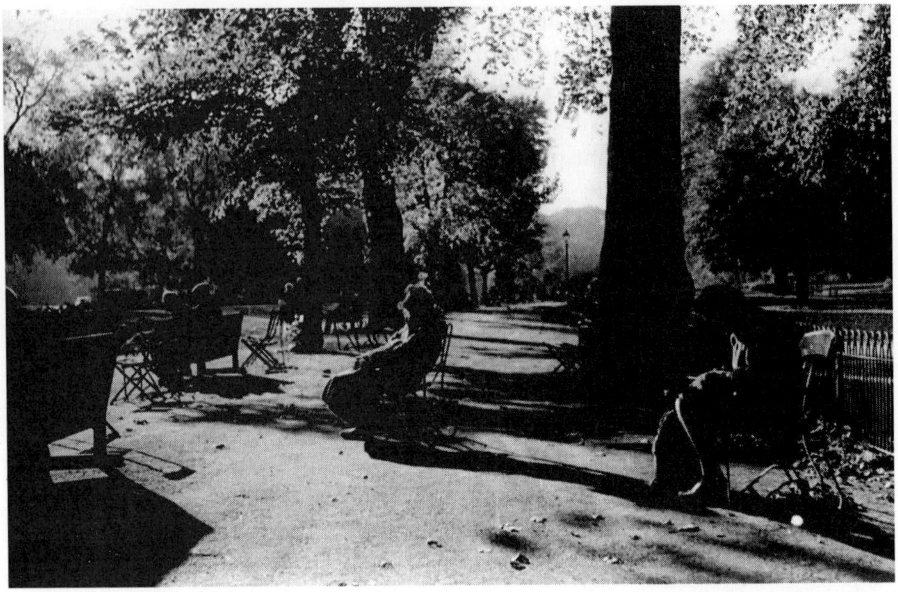

Figure 7. Debalina Mazumder, Photograph, c.1960. Courtesy Kamalini Mazumder.

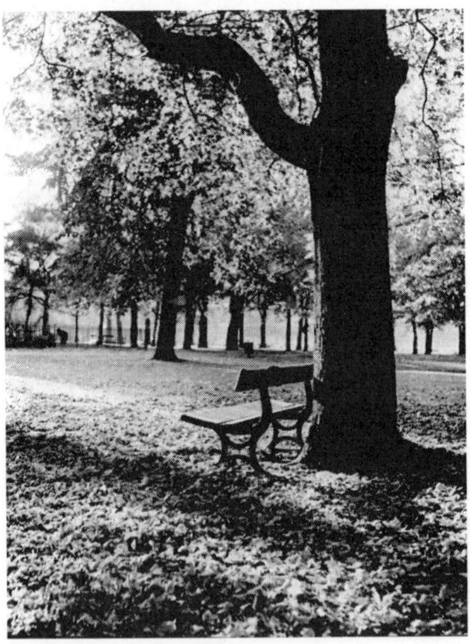

Figure 8. Debalina Mazumder, Photograph, c.1960. Courtesy Kamalini Mazumder.

woman's reading as by the way in which the light was reflecting off the white handkerchief she clutched between her fingers, the wooden bench she was seated on and the park in the background.

Debalina's photograph likely anticipated two others nestled in the stack of prints Kamalini had given me to peruse: the first featuring numerous people on numerous benches and which she titled 'September Afternoon' (Figure 7); the second, an empty bench (Figure 8). According to Kamalini, it had been 'very difficult to find an empty bench … [but] she had this preconceived photograph in her mind, that this is what she wanted. She chose the spot and then just sat there, stayed put. And she got what she wanted.'[86] From the resulting

[86] Mazumder, Kamalini. Personal correspondence with author. 15 November 2016.

image, it is possible to retrace this slow prickling of Debalina's senses as time passed, her posture very still except for her eye travelling upwards, taking in the trees and following the play of light through them from left to right, top to bottom, gauging precisely the moment in which it illuminated the leaves bunched together on the ground in front of her. That is, one can feel the obsessive compulsion that moved her to forget time and all other priorities (perhaps even propriety) working its way into an image of perfect peace and quiet. One can appreciate why, although it was initially titled 'The Deserted Park', these words were returned to and scratched out in favour of 'Solitude'.

It is this atmospheric quality that pervades the twins' images of shop windows, market stalls and newsstands. In these, it is as if the twins' movement through urban spaces was arrested, and the scene before them dramatised by a table of second-hand books and quaint knick-knacks, the front pages of newspapers screaming bloody murder, a wide sheet of glass. Debalina made a series of photographs of the preparatory stages of the autumn sale for women's wear on Oxford Street. In one digitised by the CSSS under the title 'All about Eve', a shop assistant is preparing a mannequin; in another, a group of women have stopped to look at what's on offer (Figure 9). Manobina also made several such photographs. Looking at them, I'm reminded of a passage from the Italian novelist Natalia Ginzburg's essay, 'England: Eulogy and Lament'. Ginzburg arrived in the city in 1960, having experienced fascism, war and exile in the Italian countryside, wrote of feeling 'dizzy' at the sight of 'shop-windows filled to overflowing with shoes that all have the same pointed toes and stiletto heels' and 'windows brimming over with women's underclothes – so stuffed with

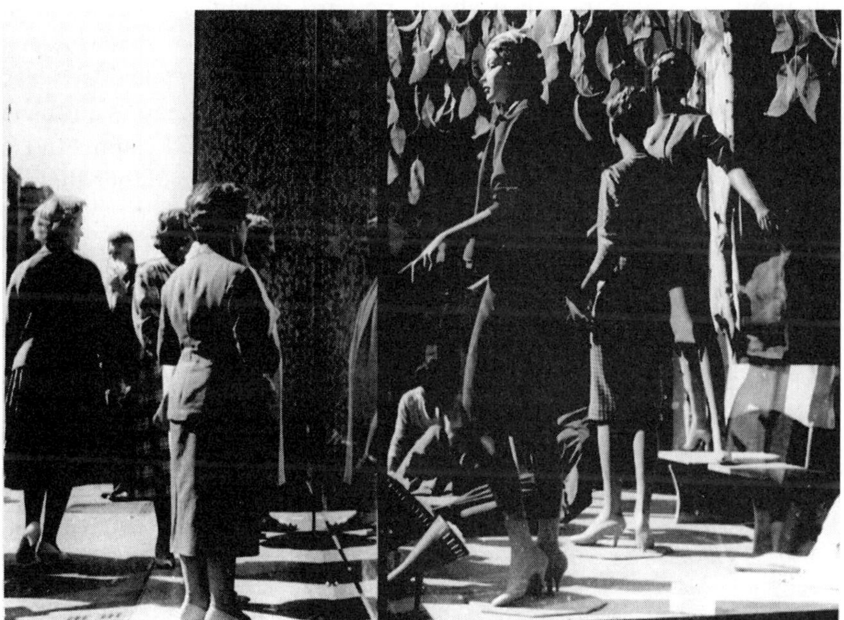

Figure 9. Debalina Mazumder, Photograph, c.1960. Courtesy Kamalini Mazumder.

merchandise that my eyes feel sated with it and any desire to buy a slip or a pair of stockings is completely destroyed'.[87]

The twins, whose retail experiences had hitherto been formed by the strict economic policies of the postcolonial Indian state pre-1991, were evidently also drawn to and repelled by how vendors had set objects out in ways that ranged from the picturesque, to the visually arresting, to the grotesque. Where Ginzburg sought comfort in words, they seem to have turned to their cameras to process this overwhelming yet hollow plenitude.

Such displays, moreover, allowed the twins to observe and photograph others without being seen themselves, the people in these photographs being so occupied in acts of looking, talking and bargaining, and the streets being much busier than a quiet corner of the park. These images of 'dizziness' are thus made calm by the very fact of seeing double, and might be thought of as companions to Vivian Maier's street photography in New York. For Maier, who was an amateur photographer active in exactly the same years as the twins, continuously returns to glass windows and mirrors as a way of stealthily turning her camera on others while always, whether secretly, poignantly or playfully, acknowledging her own presence.[88]

I often find myself coming back to a photograph (Figure 10) of two women, facing each other in a street of shop windows, protected from the elements, and my curious gaze, by the shrouding, abstracting effect of their long, robust-looking coats, their hats, glasses and the shadows these and the buildings around them cast. The twins, as two other women in long coats and spectacles had, in the course of their wanderings through London, chanced upon them and, perhaps taken aback, perhaps delighted by in some way, seeing themselves, stopped in their tracks, looked down into the viewfinders of their Rollis, adjusted the shutter speed, tensed the shutter on one side, released the knob on the other, and thereby incorporated these lines, layers and shapes into a black-and-white composition to which they both laid claim. And yet, I would not say that they 'captured' these two women, but rather that their photography produced a kind of kinship with and for them.

On the back of the print housed amongst Manobina's photographs with her son Joy in Bombay, she has written 'Two old ladies meet on the road in

[87] Ginzburg, Natalia. "England: Eulogy and Lament", in *The Little Virtues*, London: Daunt Books Publishing, 2018, pp. 35-47, p. 37. Print.

[88] Maier's apparent androgyny and habits of hoarding newspapers, images and negatives, including many of her own, which she never developed, points not only to the way in which photography constitutes madness, but also to how it is seen as such by its present commentators and custodians. The compulsion to 'uncover' and explain Vivian Maier involves pathologising her character and motivations via labels of 'androgyny', 'bizarreness', 'strangeness' and 'irresponsible'. Vivian Maier's afterlife suggests that the twins knew what they were doing, and played a long game in the consistent way in which they removed their biographical connections and legacies from their photography in public articulations of it (both to journalists and descendants). See *Finding Vivian Maier*. 2014. Directed by John Maloof and Charlie Siskel. Ravine Pictures and Maloof, John. ed. 2011. *Vivian Maier – Street Photographer* (New York: Powerhouse Books).

London just to say "what a lovely day" – they are so lonely – that just to be able to talk to someone – is a relief'.[89] The print inscribed in Debalina's handwriting and now in Kamalini's safekeeping in Calcutta, more simply and light-heartedly reads 'Roadside gossip'. Both, in different tones, involve the twins placing themselves as observers of a foreign culture and of other people, whilst also coming face to face with, or preempting, a vision of themselves. Alongside conceptualisations and histories of photography as normalising, if not outright exploitative and violent, photography thus also emerges along the more ethically portentous lines recently explored by Kaja Silverman in *The Miracle of Analogy*, as a way of being in the world, as a form of orientation towards others.[90] Or, following Donna Haraway in *Staying with the Trouble: Making Kin in the Chthulucene*, a book that is not about photography but all about relationality and radical encounter, as a 'becoming-with'.[91]

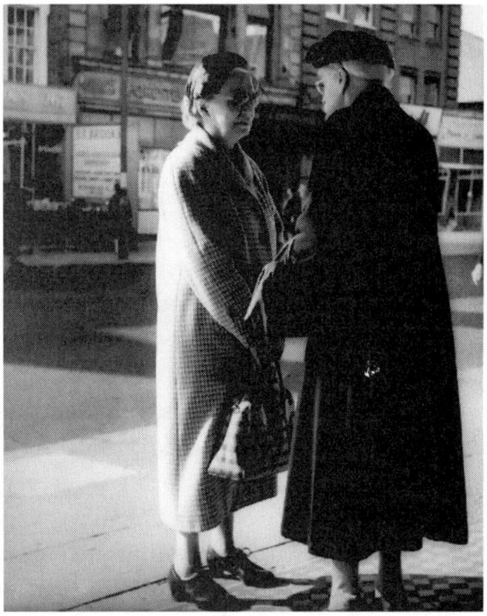

Figure 10. Manobina Roy, Photograph, c.1960. Courtesy Joy Roy.

Fog over London

However, lest we too get too carried away by the camera's promise of kinship, it is important to note that many of the twins' European photographs also speak of impenetrability and alienation. Many of Manobina's photographs feature heavy fog, dark lighting, solid and obscuring arches, unsociable street corners, and passers-by whose backs are turned to the camera, either because they were figures she was keen to keep her distance from, or simply could not get close to. All of these are present in a photograph titled 'A Mild "Pea-Souper"', taken at 'Aldwych opp. B.B.C.' with an aperture of 6¾ on a 'November Afternoon in London', where, as specified via a repetition that suggests incredulity, 'Dusk sets in at about 3 pm in the afternoon'.

---

[89] Manobina's inscription echoes Natalia Ginzburg's description of how '[e]very place where the English gather to chat with one another exudes melancholy. Indeed, nothing in the world is sadder than an English conversation.' Ginzburg. 'England'. p. 43.

[90] Silverman, Kaja. 2015. *The Miracle of Analogy, or The History of Photography, Part 1* (Stanford: Stanford University Press).

[91] Haraway, Donna. 2016. *Staying with the Trouble: Making Kin in the Chthulucene* (Durham: Duke University Press). p. 128.

This melancholic affect is more than a return to, or continuation of the soft-focus, pictorialist emphasis of the early twentieth-century amateur photography Debalina and Manobina were raised on. It is a visual registration of/reckoning with London as an uncomfortable, inaccessible and alienating space, which as visual histories sourced from documentary, press and personal photographs, such as *Black Britain* and *Asian Britain* have begun to establish, was especially the case for persons of colour, refugees and otherwise vulnerable people, such as the elderly or the unemployed.[92] Moreover, it is an aesthetic that was also being developed by literary migrants and visitors to London in those very years.

Fog is, for instance, a recurring metaphor in Sam Selvon's 1956 novel *The Lonely Londoners*, which tells the story of a motley crew of African-Caribbean 'Windrush' arrivals, that is, men and women who were encouraged by the British government to migrate from the former colonies to the United Kingdom to fill labour shortages after WWII. Under the British Nationality Act of 1948, they were technically given British citizenship but this welcome officially ended with the Commonwealth Immigrants Act of 1962. In any case, their welcome was always thin and no competition for the fog, which hangs thickly and menacingly over Selvon's characters. It never allows them to be comfortable or see clearly, and it makes Sir Galahad, the protagonist, feel hot in winter and cold in summer and therefore casts him as a misfit, always out of season, out of place, out of time.[93] In 'England: Eulogy and Lament', Natalia Ginzburg wrote about how the 'openly gloomy' and 'desolate' character of the city undercuts its reputation for providing refuge and civility. Ginzburg also references the rows upon rows of terraced houses, each with their little fenced-in back garden, which Manobina photographed (Figure 11). For her, they form the built environment through which white, middle-class British notions of privacy and 'every man to himself' attitudes keep out foreigners, especially those used to other, more communal ways of relating to each other and to their surroundings.[94]

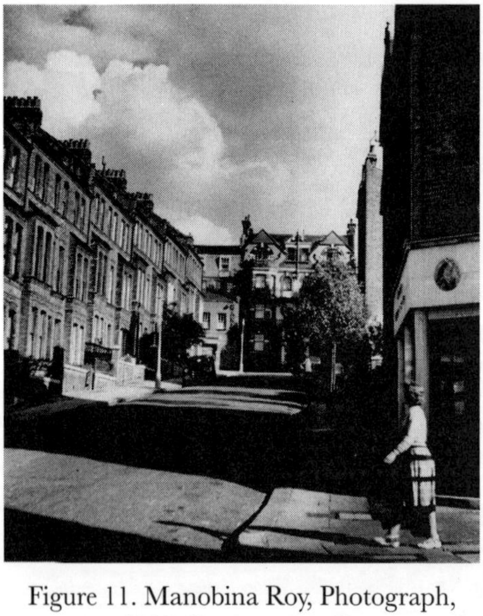

Figure 11. Manobina Roy, Photograph, c.1960. Courtesy Joy Roy.

[92] See Nashta, Susheila. 2013. *Asian Britain: A Photographic History* (London: The Westbourne Press) and Gilroy, Paul. 2011. *Black Britain: A Photographic History* (London: Saqi Books).

[93] Selvon, Sam. 2006 [1956]. *The Lonely Londoners* (London: Penguin Books).

[94] Ginzburg. 'England'. pp. 35–47 and 36–37.

Even in those photographs where the fog has lifted, the sun is out and the mood is lively, there is an insurmountable distance and feeling of discord, as in Manobina's images of people congregating at the Speaker's Corner in Hyde Park. In her article for *The Illustrated Weekly*, Manobina writes how she

> happened to visit … on a bright autumn afternoon with my camera … I was amused to see a couple of old women (surely in their seventies) sprawled on the grass, reading avidly some blood-curdling murder report in an evening paper – through a magnifying glass! Near them was a fiery orator, with a large group of people around him, shouting about the injustices of the Conservative Government. But he did not seem to disturb the old women in the least. There was a Negro speaker who was hooted as a liar as he recounted his bitter experiences with the white people. A Hindu orator was also jeered at by some as he talked on Vedanta ('Just rot!'). I was particularly annoyed to see two youngsters, of about ten or twelve, leering at the elderly speaker and asking him who taught him to wear a suit and from whom he got his shoes. Some of the listeners encouraged the boys by joining in the laughter. I was so angry that I cried out, to the amazement of by-standers: 'How very badly these children are brought up! Insulting an elderly man … We wouldn't have tolerated it in our country!' At this outburst those around me suddenly looked sheepish and stopped laughing.[95]

Manobina's words make no bones about the racist environment in which the last two speakers attempted to speak up for themselves, while also under pressure to appear before a public as postcolonial subjects. Moreover, they draw attention to the righteous and patriotic stance she took in response, using the language of civility so commonly associated with and used by the British, to shame them. Yet she also mobilises photography, using her camera to highlight how what was happening right in front of those nonchalant members of the public so literally focused on sensational news stories in print, was itself 'blood-curdling'. She placed, for instance, her image of the Hindu orator in the top left hand corner of the first page of her article. He thus appears in dignified animation, his strong, gesticulating hand held up against a muted crowd underneath him, the black bowler hat in one man's hand exactly hiding his face in a visible gesture of shame.

The photograph (Figure 12) she made of the black speaker and captioned 'A Negro Orator at Hyde Park' notably did not make it into the pages of *The Illustrated Weekly*. It suggests, alongside her extensive defence of the Hindu orator, that the postcolonial nationalism and citizenship that the twins were part of forging had certain priorities. In her opening paragraph, Manobina had, after all, also alleged that

> a pavement artist, claiming to be the oldest in the profession in London, objected vehemently when I tried to photograph him … with his interesting collection of paintings. He was so rude to me that I came away in a huff from the gaping

[95] Roy, Manobina. 'A Sunday Afternoon'.

crowd – which was apparently quite startled to see an Indian woman in this angry mood. I was more successful with the next artist, but just as I snapped him he stepped in front with his back to me, obscuring the view of his paintings. (I could not help thinking how willingly people in India allow themselves or their surroundings, however sordid, to be photographed by foreigners).[96]

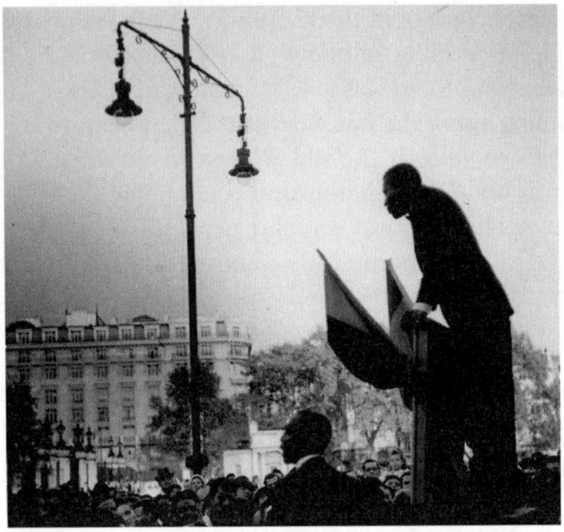

Figure 12. Manobina Roy, Photograph taken c.1960. Courtesy Joy Roy.

Manobina's upset at realising that, as an Indian woman, she is herself 'a spectacle of empire', is deftly channelled into an articulate postcolonial critique of white/Western privilege. Yet this channelling carries an elitist conceit—for she, too, would surely have objected vehemently to a stranger's desire to photograph her and she, too, was amongst those photographers whose urban, middle-class, upper-caste Hindu positionality and mobility allowed them to name and claim as photographic subjects a diverse, secular and coherent national landscape and subaltern Indians, as in her 'pictures of [the] Doga tribe in Ooty'.[97]

The photograph nonetheless contains the sparks of a transcendental solidarity which Manobina felt towards its subject, and her anger at a British public (culture) that on the surface seems so civil and even amiable, but under which lurks all manner of racism, prejudice and intolerance. The upward-tilting angle of the camera effects a symbolically rich stand-off between the black orator and the towering Victorian lamp-post, backed by the grand edifice of the Marriott Hotel on the corner of Park Lane, reminiscent of David vs. Goliath. Under them, the crowd appears as a sea of faces that individually bear a range of expressions including the amiable and sympathetic, yet morph into a larger, unfathomable and threatening mass with whom there is no obvious point of connect, and certainly no refuge.

Another view of what this stand-off looked, felt and sounded like confronted me in the form of a visceral scene in *The Lonely Londoners*, where Sir Galahad is jostled and egged on by his mates, in particular a man called Big City, to step up onto the platform and speak on 'the colour problem':

---

[96] Ibid.

[97] Devi. 'In Black and White'.

> 'Ladies and gentlemen –' he began.
>
> 'Talk louder man,' Big City say. 'We can't hear you.'
>
> 'The truth about this whole question,' Galahad went on desperately, 'is that we want work to do. I here in this country a long time and I can't get a regular work-'
>
> 'The people can't understand you boy,' Big City was out to make it hard for Galahad. 'Talk good English.'
>
> 'Give me a chance, Big City,' Galahad say, finding it easier to address one man in the crowd, and everybody start to laugh.
>
> 'Tell them about the time the foreman call you a nigger,' Big City say.
>
> 'Give me a chance, Big City,' Galahad say.
>
> But Big City start to exchange words with Galahad, and all the people looking at the two of them and laughing, and Galahad getting more and more vex, until at last he fly down from the platform as if he going to attack Big City.[98]

While Selvon's description of Galahad's fumbling movements as he desperately tries to live up to multiple expectations ends with (his) defeat and his deflation in front of a public, Manobina's photograph keeps the speaker earnestly, and elegantly upright, leaning towards the crowd from a platform that becomes nothing short of a moral high-ground. In some way, the speaker thus finds in Manobina's photography the space and time denied to him in real-life—and shown up as impossible in Selvon's upsetting document of subaltern life in postcolonial London—to hold forth.

Conclusion

Given such instances, it is no wonder that Manobina would tell Sabeena Gadihoke in an interview, firmly and emotionally, 'Wherever I go, the camera goes with me.'[99] Debalina, meanwhile, chose to reflect on her photography through the uncanny framework of a dream. At the age of eighty-one, she told Gadihoke,

> I used to dream that I am going to London or somewhere, and then after going to the airport, on the plane, I discover I haven't got my camera. I begin to cry. What will I do without my camera? I had that sort of an attachment with it. Somebody once told me that the eye is better than the camera. I said, that is all fine, but I would like to go over memories. Things as I saw them then.[100]

The twins' attachment to the camera as a part of themselves, as constituting their subjectivity, their memories, their mobility, their subconscious; without which they are disoriented, brings us back full circle not only to Walter Benjamin's instinctive grasp of the camera as a historical force to be reckoned with, but also to Jhumpa Lahiri's invocation of the relations her Italian dictionary was capable of generating, perhaps was also burdened with:

---

[98] Selvon. 2006. *The Lonely Londoners*. pp. 89–90.

[99] Gadihoke, Sabeena. 2022. 'Sisters, Cameras and Amateur Photography'.

[100] Gadihoke. 2003. 'The Home and Beyond'. p. 61.

> I always put it in my purse. I look up words when I'm in the street, when I return to the hotel after an outing, when I try to read an article in the newspaper. It guides me, protects me, explains everything. It becomes both a map and a compass, and without it I know I'd be lost.[101]

Indeed, when she forgot to take it with her, she felt 'slightly uneasy'. When a friend suggested she could do without it, or at least upgrade to a better dictionary, for instance, a phone app, she opposed this, describing how over the years it has morphed from a parental figure into a sibling, and yet, or therefore, 'remains full of secrets. This little book will always be bigger than I am.'[102]

To conclude on this note is not to insist that the twins' cameras and Jhumpa Lahiri's dictionary are interchangeable objects, or entities in and of themselves, but to emphasise how they attest to an amateurism worth thinking over, even taking on. As Sean Cubbitt writes in his manifesto for an 'Amateur Aesthetics', there is something radically precious in such readiness 'to transform every material, to show respect through manipulating and changing what comes to hand, seizing a technology, a technique, a shape or melody or image and making it anew. The process is future-directed and open-ended.'[103]

---

[101] Lahiri. 2016. *In Other Words*. p. 9.

[102] Ibid. p. 11.

[103] Cubitt, Sean. September 2008. 'Amateur Aesthetics'. Paper presented to the colloquium 'Beyond the End of Art', National Gallery of Victoria, Melbourne, Australia. www.academia.edu/574424/Amateur_aesthetics. Last viewed on 19 July 2018.

Yaatra Chitra/Parivar Chitra

Mrs. Gupta's Photographic Archive of a Family Amidst a Changing Nation

Suryanandini Narain

'Look after these trees that I planted, for they will outlast me, and when you look at them, you will remember me.'

—Mrs. Gupta, c. 2000, Mathura-Vrindavan

This essay dwells on photographic albums, framed family portraits and a diary left by Mrs. Gupta (1933–2013), who with her family, resided across the cities and towns of Uttar Pradesh in India. It is an attempt to reconstruct her occupation of public and private realms of existence from the 1950s to the 2000s, her archive evidencing a comparative view on the biographical temporalities of her life. It is a reflection on how she moved deeper into or further away from familial life, while consistently referencing the changing state of a nation post independence.

A postgraduate in Sanskrit literature and a politically active Gandhian, she negotiated her family life within a time of Nehruvian nation-building, reconciling the family and nation as extensions of each other. Her archival documents reveal how she debated the core political, economic and social values of a newly independent India, as she oscillated between being a critical and compliant citizen. Of Mrs. Gupta's many documents, I examine a selection of two photographic albums, a travel diary and six framed portraits that reflect upon her desire to locate herself simultaneously as householder and activist, mother and scholar, pilgrim and pragmatist. I hypothesise that Mrs. Gupta's self-positioning in the history of her time was highly self-conscious, as seen in the painstaking maintenance of this personal archive. Like the neem trees that she planted in her garden, she documented her life in a bid to be remembered on her own terms. By further textualising her personal history ensconced in this archive, I can but present only one perspective on the late Mrs. Gupta's reflections, limited by my own interpretative framework.[1]

[1] Jaimie Baron's essay broadly discusses the crises-ridden relationship between history and the archive, and the limiting or redemptive role of textual history in relation to audio-visual archival material. She proposes the idea of 'interpretative frameworks', especially important when family histories are textualised by later generations. This is because the personal cannot be discounted from influencing the reading of archival material and the attempt at meaning-making.

Recent international scholarship has regarded family photographs as the means of insight into feminine engagements in private and public realms of life.[2] These works examine emerging histories from the margins while also reflecting upon the medium's technological and aesthetic specificities. My study locates family photographs as they articulate the familial/domestic and the public/exterior as non-divergent domains straddled by women such as Mrs. Gupta, who through their engagement with images are able to establish a continuum between these different worlds. The domestic and the public often appear embedded within one another in the photographs considered here, explicating her attempts to merge the two worlds on her terms. Academically, Karen Stein's work explores the assumed binary between the worlds of 'home' and 'away' in the context of travel, and I build upon her scholarship to explore this collation through Mrs. Gupta's travel photographs.[3] I hypothesise that travel, both as the recreational family vacation as well as the religious pilgrimage or yatra, provides the female householder with special circumstances to reinvent her own identity and worldview. At such events, the domestic context is not abandoned, but infused with novel flexibility as it adapts to circumstances beyond the realm of the home. These albums evidence and explicate the coming together of seemingly divergent interior and exterior worlds as Mrs. Gupta acquires a fluid identity during her travels. The two specific travel documents, namely the photographic Touring Album and the diary of her yatra further classify the different types of mobility she espoused and expressed.

I evoke David Morgan's concept of 'family practices' as a method of studying family away from familiar sites of home and household, granting perspective on the everyday and routine activities 'seen through new pairs of spectacles that make us reflect on their significance' (2011:6).[4] Travel, I argue, is one context where 'family practices' can be observed away from the everyday. To sharpen this perspective, travel accounts in the form of photographs ('Touring Album') and the yatra diary have been juxtaposed with counterpart images ('Parivar Chitra' and six framed family portraits) that remain embedded within everyday and familial contexts of the home. In the first part of this essay, I

Mrs. Gupta is part of my own extended family, making access to this material, narratives by her children and my immersion in her world possible for this essay, within a personally determined 'interpretative framework'. (Jaimie Baron, 'The Digital Archive Effect: Historiographies and histories for the digital era', *The Archive Effect: Found Footage and the Audiovisual Experience of History*, London and New York, Rutledge, 2014, 138-172

[2] Malavika Karlekar presents a close analysis of the changing feminine figure in modern Indian photographs, in her work *Re-Visioning the Past: Early Photography in Bengal 1875 – 1915.* Oxford University Press, New Delhi; also Rochona Majumdar, *Marriage and Modernity: Family Values in Colonial Bengal,* 2009 Oxford University Press, New Delhi and Gillian Rose, *Doing Family Photography: The Domestic, the Public and the Politics of Sentiment.* 2010, Ashgate Publishing Ltd.

[3] Stein, Karen. Spring 2011. 'Getting Away from It All: The Construction and Management of Temporary Identities on Vacation'. *Symbolic Interaction.* 34: 2. pp. 290–308.

[4] Morgan, David H. 14 November 2011. 'Locating "Family Practices"'. *Sociological Research Online.* 16:4. p. 6.

examine the two photographic albums for readings on how holiday images map a geography of leisure and familial conviviality onto the topography of a nation, articulating in mutual reference, public, private and imagined identities. In the second part, I dwell upon Mrs. Gupta's diary of a religious pilgrimage or yatra that she undertook without her family, more than 30 years later. The latter bears a thick description of her experiences, and although there is only one group photograph to go by, the rich text itself visualises this tour in great detail. In the third and concluding part of the essay, I examine a set of framed family portraits that currently hang on Mrs. Gupta's drawing room wall, anchoring genealogical continuities following patriarchal norms in identity construction.

The Albums

A 'Touring Album', also titled '*Yatra Chitra*' (lit. 'Travel Images') compiled by Mrs. Gupta and her eldest son Guddu, documents the family's vacation photographs made between the years 1969 and 1976. The nuclear family at the time comprised of Mr. and Mrs. Gupta and their three children, Guddu, Guddi and Dabboo, aged between six and thirteen years. When seen alongside another of their family albums titled 'Parivar Chitra' (lit. 'Family Images') (1953–1981), certain aesthetic and formal comparisons can be identified. Both albums offer readings into private and public worlds inhabited by the Gupta family, their overlaps surfacing in the visual affordances steered by Mrs. Gupta as the main producer and archivist of the images. This section of the essay analyses the visual and material details of the Touring Album and positions it in conversation with the 'Parivar Chitra' album, reading into visceral qualities of familial performativity, the portrayal of its togetherness and the larger socio-political implications of mapping the cultural geography of a nation aligned with the socialist motto of 'unity in diversity'.

The Touring Album bears a horizontal format, with pink paper pages punched and tied together with string. The pages bear metallic corners to keep photographs in place; the black-and-white images range between 4x6 cm and 9x6 cm. The album's body was actually made by Guddu in his high school craft class, each page bearing carefully hand-cut flaps of tracing paper to prevent the sticking of photographs on adjacent leaves. Hardbound and covered in synthetic paper by a local bookmaker in Moradabad, with time and use, some pages threaten to come loose, yet the photos remain remarkably well placed in elaborate arrangements. The verso of the album cover bears the holographic image of a ship sailing in stormy waters, emphasising the fact that this is an album of travel-related photographs. Each page bears the names of places visited and the year of the trip in correspondence to the images. These are neatly inscribed in Hindi, first with pencil and then with a sharp-nib fountain pen in red ink, the top line combining the letters of each word is decoratively scalloped. The design and layout of the album

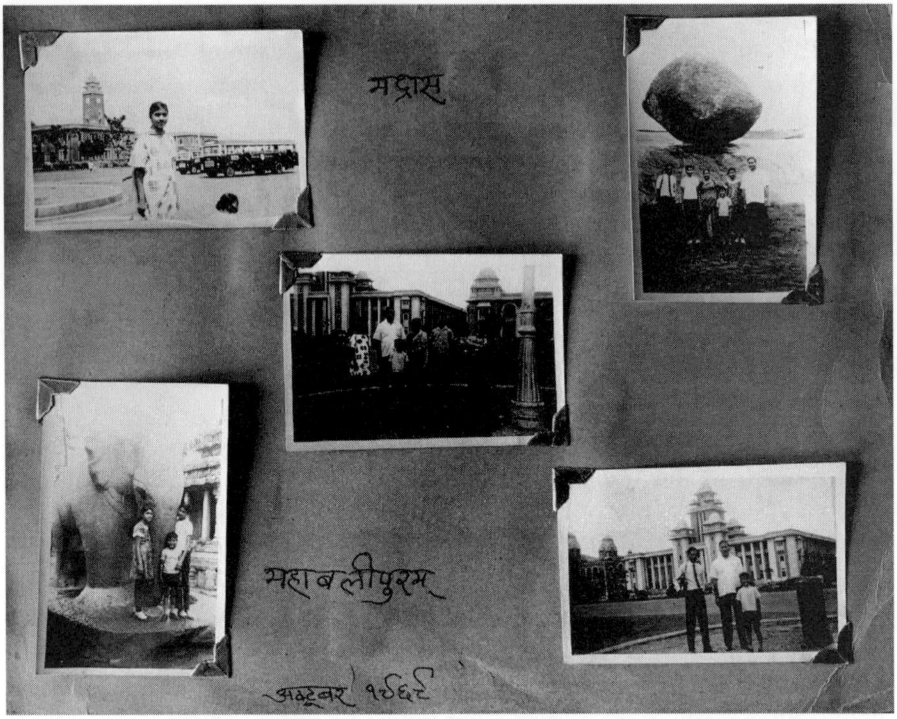

Touring Album/ 'Yatra Chitra', 1969-76, Gupta Family

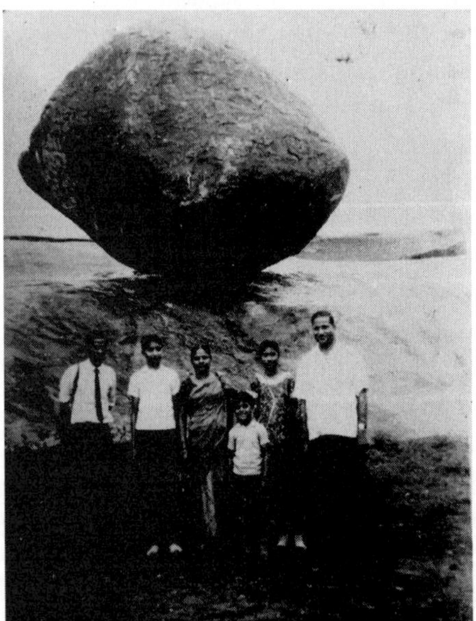

Touring Album/ 'Yatra Chitra', 1969-76, Gupta Family

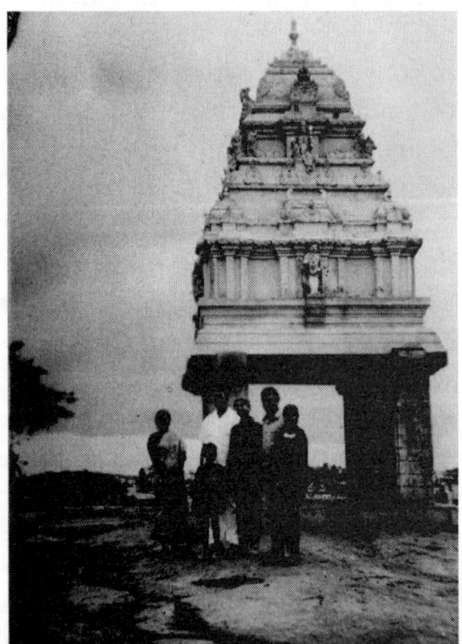

Touring Album/ 'Yatra Chitra', 1969-76, Gupta Family

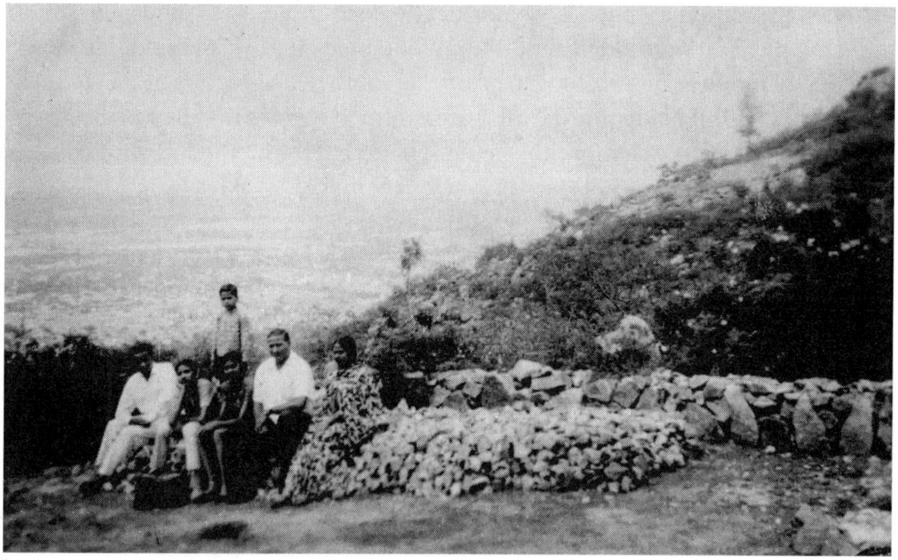

Touring Album/ 'Yatra Chitra', 1969-76, Gupta Family

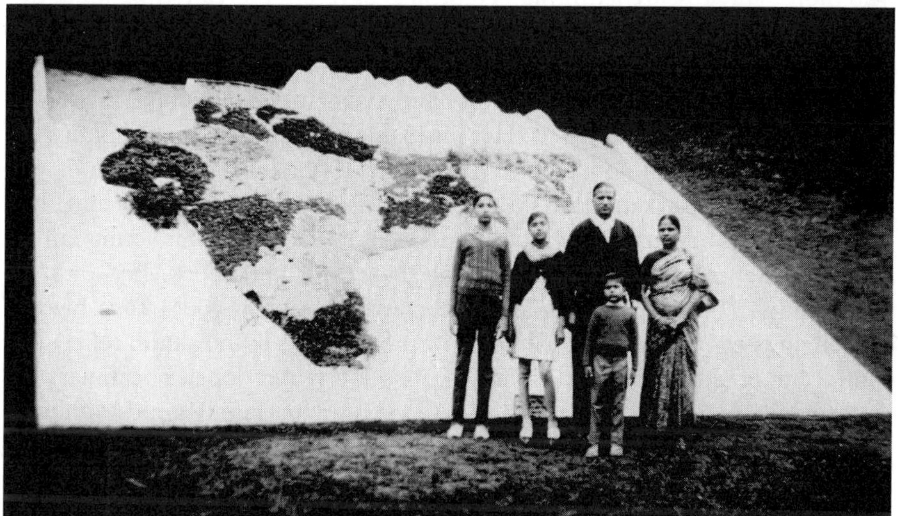

Touring Album/ 'Yatra Chitra', 1969-76, Gupta Family

are highly deliberate; no images are left without textualised affiliations to time and place. The photographs themselves are positioned in elaborate circular, stepped or diamond arrangements, vertical and horizontal orientations being treated symmetrically (see images). This dynamic arrangement activates the individual content and collective narratives of the photos on each page. There is an element of play, of listening to the resonance between images as they are angled towards each other, as if in dialogue.

Thematically, each page does not neatly correspond to a single site, often the same page accommodates more than one place that was visited. However, the Gupta family's month-long trip to the southern states of India, namely Karnataka, Tamil Nadu and Kerala, are grouped together at the beginning of the album, indicating a temporal scheme. The rest of the album has photographs of trips to North India's hill stations, such as Srinagar, Mukteshwar, Mussoorie and Nainital, and destinations in the planes where extended family had residences, such as Lucknow, Agra, Mumbai and Delhi. Historic and sacred cities, such as Allahabad, Amritsar, Chitrakoot and Varanasi, and the ruined temples of Khajuraho and Ellora make this seven-year period a busy one with much recreational travel. Each year saw multiple trips during school holidays, indicating Mrs. Gupta's practicality and convenience in travelling with children of manageable age. Later trips in fact excluded Guddu and Guddi as they prepared for school-leaving examinations back home, and only little Dabboo is seen accompanying his parents in these photographs.

The range of sites for vacationing spells Mrs. Gupta's breadth of interests, for she was the protagonist choosing destinations, planning itineraries, packing and providing childcare. As recalled by her children, she was a bibliophile who thoroughly researched India's cultural geography, thereafter planning the family's travel to the sites she wished to explore. This was thus a period of intense study for Mrs. Gupta, as she engaged with the world outside of her home through Hindi and English books and magazines, bought and borrowed from shops, friends and libraries. Her insatiable curiosity about the country in a pre-televisual world motivated her to physically explore the breadth of the nation, but it is remarkable that she did so while simultaneously performing her familial roles as mother and wife. With the will to document her young family along with new and historical monuments, cities and landscapes, she straddled the duality of being a householder and traveller in what could have been a challenging negotiation. One can see how most images in the album reflect the confluence of these two worlds, how a consciously developed vocabulary of the camera and albums embedded Mrs Gupta and her family amidst multiple personal and public contexts.

Domesticity was very much a part of the Gupta family's travels in those days, as an attendant frequently accompanied them to help with food, transport and lodging arrangements in new places. The family travelled by rail and car, and local food was often not to the children's liking. The trip to South India in 1969, for instance, was the first for a family from Moradabad. Guddu recalls how the family would anticipate the presence of a Marwari *bhojanalaya* (dining hall) in major cities, catering to visiting Marwari businessmen, for familiar North Indian food. Mrs. Gupta travelled with a complicated wooden box with a wire mesh, bearing dry snacks, powdered milk, a small immersion rod to heat water, utensils and basic spices to cook on the move. Interestingly, the camera was not a part of this travel paraphernalia, for the family never owned one until the 1980s. Their photos were made on borrowed cameras, often wielded by hired attendants, fluidly doubling duties as per the family's requirements. The attendant was part-cook, part-guide, part-photographer. Unlike other skills that needed training, the point-and-shoot camera did not need an expert to operate it, leaving the photographer's identity indeterminate and changeable. Often a research assistant or junior faculty from the local university accompanied the family, sourced by Mr. Gupta, who was the principal and vice chancellor of various colleges and universities in Uttar Pradesh. A semi-academic engagement with the monuments and sites of tourism was thus enhanced by this temporary association, as the local university contact also became the bearer and, in some cases, the subject of the photographic lens. The borrowed camera, whose photographs were subsequently posted to the family, was thus an additional but crucial arrangement made by Mrs. Gupta as part of her travel plans.

Delving deeper into the visuality of the album, it is worthwhile to look at the construction of the photographs into which I read a conscious effort by Mrs. Gupta to bring together the family's public and private presences. On the very first page, five photographs of the family in Madras (now Chennai) and Mahabalipuram show different arrangements of bodies and backgrounds. At the top left is Guddi, standing at a busy intersection with the clock tower atop Chennai Central Station in the background. The next two images show the family in front of Victoria Memorial Hall, followed by Mr. Gupta, Dabboo and their local contact Mr. Saharia posing against the same backdrop. At Mahabalipuram, the family stands under the geological wonder of Krishna's Butter Ball and a famous elephant statue next to the frieze popularly called the 'Descent of the Ganges'. In each image, the history and mythology of landmark sites are given visual importance, filling the frame with the family standing before it. Often this meant that the family was reduced in scale, miniaturised against the largesse and grandeur of the site. The next page has five out of eight images picturing the famous Shiva temple, the *rathas* (lit. chariots) and the *mandalas* of Pallava architecture also at Mahabalipuram, photographed from carefully chosen angles. In a bid to include the entire 27x9 metre frieze of the 'Descent of the Ganges' with the Gupta family of five, as well as Mr. Saharia in the same frame, everyone is miniaturised.

This urgent impulse to include backgrounds and bodies in the same visual scape can be gleaned from most photos in the album. There is no attempt at closeup shots of the children's faces, or of Mr. and Mrs. Gupta as a couple that may have excluded the topography and architecture of the site. Instead, a conscious balance is struck between human and inanimate architectural/ geographical elements as subject matters. The family was never pictured to the exclusion of the noteworthy touristic markers, possibly fulfilling Mrs. Gupta's desire to fully document the sites that she had laboriously read about and had made tremendous efforts to travel to. These images index Mrs. Gupta's aspirations of truly looking at the family and the nation as part of the same continued trajectory, embedding her own kin within the India's history and geography that she was so curious to explore. This inclusion and importance given to the natural or architectural attractions in the Gupta family photos challenge Rojek and Urry's claim in their landmark text, *Touring Cultures*, where they propose that the attraction's 'socially constructed aura' is merely to 'stage the family' rather than grant any value that is intrinsic to the site itself, when devoid of the visiting family.[5] Perceptibly, Mrs. Gupta's intentions are to visually balance her family and the sites they were visiting, in each frame. The attraction is not treated as a mere background, but as a central and essential reason for the image to exist, as important as the family itself.

There is a remarkable consistency in framing the images, considering that the camera was wielded by different people on each trip. In a conversation,[6] Guddu explains that the photographers were mainly attendants, guides, but also sometimes Mrs. Gupta herself, but never the children or Mr. Gupta. This explains Mrs. Gupta's prerogative in laying down the guidelines for the way all the photographs were composed, carefully positioning her children and husband, choosing the angles and frames of the photographs, including archaeological backgrounds to the fullest capacity. The bearer of the lens in each case followed the same mandate of framing the family against the landmark sites of and near Madras. Even at the cost of miniaturising the details of black-and-white 3x2 inch photographs, calling for a magnifying glass to view them properly, the subject matter compromised neither family nor site, bearing evidence of Mrs. Gupta's attempt to visually itemise an encyclopaedic account of the India she visited. Even when there is no architectural element, the frame includes natural delineations of horizons, seashores and mountain tops, highlighting regional topographies unfamiliar to her, embedding the family as a motif in the landscape. There are, for instance, photographs of the children next to a bridge in Mysore, the family sitting by the banks of the Kaveri river, or the unpopulated images of the seashore at Kanyakumari and the lake of Nainital. Mrs Gupta's desire to co-visualise her family with the cultural geography of their travels manifests in an alternative mode of 'familyness' in the Touring Album.[7]

In order to explore another expression of 'familyness', I now turn to the Gupta 'Parivar Chitra' album for a comparative point of view. This larger album with many more pages and images focuses on the family's rites of passage such as birthdays and weddings, festivals, occasional dress-ups, and visits from extended family. The album begins with matrimonial portraits of Mr. and Mrs. Gupta, and a few images from their wedding. Guddu, Guddi and Dabboo

---

[5] Chris Rojek and John Urry, *Touring Cultures: Transformations of Travel and Theory*, New York: Routledge, 1997: 91

[6] Conversation with the author, June-July, 2020, Mathura-Vrindavan.

[7] Haldrup, Michael and Jonas Larsen. 2003.'The Family Gaze'. *Tourist Studies* (London: Sage Publications). pp. 25–26. Haldrup and Larsen argue that the key role of tourist photography is to construct a sense of family: 'Rather than being an alienating add-on, photographing is an integral component in producing identity, social relations and "familyness".'

then appear as babies occupying the whole frame, smiling charmingly at the camera, each detail of their clothes, faces and limbs in clear view. Most of the photographs have been taken within their childhood home, a large, well lit, multi-storey house in Khurja where Mr. Gupta was the principal of a college. One sees Guddu and Guddi, closer in age than their third sibling Dabboo, posing in fancy dress costumes in a sunny veranda. Here Guddu wears a sari and holds a doll, there Guddi dons a hat and sunglasses. An adolescent Guddu poses against a bamboo trellis, wearing long hair, bell bottoms, holding a far away gaze as his arm reaches above his head, one foot resting back. In the next image, Guddi with long hair streaming down her shoulders poses in exactly the same way. There are several individual portraits of Mrs. Gupta: one of her in a fashionable chequered blouse, another in a couple portrait with her husband, yet another in the company of her extended family, with the children crowding onto her lap or leaning on her chair. In a typical family tableau, the couple is surrounded by their three children in front of a mantlepiece in the drawing room, firmly embedding them in their domestic interiority.

As such, in the 'Parivar Chitra' album, Mrs. Gupta's familial identity is entirely that of a wife, mother and householder. There is no indication of her pursuits as a reader, a political activist, or her intellectual inquiries. What the emblems of India's cultural wealth—its heritage sites, monuments and landscape—could grant her in the Touring Album, indexing her curiosity and research, her family overrides in the 'Parivar Chitra' album. The arrangement of images in the latter album follows a broad chronology, but there are deviations and duplications, with no labelling or consistency in format. Images include those taken at studios, by friends and relatives in varied formats, in black and white, and colour during the 1980s when the family acquired their own Agfa camera. There are hand-coloured, professionally taken portraits of the children as toddlers, or homemade ones against makeshift backdrops of printed bedsheets, emulating a photo studio's aesthetic. The absence of labels indicates confidence on the persistent accuracy of familial memorialisation, resulting in a non-textual engagement with this album, unlike the heavily annotated Touring Album. It is as if the 'Parivar Chitra' album, in its aesthetic and chronological chequering embodies the transforming nature of the family, its unwieldiness, as it refuses to stabilise along a larger historical narrative. Even in the bid to archive the family as it changed and grew over the years, it is essentially difficult for narratives from the 'Parivar Chitra' album to pin down identities, locations and contexts in a precise manner. Freed from the cultural geographies of the Touring Album, these family photographs appear at will, and Mrs. Gupta's singular authorship is diluted. The Touring Album gave its makers a viable logic according to which the family could be meaningfully plotted in time and in space. Mrs. Gupta's desire for personally making this album perhaps lay in casting anew her familial reality as an alternative to the fluidity of everyday life. She therefore jettisoned the family onto more graspable mappings that India's cultural geography could provide. In turn, the diversity and the breadth of a young nation, only twenty or so years after its independence, could be understood through the familiar motif of her family dotting its famous sites. In the novelty of experience and the historicity of the sites they visited, Mrs. Gupta found firmer frames of reference and anchorage in India's heritage, than in the space of her home, which remained in a state of transformation in the way it accommodated a growing and transforming family. This, no doubt, imposed demands on her as householder and provider, amidst which she had an unstructured engagement with her studies and political interests.

The Yatra Diary

I now move on to a phase in Mrs. Gupta's life, when free of the demands of young children, most household responsibilities and a husband's transferable job, she undertook her first solo trip. Mr. Gupta passed away of a cardiac arrest in June 1999. In November, the same year, Mrs. Gupta undertook a religious pilgrimage to the Braj area in North India, in and around Mathura-Vrindavan, where she lived. In that sense, the topography of the region was not entirely unfamiliar to her. Known by the name of *Braj Chaurasi Kos Yatra* or the *Shri Brajmandal Parikrama*, the group tour promised her darshan of the sacred sites and *lila sthalis* of the divine couple, Radha and Krishna, in a matter of 43 days. Various religious groups are known to periodically organise such tours for their devotees, and this one was led by Sadguru Karshni Gurusharananandji Maharaj and his disciples between 17 November and 30 December 1999. The idea behind a Hindu pilgrimage is to live in an austere state and immerse oneself in devotion while visiting places of worship along a sacred geography. The Shri Brajmandal Parikrama and its lila sthalis are part of 'the network of *tirthas* thus sketch(ing) out a holy geography covering the entire space of Hindu civilisation'.[8] As a 'space codified by the Brahmanic tradition',[9] such tirthas map the nation according to a sacred logic, rendering the occupants of the land into devotees.[10] Yet again, the idea of the nation manifests for Mrs Gupta, but this time in spiritual terms.

The Brajmandal Parikrama occupies 84 *kos* or a 5,000 square kilometre area, dotted with temples, sacred groves, ancient water bodies and hills that

[8] Jaffrelot, Christopher. 2009. 'The Hindu nationalist reinterpretation of pilgrimage in India: The limits of Yatra politics'. *Nations and Nationalism*. 15:1. p. 4.

[9] Ibid. p. 5.

[10] The ultimate yatra or pilgrimage consists of 'encircling the universe' by touring India through Puri, Rameshvaram, Dwarka and Badrinath—the four *dhams* that between them spell the boundaries of the country, i.e. they 'mark out a sacred geography delimiting a civilisation'. By virtue of including the sacred space to which the supposedly Hindu population belongs, such demarcations also exclude the geographies to which they do not belong, or that which belongs to 'others'. The politically understood congruence of nation and sacred Hindu land in the case of India has been discussed by several scholars, and remains beyond the scope of this essay. Here, we explore the imagination and comprehension of family, nation and identity for Mrs. Gupta, through documents that repeatedly evoke these axes. See Jaffrelot. 2009. 'The Hindu nationalist reinterpretation of pilgrimage in India'. pp. 1–19.

feature in the popular mythologies of Krishna and Radha. Mrs. Gupta mentions in her diary how going on this yatra was a long held desire which she couldn't fulfil due to her domestic duties. After the passing of her husband, she thought this to be a fitting way to grieve, as well as to move onto a more spiritually attuned life. After 1999, she devoted herself to the *seva* or service of saints in Vrindavan where she lived, and to a small temple in her own home, which housed the deity Bal Gopal, or Krishna in child form. As a moment that heralded Mrs. Gupta's ascetic life as a Vaishnav devotee, this yatra played a pivotal role. Jaffrelot in his essay[11] dwells on the crucial transformation of social identities, especially across the lines of caste, class and gender, during the sacred Hindu yatra. Mrs. Gupta's shift in identity from being a householder to an almost ascetic devotee, moving from a private space into a public one, is marked by this yatra, and her diary attests to the details of this transformation. In this section, I focus on her diary in the attempt to gauge the details of this shift.

The yatra diary is written in a notebook, priced at ₹3 and printed at Pathak Paper Industries, Muradgunj, Jaunpur in Uttar Pradesh. Mr. Gupta had been the vice chancellor at the University of Jaunpur, where this notebook may have been procured, although it was inscribed by Mrs. Gupta, several years later. On its cover is a polychromatic print, bearing the title 'Mahabharat' after the Indian epic, and three photographic images of the televisual series produced by B.R. Chopra in 1988 for the national television channel, Doordarshan. Even though the contents of the diary were not meant to relate to the theme of its cover, a broad logic connects the sacred nature of Mrs. Gupta's yatra to the divine characters on the cover. The iconisation of the TV series in the Hindu imagination is not unlike the *lilas* or local theatrical productions of Krishna's life episodes that Mrs. Gupta viewed every evening during the yatra. A certain acknowledgment of the enactment of worship, and the performative quality of sacred engagement resonates between the cover and the contents of the diary. Even though the *Mahabharata* images on the cover narrate a time in the life of adult Krishna's engagement with Arjun at the battle of Kurukshetra, while Mrs. Gupta's yatra engaged with his pastimes as a child and adolescent in the Braj area, the larger containment of the Hindu imaginary brings them together in a continuum in popular usage.

The diary begins with Mrs. Gupta's account of her preparations on the eve of the yatra. She subsequently narrates each day's itinerary, marking the time that the yatra begins (usually 9 a.m.), when they break for a meal and when she retires in the evening (usually 9 p.m.). On each day the group of thirty-odd *yatris* or devotees follow a pre-planned route on foot, rickshaw or horse-drawn carriage, visiting sites of worship along Krishna's *lila sthalis*. Mrs. Gupta's corporeal experiences of the travel account for her alternately feeling spiritual gratification and grief, fatigue and rest, interspersed with descriptions of the

[11] Ibid.

living arrangements provided en route, the friendships and conversations she struck with fellow devotees. She lists the items she ate during each meal, some that she enjoyed while others that left her ill. These are embedded within a larger account of the sites that were visited, their sacred significance and the receptions they got by local hosts. For instance, Mrs. Gupta describes how it was preferable to cover the journey on foot, as per the prescriptions of austerity by Sadguru Karshni Gurusharananandji who was leading the group, but because of her age and an aching leg, or on account of losing her slippers, she often took a horse-drawn carriage. Her writing emphasises the importance of *seva* or service to pilgrims which is part of Hindu practice. The personal, the bodily and the emotional, however, are never far away, as she ties in the themes on which the Sadguru gives lectures every day with memories of her late husband, and her feelings of grief marking this time as a threshold into the next phase of her life.

As such, the *yatra* diary indicates that Mrs. Gupta believed this tour to be her personal journey as much as a part of religious prescriptions for a Vaishnav devotee to undertake periodic pilgrimages. It is noteworthy that Mrs. Gupta's highly detailed account bears a visually textured language, so even though the diary has only one accompanying group photograph, a visual reconstruction of her experiences is possible through her writing. For someone who undertook great pains to arrange for borrowed cameras on previous holidays with her family, it would not have been unusual to arrange one for this *yatra* too, especially since by the 1990s her adult children possessed cameras of their own. The reason for the camera's absence could not have been that Mrs. Gupta was disengaged from her surroundings, nor was she undesirous of keeping a detailed account of her journey, as indicated by her diary; so then why the non-existence of photographs? I attribute this to the absence of her family at a stage when her life became marked by solitude. Having recently lost her husband, her children living away as independent adults with their own nuclear families, Mrs. Gupta's chief subjects had disappeared, rendering the camera redundant. It was as if the family and camera went together in mutual visualisation, and disappeared together from her horizon at this later point in time. Folded within the intention of mapping the nation's cultural geography in the Touring Album, had been the family whom she always carried with her, including them in most frames with India's cultural landmarks. With all the demands that her family could have placed on her, they were also her facilitators in completing her imagination of the nation. Her recreational travels had mapped this familial and national identity, as well as her own self-identity within these contexts. In their absence, perhaps Mrs. Gupta's own vision had refocused towards textually accounting for the esoteric rather than the historical, the material and the familial.

Mrs. Gupta mourns this shift as an inevitable loss. On her birthday on 9 December, the yatra halted at Barsana, believed to be the village from where Radha hailed. Mrs. Gupta writes (translation mine):

> Like every day, I was ready early in the morning. Today is my birthday. Last year in Moradabad, he (Mr. Gupta) had insisted on buying me a sari. It was a dull yellow, and I wondered why he was insisting we buy it, knowing that I don't like such dull colours. I had then thought that since he liked it, I'd buy it anyway. How was I to know that this was to be the last sari I would receive from him! In June while he was ill, he had once asked whether I had worn the sari he had gifted me on my birthday. I told him that he had perhaps forgotten that I had worn it the very day he had given it to me, even though the sari hadn't got a fall on it. I have been weeping at this memory since morning, today. I wore the same sari today after my prayers, during which I had placed his photograph in front of me. I then ate breakfast, and changed out of that sari. I shall now only have this same sari to wear on all subsequent birthdays, and shed tears at my memories.
>
> At 9 a.m., we left Barsana. I took a tonga for the first four kilometres, after which we stopped at Prem Sarovar. We then took darshan at Sanket Bihari Ji in Sanketvan. I then walked on foot. On the way, dau-daha played holi with brajraj. Stopping by at Shri Yashoda kund and Dau kund, we circumambulated Nandagram covering 7-8 km. We then took darshan at Mansarovar, and then I took a lift in a car for the next 4 km. We then witnessed a *lila*, after which we ate lunch. Thakurji and the cowherds received food first, then we got *roti*, *saag*, *halva*, apple, *cheekoo*, *petha* and *dalmoth*. I returned by tonga and feeling tired, retired early to bed. I couldn't watch the evening's performance of the lila.

Mrs. Gupta's precise visualisations of everyday objects such as clothing and food, her activities and the sites she visited, make her diary richly descriptive. She mentions that she carries Mr. Gupta's photograph with her and looks at it periodically, confirming her continued visual engagement with family. During the *yatra* she doesn't turn the lens upon herself, choosing text as the mode of private expression of her feelings as well as chronicling. There is no deliberate act of self-insertion in the frame, which now the family had emptied, also obliterating part of her own selfhood. Perhaps this is also because she enumerates several points of discomfort during the *yatra*. She describes her fatigued, ageing body which ideally should have covered the *yatra* on foot, but was compelled to take tongas and other modes of transport to cover distances. She speaks of broken buckets, bags and slippers which were duly replaced by friends and extended family who visited her during the *yatra*, although help came at intervals of several days when she was able to reach a payphone and call for it. Mrs. Gupta's mournful recollections of her husband dot the diary at several places, as she comes to terms with her solitude and regrets even the desire to come away from him to *yatras* such as this one while he was still alive. Perhaps photographs would not have done enough to capture these realms of sentiment and experience for a woman who had known the camera mostly for its role at times of celebration, travel and spectacles foregrounding the family. Photography's conventions in terms of familial portrayal endorse predictable formats, limiting the use of the camera especially for the pre-digital generation. Mrs. Gupta's exclusion of the camera from the *yatra* was not to undermine the importance of the time, but a disconnect between personal experience and this mode of expression; the camera she no longer felt she could speak to.

Family Portraits

In a bid to look at which type of photographs may have persisted through Mrs. Gupta's episodic relationship with the camera, I analyse the family portraits on the walls of her home in Vrindavan. These framed portraits, numbering six, range between the years 1905 and 2010, preceding and succeeding her own lifetime, while following the Gupta patrilineage. It is remarkable that the first two photographs are taken twenty-four years apart, but the last two are taken merely eight years apart. This reflects the relative rarity of the photographic moment in the early twentieth century, the uneven access and economics of the medium across generations.

These photographs reflect on the Gupta lineage but also the changing technology, conventions and aesthetics of family photography itself. Mrs. Gupta would have encountered these images on a daily basis in her home, she herself appearing in three of the six frames. Remarkably, the third image that dates to her own wedding day in 1953, features her husband and his six brothers, with no sign of her as the bride. Such were the conventions regarding spatial separations between the genders in domestic settings, that a newly married couple would not be visualised within the same portrait. This is confirmed by another family montage that immediately precedes this one, dating to 1930, when Mr. Gupta's father, an engineer with the Railways, was being transferred out of Jaipur to another location. This is an image of a farewell party at the *Zanana-khana* (lit. female quarters), portraying Mr. Gupta's mother, her sister and sister-in-law. The little boys wearing hunting hats and holding bouquets are the sons and brothers of these women, one of whom is Mr. Gupta himself. The girls are the daughters of the family, and wear saris at a young age. This group portrait excludes the men of the family, except for the very youngest.

The use of objects of cultural refinement and bourgeois taste, such as hats, bouquets, books, carpets and backdrops, reflect the social aspirations of the sitters. The colonial legacy had inscribed itself in the accoutrements surrounding the figures, who for the sake of the photograph don Western garments and bear cultural objects of education and bourgeois living. Two other photographs dating from 2002 and 2010 are set against the backdrop of the family home in Vrindavan. Replacing the studio setting, the façade of the home anchors the family in its domestic context. All the photographs succeeding the 1953 family group radically challenge older conventions of studio photography, portraying Guddu on his wedding day in 1981, with his wife and both sides of their immediate family, followed by his niece's ear piercing ceremony in 2002 and his own son's wedding in 2010. Men and women intermix without the gendering of photographic spaces. Mrs. Gupta appears in the last three images as mother and grandmother. These family photographs have notably only been taken at rites of passage—weddings, an ear-piercing ceremony, a change in jobs. Sociologically, at these moments of transition, families are most fragile and in need of a reaffirmation of their cohesiveness. It is as if photographs perform the adhesive function of reminding the growing and transforming family that they still very much belong together.

A last pair of historic images from Mrs. Gupta's paternal line are on the walls of the dining room. Shyamlal Govil, Mrs Gupta's father, was a graduate of Allahabad University in 1927, having studied Economics and the Law. He was the secretary of the UP Legislative Council in pre-Independence India, and this photograph from 1948 shows him standing in the top row with Lal Bahadur Shastri, Sarojini Naidu and others in the front row, who became members of India's first independent government's cabinet. This photograph predates the adoption of the Indian Constitution, and is taken just weeks after the Constitution had been drafted, in 1950, portraying Shyamlal Govil as Secretary of the UP Legislative Council. It is a firm marker of Mrs. Gupta's patrilineage comprising erudite figures in the government at a time of the nation's awakening; a moment that would have etched itself in her own outlook as a politically aware and socially conscious person. Yet again, a nation in the making has inscribed its presence into the images of the Gupta ancestors, inextricably entwining private and public histories.

At the outset, these portraits are remarkable for their centrality and hyper-visibility in the Gupta household. They are placed on the drawing room wall, each in a broad black wooden frame with the year of the photograph at the bottom of the image in bold typeface. Visiting family and friends have often been 'introduced' to those in the photographs, described by their jobs, the places they lived in, the spouses and children that they had, and the personal characteristics they bore. Unlike the Touring Album, the 'Parivar Chitra' Album, or Mrs. Gupta's *yatra* diary that belong to a more private realm, brought out for contemplative conversations with fewer people, the framed images enjoy a certain exteriority of self-presentation, a portrayal of their 'familyness'. The *yatra* diary belongs to a further realm of interiority as it has rarely been shared with anyone outside Guddu's immediate family. Perhaps this is so because it bears an account of grief and a personal journey of Mrs. Gupta's rather than a collective one relevant to the family. It has a degree of unmatched spontaneity in the way diaries tend to possess, and carefully composed family portraits do not.

In conclusion, the Gupta family archives represent a range of intimacies, positioning the family unit as both a publicly presentable montage on the one hand and a personally held motif on the other. The more carefully constructed documents such as the Touring Album, or family portraits on the walls of the Vrindavan Gupta home, are attuned to public display. But the more intuitive and reflexive accounts, such as the diary, circumvent direct visualisation, belonging instead to the private realm known only to a few. Mrs Gupta understood the functional range mapped by family images and invested in their organisation

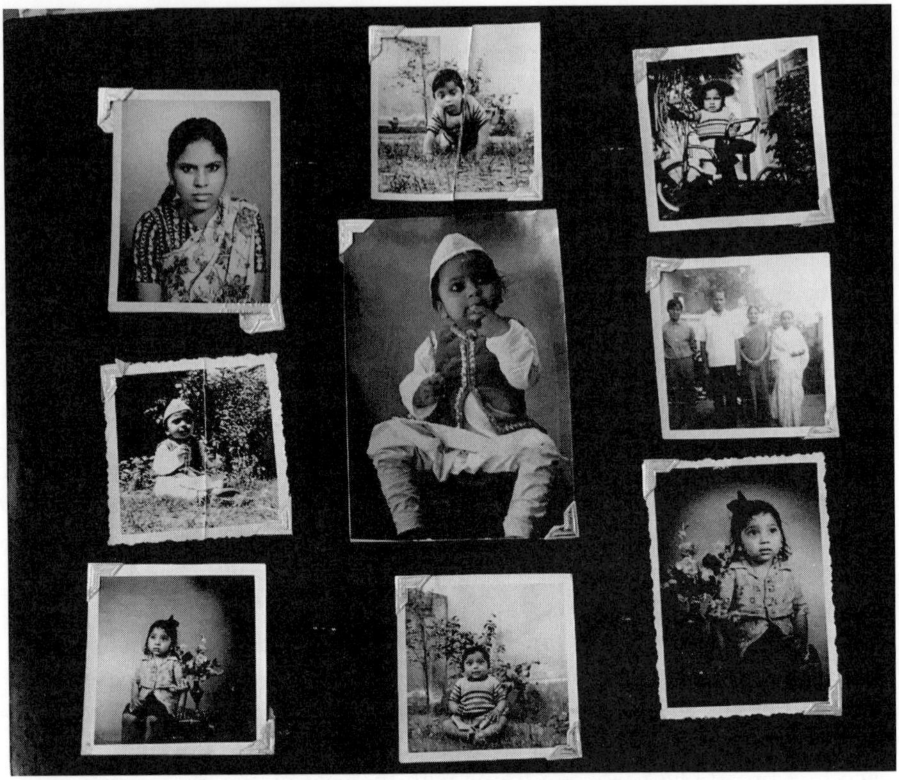

'Parivar Chitra', 1953-81, Gupta Family

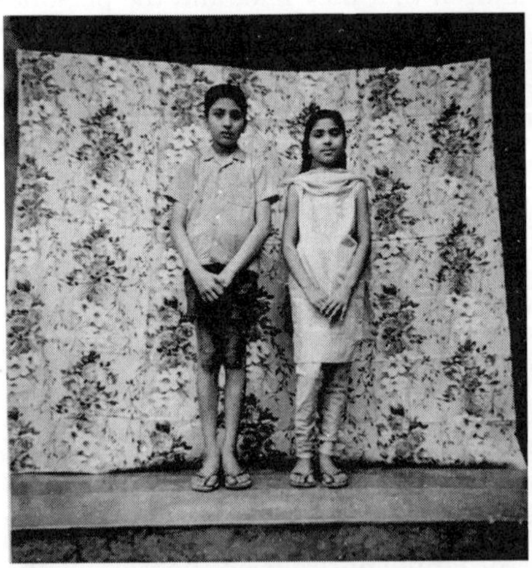

'Parivar Chitra', 1953-81, Gupta Family

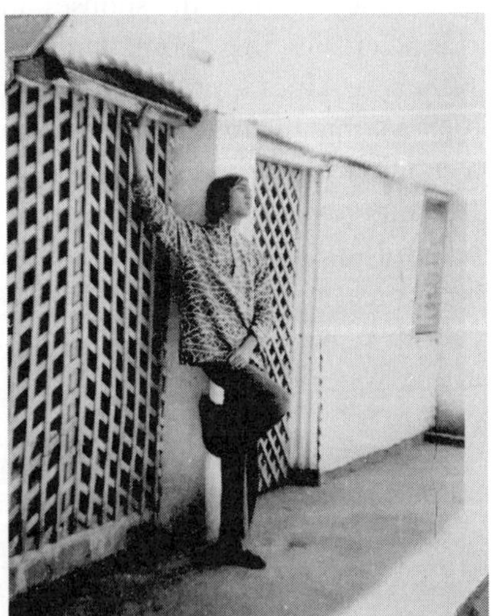

'Parivar Chitra', 1953-81, Gupta Family

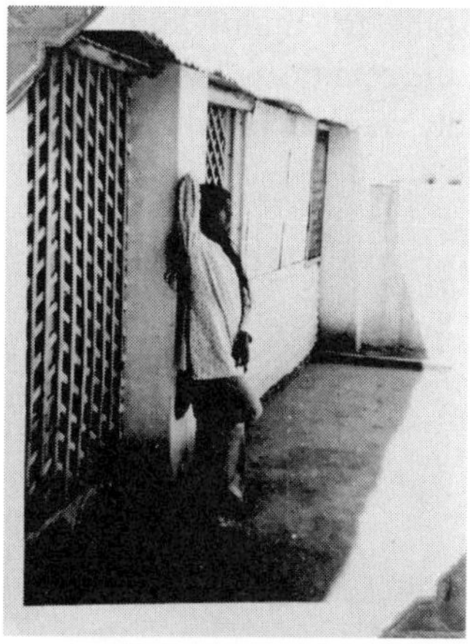

'Parivar Chitra', 1953-81, Gupta Family

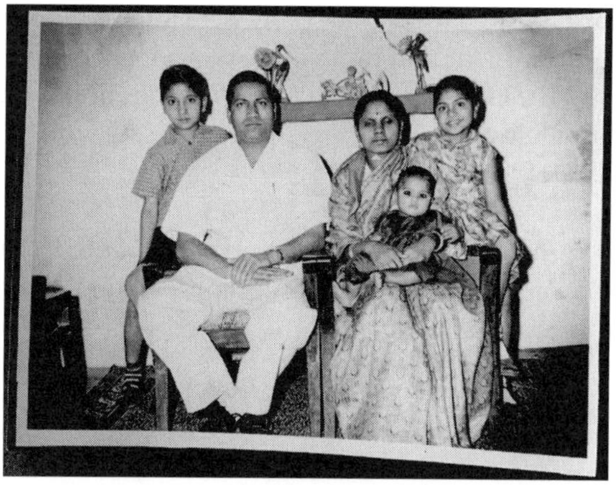

'Parivar Chitra', 1953-81, Gupta Family

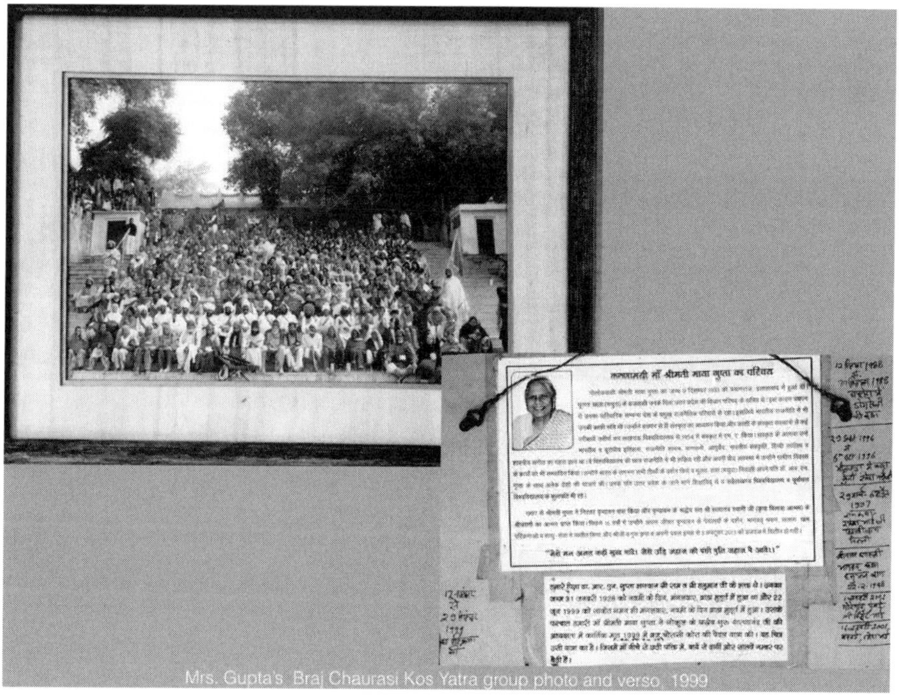

Yatra group portrait, 1999, Mrs. Gupta

and presentation in a way that corresponded to different markers of time in her own life, alternating between her familial embeddedness, spiritual solitude and national consciousness. As such, the albums, the diary and framed images fill out the facts in Mrs. Gupta's biography not only by virtue of their content but by their intent, organisation, physical mode of presentation and subsequent preservation, addressing social, geographical and gendered understandings of family and nation. This essay is an attempt to lay parallel the nation and family as institutions that mutually explained each other in the reality and imagination of Mrs. Gupta, neither complete without periodically referencing the other in her archive.

I wish to thank the Gupta, Poddar and Narain families for so generously sharing Mrs. Gupta's photographs, albums, diary and associated narratives for this essay.

8

Politics (re)articulated: Familial responses to State positions:

Revisiting Chyaasi – 1986

Family Albums and Women's Memories from the Darjeeling Hill's Political Agitation

Dipti Tamang and Ruchika Gurung

> 'Gender is an inescapable dimension of differential power relations, and cultural memory is always about the distribution of and contested claims of power. What a culture remembers and what it chooses to forget are intricately bound up with issues of power and hegemony, and thus with gender.'
>
> — Hirsch and Smith, 2002[1]

The need for an archive led by narratives of women in the Darjeeling Hills drives this essay. The Darjeeling Hills includes Kalimpong, Mirik and nearby areas, and specifically the stories of our mothers are located in Kalimpong and Mungpoo. It proposes a visual space where the stories of women, their history and culture can be documented for public access. There is a critical need to engage with the dominant patriarchal narratives around the Gorkhaland Movement[2] and a visual archive of family photographs supplemented by oral narratives of women. We believe that this would be crucial to a cultural and historical understanding of the movement and people's engagement during this period. We revisit the 1986 period (popularly remembered as *Chyaasi ko Andolan*),[3] through our mothers' eyes. This essay employs the method of photo elicitation to revive hidden memories of the andolan (protest) through our mothers, Meera Tamang and Nandita Gurung. In a conversational format, we share what we learnt about our own familial pasts, as everyday life became a conduit to understand the extraordinary political events of 1986 and its immediate aftermath. We have also chosen to refer to both our mothers by their names, after an initial introduction; the aim is to distance their narratives from their maternal sides and focus on their participation and understanding of the andolan as women and keepers of cultural knowledge.

Scholars like Chhetri write that the issues of gender need to be explored in identity-based movements in order to understand the different social structures

---

[1] Hirsch, M. (2008) 'The Generation of Postmemory', *Poetics Today*, 29(1), pp. 103-128.

[2] The Gorkhaland Movement is one of the oldest ethno-nationalist political movements for statehood in the Darjeeling Hills.

[3] The Agitation of 1986.

at play, leading to a more nuanced understanding of the ideologies that impact the differential participation of women.[4] Women who occupied positions in political bodies or in their own domestic spaces bring different perspectives into an otherwise male dominated account of the andolan, highlighting gendered imbalances in the significance given to narratives of the agitation. Chettri notes that the 'repertoire of the movement was gendered since its inception',[5] for the speeches made by the leader of the Gorkhaland movement, Subhash Ghisingh,[6] referred to the Gorkha homeland or *mato* (soil/land), drawing on nationalistic imaginings of the figure of the motherland.[7] While it is common knowledge that women actively participated in various capacities during the Gorkhaland movement, their personal stories remain confined to domestic spaces and removed from the political, and emerge as a powerful repository of knowledge allowing us to understand their engagement with the movement and the oral tradition of preserving cultural knowledge.

This piece throws light on such narratives of the lived experiences of two women, and how their accounts continue to add to a wider cultural understanding of the movement in public and private spaces. In constructing this essay, we started our dialogue close to home, unravelling what the agitation period meant to Meera and Nandita, and how they found themselves engaging with the Gorkhaland movement. Our next task was to dive head-on into our family photo albums to find visually perceivable impacts of the movement. In a series of informal and formal discussions, we sat down with both Meera and Nandita, and pieced together both oral and visual narratives along with how they in turn reshaped our own understanding of not just the andolan but also helped us locate the silences around women's engagement with it. In this sense, we engage with the concept of postmemory[8] proposed by the photography historian Marianne Hirsch, who writes of the intergenerational transference of memories of trauma through photography and oral recollections.

In centering women's experiences of the period from 1985–87, a time of intense transformation in the Darjeeling Hills embroiled in political conflict, militarisation and violence, our purpose is to foreground gendered recollections of these events, framed by family photographs as the negotiating

[4] Chhetri, N. 2021. 'Gendered Frames of Mobilization: Differential Participation of Women in Ethnopolitics of Darjeeling'. *Indian Journal of Gender Studies*. 28:1. p. 47.

[5] Ibid. p. 51.

[6] Traces of the demand for a separate administration for the Hill people can be found in the colonial period, but the Gorkhaland Movement was launched in an organised political manner in the 1980s by Subhash Ghising and his party, the Gorkha National Liberation Front (GNLF).

[7] Ibid.

[8] On postmemory, Hirsch writes, 'it reflects an uneasy oscillation between continuity and rupture … [it is] not a movement, method, or idea; I see it, rather, as a structure of inter- and trans-generational transmission of traumatic knowledge and experience. It is a consequence of traumatic recall but (unlike post-traumatic stress disorder) at a generational remove.' Hirsch, Marianne. 2008. 'The Generation of Postmemory'. Poetics Today. 29:1. p. 106.

agency between these events and everyday lives. Conversely, deeply personal conversations inevitably spill into larger political references, and are therefore significant in the collective remembrance of history.

This essay occupies an uncharted space for both authors approaching an intimate space through a critical lens, deconstructing the narratives that we have found ourselves interwoven into. Given the nature of our method, we have employed a more conversational style in our writing, moving back and forth between our discussions with Nandita and Meera, and linking them to the construction of memory and the notion of the everyday at a challenging point in the history of our community. In juxtaposing their narratives, we attempt to create for our readers a free-flowing way to engage with two perspectives that are different and yet similar in their processing of a period of conflict, fear and uncertainty. The photographs we discuss run parallel in many ways to the memories of conflict our mothers talk about. We explore an amalgamation of the everyday infused with violent memories of the agitation, reminiscences that sound strangely nonchalant, despite the trauma they might have inflicted. The result is an essay that pays homage to the undocumented narratives of women who have lived through the 1986 agitation that manifest as stories passed on from mothers to their daughters here.

Conversations Between Mothers and Daughters

RUCHIKA: Nandita was always surrounded by stories. An English teacher for a significant period of her life, she excelled at crafting stories that became an integral part of my life as well. She managed to breathe life into the worlds and characters she narrated. The stories ranged from the everyday and the mythical to more popular children's stories. I always wondered why stories were so important to her and about her need to have them be passed on to her daughters. This opened up a space of questioning: are women inherently nurtured to be storytellers, is it through them that cultural knowledge gets preserved and passed on? As Tilly Vriend writes, 'Women have collected and disseminated information for many years.'[9] This was keeping in mind comparisons made with my father Udai, who never indulged in telling stories of our histories while I was growing up. I witnessed women's affinity for storytelling through the cultural information passed on intergenerationally by women in our household, especially by grandmothers, mothers and sisters to daughters, granddaughters and nieces.

Vriend writes that it is only since the twentieth century onwards that we see archives[10] being set up to collect and document what she terms as 'women's

[9] Vriend, T. 2011. 'Women's Memory, Whose Memory?'. Keşoğlu, B.T. and D.F. Ture. eds. *Women's Memory: The Problem of Sources* (Newcastle upon Tyne: Cambridge Scholars Publishing). p. 2.

[10] Some examples include organisations in India such as Sound & Picture Archives for Research on Women (SPARROW) based in Mumbai. Vriend cites European libraries (such as

information'.[11] They have come into being with the belief that that if there are no records of women's lives, 'then future generations cannot be inspired by them' and they 'may think these issues were not relevant to our times'.[12] Much of my familial and cultural understanding has stemmed from the stories contained within and outside of these formal archives, influencing my understanding of gender, history and power in the telling and retelling of stories by the women in my family. Local museums such as the Dr. Graham's Homes School Museum and the Lepcha Museum are limited in the historical trajectory they project; their stories do not centre local women and the cultural knowledge they are gatekeepers of—stories which are orally shared amongst community members from generation to generation. The conversations mentioned in this piece span a period of time, a culmination of stories told to me by family members and Nandita but are particularly grounded on one formal interview on the 2 February 2021 that revived stories recounted by her to me. The recounting of events through the photographs initially took place over several informal family events and then resulted in a mapping event over the same formal interview.

For someone like Nandita, who prided herself in telling stories, it seemed strange that those from the '86 andolan were not widely discussed. Das citing Cavell writes, 'Voice is not that of speech or utterance but as that which might animate words, give them life, so to say.'[13] The implication of voicing a narrative would imply giving those words and memories a life, and with the incidents following '86, a lot of those memories had lain dormant with people who were unsure as to what and where their voices lay. While Das's work revolves around the events of the Partition in 1947 and the assassination of the then Prime Minister Indira Gandhi in 1984, her writing strikes a resounding chord with the narratives of the andolan as well. She questions, 'What happens to the subject and world when the memory of such events is folded into ongoing relationships?'[14] I wonder if my worldview of the State and the region would have been different had these stories been narrated to me when I was younger. Would saying it out loud have impacted Nandita's interaction with the community and region? This is where Das draws on her notion of the 'voiceless', clarifying, 'not in the sense that one does not have words—but that these words become frozen, numb, without life.'[15] She goes on to write that when asked, women and men narrate their stories about the

---

Amsterdam Women's Library and Archive) concentrating on women's materials, springing out of the suffrage movement or out of second-wave feminism. Her examples also point to women's centres situated all over the world (2011:2-3).

[11] Ibid.

[12] Ibid. p. 4.

[13] Das, V. 2007. *Life and Words: Violence and the Descent into the Ordinary* (Berkley: University of California Press). p. 6.

[14] Ibid. p. 8.

[15] Ibid.

violence they had either seen or endured, adding that 'My thought was that perhaps they had speech but not voice.'[16] This sheds some light on the inability of family members to recount their traumatic memories of the andolan beyond an odd mention in conversation. Having witnessed a period of violent political struggle in the region, their inability to articulate their memories resonate with this idea of being voiceless.

DIPTI: Whose stories fit or whose voices matter, and whose voices came to be silenced in India's history, have been a matter of concern for scholars and practitioners working across different fields of interest. Feminist academics such as Urvashi Butalia[17] and others have provided crucial interventions, offering new ways of reimagining known narratives. Such interrogations have provided us with spaces to reimagine our histories from the decolonised perspective of multiple voices, offering counterpoints to existing narratives. As Linda Tuhiwa Smith (1999) reminds us, history is the story of the powerful resulting in the exclusion of the marginalised and the Others.[18] Revisiting histories through the vantage point of the silenced, one is forced to engage with the idea of silence itself as a matter of greater retrospection.[19]

As a child, I grew up listening to stories about my mother's life and journey as an upper-caste Brahmin Nepali woman who grew up in Bhutan and later migrated to a small town called Jhaldhaka in the Doars-Terai region, finally settling down in Darjeeling after marriage. My mother[20] Meera explained how this journey unfolded in multiple ways over the years and I grew up listening to her revealing, insightful and intimate accounts often rendered invisible like the female figures in our histories. The fact that Chyaasi is so embedded into the everyday spaces that we often take these spaces as the everyday normal, only finding meaning when I re-enter and engage with these stories as important sites of socio-cultural and political histories. Drawing from Ather Zia's (2020) concept of 'counter memory'[21] I re-engage with these conversations through renewed perspectives as crucial sites of history, otherwise so powerfully and violently erased from public memory.

---

[16] Ibid.

[17] Butalia, Urvashi. 2000. *The Other Side of Silence: Voices from Partition of India* (Durham: Duke University Press).

[18] Smith, Tuhiwai Linda. 1999. *Decolonizing Methodologies: Research and Indigenous Peoples* (London: Zed Books).

[19] Parpart, Jane and Swati Parashar. 2019. *Rethinking Silence, Voice and Agency in Contested Gendered Terrains* (London: Routledge).

[20] The author Dipti uses both her mother's identity as Meera and 'my mother' because of how her identity for a long time has primarily been as *'aama'(mother),* only recently through these conversations working in undoing this practice to place her as Meera – the narrator.

[21] Zia, Ather. 2020. *Resisting Disappearance, Military Occupation and Women's Activism in Kashmir* (New Delhi: Zubaan Publishers).

RUCHIKA IN CONVERSATION WITH NANDITA (R&N)[22]: When we began to discuss the possibility of a women's visual and oral archive in the Hills, especially focusing on the '86 andolan, I found myself questioning Nandita about her understanding of the fight for a separate state and the violent history that was involved. It was a strange experience interviewing her, although unsurprisingly, it turned into a storytelling session with her recounting this particular memory of the andolan that proved to be the most significant to her. Despite the lack of imagery of these events, Nandita's recollections were strikingly visual in their construction of a memory for me. I was impressed at the clarity of her memory; her account was almost photographic, but as we progressed with the interview, I began to understand that this was a memory both focused and yet lacking clarity on the political motivations of the event, or how public participation had been encouraged.

On 27 July 1986, Subhas Ghisingh, the leader of the GNLF, called for members from each household to rise and peacefully protest against the diktats of the State. It appeared there was a blanket understanding that all people were to support the GNLF, and no questions were asked. Nandita remembered how people believed that Ghisingh would deliver on his promise of Gorkhaland, and that 'there was a lot of excitement, a lot of enthusiasm'.[23] She recounts that Udai, her sixteen-year-old younger sister, her sister-in-law and my three-year-old elder sister Tanya were all a part of this march to the Mela ground.[24] With a smile, she reminisces, 'it was a very festive occasion, and the entire village was there.'[25] Nandita remembers how it felt like an outing during Dashain, everyone was 'yapping and talking and meeting each other'[26] and there were contingents from every village. People had gathered from all over Kalimpong district to showcase their solidarity. Even though people marched on merrily to peacefully support the call for a separate state, on reaching the tenth mile, she suddenly had a sinking feeling, and sent her sister and daughter back home.

She distinctly remembers how the jovial atmosphere of people cheering 'Gorkhaland!' immediately changed as they approached the Haart Bazaar road, where there was a massive crowd and people had begun to wave their *khukuris*[27] around. The chants became angrier and louder. As they got closer to Hind Bakery, there was a loud stuttering noise and the crowd dispersed in panic. What followed was chaos and several voices from the crowd shouting '*pateka ho*' (those are fireworks) and 'blank fire, blank fire'. Assured to some

[22] Gurung, N. (2021) 'Interview of Nandita Gurung'. Interviewed by Ruchika Gurung, 2 February.

[23] Gurung, N. 2 February 2021. Interview with Nandita Gurung. By Ruchika Gurung.

[24] The Mela ground or fair ground in Kalimpong is located centrally and is a space used for communal sporting and cultural activities.

[25] Ibid.

[26] Ibid.

[27] A khukuri is a traditional machete/knife associated with Nepalese and Gorkha people.

degree, people regrouped, and Nandita found herself right up front, separated from Udai and everyone familiar to her.

What struck me about her narrative was the fearlessness with which she was narrating the incident and her memory of not feeling any fear while the chaos was unfolding around her. In many ways, this was tied into her engagement with the political turmoil: the community felt they were safe and supported by the party in power. She nonchalantly added, 'I didn't know Kalimpong that well'. Here, she was both an insider and an outsider to the community in the midst of a revolution. Assuming everyone would end up at the same destination, she followed the crowd, crossing the motor stand area, as they climbed up the road that led to the police station. The road was lined with small eateries and shops. As the crowd walked up the road, she recalls hearing the sound of glass exploding behind her and wondering why people were throwing stones. Slowly, people began to realise that the Central Reserve Police Force (CRPF) had opened fire from above. As people began to run for shelter, she found herself stuck, not knowing where to run. She laughs and tells me she just stood there near the Mela ground, peeking out and trying to see what was happening. Meanwhile, two boys from the village had been sent by Udai to find her. On locating her, they picked her up and were rushing when a lady near her, in her fifties, just fell on the ground. The boys lifted her as well and they rushed to find Udai, who was waiting by a side lane. In her retelling of the incident, she does not express fear; instead there is humour at her own innocence. Her lack of knowledge about the layout of the town and possibly the confusion during the time, explain her confidence in her ability to cope with the situation, and in her faith at being located by Udai eventually. She recounts feeling confusion and curiosity at the surrounding events; her lack of understanding of the larger political implications of the march strangely shielding her.

Through her telling and retelling of this story, I have found myself amazed at the visually precise details that have sprung up in our conversations. She remembers that this lady, who had fallen on the ground, was wearing a red cardigan, *chaubandi cholo*[28] and a saree underneath. Udai, a doctor, asked her what had happened, and she pointed to her back saying it was hurting. When he lifted her cardigan to have a look, Nandita noticed that inside her *potakki*,[29] the woman was carrying a big sickle. A bullet was lodged in her shoulder blade, proving that the CRPF had not been firing blanks. They quickly rushed the woman to the government hospital nearby, located across the town about a kilometre away, up a steep road, that took them eight to ten minutes. On their way there, in a lane near Damber Chowk, Nandita saw an elderly lady standing all alone. She had surrounded herself with stones and was throwing them at the CRPF, catching hold of men and women running for their lives, urging them to fight. Unknown to Nandita and Udai at the time, the CRPF

[28] Traditional blouse worn by Gorkhali and Nepalese women.

[29] Belt/sash worn around the waist over the draped saree.

had opened fire in the main town road and people had died. There are numerous times where Nandita points out not knowing what was going on or the role people like her played in the larger political landscape of Gorkhaland. She recalls never questioning the ideology or commands of the GNLF, and instead the acceptance that they would deliver on a separate state for the community. For Nandita, that fateful day was not a memory of hatred and fear, but of the courage shown by two ordinary women, ready to fight for their ideals, community and land. She recalls, 'Whenever I think of the andolan, I think of that lady: the lady who next to me collapsed, and that lady alone in Damber Chowk with those little-little stones she had gathered near her.' The history of our andolan has sadly muted many of these voices; stories of women surviving a period of conflict and protecting their families, harbouring unique experiences of the moment.

On making it to the hospital operation theatre, Udai rushed upstairs to get help for the lady while Nandita and their companions waited below. That was when she began to understand the gravity of the situation, seeing all the bodies come in. She remembers not feeling fear but just standing there, shocked, watching everything. She recounts a story Udai had told her later, of a sixteen- or eighteen-year-old girl who had been shot in her forehead. The bullet had entered from the front and exited from the back of her head—an instant death. Her brains had splattered out the back. She had been brought to the operation theatre declared dead. Subsequently, a man called King Kong had gone on his motorbike through the chaos on the main road and collected her brains from the ground. He quickly brought it back to the hospital in his hands and showed it to Udai, asking him if it would help. These are the stories my mother has held onto through the years; brutal events that she narrates with such a sense of normalcy. She says, 'I don't know why it didn't make more of an impact on me because after that there was a clamp down … Then we had a whole lot of raids and I still remember that all the boys used to run away to the forest because the CRPF would come and catch people and send them to jails.'[30] There were numerous incidents of men being sent to distant jails around West Bengal to be tortured and beaten. Nothing was ever officially declared.

Dipti in conversation with Meera (D&M)[31]: 'Why does my story matter?' asked Meera. This reaction on her part is reflective of the normalised silencing of women's voices, who are often made to believe that their stories do not matter. It is not uncommon that women's stories have failed to find voices in the 'bigger, important' matters of politics convincing women to internalise this patriarchal logic of being silenced, of not mattering. Dolly Phukon (2017) succinctly elaborates on this in the context of the political movement in Assam,

---

[30] Ibid.

[31] Tamang, M. December, 19th, (2020) 'Interview of Meera Tamang'. Interviewed by Dipti Tamang,

where through such internalisation, women have convinced themselves of 'not mattering'.[32] I felt the discomfort and a strong sense of sadness, for all of us—including me—have been complicit in making Meera feel like her stories do not matter, when in reality it is her stories that have been the sources of rich conversations on the socio-political life of the place in guiding and giving shape to much of my research on gender, feminism and more.

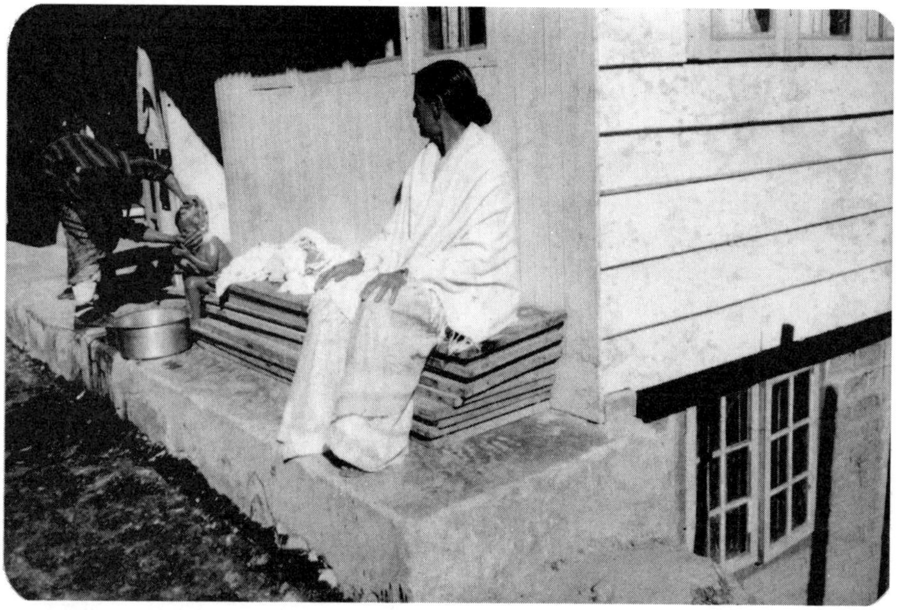

Figure 1. Left to right: Meera Tamang is seen bathing her elder child-Devashish Tamang and seated on the right is her late mother Mungpoo, 1987–88. Source: Meera Tamang's family album.

In this image, Meera is seen bathing her elder child—my sibling—while my grandmother sits nearby and watches us. When asked about the specific date or time, she vaguely remembers it being sometime around 1987–88. As we sat down to work on this project, one of the challenges we confronted was bringing the visual and the oral elements to agree in her narratives. Photography likewise was also a luxury unavailable to many, and our family did not own a camera until as recently as 2005. Studio photography is a much popular practice in the Hill regions and owning cameras is considered a symbol of a certain class and luxury. Family albums comprised of a limited number of images taken by relatives or family friends who owned cameras. Most pictures of my family from this period were either taken by the local photographer, who was also a family friend, or by our relatives.

[32] Phukon, Dolly. 2017. 'Contested Space of Democracy and Women's Agency for Change in Assam'. Kolas, Ashild. ed. *Women, Peace and Security in Northeast India* (New Delhi: Zubaan Publishers). pp. 48–67.

My childhood was about growing up listening to stories of my mother, her struggles and challenges as she negotiated her reality amidst politically instigated fear, danger and tensions. She tried to create a sense of normalcy through everyday routines of managing the house and her two children, sometimes with help from her mother or other family members, and sometimes alone. Her story is reminiscent of the everyday roles ordinary women were engaged in, in the backdrop of political conflict. These roles included running the household, holding jobs (Meera was responsible for running a shop), and keeping the family safe during the violence that engulfed the Darjeeling Hills in 1986. While the stories of male figures contributing to the cause, sacrificing their lives for the agitation while being away from their families are valorised, the stories of women navigating the harsh realities of a highly militarised society remain silenced. It is to the everyday that our family photographs belong, and for me, they formulate a personal history that bears the dominant narrative, as compared to the political ongoings of 1986.

The background of the house is significant in this image, as it constantly figures in her narratives. 'I used to wake up at four or sometimes even earlier,' she reminisces, 'otherwise I wouldn't have time. I had two small children to take care of—bathing them, feeding them and having everything done before 7 a.m., then open the shop. Your father would barely be available, always away on some tour or the other, doing something.'[33] My father was actively engaged in the political agitation of 1986 in his capacity as a member of the GNLF, along with most men in the area. There is no hint of resentment or disappointment in her voice when she recollects these memories; on the contrary, she takes pride in how she managed and performed these laborious and challenging duties singlehandedly. 'The girls nowadays can't even imagine doing such tasks, our realities will seem like nothing but a concocted tale,' she says merrily as I walk behind her while she still rushes about performing multiple chores in the house. Similar sentiments from that period have emerged in the different conversations I have had with other women of my mother's generation. Women and men likewise believe that without women, the struggle for Gorkhaland is incomplete, for it was them who provided the fundamental support that made it possible for men to go out and fight a larger battle. I contest the rendering of such 'sacrifices' as secondary and merely 'supportive' roles, turning to critically engage with the parochial, patriarchal realities of the Hill society.

R&N: While looking at available photographs and visual documents, it was surprising that this period of conflict and resilience was not documented in the albums lying at home. There were barely any photographs from the period, and it seemed strange that those that were, depicted regular lives untouched by the andolan. Martha Langford (2006) writes that in the telling of stories the

[33] Tamang, M. 2020. Interview of Meera Gurung. By Dipti Tamang.

setting is either familiar or inherently strange.[34] My mother and I encounter both familiarity and strangeness when we look at the few photographs of this time, and as a family reconstructing our own history, we begin to craft stories from the events that we know transpired in the andolan, even when they have not been visualised. We do so by adding observations made for the first time while revisiting these photographs, referring to occurrences outside of the frame of the image.

Langford further writes, 'Albums are full of repetitions: situations are revisited or recreated with slight variations; actual images are often repeated in different arrangements.'[35] The act of looking at a photograph from the family album and engaging in a discussion of that memory becomes a synchronised affair. As we examined the few photographs taken during the period of conflict, I found myself unconsciously participating in the storytelling process, including references to both, the everyday and the larger political crisis, sharing my observations and collaborating with a memory that I was not a part of.

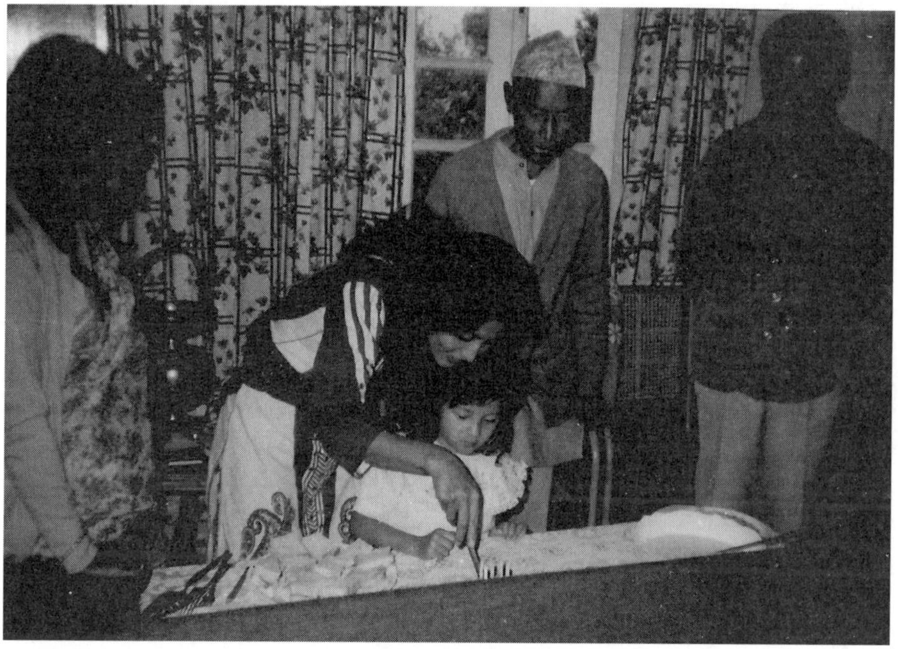

Figure 2. From left to right: Sarah Gurung, Nandita Gurung, Tanya Gurung, K.B. Gurung and Brigadier Gurung. 31 March 1987. Source: Nandita Gurung's family album.

[34] Langford, M. 2006. 'Speaking the Album: An Application of the Oral-Photographic Framework'. Kuhn, A and K.E. McAllister. eds. *Locating Memory: Photographic Acts* (New York: Berghahn Books). pp. 223–246.

[35] Ibid. p. 225.

Figures 2 and 3 feature photographs taken on 31 March 1987. The period of agitation for a separate state continued from 1985 to 1988, with several *bandhs*[36] and clamp downs during the time. This was the time period my search for photographs centred on, and while it was difficult to find pictures from this period, I was able to find a few from after I was born at the end of 1988. By then the Darjeeling Gorkha Hill Council Agreement had been signed by the West Bengal government and the GNLF. The two photographs in Figure 2 and Figure 3 document the family coming together to celebrate my sister Tanya's birthday, an event far removed from the conflict that had seized the Hills for almost a year. These photographs throw light on a life unknown to me, a different house and people who are no longer in our lives. Nandita can be seen bending down to cut the cake with Tanya tucked safely under her. She remembers the birthday celebration and fondly recalls the old house, Udai's family members flocking around for the celebration, keeping her busy with preparing snacks, ordering a birthday cake and getting the house ready for a party. The cake and sandwiches in the photograph were a staple at every birthday party growing up, and Nandita recounts fond memories of these events filled with the food items that she had prepared. The absence of her own side of the family in these celebrations never appeared to bother her, a circumstance also of the inability to travel freely during the agitation period.

Appearing second from the right is Udai's granduncle, Krishna Bahadur Gurung, and on the extreme left is his daughter Sarah Gurung, and although they are my baje (grandfather) and phupu (aunt), I have not had the opportunity to know them well. This photograph was taken on the lower floor of Gurung Lodge, the *mool ghar* (family home), an unfamiliar space to me but one that features significantly in my parents' memories and that I, by default, have postmemory of. Articulated in Nandita's stories, the house constructs itself like a fortress in my mind, a space where our family was protected and shielded from the conflict; yet it was a space that would be sporadically raided by the CPRF in their hunt for party members of the GNLF. These stories of raids and disappearing men have cropped up in other stories involving family and community members, in social gatherings and recollections of the andolan—a fact that is both known but has remained hidden and undocumented in its reality, and impacts a generation of young people growing up in the shadow of these memories.

These records have been erased from our histories and collective memories through violence, and they now lay dormant in oral narratives. They have formed a memory culture that people in the region draw on when talking about conflict, politics and despair over the political situation of the Hills. Hirsch writes that the 'growth of memory culture may, indeed, be a symptom of a need for inclusion in a collective membrane forged by a shared inheritance of multiple traumatic histories and the individual and social responsibility we

[36] State-enforced lockdowns.

feel toward a persistent and traumatic past.'[37] These memories of the andolan narrated by the women in my community have sprung from a need to conserve stories of resistance and in their process of retelling, showcase how memory culture has been vital in preserving the stories of resistance in places like Kalimpong.

During the time of scarce resources and a fear of venturing into public spaces, Nandita must have struggled with arranging things, but that does not feature in her narrative. What is apparent is a lack of young children in the frame. Our family albums are otherwise filled with us standing with our friends and the friends of my parents. The political curfews and uncertainty significantly impacted the shaping of this photograph, but this is an observation she glosses over. Going back and forth between the political crisis of the time and these mundane events, she does not appear to notice how easily she shifts between the memory of people being shot and the memory of my sister's birthday. The period between 1985–87 merges into a long period of collective political crisis, as she does not differentiate between the years that appear fluid and only certain memories stand out.

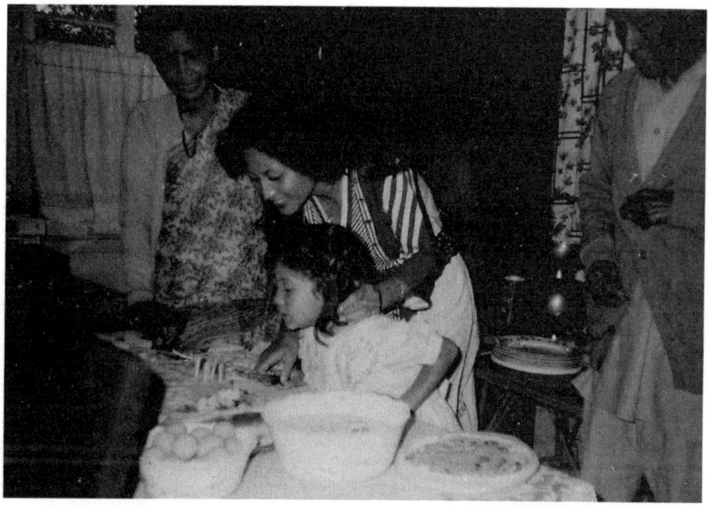

Figure 3. From left: Sarah Gurung, Nandita Gurung, Tanya Gurung and K.B. Gurung. 31 March 1987. Source: Nandita Gurung's family album.

Langford's observation on albums being full of repetitions can be witnessed here, as a change in the angle between the two images brings added perspective to the same narrative. Figure 3 draws my focus to a cherished antique that still sits in our house. Passed on to Udai by his father, it is a larger version of a sacred brass pot known as a *kamandal*[38]. Other details strike me, such as the

[37] Ibid. p. 111.

[38] Water pot often carried around by yogis.

cake bearing five candles that determine the year this photo was taken, while accounting for the one extra candle for luck. The plates on the table behind Nandita are still in our house; items collected and preserved by her through the years. The rasagullas (dessert made from milk and semolina) and kheer (rice pudding) on the table, are other staple birthday items. Even though these pictures were taken by Udai, I have always attributed the ownership of family albums to Nandita. She was the one who looked after them, preserved them and took part in the oral narratives surrounding the photographs.

Rose writes that family photographs have been 'criticised for perpetuating an idyllic image of the nuclear family'.[39] In my family's case, photographs upheld the idea of a close family that included extended family members, cementing dominant ideas of class, gender and race. Despite such values that we imbibed in our lives, a lot of our family photographs taken by Udai featured Nandita and us as the central figures. While some family photographs do include him, most of the pictures centre around Nandita and the children on trips, birthdays and special occasions. In these pictures, we appear in familiar and predictable poses that are 'not visually innovative', as pointed out by Rose, citing scholarship on the matter of the 'less than positive critical reception' of family photographs.[40] The question then is, does this banality, along with the repetitive nature of family photographs, diminish their significance? After all, family photographs do portray selective, repetitive moments of our lives. The 'not visually innovative' aspect of the pictures, Rose notes, did not bother her participants. Similarly, this aspect does not bother my family members because their focus is on the larger memories the photos preserve and the stories that unravel from them, spilling beyond the frame. It was interesting to note that between 1985–87, Nandita had managed to maintain this curated version of her family history in the few photographs from the time, and the memories showcased were happy moments and not the political turbulence of her surroundings.

D & M: This image of Meera and my elder sibling was taken at a former friend's home in 1985. 'In those days, we all had time for each other. Despite hardships and difficulties, it was nice to meet with friends and talk, nowadays we barely get time to see anyone,' explains Meera. If looked at closely, one can see the presence of another person in the image: Meera's friend's arm in the lower left corner. 'The men were in the other room and we were in another,' she explains. This practice of gender-based segregation is familiar as men and women still find separate spaces to sit and converse about topics ranging from their everyday lives to larger debates on 'Hill politics'. Through these conversations, I have significantly understood the socio-political and cultural

---

[39] Rose, G. 2010. *Doing Family Photography: The Domestic, The Public and The Politics of Sentiment* (Farnham: Ashgate Press). p. 11.

[40] Ibid.

realities of the Hills. Women's conversations in kitchen spaces remain segregated from organised 'public' spaces, hence heard and passed on only by other women and their children.

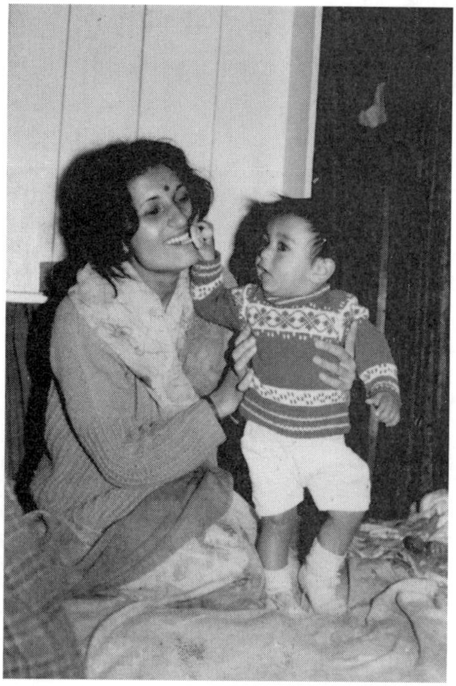

Figure 4. Meera Tamang with her eldest child, Devashish Tamang. 1985. Source: Meera Tamang's family album.

Most of Meera's images from this period are either of her with me and/or with my brother, with the house and her shop in the backdrop, a telling detail of her life in the absence of my father. This invisibility is also reflected in the stories I grew up listening to, of Meera singlehandedly bearing through endless struggles to give us a secure and safe childhood. Meera begins by telling me about my brother being very weak following his birth and how difficult it was for her to manage the household with my father being away most of the time. It was around this time, sometime during the 1987 period, that she had also taken up teaching at a small, private nursery school in the locality. Along with managing the household and the children, she was also successfully working as a teacher in a private nursery school and providing private tuitions. 'Now that I think of it—I do not know how I managed all of it,' she laughs, 'your father would help when he was around, but he was always travelling at that time,' she recollects. In the years to come, my mother would have her own private school to run, but eventually she put her career aside for the family, a familiar reality for many women.

These two images (Figures 4 and 5) of Meera at her most intimate, in her personal space with her child, spoke to me in a different manner. As succinctly put by Mridu Rai,[41] it is this 'insane urge to make sense' of what was she doing at this time, what was her positionality vis à vis my father—an active member of the GNLF, fighting the 'big' fight. His and other stories of men fighting for the cause have found meaning and relevance in the discourse around the andolan, but women's stories continue to be historically silenced, simply for being 'ordinary' and embedded in the mundane. In the absence of

---

[41] Rai, Mridu. 'Reconnecting and Learning to Let Go My Great-grandmothers through Images'. The Confluence Collective. Available at: www.theconfluencecollective.com/post/reconnecting-and-learning-to-let-go-my-great-grandmothers-through-images.

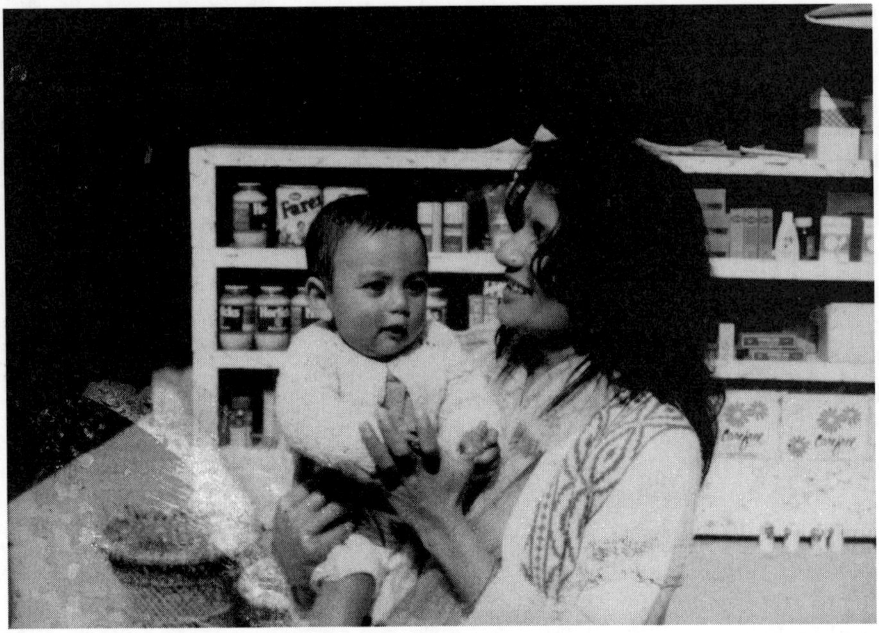

Figure 5. Meera Tamang with her son, Devashish Tamang. 1985–86. Source: Meera Tamang's family album.

my father, it was my mother Meera who held the house together, established and created a community of family, friends, relatives, who kept her going. In her recollection of the everyday, which includes stories of banter, laughter and small social gatherings, one would be forced to imagine them as being everyday, normal affairs in a 'peaceful' place, and that is precisely how we approach the andolan—not as an abstract event, but as constantly playing in the background, while life moved on for the people amidst police and military raids, arson and violence. I understand why Meera would feel her stories did not matter; these were ordinary stories of the everyday spaces, and yet it is here we find evidences of a history of militarisation, conflict and violence, otherwise erased from public memory. Yet it is Meera who is rendered invisible from these sites of history and without an identity of her own—from being Meera Chettri to being very fondly recognised as my father's wife, Sagar daju's bhauju.[42]

'Your brother was my third child,' she reveals softly. This was new information for me as I had always thought that it had always been only the two of us—my brother and myself. 'I had two miscarriages before him, one at childbirth, while the other one died nineteen days after she was born.' As I now look back at pictures of my mother from our family album, I cannot but help notice how frail and weak she looks; it is almost a miracle that she survived those repeated miscarriages, happening so close in time. I hesitated to probe

[42] Sagar is my father's name, and 'Sagar daju's bhauju' translates as 'Sagar brother's wife'.

further, worried that it would trigger painful memories, but she looks fondly at my brother's image and tells me another difficult tale of how they almost lost him too, in their struggle to keep him alive. In these ordinary struggles of seeking access to basic healthcare during emergencies, one is forced to think about the difficulties of conflicts, of how life truly 'goes on' in the backdrop of a raging conflict, where travelling to distant places for healthcare makes for a harrowing tale of immense hardship and serious challenge, fraught with risks and dangers.

Pain, difficulties and hardship continue to form a grim backdrop for most of her stories, but she says with a smile, 'The time was such, and it was worse apparently for women in far-flung villages and the tea gardens. I would be scared, sometimes I would be alone with my two small children and I wished that night never came.' A fear of the dark is another element that remains a recurrent theme in most feminine narratives, as I have also documented elsewhere.[43] She narrated another unsettling tale of how she once travelled alone to Siliguri, the closest city to the Hills, to get supplies for the shop. This was during the 40 days of political bandh called by the GNLF in 1986 while demanding for the creation of the political state of Gorkhaland. 'I travelled halfway in the back of a truck and then walked halfway from this point called Rambhi towards Mungpoo. As I think of it now, I myself am amazed at my own courage,' she says.

I wonder, did she or any other woman like her even have a choice but to be resilient, given that our basic needs were at stake? It is in such personalised narratives of women, that we find mentions of rape, sexual abuse and violence. She adds, 'As a lone female in the house, I was scared. I had heard of the CRPF raping young women in areas such as Bijanbari[44] and Kalimpong.' Of these recollections, there is no evidence or official documentation, no committees that had been set up to enquire into such crimes despite the oral testimonies of the people. Whether it was the 1986 period or the later movements—especially during the 2017 political agitation—the Darjeeling Hills remain an area which is yet to see the setting up of public bodies to investigate the consequences of violence in the region. On the other hand, we have been forced to personally confront these realities through kitchen conversations, as almost every household has a story to tell of the Chyasi ko Andolan. We realised how deeply interconnected the idea of the 'personal' has been with the 'political'.

R&N: I grew up in Mandal Gaon, a village located just above an area called Tirpai. Nandita recounts that during the CRPF raids in 1986, the men from Tirpai and Mandal Gaon would run into the forest located beyond the village,

---

[43] Tamang. 2020. Interview.

[44] Bijanbari is another small town in Darjeeling Hills with undocumented histories of intra-party violence, state sponsored violence. The place is also supposed to have witnessed the most cases of sexual violence against women in the 1986-87 period.

to an area called Bhalukhop. Only a few men stayed back in the village, their professions as doctors (like Udai) or brigadiers functioning as coats of privilege. Nandita remembers how she and the other women would carry chilli powder in their pockets/garments while they were at home, in case the CRPF came and attacked them. She says they were made to believe that the CRPF would rape and kill them. A lot of my parent's friends from Tirpai and beyond would come and hide in our house, the Gurung Lodge. She laughs, remembering how they would play mahjong[45] the entire day while staying indoors. My parents were not financially well off at the time, but she remembers the house as always being full of people and the table always full of food. 'Everybody brought something to the table,' she declares proudly. The community rallied together, and this is how they protected themselves; the women staying back, guarding the houses, while the men left for safer hideouts. Possibly, the danger of the forest and unknown men hiding there was just as much as that posed by the CPRF, so the women and children stayed back in their houses. Between the divided politics of the GNLF, the Gorkha Volunteer Cell (GVC) and the CRPF, the people of the Hills found themselves vulnerable and exposed.

Recounting the domestic everyday, Nandita talks about how she spent her time tending to her vegetable garden and with Udai's family, content in her domestic life and accepting of the political matters unfolding in the region. Her memories and photographs of the time centre around domestic spaces, on a life removed from her career or aspirations of a career. I point out how odd it is to know about the violent history of the Hills, the oppression, and to then hear such normal stories in simultaneity. She mentions that people living in town had it much tougher, that being in a small village away from the epicentre helped them stay protected. Middle-class households tucked away in small villages would have found themselves away from the ire of the CRPF. 'They used to come at night and evening, with injuries,' she says referring to how 'our people' would take Udai to their hideouts to tend to their injuries either from being shot at by the CRPF or sustained while building homemade bombs. None of her stories mention members from other non-Gorkhali/ Nepali communities, but her language demarcates an 'us' versus 'them'. Casually, she notes, 'We romanticise many things, you know, we never play it out as normally as it was.' These stories are a far cry from normalcy, but she was recounting them like they weren't. Is this how communities cope with conflict and brutality, by normalising their lives even amidst the most horrific of events? Nandita appears to believe so; she later remarks that behaving normally was how they coped and did not let themselves dwell on the negative turns their lives could have taken.

This picture was taken by Udai between 1985–86. It shows my three-year-old elder sister, Tanya, and the family dog Zeeba. It was taken in front of the mool ghar, and in the far right, you can spot a chicken coop. Nandita mentions

[45] A tile-based four player game originating in China.

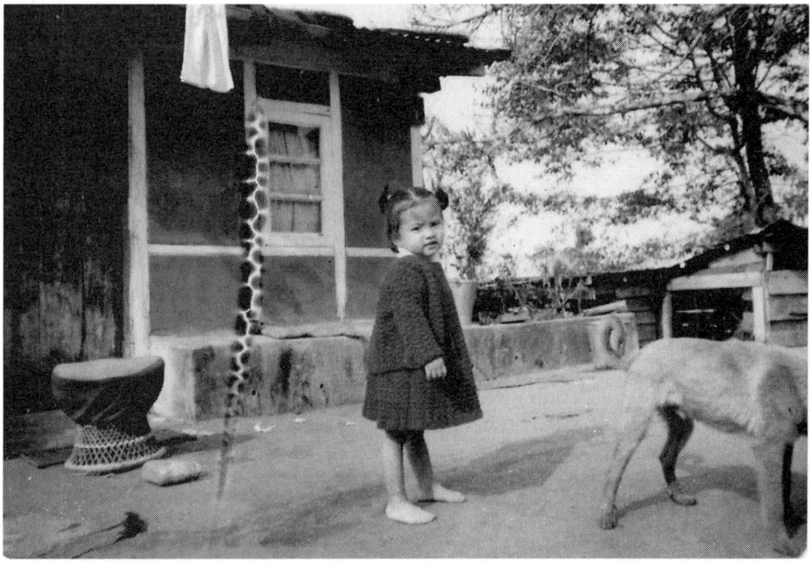

Figure 6. Tanya Gurung and Zeeba. 1986. Source: Nandita Gurung's family album.

how the family tried to be as self-sufficient as possible, growing their own vegetables and rearing poultry. She mentions that photographs were limited because of the expense of developing them, and so moments of celebration were prioritised and documented. My first question on finding this photograph was of its relevance, as it did not appear to mark a celebration. To which she instantly answered that Udai's youngest sister had come to visit them, so the photograph had been taken to commemorate that day, even though the visitor was not in the frame. Other photographs of the day may have existed, but over time, they were misplaced or damaged due to poor storage practices. Many family albums appear to lack value in the eyes of the family and so are placed in dark corners of shelves or in drawers that are seldom opened; the photographs that preserve so many memories themselves live on borrowed time.

D&M: This image of my elder brother Devashish Tamang, me and our mother Meera was taken in front of the house and the main road between 1987 and 1989. Although this period falls outside of the timeframe of 1986, Chyaasi ko Andolan is remembered by the people of the Hills as a time that extends well into the late 1980s, upto 1992, when the first phase of the political movement ended with the signing of an agreement for the formation of an autonomous Hill Council. Well into the second half of the 1980s, this was still a period where the larger political situation of the Hills was delicate, but with relatively lesser violence, as negotiations on peace were underway with the leadership of the GNLF.

In this image (Meera recollects this being taken somewhere between 1986–87), we can see a visibly more relaxed environment, with more people included

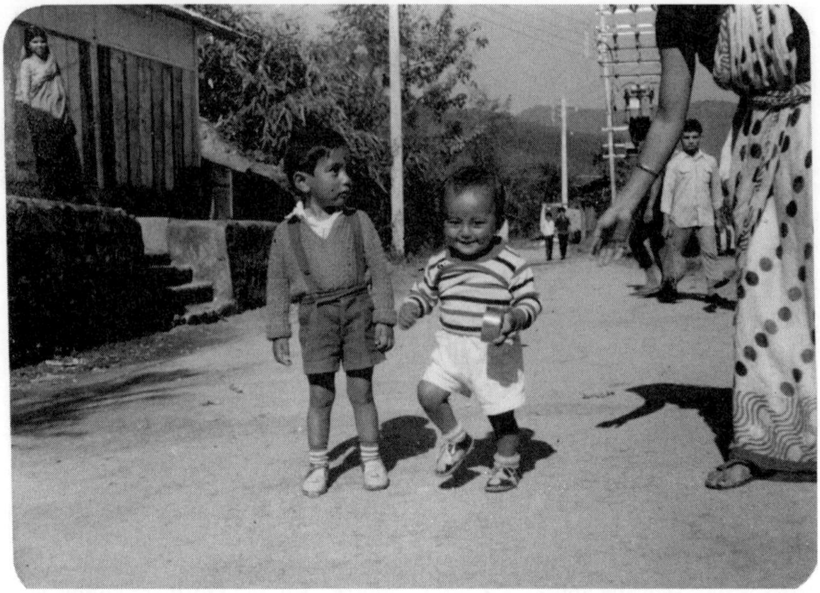

Figure 7. From the left: Devashish Tamang, Dipti Tamang, Meera Tamang. 1987–89. Source: Meera Tamang's family album.

in the frame. Our earlier house by now had a new tenant, a Bihari migrant family of four members, the father being the only carpenter in the village, till date known as Mistiri Mama. The woman standing on top of the stairs watching us from a distance is his wife, whom we called Maami. She later left for her hometown, with Mama staying back for work . 'See how empty these spaces were?' says Meera pointing to the stretches of spaces behind us in the image. Over almost forty years since the andolan, the landscape has changed into a bustling neighbourhood with rows of buildings replacing the vast wilderness in the image. 'It was not as crowded before,' she recollects, 'which is why it was very scary for a lone woman. It is a miracle how I survived that time; it haunts me when I think of that time now. Those were times when we lived in fear—people fighting against each other, being abducted and killed by the CRPF were ordinary, everyday realities; it is nothing compared to the political agitation now,' she remembers. Chyaasi, as we come to see, is deeply etched into these lived memories which allow us in the present times to locate Darjeeling Hills in a period of violent conflict, remnants of which can only be found in razed buildings falling prey to arson, stories of people murdered, and families yet to find closures for their trauma and loss.

Meera's conversations with me through these photographs allowed her—and through her recollections, me—to revisit those times. She reminisces these memories with a sense of fondness, love and warmth. I see it as a story of resilience and courage. She must have barely been twenty-four years old at that time with no clue of what life was throwing at her; she was physically frail but inwardly immensely strong, somehow finding the courage to confront her fears and manage as best as she could. I felt both a sense of awe, admiration, renewed respect and a sense of 'feminist despair'[46] in my engagement with her. Despair at being complicit in forgetting her stories, her history, her reality and her courage. I always grew up hearing my mother narrate these stories, but never really 'listening'. As I engage with her story, positioned as an 'objective' researcher, I now understand how in failing to 'listen' to these stories; we are complicit in perpetuating the culture of silence. And in doing so, we perhaps also contribute to the practice of upholding structures that hold some stories important while excluding so many more.

R&N: Nandita's memories do not follow a linear trajectory, she jumps back and forth in time, recounting events based on their intensity and her association with them. Her place as an outsider to the community is something that I find myself fixated upon. She grew up as an army child, far removed from the politics of Gorkhaland. She was twenty-one when she married Udai, moving from Durgapur, West Bengal, to the small hill station of Kalimpong, with a different life, culture, and a different dialect. She would often tell me how Udai's family members would place her in the centre of the room, sit around her and ask her to pronounce certain Nepali words. They were thoroughly amused and welcomed her with open arms. Growing up, she had moved around and spent her formative years in Dehradun, Uttarakhand, where Nepali was heavily interspersed with Hindi. It is probably while nurturing a family that she understood the significance of her stories and the value of photographs in preserving her memories.

This photograph was one Nandita could not place immediately, and she identified it as belonging to the 1987 Dashain celebrations on the basis of the saree, which she vividly remembers. The photograph was taken by Udai's cousin in the same room as indicated in Figures 2 and 3, the curtains signalling the space. She points to the bottle of Old Tavern whiskey, a popular drink of the time, accompanied by gambling using playing cards. The icebox and snacks seen on the table are familiar items during social gatherings with family even today.

These photographs showcase a very normal household, far removed from the political turmoil tearing the Hills apart outside its walls. They contradict the stories of horror and unease that shadow the stories told by Nandita. They show people celebrating birthdays and religious festivals, and a family member's visit. The stories of the time told by my mother—of her getting a job and teaching under a lockdown, students being rushed to Kolkata to sit for the board exams, women fighting and losing their lives—are not the stories that my family album portrays. These stories run parallel to each other, almost daring the other to cross paths.

---

[46] Ahmed, Sara. 25 August 2014. 'Self-care as warfare'. feministkilljoys. Available at: feministkilljoys.com/2014/08/25/selfcare-as-warfare/

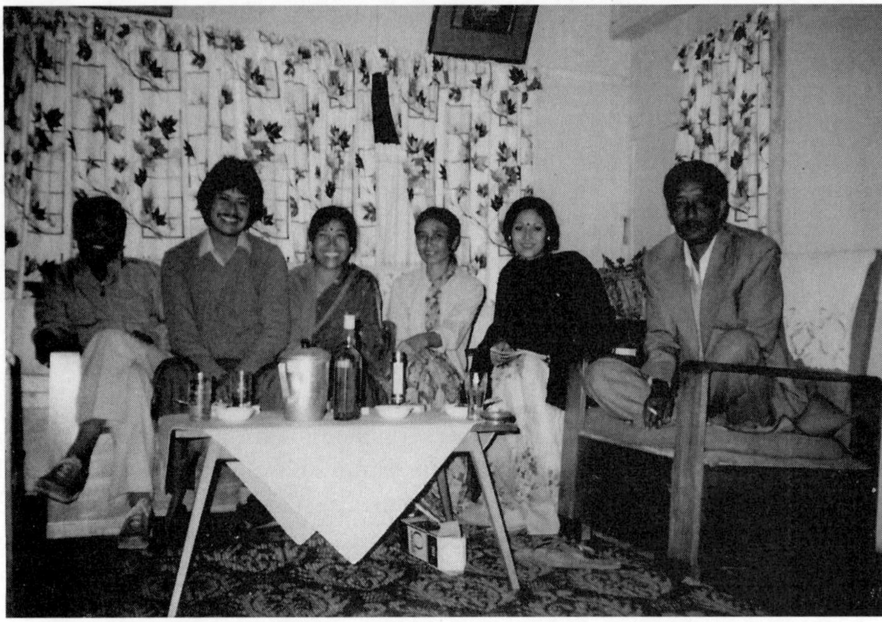

Figure 8. From left: Narain Gurung, Udai Gurung, Saru Gurung, Philomena Gurung, Nandita and Chand Gurung. Dassai 1987. Source: Nandita Gurung's family album.

Memories that Construct the 'Everyday'

When we came together to work on this essay, we were still having conversations around the 'need to build an archive' of the Hills, where conversations and experiences would be central to the narrative. Working on this project has been challenging, for we were conscious of not treating our respective mothers simply as 'subjects' while at the same time not being merely 'objective' in bringing forth their stories. As we were preparing this essay, both of us realised our own subjective and authorial positions in these conversations, and our different stylistic approaches to oral and visual material in families. Ruchika worked with the idea of distancing herself from her subject and using her mother's name, abstaining from using the term 'my mother' as much as possible, while Dipti was less objective in maintaining distance from her mother's narrative. We came to a common ground of referring to our mothers by their names and distancing from their maternal identities. These approaches and our different writing styles made us reflect on how we navigate around questions of memory and spaces we were so intimate and familiar with to bring forth stories of lived experiences while maintaining a sense of objectivity to the same. Research in the humanities often finds itself steering towards discourse from objective standpoints, concrete evidence and reliability. Dealing with family photographs opens a platform to talk about the subjectivity of memories and their emotionality amidst political climates that change the landscape of the family as documented in photographs.

In engaging with the stories of our mothers, what caught our imagination was the construction of the everyday, its absence from historical narratives and replete presence among family photographs. Our mother's stories constructed a barrier between their everyday survival and the overall support and understanding of a statehood that benefitted 'our people'. Their memories of 1986 helped us revisit a period where the everyday and political conflict went hand in hand; evident in their retelling of these parallel narratives which appear to be heavily influenced by each other. Their reflection of that period is testimony to overwhelming violence experienced by the people in the Hills; otherwise erased from public memory. And in centering their memories and experiences of their domestic lives in the backdrop of such extreme political violence and conflict, we seek to offer a broader understanding of statehood. Family photographs especially construct a narrative of the everyday and the domestic, the idyllic and the mundane as part of their aesthetic.

These conversations are a beginning in the direction of rebuilding a more inclusive narrative of the andolan that gripped the Darjeeling Hills during 1986. It is our effort to include the lost and silenced voices not as personal, isolated events but as a significant part of the collective whole. By documenting the oral and visual narratives of women, we can begin to develop a more nuanced understanding of the politics of the region, highlighting how the gendered role of storytelling can be political praxis in its own right. As mentioned earlier in the piece, Das (2007) discusses the implication of identifying a narrative and developing a voice to recount that narrative. This would give those words a life, or instil life into those memories. We hope that through this work, and subsequently a larger archival project, women like our mothers are able to identify with and develop their voices to add to the wider discourse around the Gorkhaland agitation and its impact on the history and culture of the Darjeeling Hills.

The New 'Family Albums'

Studying Anti-CAA Protest Photographs in India

Jigisha Bhattacharya

Introduction

What makes a family album? Is it the artefact of the album itself, the act of touching and flipping through it, moving from one photograph to another, and reminiscing about olden days? Is it the awe of faded black-and-white photographs carefully preserved with corner-marks? Is it the act of removing the tracing paper sheets from each page, and peeping into what it offers? Is it the people, near and dear ones whom we know directly, or through family lore passed on from generation to generation? Is it the possibility of locating one's roots as one flips through the young faces of the now old, now deceased members? In most of the discussions around family photographs, it is the domestic that dominates the discourse. It is the lives, actions, relationships and the fissures within the confines of the house per se, or activities that include and/or affirm the familial ties, practically in an extension of the home space, that typically constitute family albums. We see children at play, couples at marital occasions and relatives and friends on family occasions in the photographs that a family carefully preserves. We see the different functions of what a 'family' should entail being ratified, memorialised and preserved by these valuable visuals. As Mary Bouquet suggests, 'family and kinship are actually constituted by and through photography.'[1] Photographs of family have a material and visual existence that is worthy of being preserved and exhibited, but they also bear a social image that they collectively project to the world.

Not all family photographs are the same; not all families have the material and socio-cultural privileges of owning photographs of their near and dear ones from the past. Even in the existing oeuvre of family photographs, not all family members or familial relationships make an appearance. There is always that absent photograph of an uncle lost to political violence, the aunt who married outside her caste, or the distant brother who cut all ties with the family in his pursuit of the world. These people live in the memories of those who tried to negotiate with their own feelings regarding their deviance. Occasionally, they live in hidden photographs in the middle of diary pages and folded clothes.

---

[1] Bouquet, Mary. 2000. 'The Family Photographic Condition'. *Visual Anthropology Review*. 16:1. p. 8.

Therefore, family photographs become as much about forgetting as they are about remembrance; as much about the omission and abandonment of images as they are about their preservation. Family photographs are the product of a careful curation of memories from the past of a family, the lineages of which it wants to celebrate and preserve. Such photographs shape the gaze through which a family's *image* could potentially be elicited, constructed, and projected.

However, fissures still exist within the dominant image that family photographs want to portray. As perhaps with all hegemonic narratives, it is the act of reading *against the grain*, of finding the gaps in family narratives, the associative displacements of certain photographs, the visual staging[2] entailed in constructing family photographs and the deliberate placement of members of a family in it in which one can locate certain fault lines. Especially since photographs became widely produced and circulated with the rise of twenty-first-century social and participatory media, new calibrations were made possible in the very way we think about family photographs. For photographs, the economy of their preservation and exhibition changed, as did the contours of the intended viewing agents even the very status and purpose of the family photographs went through several changes with changing forms of archiving, memorialisation and dissemination. There is a wider consideration of what constitutes the domestic and the public for family photographs, especially as family photographs are now circulated in a public domain with potentially a much larger viewership on the internet.

On the other hand, when one looks at the history of public photographic documentation or photojournalism, their discursive understanding becomes that of anonymous, amorphous individuals, communities and collectives bearing witness to a past, or allowing the viewer an extension to that (often traumatic) past. Photographic documentation of significant political events of violence, trauma or conflict often embody the 'signpost' visual metaphors of these events, directing the viewers towards specific templates for commemorating the past.[3] Amongst the photojournalists working with contemporary events of political significance, many have tried to induce through their works the 'consciousness of a distracted people and a sometimes oblivious government'.[4] While the field of photojournalism is still dominated by appointed professionals, there is now a rise of amateurs or citizen photographers, and their visuals become the sources for news and information for many across social media. In both these domains of authorship, there is 'a new form of encounter' that enables 'new

[2] Family-photographs, captured in the studio and beyond, often have been noted to have a performative 'staging' of the photographic event that is characterised by a certain kind of 'planned spontaneity.' See Sinha (2010), 51; Allana (2013), 51.

[3] Zelizer, Barbie. 2002. 'Photography, Journalism and Trauma'. Zelizer, Barbie and Stuart Allan. eds. *Journalism after September 11* (London and NY: Routledge). p. 711.

[4] Ritchen, Fred. 2013. *Bending the Frame: Photojournalism, Documentary and the Citizen* (New York: Aperture). pp. 29–30.

possibilities of political action' and engenders 'new conditions' for the visibility of the photographic subjects.[5]

Drawing from the new ways of understanding documentary and family photographs, new ways of making, disseminating and viewing photographs, this essay wants to probe the dichotomy of journalistic and private album photographs of the family. To situate this query, this essay concerns itself with the binary questions of presences and absences, exhibition and secrecy, domestic and public through a study of the photographic documentation of the Anti-Citizenship Bill Protests in India. These protests hinged around the Citizenship Amendment Act (CAA), 2019,[6] that effectively enforces strict criteria of Indian citizenship, putting the onus of proving one's citizen status on the individual, sparking widespread dissent by communities, civil societies, activists, and human rights organisations. The Act has been widely criticised for its divisive, communal and punitive agenda, and resulted in mass protests around India in multiple convergent and divergent forms of protest actions in the year 2019. In protest sites like Delhi's Shaheen Bagh, Seelampur, or Kolkata's Park Circus, predominantly Muslim families lived for months on end at protest sites, enmeshing their regular family activities with protest activities. These were documented by a wide range of journalistic photographs produced for mass circulation. These photographs attempted to portray the formation of new spaces of protest, and invariably ended up foregrounding what we traditionally call the 'domestic' or 'familial' aspects present within it. By the very nature of the photographic subjects here, there happens a negotiation between the ideas of documentary photographs for mass circulation and those of private family photographs.

By hinging on the duality of the domestic and the public in these particular photographs, this essay tries to problematise and expand the existing contours of 'family photography'. Exploring the photographic subject, the photographing agencies, looking at the processes of their dissemination, and finally, situating this photographic archive vis-à-vis photojournalistic and family images, this essay attempts to argue that these images reinstate the idea of family as being connected to the political goals of protest movements, and therefore, offers a new understanding of what a family photograph is. It is important to note here that the reflections in this essay stem from my perspective as a non-Muslim viewer of these publicly circulated photographic images, and I solely focus on the visual discourse such images produced. This essay is reflective of my broader research on political movements and their cultural implications. I do not have the lived experience, nor the expertise to reflect on the debilitating violence this Act, the ensuing protests, or their brutal aftermath produced on the bodies of marginalised Muslim women that these photographic images document.

[5] Azoulay, Ariella. 2014. *The Civil Contract of Photography* (New York: Zone Books). p. 22.

[6] Referred to as 'the Act' henceforth.

The Anti-Citizenship Bill Protests

The Citizenship Amendment Act was passed in the Parliament on 11 December 2019. The CAA was passed in the backdrop of a turbulent, divisive and communal political atmosphere enabled by the majoritarian Hindu nationalist party at the Centre, and its allied organisations. Further, the CAA was passed shortly after the National Register of Indian Citizens (NRIC) was implemented in Assam, and the National Population Register (NPR) was being implemented or being announced to be implemented in several states across India. Ever since, several states including Delhi, Uttar Pradesh, West Bengal, Maharashtra, Kerala and others saw peaceful protest demonstrations by its citizens.[7] The CAA proposed an expedited process of providing citizenship rights to the persecuted religious minority communities from India's neighbouring states. However, the detailed mandates of the CAA only offered this provision to the non-Muslim 'refugees' from three Muslim-majority neighbouring nation states. Through the CAA, for the first time, a religious criterion was introduced to the mandates of Indian citizenship, sparking serious fear and suspicion across several sections of society.

As early as 7 September 2015, the Ministry of Home Affairs had issued a directive ('Exemptions' 2015) allowing non-Muslim immigrants from Pakistan and Bangladesh to stay in India indefinitely. Through CAA, this mandate was formally extended to those from Afghanistan as well. In the aftermath of the passing of the Act, several questions highlighted the fallacies of the 'humanitarian' consideration that the Act proposed. The same provisions were not extended to neighbouring states like Myanmar that had a recent history of persecution of Rohingya Muslim minorities, or to Sri Lanka, also with a history of community persecution (Venkataramakrishnan 2019).[8] The Bill most notably left out persecuted Muslims and included only those neighbouring nation states with a Muslim-majority demographic constituency. Therefore, the Bill cast a shadow of widespread doubt and panic over the minority communities across India, especially considering that communal conflicts were commonplace, and the shadow of violent riots that characterised the Partition (first the British India Partition of 1947, and then the East Pakistan Partition in 1971) was not in the distant past. In the states most heavily affected by the Partition, like West Bengal, the experiences of being disenfranchised from citizenship rights, or spending years in refugee settlements were brought alive, prompting a series of different protest activities. In Uttar Pradesh, the

[7] Danial, Shoaib. 17 December 2019. 'Scroll Investigation: Amit Shah's all-India NRC has already begun – with the NPR'. Scroll. scroll.in/article/947116/scroll-investigation-amit-shahs-all-india-nrc-has-already-begun-with-the-npr. Last viewed on 15 August 2021.

[8] Venkataramakrishnan, Rohan. 23 December 2019. 'The Political Fix: The BJP's sneaky electoral tactic that led to massive week-long protests in India'. Scroll. scroll.in/article/947638/the-political-fix-the-bjps-sneaky-electoral-tactic-that-led-to-massive-week-long-protests-in-india. Last viewed on 15 August 2021.

recent histories of communal riots and pogroms[9] sparked widespread dissent following the introduction of the Bill, which met with strict police action and prohibitory government directives. In several other states, protests were staged with Muslim communities at the forefront of the demonstrations, wanting to preserve the dignity of their own selves, families and communities.

It is in this socio-political context that the visual imagery surrounding the protests started to emerge. As photojournalists documented the protestors and protest spaces for various media outlets, as participants and allies of the protests started circulating their photographs through social and participatory media websites, there was a certain visual construction of the protests that took place. Photojournalism has traditionally associated itself with the claim of objectively representing reality since the inception of mass-circulated photographs through print media.[10] In the interocular age of the print, electronic and virtual media, it has further enabled a window to see, engage with, imagine and even participate in these protests. Inevitably, the anti-CAA protests situated in the heart of the national capital garnered more prominent, nation-wide coverage whereas the protests in the other states including in West Bengal and Kerala (which also witnessed protest *dharnas* for months) predominantly received the attention of the local and regional media. However, within the photojournalistic documentation of these events, a conversation could be forged between these different protest sites and their modes of agitation. Many have pointed out[11] how there was a new calibration in the idea of what a protest space looks like as the Muslim community became the central visual cue in a majority of these photographs, particularly the wide participation of Muslim women in these protests, which became the central subject. Against the hegemonic gaze that excludes the visuality of the Muslim woman from the nation's popular eye, there was a confronting visual narrative that was unfolding.

What did these photographs embody? Who and what did these photographs want to represent? What were the possible associations that these photographs were leading their viewers towards? How was photographic documentation interacting with the politics of these protests? How does the 'family' feature in these decidedly public photographs of public spaces and actions?

---

[9] According to the 2019 National Crime Records Bureau data, there were 5,714 cases of rioting in UP; in the previous year, 2018, it had 8,908 instances of rioting (Gupta 2022). These events most notably include the Muzaffarnagar riots in 2013.

[10] Roychoudhuri, Ranu. 2015. 'The Public Lives of Photographs: Aesthetic Conventions and Sociocultural Change in Twentieth-Century India'. PhD thesis, University of Chicago. pp. 12–13.

[11] Bhatia, Kiran Vinod and Radhika Gajjala. 2020. 'Examining Anti-CAA Protests at Shaheen Bagh: Muslim Women and Politics of the Hindu India'. *International Journal of Communication.* 14:18. pp. 1932–8036.

Photographic Documentation of Anti-Citizenship Bill Protest Demonstrations

The practice of photographically documenting protest demonstrations such as dharnas[12] or *satyagraha*[13] dates back to the earliest acts of protest in India during the British Raj. From Gandhi's Satyagraha, the Non-Cooperation and Quit India Movements, to the protests against the Emergency, the Mandal Commission Protests or the anti-corruption protests led by Anna Hazare, there have been various photographs in public circulation and archives that corroborate the historicity of these events. In these images, we see large-scale mobilisations of anonymous people. Sometimes a familiar or an unfamiliar individual is in focus, sometimes the photographs would only provide us with a sense of the scale of the protests by framing the crowd. However, in the case of the photographic documentation of the Anti-Citizenship Bill protests, the changing forms of protest activities resulted in changing visual registers. Photojournalistic documentation of protest sites including Delhi's Shaheen Bagh, Seelampur, or Kolkata's Park Circus, amongst others, captured Muslim families protesting for months on end. The very nature of these protest-gatherings, which included entire families having to conduct their 'domestic' activities in public view, generate new questions about what constitutes protest photographs, and what constitutes family-albums.

Some of these photographs look at the protestors involved in various forms of domestic housework, like cooking, stitching, feeding or teaching children. Some of the people in them are seen sleeping, gossiping, or singing and laughing. Some of them are in 'protest' as well, raising demands, sloganeering, giving speeches or organising themselves. We see political activists and organisers interacting with the local inhabitants forming new structures of kinship within the protest site. The family is placed at the very core of these photographs, emerging as a representative visual cue for the public, as a publicly produced phenomenon. These are not private family albums for consumption by extended family members and friends. It is not the public life of private photographs, nor is it the occasional 'public' family photograph we find within news media, where celebrities are having babies, or sharing a meal, or travelling to exotic destinations. This archive instead is a public testament to the continued presence of familial privacies in the face of political contestation.

Alan Sekula suggests that the communication by a 'photographic message' is 'necessarily context determined', that is, the photograph does not carry an intrinsic predisposition present universally in photographs but is shaped by socio-culturally defined semantic cues.[14] The photographs of these protests

[12] 'Dharna' refers to a peaceful protest demonstration or sit-in in demand of something.

[13] 'Satyagraha' literally translates to 'holding onto the truth' and suggests a passive mode of protest as political action. This was most famously introduced by Gandhi in early twentieth century as a means of non-violent resistance to British rule.

[14] Sekula, Allan. 1975. 'On the Invention of Photographic Meaning'. *Art Forum*. 13:5. p. 4.

which were printed in newspapers or digital media portals often derive their meaning from their historical and cultural contexts. They are doubly characterised by conventions of family photographs and those of journalistic photographs produced for mass circulation. These photographs, then, do not embody a celebration of family occasions, but portray families and their members in a moment of precarity; of forming solidarities and performing resistance against the State. These are not situations that are preserved intentionally in the traditional archives of family photographs. And yet, we find regular family activities present in these photographs, much like in family albums. A mother tending to a baby, the occasions of collective sharing of meals, children drawing, painting, reading and dancing, an occasional romantic conjugal moment of sweets being shared. These photographs do not entirely become journalistic documentations of amorphous faces within a rally, or an indistinguishable crowd gathering with leaders and participants. Mushtaq (name changed), on duty to photographically document the moment for a leading daily newspaper, recalls, 'It was my duty as a photojournalist to capture these protests, to show the world the truth of the people who were fighting for an idea of India they nurtured. And they were willing to uproot themselves from their comfortable confines of the home to prevent being uprooted from the land.'[15] The photographs were produced again and again publicly, as the people at the sites were busy foregrounding their identity as people, as individuals, as citizens. They are not entirely anonymous; neither are they entirely singular, the two common approaches that we find within photojournalistic works.

In Figures 1 and 2, for example, we see protesting women at the Shaheen Bagh protest site, engaging in their maternal duties. Looked at closely, we see the presence of the same two women in both photographs, with their children, inset among other protestors. In Figure 1, we see a conglomeration of people, primarily women, sitting with children of various ages. There are three women who sit in the front, holding their toddlers. While the woman in a teal sweater and pink head covering holds a sleeping toddler, the woman in the middle fondly holds her child, who in turn looks at the third child. The woman on the extreme right is shown adjusting the woollen cap of the child she holds, smiling. In the backdrop, we see several women sitting in an ongoing demonstration with their children, engaging in conversations with each other, looking at each other as the children become a part of the action. In Figure 2, we see a close-up of the same situation depicted in Figure 1. The woman in a black burqa and a red-and-white headscarf in the front feeds her toddler. There are two children from the earlier photograph who engage with each other in play. The other woman, clad in a black burqa and a black headscarf looks away from the camera. While there were no visual cues that denote a protest space, apart from

[15] Personal interview with Mushtaq (Name changed on request). 22 February 2021. New Delhi.

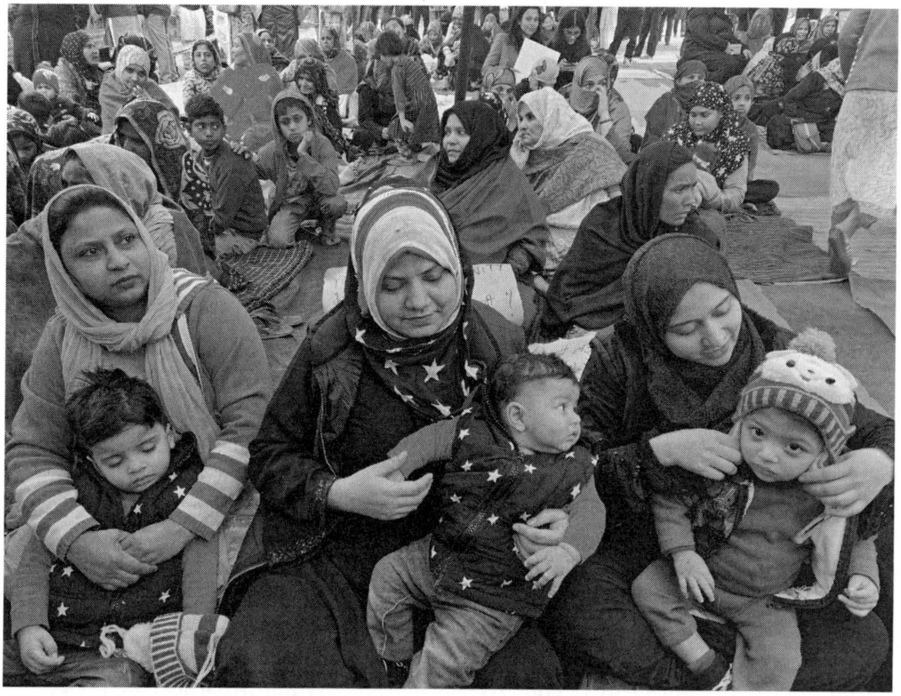

Figure 1. Image Courtesy: Jaishree Kumar, Jyoti Thakur, 'Day 24 of Shaheen Bagh Protest: Women Refuse to Move Despite Threats'. *The Citizen*. 6 January 2020. www.thecitizen.in/index.php/en/NewsDetail/index/7/18119/Day-24-of-Shaheen-Bagh-Protest:-Women-Refuse-to-Move-Despite-Threats---

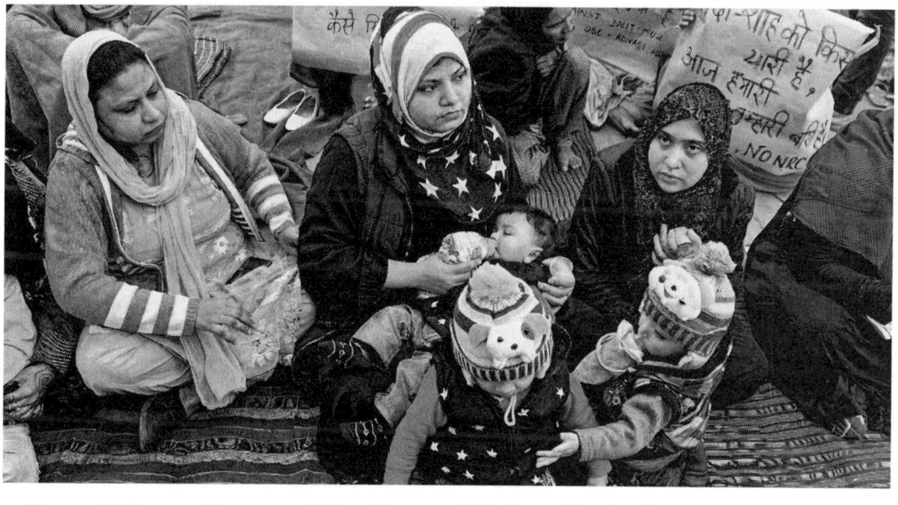

Figure. 2. Image Courtesy: Saket Suman, 'Shaheen Bagh: "Dabang Dadis" Brave Winter Cold as Protests Against CAA Show No Signs of Slowing Down'. *India Times*. 12 January 2020. www.indiatimes.com/news/india/shaheen-bagh-dabang-dadis-brave-winter-cold-as-protests-against-caa-show-no-signs-of-slowing-down-504065.html

the associative narrative and fragmented texts from the report which the first photograph accompanies, in the second photograph, we see other women in the background holding posters with slogans written on them. The full slogan is not legible in the photograph itself, but the 'No NRC' scribbling is. Thus, in the second photo, there is a definite insertion of the protest itself beside the depicted maternal activities, or children's play.

These two photographs (Figures 1 and 2) show women in their maternal roles of tending to children, a motif that is common to most family photographic archives. Most families try to capture the earliest days of a toddler, the growing up of children and the tending mothers who often become the backdrop of the photographs. While in the first photograph, the faces of the three women bear recognisable fondness towards the children they are nurturing, in the second photograph, two out of those women seem to embody a certain resolute emotion. There seems to be a certain exhaustion and a resolve in their gazes as both of them look away from the camera. As per Barthes' concept of *punctum*,[16] this shift in the gaze seems to be the piercing visual cue that relocates the otherwise familial activities of motherhood into the political space of the protest.

> Of course, it was a political strategy for the protestors to put the women in the fore. But that strategy was generated because of the persistent fear of police action. Riots were breaking out in UP, Section 144 was being put up, news was being buried. Our friends who were reporters from specific regions informed us daily of these incidents. That's also what caused the protestors in these big gatherings to put the women in the fore. But it was not that the women participants were being instructed—they were not trained activists. They came to fight their own battles—for themselves, their children and their families.

Thus proclaimed Nisar, a student of journalism who undertook photographic documentation of the Shaheen Bagh protests.[17]

Much like the album of a family, in these two photographs, we see the repetition of faces and people. As the protestors made the sites into their living space, it was not uncommon for photographic documentation to circulate visuals of the same people. Through these photographs, they became familiar faces to the viewing public, as exemplified by the figure of Bilkis Dadi[18] of Shaheen Bagh. Even though we do not know these women's individual narratives, we see them simultaneously as Muslims, mothers and protestors. As they engage in the domestic act of nurturing their children, it is not merely the insertion of the protest posters that make this act a public one. Through

---

[16] Barthes, Roland. 1981. *Camera Lucida: Reflections on Photography* (New York: Hill and Wang). p. 27.

[17] Personal interview with Nisar (Name changed on request). 5 July 2021. New Delhi.

[18] Bilkis Dadi (Grandmother Bilkis) is an elderly activist who was at the forefront of the protests at Shaheen Bagh and became the face of the anti-CAA protests. She was subsequently recognised by *TIME* magazine as one of the 100 most influential people worldwide in 2020.

the gaze that they embody, which oscillates between a fond loving look to their children and an exhaustion engendered by their participation in the long and tiring protest activities, one can locate a foregrounding of a certain 'ethic of care'.[19] that commonly characterises family albums. These women, either actively avoiding or oblivious to the camera device, simultaneously engage in their domestic and public activities. In the viewer's 'culturally determined'[20] visual experience, these photographic subjects do not bifurcate between these chores, or separately allocate spaces of the home and the outside, because the protest space enables them to be present within the functions of protest, but also as mothers, as women, as people who undertake incessant domestic activities.

The presence of children of various ages in these photographs demands further attention. In Figures 3, 4 and 5, we see children engaging in various activities in the protest space. In the first two images, we get a window into the activities of young girls. In Figure 3, we see three girls, clad in salwar suits with their heads covered, reading aloud or reciting as they hold open books in their hands. Figure 4 is a picture of four young girls, similarly dressed, speaking into a microphone with shy smiles on their faces. In Figure 5, we see who seem like a mother and a daughter engaging in studies; the mother points to a section in the open book possibly taken out of the schoolbag next to her, while the girl writes with utmost attention. While Figures 5 precludes any particularities of the protest space as such, the associative report that narrates the 'kitchen revolution' in the Park Circus protest demonstration in West Bengal places the image at the site of the protest demonstration. In the previous two images (Figures 3 and 4), however, there are certain visual cues apart from the reportage that accompany the images, which lead the viewer to associate these photographs to the protest spaces. In Figure 4, the girls, visibly elated perhaps at the opportunity of finally securing the space usually reserved for adults, of speaking into the microphone, have 'NRC' written on a banner in the backdrop. In Figure 3, the girl in the front has the Indian flag painted on her cheek, suggesting the awareness of and claim to her challenged Indian identity.

The young girls here, engage in activities, recall a familiar trope in family photographs; activities that demand to be visually preserved. The images of children reading, of learning, or of performing in front of a crowd, are reminiscent of photographs from various family archives which demonstrate a slice of their lives which the family has attempted to freeze in time, to look back at when the kids grow up, to provide a visuality to fond memories of childhood that the family wants to cherish. What differentiates these photographs from the traditional family photographs is their provenance, and of being documentations published in various media outlets for public consumption. As

[19] Bhatia and Gajjala. 2020. 'Examining Anti-CAA Protests at Shaheen Bagh'. p. 6291.

[20] Sekula. 1975. 'On the Invention of Photographic Meaning'. p. 5.

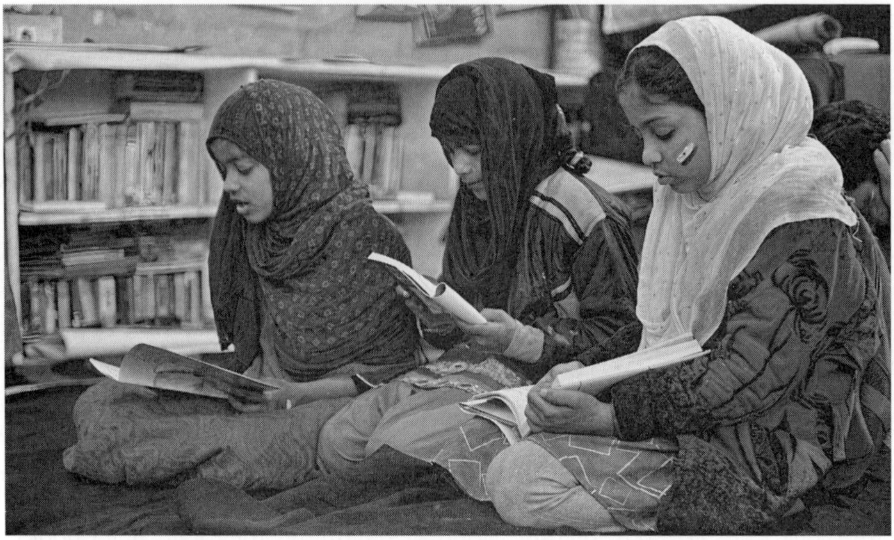

Figure 3. "Children at the roadside library in Shaheen Bagh." Image Courtesy: Photographer Salil Bera. Sneha Bhura, 'The story behind the library at Shaheen Bagh'. *The Week*. 18 February 2020. www.theweek.in/news/india/2020/02/17/the-story-behind-the-library-at-shaheen-bagh.html#:~:text=He%20has%20aptly%20named%20it,brave%20women%20of%20Shaheen%20Bagh.

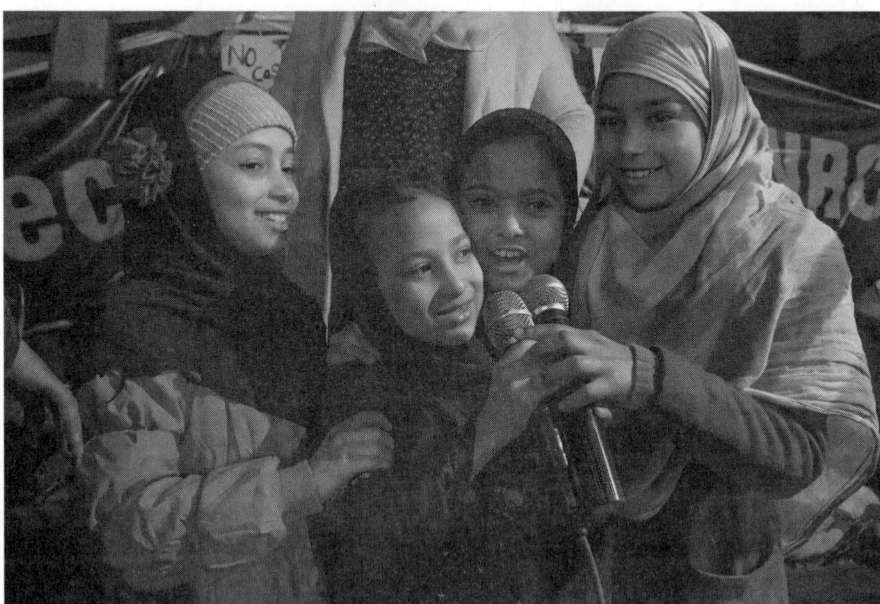

Figure 4. Image Courtesy: Money Sharma via Getty Images. Piyasree Dasgupta, 'NCPCR Chief Tried Explaining Why Shaheen Bagh Kids May Be "Traumatised"'. *HuffPost*. 25 January 2020. www.huffpost.com/archive/in/entry/shaheen-bagh-children-counselling-ncpcr_in_5e2ae361c5b6779e9c315556

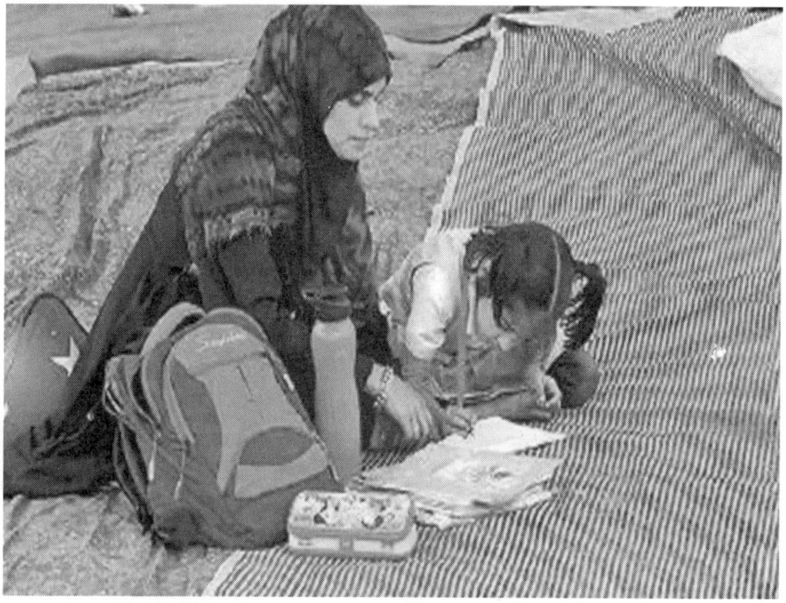

Figure 5. Image Courtesy: Zeeshan Javed/ TNN. 'West Bengal: Anti-CAA protests stir up kitchen revolution'. *Times of India*. 25 January 2020. timesofindia.indiatimes.com/city/kolkata/anti-caa-protests-stir-up-kitchen-revolution/articleshow/73594213.cms

much as Figure 3 is about the library that was set up at Shaheen Bagh, it is also about the participation of these girls and other protestors that engendered the need for a library. Because they were displaced from their everyday activities presumably enabled by their families and households, there was a need to create a similar space (even if makeshift) to nurture a different variety of protest participation from children and youngsters. As much as Figure 4 is about the four girls finding a sudden fascination with the microphone (a marked tool of protest demonstrations), it is also about a space that included different age groups of children, enabling them to assume the stage and speak; to address the public at large.

These children engage in familiar activities, and they are often seen in close proximity to the adults of their families, especially their mothers. Yet, they also enter the political space of protest and mark that space with their own embodied activities, characteristics and quirks. We do not know whether they are oblivious to the photographic camera, or whether they often choose not to return its gaze. But, as viewers looking at these photographs in their various afterlives, we do see children engaging with political activities in their own ways. While the act of speaking into the microphone might seem to directly correspond with the ongoing political activities, the act of reading in a makeshift public library, or the act of reading in a public space also entails a certain kind of politics; the politics of a complex negotiation between the discursive space enabled by

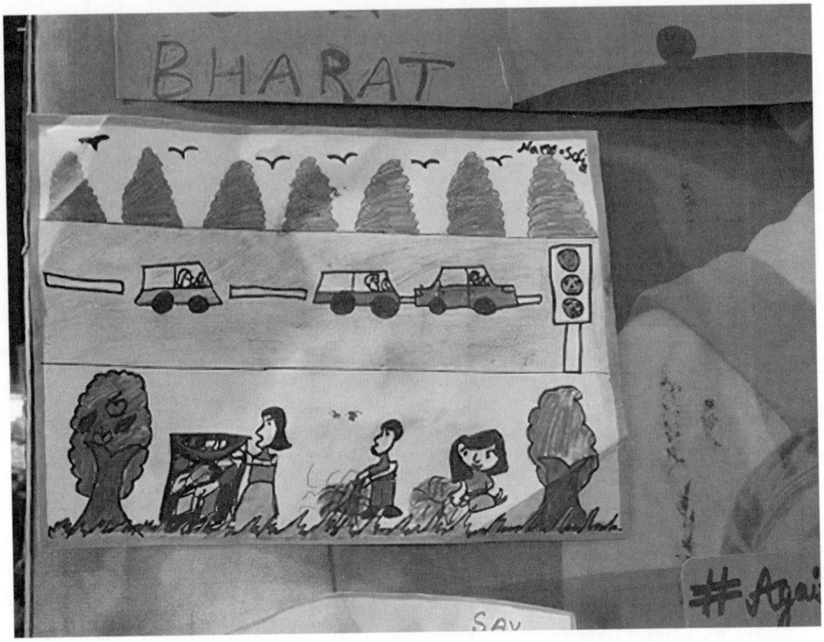

Figure 6. Image Courtesy: Ismat Ara. 'In pictures: The "kids' corner" at the Shaheen Bagh protest'. *News Laundry*. 6 January 2020. www.newslaundry.com/2020/01/06/in-photos-the-kids-corner-at-the-shaheen-bagh-protest

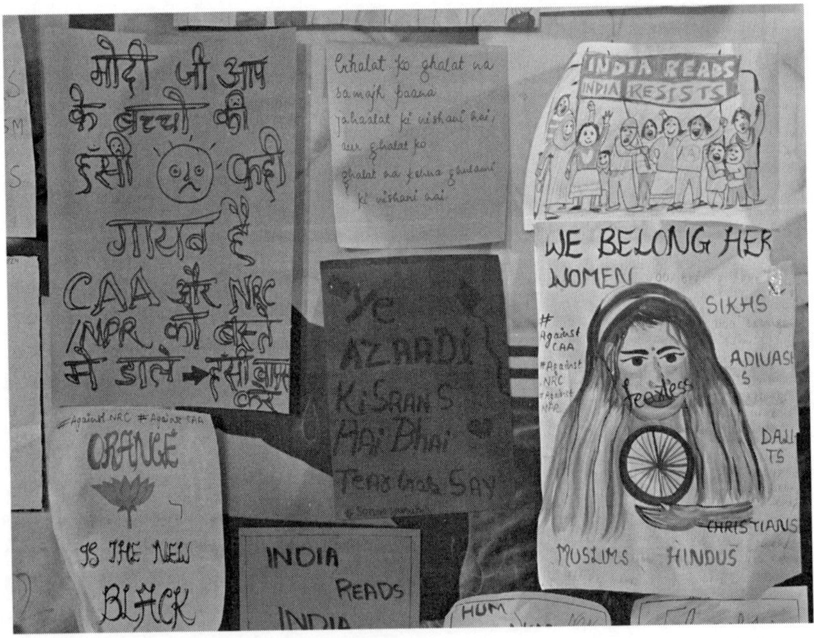

Figure 7. Image Courtesy: Aniruddha Dhar/ News Nation. 'Determined Mothers, Unfazed Children and Chants Of "Azadi": An Evening in Shaheen Bagh'. *News Nation*. 11 January 2020. english.newsnationtv.com/cities/delhi-and-ncr/azadi-shaheen-bagh-caa-citizenship-amendment-act-kanhaiya-kumar-manoj-jha-sharmistha-mukherjee-250525.html

the family and by public demonstrations. The children calibrate the nature of their activities depending on the physical locations of protest, and the diverse everyday actions enabled by these spaces. On the other hand, as they engage in different activities common to the children of their age, they also exercise a certain kind of insertion into the spaces of these protests, challenging their strictly political frameworks. The images portray that protest space belongs to children as much as the children belong in spaces of demonstration.

Similarly, while painting the image of the *tiranga* on one's cheek might recall the various activities children are found doing, especially in response to the craze of sports matches, or annual events in celebration of patriotism, another image of drawings made by the children leads the viewer in a different direction (Figures 6 and 7). The drawings made by the 'unfazed children', as the report terms them, depict familiar places and activities that they see around them; cars passing by traffic signals, trees with fruits or people coming together. Alongside the familiar tropes, these images also showcase the decidedly political activities that they see around themselves as they experience the new protest space. A female figure upholds a banner, a girl waters the plants, and a male figure possibly lights a fire (Figure 6); in the same image, we also see the inscription of 'Bharat' peeping from behind the drawing, further announcing the nature of the artwork the children in these protest spaces were producing as they got exhibited in the makeshift galleries around the sites. While Figure 7 offers us lines, colours and executions common to the early paintings of children, Figure 6 does not offer such definitive hints towards the possible artists. This image shows an artwork portraying a young girl with a headband, her hair bearing the colours of the nation's flag; another of a group of protestors hoisting a banner, and other slogans bearing poems and doodles of protest on posters.

In the Shatila refugee camp in Beirut, the drawings by the children in the Gaza Strip depicted images of bombings, of drones and bomber jets, of barbed wires, blood on the streets and Palestinian flags (Bhattacharya 2012).[21] While in a usual household, children's drawings would possibly include images of flowers, birds, trees and family members—the first images a child is traditionally instructed to learn—in the drawings of Shaheen Bagh, they painted what they saw around them. They engaged in their childhood activities of drawing and painting, yet the subject-matters spoke of a certain affective transformation as they drew the flags, the banners and the people. The negotiation that the children have with the space of protest is complex and multidimensional. They do not simply replace their familiar spaces with the space of the protest; they do not merely get placed within the sites of demonstration as their family members participate in the protests. Unlike Rose's realisation of children in photographs often being produced in relation to the mothers who do not enter

[21] Bhattacharya, Tithi. 20 November 2012. 'The Children of Gaza Have Names'. *Raising Cain*. www.tithibhattacharya.net/blogs/2012/11/20/the-children-of-gaza-have-names. Last viewed on 15 August 2021.

the frame, but still operate the framing of the photographs.[22] Here, we have mothers and children cohabiting the visual construction of the protest space through the photographs. We see mothers and children in their independent pursuits as well as in their associative activities. The protest space, with its cultural, political and social aspects, force the children into an interaction with it. The site of protest becomes a regular subject of engagement for these children as they continue to spend their time alongside their families, the familiar and unfamiliar faces from their communities, and as they make new friends and learn new lexical and visual vocabularies, as they try to make sense of the protests on their own.

As the category of the 'Muslim women' is highlighted and lauded in the report narratives, we see women protestors inhabiting the sites while engaging in activities that vary from the strictly domestic to ones in between the domestic and the public, and to the very public act of protesting. In Figure 8, we see two women, carrying the visual markers of Muslim identity via their clothing, engaging in a conversation as they eat, possibly sharing their meal. The meal, evidently sourced from a roadside stall or the community kitchens set up at the protest sites, speak of the makeshift nature of such provisions. It is not a photograph of a meal traditionally enjoyed in the family household on occasions of dining, which are specially photographed for memorialisation. Yet, that does not take away the moment from the two women exchanging words over a meal, their postures hinting at a sense of urgency or a sense of break from the realities of protest activities. On the other hand, in Figure 9, we see numerous women sitting in successive rows as they eat their meals, exchanging snippets of conversations with each other. Figure 9 effectively recalls the familiar photographs of religious and other celebratory occasions—a marriage, a birthday bash, a family dinner—that usually find their way into family photographs. Additionally, this image also recalls some of the public photographs one finds circulating as associative images, providing an often-anonymous stock photographic reference to ethnic communities and their rituals.

What differentiates these two photographs is the way in which they negotiate their space within the oeuvre of 'protest photographs' that are mass-circulated through the media. The overwhelming presence of the Muslim women at these protest sites, including Shaheen Bagh, Park Circus and other sites, enforces a certain kind of recognition of the photodocumentary eye. Their seemingly mundane acts of conversing, of having community meals, or simply appearing with their children, become a visual register of these protest spaces and protest activities. As these photographs find their way into various media reports and stories, they cohabit, if not partially displace, the understanding of women's political activities, and protest activities as such. While community

[22] Rose, Gillian. 2016. *Doing Family Photography: The Domestic, The Public and The Politics of Sentiment* (London: Routledge). p. 55.

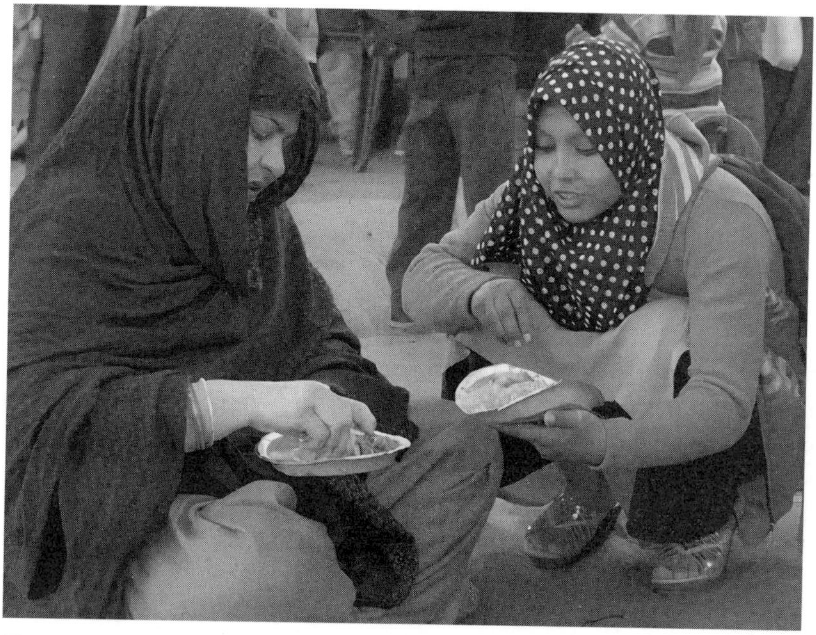

Figure 8. "Two women protestors at Shaheen Bagh sharing biryani." Image Courtesy: Anoothi Vishal/ TNN. 'Shaheen Bagh anti-CAA stir: Protest on their lips, solidarity on their plate'. *Times of India*. 20 January 2020. timesofindia.indiatimes.com/city/delhi/shaheen-bagh-anti-caa-stir-protest-on-their-lips-solidarity-on-their-plate/articleshow/73432011.cms

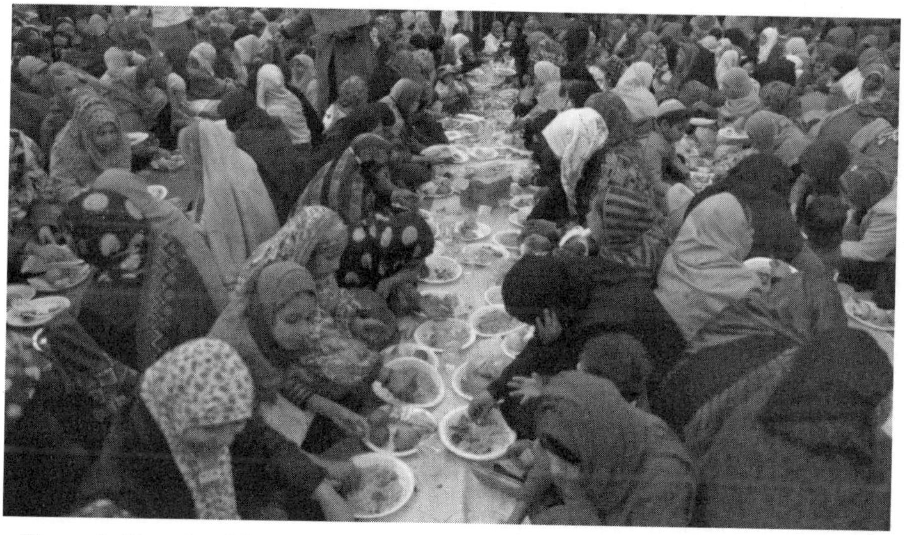

Figure 9. "Local residents break their day-long fast as they attend a protest against a new citizenship law, New Delhi." Image Courtesy: Reuters. 'Shaheen Bagh sit-in: How Muslim women have taken the lead at Delhi CAA protest'. *India Today*. 25 December 2019. www.indiatoday.in/india/story/biryani-bankers-and-burqas-inside-a-sit-in-protest-on-an-indian-highway-1631297-2019-12-25

dining becomes an act of forging, celebrating and upholding the sense of the community that the anti-Citizenship Bill protests are marked with, these women seem to participate in these activities as a part of their everyday routines, without making protesting and everyday living seem like disjunctive domains. These photographs are also often coupled with reports[23] that call these women, who are not seen here to be engaging in traditional protest activities of speeches, demonstrations or sloganeering, as the leadership of these protests. These reports specifically highlight the inclusion of seemingly domestic activities into the seemingly political (and therefore public) ones, and on the basis of the definitive presence of the former, establish the women at the forefront of the protests. If these photographs indeed perform the 'representational task'[24] of documenting the protest events, they do that through offering an alternative frame for imagining the Muslim woman; of their domestic, familial and protest activities together.

In Figure 10, we see a group of women engaging in the act of offering *namaaz* as the state and police forces keep them under strict supervision. While announcing the resilience of the protestors braving open fires at the protest site, the report is accompanied with a photograph of a group of women, again visibly marked as Muslim in their attires, engaging in a difficult spatial negotiation with the police. Even though there are existing public photographs of mass prayers during Eid or other occasions celebrated at mosque sites, this image of women cumulatively offering namaaz in the form of a public spectacle, is scarcely found. In a significant departure from both the family photographic archives of women and the public archives of religious rituals, then, this particular photograph (Figure 10) enables a certain kind of indirect political confrontation with the State. It is through their everyday actions that this confrontation thus happens. It is through the innocuous act of publicly offering of prayers, without bothering about the police presence, that this photograph becomes a visual metaphor of ownership over spaces and places. These women do not address the police presence behind them, but are seen

---

[23] Sengupta, Nandita. 1 February 2020. 'Core group of women who are real Shaheen Bagh organisers'. *Times of India*. timesofindia.indiatimes.com/city/delhi/core-group-of-women-who-are-real-shaheen-bagh-organisers/articleshow/73711808.cms. Last viewed 7 July 2022.

Mirza, Saeed Akhtar. 17 May 2020. 'Remembering the women of Shaheen Bagh, who showed how poetry can overpower violence and hate'. Scroll. scroll.in/article/960659/remembering-the-women-of-shaheen-bagh-who-showed-how-poetry-can-overpower-violence-and-hate. Last viewed 8 July 2022.

Roy Barman, Sourav. 25 December 2019. 'Women take the lead at Delhi's Shaheen Bagh sit-in: NRC will have devastating impact on families'. *The Indian Express*. indianexpress.com/article/cities/delhi/women-take-the-lead-at-delhis-shaheen-bagh-sit-in-nrc-will-have-devastating-impact-on-families-6183409/. Last viewed 7 July 2022.

Aiyar, Mani Shankar. 19 April 2020. 'Women who lead'. *The Telegraph*. www.telegraphindia.com/opinion/shaheen-bagh-women-who-lead/cid/1766340. Last viewed 8 July 2020.

[24] Sekula. 1975. 'On the Invention of Photographic Meaning'. p. 5.

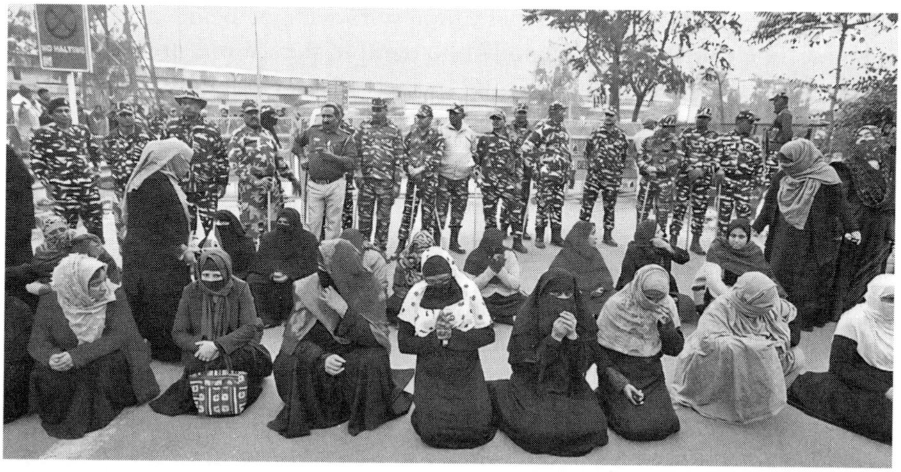

Figure 10. "After a person allegedly opened fire in Shaheen Bagh, women protesters gathered to pray at the spot where the incident took place." Image Courtesy: Shekhar Yadav. 'Puzzled but not going to give up: Shaheen Bagh Protestor after Firing'. *The New Indian Express*. 2 February 2020. www.newindianexpress.com/cities/delhi/2020/Feb/02/puzzled-but-not-going-to-give-up-shaheen-bagh-protestor-after-firing-2097749.html

talking to each other, also not looking at the camera that witnesses them in the act.

In a curious negotiation of the public and the private, the protest space is transformed to belong simultaneously to the individual, the family and the community. The visuals of these women inscribe the hegemonic idea of the protest space with a certain kind of domesticity that is not afraid to announce its ownership over familial functions, or the protest actions. In fact, the familial and domestic act becomes an act of protest. While in comparable photographs of protest demonstrations in other contexts there would be scarce photographs of women or children, in the case of these photographs, they become a key visual motif that is established time and again, becoming a new space and a new way of protest in the public eye. As stories of friendships and kinships meet the viewer's eye, these photographs also enable a certain insertion of the familial activities such as cooking, eating, nurturing, feeding, drawing or playing into the protest space which often showcases different forms of solidarity that are not necessarily familial as such. As this set of images embody a certain kind of nonchalance or oblivion towards the photographic eye, as none of the subjects look at the camera or return the gaze of the photographer, they further accentuate the quotidianness of the activities that absorb them fully. While it could be argued that such an ambivalence towards the photographer could also come from the overwhelming presence of photojournalists and camera devices which enable a certain kind of fatigue, it also offers to the viewers an opportunity to engage with the photographs almost as a window into the everyday activities of these protestors without being reminded of the mediating camera. Like a family photograph, the viewers are offered the people, the activities, the occasions and special events of a family through these photographs.

The Public, the Domestic and the Family

Family photographs have public lives to varying degrees. Some photographs are preserved for the consumption of the family, some for the extended structures of kinship and social bonds, and some are public photographs of celebrities, politicians and other noted personalities that are routinely produced in the media. Yet, this particular set of photographs cannot be neatly placed into any of these categories. Mary Bouquet, while speaking on public circulation of family photographs, suggests that the camera does not find 'ready made families', but photography has an 'active hand in making them [families] appear'.[25] (Bouquet 2000, 16). The photographs from India's anti-CAA protests, which are primarily intended to capture not the family per se, but the protest space, end up making the family *appear* in and through the protest photographs. Especially in these sites, where no semblance of a 'readymade' family can be possible due to the exigency of the collectivity of the protests, the photographs nevertheless make it possible for the public to really *see* the family. If photography does indeed possess the 'power to make visible',[26] these protest photographs make visible the anxiety that is at the heart of these protests—of being torn away from the kinship ties and being uprooted from families.

If we think about the family, there are several ways in which it is produced in intersections of class, caste, gender, religion, and so on. But family as a legal category is recognised as a 'family' through various laws, rules and documentation by the state. Now those very sanctions regarding what constitutes the family are threatened. By the mandates of the CAA bill, the individual citizen and the citizen members of their family are now at the risk of being disenfranchised, of being uprooted from their familial spaces, and eventually, of being put into camps, or deported. The question of the Citizenship Bill and the horrific possibilities of its aftermath, really puts individuals not only in a situation where they are socially threatened, but also threatens to displace political and legal subjects. Indeed, all our lives are marred with an oscillation between the public and the private, the social and the political, the personal and the collective and so on. But, in the context of the Bill, there is a legal and political formation that threatens the very core of the family—in the way we commonly understand it as the heterosexual, normative, traditional family. Here, we have the possibility of citizens suddenly becoming non-citizens. People suddenly becoming non-people. It is not only a socio-political question

[25] Bouquet. 2000. 'The Family Photographic Condition'. p. 16.

[26] Frosh, Paul. 2001. 'The Public Eye and the Citizen-Voyeur: Photography as Performance of Power'. *Social Semiotics*. 11:1. p. 43.

of houses being demolished, people being uprooted and displaced, or certain forms of families being made more acceptable than others; here the 'family' is threatened differently.

Gillian Rose argues about the complex visual economy of domesticity and family photographs, and suggests that the presence of the subject of a family photograph is perhaps most valued when the actual person is 'absent, or changed'.[27] It is this change, she argues, that effectively stretches the spatio-temporal ambits of domesticity beyond the moment of producing a particular family photograph.[28] In this case, as public photographs transform into family photographs, there is a wider extension of the domestic spatio-temporality. Even if it does not become materially possible to trace the genealogy of individual persons and their families through the photographs of the anti-CAA protests, what becomes possible is to get a sense of the very space of the family that is absent, or changed, preempting their physical displacement from homes that the Bill would bring about. It is by looking at the subjects in a removal from their familial domain, that these photographs reinforce the idea of the family; by extending the sense of the domestic over different visual registers. If these public photographs indeed create a 'mnemonic frame'[29] of the event of the collective citizen protests across spatial locations, it is the frame of the family that is centrally placed within it. The photographs which attempted to capture this phenomenon, unable to find any readymade communities of protestors, confronted the new reality of these protests, and further shaped the visual metaphor for these protests for the public.

If the task is to 'assume responsibility for how what is visible is articulated into discourse',[30] then one has to place these public photographs against the backdrop of the particularities of the protests, as well as the larger canvas of the hegemonic framing of dissent. As early as December 2019, soon after the protests erupted, there was news of police brutality, arrests and violence from around India. The majoritarian Hindu Right outfits further ignited the communal tension by circulating images of Muslims with arms and ammunition, sometimes superimposing figures from old photographs onto the images of the protest sites, sometimes simply circulating other photographs as ones of the protest sites. The figure of the Muslim 'jihadi' that is visually inscribed in people's minds following the Islamophobia engendered post 9/11 (Halim Rane, Jacqui Ewart & John Martinkus 2014),[31] was thus invoked time and again to delegitimise these protests, hence provoking untoward responses from the protestors. The protestors, however, responded to these threats

[27] Rose. 2016. *Doing Family Photography*. p. 54.

[28] Ibid. p. 54.

[29] Zelizer. 2002. 'Photography, Journalism and Trauma'. p. 699.

[30] Azoulay. 2014. *The Civil Contract of Photography*. p. 182.

[31] Halim Rane, Jacqui Ewart & John Martinkus. 2014. *Media Framing of the Muslim World*. p. 30.

with a stern yet non-reactionary urgency as they inhabited public spaces with their families and friends, and practically shifted their daily chores and habits onto the protest space. They were claiming ownership through their presence over the sites of the protests as if to show that life carries on uninterrupted, and thus almost exercised a symbolic ownership over the land from which they now risked disenfranchisement. Such a resolute presence of these marginalised bodies not only destabilises the common norms of women's participation in politics, but also democratises the protest sites by making them more inclusive.[32] These photographs, through establishing a new visual grammar of imaging the protesting Muslim, then curate a new 'iconographic terrain'[33] that nurtures the possibility of creating a dent in the mainstream visuals, in framing the protest spaces as also domestic (but not domesticated) and therefore engendering a new imagination of protest spaces and protesting communities.

A public that is already accustomed to the trauma of the 1947 Partition, has had to face a stringent legal aftermath again, albeit to differing degrees. It does not come across as a surprise, therefore, that entire families participated in these protests. We see the 'domestic' habits, chores and kinship ties entering the public space of the protest, questioning our idea of the protest spaces, and we see protest spaces being transformed through such interactions between the domestic and the public. It is not only that the photographs capture protest spaces and activities where the communities participate with their community ties, engaging in communal meals, or cooking in community kitchens, or sharing protest activities. It is also a foregrounding and celebration of the so-called 'domestic' activities that are traditionally unseen in the protest spaces, involving family members and invoking familial ties. While these photographs very much exclude the personal narratives or memories of the protesting subjects—in sync with the conventionalised forms of anonymous photographic documentation—there emerges a sense of association through these intimate activities that the photographs frame. Especially in the digital age, such images helped generate a certain idea of belonging[34] to an everyday readership potentially much larger than the communities participating in the protests. This is not merely the visual construction of an *imagined community* of protestors who have been wronged by the politics of the Act, but it is also a destabilisation of what such protest communities are. Additionally, as against the lack of intimacy that the documentary photographs usually embody, there is a certain insertion of intimate bonds and kinship ties that these photographs demonstrate.

[32] Bhatia and Gajjala. 2020. 'Examining Anti-CAA Protests at Shaheen Bagh'. p. 6292.

[33] Sekula. 1975. 'On the Invention of Photographic Meaning'. p. 6.

[34] Bhatia and Gajjala. 2020. 'Examining Anti-CAA Protests at Shaheen Bagh'. p. 6296.

Conclusion

This is the new emergence of family photographs as 'public photographs', where protest photographs offer us new imaginations of family frames. It is a new visuality being determined for the family as a public phenomenon. The political climate that engendered the protests invoked such exceptional modes of resistance as a response. The strategic as well as spontaneous change in the protest activities which foregrounded the family resulted in the blurring of lines between the conventions of photojournalism and family photography. The family photograph emerged as a public phenomenon not by accident, but as a necessity enabled by these protests. A new visual language is being set here, where the imagination of the protest space also changes through such photographs, thereby allowing excluded members of society to boldly come forth and participate in voicing their concerns in a public forum. These photographs act as an intervention in how we see protest photographs and family photographs, both. These photographs, in their public lives, capture the crisis of belongingness, of home and nation. They embody collectivity and domesticity, loud dissents and silent presences. They frame the protest space, the communities and the families as interconnected against a dominant 'visual regime'.[35] Drawing on Sontag, one can rephrase the question of photography on the Spanish Civil War and ask, 'How can we best contribute to the defence of the fabric of the family, of citizenship, of communal harmony against this political onslaught?'[36] The answer might be in the alternative visual framing of these protests, where intimate markers of familial life activities are collectively achieved. In the quest for new languages for freedom and belonging, within such decidedly public photographs of public spaces and events, there emerges a new visual language which had thus far remained largely confined to the privacy of the family album.

Further Reading

Aiyar, Mani Shankar. "Women who lead." *The Telegraph*: April 19, 2020. Online. Last viewed July 8, 2020.

Allana, Rahaab. "Statuesque Enthralment: The Body in Early South Asian Photography." *Allegory and Illusion: Early Portrait Photography from South Asia.* New Delhi: The Alkazi Collection of Photography and Mapin Publishing, 2013. Print.

Azoulay, Ariella. *The Civil Contract of Photography.* New York: Zone Books, 2014. Print.

Barthes, Roland. *Camera Lucida: Reflections on Photography*. New York: Hill and Wang, 1981. Print.

Bhatia, Kiran Vinod, Radhika Gajjala. "Examining Anti-CAA Protests at Shaheen Bagh: Muslim Women and Politics of the Hindu India." *International Journal of Communication.* 14/18 (2020): 1932-8036. Online. Last viewed July 28, 2022.

Bhattacharya, Tithi. "The Children of Gaza Have Names." *Raising Cain:* November 20, 2012. Online. Last viewed August 15, 2021.

[35] Azoulay. 2014. *The Civil Contract of Photography*. p. 177.

[36] Sontag, Susan. 2003. *Regarding the Pain of Others* (London: Penguin Books). p. 10.

Bouquet, Mary, "The Family Photographic Condition." *Visual Anthropology Review*. Issue 16, No. 1 (2000): 2-19. Print.

Danial, Shoaib. "Scroll Investigation: Amit Shah's all-India NRC has already begun – with the NPR." *Scroll*: December 17, 2019. Online. Last viewed August 15, 2021.

"Exemptions to minority community nationals from Bangladesh and Pakistan in regularization of their entry and stay in India" *Press Information Bureau, Government of India, Ministry of Home Affairs*: September 7, 2015. Online. Last viewed August 15, 2021.

Frosh, Paul. "The Public Eye and the Citizen-Voyeur: Photography as Performance of Power." *Social Semiotics 11*, No. 1 (2001): 43–49. Print.

Gupta, Sonal. "CM Yogi Turns Blind Eye to Facts, Falsely Claims 'No Riots in UP'." *Quint*: January, 2022. Online. Last viewed July 7, 2022.

Mirza, Saeed Akhtar. "Remembering the women of Shaheen Bagh, who showed how poetry can overpower violence and hate." *Scroll*: May 17, 2020. Online. Last viewed July 8, 2022.

Halim Rane, Jacqui Ewart & John Martinkus. *Media Framing of the Muslim World*. London: Palgrave Macmillan London, 2014. Print.

Ritchen, Fred. *Bending the Frame: Photojournalism, Documentary and the Citizen*. New York: Aperture, 2013. Print.

Rose, Gillian. *Doing Family Photography: The Domestic, The Public and The Politics of Sentiment*. London: Routledge, 2016. Print.

Roy Barman, Sourav. "Women take the lead at Delhi's Shaheen Bagh sit-in: NRC will have devastating impact on families." *The Indian Express*: December 25, 2019. Online. Last viewed July 7, 2022.

Roychoudhuri, Ranu. 'The Public Lives of Photographs: Aesthetic Conventions and Sociocultural Change in Twentieth-Century India.' PhD thesis, University of Chicago, 2015.

Sekula, Allan. "On the Invention of Photographic Meaning." *Art Forum*, Vol. 13, No. 5 (1975): 3-21. Online. Last viewed August 15, 2021.

Sengupta, Nandita. "Core group of women who are real Shaheen Bagh organisers." *Times of India*: February 1, 2020. Online. Last viewed July 7, 2022.

Sinha, Suryanandini, "Facing the lens: women in Bombay's photographic studios," in *The Artful Pose: Early Studio Photography in Mumbai (1855-1940)*. Mumbai: The Alkazi Collection of Photography, Dr. Bhau Daji Lad, Mapin Publishing, 2010. Print.

Sontag, Susan. *Regarding the Pain of Others*. London: Penguin Books, 2003. Print.

Venkataramakrishnan, Rohan. "The Political Fix: The BJP's sneaky electoral tactic that led to massive week-long protests in India." *Scroll*: December 23, 2019. Online. Last viewed August 15, 2021.

Zelizer, Barbie. "Photography, Journalism and Trauma." Ed. Barbie Zelizer and Stuart Allan, *Journalism after September 11*, London and NY: Routledge, 2002. Print.

Notes on Contributors

Adira Thekkuveettil is an artist, researcher and designer working primarily with photography. She is also currently the Course Director of Aesthetics, Criticism and Theory at Jnanapravaha, Mumbai. She is a graduate of the National Institute of Design.

Aditi Kumar is an art historian and cultural practitioner. She is working as a postdoctoral RA on 'Migrant Memory and the Postcolonial Imagination', a Leverhulme-funded project at Loughborough University. Additionally, she holds a visiting research fellowship at WICID-Political and International Studies, University of Warwick.

Ajay Salunkhe specialises in museum practices in modern South Asia. He is currently pursuing his PhD at the Indian Institute of Technology, Guwahati. Ajay serves as faculty in History at Azim Premji University, Bhopal, where he is dedicated to developing a practice-based Museum Studies programme. Previously, he has worked at the Chhatrapati Shivaji Maharaj Vastu Sangrahalaya (CSMVS), Mumbai.

Anna Sireiliu Charenamei is a PhD candidate in visual studies at the School of Arts and Aesthetics, JNU. Her field of interest lies in visual anthropology, popular photographic practices, indigenous movements and self-representation. Her current research is centred on examining contemporary "tribal" Naga selfhood and representation through wedding photographs.

Annalisa Mansukhani is a writer-curator, studying histories of photography and notions of the image in contemporary art and curatorial practices. She has a Master's in art history from Nalanda University. Annalisa is a contributing writer for ASAP | art, and has been published in *Hakara Journal*, *Take on Art*, *Shared Ecologies* by Serendipity Arts Foundation. She is also one of the recipients of the first Critical Collective-PhotoSouthAsia Young Writer's Award for lens-based practices.

Charan Singh has a PhD from the Royal Colleged of Art and an MFA from the University for the Creative Arts. His research-based practice uses the mediums of photography, video, and text to explore how language shapes queer landscapes, the politics of representation and legitimacies of a queer history. His work has been seen at the Kochi-Muziris Biennale, India 2018, the Contemporary Art Museum Houston, (catalogue), 2018. He won a

Magnum/Photo London award in 2016. He co-authored *Delhi: Communities of Belonging* (2016).

Chinar Shah is an artist based in Bangalore. She is interested in documentary practices and uses her screen as a site of navigation. She is the founder of Home Sweet Home Studio, a research and publication platform to investigate self-organised, artist-led, and curatorial projects in India. She has co-edited *Photography in India: From Archives to Contemporary Practice* (2018).

Dipti Tamang is faculty at the General Government Degree College, Pedong. She is a recipient of the Fulbright-Nehru postdoctoral research grant. Her areas of interest lie at the intersection of gender, politics and governance. She is a member of the Confluence Collective, composed of photographers and researchers from the Darjeeling-Sikkim Himalayas working on curating localised, organic archives of the region.

Divya Gauri is a visual studies research scholar who recently submitted her PhD thesis titled "Servants in the Colonial Household: A study of their portrayal in the visual materials of 18th- and 19th-century India" at the School of Arts and Aesthetics, Jawaharlal Nehru University, New Delhi. Her research focuses on how domestic servants were depicted in colonial households in India, providing insight into their prominent yet concealed existence during the colonial period.

Diya Dutta holds a PhD in Sociology from Jawaharlal Nehru University and an MPhil in Development Studies from Oxford University. She has been working in the International Development sector for 17 years and is currently Head of Monitoring, Evaluation, Accountability and Learning (MEAL) at Oxfam America.

Hardik Brata Biswas was trained in Comparative Literature and Women's Studies, and moved to the latter to pursue research on middle-class women and photographic cultures in West Bengal. He collaborated with the India Foundation for the Arts in establishing a digital archive of family photographs from Bengal. He teaches at St. Xavier's College, Kolkata and recently has been Mellon postdoctoral fellow in Cultural Studies at the Centre for Studies in Social Sciences, Calcutta. He is co-editing an online journal published in Kolkata, merujeen.in.

Jaisingh Nageswaran is a self taught Photographer, Filmmaker and Curator from South India. His work focuses on the Dalit resistance and resilience through documenting his own childhood memories and tracing his family histories across four generations.His project 'I Feel Like a Fish' was exhibited at the 13th African Biennale of Photography in 2023. The same year, he won the Grand Prix KG+ select in the Kyotography Festival (Japan), participated in the Khoj Curatorial Intensive South Asia Fellowship (India), and received the Musée du Quai Branly Jacques Chirac Photography award (France).

Jayanti Dutta was born in Calcutta, in July 1954, to a middle-class family of intellectuals. After passing Higher Secondary from Gokhale Memorial Girls School, she graduated in Economics Honours from Lady Brabourne College. Soon after in May 1975, she married an advertising executive. Her only daughter Diya was born in 1982, while they lived in Delhi. In 1985, having settled back in Calcutta, she started a career as a software developer. The high point of her career was the years she worked with Brooke Bond India Ltd.

Jigisha Bhattacharya is a Gates Cambridge doctoral researcher at the Faculty of English, University of Cambridge. Her dissertation focuses on the literatures and cultures of political incarceration in South Asia.

Mallika Leuzinger is a historian of everyday media and technology. She obtained her MPhil in Gender Studies from Cambridge University and PhD in Art History from University College London, and has been a postdoctoral fellow at Princeton University, the Institute for Asian and African Studies at HU-Berlin, the University of Edinburgh and most recently, the International Centre of Advanced Studies in New Delhi.

Nadia Nooreyezdan is an independent journalist and writer, covering issues at the intersection of identity, politics, and culture. Her work has appeared in *Vice*, *Rest of World*, *Hyperallergic*, *Delayed Gratification*, *Atlas Obscura*, and *Critical Collective*. She was the recipient of the 2021 National Gender Fellowship to report on gender and the digital economy for IT For Change.

Rajyashri Goody was born in 1990 in Pune, India. She lives and works between the Netherlands and India. Goody completed her BA in Sociology at Fergusson College in Pune in 2011, and an MA in Visual Anthropology at the Granada Centre for Visual Anthropology at the University of Manchester, UK in 2013. In 2023, she completed a two-year residency at the Rijksakademie Van Beeldende Kunsten, Amsterdam. Her research interests include food culture, religious conversion, literacy and literature, mobility and space-making in the context of caste-based violence and Dalit resistance in India. Her mediums are primarily pulp, clay, text, photography and printmaking. Goody's work has been presented at numerous spaces including National Museum for Women in the Arts, Washington DC (2024), GALLERYSKE, New Delhi (2022), Jogja Fotografis Festival, Indonesia (2023), Breda Photo, Netherlands (2022), Savvy Contemporary, Germany (2022), Goethe Institut, India (2022), and Recontres de Bamako, Mali (2022).

Ranu Roychoudhuri is assistant professor in Performing and Visual Arts in the School of Arts and Sciences at Ahmedabad University. Her research has been supported by the Photography Network, the Foundation for Indian Contemporary Art (FICA), Yale Institute of Sacred Music, and the University of Chicago, from where she received her PhD. She has published in peer-reviewed journals, edited volumes, and art magazines, and her co-edited volume titled *Documenting Industry: Photography, Aesthetics, and Labor in India* is forthcoming.

Ruchika Gurung is a Curator of Community and Partnerships at Tate Britain, London. She is an educator and researcher, from Kalimpong, who strongly champions participatory and creative models of learning. She has led community engagement for the Legacies of Empire and Enslavement project at the University of Cambridge Museums, has been a faculty member at the School of Media and Communication, Whistling Woods International, Mumbai and School of Photography, Symbiosis International University and has taught Media and Cultural Studies at the University of East Anglia, Norwich.

Sarojini Lewis has a background in Fine Art (MFA Fine Art Edinburgh University) with a specialisation in archival photography, video art and book arts. She is currently working as a researcher and artist. Her PhD in visual studies at Jawaharlal Nehru University examined (using an interdisciplinary approach) the indentured labour archive through a contemporary lens.

Sharbendu De is a contemporary lens-based artist, academic and writer. He was the 2022 Visiting Artist Fellow at Harvard University. He has contributed to several books including *108 Portraits of Indian Photography* (2024), *Multispecies Speculations* (2022), and *Folk Costumes, Indo-Pacific Air* (2022). He has taught and delivered artist talks and lectures on photography and visual communications for the last 12 years.

Shilpi Goswami is an independent editor, researcher and curator with a PhD in Cultural Studies. She has been an archivist for the Alkazi Foundation for the Arts, a curator at the Kiran Nadar Museum of Art, Artistic Director of Gallery Nature Morte, Project Manager for Qatar Museums and What About Art?. She has co-authored *Mastering the Lens: Before and After Henri Cartier-Bresson in Pondicherry* (2013), and has contributed to *Allegory and Illusion: Early Portrait Photography from South Asia* (2013), *Unveiling India: The Early Lensmen, 1850-1910*. She is also a core team member of the Katkatha Puppet Arts Trust for their festivals and academic endeavours.

Suryanandini Narain is assistant professor of Visual Studies at the School of Arts and Aesthetics, Jawaharlal Nehru University, New Delhi. Her doctoral thesis addressed the feminine figure in family photographs from Delhi. She has written extensively on photography in India, especially around themes of women, the family, the home and the studio photography. At SAA, JNU, she teaches courses on Indian visual culture, photography, aesthetic theory and critical writing.

Uzma Mohsin, a recipient of the Alkazi Foundation Grant for Documentary Photography 2017, uses photography to unravel narratives of people and places. Among her group shows are *India today* (Ente Regionale per il Patrimonio Cultural del Friuli Venezia Giulia, 2023-24), *Kaghazi Pairahan: Publishing & Resistance in South Asia* (Double Dummy, Arles, France 2023, the *Maze Collective Studio Showcase* (Wet Plate Collodion process residency programme, New Delhi 2022, *Girl Gaze: Journeys Through the Punjab & the Black Country, UK* (the British Council's 'Re-imagine India' initiative at the Blast Festival, West Bromwich 2019). She also presented a solo show, *Trees Can't Walk* at the Forum Schlossplatz, as part of an artist residency at the Working Group Gästeatelier Krone, Aarau, Switzerland (2011).

Vijay Kumar is assistant professor in the History Department at Miranda House. He completed his PhD from the University of Delhi. His specialisation is in the history of modern India. His research work focusses on Dalit history, labour history and popular culture in modern north India. He has contributed his research articles to *Modern Asian Studies* and *Studies in People's History*.

A Note of Acknowledgement

This book has taken nearly five years to produce. It began with a conversation between the two editors about the lack of writing in India's visual histories about the personal, the middle class and what we otherwise see as the mundane. This dialogue became a point of departure for this project, which focused on everyday photography. Another major concern that we both noted was the lack of avenues for academic representation, especially in visual studies, in our country. Unlike the West, our country lacks university presses (barring one or two) and peer-reviewed academic journals, nor do we have adequate research bursaries and government endowments which allow competent research and scholarship to get published with relative ease and frequency. This book has been an attempt to redeem the academic interest in a field on the margins of mainstream support and funding.

Our journey has not been straightforward or comfortable at any level, but since we can finally see the book as a whole, we have to take a moment to mention all those without whom this book would not have been possible. It is only fair to say that a community came together to help us through this publication.

We must begin by thanking our publisher and the entire team at Zubaan. We had approached Urvashi Butalia personally to seek advice regarding our idea for an academic book on family photographs and the possible way forward. After spending a substantial time meticulously inquiring about various factors regarding the content, she offered to put the idea to her team and soon reverted with a positive response that jumpstarted our project almost immediately. Ever since then, Urvashi and everyone else at Zubaan have worked tirelessly to put together this volume together. We would like to mention Ishani Butalia, Jojy Philip, Udyotna Kumar, Melissa Fernandes, Moumita Pal, Amanda D'souza and everyone else on the Zubaan team. Sincere thanks to all of you.

Our heartfelt gratitude goes to the MurthyNAYAK Foundation, especially Vasant Nayak and Anita Khemka, who gave us a production grant which eased the book's financial concerns. In the ensuing years, the patience and understanding that they showed with every roadblock we faced due to the pandemic and other problems allowed us to complete the book without any pressure. For their empathy, we are truly grateful.

This book would not have taken its current shape without the support of the India Foundation for the Arts (IFA, Bangaluru), especially of Arundhati Ghosh and Tanveer Ajsi. Their review of our proposal for a closed-door conference became pertinent to the politics of representation that both of us were trying to address. They insisted that we consider giving academic space to newer and younger voices. This did increase our work as editors, as we had to first identify and then nurture fresh scholarship into academic writing. The result and experience of this process have been exhilarating. Although both Tanveer and Arundhati have now moved on from the organisation, their successors, Menaka Rodriguez and Harshita Bathwal, have seen this book through with much enthusiasm.

We must take this opportunity to thank the work done by The Family Camera Network (FAMCAM), Canada, for setting a precedent for us. Both of us had the opportunity to interact with the members of their steering team in 2019 —Dr Deepali Dewan, Curator of South Asian Art and Culture, Royal Ontario Museum; Dr. Thy Phu, Professor and Departmental Chair, Department of Art, Culture and Media, University of Toronto; Dr. Elspeth H. Brown, Professor, Department of Historical Studies, University of Toronto. This was at a crucial time when both of us were trying to grapple with our method, process and intended outcome through this endeavour. Our special thanks to the School of Arts and Aesthetics, Jawaharlal Nehru University, New Delhi, where we held a round table discussion on family photographs with the School's faculty and the members of FAMCAM in 2019. Our conversations with them and their willingness to share their experiences helped us chart our journey.

In 2020-21, Dr Surajit Sarkar, Sarnath Banerjee and Urvashi Butalia readily agreed to take masterclasses on visual research for our diverse contributors and were very forthcoming in sharing their knowledge and experiences. Further, we thank Professor Tapati Guha-Thakurta and Professor Malavika Karlekar for being keen observers during our closed-door workshops and conferences and giving their insights on each contributing author's ideas as they were developing into essays. At various points, we felt that these senior advisors to our project held it together, giving us all the tools and the faith to go forward with our research in constructive ways.

We do not have words to express what we feel towards all our authors. This project took flight when the world came to a standstill due to the pandemic. Over the last five years, India has seen a number of other disasters, man-made and natural. Many of our authors were in life-threatening conditions in various parts of the country. We truly admire you for braving these situations and submitting and revising your papers for the volume. We also thank all others who patiently waited and gave time and space to others in the project to cope with the unforeseeable. We take this opportunity to express how encouraging it has been for us to be part of a cohort made up of people of such excellent intellectual calibre, and we thank you for placing your confidence in this project. We would never have been able to get this book to where it is without the dedication of each and every one of you.

For the cover of our book, we are indebted to Dayanita Singh, whose work with family portraits has been definitive. The image used for the cover shows her in her grandmother's lap, as she looks up at her mother, Noni Singh, bearer of the camera. This is the way family and family photos gaze back at us, through time, emplacing us in our identities as much as we seek to locate them in theirs.

Last but not least, we want to thank our families: the reason why we think personal photography is an important genre in the first place. Our families first exposed us to the role and possibilities of the camera, and being children from the 1980s, we witnessed the important shift from the analogue family camera to the digital personal mobile camera. Our own portraits and albums have spoken to us about our histories and memories, both contingent and often delightful, but also incomplete and disturbing. We thank the parents, partners, children and the extended families we belong to for having seen us through this project. We also thank the community of friends and supporters of our writers and their essays, whose names cannot be mentioned due to paucity of space. This work is dedicated to all those who still believe in the familial system in the widest sense despite its fragilities in the contemporary context.

Shilpi Goswami
Suryanandini Narain

New Delhi, 30 July 2024